Henry Mallam

The constitutional history of England

from the accession of Henry 7. to the death of George 2. - Vol. 3

Henry Mallam

The constitutional history of England
from the accession of Henry 7. to the death of George 2. - Vol. 3

ISBN/EAN: 9783742868466

Manufactured in Europe, USA, Canada, Australia, Japa

Cover: Foto ©ninafisch / pixelio.de

Manufactured and distributed by brebook publishing software (www.brebook.com)

Henry Mallam

The constitutional history of England

THE

CONSTITUTIONAL

HISTORY OF ENGLAND

FROM THE ACCESSION OF HENRY VII. TO
THE DEATH OF GEORGE II.

BY HENRY HALLAM, LL.D., F.R.A.S.,
FOREIGN ASSOCIATE OF THE INSTITUTE OF FRANCE.

IN THREE VOLUMES.—VOL. III.

ELEVENTH EDITION.

LONDON:
JOHN MURRAY, ALBEMARLE STREET.
1866.

The Right of Translation is reserved.

CONTENTS

OF

THE THIRD VOLUME.

CHAPTER XIII.

ON THE STATE OF THE CONSTITUTION UNDER CHARLES II.

Effect of the Press — Restrictions upon it before and after the Restoration — Licensing Acts — Political Writings checked by the Judges — Instances of illegal Proclamations not numerous — Juries fined for Verdicts — Question of their Right to return a general Verdict — Habeas Corpus Act passed — Differences between Lords and Commons — Judicial Powers of the Lords historically traced — Their Pretensions about the Time of the Restoration — Resistance made by the Commons — Dispute about their original Jurisdiction — and that in Appeals from Courts of Equity — Question of the exclusive Right of the Commons as to Money Bills — Its History — The Right extended farther — State of the Upper House under the Tudors and Stuarts — Augmentation of the Temporal Lords — State of the Commons — Increase of their Members — Question as to Rights of Election — Four different Theories as to the original Principle — Their Probability considered . . . . . . Page 1

CHAPTER XIV.

THE REIGN OF JAMES II.

Designs of the King — Parliament of 1685 — King's intention to Repeal the Test Act — Deceived as to the Dispositions of his Subjects — Prorogation of Parliament — Dispensing Power confirmed by the Judges — Ecclesiastical Commission — King's Scheme of establishing Popery — Dismissal of Lord Rochester — Prince of Orange alarmed — Plan of setting the Princess aside — Rejected by the King — Overtures of the Malcontents to Prince of Orange — Declaration for Liberty of Conscience — Addresses in favour of it — New-modelling of the Corporations — Affair of Magdalen College — Infatuation of the King — His Coldness towards Louis — Invitation signed to the Prince of Orange — Birth of Prince of Wales — Justice and Necessity of the Revolution — Favourable Circumstances attending it — Its salutary Consequences — Proceedings of the Convention — Ended by the Elevation of William and Mary to the Throne . . . . Page 48

CHAPTER XV.

ON THE REIGN OF WILLIAM III.

Declaration of Rights — Bill of Rights — Military Force without Consent declared illegal — Discontent with the new Government — Its Causes — Incompatibility of the Revolution with received Principles — Character and Errors of William — Jealousy of the Whigs — Bill of Indemnity — Bill for restoring Corporations — Settlement of the Revenue — Appropriation of Supplies — Dissatisfaction of the King — No Republican Party in Existence — William employs Tories in Ministry — Intrigues with the late King — Schemes for his Restoration — Attainder of Sir John Fenwick — Ill Success of the War — Its Expenses — Treaty of Ryswick — Jealousy of the Commons — Army reduced — Irish Forfeitures resumed — Parliamentary Inquiries — Treaties of Partition — Improvements in Constitution under William — Bill for Triennial Parliaments — Law of Treason — Statute of Edward III. — Its constructive Interpretation — Statute of William III. — Liberty of the Press — Law of Libel — Religious Toleration — Attempt at Comprehension — Schism of the Non-jurors — Laws against Roman Catholics — Act of Settlement — Limitations of Prerogative contained in it — Privy Council superseded by a Cabinet — Exclusion of Placemen and Pensioners from Parliament — Independence of Judges — Oath of Abjuration 102

CHAPTER XVI.

ON THE STATE OF THE CONSTITUTION IN THE REIGNS OF ANNE, GEORGE I., AND GEORGE II.

Termination of Contest between the Crown and Parliament — Distinctive Principles of Whigs and Tories — Changes effected in these by Circumstances — Impeachment of Sacheverell displays them again — Revolutions in the Ministry under Anne — War of the Succession — Treaty of Peace broken off — Renewed again by the Tory Government — Arguments for and against the Treaty of Utrecht — The Negotiation mismanaged — Intrigues of the Jacobites — Some of the Ministers engage in them — Just Alarm for the Hanover Succession — Accession of George I. — Whigs come into Power — Great Disaffection in the

Kingdom — Impeachment of Tory Ministers — Bill for Septennial Parliaments — Peerage Bill — Jacobitism among the Clergy — Convocation — its Encroachments — Hoadley — Convocation no longer suffered to sit — Infringements of the Toleration by Statutes under Anne — They are repealed by the Whigs — Principles of Toleration fully established — Banishment of Atterbury — Decline of the Jacobites — Prejudices against the Reigning Family — Jealousy of the Crown — Changes in the Constitution whereon it was founded — Permanent Military Force — Apprehensions from it — Establishment of Militia — Influence over Parliament by Places and Pensions — Attempts to restrain it — Place Bill of 1743 — Secret Corruption — Commitments for Breach of Privilege — of Members for Offences — of Strangers for Offences against Members — or for Offences against the House — Kentish Petition of 1701 — Dispute with Lords about Aylesbury Election — Proceedings against Mr. Murray in 1751 — Commitments for Offences unconnected with the House — Privileges of the House not controllable by Courts of Law — Danger of stretching this too far — Extension of Penal Laws — Diminution of Personal Authority of the Crown — Causes of this — Party Connexions — Influence of Political Writings — Publication of Debates — Increased Influence of the Middle Ranks.

Page 198

CHAPTER XVII.

ON THE CONSTITUTION OF SCOTLAND.

Early State of Scotland — Introduction of Feudal System — Scots Parliament — Power of the Aristocracy — Royal Influence in Parliament — Judicial Power — Court of Session — Reformation — Power of the Presbyterian Clergy — Their Attempts at Independence on the State — Andrew Melville — Success of James VI. in restraining them — Establishment of Episcopacy — Innovations of Charles I. — Arbitrary Government — Civil War — Tyrannical Government of Charles II. — Reign of James VII. — Revolution and Establishment of Presbytery — Reign of William III. — Act of Security — Union — Gradual Decline of Jacobitism 305

CHAPTER XVIII.

ON THE CONSTITUTION OF IRELAND.

Ancient State of Ireland — Its Kingdoms and Chieftainships — Law of Tanistry and Gavel-kind — Rude State of Society — Invasion of Henry II. — Acquisitions of English Barons — Forms of English Constitution established — Exclusion of native Irish from them — Degeneracy of English Settlers — Parliament of Ireland — Disorderly State of the Island — The Irish regain Part of their Territories — English Law confined to the Pale — Poyning's Law — Royal Authority revives under Henry VIII. — Resistance of Irish to Act of Supremacy — Protestant Church established by Elizabeth — Effects of this Measure — Rebellions of her Reign — Opposition in Parliament — Arbitrary Proceedings of Sir Henry Sidney — James I. — Laws against Catholics enforced — English Law established throughout Ireland — Settlements of English in Munster, Ulster, and other Parts — Injustice attending them — Constitution of Irish Parliament — Charles I. promises Graces to the Irish — Does not confirm them — Administration of Strafford — Rebellion of 1641 — Subjugation of Irish by Cromwell — Restoration of Charles II. — Act of Settlement — Hopes of Catholics under Charles and James — War of 1689, and final Reduction of Ireland — Penal Laws against Catholics — Dependence of Irish on English Parliament — Growth of a patriotic party in 1753 . . . . Page 342

INDEX 409

THE
CONSTITUTIONAL HISTORY
OF
ENGLAND
FROM
HENRY VII. TO GEORGE II.

CHAPTER XIII.

ON THE STATE OF THE CONSTITUTION UNDER CHARLES II.

Effect of the Press — Restrictions upon it before and after the Restoration — Licensing Acts — Political Writings checked by the Judges — Instances of Illegal Proclamations not numerous — Juries fined for Verdicts — Question of their Right to return a General Verdict — Habeas Corpus Act passed — Differences between Lords and Commons — Judicial Powers of the Lords historically traced — Their Pretensions about the Time of the Restoration — Resistance made by the Commons — Dispute about their original Jurisdiction — And that in Appeals from Courts of Equity — Question of the Exclusive Right of the Commons as to Money Bills — Its History — The Right extended farther — State of the Upper House under the Tudors and Stuarts — Augmentation of the Temporal Lords — State of the Commons — Increase of their Members — Question as to Rights of Election — Four different Theories as to the Original Principle — Their Probability considered.

It may seem rather an extraordinary position, after the last chapters, yet is strictly true, that the fundamental privileges of the subject were less invaded, the prerogative swerved into fewer excesses, during the reign of Charles II. than in any former period of equal length. Thanks to the patriotic energies of Selden and Eliot, of Pym and Hampden, the constitutional boundaries of royal power had been so well established that no minister was daring enough to attempt any flagrant and general violation of them. The frequent session of parliament, and its high estimation of its own privileges, furnished a security against illegal taxation. Nothing of this sort has been imputed to the government of Charles, the first king of England, perhaps, whose reign was wholly free from such a charge. And as the nation happily escaped the attempts that were made after the Restoration to revive the star-chamber and high commission courts, there were no means of chastising political delinquencies except through the regular tribunals of justice and through the verdict of a jury. Ill as the one were often constituted, and submissive as the other might often be found, they afforded something more of a guarantee, were it only by the publicity of their proceedings, than the dark and silent divan of courtiers and prelates who sat in judgment under the two former kings of the house of Stuart. Though the bench was frequently subservient, the bar contained high-spirited advocates whose firm defence of their clients the judges often reproved, but no longer affected to punish. The press, above all, was in continual service. An eagerness to peruse cheap and ephemeral tracts on all subjects of passing interest had prevailed ever since the Reformation. These had been extraordinarily multiplied from the meeting of the long parliament. Some thousand pamphlets of different descriptions, written between that time and the Restoration, may be found in the British Museum; and no collection can be supposed to be perfect. It would have required the summary process and stern severity of the court of star-chamber to repress this torrent, or reduce it to those bounds which a government is apt to consider as secure. But the measures taken with this view under Charles II. require to be distinctly noticed.

In the reign of Henry VIII., when the political importance of the art of printing, especially in the great question of the Reformation, began to be apprehended, it was thought necessary to assume an absolute control over it, partly by the king's general prerogative, and still more by virtue of his ecclesiastical supremacy.* Thus

Effect of the press. Restrictions upon it before and after the Restoration.

---

* It was said in 18 Car. 2 (1666) that "the king by the common law hath a general prerogative over the printing-press; so that none ought to print a book for public use without his licence." This seems, however, to have been in the argument of counsel; but the court held that a patent to print law-books exclusively was no monopoly. Carter's Reports, 89. "Matters of state and things that concern the government," it is said in another case, "were never left to any

it became usual to grant by letters patent the exclusive right of printing the Bible or religious books, and afterwards all others. The privilege of keeping presses was limited to the members of the stationers' company, who were bound by regulations established in the reign of Mary by the star-chamber, for the contravention of which they incurred the speedy chastisement of that vigilant tribunal. These regulations not only limited the number of presses, and of men who should be employed on them, but subjected new publications to the previous inspection of a licenser. The long parliament did not hesitate to copy this precedent of a tyranny they had overthrown; and, by repeated ordinances against unlicensed printing, hindered, as far as in them lay, this great instrument of political power from serving the purposes of their adversaries. Every government, however popular in name or origin, must have some uneasiness from the great mass of the multitude, some vicissitudes of public opinion to apprehend; and experience shows that republics, especially in a revolutionary season, shrink as instinctively, and sometimes as reasonably, from an open licence of the tongue and pen, as the most jealous court. We read the noble apology of Milton for the freedom of the press with admiration; but it had little influence on the parliament to whom it was addressed.

It might easily be anticipated, from the general spirit of lord Clarendon's administration, that he would not suffer the press to emancipate itself from these established shackles.[b] A bill for the regulation of printing failed in 1661, from the commons' jealousy of the peers, who had inserted a clause exempting their own houses from search.[c] But next year a statute was enacted, which, reciting "the well-govern-

Licensing acts.

man's liberty to print that would." 1 Mod. Rep. 258. Kennet informs us that, several complaints having been made of Lilly's Grammar, the use of which had been prescribed by the royal ecclesiastical supremacy, it was thought proper in 1664 that a new public form of grammar should be drawn up and *approved in convocation*, to be enjoined by the royal authority. One was accordingly brought in by bishop Pearson, but the matter dropped. Life of Charles II., 274.

[b] We find an order of council, June 7, 1660, that the stationers' company do seize and deliver to the secretary of state all copies of Buchanan's History of Scotland, and De Jure Regni apud Scotos, "which are very pernicious to monarchy, and injurious to his majesty's blessed progenitors." Kennet's Register, 176. This was beginning early.

[c] Commons' Journals, July 29, 1661.

ment and regulating of printers and printing-presses to be matter of public care and concernment, and that by the general licentiousness of the late times many evil-disposed persons had been encouraged to print and sell heretical and seditious books," prohibits every private person from printing any book or pamphlet, unless entered with the stationers' company, and duly licensed in the following manner: to wit, books of law by the chancellor or one of the chief-justices, of history and politics by the secretary of state, of heraldry by the kings at arms, of divinity, physic, or philosophy, by the bishops of Canterbury or London, or, if printed at either university, by its chancellor. The number of master printers was limited to twenty; they were to give security, to affix their names, and to declare the author, if required by the licenser. The king's messengers, by warrant from a secretary of state, or the master and wardens of the stationers' company, were empowered to seize unlicensed copies wherever they should think fit to search for them, and, in case they should find any unlicensed books suspected to contain matters contrary to the church or state, they were to bring them to the two bishops before mentioned, or one of the secretaries. No books were allowed to be printed out of London, except in York and in the universities. The penalties for printing without licence were of course heavy.[d] This act was only to last three years; and, after being twice renewed (the last time until the conclusion of the first session of the next parliament), expired consequently in 1679; an era when the house of commons were happily in so different a temper that any attempt to revive it must have proved abortive. During its continuance the business of licensing books was intrusted to sir Roger L'Estrange, a well-known pamphleteer of that age, and himself a most scurrilous libeller in behalf of the party he espoused, that of popery and despotic power. It is hardly necessary to remind the reader of the objections that were raised to one or two lines in Paradise Lost.

Though a previous licence ceased to be necessary, it was held by all the judges, having met for this purpose (if we believe chief-justice Scroggs), by the king's command, that all books scan-

Political writings checked by the judges.

[d] 14 Car. 2, c. 33.

dalous to the government or to private persons may be seized, and the authors or those exposing such books punished; and that all writers of false news, though not scandalous or seditious, are indictable on that account.ᵉ But in a subsequent trial he informs the jury that, "when by the king's command we were to give in our opinion what was to be done in point of regulation of the press, we did all subscribe that to print or publish any news, books, or pamphlets of news whatsoever, is illegal; that it is a manifest intent to the breach of the peace, and they may be proceeded against by law as an illegal thing.ᶠ Suppose now that this thing is not scandalous, what then? If there had been no reflection in this book at all, yet it is *illicite;* and the author ought to be convicted for it. And that is for a public notice to all people, and especially printers and booksellers, that they ought to print no book or pamphlet of news whatsoever without authority." The pretended libel in this case was a periodical pamphlet, entitled the Weekly Pacquet of Advice from Rome; being rather a virulent attack on popery than serving the purpose of a newspaper. These extraordinary propositions were so far from being loosely advanced, that the court of king's bench proceeded to make an order that the book should no longer be printed or published by any person whatsoever.ᵍ Such an order was evidently beyond the competence of that court, were even the prerogative of the king in council as high as its warmest advocates could strain it. It formed accordingly one article of the impeachment voted against Scroggs in the next session.ʰ Another was for issuing general warrants (that is, warrants wherein no names are mentioned) to seize seditious libels and apprehend

---

ᵉ S'ate Trials, vii. 929.

ᶠ This declaration of the judges is recorded in the following passage of the London Gazette, May 5, 1680:—"This day the judges made their report to his majesty in council, in pursuance of an order of this board, by which they unanimously declare that his majesty may by law prohibit the printing and publishing of all news-books and pamphlets of news whatsoever not licensed by his majesty's authority, as manifestly tending to the breach of the peace and disturbance of the kingdom. Whereupon his majesty was pleased to direct a proclamation to be prepared for the restraining the printing of news-books and pamphlets of news without leave." Accordingly such a proclamation appears in the Gazette of May 17.

ᵍ State Trials, vii. 1127; viii. 184, 197. Even North seems to admit that this was a stretch of power. Examen, 564.

ʰ State Trials, viii. 163.

their authors.¹ But this impeachment having fallen to the ground, no check was put to general warrants, at least issued by the secretary of state, till the famous judgment of the court of common pleas in 1763.

<small>Instances of illegal proclamations not numerous.</small> Those encroachments on the legislative supremacy of parliament, and on the personal rights of the subject, by means of proclamations issued from the privy council, which had rendered former princes of both the Tudor and Stuart families almost arbitrary masters of their people, had fallen with the odious tribunal by which they were enforced. The king was restored to nothing but what the law had preserved to him. Few instances appear of illegal proclamations in his reign. One of these, in 1665, required all officers and soldiers who had served in the armies of the late usurped powers to depart the cities of London and Westminster, and not to return within twenty miles of them before the November following. This seems connected with the well-grounded apprehension of a republican conspiracy.ᵏ Another, immediately after the Fire of London, directed the mode in which houses should be rebuilt, and enjoined the lord mayor and other city magistrates to pull down whatsoever obstinate and refractory persons might presume to erect upon pretence that the ground was their own; and especially that no houses of timber should be erected for the future.ᵐ Though the public benefit of this last restriction, and of some regulations as to the rebuilding of a city which had been destroyed in great measure through the want of them, was sufficiently manifest, it is impossible to justify the tone and tenor of this proclamation; and more particularly as the meeting of parliament was very near at hand. But an act having passed therein for the same purpose, the proclamation must be considered as having had little effect. Another instance, and far less capable of extenuation, is a proclamation for shutting up coffeehouses, in December, 1675. I have already mentioned this as an intended measure of lord Clarendon. Coffeehouses were all at that time subject to a licence, granted

---

<small>¹ It seems that these warrants, though usual, were known to be against the law. State Trials, vii. 949, 956. Possibly they might have been justified under the words of the licensing act, while that was in force, and, having been thus introduced, were not laid aside.
ᵏ Kennet's Charles II., 277.
ᵐ State Trials, vi. 637.</small>

by the magistrates at quarter sessions. But, the licences having been granted for a certain time, it was justly questioned whether they could in any manner be revoked. This proclamation being of such disputable legality, the judges, according to North, were consulted, and intimating to the council that they were not agreed in opinion upon the most material questions submitted to them, it seemed advisable to recall it.[a] In this essential matter of proclamations, therefore, the administration of Charles II. is very advantageously compared with that of his father; and, considering at the same time the entire cessation of impositions of money without consent of parliament, we must admit that, however dark might be his designs, there were no such general infringements of public liberty in his reign as had continually occurred before the long parliament.

One undeniable fundamental privilege had survived the shocks of every revolution; and in the worst times, except those of the late usurpation, had been the standing record of primeval liberty—the trial by jury: whatever infringement had been made on this, in many cases of misdemeanour, by the present jurisdiction of the star-chamber, it was impossible, after the bold reformers of 1641 had lopped off that unsightly excrescence from the constitution, to prevent a criminal charge from passing the legal course of investigation through the inquest of a grand jury and the verdict in open court of a petty jury. But the judges, and other ministers of justice, for the sake of their own authority or that of the crown, devised various means of subjecting juries to their own direction, by intimidation, by unfair returns of the panel, or by narrowing the boundaries of their lawful function. It is said to have been the practice in early times, as I have mentioned from sir Thomas Smith in another place, to fine juries for returning verdicts against the direction of the court, even as to matter of evidence, or to summon them before the star-chamber. It seems that instances of this kind were not very numerous after the accession of Elizabeth; yet a small number occur in our books of reports. They were probably sufficient to keep juries in much awe.

[a] Ralph, 207; North's Examen, 139; Kennet, 337. Hume of course pretends that this proclamation would have been reckoned legal in former times.

But after the restoration, two judges, Hyde and Keeling, successively chief-justices of the king's bench, took on them to exercise a pretended power, which had at least been intermitted in the time of the commonwealth. The grand jury of Somerset, having found a bill for manslaughter instead of murder, against the advice of the latter judge, were summoned before the court of king's bench, and dismissed with a reprimand instead of a fine.º In other cases fines were set on petty juries for acquittals against the judge's direction. This unusual and dangerous inroad on so important a right attracted the notice of the house of commons; and a committee was appointed, who reported some strong resolutions against Keeling for illegal and arbitrary proceedings in his office, the last of which was, that he be brought to trial, in order to condign punishment, in such manner as the house should deem expedient. But the chief justice, having requested to be heard at the bar, so far extenuated his offence that the house, after resolving that the practice of fining or imprisoning jurors is illegal, came to a second resolution to proceed no farther against him.ᴾ

Question of their right to return a general verdict.

The precedents, however, which these judges endeavoured to establish, were repelled in a more decisive manner than by a resolution of the house of commons. For in two cases, where the fines thus imposed upon jurors had been estreated into the exchequer, Hale, then chief baron, with the advice of most of the judges of England, as he informs us, stayed process; and in a subsequent

º "Sir Hugh Wyndham and others of the grand jury of Somerset were at the last assizes bound over, by lord Ch. J. Keeling, to appear at the K. B. the first day of this term, to answer a misdemeanour for finding upon a bill of murder, 'billa vera quoad manslaughter,' against the directions of the judge. Upon their appearance they were told by the court, being full, that it was a misdemeanour in them, for they are not to distinguish betwixt murder and manslaughter; for it is only the circumstance of malice which makes the difference, and that may be implied by the law without any fact at all, and so it lies not in the judgment of a jury, but of the judge; that the intention of their finding indictments is, that there might be no malicious prosecution; and therefore, if the matter of the indictment be not framed of malice, but is verisimilis, though it be not vera, yet it answers their oaths to present it. Twisden said he had known petty juries punished in my lord chief justice Hyde's time for disobeying of the judge's directions in point of law. But, because it was a mistake in their judgments rather than an obstinacy, the court discharged them without any fine or other attendance." l'anch. 19 Car. 2. Keeling, Ch. J. Twisden, Wyndham, Morton, Justices; Hargrave MSS., vol. 339.

ᴾ Journals, 16th Oct. 1667.

case it was resolved by all the judges, except one, that it was against law to fine a jury for giving a verdict contrary to the court's direction. Yet notwithstanding this very recent determination, the recorder of London, in 1670, upon the acquittal of the quakers, Penn and Mead, on an indictment for an unlawful assembly, imposed a fine of forty marks on each of the jury.[q] Bushell, one of their number, being committed for non-payment of this fine, sued his writ of habeas corpus from the court of common pleas; and, on the return made, that he had been committed for finding a verdict against full and manifest evidence, and against the direction of the court, chief justice Vaughan held the ground to be insufficient, and discharged the party. In his reported judgment on this occasion he maintains the practice of fining jurors, merely on this account, to be comparatively recent, and clearly against law.[r] No later instance of it is recorded; and perhaps it can only be ascribed to the violence that still prevailed in the house of commons against nonconformists that the recorder escaped its animadversion.

In this judgment of the chief-justice Vaughan he was led to enter on a question much controverted in later times—the legal right of the jury, without the direction of the judge, to find a general verdict in criminal cases, where it determines not only the truth of the facts as deposed, but their quality of guilt or innocence; or, as it is commonly, though not perhaps quite accurately worded, to judge of the law as well as the fact. It is a received maxim with us, that the judge cannot decide on questions of fact, nor the jury on those of law. Whenever the general principle, or what may be termed the major proposition of the syllogism, which every litigated case contains, can be extracted from the particular circumstances to which it is supposed to apply, the court pronounce their own determination, without reference to a jury. The province of the latter, however, though it properly extend not to any general decision of the law, is certainly not bounded, at least in modern times, to a mere estimate of the truth of testimony. The intention of the litigant parties in civil matters, of the accused in crimes, is in every case a matter of inference from the testimony or from the acknowledged facts of the case;

[q] State Trials, vi. 967   [r] Vaughan's Reports. State Trials, v. 959.

and wherever that intention is material to the issue, is constantly left for the jury's deliberation. There are indeed rules in criminal proceedings which supersede this consideration; and where, as it is expressed, the law presumes the intention in determining the offence. Thus, in the common instance of murder or manslaughter, the jury cannot legally determine that provocation to be sufficient which by the settled rules of law is otherwise; nor can they, in any case, set up novel and arbitrary constructions of their own without a disregard of their duty. Unfortunately it has been sometimes the disposition of judges to claim to themselves the absolute interpretation of facts, and the exclusive right of drawing inferences from them, as it has occasionally, though not perhaps with so much danger, been the failing of juries to make their right of returning a general verdict subservient to faction or prejudice. Vaughan did not of course mean to encourage any petulance in juries that should lead them to pronounce on the law, nor does he expatiate so largely on their power as has sometimes since been usual; but confines himself to a narrow, though conclusive, line of argument, that, as every issue of fact must be supported by testimony, upon the truth of which the jury are exclusively to decide, they cannot be guilty of any legal misdemeanour in returning their verdict, though apparently against the direction of the court in point of law; since it cannot ever be proved that they believed the evidence upon which that direction must have rested.*

I have already pointed out to the reader's notice that article of Clarendon's impeachment which charges him with having caused many persons to be imprisoned against law.† These were released by the duke of Buckingham's administration, which in several respects acted on a more liberal principle than any other in this reign. The practice was not, however, wholly discontinued. Jenkes, a citizen of London on the popular or factious side, having been

<small>Habeas corpus act passed.</small>

---

* See Hargrave's judicious observations on the province of juries. State Trials, vi. 1013.

† Those who were confined by warrants were forced to buy their liberty of the courtiers;—" which," says Pepys, (July 7, 1667), " is a most lamentable thing that we do professedly own that we do these things, not for right and justice' sake, but only to gratify this or that person about the king."

committed by the king in council for a mutinous speech in Guildhall, the justices at quarter sessions refused to admit him to bail, on pretence that he had been committed by a superior court; or to try him, because he was not entered in the calendar of prisoners. The chancellor, on application for a habeas corpus, declined to issue it during the vacation; and the chief-justice of the king's bench, to whom, in the next place, the friends of Jenkes had recourse, made so many difficulties that he lay in prison for several weeks.ᵘ This has been commonly said to have produced the famous act of habeas corpus. But this is not truly stated. The arbitrary proceedings of lord Clarendon were what really gave rise to it. A bill to prevent the refusal of the writ of habeas corpus was brought into the house on April 10, 1668, but did not pass the committee in that session.ˣ But another to the same purpose, probably more remedial, was sent up to the lords in March, 1669-70.ʸ It failed of success in the upper house; but the commons continued to repeat their struggle for this important measure, and in the session of 1673-4 passed two bills, —one to prevent the imprisonment of the subject in gaols beyond the seas, another to give a more expeditious use of the writ of habeas corpus in criminal matters.ᶻ The same or similar bills appear to have gone up to the lords in 1675. It was not till 1676 that the delay of Jenkes's habeas corpus took place. And this affair seems to have had so trifling an influence that these bills were not revived for the next two years, notwithstanding the tem-

---

ᵘ State Trials, vi. 1189.

ˣ Commons' Journals. As the titles only of these bills are entered in the Journals, their purport cannot be stated with absolute certainty. They might, however, I suppose, be found in some of the offices.

ʸ Parl. Hist. 661. It was opposed by the court.

ᶻ In this session, Feb. 14, a committee was appointed to inspect the laws, and consider how the king may commit any subject by his immediate warrant, as the law now stands, and report the same to the house, and also how the law now stands touching commitments of persons by the council-table. Ralph supposes (p. 255) that this gave rise to the habeas corpus act, which is certainly not the case. The statute 16 Car. 1, c. 10, seems to recognise the legality of commitments by the king's special warrant, or by the privy council, or some, at least, of its members singly; and probably this, with long usage, is sufficient to support the controverted authority of the secretary of state. As to the privy council, it is not doubted, I believe, that they may commit. But it has been held, even in the worst of times, that a warrant of commitment under the king's own hand, without seal or the hand of any secretary or officer of state or justice, is bad. 2 Jac. 2, B. R.; 2 Shower, 484.

pests that agitated the house during that period.[a] But in the short parliament of 1679 they appear to have been consolidated into one, that, having met with better success among the lords, passed into a statute, and is generally denominated the habeas corpus act.[b]

It is a very common mistake, and that not only among foreigners, but many from whom some knowledge of our constitutional laws might be expected, to suppose that this statute of Charles II. enlarged in a great degree our liberties, and forms a sort of epoch in their history. But though a very beneficial enactment, and eminently remedial in many cases of illegal imprisonment, it introduced no new principle, nor conferred any right upon the subject. From the earliest records of the English law, no freeman could be detained in prison, except upon a criminal charge or conviction, or for a civil debt. In the former case it was always in his power to demand of the court of king's bench a writ of habeas corpus ad subjiciendum, directed to the person detaining him in custody, by which he was enjoined to bring up the body of the prisoner, with the warrant of commitment, that the court might judge of its sufficiency, and remand the party, admit him to bail, or discharge him, according to the nature of the charge. This writ issued of right, and could not be refused by the court. It was not to bestow an immunity from arbitrary imprisonment, which is abundantly provided in Magna Charta (if indeed it were not much more ancient), that the statute of Charles II. was enacted, but to cut off the abuses by which the government's lust of power, and the servile subtlety of crown lawyers, had impaired so fundamental a privilege.

There had been some doubts whether the court of common pleas could issue this writ; and the court of exchequer seems never to have done so.[c] It was also a

---

[a] In the Parliamentary History, 845, we find a debate on the petition of one Harrington to the commons in 1677, who had been committed to close custody by the council. But as his demeanour was alleged to have been disrespectful, and the right of the council to commit was not disputed, and especially as he seems to have been at liberty when the debate took place, no proceedings ensued, though the commitment had not been altogether regular. Ralph (p. 314) comments more severely on the behaviour of the house than was necessary.

[b] 31 Car. 2, c. 2.

[c] The puisne judges of the common pleas granted a habeas corpus against the opinion of chief-justice Vaughan, who denied the court to have that power. Carter's Reports 221

question, and one of more importance, as we have seen in the case of Jenkes, whether a single judge of the court of king's bench could issue it during the vacation. The statute therefore enacts that where any person, other than persons convicted or in execution upon legal process, stands committed for any crime, except for treason or felony plainly expressed in the warrant of commitment, he may during the vacation complain to the chancellor, or any of the twelve judges, who, upon sight of a copy of the warrant, or an affidavit that a copy is denied, shall award a habeas corpus directed to the officer in whose custody the party shall be, commanding him to bring up the body of his prisoner within a time limited according to the distance, but in no case exceeding twenty days, who shall discharge the party from imprisonment, taking surety for his appearance in the court wherein his offence is cognizable. A gaoler refusing a copy of the warrant of commitment, or not obeying the writ, is subjected to a penalty of 100*l.*; and even the judge denying a habeas corpus, when required according to this act, is made liable to a penalty of 500*l.* at the suit of the injured party. The court of king's bench had already been accustomed to send out their writ of habeas corpus into all places of peculiar and privileged jurisdiction, where this ordinary process does not run, and even to the island of Jersey, beyond the strict limits of the kingdom of England;[d] and this power, which might admit of some question, is sanctioned by a declaratory clause of the present statute. Another section enacts, that "no subject of this realm that now is, or hereafter shall be, an inhabitant or resiant of this kingdom of England, dominion of Wales, or town of Berwick-upon-Tweed, shall be sent prisoner into Scotland, Ireland, Jersey, Guernsey, Tangier, or into parts, garrisons, islands, or places beyond the seas, which are, or at any time hereafter shall be, within or without the dominions of his majesty, his heirs or successors," under penalties of the heaviest nature short of death which the law then knew, and an incapacity of receiving the king's pardon.

---

[d] The court of king's bench directed a habeas corpus to the governor of Jersey to bring up the body of Overton, a well-known officer of the commonwealth, who had been confined there several years. Siderfin's Reports, 386. This was in 1668, after the fall of Clarendon, when a less despotic system was introduced.

The great rank of those who were likely to offend against this part of the statute was, doubtless, the cause of this unusual severity.

But as it might still be practicable to evade these remedial provisions by expressing some matter of treason or felony in the warrant of commitment, the judges not being empowered to inquire into the truth of the facts contained in it, a further security against any protracted detention of an innocent man is afforded by a provision of great importance—that every person committed for treason or felony, plainly and specially expressed in the warrant, may, unless he shall be indicted in the next term, or at the next sessions of general gaol delivery after his commitment, be, on prayer to the court, released upon bail, unless it shall appear that the crown's witnesses could not be produced at that time; and if he shall not be indicted and tried in the second term or sessions of gaol delivery, he shall be discharged.

The remedies of the habeas corpus act are so effectual that no man can possibly endure any long imprisonment on a criminal charge, nor would any minister venture to exercise a sort of oppression so dangerous to himself. But it should be observed that, as the statute is only applicable to cases of commitment on such a charge, every other species of restraint on personal liberty is left to the ordinary remedy as it subsisted before this enactment. Thus a party detained without any warrant must sue out his habeas corpus at common law; and this is at present the more usual occurrence. But the judges of the king's bench, since the statute, have been accustomed to issue this writ during the vacation in all cases whatsoever. A sensible difficulty has, however, been sometimes felt, from their incompetency to judge of the truth of a return made to the writ. For, though in cases within the statute the prisoner may always look to his legal discharge at the next sessions of gaol delivery, the same redress might not always be obtained when he is not in custody of a common gaoler. If the person therefore who detains any one in custody should think fit to make a return to the writ of habeas corpus, alleging matter sufficient to justify the party's restraint, yet false in fact, there would be no means, at least by this summary process, of obtaining relief. An attempt was made in 1757, after an examination of the judges by the house of lords as to the extent and efficiency of the habeas corpus at common law, to render their jurisdiction more remedial.* It failed, however, for the time, of success; but a statute has recently been enacted† which not only extends the power of issuing the writ during the vacation, in cases not within the act of Charles II., to all the judges, but enables the judge before whom the writ is returned to inquire into the truth of the facts alleged therein, and, in case they shall seem to him doubtful, to release the party in custody, on giving surety to appear in the court to which such judge shall belong, on some day in the ensuing term, when the court may examine by affidavit into the truth of the facts alleged in the return, and either remand or discharge the party, according to their discretion. It is also declared that a writ of habeas corpus shall run to any harbour or road on the coast of England, though out of the body of any county; in order, I presume, to obviate doubts as to the effects of this remedy in a kind of illegal detention, more likely perhaps than any other to occur in modern times, on board of vessels upon the coast. Except a few of this description, it is very rare for a habeas corpus to be required in any case where the government can be presumed to have an interest.

The reign of Charles II. was hardly more remarkable by the vigilance of the house of commons against arbitrary prerogative than by the warfare it waged against whatever seemed an encroachment or usurpation in the other house of parliament. It has been a peculiar happiness of our constitution that such dissensions have so rarely occurred. I cannot recollect any republican government, ancient or modern (except perhaps some of the Dutch provinces), where hereditary and democratical authority have been amalgamated so as to preserve both in effect and influence, without continual dissatisfaction and reciprocal encroachments; for though, in the most tranquil

<small>Differences between lords and commons.</small>

---

* See the lords' questions and answers of the judges in Parl. Hist. xv. 898; or Bacon's Abridgment, tit. Habeas Corpus; also Wilmot's Judgments, 81. This arose out of a case of impressment, where the expeditious remedy of habeas corpus is eminently necessary.

† 56 G. III. c. 100.

and prosperous season of the Roman state, one consul, and some magistrates of less importance, were invariably elected from the patrician families, these latter did not form a corporation, nor had any collective authority in the government. The history of monarchies, including of course all states where the principality is lodged in a single person, that have admitted the aristocratical and popular temperaments at the same time, bears frequent witness to the same jealous or usurping spirit. Yet monarchy is unquestionably more favourable to the coexistence of an hereditary body of nobles with a representation of the commons than any other form of commonwealth; and it is to the high prerogative of the English crown, its exclusive disposal of offices of trust, which are the ordinary subjects of contention, its power of putting a stop to parliamentary disputes by a dissolution, and, above all, to the necessity which both the peers and the commons have often felt, of a mutual good understanding for the maintenance of their privileges, that we must in a great measure attribute the general harmony, or at least the absence of open schism, between the two houses of parliament. This is, however, still more owing to the happy graduation of ranks, which renders the elder and the younger sons of our nobility two links in the unsevered chain of society; the one trained in the school of popular rights, and accustomed, for a long portion of their lives, to regard the privileges of the house whereof they form a part, full as much as those of their ancestors;[e] the other falling without hereditary distinction into the class of other commoners, and mingling the sentiments natural to their birth and family affections with those that are more congenial to the whole community. It is owing also to the wealth

---

[e] It was ordered, 21st Jan. 1549, that the eldest son of the earl of Bedford should continue in the house after his father had succeeded to the peerage. And, 9th Feb. 1575, that his son should do so, "according to the precedent in the like case of the now earl his father." It is worthy of notice that this determination, which, at the time, seems to have been thought doubtful, though very unreasonably (Journals, 10th Feb.), but which has had an influence which no one can fail to acknowledge, in binding together the two branches of the legislature, and in keeping alive the sympathy for public and popular rights in the English nobility (that sensus communis which the poet thought so rare in high rank), is first recorded, and that twice over, in behalf of a family in whom the love of constitutional freedom has become hereditary, and who may be justly said to have deserved, like the Valerii at Rome, the surname of Publicolae.

and dignity of those ancient families who would be styled noble in any other country, and who give an aristocratical character to the popular part of our legislature, and to the influence which the peers themselves, through the representation of small boroughs, are enabled to exercise over the lower house.

The original constitution of England was highly aristocratical. The peers of this realm, when summoned to parliament (and on such occasions every peer was entitled to his writ), were the necessary counsellors and coadjutors of the king in all the functions that appertain to a government. *Judicial powers of the lords historically traced.* In granting money for the public service, in changing by permanent statutes the course of the common law, they could only act in conjunction with the knights, citizens, and burgesses of the lower house of parliament. In redress of grievances, whether of so private a nature as to affect only single persons, or extending to a county or hundred, whether proceeding from the injustice of public officers or of powerful individuals, whether demanding punishment as crimes against the state, or merely restitution and damages to the injured party, the lords assembled in parliament were competent, as we find in our records, to exercise the same high powers, if they were not even more extensive and remedial, as the king's ordinary council, composed of his great officers, his judges, and perhaps some peers, was wont to do in the intervals of parliament. These two, the lords and the privy council, seem to have formed, in the session, one body or great council, wherein the latter had originally right of suffrage along with the former. In this judicial and executive authority the commons had at no time any more pretence to interfere than the council or the lords by themselves had to make ordinances, at least of a general and permanent nature, which should bind the subject to obedience. At the beginning of every parliament numerous petitions were presented to the lords, or to the king and lords (since he was frequently there in person, and always presumed to be so), complaining of civil injuries and abuse of power. These were generally endorsed by appointed receivers of petitions, and returned by them to the proper court, where relief was be sought.[h] For an immediate inquiry and remedy seem to have been rarely granted, except in cases of an extraordinary nature, when the law was defective, or could not easily be enforced by the ordinary tribunals; the shortness of sessions, and multiplicity of affairs, preventing the upper house of parliament from entering so fully into these matters as the king's council had leisure to do.

It might perhaps be well questioned, notwithstanding the respectable opinion of Sir M. Hale, whether the statutes directed against the prosecution of civil and criminal suits before the council are so worded as to exclude the original jurisdiction of the house of lords, though their principle is very adverse to it. But it is remarkable that, so far as the lords themselves could allege from the rolls of parliament, one only instance occurs between 4 Henry IV. (1403) and 43 Eliz. (1602) where their house had entered upon any petition in the nature of an original suit; though in that (1 Ed. IV. 1461) they had certainly taken on them to determine a question cognizable in the common courts of justice. For a distinction seems to have been generally made between cases where relief might be had in the courts below, as to which it is contended by Hale that the lords could not have jurisdiction, and those where the injured party was without remedy, either through defect of the law, or such excessive power of the aggressor as could defy the ordinary process. During the latter part at least of this long interval, the council and court of star-chamber were in all their vigour, to which the intermission of parliamentary judicature may in a great measure be ascribed. It was owing also to the longer intervals between parliaments from the time of Hen. VI., extending sometimes to five or six years, which rendered the redress of private wrongs by their means inconvenient and uncertain. In 1621 and 1624 the lords, grown bold by the general disposition in favour of parliamentary rights, made orders without hesitation on private petitions of an original nature. They continued

[h] The form of appointing receivers and tryers of petitions, though intermitted during the reign of William III., was revived afterwards, and finally not discontinued without a debate in the house of lords, and a division, in 1740. Parl. Hist. xI. 1013.

to exercise this jurisdiction in the first parliaments of Charles I.; and in one instance, that of a' riot at Banbury, even assumed the power of punishing a misdemeanor unconnected with privilege. In the long parliament it may be supposed that they did not abandon this encroachment, as it seems to have been, on the royal authority, extending their orders both to the punishment of misdemeanors and to the awarding of damages.[1]

The ultimate jurisdiction of the house of lords, either by removing into it causes commenced in the lower courts, or by writ of error complaining of a judgment given therein, seems to have been as ancient, and founded on the same principle of a paramount judicial authority delegated by the crown, as that which they exercised upon original petitions. It is to be observed that the council or star-chamber did not pretend to any direct jurisdiction of this nature; no record was ever removed thither upon assignment of errors in an inferior court. But after the first part of the fifteenth century there was a considerable interval during which this appellant jurisdiction of the lords seems to have gone into disuse, though probably known to be legal.[k] They began again, about 1580, to receive writs of error from the court of king's bench; though for forty years more the instances were by no means numerous. But the statute passed in 1585, constituting the court of exchequer-chamber as an intermediate tribunal of appeal between the king's bench and the parliament, recognises the jurisdiction of the latter, that is, of the house of lords, in the strongest terms.[m] To this power, therefore, of determining in the last resort, upon writs of error from the courts of common law, no objection could possibly be maintained.

The revolutionary spirit of the long parliament brought forward still higher pretensions, and obscured all the landmarks of constitutional privilege. As the commons

---

[1] Hargrave, p. 60. The proofs are in the Lords' Journals.

[k] They were very rare after the accession of Henry V.; but one occurs in 10th Hen. VI., 1432, with which Hale's list concludes. Hargrave's Preface to Hale, p. 7. This editor justly observes that the incomplete state of the votes and early Journals renders the negative proof inconclusive; though we may be fully warranted in asserting that from Henry V. to James I. there was very little exercise of judicial power in parliament, either civilly or criminally.

[m] 27th Eliz. c. 8.

took on themselves to direct the execution of their own orders, the lords, afraid to be jostled out of that equality to which they were now content to be reduced, asserted a similar claim at the expense of the king's prerogative. They returned to their own house on the Restoration with confused notions of their high jurisdiction, rather enhanced than abated by the humiliation they had undergone. Thus, before the king's arrival, the commons having sent up for their concurrence a resolution that the persons and estates of the regicides should be seized, the upper house deemed it an encroachment on their exclusive judicature, and changed the resolution into "an order of the lords on complaint of the commons."[n] In a conference on this subject between the two houses, the commons denied their lordships to possess an exclusive jurisdiction, but did not press that matter.[o] But in fact this order was rather of a legislative than judicial nature; nor could the lords pretend to any jurisdiction in cases of treason. They artfully, however, overlooked these distinctions, and made orders almost daily in the session of 1660, trenching on the executive power and that of the inferior courts. Not content with ordering the estates of all peers to be restored, free from seizure by sequestration, and with all arrears of rent, we find in their journals that they did not hesitate on petition to stay waste on the estates of private persons, and to secure the tithes of livings from which ministers had been ejected, in the hands of the churchwardens till their title could be tried.[p] They acted, in short, as if they had a plenary authority in matters of freehold right where any member of their own house was a party, and in every

Their pretensions about the time of the Restoration.

---

[n] Lords' Journals, May 18, 1660.
[o] Commons' Journals, May 22.
[p] Lords' Journals, June 4, 6, 14, 20, 22, et alibi sæpe. "Upon information given that some person in the late times had carried away goods from the house of the earl of Northampton, leave was given to the said earl, by his servants and agents, to make diligent and narrow search in the dwelling-houses of certain persons, and to break open any door or trunk that shall not be opened in obedience to the order." June 26. The like order was made next day for the marquis of Winchester, the earls of Derby and Newport, &c. A still more extraordinary vote was passed August 16. Lord Mohun having complained of one Keigwin, and his attorney Danby, for suing him by common process in Michaelmas term 1651, in breach of privilege of peerage, the house voted that he should have damages: nothing could be more scandalously unjust, and against the spirit of the bill of indemnity. Three presbyterian peers protested.

case as full and equitable jurisdiction as the court of chancery. Though, in the more settled state of things which ensued, these anomalous orders do not so frequently occur, we find several assumptions of power which show a disposition to claim as much as the circumstances of any particular case should lead them to think expedient for the parties, or honourable to themselves.⁹

The lower house of parliament, which hardly reckoned itself lower in dignity, and was something more than equal in substantial power, did not look without jealousy on these pretensions. They demurred to a privilege asserted by the lords of assessing themselves in bills of direct taxation; and, having on one occasion reluctantly permitted an amendment of that nature to pass, took care to record their dissent from the principle by a special entry in the journal.ʳ An amendment having been introduced into a bill for regulating the press, sent up by the commons in the session of 1661, which exempted the houses of peers from search for unlicensed books, it was resolved not to agree to it; and the bill dropped for that time.ˢ Even in far more urgent circumstances, while the parliament sat at Oxford in the year of the plague, a bill to prevent the progress of infection was lost, because the lords insisted that their houses should not be subjected to the general provisions for security.ᵗ These ill-judged demonstrations of a design to exempt themselves from that equal submission to the law which is required in all well-governed states, and had ever been remarkable in our constitution, naturally raised a prejudice against the lords, both in the other house of parliament and among the common lawyers.

Resistance made by the commons.

This half-suppressed jealousy soon disclosed itself in the famous controversy between the two houses about the case of Skinner and the East India company. This began by a petition of the former to the king, wherein he complained, that, having gone as a merchant to the Indian seas at a

Dispute about their original jurisdiction.

⁹ They resolved in the case of the earl of Pembroke, Jan. 30, 1679, that the single testimony of a commoner is not sufficient against a peer.

ʳ Journals, Aug. 2 and 15, 1660.
ˢ Id. July 29, 1661.
ᵗ Id. Oct. 31, 1665.

time when there was no restriction upon that trade, the East India company's agents had plundered his property, taken away his ships, and dispossessed him of an island which he had purchased from a native prince. Conceiving that he could have no sufficient redress in the ordinary courts of justice, he besought his sovereign to enforce reparation by some other means. After several ineffectual attempts by a committee of the privy council to bring about a compromise between the parties, the king transmitted the documents to the house of lords, with a recommendation to do justice to the petitioner. They proceeded accordingly to call on the East India company for an answer to Skinner's allegations. The company gave in what is technically called a plea to the jurisdiction, which the house overruled. The defendants then pleaded in bar, and contrived to delay the inquiry into the facts till the next session, when, the proceedings having been renewed, and the plea to the lords' jurisdiction again offered and overruled, judgment was finally given that the East India company should pay 5000*l.* damages to Skinner.

Meantime the company had presented a petition to the house of commons against the proceedings of *and that in appeals from courts of equity.* the lords in this business. It was referred to a committee who had already been appointed to consider some other cases of a like nature. They made a report, which produced resolutions to this effect—that the lords, in taking cognizance of an original complaint, and that relievable in the ordinary course of law, had acted illegally, and in a manner to deprive the subject of the benefit of the law. The lords in return voted, "That the house of commons entertaining the scandalous petition of the East India company against the lords' house of parliament, and their proceedings, examinations, and votes thereupon had and made, are a breach of the privileges of the house of peers, and contrary to the fair correspondency which ought to be between the two houses of parliament, and unexampled in former times; and that the house of peers, taking cognizance of the cause of Thomas Skinner, merchant, a person highly oppressed and injured in East India by the governor and company of merchants trading thither, and overruling the plea of the said company, and adjudging

5000*l.* damages thereupon against the said governor and company, is agreeable to the laws of the land, and well warranted by the law and custom of parliament, and justified by many parliamentary precedents ancient and modern."

Two conferences between the houses, according to the usage of parliament, ensued, in order to reconcile this dispute. But it was too material in itself, and aggravated by too much previous jealousy, for any voluntary compromise. The precedents alleged to prove an original jurisdiction in the peers were so thinly scattered over the records of centuries, and so contrary to the received principle of our constitution that questions of fact are cognizable only by a jury, that their managers in the conferences seemed less to insist on the general right than on a supposed inability of the courts of law to give adequate redress to the present plaintiff; for which the judges had furnished some pretext, on a reference as to their own competence to afford relief, by an answer more narrow, no doubt, than would have been rendered at the present day. And there was really more to be said, both in reason and law, for this limited right of judicature, than for the absolute cognizance of civil suits by the lords. But the commons were not inclined to allow even of such a special exception from the principle for which they contended, and intimated that the power of affording a remedy in a defect of the ordinary tribunals could only reside in the whole body of the parliament.

The proceedings that followed were intemperate on both sides. The commons voted Skinner into custody for a breach of privilege, and resolved that whoever should be aiding in execution of the order of the lords against the East India company should be deemed a betrayer of the liberties of the commons of England, and an infringer of the privileges of the house. The lords, in return, committed sir Samuel Barnardiston, chairman of the company, and a member of the house of commons, to prison, and imposed on him a fine of 500*l.* It became necessary for the king to stop the course of this quarrel, which was done by successive adjournments and prorogations for fifteen months. But on their meeting again, in October 1669, the commons proceeded instantly to renew the dispute. It appeared that Barnardiston, on the day of the adjournment, had been released from custody without demand of his fine, which, by a trick rather unworthy of those who had resorted to it, was entered as paid on the records of the exchequer. This was a kind of victory on the side of the commons; but it was still more material that no steps had been taken to enforce the order of the lords against the East India company. The latter sent down a bill concerning privilege and judicature in parliament, which the other house rejected on a second reading. They in return passed a bill vacating the proceedings against Barnardiston, which met with a like fate. In conclusion, the king recommended an erasure from the Journals of all that had passed on the subject, and an entire cessation; an expedient which both houses willingly embraced, the one to secure its victory, the other to save its honour. From this time the lords have tacitly abandoned all pretensions to an original jurisdiction in civil suits."

They have, however, been more successful in establishing a branch of their ultimate jurisdiction which had less to be urged for it in respect of precedent, that of hearing appeals from courts of equity. It is proved by sir Matthew Hale and his editor, Mr. Hargrave, that the lords did not entertain petitions of appeal before the reign of Charles I., and not perhaps unequivocally before the long parliament.* They became very common from that time, though hardly more so than original suits; and, as they bore no analogy, except at first glance, to writs of error, which come to the house of lords by the king's express commission under the great seal, could not well be defended on legal grounds. But, on the other hand, it was reasonable that the vast power of the court of chancery should be subject to some control; and though a commission of review, somewhat in the nature of the court of delegates in ecclesiastical appeals, might have been and had been occasionally ordered by the crown,⁷ yet, if the ultimate jurisdiction of the peer-

---

" For the whole of this business, which is erased from the journals of both houses, see State Trials, v. 711; Parl. Hist. iv. 431, 443; Hatsell's Precedents, iii. 336; and Hargrave's Preface to Hale's Jurisdiction of the Lords, 101. [A slight attempt to revive the original jurisdiction was made by the lords in 1702. Id. 196.

* Hale says, " I could never get to any precedent of greater antiquity than 3 Car. I., nay, scarce before 16 Car. I., of any such proceeding in the lords' house.' C. 33; and see Hargrave's Preface, 53

⁷ Id. c. 31.

age were convenient and salutary in cases of common
law, it was difficult to assign any satisfactory reason why
it should be less so in those which are technically denominated equitable.* Nor is it likely that the commons
would have disputed this usurpation, in which the crown
had acquiesced, if the lords had not received appeals
against members of the other house. Three instances of
this took place about the year 1675; but that of Shirley
against sir John Fagg is the most celebrated, as having
given rise to a conflict between the two houses as violent
as that which had occurred in the business of Skinner.
It began altogether on the score of privilege. As members of the house of commons were exempted from legal
process during the session, by the general privilege of
parliament, they justly resented the pretension of the
peers to disregard this immunity, and compel them to
appear as respondents in cases of appeal. In these con-
tentions neither party could evince its superiority but at
the expense of innocent persons. It was a contempt of
the one house to disobey its order, of the other to obey
it. Four counsel, who had pleaded at the bar of the
lords in one of the cases where a member of the other
house was concerned, were taken into custody of the
serjeant-at-arms by the speaker's warrant. The gentleman usher of the black rod, by warrant of the lords, em-
powering him to call all persons necessary to his assistance, set them at liberty. The commons apprehended
them again; and, to prevent another rescue, sent them
to the Tower. The lords despatched their usher of the
black rod to the lieutenant of the Tower, commanding
him to deliver up the said persons. He replied that
they were committed by order of the commons, and he
could not release them without their order; just as, if
the lords were to commit any person, he could not re-

* It was ordered in a petition of Robert Roberts, esq., that directions be given to the lord chancellor that he proceed to make a speedy decree in the court of chancery, according to equity and justice, notwithstanding there be not any precedent in the case. Against this lords Mohun and Lincoln severally protested; the latter very sensibly observing, that, whereas it hath been the prudence and care of former parliaments to set limits and bounds to the jurisdiction of chancery, now this order of directions, which implies a command, opens a gap to set up an arbitrary power in the chancery, which is hereby countenanced by the house of lords to act, not according to the accustomed rules or former precedents of that court, but according to his own will. Lords' Journals, 29th Nov 1664

lease him without their lordships' order. They addressed the king to remove the lieutenant; but, after some hesitation, he declined to comply with their desire. In this difficulty they had recourse, instead of the warrant of the lords' speaker, to a writ of habeas corpus returnable in parliament; a proceeding not usual, but the legality of which seems to be now admitted. The lieutenant of the Tower, who, rather unluckily for the lords, had taken the other side, either out of conviction or from a sense that the lower house were the stronger and more formidable, instead of obeying the writ, came to the bar of the commons for directions. They voted, as might be expected, that the writ was contrary to law and the privileges of their house. But, in this ferment of two jealous and exasperated assemblies, it was highly necessary, as on the former occasion, for the king to interpose by a prorogation for three months. This period, however, not being sufficient to allay their animosity, the house of peers took up again the appeal of Shirley in their next session. Fresh votes and orders of equal intemperance on both sides ensued, till the king by the long prorogation, from November 1675 to February 1677, put an end to the dispute. The particular appeal of Shirley was never revived; but the lords continued without objection to exercise their general jurisdiction over appeals from courts of equity.[a] The learned editor of Hale's Treatise on the Jurisdiction of the Lords expresses some degree of surprise at the commons' acquiescence in what they had treated as an usurpation. But it is evident from the whole course of proceeding that it was the breach of privilege in citing their own members to appear which excited their indignation. It was but incidentally that they observed in a conference "that the commons cannot find by Magna Charta, or by any other law or ancient custom of parliament, that your lordships have any jurisdiction in cases of appeal from courts of equity." They afterwards, indeed, resolved that there lies no appeal to the judicature of the lords in parliament from courts of equity;[b] and came ultimately, as their wrath increased, to a vote, "That whosoever shall solicit, plead, or prose-

---

[a] It was thrown out against them by the commons in their angry conferences about the business of Ashby and White in 1704, but not with any serious intention of opposition.
[b] C. J. May 30.

cute any appeal against any commoner of England, from any court of equity, before the house of lords, shall be deemed and taken a betrayer of the rights and liberties of the commons of England, and shall be proceeded against accordingly;"[c] which vote the lords resolved next day to be "illegal, unparliamentary, and tending to a dissolution of the government."[d] But this was evidently rather an act of hostility arising out of the immediate quarrel than the calm assertion of a legal principle.[e]

During the interval between these two dissensions, which the suits of Skinner and Shirley engendered, another difference had arisen, somewhat less violently conducted, but wherein both houses considered their essential privileges at stake. This concerned the long-agitated question of the right of the lords to make alterations in money-bills. Though I cannot but think the importance of their exclusive privilege has been rather exaggerated by the house of commons, it deserves attention; more especially as the embers of that fire may not be so wholly extinguished as never again to show some traces of its heat.

Question of the exclusive right of the commons as to money-bills.

In our earliest parliamentary records the lords and commons, summoned in a great measure for the sake of relieving the king's necessities, appear to have made their several grants of supply without mutual communication, and the latter generally in a higher proportion than the former. These were not in the form of laws, nor did they obtain any formal assent from the king, to whom they were tendered in written indentures, entered afterwards on the roll of parliament.

Its history.

---

[c] Id. Nov. 19. Several divisions took place in the course of this business, and some rather close; the court endeavouring to allay the fire. The vote to take serjeant Pemberton into custody for appearing as counsel at the lords' bar was only carried by 154 to 146 on June 1.

[d] Lords' Journals, Nov. 20.

[e] Lords' and Commons' Journals, May and November, 1675; Parl. Hist. 721, 791; State Trials, vi. 1121; Hargrave's Preface to Hale, 135; and Hale's Treatise, c. 33.

It may be observed that the lords learned a little caution in this affair. An appeal of one Cottington from the court of delegates to their house was rejected by a vote that it did not properly belong to them, Shaftesbury alone dissentient. June 17, 1678. Yet they had asserted their right to receive appeals from inferior courts, that there might be no failure of justice, in terms large enough to embrace the ecclesiastical jurisdiction. May 6, 1675. And it is said that they actually had done so in 1628. Hargrave, 52.

The latest instance of such distinct grants from the two houses, as far as I can judge from the rolls, is in the 18th year of Edward III.[f] But in the 22nd year of that reign the commons alone granted three fifteenths of their goods, in such a manner as to show beyond a doubt that the tax was to be levied solely upon themselves.[g] After this time the lords and commons are jointly recited in the rolls to have granted them, sometimes, as it is expressed, upon deliberation had together. In one case it is said that the lords, with one assent, and afterwards the commons, granted a subsidy on exported wool.[h] A change of language is observable in Richard II.'s reign, when the commons are recited to grant with the assent of the lords; and this seems to indicate, not only that in practice the vote used to originate with the commons, but that their proportion, at least, of the tax being far greater than that of the lords (especially in the usual impositions on wool and skins, which ostensibly fell on the exporting merchant), the grant was to be deemed mainly theirs, subject only to the assent of the other house of parliament. This is, however, so explicitly asserted in a remarkable passage on the roll of 9 Hen. IV., without any apparent denial, that it cannot be called in question by any one.[i] The language of the rolls continues to be the same in the following reigns; the commons are the granting, the lords the consenting power. It is even said by the court of king's bench, in a year-book of Edward IV., that a grant of money by the commons would be binding without assent of the lords; meaning of course as to commoners alone. I have been almost led to suspect, by considering this remarkable exclusive privilege of originating grants of money to the crown, as well as by the language of some passages in the rolls of parliament relating to them, that no part of the direct taxes, the tenths or fifteenths of goods, were assessed upon the lords temporal and spiritual, except where they are positively mentioned, which is frequently the case. But, as I do not remember to have seen this anywhere asserted by those who have turned their attention to the antiquities of our constitution, it may possibly be an

[f] Rot. Parl. II. 149.
[g] Id. 200.
[h] Id. 300 (43 Edw. 3).
[i] Rot. Parl. III. 611. View of Middle Ages II. 310.

unfounded surmise, or at least only applicable to the earlier period of our parliamentary records.

These grants continued to be made as before, by the consent indeed of the houses of parliament, but not as legislative enactments. Most of the few instances where they appear among the statutes are where some condition is annexed, or some relief of grievances so interwoven with them that they make part of a new law.[k] In the reign of Henry VII. they are occasionally inserted among the statutes, though still without any enacting words.[m] In that of Henry VIII. the form is rather more legislative, and they are said to be enacted by the authority of parliament, though the king's name is not often mentioned till about the conclusion of his reign;[n] after which a sense of the necessity of expressing his legislative authority seems to have led to its introduction in some part or other of the bill.[o] The lords and commons are sometimes both said to grant, but more frequently the latter with the former's assent, as continued to be the case through the reigns of Elizabeth and James I. In the first parliament of Charles I. the commons began to omit the name of the lords in the preamble of bills of supply, reciting the grant as if wholly their own, but in the enacting words adopted the customary form of statutes. This, though once remonstrated against by the upper house, has continued ever since to be the practice.

---

[k] 14 E. 3, stat. 1, c. 21. This statute is remarkable for a promise of the lords not to assent in future to any charge beyond the old custom, without assent of the commons in full parliament. Stat. 2, same year; the king promises to lay on no charge but by assent of the lords and commons. 18 E. 3, stat. 2, c. 1: the commons grant two fifteenths of the commonalty, and two tenths of the cities and boroughs. " Et en cas que notre signeur le roi passe la mer, de paier a mesmes les tems les quinzisme et disme del second an, et nemy en autre maniere. Issint que les deniers de ce levez solent despendus, en les besoignes a eux monstez a cest parlement, par avis des grauntz a ce assignez, et que les aides de la Trent solent mys en defense de north.' This is a remarkable precedent for the usage of appropriation, which had escaped me, though I have elsewhere quoted that in 5 Rich. 2, stat. 2, c. 2 & 3. In two or three instances we find grants of tenths and fifteenths in the statutes, without any other matter, as 14 E. 3, stat. 1, c. 20; 27 E. 3, stat. 1, c. 4.

[m] 7 H. 7, c. 11; 12 H. 7, c. 12.

[n] I find only one exception, 5 H. 8, c. 17, which was in the now common form: Be it enacted by the king our sovereign lord, and by the assent, &c.

[o] In 37 H. 8, c. 25, both lords and commons are said to grant, and they pray that their grant " may be ratified and confirmed by his majesty's royal assent, so to be enacted and authorized by virtue of this present parliament as in such cases heretofore has been accustomed."

The originating power as to taxation was thus indubitably placed in the house of commons; nor did any controversy arise upon that ground. But they maintained also that the lords could not make any amendment whatever in bills sent up to them for imposing, directly or indirectly, a charge upon the people. There seems no proof that any difference between the two houses on this score had arisen before the Restoration; and in the convention parliament the lords made several alterations in undoubted money-bills, to which the commons did not object. But in 1661, the lords having sent down a bill for paving the streets of Westminster, to which they desired the concurrence of the commons, the latter, on reading the bill a first time, "observing that it went to lay a charge upon the people, and conceiving that it was a privilege inherent in their house that bills of that nature should be first considered there," laid it aside, and caused another to be brought in.[p] When this was sent up to the lords, they inserted a clause to which the commons disagreed, as contrary to their privileges, because the people cannot have any tax or charge imposed upon them, but originally by the house of commons. The lords resolved this assertion of the commons to be against the inherent privileges of the house of peers; and mentioned one precedent of a similar bill in the reign of Mary, and two in that of Elizabeth, which had begun with them. The present bill was defeated by the unwillingness of either party to recede; but for a few years after, though the point in question was still agitated, instances occur where the commons suffered amendments in what were now considered as money-bills to pass, and others where the lords receded from them rather than defeat the proposed measure. In April 1671, however, the lords having reduced the amount of an imposition on sugar, it was resolved by the other house, "That, in all aids given to the king by the commons, the rate or tax ought not to be altered by the lords."[q] This brought

[p] Commons' Journals, 24, 29 July; Lords' Journals, 30 July. See also Hatsell's Precedents, iii. 100, for this subject of supply.
[q] They expressed this with strange latitude in a resolution some years after, that all aids and supplies to his majesty in parliament are *the sole gift of the commons.* Parl. Hist. 1005. As they did not mean to deny that the lords must concur in the bill, much less that they must pay their quota, this language seems indefensible.

on several conferences between the houses, wherein the limits of the exclusive privilege claimed by the commons were discussed with considerable ability, and less heat than in the disputes concerning judicature; but, as I cannot help thinking, with a decided advantage both as to precedent and constitutional analogy on the side of the peers.' If the commons, as in early times, had merely granted their own money, it would be reasonable that their house should have, as it claimed to have, "a fundamental right as to the matter, the measure, and the time." But that the peers, subject to the same burthens as the rest of the community, and possessing no trifling proportion of the general wealth, should have no other alternative than to refuse the necessary supplies of the revenue, or to have their exact proportion, with all qualifications and circumstances attending their grant, presented to them unalterably by the other house of parliament, was an anomaly that could hardly rest on any other ground of defence than such a series of precedents as establish a constitutional usage; while, in fact, it could not be made out that such a pretension was ever advanced by the commons before the present parliament. In the short parliament of April 1640, the lords having sent down a message, requesting the other house to give precedency, in the business they were about, to matter of supply, it had been highly resented as an infringement of their privilege; and Mr. Pym was appointed to represent their complaint at a conference. Yet even then, in the fervour of that critical period, the boldest advocate of popular privileges who could have been selected was content to assert that the matter of subsidy and supply ought to begin in the house of commons.'

There seems to be still less pretext for the great ex-

' Lords' and Commons' Journals, April 17th and 22nd, 1679. Parl. Hist. iv. 480. Hatsell's Precedents, iii. 109, 368, 409.

In a pamphlet by lord Anglesea, if I mistake not, entitled 'Case stated of the Jurisdiction of the House of Lords in point of Impositions,' 1696, a vigorous and learned defence of the right of the lords to make alterations in money-bills, it is admitted that they cannot increase the rates; since that would be to originate a charge on the people, which they cannot do. But it is even said in the year-book, 33 H. 6, that, if the commons grant tonnage for four years, and the lords reduce the terms to two years, they need not send the bill down again. This of course could not be supported in modern times.

* Parl. Hist. ii. 563.

tension given by the commons to their acknowledged privilege of originating bills of supply. The principle was well adapted to that earlier period when security against misgovernment could only be obtained by the vigilant jealousy and uncompromising firmness of the commons. They came to the grant of subsidy with real or feigned reluctance, as the stipulated price of redress of grievances. They considered the lords, generally speaking, as too intimately united with the king's ordinary council, which indeed sat with them, and had, perhaps as late as Edward III.'s time, a deliberative voice. They knew the influence or intimidating ascendancy of the peers over many of their own members. It may be doubted in fact whether the lower house shook off, absolutely and permanently, all sense of subordination, or at least deference, to the upper, till about the close of the reign of Elizabeth. But I must confess that, when the wise and ancient maxim, that the commons alone can empower the king to levy the people's money, was applied to a private bill for lighting and cleansing a certain town, or cutting dikes in a fen, to local and limited assessments for local benefit (as to which the crown has no manner of interest, nor has any thing to do with the collection), there was more disposition shown to make encroachments than to guard against those of others. They began soon after the Revolution to introduce a still more extraordinary construction of their privilege, not receiving from the house of lords any bill which imposes a pecuniary penalty on offenders, nor permitting them to alter the application of such as had been imposed below.¹

These restrictions upon the other house of parliament, however, are now become, in their own estimation, the

---

¹ The principles laid down by Hatsell are: 1. That in bills of supply the lords can make no alteration but to correct verbal mistakes. 2. That in bills, not of absolute supply, yet imposing burthens, as turnpike acts, &c., the lords cannot alter the quantum of the toll, the persons to manage it, &c.; but in other clauses they may make amendments. 3. That where a charge may indirectly be thrown on the people by a bill, the commons object to the lords making amendments. 4. That the lords cannot impose pecuniary penalties in a bill, or alter those inserted by the commons. iii. 127. He seems to boast that the lords during the last century have very faintly opposed the claim of the commons. But surely they have sometimes done so in practice by returning a money-bill, or what the lower house call one, amended; and the commons have had recourse to the evasion of throwing out such bill, and bringing in another with the amendments inserted in it, which does not look very triumphant.

standing privileges of the commons. Several instances have occurred during the last century, though not, I believe, very lately, when bills, chiefly of a private nature, have been unanimously rejected, and even thrown over the table by the speaker, because they contained some provision in which the lords had trespassed upon these alleged rights." They are, as may be supposed, very differently regarded in the neighbouring chamber. The lords have never acknowledged any further privilege than that of originating bills of supply. But the good sense of both parties, and of an enlightened nation, who must witness and judge of their disputes, as well as the natural desire of the government to prevent in the outset any altercation that must impede the course of its measures, have rendered this little jealousy unproductive of those animosities which it seemed so happily contrived to excite. The one house, without admitting the alleged privilege, has generally been cautious not to give a pretext for eagerly asserting it; and the other, on the trifling occasions where it has seemed, perhaps unintentionally, to be infringed, has commonly resorted to the moderate course of passing a fresh bill to the same effect, after satisfying its dignity by rejecting the first.

It may not be improper to choose the present occasion for a summary view of the constitution of both houses of parliament under the lines of Tudor and Stuart. Of their earlier history the reader may find a brief and not, I believe, very incorrect account, in a work to which this is a kind of sequel. *State of the upper house under the Tudors and Stuarts.*

The number of temporal lords summoned by writ to the parliaments of the house of Plantagenet was exceedingly various; nor was anything more common in the fourteenth century than to omit those who had previously sat in person, and still more their descendants. They were rather less numerous, for this reason, under the line of Lancaster, when the practice of summoning those who were not hereditary peers did not so much prevail as in the pre- *Augmentation of the temporal lords.*

" The last instance mentioned by Hatsell is in 1790, when the lords had amended a bill for regulating Warwick gaol by changing the rate to be imposed from the landowners to the occupiers: iii. 131. I am not at present aware of any subsequent case, but rather suspect that such might be found.

ceding reigns. Fifty-three names, however, appear in the parliament of 1454, the last held before the commencement of the great contest between York and Lancaster. In this troublous period of above thirty years, if the whole reign of Edward IV. is to be included, the chiefs of many powerful families lost their lives in the field or on the scaffold, and their honours perished with them by attainder. New families, adherents of the victorious party, rose in their place; and sometimes an attainder was reversed by favour; so that the peers of Edward's reign were not much fewer than the number I have mentioned. Henry VII. summoned but twenty-nine to his first parliament, including some whose attainder had never been judicially reversed; a plain act of violence, like his previous usurpation of the crown. In his subsequent parliaments the peerage was increased by fresh creations, but never much exceeded forty. The greatest number summoned by Henry VIII. was fifty-one; which continued to be nearly the average in the two next reigns, and was very little augmented by Elizabeth. James, in his thoughtless profusion of favour, made so many new creations, that eighty-two peers sat in his first parliament, and ninety-six in his latest. From a similar facility in granting so cheap a reward of service, and in some measure perhaps from the policy of counteracting a spirit of opposition to the court, which many of the lords had begun to manifest, Charles called no less than one hundred and seventeen peers to the parliament of 1628, and one hundred and nineteen to that of November, 1640. Many of these honours were sold by both these princes; a disgraceful and dangerous practice, unheard of in earlier times, by which the princely peerage of England might have been gradually levelled with the herd of foreign nobility. This has, occasionally, though rarely, been suspected since the Restoration. In the parliament of 1661 we find one hundred and thirty-nine lords summoned.

The spiritual lords, who, though forming another estate in parliament, have always been so united with the temporality that the suffrages of both upon every question are told indistinctly and numerically, composed in general, before the Reformation, a majority of the upper house; though there was far more irregularity in the summonses of the mitred abbots and priors than those of the barons. But by the surrender and dissolution of the monasteries, about thirty-six votes of the clergy on an average were withdrawn from the parliament; a loss ill compensated to them by the creation of five new bishoprics. Thus, the number of the temporal peers being continually augmented, while that of the prelates was confined to twenty-six, the direct influence of the church on the legislature has become comparatively small; and that of the crown, which, by the pernicious system of translations and other means, is generally powerful with the episcopal bench, has, in this respect at least, undergone some diminution. It is easy to perceive from this view of the case that the destruction of the monasteries, as they then stood, was looked upon as an indispensable preliminary to the Reformation; no peaceable efforts towards which could have been effectual without altering the relative proportions of the spiritual and temporal aristocracy.

The house of lords, during this period of the sixteenth and seventeenth centuries, were not supine in rendering their collective and individual rights independent of the crown. It became a fundamental principle, according indeed to ancient authority, though not strictly observed in ruder times, that every peer of full age is entitled to his writ of summons at the beginning of a parliament, and that the house will not proceed on business if any one is denied it.[x] The privilege of voting by proxy, which was originally by special permission of the king, became absolute, though subject to such limitations as the house itself may impose. The writ of summons, which, as I have observed, had in earlier ages (if usage is to determine that which can rest on nothing but usage) given only a right of sitting in the parliament for which it issued, was held, about the end of Elizabeth's reign, by a construction founded on later usage, to convey an inheritable peerage, which was afterwards adjudged to descend upon heirs general,

[x] See the case of the earl of Arundel in parliament of 1626. In one instance the house took notice that a writ of summons had been issued to the earl of Mulgrave, he being under age, and addressed the king that he would be pleased to be sparing of writs of this nature for the future. 20th Oct. 1667. The king made an excuse that he did not know the earl was much under age, and would be careful for the future. 29th Oct.

female as well as male; an extension which sometimes raises intricate questions of descent, and, though no materially bad consequences have flowed from it, is perhaps one of the blemishes in the constitution of parliament. Doubts whether a peerage could be surrendered to the king, and whether a territorial honour, of which hardly any remain, could be alienated along with the land on which it depended, were determined in the manner most favourable to the dignity of the aristocracy. They obtained also an important privilege; first of recording their dissent in the journals of the house, and afterwards of inserting the grounds of it. Instances of the former occur not unfrequently at the period of the Reformation: but the latter practice was little known before the long parliament. A right that Cato or Phocion would have prized, though it may sometimes have been frivolously or factiously exercised!

State of the commons. The house of commons, from the earliest records of its regular existence in the 23rd year of Edward I., consisted of seventy-four knights, or representatives from all the counties of England, except Chester, Durham, and Monmouth, and of a varying number of deputies from the cities and boroughs; sometimes, in the earliest period of representation, amounting to as many as two hundred and sixty; sometimes, by the negligence or partiality of the sheriffs in omitting places that had formerly returned members, to not more than two thirds of that number. New boroughs, however, as being grown into importance, or from some private motive, acquired the franchise of election; and at the accession of Henry VIII. we find two hundred and twenty-four citizens and burgesses from one hundred and eleven towns (London sending four), none of which have since intermitted their privilege.

Increase of their members.

Question as to rights of election.

I must so far concur with those whose general principles as to the theory of parliamentary reform leave me far behind, as to profess my opinion that the change which appears to have taken place in the English government towards the end of the thirteenth century was founded upon the maxim that all who possessed landed or moveable property ought, as freemen, to be bound by no laws, and especially by no taxation, to which they had not consented through their representatives. If we look at the constituents of a house of commons under Edward I. or Edward III., and consider the state of landed tenures and of commerce at that period, we shall perceive that, excepting women, who have generally been supposed capable of no political right but that of reigning, almost every one who contributed towards the tenths and fifteenths granted by the parliament might have exercised the franchise of voting for those who sat in it. Were we even to admit that in corporate boroughs the franchise may have been usually vested in the freemen rather than the inhabitants, yet this distinction, so important in later ages, was of little consequence at a time when all traders, that is, all who possessed any moveable property worth assessing, belonged to the former class. I do not pretend that no one was contributory to a subsidy who did not possess a vote, but that the far greater portion was levied on those who, as freeholders or burgesses, were reckoned in law to have been consenting to its imposition. It would be difficult probably to name any town of the least consideration in the fourteenth and fifteenth centuries which did not, at some time or other, return members to parliament. This is so much the case that if, in running our eyes along the map, we find any seaport, as Sunderland or Falmouth, or any inland town, as Leeds or Birmingham, which has never enjoyed the elective franchise, we may conclude at once that it has emerged from obscurity since the reign of Henry VIII.[y]

Though scarce any considerable town, probably, was intentionally left out, except by the sheriffs' partiality, it is not to be supposed that all boroughs that made returns were considerable. Several that are currently said to be decayed were never much better than at present. Some of these were the ancient demesne of the crown; the tenants of which, not being suitors to the county courts, nor voting in the election of knights for the shire, were, still on the same principle of consent to public burthens, called upon to send their own representatives. Others received the privilege along with

[y] Though the proposition in the text is, I believe, generally true, it has occurred to me since that there are some exceptions in the northern parts of England; and that both Sheffield and Manchester are among them.

their charter of incorporation, in the hope that they would thrive more than proved to be the event; and possibly, even in such early times, the idea of obtaining influence in the commons through the votes of their burgesses might sometimes suggest itself.

That, amidst all this care to secure the positive right of representation, so little provision should have been made as to its relative efficiency, that the high-born and opulent gentry should have been so vastly outnumbered by peddling traders, that the same number of two should have been deemed sufficient for the counties of York and Rutland, for Bristol and Gatton, are facts more easy to wonder at than to explain; for though the total ignorance of the government as to the relative population might be perhaps a sufficient reason for not making an attempt at equalization, yet, if the representation had been founded on anything like a numerical principle, there would have been no difficulty in reducing it to the proportion furnished by the books of subsidy for each county and borough, or at least in a rude approximation towards a more rational distribution.

Henry VIII. gave a remarkable proof that no part of the kingdom, subject to the English laws and parliamentary burthens, ought to want its representation, by extending the right of election to the whole of Wales, the counties of Chester and Monmouth, and even the towns of Berwick and Calais. It might be possible to trace the reason why the county of Durham was passed over. The attachment of those northern parts to popery seems as likely as any other. Thirty-three were thus added to the commons. Edward VI. created fourteen boroughs, and restored ten that had disused their privilege. Mary added twenty one, Elizabeth sixty, and James twenty-seven members.

These accessions to the popular chamber of parliament after the reign of Henry VIII. were by no means derived from a popular principle, such as had influenced its earlier constitution. We may account perhaps on this ground for the writs addressed to a very few towns, such as Westminster. But the design of that great influx of new members from petty boroughs, which began in the short reigns of Edward and Mary, and continued under Elizabeth, must have been to secure the authority of government, especially in the successive revolutions of religion. Five towns only in Cornwall made returns at the accession of Edward VI.; twenty-one at the death of Elizabeth. It will not be pretended that the wretched villages, which corruption and perjury still hardly keep from famine, were seats of commerce and industry in the sixteenth century. But the county of Cornwall was more immediately subject to a coercive influence, through the indefinite and oppressive jurisdiction of the stannary court. Similar motives, if we could discover the secrets of those governments, doubtless operated in most other cases. A slight difficulty seems to have been raised in 1563 about the introduction of representatives from eight new boroughs at once by charters from the crown, but was soon waived with the complaisance usual in those times. Many of the towns which had abandoned their privilege at a time when they were compelled to the payment of daily wages to their members during the session, were now desirous of recovering it when that burthen had ceased and the franchise had become valuable. And the house, out of favour to popular rights, laid it down in the reign of James I. as a principle, that every town which has at any time returned members to parliament is entitled to a writ as a matter of course. The speaker accordingly issued writs to Hertford, Pomfret, Ilchester, and some other places, on their petition. The restorations of boroughs in this manner, down to 1641, are fifteen in number. But though the doctrine that an elective right cannot be lost by disuse is still current in parliament, none of the very numerous boroughs which have ceased to enjoy that franchise since the days of the three first Edwards have from the Restoration downwards made any attempt at retrieving it; nor is it by any means likely that they would be successful in the application. Charles I., whose temper inspired him rather with a systematic abhorrence of parliaments than with any notion of managing them by influence, created no new boroughs. The right indeed would certainly have been disputed, however frequently exercised. In 1673 the county and city of Durham, which had strangely been unrepresented to so late an era, were raised by act of parliament to the privileges of their fellow-subjects.* About the same time a charter was granted to the town of Newark, enabling it to return two burgesses. It passed with some little objection at the time; but four years afterwards, after two debates, it was carried on the question, by 125 to 73, that, by virtue of the charter granted to the town of Newark, it hath right to send burgesses to serve in parliament." Notwithstanding this apparent recognition of the king's prerogative to summon burgesses from a town not previously represented, no later instance of its exercise has occurred; and it would unquestionably have been resisted by the commons, not, as is vulgarly supposed, because the act of union with Scotland has limited the English members to 513 (which is not the case), but upon the broad maxims of exclusive privilege in matters relating to their own body, which the house was become powerful enough to assert against the crown.

It is doubtless a problem of no inconsiderable difficulty to determine with perfect exactness by what class of persons the elective franchise in ancient boroughs was ori-

Four different theories as to the original principle. ginally possessed; yet not perhaps so much so as the carelessness of some, and the artifices of others, have caused it to appear. The different opinions on this controverted question may be reduced to the four following theses: — 1. The original right, as enjoyed by boroughs represented in the parliaments of Edward I., and all of later creation, where one of a different nature has not been expressed in the charter from which they derive the privilege, was in the inhabitant householders resident in the borough, and paying scot and lot; under those words including local rates, and probably general taxes. 2. The right sprang from the tenure of certain freehold lands or burgages within the borough, and did not belong to any but such tenants. 3. It was derived from charters of incorporation, and belonged to the community or freemen of the corporate body. 4. It did not extend to the generality of freemen, but was limited to the governing part or municipal magistracy. The actual right of election, as fixed by determinations of the house of commons before

---

* 25 Car. 2, c. 9. A bill had passed the commons in 1624 for the same effect, but failed through the dissolution.

ª Journals, 26th Feb. and 25th March, 1676-7.

1772, and by committees under the Grenville Act since, is variously grounded upon some of these four principal rules, each of which has been subject to subordinate modifications which produce still more complication and irregularity.

Of these propositions the first was laid down by a celebrated committee of the house of commons in 1624, the chairman whereof was serjeant Glanville, and the members, as appears by the list in the Journals, the most eminent men, in respect of legal and constitutional knowledge, that were ever united in such a body. It is called by them the common-law right, and that which ought always to obtain where prescriptive usage to the contrary cannot be shown. But it has met with very little favour from the house of commons since the Restoration. The second has the authority of lord Holt in the case of Ashby and White, and of some other lawyers who have turned their attention to the subject. It countenances what is called the right of burgage tenure; the electors in boroughs of this description being such as hold burgages or ancient tenements within the borough. The next theory, which attaches the primary franchise to the freemen of corporations, has on the whole been most received in modern times, if we look either at the decisions of the proper tribunal, or the current doctrine of lawyers. The last proposition is that of Dr. Brady, who, in a treatise of boroughs, written to serve the purposes of James II., though not published till after the Revolution, endeavoured to settle all elective rights on the narrowest and least popular basis. This work gained some credit, which its perspicuity and acuteness would deserve, if these were not disgraced by a perverse sophistry and suppression of truth.

Their probability considered.

It does not appear at all probable that such varying and indefinite usages as we find in our present representation of boroughs could have begun simultaneously, when they were first called to parliament by Edward I. and his two next descendants. There would have been what may be fairly called a common-law right, even were we to admit that some variation from it may, at the very commencement, have occurred in particular places. The earliest writ of summons directed the sheriff to make a return from every borough within his jurisdiction, without any limitation to such as had obtained charters, or any rule as to the electoral body. Charters, in fact, incorporating towns seem to have been by no means common in the thirteenth and fourteenth centuries; and though they grew more frequent afterwards, yet the first that gave expressly a right of returning members to parliament was that of Wenlock, under Edward IV. These charters, it has been contended, were incorporations of the inhabitants, and gave no power either to exclude any of them, or to admit non-resident strangers, according to the practice of later ages. But, however this may be, it is highly probable that the word burgess (burgensis), long before the elective franchise or the character of a corporation existed, meant literally the free inhabitant householder of a borough, a member of its court-leet, and subject to its jurisdiction. We may, I believe, reject with confidence what I have reckoned as the third proposition; namely, that the elective franchise belonged, as of common right, to the freemen of corporations; and still more that of Brady, which few would be found to support at the present day.

There can, I should conceive, be little pretence for affecting to doubt that the burgesses of Domesday-book, of the various early records cited by Madox and others, and of the writs of summons to Edward's parliament, were inhabitants of tenements within the borough. But it may remain to be proved that any were entitled to the privileges or rank of burgesses who held less than an estate of freehold in their possessions. The burgage tenure, of which we read in Littleton, was evidently freehold; and it might be doubtful whether the lessees of dwellings for a term of years, whose interest, in contemplation of law, is far inferior to a freehold, were looked upon as sufficiently domiciled within the borough to obtain the appellation of burgesses. It appears from Domesday that the burgesses, long before any incorporation, held lands in common belonging to their town; they had also their guild or market-house, and were entitled in some places to tolls and customs. These permanent rights seem naturally restrained to those who possessed an absolute property in the soil. There can surely be no question as to mere tenants at will, liable to be removed from their occupation at the pleasure of the lord; and it is perhaps unnecessary to mention that the tenancy from year to year, so usual at present, is of very recent introduction. As to estates for a term of years, even of considerable duration, they were probably not uncommon in the time of Edward I.; yet far outnumbered, as I should conceive, by those of a freehold nature. Whether these lessees were contributory to the ancient local burthens of scot and lot, as well as to the tallages exacted by the king, and tenths afterwards imposed by parliament in respect of moveable estate, it seems not easy to determine; but if they were so, as appears more probable, it was not only consonant to the principle that no freeman should be liable to taxation without the consent of his representatives, to give them a share in the general privilege of the borough, but it may be inferred with sufficient evidence from several records that the privilege and the burthen were absolutely commensurate; men having been specially discharged from contributing to tallages because they did not participate in the liberties of the borough, and others being expressly declared subject to those impositions as the condition of their being admitted to the rights of burgesses.[b] It might however be conjectured that a difference of usage between those boroughs where the ancient exclusive rights of burgage tenants were maintained, and those where the equitable claim of taxable inhabitants possessing only a chattel interest received attention, might ultimately produce those very opposite species of franchise which we find in the scot and lot borough, and in those of burgage-tenure. If the franchise, as we now denominate it, passed in the thirteenth century for a burthen, subjecting the elector to bear his part in the payment of wages to the representative, the above conjecture will be equally applicable, by changing the words right and claim into liability.[c]

[b] Madox Firma, Burgi, p. 270, et post.
[c] The popular character of the elective franchise in early times has been maintained by two writers of considerable research and ability; Mr. Luders, Reports of Election Cases, and Mr. Merewether, in his Sketch of the History of Boroughs and Report of the West Looe Case. The former writer has the following observations, vol. l. p. 99:—" The ancient history of boroughs does not confirm the opinion above referred to, which lord chief justice Holt delivered in the case of Ashby v. White: viz. that in-

It was according to the natural course of things that the mayors or bailiffs, as returning officers, with some of the principal burgesses (especially where incorporating charters had given them a pre-eminence), would take to themselves the advantage of serving a courtier or neighbouring gentleman, by returning him to parliament, and virtually exclude the general class of electors, indifferent to public matters, and without a suspicion that their individual suffrages could ever be worth purchase. It is certain that a seat in the commons was an object of ambition in the time of Edward IV., and I have little doubt that it was so in many instances much sooner. But there existed not the means of that splendid corruption which has emulated the Crassi and Luculli of Rome. Even so late as 1571, Thomas Long, a member for Westbury, confessed that he had given four pounds to the mayor and another person for his return. The elections were thus generally managed, not often perhaps by absolute bribery, but through the influence of the government and of the neighbouring aristocracy; and while the freemen of the corporation, or resident householders, were frequently permitted, for the sake of form, to concur in the election, there were many places where the smaller part of the municipal body, by whatever names distinguished, acquired a sort of prescriptive right through an usage, of which it was too late to show the commencement.[d]

habitants not incorporated cannot send members to parliament but by prescription. For there is good reason to believe that the elections in boroughs were in the beginning of representation popular; yet in the reign of Edward I. there were not perhaps thirty corporations in the kingdom. Who then elected the members of boroughs not incorporated? Plainly, the inhabitants or burghers [according to their tenure or situation]; for at that time every inhabitant of a borough was called a burgess; and Hobart refers to this usage in support of his opinion in the case of Dungannon. The manner in which they exercised this right was the same as that in which the inhabitants of a town, at this day, hold a right of common, or other such privilege, which many possess who are not incorporated." The words in brackets, which are not in the printed edition, are inserted by the author himself in a copy bequeathed to the Inner Temple library. The remainder of Mr. Luders's note, though too long for this place, is very good, and successfully repels the *corporate* theory.

d The following passage from Vowell's treatise on the order of the parliament, published in 1571, and reprinted in Hollingshed's Chronicles of Ireland (vi. 315), seems to indicate that, at least in practice, the election was in the principal or governing body of the corporation. " The sheriff of every county, having received his writ, ought forthwith to send his precepts and summons to the mayors, bailiffs, and head officers of every city, town corporate, borough, and such places as have been accustomed to send burgesses within his county, that they do choose and elect among themselves two

It was perceived, however, by the assertors of the popular cause under James I., that, by this narrowing of the electoral franchise, many boroughs were subjected to the influence of the privy council, which, by restoring the householders to their legitimate rights, would strengthen the interests of the country. Hence lord Coke lays it down in his Fourth Institute, that, "if the king newly incorporate an ancient borough which before sent burgesses to parliament, and granteth that certain selected burgesses shall make election of the burgesses of parliament, where all the burgesses elected before, this charter taketh not away the election of the other burgesses. And so, if a city or borough hath power to make ordinances, they cannot make an ordinance that a less number shall elect burgesses for the parliament than made the election before; for free elections of members of the high court of parliament are pro bono publico, and not to be compared to other cases of election of mayors, bailiffs, &c., of corporations."* He adds, however, "by original grant or by custom, a selected number of burgesses may elect and bind the residue." This restriction was admitted by the committee over which Glanville presided in

citizens for every city, and two burgesses for every borough, according to their old custom and usage. And these head officers ought then to assemble themselves, and the aldermen and common council of every city or town; and to make choice among themselves of two able and sufficient men of every city or town, to serve for and in the said parliament."

Now, if these expressions are accurate, it certainly seems that at this period the great body of freemen or inhabitants were not partakers in the exercise of their franchise. And the following passage, if the reader will turn to it, wherein Vowell adverts to the form of a county election, is so differently worded in respect to the election by the freeholders at large, that we may fairly put a literal construction upon the former. In point of fact, I have little doubt that elections in boroughs were for the most part very closely managed in the sixteenth century, and probably much earlier. This, however, will not by any means decide the question of right. For we know that in the reigns of Henry IV. and Henry V.

returns for the great county of York were made by the proxies of a few peers and a few knights; and there is a still more anomalous case in the reign of Elizabeth, when a lady Packington sealed the indenture for the county of Worcester. Carew's Hist. of Elections, part ii. p. 242. But no one would pretend that the right of election was in these persons, or supposed by any human being to be so.

The difficulty to be got over by those who defend the modern decisions of committees is this. We know that in the reign of Edward I. more than one hundred boroughs made returns to the writ. If most of these were not incorporated, nor had any aldermen, capital burgesses, and so forth, by whom were the elections made? Surely by the freeholders, or by the inhabitants. And if they were so made in the reign of Edward I., how has the franchise been restrained afterwards?

* 4 Inst. 48. Glanville, p. 53, 66. That no private agreement or by-law of the borough can restrain the right of election, is laid down in the same book p. 17.

1624.[f] But both they and lord Coke believed the representation of boroughs to be from a date before what is called legal memory, that is, the accession of Richard I. It is not easy to reconcile their principle, that an elective right once subsisting could not be limited by anything short of immemorial prescription, with some of their own determinations, and still less with those which have subsequently occurred, in favour of a restrained right of suffrage. There seems, on the whole, great reason to be of opinion that, where a borough is so ancient as to have sent members to parliament before any charter of incorporation proved or reasonably presumed to have been granted, or where the word burgensis is used without anything to restrain its meaning in an ancient charter, the right of election ought to have been acknowledged either in the resident householders paying general and local taxes, or in such of them as possessed an estate of freehold within the borough. And whatever may have been the primary meaning of the word burgess, it appears consonant to the popular spirit of the English constitution that, after the possessors of leasehold interest became so numerous and opulent as to bear a very large share in the public burthens, they should have enjoyed commensurate privileges; and that the resolution of Mr. Glanville's committee in favour of what they called the common-law right should have been far more uniformly received, and more consistently acted upon, not merely as agreeable to modern theories of liberty, from which some have intimated it to have sprung, but as grounded on the primitive spirit and intention of the law of parliament.

In the reign of Charles II. the house of commons seems to have become less favourable to this species of franchise. But after the Revolution, when the struggle of parties was renewed every three years throughout the kingdom, the right of election came more continually into question, and was treated with the grossest partiality by the house, as subordinate to the main interests of the rival factions. Contrary determinations for the sole purpose of serving these interests, as each grew in its turn more powerful, frequently occurred; and at this time the ancient right of resident householders seems to

[f] Glanville's case of Bletchingly, p. 33

have grown into disrepute, and given way to that of corporations, sometimes at large, sometimes only in a limited and very small number.[g] A slight check was imposed on this scandalous and systematic injustice by the act 2 G. II., c. 2, which renders the last determination of the house of commons conclusive as to the right of election.[h] But this enactment confirmed many decisions that cannot be reconciled with any sensible rule. The same iniquity continued to prevail in cases beyond its pale; the fall of sir Robert Walpole from power was reckoned to be settled when there appeared a small majority against him on the right of election at Chippenham, a question not very logically connected with the merits of his administration; and the house would to this day have gone on trampling on the franchises of their constituents, if a statute had not been passed through the authority and eloquence of Mr. Grenville, which has justly been known by his name. I shall not enumerate the particular provisions of this excellent law, which, in point of time, does not fall within the period of my present work; it is generally acknowledged that, by transferring the judicature, in all cases of controverted elections, from the house to a sworn committee of fifteen members, the reproach of partiality has been a good deal lightened, though not perhaps effaced.[i]

[g] [I incline to suspect that it would be found on research that, in a plurality of instances, the tories favoured the right of residents, either householders or burgage tenants, to the exclusion of freemen, who, being in a great measure outvoters, were less likely to be influenced by the neighbouring gentry. In 1694 a bill was brought in to disfranchise the borough of Stockbridge for bribery. But the burgesses petitioned against it, declaring themselves resolved for the future, in all difficult cases, to consult the gentlemen of the county. Journals, 7th Feb. They by no means kept their word in the next century; no place having been more notoriously venal. The bill was thrown out by a small majority; but the whigs seem to have supported it, as far as we can judge by the tellers. Id. March 30.—1848].

[h] This clause, in an act imposing severe penalties on bribery, was inserted by the house of lords with the insidious design of causing the rejection of the whole bill; if the commons, as might be expected, should resent such an interference with their privileges. The ministry accordingly endeavoured to excite this sentiment; but those who had introduced the bill very wisely thought it better to sacrifice a point of dignity rather than lose so important a statute. It was, however, only carried by two voices to agree with the amendment. Parl. Hist. viii. 754.

[i] These pages were first published in 1827. The Reform bill of 1832 has of course rendered a disquisition on the ancient rights of election in boroughs a matter of merely historical interest.

CHAPTER XIV.

THE REIGN OF JAMES II.

Designs of the King — Parliament of 1685 — King's Intention to repeal the Test Act — Deceived as to the Dispositions of his Subjects — Prorogation of Parliament — Dispensing Power confirmed by the Judges — Ecclesiastical Commission — King's Scheme of establishing Popery — Dismissal of Lord Rochester — Prince of Orange alarmed — Plan of setting the Princess aside — Rejected by the King — Overtures of the Malecontents to Prince of Orange — Declaration for Liberty of Conscience — Addresses in favour of it — New Modelling of the Corporations — Affair of Magdalen College — Infatuation of the King — His Coldness towards Louis - Invitation signed to the Prince of Orange — Birth of Prince of Wales — Justice and Necessity of the Revolution — Favourable Circumstances attending it — Its Salutary Consequences — Proceedings of the Convention — Ended by the Elevation of William and Mary to the Throne.

THE great question that has been brought forward at the end of the last chapter, concerning the right and usage of election in boroughs, was perhaps of less practical importance in the reign of Charles II. than we might at first imagine, or than it might become in the present age. Whoever might be the legal electors, it is undoubted that a great preponderance was virtually lodged in the select body of corporations. It was the knowledge of this that produced the corporation act soon after the Restoration, to exclude the presbyterians, and the more violent measures of quo warranto at the end of Charles's reign. If by placing creatures of the court in municipal offices, or by intimidating the former corporators through apprehensions of forfeiting their common property and lucrative privileges, what was called a loyal parliament could be procured, the business of government, both as to supply and enactment or repeal of laws, would be carried on far more smoothly and with less scandal than by their entire disuse. Few of those who assumed the name of tories were prepared to sacrifice the ancient fundamental forms of the constitution. They thought it equally necessary that a parliament should exist, and that it should have no will of its own, or none, at least, except for the preservation of that ascendancy of the established religion which even their loyalty would not consent to surrender.

It is not easy to determine whether James II. had resolved to complete his schemes of arbitrary government by setting aside even the nominal concurrence of the two houses of parliament in legislative enactments, and especially in levying money on his subjects. Lord Halifax had given him much offence towards the close of the late reign, and was considered from thenceforth as a man unfit to be employed, because in the cabinet, on a question whether the people of New England should be ruled in future by an assembly or by the absolute pleasure of the crown, he had spoken very freely against unlimited monarchy.[a] James, indeed, could hardly avoid perceiving that the constant acquiescence of an English house of commons in the measures proposed to it, a respectful abstinence from all intermeddling with the administration of affairs, could never be relied upon or obtained at all, without much of that dexterous management and influence which he thought it both unworthy and impolitic to exert. It seems clearly that he had determined on trying their obedience merely as an experiment, and by no means to put his authority in any manner within their control. Hence he took the bold step of issuing a proclamation for the payment of customs, which by law expired at the late king's death;[b]

---

[a] Fox, Appendix, p. 8.

[b] "The legal method," says Burnet, "was to have made entries, and to have taken bonds for those duties to be paid when the parliament should meet and renew the grant." Mr. Onslow remarks on this, that he should have said, the least illegal and the only justifiable method. To which the Oxford editor subjoins that it was the proposal of lord-keeper North, while the other, which was adopted, was suggested by Jefferies. This is a mistake. North's proposal was to collect the duties under the proclamation, but to keep them apart from the other revenues in the exchequer until the next session of parliament. There was surely little difference in point of illegality between this and the course adopted. It was alleged that the merchants, who had paid duty, would be injured by a temporary importation duty free; and certainly it was inconvenient to make the revenue dependent on such a contingency as the demise of the crown. But this neither justifies the proclamation nor the disgraceful acquiescence of the next parliament in it.

The king was thanked in several addresses for directing the customs to be levied, particularly in one from the benchers and barristers of the Middle Temple. London Gazette, March 11. This was drawn by sir Bartholomew Shower, and presented by sir Humphrey Mackworth. Life of James, vol. ii. p. 17. The former was active as a lawyer in all the worst measures of these two reigns. Yet, after the Revolution, they both became tory patriots and jealous assertors of freedom against the government of William III. Barillon, however, takes notice that this illegal continuance of the revenue produced much discontent.

and Barillon mentions several times that he was resolved to continue in the possession of the revenue, whether the parliament should grant it or no. He was equally decided not to accept it for a limited time. This, as his principal ministers told the ambassador, would be to establish the necessity of convoking parliament from time to time, and thus to change the form of government by rendering the king dependent upon it; rather than which it would be better to come at once to the extremity of a dissolution, and maintain the possession of the late king's revenues by open force.[c] But the extraordinary conduct of this house of commons, so unlike any that had met in England for the last century, rendered any exertion of violence on this score quite unnecessary.

Parliament of 1685. The behaviour of that unhonoured parliament which held its two short sessions in 1685, though in a great measure owing to the fickleness of the public mind and rapid ascendancy of tory principles during the late years, as well as to a knowledge of the king's severe and vindictive temper, seems to confirm the assertion strongly made at the time within its walls, that many of the members had been unduly returned.[d] The notorious facts, indeed, as to the forfeiture of corporations throughout the kingdom, and their re-grant under such restrictions as might serve the purpose of the crown, stand in need of no confirmation. Those who look at the debates and votes of this assembly, their large grant of a permanent revenue to the annual amount of two millions, rendering a frugal prince, in time of peace, entirely out of all dependence on his people; their timid departure from a resolution taken to address the king on the only matter for which they were really solicitous, the enforcement of the penal laws, on a suggestion of his displeasure;[e] their bill en-

---

Fox's Appendix, 39. And Rochester told him that North and Halifax would have urged the king to call a parliament, in order to settle the revenue on a lawful basis, if that resolution had not been taken by himself. Id. p. 20. The king thought it necessary to apologise to Barillon for convoking parliament. Id. p. 18. Dalrymple, p. 100.

[c] Dalrymple, p. 142. The king alludes to this possibility of a limited grant with much resentment and threatening, in his speech on opening the session.

[d] Fox, Appendix, p. 93; Lonsdale, p. 5; Ralph, 860; Evelyn, i. 561.

[e] For this curious piece of parliamentary inconsistency, see Reresby's Memoirs, p. 113; and Barillon, in the Appendix to Fox, p. 95. "Il s'est passé avant hier une chose de grande conséquence dans la chambre basse: Il fut proposé le matin que la chambre se met-

titled 'For the preservation of his majesty's person, full of dangerous innovations in the law of treason, especially one most unconstitutional clause, that any one moving in either house of parliament to change the descent of the crown should incur the penalties of that offence;' their supply of 700,000*l*., after the suppression of Monmouth's rebellion, for the support of a standing army;⁵ will be inclined to believe that, had James been as zealous for the church of England as his father, he would have succeeded in establishing a power so nearly despotic, that neither the privileges of parliament, nor much less those of private men, would have stood in his way. The prejudice which the two last Stuarts had acquired in favour of the Roman religion, so often deplored by thoughtless or insidious writers as one of the worst consequences of their father's ill fortune, is to be accounted rather among the most signal links in the chain of causes through which a gracious Provi-

---

toit en comité l'après dîner pour considérer la harangue du roy sur l'affaire de la religion, et savoir ce qui devoit être entendu par le terme *de religion protestante*. La résolution fut prise unanimement, et sans contradiction, de faire une adresse au roy pour le prier de faire une proclamation pour l'exécution des loix contre tous les non-conformistes généralement, c'est-à-dire, contre tous ceux qui ne sont pas ouvertement de l'église Anglicane; cela enferme les presbytériens et tous les sectaires, aussi bien que les catholiques Romains. La malice de cette résolution fut aussitôt reconnu du roy d'Angleterre, et de ses ministres; les principaux de la chambre basse furent mandés, et ceux que sa majesté Britannique croit être dans ses intérêts; il leur fit une réprimande sévère de s'être laissés séduire et entraîner à une résolution si dangereuse et si peu admissible. Il leur déclara que, si l'on persistoit à lui faire une pareille adresse, il répondroit à la chambre basse en termes si décisifs et si fermes qu'on ne retourneroit pas à lui faire une pareille adresse. La manière dont sa majesté Britannique s'explique produisit son effet hier matin; et la chambre basse rejeta tout d'une voix ce qui avoit été résolu en comité le jour auparavant."

The only man who behaved with distinguished spirit in this wretched parliament was one in whose political life there is little else to praise, sir Edward Seymour. He opposed the grant of the revenues for life, and spoke strongly against the illegal practices in the elections. Fox, 90, 93.

f Fox, Appendix, p. 156. " Provided always, and be it further enacted, that if any peer of this realm, or member of the house of commons, shall move or propose in either house of parliament the disherison of the rightful and true heir of the crown, or to alter or change the descent or succession of the crown in the right line, such offence shall be deemed and adjudged high treason, and every person being indicted and convicted of such treason shall be proceeded against, and shall suffer and forfeit as in other cases of high treason mentioned in this act."
See what lord Lonsdale says, p. 8 of this bill, which he, among others, contrived to weaken by provisoes, so that it was given up.

⁵ Parl. Hist. 1372. The king's speech had evidently shown that the supply was only demanded for this purpose. The speaker, on presenting the bill for settling the revenue in the former session, claimed it as a merit that they had not inserted any appropriating clauses. Parl. Hist. 1359.

dence has favoured the consolidation of our liberties and welfare. Nothing less than a motive more universally operating than the interests of civil freedom would have stayed the compliant spirit of this unworthy parliament, or rallied, for a time at least, the supporters of indefinite prerogative under a banner they abhorred. We know that the king's intention was to obtain the repeal of the habeas corpus act, a law which he reckoned as destructive of monarchy as the test was of the catholic religion.[h] And I see no reason to suppose that he would have failed of this, had he not given alarm to his high-church parliament by a premature manifestation of his design to fill the civil and military employments with the professors of his own mode of faith.

King's intention to repeal the habeas corpus act.

It has been doubted by Mr. Fox whether James had, in this part of his reign, conceived the projects commonly imputed to him, of overthrowing, or injuring by any direct acts of power, the protestant establishment of this kingdom. Neither the copious extracts from Barillon's correspondence with his own court, published by sir John Dalrymple and himself, nor the king's own memoirs, seem, in his opinion, to warrant a conclusion that anything farther was intended than to emancipate the Roman catholics from the severe restrictions of the penal laws, securing the public exercise of their worship from molestation, and to replace them upon an equality as to civil offices by abrogating the test act of the late reign.[i] We find nevertheless a remarkable conversation of the king himself with the French ambassador, which leaves an impression on the mind that his projects were already irreconcilable with that pledge of

[h] Reresby, p. 110. Barillon, in Fox's Appendix, p. 93, 127, &c. " Le feu roi d'Angleterre et celui-ci m'ont souvent dit, qu'un gouvernement ne peut subsister avec une telle loi." Dalrymple, p. 171.

[i] This opinion has been well supported by Mr. serjeant Heywood (Vindication of Mr. Fox's History, p. 154). In some few of Barillon's letters to the king of France he speaks of James's intention établir la religion catholique; but these perhaps might be explained by a far greater number of passages, where he says only établir le libre exercice de la religion catholique, and by the general tenor of his correspondence. But though the primary object was toleration, I have no doubt but that they conceived this was to end in establishment. See what Barillon says, p. 84; though the legal reasoning is false, as might be expected from a foreigner. It must at all events be admitted that the conduct of the king, after the formation of the catholic junto in 1686, demonstrates an intention of overthrowing the Anglican establishment.

support he had rather unadvisedly given to the Anglican church at his accession. This interpretation of his language is confirmed by the expressions used at the same time by Sunderland, which are more unequivocal, and point at the complete establishment of the catholic religion.[k] The particular care displayed by James in this conversation, and indeed in so many notorious in-

[k] " Il [le roy] me répondit à ce que je venois de dire, que je connoissois le fond de ses intentions pour l'établissement de la religion catholique; qu'il n'esperoit en venir à bout que par l'assistance de V. M.; que je voyois qu'il venoit de donner des emplois dans ses troupes aux catholiques aussi bien qu'aux protestans; que cette égalité fâchoit beaucoup de gens, mais qu'il n'avoit pas laissé passer une occasion si importante sans s'en prévaloir; qu'il feroit de même à l'égard des choses praticables; et que je voyois plus clair sur cela dans ses desseins que ses propres ministres, s'en étant souvent ouvert avec moi sans reserve." P. 104. In a second conversation immediately afterwards the king repeated, " que je connoissois le fond de ses desseins, et que je pouvois répondre que tout son but étoit d'établir la religion catholique; qu'il ne perdroit aucune occasion de la faire . . . que peu à peu il va à son but; et que ce qu'il fait présentement emporte nécessairement l'exercice libre de la religion catholique, qui se trouvera établi avant qu'un acte de parlement l'autorise; que je connoissois assez l'Angleterre pour savoir que la possibilité d'avoir des emplois et des charges fera plus de catholiques que la permission de dire des messes publiques; que cependant il s'attendoit que V. M. ne l'abandonneroit pas," &c. P. 106. Sunderland entered on the same subject, saying, " Je ne sais pas si l'on voit en France les choses comme elles sont ici; mais je défie ceux qui les voyent de près de ne pas connoître que le roy mon maitre n'a rien dans le cœur si avant que l'envie d'établir la religion catholique; qu'il ne peut même, selon le bon sens et la droite raison, avoir d'autre but; que sans cela il ne sera jamais en sûreté, et sera toujours exposé au zèle indiscret de ceux qui échaufferont les peuples contre la catholicité, tant qu'elle ne sera pas plus pleinement établie. Il y a un autre chose certaine, c'est que ce plan là ne peut réussir que par un concert et une liaison étroite avec le roi votre maitre; c'est un projet qui ne peut convenir qu'à lui, ni réussir que par lui. Toutes les autres puissances s'y opposeront ouvertement, ou le traverseront sons main. On sait bien que cela ne convient point au prince d'Orange; mais il ne sera pas en état de l'empêcher si on veut se conduire en France comme il est nécessaire, c'est-à-dire ménager l'amitié du roy d'Angleterre, et le contenir dans son projet. Je vois clairement l'appréhension que beaucoup de gens ont d'une liaison avec la France, et les efforts qu'on fait pour l'affoiblir; mais cela ne sera au pouvoir de personne, si on n'en a pas envie de France; c'est sur quoi il faut que vous vous expliquiez nettement, que vous fassiez connoître que le roi votre maitre veut aider de bonne foi le roi d'Angleterre à établir fermement la religion catholique."

The word *plus* in the above passage is not in Dalrymple's extract from this letter, vol. ii. part ii. p. 174, 187. Yet for omitting this word serjeant Heywood (not having attended to Dalrymple) censures Mr. Rose as if it had been done purposely. Vindic. of Fox, p. 154. But this is not quite judicious or equitable, since another critic might suggest that it was purposely interpolated. No one of common candour would suspect this of Mr. Fox; but his copyist, I presume, was not infallible. The word *plus* is evidently incorrect. The catholic religion was not established at all in any positive sense; what room could there be for the comparative? M. Mazure, who has more lately perused the letters of Barillon at Paris, prints the passage without *plus*. Hist. de la Révol. ii. 36. Certainly the whole conversation here ascribed to Sunderland points at something far beyond the free exercise of the Roman catholic religion.

stances, to place the army, as far as possible, in the command of catholic officers, has very much the appearance of his looking towards the employment of force in overthrowing the protestant church, as well as the civil privileges of his subjects. Yet he probably entertained confident hopes, in the outset of his reign, that he might not be driven to this necessity, or at least should only have occasion to restrain a fanatical populace. He would rely on the intrinsic excellence of his own religion, and still more on the temptations that his favour would hold out. For the repeal of the test would not have placed the two religions on a fair level. Catholics, however little qualified, would have filled, as in fact they did under the dispensing power, most of the principal stations in the court, law, and army. The king told Barillon he was well enough acquainted with England to be assured that the admissibility to office would make more catholics than the right of saying mass publicly. There was, on the one hand, a prevailing laxity of principle in the higher ranks, and a corrupt devotedness to power for the sake of the emoluments it could dispense, which encouraged the expectation of such a nominal change in religion as had happened in the sixteenth century. And, on the other, much was hoped by the king from the church itself. He had separated from her communion in consequence of the arguments which her own divines had furnished; he had conversed with men bred in the school of Laud; and was slow to believe that the conclusions which he had, not perhaps unreasonably, derived from the semi-protestant theology of his father's reign, would not appear equally irresistible to all minds when free from the danger and obloquy that had attended them. Thus, by a voluntary return of the clergy and nation to the bosom of the catholic church, he might both obtain an immortal renown, and secure his prerogative against that religious jealousy which had always been the aliment of political factions.[m]

[m] It is curious to remark that both James and Louis considered the re-establishment of the catholic religion and of the royal authority as closely connected, and parts of one great system. Barillon in Fox, Append. 19, 57. Mazure, i. 346. Mr. Fox maintains (Hist. p. 102) that the great object of the former was absolute power rather than the interests of popery. Doubtless, if James had been a protestant, his encroachments on the rights of his subjects would not have been less than they were, though not exactly of the same nature; but the

Till this revolution, however, could be brought about, he determined to court the church of England, whose boast of exclusive and unlimited loyalty could hardly be supposed entirely hollow, in order to obtain the repeal of the penal laws and disqualifications which affected that of Rome. And though the maxims of religious toleration had been always in his mouth, he did not hesitate to propitiate her with the most acceptable sacrifice, the persecution of nonconforming ministers. He looked upon the dissenters as men of republican principles; and if he could have made his bargain for the free exercise of the catholic worship, I see no reason to doubt that he would never have announced his general indulgence to tender consciences."

But James had taken too narrow a view of the mighty people whom he governed. The laity of every class, the tory gentleman almost equally with the presbyterian artisan, entertained an inveterate abhorrence of the Romish superstition. Their first education, the usual tenor of preaching, far more polemical than at present, the books most current, the tradition of ancient cruelties and conspiracies, rendered this a cardinal point of

James deceived as to the dispositions of his subjects.

---

main object of his reign can hardly be denied to have been either the full toleration, or the national establishment, of the church of Rome. Mr. Fox's remark must, at all events, be limited to the year 1686.

" Fox, Appendix, p. 33. Ralph, 869. The prosecution of Baxter, for what was called reflecting on the bishops, is an instance of this. State Trials, ii. 494. Notwithstanding James's affected zeal for toleration, he did not scruple to congratulate Louis on the success of his very different mode of converting heretics. Yet I rather believe him to have been really averse to persecution; though with true Stuart insincerity he chose to flatter his patron. Dalrymple, p. 177. A book by Claude, published in Holland, entitled " Plaintes des Protestans cruellement opprimés dans le royaume de France," was ordered to be burnt by the hangman on the complaint of the French ambassador, and the translator and printer to be inquired after and prosecuted. Lond. Gazette, May 8, 1686. Jefferies objected to this in council as unusual; but the king was determined to gratify his most christian brother. Mazure, ii. 122. It is said also that one of the reasons for the disgrace of lord Halifax was his speaking warmly about the revocation of the edict of Nantes. Id. p. 55. Yet James sometimes blamed this himself, so as to displease Louis. Id. p. 56. In fact, it very much tended to obstruct his own views for the establishment of a religion which had just shown itself in so odious a form. For this reason, though a brief was read in churches for the sufferers, special directions were given that there should be no sermon. It is even said that he took on himself the distribution of the money collected for the refugees, in order to stop the subscription, or, at least, that his interference had that effect. The enthusiasm for the French protestants was such that single persons subscribed 500 or 1000 pounds, which, relatively to the opulence of the kingdom, almost equals any munificence of this age. Id. p. 123.

religion even with those who had little beside. Many still gave credit to the popish plot; and with those who had been compelled to admit its general falsehood, there remained, as is frequently the case, an indefinite sense of dislike and suspicion, like the swell of waves after a storm, which attached itself to all the objects of that calumny.° This was of course enhanced by the insolent and injudicious confidence of the Romish faction, especially the priests, in their demeanour, their language, and their publications. Meanwhile a considerable change had been wrought in the doctrinal system of the Anglican church since the Restoration. The men most conspicuous in the reign of Charles II. for their writings, and for their argumentative eloquence in the pulpit, were of the class who had been denominated Latitudinarian divines; and, while they maintained the principles of the Remonstrants in opposition to the school of Calvin, were powerful and unequivocal supporters of the protestant cause against Rome. They made none of the dangerous concessions which had shaken the faith of the duke and duchess of York; they regretted the disuse of no superstitious ceremony; they denied not the one essential characteristic of the Reformation, the right of private judgment; they avoided the mysterious jargon of a real presence in the Lord's Supper. Thus such an agreement between the two churches as had been projected at different times was become far more evidently impracticable, and the separation more broad and defined.ᵖ These men, as

° It is well known that the house of commons in 1685 would not pass the bill for reversing Lord Stafford's attainder, against which a few peers had entered a very spirited protest. Parl. Hist. 1361. Barillon says, this was "parce que dans le préambule il y a des mots insérés qui semblent favoriser la religion catholique; cela seul a retardé la réhabilitation du comte de Stafford, dont tous sont d'accord à l'égard du fond." Fox, App. p. 110. But there was another reason which might have weight. Stafford had been convicted on the evidence, not only of Oates, who had been lately found guilty of perjury, but of several other witnesses, especially Dugdale and Turberville. And these men had been brought forward by the government against Lord Shaftesbury and College, the latter of whom had been hanged on their testimony. The reversal of Lord Stafford's attainder, just as we now think it, would have been a disgrace to these crown prosecutions; and a conscientious tory would be loth to vote for it.

ᵖ " In all the disputes relating to that mystery before the civil wars, the church of England protestant writers owned the real presence, and only abstracted from the *modus* or manner of Christ's body being present in the eucharist, and therefore durst not say but it might be there by transubstantiation as well as by any other way.... It was only of late years that such principles have crept into the

well as others who do not properly belong to the same class, were now distinguished by their courageous and able defences of the Reformation. The victory, in the judgment of the nation, was wholly theirs. Rome had indeed her proselytes, but such as it would have been more honourable to have wanted. The people heard sometimes with indignation, or rather with contempt, that an unprincipled minister, a temporising bishop, or a licentious poet, had gone over to the side of a monarch who made conformity with his religion the only certain path to his favour.

The short period of a four years' reign may be divided by several distinguishing points of time, which make so many changes in the posture of government. From the king's accession to the prorogation of parliament on November 30, 1685, he had acted apparently in concurrence with the same party that had supported him in his brother's reign, of which his own seemed the natural and almost undistinguishable continuation. This party, which had become incomparably stronger than the opposite, had greeted him with such unbounded professions,[q] the

Prorogation of parliament.

---

church of England, which, having been blown into the parliament house, had raised continual tumults about religion ever since. Those unlearned and fanatical notions were never heard of till doctor Stillingfleet's late invention of them, by which he exposed himself to the lash, not only of the Roman catholics, but to that of many of the church of England controvertists too." Life of James, ii. 146.

[q] See London Gazettes, 1685, passim; the most remarkable are inserted by Ralph and Kennet. I am sure the addresses which we have witnessed in this age among a neighbouring people are not on the whole more fulsome and disgraceful. Addresses, however, of all descriptions, as we well know, are generally the composition of some zealous individual, whose expressions are not to be taken as entirely those of the subscribers. Still these are sufficient to manifest the general spirit of the times.

The king's popularity at his accession, which all contemporary writers attest, is strongly expressed by lord Lonsdale. "The great interest he had in his brother, so that all applications to the king seemed to succeed only as he favoured them, and the general opinion of him to be a prince steady above all others to his word, made him at that time the most popular prince that had been known in England for a long time. And from men's attempting to exclude him, they, at this juncture of time, made him their darling; no more was his religion terrible; his magnanimous courage, and the hardships he had undergone, were the discourse of all men. And some reports of a misunderstanding betwixt the French king and him, occasioned originally by the marriage of the lady Mary to the prince of Orange, industriously spread abroad to arouse the ignorant, put men in hopes of what they had long wished; that, by a conjunction of Holland and Spain, &c., we might have been able to reduce France to the terms of the Pyrenean treaty, which was now become the terror of Christendom, we never having had a prince for many ages that had so great a reputation for experience and a martial spirit." P. 3. This last sentence is a truly amusing contrast to the real truth.

temper of its representatives had been such in the first session of parliament, that a prince less obstinate than James might have expected to succeed in attaining an authority which the nation seemed to offer. A rebellion speedily and decisively quelled confirms every government; it seemed to place his own beyond hazard. Could he have been induced to change the order of his designs, and accustom the people to a military force, and to a prerogative of dispensing with statutes of temporal concern, before he meddled too ostensibly with their religion, he would possibly have gained both the objects of his desire. Even conversions to popery might have been more frequent, if the gross solicitations of the court had not made them dishonourable. But, neglecting the hint of a prudent adviser, that the death of Monmouth left a far more dangerous enemy behind, he suffered a victory that might have insured him success to inspire an arrogant confidence that led on to destruction. Master of an army, and determined to keep it on foot, he naturally thought less of a good understanding with parliament.[r] He had already rejected the proposition of employing bribery among the members, an expedient very little congenial to his presumptuous temper and notions of government.[s] They were assembled, in his opinion, to testify the nation's

[r] "On voit qu'insensiblement les catholiques auront les armes à la main; c'est un état bien différent de l'oppression où ils étoient, et dont les protestans zélés reçoivent une grande mortification: ils voyent bien que le roy d'Angleterre fera le reste quand il le pourra. La levée des troupes, qui seront bientôt complètes, fait juger que le roy d'Angleterre veut être en état de se faire obéir, et de n'être pas gêné par les loix qui se trouveront contraires à ce qu'il veut établir." Barillon, in Fox's Appendix, 111. "Il me paroit," he says, June 25, " que le roy d'Angleterre a été fort aisé d'avoir une prétexte de lever des troupes, et qu'il croit que l'entreprise de M. le duc de Monmouth ne servira qu'à le rendre plus maître de son pays." And on July 30, " Le projet du roy d'Angleterre est d'abolir entièrement les milices, dont il a reconnu l'inutilité et le danger en cette dernière occasion; et de faire, s'il est possible, que le parlement établisse le fond destiné pour les milices à l'entretien des troupes réglées. Tout cela change entièrement l'état de ce pays ici, et met les Anglois dans une condition bien différente de celle où ils ont été jusques à présent. Ils le connoissent, et voyent bien qu'un roy de différente religion que celle du pays, et qui se trouve armé, ne renoncera pas aisément aux avantages que lui donne la défaite des rebelles, et les troupes qu'il a sur pied." And afterwards: " Le roi d'Angleterre m'a dit que, quoiqu'il arrive, il conservera les troupes sur pied, quand même le parlement ne lui donneroit pour les entretenir. Il connoit bien que le parlement verra mal volontiers cet établissement; mais il veut être assuré du dedans de son pays, et il croit ne le pouvoir être sans cela." Dalrymple, 169, 170.

[s] Fox's App. 69. Dalrymple, 152.

loyalty, and thankfulness to their gracious prince for
not taking away their laws and liberties. But, if a
factious spirit of opposition should once prevail, it could
not be his fault if he dismissed them till more becoming
sentiments should again gain ground.' Hence he did
not hesitate to prorogue, and eventually to dissolve, the
most compliant house of commons that had been returned since his family had sat on the throne, at the
cost of 700,000*l.*, a grant of supply which thus fell to
the ground, rather than endure any opposition on the
subject of the test and penal laws. Yet, from the
strength of the court in all divisions, it must seem not
improbable to us that he might, by the usual means of
management, have carried both of those favourite
measures, at least through the lower house of parliament. For the crown lost the most important division
only by one vote, and had in general a majority. The
very address about unqualified officers, which gave the
king such offence as to bring on a prorogation, was
worded in the most timid manner; the house having
rejected unanimously the words first inserted by their
committee, requesting that his majesty would be pleased
not to continue them in their employments, for a vague
petition that "he would be graciously pleased to give such
directions that no apprehensions or jealousies may remain
in the hearts of his majesty's good and faithful subjects."[u]

The second period of this reign extends from the prorogation of parliament to the dismissal of the earl of

[t] It had been the intention of Sunderland and the others to dissolve parliament as soon as the revenue for life
should be settled, and to rely in future
on the assistance of France. Fox's App.
59, 60. Mazure, i. 432. But this was
prevented, partly by the sudden invasion
of Monmouth, which made a new session
necessary, and gave hopes of a large supply for the army; and partly by the unwillingness of the king of France to
advance as much money as the English
government wanted. In fact, the plan
of continual prorogations answered as
well.

[u] Journals, Nov. 14. Barillon says
that the king answered this humble address " avec des marques de fierté et de
colère sur le visage, qui faisoit assez connoître ses sentimens." Dalrymple, 172.
See, too, his letter in Fox, 139.

A motion was made to ask the lords'
concurrence in this address, which, according to the Journals, was lost by 212
to 138. In the Life of James, ii. 55, it
is said that it was carried against the
motion by only four voices; and this I
find confirmed by a manuscript account
of the debates (Sloane MSS. 1470), which
gives the numbers 212 to 208. The
journal probably is misprinted, as the
court and country parties were very equal.
It is said in this manuscript that those
who opposed the address opposed also
the motion for requesting the lords' concurrence in it; but James represents it
otherwise, as a device of the court to
quash the proceeding.

Rochester from the treasury in 1686. During this time James, exasperated at the reluctance of the commons to acquiesce in his measures, and the decisive opposition of the church, threw off the half restraint he had imposed on himself; and showed plainly that, with a bench of judges to pronounce his commands, and an army to enforce them, he would not suffer the mockery of constitutional limitations to stand any longer in his way. Two important steps were made this year towards the accomplishment of his designs, by the judgment of the court of king's bench in the case of sir Edward Hales, confirming the right of the crown to dispense with the test act, and by the establishment of the new ecclesiastical commission.

The kings of England, if not immemorially, yet from a very early era in our records, have exercised a prerogative unquestioned by parliament, and recognised by courts of justice, that of granting dispensations from the prohibitions and penalties of particular laws.

Dispensing power confirmed by the judges.

The language of ancient statutes was usually brief and careless, with few of those attempts to regulate prospective contingencies, which, even with our pretended modern caution, are so often imperfect; and, as the sessions were never regular, sometimes interrupted for several years, there was a kind of necessity, or great convenience, in deviating occasionally from the rigour of a general prohibition; more often perhaps some motive of interest or partiality would induce the crown to infringe on the legal rule. This dispensing power, however, grew up, as it were, collaterally to the sovereignty of the legislature, which it sometimes appeared to overshadow. It was, of course, asserted in large terms by councillors of state, and too frequently by the interpreters of law. Lord Coke, before he had learned the bolder tone of his declining years, lays it down, that no act of parliament can bind the king from any prerogative which is inseparable from his person, so that he may not dispense with it by a non obstante; such is his sovereign power to command any of his subjects to serve him for the public weal, which solely and inseparably is annexed to his person, and cannot be restrained by any act of parliament. Thus, although the statute 23 H. VI. c. 8, provides that all patents to hold the office of sheriff for more than one year shall be void, and even enacts that the king shall not dispense with it, yet it was held by all the judges in the reign of Henry VII., that the king may grant such a patent for a longer term on good grounds, whereof he alone is the judge. So also the statutes which restrain the king from granting pardons in case of murder have been held void; and doubtless the constant practice has been to disregard them.*

This high and dangerous prerogative, nevertheless, was subject to several limitations, which none but the grosser flatterers of monarchy could deny. It was agreed among lawyers that the king could not dispense with the common law, nor with any statute prohibiting that which was *malum in se*, nor with any right or interest of a private person or corporation.ʸ The rules, however, were still rather complicated, the boundaries indefinite, and therefore varying according to the political character of the judges. For many years dispensations had been confined to taking away such incapacity as either the statutes of a college, or some law of little consequence, perhaps almost obsolete, might happen to have created. But when a collusive action was brought against sir Edward Hales, a Roman catholic, in the name of his servant, to recover the penalty of 500*l.* imposed by the test act, for accepting the commission of

---

* Coke, 12 Rep. 18.

ʸ Vaughan's Reports. Thomas v. Sorrell, 333. [Lords' Journals, 29th Dec. 1666. "The commons introduced the word 'nuisance' into the Irish bill, in order to prevent the king's dispensing with it. The lords did argue that it was an ill precedent, and that which will ever hereafter be held as a way of preventing the king's dispensation with acts, and therefore rather advise to pass the bill without that word, and let it go accompanied with a petition to the king that he will not dispense with it, this being a more civil way to the king. They answered well, that this do imply that the king should pass their bill, and yet with design to dispense with it; which is to suppose the king guilty of abusing them. And more, they produce precedents for it; namely, that against new buildings, and about leather, when the word nuisance is used to the purpose; and farther, that they do not rob the king of any right he ever had: for he never had a power to do hurt to his people, nor would exercise it; and therefore there is no danger in the passing this bill of imposing on his prerogative; and concluded that they think they ought to do this, so as the people may really have the benefit of it when it is passed, &c. The lords gave way soon after wards." Pepys's Diary, Jan. 9, 1666-7. Clarendon speaks of this precaution against the dispensing power as derogatory to the king's prerogative, "divesting him of a trust that was inherent in him from all antiquity." Life of Clarendon, p. 380.]

colonel of a regiment, without the previous qualification of receiving the sacrament in the church of England, the whole importance of the alleged prerogative became visible, and the fate of the established constitution seemed to hang upon the decision. The plaintiff's advocate, Northey, was known to have received his fee from the other side, and was thence suspected, perhaps unfairly, of betraying his own cause;[a] but the chief justice Herbert showed that no arguments against this prerogative would have swayed his determination. Not content with treating the question as one of no difficulty, he grounded his decision in favour of the defendant upon principles that would extend far beyond the immediate case. He laid it down that the kings of England were sovereign princes; that the laws of England were the king's laws; that it was consequently an inseparable prerogative of the crown to dispense with penal laws in particular cases, for reasons of which it was the sole judge. This he called the ancient remains of the sovereign power and prerogative of the kings of England, which never yet was taken from them, nor could be. There was no law, he said, that might not be dispensed with by the supreme lawgiver (meaning evidently the king, since the proposition would otherwise be impertinent); though he made a sort of distinction as to those which affected the subject's private right. But the general maxims of slavish churchmen and lawyers were asserted so broadly, that a future judge would find little difficulty in making use of this precedent to justify any stretch of arbitrary power.[a]

It is by no means evident that the decision in this particular case of Hales, which had the approbation of eleven judges out of twelve, was against law.[b] The course of former precedents seems rather to furnish its justification. But the less untenable such a judgment in favour of the dispensing power might appear, the more necessity would men of reflection perceive of making some great change in the relations of the people

[a] Burnet and others. This hardly appears by Northey's argument.
[a] State Trials, xi. 1165-1280. Shower's Reports, 475.
[b] The dissentient judge was Street, and Powell is said to have doubted. The king had privately secured this opinion of the bench in his favour before the action was brought. Life of James, ii. 78.

towards their sovereign. A prerogative of setting aside the enactments of parliament, which in trifling matters, and for the sake of conferring a benefit on individuals, might be suffered to exist with little mischief, became intolerable when exercised in contravention of the very principle of those statutes which had been provided for the security of fundamental liberties or institutions. Thus the test act, the great achievement, as it had been reckoned, of the protestant party, for the sake of which the most subservient of parliaments had just then ventured to lose the king's favour, became absolutely nugatory and ineffective, by a construction which the law itself did not reject. Nor was it easy to provide any sufficient remedy by means of parliament; since it was the doctrine of the judges that the king's inseparable and sovereign prerogatives in matters of government could not be taken away or restrained by statute. The unadvised assertion in a court of justice of this principle, which, though not by any means novel, had never been advanced in a business of such universal concern and interest, may be said to have sealed the condemnation of the house of Stuart. It made the co-existence of an hereditary line, claiming a sovereign prerogative paramount to the liberties they had vouchsafed to concede, incompatible with the security or probable duration of those liberties. This incompatibility is the true basis of the Revolution in 1688.

But, whatever pretext the custom of centuries or the authority of compliant lawyers might afford for these dispensations from the test, no legal defence could be made for the ecclesiastical commission of 1686. The high-commission court of Elizabeth had been altogether taken away by an act of the long parliament, which went on to provide that no new court should be erected with the like power, jurisdiction, and authority. Yet the commission issued by James II. followed very nearly the words of that which had created the original court under Elizabeth, omitting a few particulars of little moment.ᵉ It is not known,]

Ecclesiastical commission.

ᵉ State Trials, xi. 1132, et seq. The members of the commission were the primate Sancroft (who never sat), Crew and Sprat, bishops of Durham and Rochester, the chancellor Jefferies, the earls of Rochester and Sunderland, and chief justice Herbert. Three were to form a quorum, but the chancellor necessarily to be one. Ralph, 929. The earl of Mulgrave was introduced afterwards.

believe, at whose suggestion the king adopted this measure. The pre-eminence reserved by the commission to Jefferies, whose presence was made necessary to all their meetings, and the violence with which he acted in all their transactions on record, seem to point him out as its great promoter; though it is true that, at a later period, Jefferies seems to have perceived the destructive indiscretion of the popish counsellors. It displayed the king's change of policy and entire separation from that high-church party to whom he was indebted for the throne, since the manifest design of the ecclesiastical commission was to bridle the clergy, and silence the voice of protestant zeal. The proceedings against the bishop of London, and other instances of hostility to the established religion, are well known.

Elated by success and general submission, exasperated by the reluctance and dissatisfaction of those on whom he had relied for an active concurrence with his desires, the king seems at least by this time to have formed the scheme of subverting, or impairing as far as possible, the religious establishment. He told Barillon, alluding to the ecclesiastical commission, that God had permitted all the statutes which had been enacted against the catholic religion to become the means of its re-establishment.[d] But the most remarkable evidence of this design was the collation of Massey, a recent convert, to the deanery of Christ Church, with a dispensation from all the statutes of uniformity and other ecclesiastical laws, so ample that it made a precedent, and such it was doubtless intended to be, for bestowing any benefices upon members of the church of Rome. This dispensation seems to have been not generally known at the time. Burnet has stated the circumstances of Massey's promotion inaccurately; and no historian, I believe, till the publication of the instrument after the middle of the last century, was fully aware of the degree in which the king had trampled upon the securities of the established church in this transaction.[e]

Marginal note: King's scheme of establishing popery.

[d] Mazure, ii. 130.
[e] Henry Earl of Clarendon's Papers, ii. 278. In Gutch's Collectanea Curiosa, vol. i. p. 287, we find not only this licence to Massey, but one to Obadiah Walker, master of University College, and to two fellows of the same, and one of Brazen-nose College, to absent themselves from church, and not to take the oaths of supremacy and allegiance, or do

A deeper impression was made by the dismissal of Rochester from his post of lord treasurer; so nearly consequent on his positive declaration of adherence to the protestant religion, after the dispute held in his presence at the king's particular command, between divines of both persuasions, that it had much the appearance of a resolution taken at court to exclude from the high offices of the state all those who gave no hope of conversion.[f] Clarendon had already given way to Tyrconnel in the government of Ireland; the privy seal was bestowed on a catholic peer, lord Arundel; lord Bellasis, of the same religion, was now placed at the head of the commission of the treasury; Sunderland, though he did not yet cease to conform, made no secret of his pretended change of opinion; the council-board, by virtue of the dispensing power, was filled with those who would refuse the test; a small junto of catholics, with father Petre, the king's confessor, at their head, took the management of almost all affairs upon themselves;[g] men whose known want of principle gave reason to expect their compliance

Dismissal of lord Rochester.

---

any other thing to which, by the laws and statutes of the realm, or those of the college, they are obliged. There is also in the same book a dispensation for one Sclater, curate of Putney and rector of Esher, from using the common prayer, &c. &c. Id. p. 290. These are in May, 1686, and subscribed by Powis, the solicitor-general. The attorney-general, Sawyer, had refused; as we learn from Reresby, p. 133, the only contemporary writer, perhaps, who mentions this very remarkable aggression on the established church.

[f] The catholic lords, according to Barillon, had represented to the king that nothing could be done with parliament so long as the treasurer caballed against the designs of his majesty. James promised to dismiss him if he did not change his religion. Mazure, ii. 170. The queen had previously been rendered his enemy by the arts of Sunderland, who persuaded her that lord and lady Rochester had favoured the king's intimacy with the countess of Dorchester in order to thwart the popish intrigue. Id. 149. "On voit," says Barillon on the treasurer's dismissal,

"que la cabale catholique a entièrement prévalu. On s'attendoit depuis quelque temps à ce qui est arrivé au comte de Rochester; mais l'exécution fait encore une nouvelle impression sur les esprits." P. 191.

[g] Life of James, 74. Barillon frequently mentions this cabal as having in effect the whole conduct of affairs in their hands. Sunderland belonged to them; but Jefferies, being reckoned on the protestant side, had, I believe, very little influence for at least the two latter years of the king's reign. "Les affaires de ce pays-ci," says Bonrepos in 1686, "ne roulent à présent que sur la religion. Le roi est absolument gouverné par les catholiques. My lord Sunderland ne se maintient que par ceux-ci, et par son dévouement à faire tout ce qu'il croit être agréable sur ce point. Il a le secret des affaires de Rome." Mazure, ii. 124. "On feroit ici," says Barillon, the same year, "ce qu'on fait en France" [that is, I suppose, dragonner et fusiller les hérétiques], "si l'on pouvoit espérer de réussir." P. 127.

were raised to bishoprics; there could be no rational doubt of a concerted scheme to depress and discountenance the established church. The dismissal of Rochester, who had gone great lengths to preserve his power and emoluments, and would in all probability have concurred in the establishment of arbitrary power under a protestant sovereign,[b] may be reckoned the most unequivocal evidence of the king's intentions; and from thence we may date the decisive measures that were taken to counteract them.

Prince of Orange alarmed.
It was, I do not merely say the interest, but the clear right and bounden duty, of the prince of Orange to watch over the internal politics of England, on account of the near connexion which his own birth and his marriage with the presumptive heir had created. He was never to be reckoned a foreigner as to this country, which, even in the ordinary course of succession, he might be called to govern. From the time of his union with the princess Mary he was the legitimate and natural ally of the whig party; alien in all his sentiments from his two uncles, neither of whom, especially James, treated him with much regard, on account merely of his attachment to religion and liberty, for he might have secured their affection by falling into their plans. Before such differences as subsisted between these personages, the bonds of relationship fall asunder like flax; and William would have had at least the sanction of many precedents in history if he had employed his influence to excite sedition against Charles or James, and to thwart their administration. Yet his conduct appears to have been merely defensive; nor had he the remotest connexion with the violent and factious proceedings of Shaftesbury and his partisans. He

---

[b] Rochester makes so very bad a figure in all Barillon's correspondence, that there really seems no want of candour in this supposition. He was evidently the most active co-operator in the connection of both the brothers with France, and seems to have had as few compunctious visitings, where the church of England was not concerned, as Sunderland himself. Godolphin was too much implicated, at least by acquiescence, in the counsels of this reign; yet we find him suspected of not wishing "se passer entièrement de parlement, et à rompre nettement avec le prince d'Orange." Fox, Append. p. 60.

If Rochester had gone over to the Romanists, many, probably, would have followed: on the other hand, his steadiness retained the wavering. It was one of the first great disappointments with which the king met. But his dismissal from the treasury created a sensible alarm. Dalrymple, 179.

played a very dexterous, but apparently very fair, game throughout the last years of Charles, never losing sight of the popular party, through whom alone he could expect influence over England during the life of his father-in-law, while he avoided any direct rupture with the brothers, and every reasonable pretext for their taking offence.

It has never been established by any reputable testimony, though perpetually asserted, nor is it in the least degree probable, that William took any share in prompting the invasion of Monmouth.[1] But it is nevertheless manifest that he derived the greatest advantage from this absurd rebellion and from its failure, not only as it removed a mischievous adventurer, whom the multitude's idle predilection had elevated so high that factious men would, under every government, have turned to account his ambitious imbecility; but as the cruelty with which this unhappy enterprise was punished rendered the king odious,[k] while the success of his arms

---

[1] Lord Dartmouth wrote to say that Fletcher told him there were good grounds to suspect that the prince, underhand, encouraged the expedition, with design to ruin the duke of Monmouth; and this Dalrymple believes, p. 136. It is needless to observe that such subtle and hazardous policy was totally out of William's character: nor is there much more reason to believe what is insinuated by James himself (Macpherson's Extracts, p. 144; Life of James, ii. 34), that Sunderland had been in secret correspondence with Monmouth, unless, indeed, it were, as seems hinted in the latter work, with the king's knowledge.

[k] The number of persons who suffered the sentence of the law, in the famous western assize of Jefferies, has been differently stated; but according to a list in the Harleian Collection, n. 4689, it appears to be as follows: at Winchester, one (Mrs. Lisle) executed; at Salisbury, none; at Dorchester, 74 executed, 171 transported; at Exeter, 14 executed, 7 transported; at Taunton, 144 executed, 284 transported; at Wells, 97 executed, 393 transported. In all, 330 executed, 855 transported; besides many that were left in custody for want of evidence. It may be observed that the prisoners sentenced to transportation appear to have been made over to some gentlemen of interest at court, among others to sir Christopher Musgrave, who did not blush to beg the grant of their unfortunate countrymen to be sold as slaves in the colonies.

The apologists of James II. have endeavoured to lay the entire blame of these cruelties on Jefferies, and to represent the king as ignorant of them. Roger North tells a story of his brother's interference, which is plainly contradicted by known dates, and the falsehood of which throws just suspicion on his numerous anecdotes. See State Trials, xi. 303. But the king speaks with apparent approbation of what he calls Jefferies's campaign, in writing to the prince of Orange (Dalrymple, 165); and I have heard that there are extant additional proofs of his perfect acquaintance with the details of those assizes: nor, indeed, can he be supposed ignorant of them. Jefferies himself, before his death, declared that he had not been half bloody enough for him by whom he was employed. Burnet, 651 (note to Oxford edition, vol. iii.). The king, or his biographer in his behalf, makes a very awkward apology for the execution of major Holmes, which is

inspired him with false confidence and neglect of caution. Every month, as it brought forth evidence of James's arbitrary projects, increased the number of those who looked for deliverance to the prince of Orange, either in the course of succession, or by some special interference. He had, in fact, a stronger motive for watching the councils of his father-in-law than has generally been known. The king was, at his accession, in his fifty-fifth year, and had no male children; nor did the queen's health give much encouragement to expect them. Every dream of the nation's voluntary return to the church of Rome must have vanished, even if the consent of a parliament could be obtained, which was nearly vain to think of; or if open force and the aid of France should enable James to subvert the established religion, what had the catholics to anticipate from his death but that fearful reaction which had ensued upon the accession of Elizabeth? This had already so much disheartened the moderate part of their body that they were most anxious not to urge forward a change for which the kingdom was not ripe, and which was so little likely to endure, and used their influence to promote a reconciliation between the king and prince of Orange, contenting themselves with that free exercise of their worship which was permitted in Holland.ᵐ But the ambitious priesthood who surrounded the throne had bolder projects. A scheme was formed early in the

---

shown by himself to have been a gross breach of faith. Life of James, II. 43.

It is unnecessary to dwell on what may be found in every history—the trials of Mrs. Lisle, Mrs. Gaunt, and alderman Cornish; the former before Jefferies, the two latter before Jones, his successor as chief justice of K. B., a judge nearly as infamous as the former, though not altogether so brutal. Both Mrs. Lisle's and Cornish's convictions were without evidence, and consequently were reversed after the Revolution. State Trials, vol. xi.

ᵐ Several proofs of this appear in the correspondence of Barillon. Fox, 135; Mazure, II. 22. The nuncio, M. d'Adda, was a moderate man, and united with the moderate catholic peers, Bellasis, Arundel, and Powis. Id. 127. This party urged the king to keep on good terms with the prince of Orange, and to give way about the test. Id. 184, 255. They were disgusted at father Petre's introduction into the privy council; 308, 353. But it has ever been the misfortune of that respectable body to suffer unjustly for the follies of a few. Barillon admits very early in James's reign that many of them disliked the arbitrary proceedings of the court: "Ils prétendent être bons Anglois, c'est-à-dire, ne pas désirer que le roi d'Angleterre ôte à la nation ses privilèges et ses libertés." Mazure, I. 404.

William openly declared his willingness to concur in taking off the penal laws, provided the test might remain. Burnet, 694; Dalrymple, 184; Mazure, II. 216, 250, 346. James replied that he must have all or nothing. Id. 953.

king's reign to exclude the princess of Orange from the succession in favour of her sister Anne, in the event of the latter's conversion to the Romish faith. The French ministers at our court, Barillon and Bonrepos, gave ear to this hardy intrigue. They flattered themselves that both Anne and her husband were favourably disposed. But in this they were wholly mistaken. No one could be more unconquerably fixed in her religion than that princess. The king himself, when the Dutch ambassador, Van Citers, laid before him a document, probably drawn up by some catholics of his court, in which these audacious speculations were developed, declared his indignation at so criminal a project. It was not even in his power, he let the prince afterwards know by a message, or in that of parliament, according to the principles which had been maintained in his own behalf, to change the fundamental order of succession to the crown.ª Nothing indeed can more forcibly paint the desperation of the popish faction than their entertainment of so preposterous a scheme. But it naturally increased the solicitude of William about the intrigues of the English cabinet. It does not appear that any direct overtures were made to the prince of Orange, except by a very few malcontents, till the embassy of Dykvelt from the States in the spring of 1687. It was William's object to ascertain, through that minister, the real state of parties in England. Such assurances as he carried back to Holland gave encouragement to an enterprise that would have been equally injudicious and unwarrantable without them.ᵇ Danby, Halifax, Nottingham, and others of the tory as well as whig factions, entered into a secret correspondence with the prince of Orange; some from a real attachment to the constitutional limitations of monarchy; some from a conviction

Plan of setting the princess aside;

rejected by the king.

Overtures of the malcontents to the prince of Orange.

ª I do not know that this intrigue has been brought to light before the recent valuable publication of M. Mazure, certainly not with such full evidence. See i. 417; II. 129, 160, 165, 167, 182, 188, 192. Barillon says to his master in one place,—" C'est une matière fort délicate à traiter. Je sais pourtant qu'on en parle au roi d'Angleterre; et qu'avec le temps on ne désespère pas de trouver des moyens pour faire passer la couronne sur la tête d'un héritier catholique. Il faut pour cela venir à bout de beaucoup de choses qui ne sont encore que commencées."

ᵇ Burnet; Dalrymple; Mazure.

that, without open apostasy from the protestant faith, they could never obtain from James the prizes of their ambition. This must have been the predominant motive with Lord Churchill, who never gave any proof of solicitude about civil liberty; and his influence taught the princess Anne to distinguish her interests from those of her father. It was about this time also that even Sunderland entered upon a mysterious communication with the prince of Orange; but whether he afterwards served his present master only to betray him, as has been generally believed, or sought rather to propitiate, by clandestine professions, one who might in the course of events become such, is not perhaps what the evidence already known to the world will enable us to determine.ᵖ The apologists of James have often represented Sunderland's treachery as extending back to the commencement of this reign, as if he had entered upon the king's service with no other aim than to put him on measures that would naturally lead to his ruin. But the simpler hypothesis is probably nearer the truth; a corrupt and artful statesman could have no better prospect for his own advantage than the power and popularity of a government which he administered; it was a conviction of the king's incorrigible and infatuated adherence to designs which the rising spirit of the nation rendered utterly infeasible, an apprehension that, whenever a free parliament should be called, he might experience the fate of Strafford as an expiation for the sins of the crown, which determined him to secure as far as possible his own indemnity upon a revolution that he could not have withstood.ᵠ

ᵖ The correspondence began by an affectedly obscure letter of lady Sunderland to the prince of Orange, dated March 7, 1687: Dalrymple, 187. The meaning, however, cannot be misunderstood. Sunderland himself sent a short letter of compliment by Dykvelt, May 28, referring to what that envoy had to communicate. Churchill, Nottingham, Rochester, Devonshire, and others, wrote also by Dykvelt. Halifax was in correspondence at the end of 1686.

ᵠ Sunderland does not appear, by the extracts from Barillon's letters published by M. Mazure, to have been the adviser of the king's most injudicious measures. He was united with the queen, who had more moderation than her husband. It is said by Barillon that both he and Petre were against the prosecution of the bishops: ii. 448. The king himself ascribes this step to Jefferies, and seems to glance also at Sunderland as its adviser. Life of James, ii. 156. He speaks more explicitly as to Jefferies in Macpherson's Extracts, 151. Yet lord Clarendon's Diary, ii. 49, tends to acquit Jefferies. Probably the king had nobody to blame but himself. One cause of Sunderland's continuance in the apparent

The dismissal of Rochester was followed up, at no great distance of time, by the famous declaration for liberty of conscience, suspending the execution of all penal laws concerning religion, and freely pardoning all offences against them, in as full a manner as if each individual had been named. He declared also his will and pleasure that the oaths of supremacy and allegiance, and the several tests enjoined by statutes of the late reign, should no longer be required of any one before his admission to offices of trust. The motive of this declaration was not so much to relieve the Roman catholics from penal and incapacitating statutes (which, since the king's accession and the judgment of the court of king's bench in favour of Hales, were virtually at an end), as, by extending to the protestant dissenters the same full measure of toleration, to enlist under the standard of arbitrary power those who had been its most intrepid and steadiest adversaries. It was after the prorogation of parliament that he had begun to caress that party, who in the first months of his reign had endured a continuance of their persecution.' But the clergy in general detested the nonconformists hardly less than the papists, and had always abhorred the idea of even a parliamentary toleration. The present declaration went much farther than the recognised prerogative of dispensing with prohibitory statutes. Instead of removing the disability from individuals by letters patent, it swept away at once, in effect, the solemn ordinances of the legislature. There was, indeed, a reference to the future concurrence of the two houses, whenever he should think it convenient for them to meet; but so expressed as rather to insult, than pay respect to, their authority.* And no

Declaration for liberty of conscience.

support of a policy which he knew to be destructive was his poverty. He was in the pay of France, and even importunate for its money. Mazure, 372; Dalrymple, 270, et post. Louis only gave him half what he demanded. Without the blindest submission to the king, he was every moment falling; and this drove him into a step as injudicious as it was unprincipled, his pretended change of religion, which was not publicly made till June, 1688, though he had been privately reconciled. It is said (Mazure, ii. 463),
more than a year before by father Petre.

ʳ "This defection of those his majesty had hitherto put the greatest confidence in [Clarendon and Rochester], and the sullen disposition of the church of England party in general, made him think it necessary to reconcile another; and yet he hoped to do it in such a manner as not to disgust quite the churchman neither." Life of James, ii. 102.

ˢ London Gazette, March 18, 1687. Ralph, 945.

one could help considering the declaration of a similar nature just published in Scotland as the best commentary on the present. In that he suspended all laws against the Roman catholics and moderate presbyterians, " by his sovereign authority, prerogative royal, and absolute power, which all his subjects were to obey without reserve ;" and its whole tenor spoke, in as unequivocal language as his grandfather was accustomed to use, his contempt of all pretended limitations on his will.' Though the constitution of Scotland was not so well balanced as our own, it was notorious that the crown did not legally possess an absolute power in that kingdom; and men might conclude that, when he should think it less necessary to observe some measures with his English subjects, he would address them in the same strain.

Addresses in favour of it. Those, indeed, who knew by what course his favour was to be sought, did not hesitate to go before and light him, as it were, to the altar on which their country's liberty was to be the victim. Many of the addresses which fill the columns of the London Gazette in 1687, on occasion of the declaration of indulgence, flatter the king with assertions of his dispensing power. The benchers and barristers of the Middle Temple, under the direction of the prostitute Shower, were again foremost in the race of infamy." They thank him " for asserting his own royal prerogatives, the very life of the law, and of their profession; which prerogatives, as they were given by God himself, so no power upon earth could diminish them, but they must always remain entire and inseparable from his royal person; which prerogatives, as the addressers had studied to know, so they were resolved to defend by asserting with their lives and fortunes that divine maxim, *à Deo rex, à rege lex*."*

---

t Ralph, 943. Mazure, ii. 207.

u [But these addresses from the Middle and Inner Temple, we are informed by sir James Mackintosh, " from recent examination of the records of those bodies, do not appear to have been voted by either. The former, eminent above others for fulsome servility, is traditionally said to be the clandestine production of three of the benchers, of whom Chauncy, the historian of Hertfordshire, was one." Hist. of James II., p. 177.]

x London Gazette, June 9, 1687. Shower had been knighted a little before, on presenting, as recorder of London, an address from the grand jury of Middlesex, thanking the king for his declaration. Id. May 12.

These addresses, which, to the number of some hundreds, were sent up from every description of persons, the clergy, the nonconformists of all denominations, the grand juries, the justices of the peace, the corporations, the inhabitants of towns, in consequence of the declaration, afford a singular contrast to what we know of the prevailing dispositions of the people in that year, and of their general abandonment of the king's cause before the end of the next. Those from the clergy, indeed, disclose their ill-humour at the unconstitutional indulgence, limiting their thanks to some promises of favour the king had made towards the established church. But as to the rest, we should have cause to blush for the servile hypocrisy of our ancestors, if there were not good reason to believe that these addresses were sometimes the work of a small minority in the name of the rest, and that the grand juries and the magistracy in general had been so garbled for the king's purposes in this year that they formed a very inadequate representation of that great class from which they ought to have been taken.[y] It was however very natural that they should deceive the court. The catholics were eager for that security which nothing but an act of the legislature could afford; and James, who, as well as his minister, had a strong aversion to the measure, seems about the latter end of the summer of 1687 to have made a sudden change in his scheme of government, and resolved once more to try the disposition of a parliament. For this purpose, having dissolved that from which he could expect nothing hostile to the church, he set himself to manage the election of

---

[y] London Gazette of 1687 and 1688, passim. Ralph, 946, 368. These addresses grew more ardent after the queen's pregnancy became known. They were renewed, of course, after the birth of the prince of Wales. But scarce any appear after the expected invasion was announced. The tories (to whom add the dissenters) seem to have thrown off the mask at once, and deserted the king, whom they had so grossly flattered, as instantaneously as parasites on the stage desert their patron on the first tidings of his ruin.

The dissenters have been a little ashamed of their compliance with the declaration, and of their silence in the popish controversy during this reign. Neal, 755, 768; and see Biog. Brit, art. Alsop. The best excuses are, that they had been so harassed that it was not in human nature to refuse a mitigation of suffering almost on any terms; that they were by no means unanimous in their transitory support of the court; and that they gladly embraced the first offers of an equal indulgence held out to them by the church.

another in such a manner as to ensure his main object, the security of the Romish religion.*

New-modelling of the corporations. "His first care," says his biographer Innes, "was to purge the corporations from that leaven which was in danger of corrupting the whole kingdom; so he appointed certain regulators to inspect the conduct of several borough towns, to correct abuses where it was practicable, and where not, by forfeiting their charters, to turn out such rotten members as infected the rest. But in this, as in most other cases, the king had the fortune to choose persons not too well qualified for such an employment, and extremely disagreeable to the people; it was a sort of motley council made up of catholics and presbyterians, a composition which was sure never to hold long together, or that could probably unite in any method suitable to both their interests; it served therefore only to increase the public odium by their too arbitrary ways of turning out and putting in; and yet those who were thus intruded, as it were, by force, being of the presbyterian party, were by this time become as little inclinable to favour the king's intentions as the excluded members." ᵃ

This endeavour to violate the legal rights of electors, as well as to take away other vested franchises, by new-modelling corporations through commissions granted to regulators, was the most capital delinquency of the king's government; because it tended to preclude any reparation for the rest, and directly attacked the fundamental constitution of the state.ᵇ But, like all his other measures, it displayed not more ill-will to the liberties of the nation than inability to overthrow them.

ᶻ "The king, now finding that nothing which had the least appearance of novelty, though never so well warranted by the prerogative, would go down with the people unless it had the parliamentary stamp on it, resolved to try if he could get the penal laws and test taken off by that authority." Life of James, ii. 134. But it seems, by M. Mazure's authorities, that neither the king nor lord Sunderland wished to convoke a parliament, which was pressed forward by the eager catholics: ii. 399, iii. 65. [The proclamation for a new parliament came out Sept. 21, 1688. The king intended to create new peers enough to insure the repeal of the test; Mazure, iii. 81; but intimates in his proclamation that he would consent to let Roman catholics remain incapable of sitting in the lower house. Id. 82; Ralph, 1010. But this very proclamation was revoked in a few days.]

ᵃ Life of James, p. 139.

ᵇ Ralph, 965, 966. The object was to let in the dissenters. This was evidently a desperate game: James had ever mortally hated the sectaries as enemies to monarchy; and they were irreconcilably adverse to all his schemes.

The catholics were so small a body, and so weak, especially in corporate towns, that the whole effect produced by the regulators was to place municipal power and trust in the hands of the nonconformists, those precarious and unfaithful allies of the court, whose resentment of past oppression, hereditary attachment to popular principles of government, and inveterate abhorrence of popery, were not to be effaced by an unnatural coalition. Hence, though they availed themselves, and surely without reproach, of the toleration held out to them, and even took the benefit of the scheme of regulation, so as to fill the corporation of London and many others, they were, as is confessed above, too much of Englishmen and protestants for the purposes of the court. The wiser part of the churchmen made secret overtures to their party; and by assurances of a toleration, if not also of a comprehension within the Anglican pale, won them over to a hearty concurrence in the great project that was on foot.[c] The king found it necessary to descend so much from the haughty attitude he had taken at the outset of his reign, as personally to solicit men of rank and local influence for their votes on the two great measures of repealing the test and penal laws. The country gentlemen, in their different counties, were tried with circular questions, whether they would comply with the king in their elections, or, if themselves chosen, in parliament. Those who refused such a promise were erased from the lists of justices and deputy lieutenants.[d] Yet his biographer admits that he received little encouragement to proceed in the experiment of a parliament;[e] and it is said by the French ambassador that evasive answers were returned

[c] Burnet; Life of James, 169; D'Oyly's Life of Sancroft, L 326. Lord Halifax, as is supposed, published a letter of advice to the dissenters, warning them against a coalition with the court, and promising all indulgence from the church. Ralph, 950; Somers Tracts, viii. 50.

[d] Ralph, 967; Lonsdale, p. 15. "It is to be observed," says the author of this memoir, "that most part of the offices in the nation, as justices of the peace, deputy-lieutenants, mayors, aldermen, and freemen of towns, are filled with Roman catholics and dissenters, after having suffered as many regulations as were necessary for that purpose. And thus stands the state of this nation in this month of September, 1688." P 34. Notice is given in the London Gazette for December 11, 1687, that the lists of justices and deputy-lieutenants would be revised.

[e] Life of James, 183.

to these questions, with such uniformity of expression as indicated an alarming degree of concert.[f]

<small>Affair of Magdalen College.</small> It is unnecessary to dwell on circumstances so well known as the expulsion of the fellows of Magdalen College.[g] It was less extensively mischievous than the new-modelling of corporations, but perhaps a more glaring act of despotism. For though the crown had been accustomed from the time of the Reformation to send very peremptory commands to ecclesiastical foundations, and even to dispense with their statutes at discretion, with so little resistance that few seemed to doubt of its prerogative; though Elizabeth would probably have treated the fellows of any college much in the same manner as James II., if they had proceeded to an election in defiance of her recommendation; yet the right was not the less clearly theirs, and the struggles of a century would have been thrown away, if James II. was to govern as the Tudors, or even as his father and grandfather, had done before him.[h] And though Parker, bishop of Oxford, the first president whom the ecclesiastical commissioners obtruded on the college, was still nominally a protestant,[i] his successor Giffard was an avowed member of the church of Rome. The college was filled with persons of the same persuasion; mass was said in the chapel, and the established religion was excluded with a degree of open force which entirely took away all security for its preservation in any other place. This latter act, especially, of the Magdalen drama, in a still greater degree than the nomination of Massey to the deanery of Christ Church, seems a decisive proof that the king's repeated promises of contenting himself with a toleration of his

---

[f] Mazure, ii. 302.

[g] The reader will find almost everything relative to the subject in that incomparable repertory, the State Trials, xli. 1; also some notes in the Oxford edition of Burnet.

[h] [This is the only ground to be taken in the great case of Magdalen College, as in that of Francis, at Cambridge, a little earlier; for the precedents of dispensing with college statutes by the royal authority were numerous. See Ralph, 958. But it is one thing to do an irregular act, and another to enforce it. A vindication of the proceedings of the ecclesiastical commission was published, wherein it is said that "the legislative power in matters ecclesiastical was lodged in the king, and too ample to be limited by act of parliament." Id. 971.—1845.]

[i] Parker's Reasons for Abrogating the Test are written in such a tone as to make his readiness to abandon the protestant side very manifest, even if the common anecdotes of him should be exaggerated.

own religion would have yielded to his insuperable bigotry and the zeal of his confessor. We may perhaps add to these encroachments upon the act of uniformity, the design imputed to him of conferring the archbishopric of York on father Petre; yet there would have been difficulties that seem insurmountable in the way of this, since, the validity of Anglican orders not being acknowledged by the church of Rome, Petre would not have sought consecration at the hands of Sancroft; nor, had he done so, would the latter have conferred it on him, even if the chapter of York had gone through the indispensable form of an election.[k]

The infatuated monarch was irritated by that which he should have taken as a terrible warning, this resistance to his will from the university of Oxford. That sanctuary of pure unspotted loyalty, as some would say,—that sink of all that was most abject in servility, as less courtly tongues might murmur, —the university of Oxford, which had but four short years back, by a solemn decree in convocation, poured forth anathemas on all who had doubted the divine right of monarchy, or asserted the privileges of subjects against their sovereigns, which had boasted in its addresses of an obedience without any restrictions or limitations, which but recently had seen a known convert to popery, and a person disqualified in other ways, installed by the chapter without any remonstrance in the deanery of Christ Church, was now the scene of a firm though temperate opposition to the king's positive command, and soon after the willing instrument of his ruin. In vain the pamphleteers, on the side of the court, upbraided the clergy with their apostasy from the principles they had so much vaunted. The imputation it was hard to repel; but, if they could not retract their course without shame, they could not continue in it without destruction.[m] They were driven to extremity

Infatuation of the king.

[k] It seems, however, confirmed by Mazure, ii. 390, with the addition that Petre, like a second Wolsey, aspired also to be chancellor. The pope, however, would not make him a bishop, against the rules of the order of Jesuits, to which he belonged. Id. 241. James then tried, through Lord Castelmain, to get him a cardinal's hat, but with as little success.

[m] "Above twenty years together," says sir Roger L'Estrange, perhaps himself a disguised catholic, in his reply to the reasons of the clergy of the diocese of Oxford against petitioning (Somers Tracts, viii. 45), "without any regard to the nobility, gentry, and commonalty, our clergy have been publishing to the world that the king can do greater things than

by the order of May 4, 1688, to read the declaration of indulgence in their churches.ⁿ This, as is well known, met with great resistance, and, by inducing the primate and six other bishops to present a petition to the king against it, brought on that famous prosecution, which, more perhaps than all his former actions, cost him the allegiance of the Anglican church. The proceedings upon the trial of those prelates are so familiar as to require no particular notice.º What is most worthy of remark is, that the very party who had most extolled the royal prerogative, and often in such terms as if all limitations of it were only to subsist at pleasure, became now the instruments of bringing it down within the compass and control of the law. If the king had a right to suspend the execution of statutes by proclamation, the bishops' petition might not indeed be libellous, but their disobedience and that of the clergy could not be warranted; and the principal argument both of the bar and the bench rested on the great question of that prerogative.

The king, meantime, was blindly hurrying on at the instigation of his own pride and bigotry, and of some ignorant priests; confident in the fancied obedience of the church, and in the hollow support of the dissenters, after all his wiser counsellors, the catholic peers, the nuncio, perhaps the queen herself, had grown sensible of the danger, and solicitous for temporising measures. He had good reason to perceive that neither the fleet nor the army could be relied upon; to cashier the most rigidly protestant officers, to draft Irish troops into the regiments, to place all important commands in the hands of catholics, were difficult and even desperate measures, which rendered his designs more notorious, without rendering them more feasible. It is among the most astonishing parts of this unhappy sovereign's impolicy, that he sometimes neglected, even offended,

are done in his declaration; but now the scene is altered, and they are become more concerned to maintain their reputation even with the commonalty than with the king." See also in the same volume, p. 19, 'A remonstrance from the church of England to both houses of parliament,' 1685; and p. 145, 'A new test of the church of England's loyalty;' both, especially the latter, bitterly reproaching her members for their apostasy from former professions.

ⁿ Ralph, 982.

º See State Trials, xil. 183. D'Oyly's Life of Sancroft, i. 250.

never steadily and sufficiently courted, the sole ally that could by possibility have co-operated in his scheme of government. In his brother's reign James had been the most obsequious and unhesitating servant of the French king. Before his own accession, his first step was to implore, through Barillon, a continuance of that support and protection, without which he could undertake nothing which he had designed in favour of the catholics. He received a present of 500,000 livres with tears of gratitude; and telling the ambassador he had not disclosed his real designs to his ministers, pressed for a strict alliance with Louis, as the means of accomplishing them.[p] Yet, with a strange inconsistency, he drew off gradually from these professions, and not only kept on rather cool terms with France during part of his reign, but sometimes played a double game by treating of a league with Spain.

The secret of this uncertain policy, which has not been well known till very lately, is to be found in the king's character. James had a real sense of the dignity pertaining to a king of England, and much of the national pride as well as that of his rank. He felt the degradation of importuning an equal sovereign for money, which Louis gave less frequently and in smaller measure than it was demanded. It is natural for a proud man not to love those before whom he has abased himself. James, of frugal habits, and master of a great revenue, soon became more indifferent to a French pension. Nor was he insensible to the reproach of Europe, that he was grown the vassal of France and had tarnished the lustre of the English crown.[q] Had he been himself pro-

James's coldness towards Louis.

[p] Fox, App. 29; Dalrymple, 107; Mazure, i. 396, 433.

[q] Several proofs of this occur in the course of M. Mazure's work. When the Dutch ambassador, Van Citers, showed him a paper, probably forged to exasperate him, but purporting to be written by some catholics, wherein it was said that it would be better for the people to be vassals of France than slaves of the devil, he burst out into rage. "'Jamais! non, jamais! je ne ferai rien qui me puisse mettre au-dessous des rois de France et d'Espagne. Vassal! vassal de la France!' s'écria-t-il avec emportement. 'Monsieur! si le parlement avoit voulu, s'il vouloit encore, j'aurois porté, je porterois encore la monarchie à un degré de considération qu'elle n'a jamais eu sous aucun des rois mes prédécesseurs, et votre état y trouveroit peut-être sa propre sécurité.'" Vol. ii. 165. Sunderland said to Barillon, "Le roi d'Angleterre se recache de ne pas être en Europe tout ce qu'il devroit être; et souvent il se plaint que le roi votre maître n'a pas pour lui

testant, or his subjects catholic, he would probably have given the reins to that jealousy of his ambitious neighbour, which, even in his peculiar circumstances, restrained him from the most expedient course; I mean expedient, on the hypothesis that to overthrow the civil and religious institutions of his people was to be the main object of his reign. For it was idle to attempt this without the steady co-operation of France; and those sentiments of dignity and independence, which at first sight appear to do him honour, being without any consistent magnanimity of character, served only to accelerate his ruin, and confirm the persuasion of his incapacity.¹ Even in the memorable year 1688, though the veil was at length torn from his eyes on the verge of the precipice, and he sought in trembling the assistance he had slighted, his silly pride made him half unwilling to be rescued; and, when the French ambassador at the Hague, by a bold manœuvre of diplomacy, asserted to the States that an alliance already subsisted between his master and the king of England, the latter took offence at the unauthorised declaration, and complained privately that Louis treated him as an inferior.²

assez de considération." Id. 313. On the other hand, Louis was much mortified that James made so few applications for his aid. His hope seems to have been that by means of French troops, or troops at least in his pay, he should get a footing in England; and this was what the other was too proud and jealous to permit. "Comme le roi," he said, in 1687, " ne doute pas de mon affection et du désir que j'ai de voir la religion catholique bien établie en Angleterre, il faut croire qu'il se trouve assez de force et d'autorité pour exécuter ses desseins, puisqu'il n'a pas recours à moi." P. 258; also 174, 225, 326.

¹ James affected the same ceremonial as the king of France, and received the latter's ambassador sitting and covered. Louis only said, smiling, "Le roi mon frère est fier, mais il aime assez les pistoles de France." Mazure, i. 423. A more extraordinary trait of James's pride is mentioned by Dangeau, whom I quote from the Quarterly Review, xix. 470. After his retirement to St. Germains he wore violet in court mourning, which,

by etiquette, was confined to the kings of France. The courtiers were a little astonished to see *solem geminum*, though not at a loss where to worship. Louis, of course, had too much magnanimity to express resentment. But what a picture of littleness of spirit does this exhibit in a wretched pauper, who could only escape by the most contemptible insignificance the charge of most ungrateful insolence!

² Mazure, iii. 50. James was so much out of humour at D'Avaux's interference that he asked his confidants "if the king of France thought he could treat him like the cardinal of Furstenburg," a creature of Louis XIV. whom he had set up for the electorate of Cologne. Id. 69. He was, in short, so much displeased with his own ambassador at the Hague, Skelton, for giving in to this declaration of D'Avaux, that he not only recalled, but sent him to the Tower. Burnet is therefore mistaken, p. 769, in believing that there was actually an alliance, though it was very natural that he should give credit to what an ambassador asserted in a matter of such importance. In fact, a

It is probable that a more ingenuous policy in the court of Whitehall, by determining the king of France to declare war sooner on Holland, would have prevented the expedition of the prince of Orange.¹

The latter continued to receive strong assurances of attachment from men of rank in England; but wanted that direct invitation to enter the kingdom with force which he required both for his security and his justification. No men who thought much about their country's interests or their own would be hasty in venturing on so awful an enterprise. The punishment and ignominy of treason, the reproach of history, too often the sworn slave of fortune, awaited its failure. Thus Halifax and Nottingham found their conscience or their courage unequal to the crisis, and drew back from the hardy conspiracy that produced the Revolution.ᵘ Nor, perhaps, would the seven eminent persons, whose names are subscribed to the invitation addressed on the 30th. of June, 1688, to the prince of Orange, the earls of Danby, Shrewsbury, and Devonshire, lord Lumley, the bishop of London, Mr. Henry Sidney, and admiral Russell, have committed themselves so far, if the recent birth of a prince of Wales had not made some measures of force absolutely necessary for the common* interests of the nation and the prince of Orange.ˣ It cannot be said without absurdity that

Invitation signed to the prince of Orange.

Birth of the prince of Wales.

---

treaty was signed between James and Louis, Sept. 13, by which some French ships were to be under the former's orders. Mazure, iii. 67.

¹ Louis continued to find money, though despising James, and disgusted with him, probably with a view to his own grand interests. He should nevertheless have declared war against Holland in October, which must have put a stop to the armament. But he had discovered that James, with extreme meanness, had privately offered about the end of September to join the alliance against him as the only resource. This wretched action is first brought to light by M. Mazure, iii. 104. He excused himself to the king of France by an assurance that he was not acting sincerely towards Holland,

Louis, though he gave up his intention of declaring war, behaved with great magnanimity and compassion towards the falling bigot.

ᵘ Halifax all along discouraged the invasion, pointing out that the king made no progress in his schemes. Dalrymple, passim. Nottingham said he would keep the secret, but could not be a party to a treasonable undertaking (id. 228; Burnet, 764), and wrote as late as July to advise delay and caution. Notwithstanding the splendid success of the opposite counsels, it would be judging too servilely by the event not to admit that they were tremendously hazardous.

ˣ The invitation to William seems to have been in debate some time before the prince of Wales's birth; but it does not

James was guilty of any offence in becoming father of this child; yet it was evidently that which rendered his other offences inexpiable. He was now considerably advanced in life; and the decided resistance of his subjects made it improbable that he could do much essential injury to the established constitution during the remainder of it. The mere certainty of all reverting to a protestant heir would be an effectual guarantee of the Anglican church. But the birth of a son to be nursed in the obnoxious bigotry of Rome, the prospect of a regency under the queen, so deeply implicated, according to common report, in the schemes of this reign, made every danger appear more terrible. From the moment that the queen's pregnancy was announced, the catholics gave way to enthusiastic unrepressed exultation; and, by the confidence with which they prophesied the birth of an heir, furnished a pretext for the suspicions which a disappointed people began to entertain.^y These suspicions were very general: they extended to the highest ranks, and are a conspicuous instance of that prejudice which is chiefly founded on our wishes. Lord Danby, in a letter to William, of March 27, insinuates his doubt of the queen's pregnancy. After the child's birth, the seven subscribers to the association inviting the prince to come over, and pledging themselves to join him, say that not one in a thousand believe it to be the queen's; lord Devonshire separately held language to the same effect.^z The princess Anne talked with little restraint of her suspicions, and made no scruple of imparting them to her sister.^a Though no one can hesitate at present to acknowledge that the prince of Wales's legitimacy is out of all question, there was enough to raise a

---

follow that it would have been despatched if the queen had borne a daughter, nor do I think that it should have been.

^y Ralph, 980; Mazure, ll. 387.

^z Dalrymple, 216, 228. The prince was urged in the memorial of the seven to declare the fraud of the queen's pregnancy to be one of the grounds of his expedition. He did this: and it is the only part of his declaration that is false.

^a State Trials, xii. 161. Mary put some very sensible questions to her sister which show her desire of reaching the truth in so important a matter. They were answered in a style which shows that Anne did not mean to lessen her sister's suspicions. Dalrymple, 305. Her conversation with lord Clarendon on this subject, after the depositions had been taken, is a proof that she had made up her mind not to be convinced. Henry Earl of Clarendon's Diary, 77, 79. State Trials, ubi supra.

reasonable apprehension in the presumptive heir, that a party not really very scrupulous, and through religious animosity supposed to be still less so, had been induced by the undoubted prospect of advantage to draw the king, who had been wholly their slave, into one of those frauds which bigotry might call pious.[b]

The great event, however, of what has been emphatically denominated in the language of our public acts the Glorious Revolution stands in need of no vulgar credulity, no mistaken prejudice, for its support. It can only rest on the basis of a liberal theory of government, which looks to the public good as the great end for which positive laws and the constitutional order of states have been instituted. It cannot be defended without rejecting the slavish principles of absolute obedience, or even that pretended modification of them which imagines some extreme case of intolerable tyranny, some, as it were, lunacy of despotism, as the only plea and palliation of resistance. Doubtless the administration of James II. was not of this nature. Doubtless he was not a Caligula, or a Commodus, or an Ezzelin, or a Galeazzo Sforza, or a Christiern II. of Denmark, or a Charles IX. of France, or one of those almost innumerable tyrants whom men have endured in the wantonness of unlimited power. No man had been deprived of his liberty by any illegal warrant. No man, except in the single though very important instance of Magdalen College, had been despoiled of his property. I must also add that the government of James II. will lose little by comparison with that of his father. The judgment in favour of his prerogative to dispense with the test was far more according to received notions of law, far less injurious and unconstitutional, than that which gave a sanction to ship-money. The injunction to read the declaration of indulgence in churches was less offensive to scrupulous men than the similar command to read the declaration of Sunday sports in the time of Charles I. Nor was any one punished for a refusal to comply with the

Justice and necessity of the Revolution.

---

[b] M. Mazure has collected all the passages in the letters of Barillon and Bonrepos to the court of France relative to the queen's pregnancy, ii. 366, and those relative to the birth of the prince of Wales, p. 547. It is to be observed that this took place more than a month before the time expected.

one; while the prisons had been filled with those who had disobeyed the other. Nay, what is more, there are much stronger presumptions of the father's than of the son's intention to lay aside parliaments, and set up an avowed despotism. It is indeed amusing to observe that many who scarcely put bounds to their eulogies of Charles I. have been content to abandon the cause of one who had no faults in his public conduct but such as seemed to have come by inheritance. The characters of the father and son were very closely similar; both proud of their judgment as well as their station, and still more obstinate in their understanding than in their purpose; both scrupulously conscientious in certain great points of conduct, to the sacrifice of that power which they had preferred to everything else; the one far superior in relish for the arts and for polite letters, the other more diligent and indefatigable in business; the father exempt from those vices of a court to which the son was too long addicted; not so harsh, perhaps, or prone to severity in his temper, but inferior in general sincerity and adherence to his word. They were both equally unfitted for the condition in which they were meant to stand—the limited kings of a wise and free people, the chiefs of the English commonwealth.

The most plausible argument against the necessity of so violent a remedy for public grievances as the abjuration of allegiance to a reigning sovereign was one that misled half the nation in that age, and is still sometimes insinuated by those whose pity for the misfortunes of the house of Stuart appears to predominate over every other sentiment which the history of the revolution should excite. It was alleged that the constitutional mode of address by parliament was not taken away; that the king's attempts to obtain promises of support from the electors and probable representatives showed his intention of calling one; that the writs were in fact ordered before the prince of Orange's expedition; that after the invader had reached London, James still offered to refer the terms of reconciliation with his people to a free parliament, though he could have no hope of evading any that might be proposed; that by reversing illegal judgments, by annulling unconstitutional dis-

pensations, by reinstating those who had been unjustly
dispossessed, by punishing wicked advisers, above all,
by passing statutes to restrain the excesses and cut off
the dangerous prerogatives of the monarchy (as efficacious, or more so, than the bill of rights and other
measures that followed the revolution), all risk of arbitrary power, or of injury to the established religion,
might have been prevented, without a violation of that
hereditary right which was as fundamental in the constitution as any of the subject's privileges. It was not
necessary to enter upon the delicate problem of absolute non-resistance, or to deny that the conservation of
the whole was paramount to all positive laws. The
question to be proved was, that a regard to this general
safety exacted the means employed in the revolution,
and constituted that extremity which could alone justify
such a deviation from the standard rules of law and
religion.

It is evidently true that James had made very little
progress, or rather experienced a signal defeat, in his
endeavour to place the professors of his own religion
on a firm and honourable basis. There seems the
strongest reason to believe that, far from reaching his
end through the new parliament, he would have experienced those warm assaults on the administration
which generally distinguished the house of commons
under his father and brother. But, as he was in no
want of money, and had not the temper to endure what
he thought the language of republican faction, we may
be equally sure that a short and angry session would
have ended with a more decided resolution on his side
to govern in future without such impracticable counsellors. The doctrine imputed of old to lord Strafford,
that, after trying the good-will of parliament in vain, a
king was absolved from the legal maxims of government, was always at the heart of the Stuarts. His
army was numerous, according at least to English
notions; he had already begun to fill it with popish
officers and soldiers; the militia, though less to be depended on, was under the command of lord and deputy
lieutenants carefully selected; above all, he would at
the last have recourse to France; and though the
experiment of bringing over French troops was very

hazardous, it is difficult to say that he might not have succeeded, with all these means, in preventing or putting down any concerted insurrection. But at least the renewal of civil bloodshed and the anarchy of rebellion seemed to be the alternative of slavery, if William had never earned the just title of our deliverer. It is still more evident that, after the invasion had taken place, and a general defection had exhibited the king's inability to resist, there could have been no such compromise as the tories fondly expected, no legal and peaceable settlement in what they called a free parliament, leaving James in the real and recognised possession of his constitutional prerogatives. Those who have grudged William III. the laurels that he won for our service are ever prone to insinuate that his unnatural ambition would be content with nothing less than the crown, instead of returning to his country after he had convinced the king of the error of his counsels, and obtained securities for the religion and liberties of England. The hazard of the enterprise, and most hazardous it truly was, was to have been his; the profit and advantage our own. I do not know that William absolutely expected to place himself on the throne; because he could hardly anticipate that James would so precipitately abandon a kingdom wherein he was acknowledged, and had still many adherents. But undoubtedly he must, in consistency with his magnanimous designs, have determined to place England in its natural station, as a party in the great alliance against the power of Louis XIV. To this one object of securing the liberties of Europe, and chiefly of his own country, the whole of his heroic life was directed with undeviating, undisheartened firmness. He had in view no distant prospect, when the entire succession of the Spanish monarchy would be claimed by that insatiable prince, whose renunciation at the treaty of the Pyrenees was already maintained to be invalid. Against the present aggressions and future schemes of this neighbour the league of Augsburg had just been concluded. England, a free, a protestant, a maritime kingdom, would, in her natural position, as a rival of France, and deeply concerned in the independence of the Netherlands, become a leading member of this confederacy. But the sinister attachments of the house of Stuart had long diverted her from her true interests, and rendered her councils disgracefully and treacherously subservient to those of Louis. It was therefore the main object of the prince of Orange to strengthen the alliance by the vigorous co-operation of this kingdom; and with no other view, the emperor, and even the pope, had abetted his undertaking. But it was impossible to imagine that James would have come with sincerity into measures so repugnant to his predilections and interests. What better could be expected than a recurrence of that false and hollow system which had betrayed Europe and dishonoured England under Charles II.; or rather, would not the sense of injury and thraldom have inspired still more deadly aversion to the cause of those to whom he must have ascribed his humiliation? There was as little reason to hope that he would abandon the long-cherished schemes of arbitrary power, and the sacred interests of his own faith. We must remember that, when the adherents or apologists of James II. have spoken of him as an unfortunately misguided prince, they have insinuated what neither the notorious history of those times, nor the more secret information since brought to light, will in any degree confirm. It was indeed a strange excuse for a king of such mature years, and so trained in the most diligent attention to business. That in some particular instances he acted under the influence of his confessor, Petre, is not unlikely; but the general temper of his administration, his notions of government, the objects he had in view, were perfectly his own, and were pursued rather in spite of much dissuasion and many warnings than through the suggestions of any treacherous counsellors.

Both with respect therefore to the prince of Orange and to the English nation, James II. was to be considered as an enemy whose resentment could never be appeased, and whose power consequently must be wholly taken away. It is true that, if he had remained in England, it would have been extremely difficult to deprive him of the nominal sovereignty. But in this case, the prince of Orange must have been invested, by some course or other, with all its real attributes. He undoubtedly intended to remain in this country; and could not otherwise have preserved that entire ascendancy which was necessary for his ultimate purposes. The king could not have been permitted, with any common prudence, to retain the choice of his ministers, or the command of his army, or his negative voice in laws, or even his personal liberty; by which I mean that his guards must have been either Dutch, or at least appointed by the prince and parliament. Less than this it would have been childish to require; and this would not have been endured by any man even of James's spirit, or by the nation when the reaction of loyalty should return, without continued efforts to get rid of an arrangement far more revolutionary and subversive of the established monarchy than the king's deposition.

In the Revolution of 1688 there was an unusual combination of favouring circumstances, and some of the most important, such as the king's sudden flight, not within prior calculation, which renders it no precedent for other times and occasions in point of expediency, whatever it may be in point of justice. Resistance to tyranny by overt rebellion incurs not only the risks of failure, but those of national impoverishment and confusion, of vindictive retaliation, and such aggressions (perhaps inevitable) on private right and liberty as render the name of revolution and its adherents odious. Those, on the other hand, who call in a powerful neighbour to protect them from domestic oppression, may too often expect to realise the horse of the fable, and endure a subjection more severe, permanent, and ignominious, than what they shake off. But the revolution effected by William III. united the independent character of a national act with the regularity and the coercion of anarchy which belong to a military invasion. The United Provinces were not such a foreign potentate as could put in jeopardy the independence of England; nor could his army have maintained itself against the inclinations of the kingdom, though it was sufficient to repress any turbulence that would naturally attend so extraordinary a crisis. Nothing was done by the multitude; no new men, either soldiers or demagogues, had their talents brought forward by this rapid and pacific revolution; it cost no blood, it violated no right, it was hardly to

Favourable circumstances attending the Revolution.

be traced in the course of justice; the formal and exterior character of the monarchy remained nearly the same in so complete a regeneration of its spirit. Few nations can hope to ascend up to the sphere of a just and honourable liberty, especially when long use has made the track of obedience familiar, and they have learned to move as it were only by the clank of the chain, with so little toil and hardship. We reason too exclusively from this peculiar instance of 1688 when we hail the fearful struggles of other revolutions with a sanguine and confident sympathy. Nor is the only error upon this side. For, as if the inveterate and cankerous ills of a commonwealth could be extirpated with no loss and suffering, we are often prone to abandon the popular cause in agitated nations with as much fickleness as we embraced it, when we find that intemperance, irregularity, and confusion, from which great revolutions are very seldom exempt. These are indeed so much their usual attendants, the reaction of a self-deceived multitude is so probable a consequence, the general prospect of success in most cases so precarious, that wise and good men are more likely to hesitate too long than to rush forward too eagerly. Yet, "whatever be the cost of this noble liberty, we must be content to pay it to Heaven."^c

It is unnecessary even to mention those circumstances of this great event which are minutely known to almost all my readers. They were all eminently favourable in their effect to the regeneration of our constitution; even one of temporary inconvenience, namely, the return of James to London, after his detention by the fishermen near Feversham. This, as Burnet has observed, and as is easily demonstrated by the writings of that time, gave a different colour to the state of affairs, and raised up a party which did not before exist, or at least was too disheartened to show itself.^d His first desertion of the kingdom had dis-

---

^c Montesquieu.
^d Some short pamphlets, written at this juncture to excite sympathy for the king and disapprobation of the course pursued with respect to him, are in the Somers Collection, vol. ix. But this force put upon their sovereign first wounded the consciences of Sancroft and the other bishops, who had hitherto done as much as in their station they well could to ruin the king's cause and paralyse his arms. Several modern writers have endeavoured to throw an interest about James at the moment of his fall,

gusted every one, and might be construed into a voluntary cession. But his return to assume again the government put William under the necessity of using that intimidation which awakened the mistaken sympathy of a generous people. It made his subsequent flight, though certainly not what a man of courage enough to give his better judgment free play would have chosen, appear excusable and defensive. It brought out too glaringly, I mean for the satisfaction of prejudiced minds, the undeniable fact, that the two houses of convention deposed and expelled their sovereign. Thus the great schism of the Jacobites, though it must otherwise have existed, gained its chief strength; and the revolution, to which at the outset a coalition of whigs and tories had conspired, became, in its final result, in the settlement of the crown upon William and Mary, almost entirely the work of the former party.

But while the position of the new government was thus rendered less secure, by narrowing the basis of public opinion whereon it stood, the liberal principles of policy which the whigs had espoused became incomparably more powerful, and were necessarily involved in the continuance of the revolution-settlement. The ministers of William III. and of the house of Brunswick had no choice but to respect and countenance the doctrines of Locke, Hoadley, and Molesworth. The assertion of passive obedience to the crown grew obnoxious to the crown itself. Our new line of sovereigns scarcely ventured to hear of their hereditary right, and dreaded the cup of flattery that was drugged with poison. This was the greatest change that affected our monarchy by the fall of the house of Stuart. The laws were not so materially altered as the spirit and senti-

either from a lurking predilection for all legitimately crowned heads, or from a notion that it becomes a generous historian to excite compassion for the unfortunate. There can be no objection to pitying James, if this feeling is kept unmingled with any blame of those who were the instruments of his misfortune. It was highly expedient for the good of this country, because the revolution-settlement could not otherwise be attained.

to work on James's sense of his deserted state by intimidation; and for that purpose the order conveyed by three of his own subjects, perhaps with some rudeness of manner, to leave Whitehall, was necessary. The drift of several accounts of the Revolution that may be read is to hold forth Mulgrave, Craven, Arran, and Dundee to admiration, at the expense of William and of those who achieved the great consolidation of English liberty. .

ments of the people. Hence those who look only at the former have been prone to underrate the magnitude of this revolution. The fundamental maxims of the constitution, both as they regard the king and the subject, may seem nearly the same; but the disposition with which they were received and interpreted was entirely different.

It was in this turn of feeling, in this change, if I may so say, of the heart, far more than in any positive statutes and improvements of the law, that I consider the Revolution to have been eminently conducive to our freedom and prosperity. Laws and statutes as remedial, nay, more closely limiting the prerogative than the bill of rights and act of settlement, might possibly have been obtained from James himself, as the price of his continuance on the throne, or from his family as that of their restoration to it. But what the Revolution did for us was this; it broke a spell that had charmed the nation. It cut up by the roots all that theory of indefeasible right, of paramount prerogative, which had put the crown in continual opposition to the people. A contention had now subsisted for five hundred years, but particularly during the last four reigns, against the aggressions of arbitrary power. The sovereigns of this country had never patiently endured the control of parliament; nor was it natural for them to do so, while the two houses of parliament appeared historically, and in legal language, to derive their existence as well as privileges from the crown itself. They had at their side the pliant lawyers, who held the prerogative to be uncontrollable by statutes, a doctrine of itself destructive to any scheme of reconciliation and compromise between the king and his subjects; they had the churchmen, whose casuistry denied that the most intolerable tyranny could excuse resistance to a lawful government. These two propositions could not obtain general acceptance without rendering all national liberty precarious.

It has been always reckoned among the most difficult problems in the practical science of government to combine an hereditary monarchy with security of freedom, so that neither the ambition of kings shall undermine the people's rights, nor the jealousy of the people

Its salutary consequences.

overturn the throne. England had already experience of both these mischiefs. And there seemed no prospect before her, but either their alternate recurrence, or a final submission to absolute power, unless by one great effort she could put the monarchy for ever beneath the law, and reduce it to an integrant portion instead of the primary source and principle of the constitution. She must reverse the favoured maxim, "A Deo rex, à rege lex;" and make the crown itself appear the creature of the law. But our ancient monarchy, strong in a possession of seven centuries, and in those high and paramount prerogatives which the consenting testimony of lawyers and the submission of parliaments had recognised, a monarchy from which the house of commons and every existing peer, though not perhaps the aristocratic order itself, derived its participation in the legislature, could not be bent to the republican theories which have been not very successfully attempted in some modern codes of constitution. It could not be held, without breaking up all the foundations of our polity, that the monarchy emanated from the parliament, or, in any historical sense, from the people. But by the Revolution, and by the act of settlement, the rights of the actual monarch, of the reigning family, were made to emanate from the parliament and the people. In technical language, in the grave and respectful theory of our constitution, the crown is still the fountain from which law and justice spring forth. Its prerogatives are in the main the same as under the Tudors and the Stuarts; but the right of the house of Brunswick to exercise them can only be deduced from the convention of 1688.

The great advantage therefore of the Revolution, as I would explicitly affirm, consists in that which was reckoned its reproach by many, and its misfortune by more—that it broke the line of succession. No other remedy could have been found, according to the temper and prejudices of those times, against the unceasing conspiracy of power. But when the very tenure of power was conditional, when the crown, as we may say, gave recognizances for its good behaviour, when any violent and concerted aggressions on public liberty would have ruined those who could only resist an in-

veterate faction by the arms which liberty put in their
hands, the several parts of the constitution were kept in
cohesion by a tie far stronger than statutes, that of a
common interest in its preservation. The attachment
of James to popery, his infatuation, his obstinacy, his
pusillanimity, nay even the death of the duke of Gloucester, the life of the prince of Wales, the extraordinary
permanence and fidelity of his party, were all the destined means through which our present grandeur and
liberty, our dignity of thinking on matters of government, have been perfected. Those liberal tenets, which
at the era of the Revolution were maintained but by one
denomination of English party, and rather perhaps on
authority of not very good precedents in our history
than of sound general reasoning, became in the course
of the next generation almost equally the creed of the
other, whose long exclusion from government taught
them to solicit the people's favour; and by the time
that Jacobitism was extinguished had passed into received maxims of English politics. None at least would
care to call them in question within the walls of parliament; nor have their opponents been of much credit in
the paths of literature. Yet, as since the extinction of
the house of Stuart's pretensions, and other events of
the last half-century, we have seen those exploded doctrines of indefeasible hereditary right revived under
another name, and some have been willing to misrepre-
sent the transactions of the Revolution and the act of
settlement as if they did not absolutely amount to a
deposition of the reigning sovereign, and an election of
a new dynasty by the representatives of the nation in
parliament, it may be proper to state precisely the
several votes, and to point out the impossibility of
reconciling them to any gentler construction.

The lords spiritual and temporal, to the number of
about ninety, and an assembly of all who *Proceedings*
had sat in any of king Charles's parliaments, *of the con-*
with the lord mayor and fifty of the common *vention.*
council, requested the prince of Orange to take upon
him the administration after the king's second flight,
and to issue writs for a convention in the usual manner.*

* Parl. Hist. v. 26. The former ad- signed by the peers and bishops, who met
dress on the king's first quitting London, at Guildhall, Dec. 11, did not, in express

This was on the 26th of December; and the convention met on the 22nd of January. Their first care was to address the prince to take the administration of affairs and disposal of the revenue into his hands, in order to give a kind of parliamentary sanction to the power he already exercised. On the 28th of January the commons, after a debate in which the friends of the late king made but a faint opposition,[f] came to their great vote: That king James II., having endeavoured to subvert the constitution of this kingdom, by breaking the original contract between king and people, and by the advice of Jesuits and other wicked persons having violated the fundamental laws, and having withdrawn himself out of the kingdom, has abdicated the government, and that the throne is thereby vacant. They resolved unanimously the next day, That it hath been found by experience inconsistent with the safety and welfare of this protestant kingdom to be governed by a popish prince.[g] This vote was a remarkable triumph of the whig party, who had contended for the exclusion bill; and, on account of that endeavour to establish a principle which no one was now found to controvert, had been subjected to all the insults and reproaches of the opposite faction. The lords agreed with equal unanimity to this vote; which, though it was expressed only as an abstract proposition, led by a practical inference to the whole change that the whigs had in view. But upon the former resolution several important divisions

---

terms, desire the prince of Orange to assume the government, or to call a parliament, though it evidently tended to that result, censuring the king and extolling the prince's conduct. Id. 19. It was signed by the archbishop, his last public act. Burnet has exposed himself to the lash of Ralph by stating this address of Dec. 11 incorrectly. [The prince issued two proclamations, Jan. 16 and 21, addressed to the soldiers and sailors, on which Ralph comments in his usual invidious manner. They are certainly expressed in a high tone of sovereignty, without the least allusion to the king, or to the request of the peers, and some phrases might give offence to our lawyers. Ralph, ii. 10.—1845.]

[f] [It appears by some notes of the debate in the convention, published in the Hardwicke Papers, ii. 401, that the vote of abdication was carried with only three negatives. The tide ran too high for the tories, though some of them spoke; they recovered their spirits after the lords' amendments. This account of the debate is remarkable, and clears up much that is obscure in Grey, whom the Parliamentary History has copied. The declaration of right was drawn up rather hastily, serjeant Maynard, as well as younger lawyers, pressing for no delay in filling the throne. I suppose that the wish to screen themselves under the statute of Henry VII. had something to do with this, which was also very expedient in itself.—1845.]

[g] Commons' Journals; Parl. Hist.

took place. The first question put, in order to save a nominal allegiance to the late king, was, whether a regency, with the administration of regal power under the style of king James II. during the life of the said king James, be the best and safest way to preserve the protestant religion and the laws of this kingdom? This was supported both by those peers who really meant to exclude the king from the enjoyment of power, such as Nottingham, its great promoter, and by those who, like Clarendon, were anxious for his return upon terms of security for their religion and liberty. The motion was lost by fifty-one to forty-nine; and this seems to have virtually decided, in the judgment of the house, that James had lost the throne.[b] The lords then resolved that there was an original contract between the king and the people, by fifty-five to forty-six; a position that seems rather too theoretical, yet necessary at that time, as denying the divine origin of monarchy, from which its absolute and indefeasible authority had been plausibly derived. They concurred, without much debate, in the rest of the commons' vote, till they came to the clause that he had abdicated the government, for which they substituted the word "deserted." They next omitted the final and most important clause, that the throne was thereby vacant, by a majority of fifty-five to forty-one. This was owing to the party of lord Danby, who asserted a devolution of the crown on the princess of Orange. It seemed to be tacitly understood by both sides that the infant child was to be presumed spurious. This at least was a necessary supposition for the tories, who sought in the idle rumours of the time an excuse for abandoning his right. As to the whigs, though they were active in discrediting this unfortunate boy's legitimacy, their own broad principles of changing the line of succession rendered it, in point of argument, a superfluous inquiry. The tories, who had made little resistance to the vote of abdication, when it was proposed in the commons, recovered courage by this difference be-

[b] Somerville and several other writers have not accurately stated the question, and suppose the lords to have debated whether the throne, on the hypothesis of its vacancy, should be filled by a king or a regent. Such a mode of putting the question would have been absurd. I observe that M. Mazure has been deceived by these authorities.

tween the two houses; and, perhaps by observing the
king's party to be stronger out of doors than it had
appeared to be, were able to muster 151 voices against
282 in favour of agreeing with the lords in leaving out
the clause about the vacancy of the throne.¹ There was
still, however, a far greater preponderance of the whigs
in one part of the convention than of the tories in the
other. In the famous conference that ensued between
committees of the two houses upon these amendments,
it was never pretended that the word "abdication" was
used in its ordinary sense, for a voluntary resignation
of the crown. The commons did not practise so pitiful
a subterfuge. Nor could the lords explicitly maintain,
whatever might be the wishes of their managers, that
the king was not expelled and excluded as much by
their own word "desertion" as by that which the lower
house had employed. Their own previous vote against
a regency was decisive upon this point.ᵏ But as abdication was a gentler term than forfeiture, so desertion
appeared a still softer method of expressing the same
idea. Their chief objection, however, to the former
word was that it led, or might seem to lead, to the
vacancy of the throne, against which their principal
arguments were directed. They contended that in our
government there could be no interval or vacancy, the
heir's right being complete by a demise of the crown;
so that it would at once render the monarchy elective,
if any other person were designated to the succession.
The commons did not deny that the present case was
one of election, though they refused to allow that the
monarchy was thus rendered perpetually elective. They
asked, supposing a right to descend upon the next heir,
who was that heir to inherit it? and gained one of their
chief advantages by the difficulty of evading this question. It was indeed evident that, if the lords should
carry their amendments, an inquiry into the legitimacy
of the prince of Wales could by no means be dispensed
with. Unless that could be disproved more satisfac-

¹ Parl. Hist. 61. The chief speakers on this side were old sir Thomas Clarges, brother-in-law of general Monk, who had been distinguished as an opponent of administration under Charles and James, and Mr. Finch, brother of lord Notting-ham, who had been solicitor-general to Charles, but was removed in the late reign.

ᵏ James is called "the late king" in a resolution of the lords on Feb. 2.

torily than they had reason to hope, they must come back to the inconveniences of a regency, with the prospect of bequeathing interminable confusion to their posterity. For, if the descendants of James should continue in the Roman catholic religion, the nation might be placed in the ridiculous situation of acknowledging a dynasty of exiled kings, whose lawful prerogative would be withheld by another race of protestant regents. It was indeed strange to apply the provisional substitution of a regent in cases of infancy or imbecility of mind to a prince of mature age, and full capacity for the exercise of power. Upon the king's return to England this delegated authority must cease of itself, unless supported by votes of parliament as violent and incompatible with the regular constitution as his deprivation of the royal title, but far less secure for the subject, whom the statute of Henry VII. would shelter in paying obedience to a king de facto, while the fate of sir Henry Vane was an awful proof that no other name could give countenance to usurpation. A great part of the nation not thirty years before had been compelled by acts of parliament[m] to declare upon oath their abhorrence of that traitorous position, that arms might be taken up by the king's authority against his person or those commissioned by him, through the influence of those very tories or loyalists who had now recourse to the identical distinction between the king's natural and political capacity, for which the presbyterians had incurred so many reproaches.

In this conference, however, if the whigs had every advantage on the solid grounds of expediency, or rather political necessity, the tories were as much superior in the mere argument, either as it regarded the common sense of words, or the principles of our constitutional law. Even should we admit that an hereditary king is competent to abdicate the throne in the name of all his posterity, this could only be intended of a voluntary and formal cession, not such a constructive abandonment of his right by misconduct as the commons had imagined. The word "forfeiture" might better have answered this purpose; but it had seemed too great a

---

[m] 13 Car. II. c. 1; 17 Car. II. c. II.

violence on principles which it was more convenient to undermine than to assault. Nor would even forfeiture bear out by analogy the exclusion of an heir whose right was not liable to be set aside at the ancestor's pleasure. It was only by recurring to a kind of paramount, and what I may call hyper-constitutional law, a mixture of force and regard to the national good, which is the best sanction of what is done in revolutions, that the vote of the commons could be defended. They proceeded not by the stated rules of the English government, but the general rights of mankind. They looked not so much to Magna Charta as the original compact of society, and rejected Coke and Hale for Hooker and Harrington.

The house of lords, after this struggle against principles undoubtedly very novel in the discussions of parliament, gave way to the strength of circumstance and the steadiness of the commons. They resolved not to insist on their amendments to the original vote; and followed this up by a resolution, that the prince and princess of Orange shall be declared king and queen of England, and all the dominions thereunto belonging.ᵃ But the commons with a noble patriotism delayed to concur in this hasty settlement of the crown, till they should have completed the declaration of those fundamental rights and liberties for the sake of which alone they had gone forward with this great revolution.ᵒ That declaration, being at once an exposition of the misgovernment which had compelled them to dethrone the late king, and of the conditions upon which they elected his successors, was incorporated in the final resolution to which both houses came on the 13th of February, extending the limitation of the crown as far

---

ᵃ This was carried by sixty-two to forty-seven, according to lord Clarendon; several of the tories going over, and others who had been hitherto absent coming down to vote. Forty peers protested, including twelve bishops out of seventeen present. Trelawney, who had voted against the regency, was one of them, but not Compton, Lloyd of St. Asaph, Crewe, Sprat, or Hall; the three former, I believe, being in the majority. Lloyd had been absent when the vote passed against a regency, out of unwillingness to disagree with the majority of his brethren; but he was entirely of Burnet's mind. The votes of the bishops are not accurately stated in most books, which has induced me to mention them here. Lords' Journals, Feb. 6.

ᵒ It had been resolved, Jan. 29, that, before the committee proceed to fill the throne now vacant, they will proceed to secure our religion, laws, and liberties.

as the state of affairs required: "That William and Mary, prince and princess of Orange, be, and be declared, king and queen of England, France, and Ireland, and the dominions thereunto belonging, to hold the crown and dignity of the said kingdoms and dominions to them, the said prince and princess, during their lives, and the life of the survivor of them; and that the sole and full exercise of the regal power be only in, and executed by, the said prince of Orange, in the names of the said prince and princess, during their joint lives; and after their decease the said crown and royal dignity of the said kingdoms and dominions to be to the heirs of the body of the said princess; for default of such issue, to the princess Anne of Denmark, and the heirs of her body; and for default of such issue, to the heirs of the body of the said prince of Orange."

Elevation of William and Mary to the throne.

Thus, to sum up the account of this extraordinary change in our established monarchy, the convention pronounced, under the slight disguise of a word unusual in the language of English law, that the actual sovereign had forfeited his right to the nation's allegiance. It swept away by the same vote the reversion of his posterity and of those who could claim the inheritance of the crown. It declared that, during an interval of nearly two months, there was no king of England; the monarchy lying, as it were, in abeyance from the 23rd of December to the 13th of February. It bestowed the crown on William, jointly with his wife indeed, but so that her participation of the sovereignty should be only in name.ᵖ It postponed the succession of the princess

---

ᵖ See Burnet's remarkable conversation with Bentinck, wherein the former warmly opposed the settlement of the crown on the prince of Orange alone, as Halifax had suggested. But nothing in it is more remarkable than that the bishop does not perceive that this was virtually done; for it would be difficult to prove that Mary's royalty differed at all from that of a queen consort, except in having her name in the style. She was exactly in the same predicament as Philip had been during his marriage with Mary I. Her admirable temper made her acquiesce in this exclusion from power, which the sterner character of her husband demanded; and with respect to the conduct of the convention, it must be observed that the nation owed her no particular debt of gratitude, nor had she any better claim than her sister to fill a throne by election which had been declared vacant. In fact, there was no middle course between what was done, and following the precedent of Philip, as to which Bentinck said he fancied the prince would not like to be his wife's gentleman usher; for a divided

Anne during his life. Lastly, it made no provision for
any future devolution of the crown in failure of issue
from those to whom it was thus limited, leaving that to
the wisdom of future parliaments. Yet only eight years
before, nay much less, a large part of the nation had
loudly proclaimed the incompetency of a full parliament, with a lawful king at its head, to alter the lineal
course of succession. No whig had then openly professed the doctrine, that not only a king, but an entire
royal family, might be set aside for public convenience.
The notion of an original contract was denounced as a
republican chimera. The deposing of kings was branded
as the worst birth of popery and fanaticism. If other
revolutions have been more extensive in their effect on
the established government, few perhaps have displayed
a more rapid transition of public opinion. For it cannot, I think, be reasonably doubted that the majority
of the nation went along with the vote of their representatives. Such was the termination of that contest
which the house of Stuart had obstinately maintained
against the liberties, and of late against the religion, of
England; or rather, of that far more ancient controversy between the crown and the people which had
never been wholly at rest since the reign of John.
During this long period, the balance, except in a few
irregular intervals, had been swayed in favour of the
crown; and though the government of England was
always a monarchy limited by law, though it always, or
at least since the admission of the commons into the
legislature, partook of the three simple forms, yet the
character of a monarchy was evidently prevalent over
the other parts of the constitution. But, since the Re-

sovereignty was a monstrous and impracticable expedient in theory, however
the submissive disposition of the queen
might have prevented its mischiefs. Burnet seems to have had a puzzled view
of this: for he says afterwards "It
seemed to be a double-bottomed monarchy, where there were two joint sovereigns; but those who know the queen's
temper and principles had no apprehensions of divided counsels or of a distracted
government." Vol. ii. p. 2. The convention had not trusted to the queen's
temper and principles It required a
distinct act of parliament (2 W. & M.
c. 6) to enable her to exercise the regal
power during the king's absence from
England. [It was urged by some, not
without plausible grounds, on Mary's
death, that the parliament was dissolved
by that event, the writs having been
issued in her name as well as the king's.
A paper printed, but privately handed
about, with the design to prove this, will
be found in Parl. Hist. v. 867. But it
was not warmly taken up by any party
—1845.]

volution of 1688, and particularly from thence to the death of George II., after which the popular element grew much stronger, it seems equally just to say that the predominating character has been aristocratical; the prerogative being in some respects too limited, and in others too little capable of effectual exercise, to counterbalance the hereditary peerage, and that class of great territorial proprietors who, in a political division, are to be reckoned among the proper aristocracy of the kingdom. This, however, will be more fully explained in the two succeeding chapters.

CHAPTER XV.

ON THE REIGN OF WILLIAM III

Declaration of Rights — Bill of Rights — Military Force without Consent declared illegal — Discontent with the new Government — Its Causes — Incompatibility of the Revolution with received Principles — Character and Errors of William — Jealousy of the Whigs — Bill of Indemnity — Bill for restoring Corporations — Settlement of the Revenue — Appropriation of Supplies — Dissatisfaction of the King — No Republican Party in Existence — William employs Tories in Ministry — Intrigues with the late King — Schemes for his Restoration — Attainder of Sir John Fenwick — Ill Success of the War — Its Expenses — Treaty of Ryswick — Jealousy of the Commons — Army reduced — Irish forfeitures resumed — Parliamentary Inquiries — Treaties of Partition — Improvements in Constitution under William — Bill for Triennial Parliaments — Law of Treason — Statute of Edward III. — Its constructive Interpretation — Statute of William III. — Liberty of the Press — Law of Libel — Religious Toleration — Attempt at Comprehension — Schism of the Nonjurors — Laws against Roman Catholics — Act of Settlement — Limitations of Prerogative contained in it — Privy Council superseded by a Cabinet — Exclusion of Placemen and Pensioners from Parliament — Independence of Judges — Oath of Abjuration.

THE Revolution is not to be considered as a mere effort of the nation on a pressing emergency to rescue itself from the violence of a particular monarch; much less as grounded upon the danger of the Anglican church, its emoluments, and dignities, from the bigotry of a hostile religion. It was rather the triumph of those principles which, in the language of the present day, are denominated liberal or constitutional, over those of absolute monarchy, or of monarchy not effectually controlled by stated boundaries. It was the termination of a contest between the regal power and that of parliament, which could not have been brought to so favourable an issue by any other means. But, while the chief renovation in the spirit of our government was likely to spring from breaking the line of succession, while no positive enactments would have sufficed to give security to freedom with the legitimate race of Stuart on the throne, it would have been most culpable, and even preposterous, to permit this occasion to pass by without asserting and defining those rights and liberties which the very indeterminate nature of the king's prerogative at common law, as well as the unequivocal extension it had lately received, must continually place in jeopardy. The house of lords, indeed, as I have observed in the last chapter, would have conferred the crown on William and Mary, leaving the redress of grievances to future arrangement; and some eminent lawyers in the commons, Maynard and Pollexfen, seem to have had apprehensions of keeping the nation too long in a state of anarchy.* But the great majority of the commons wisely resolved to go at once to the root of the nation's grievances, and show their new sovereign that he was raised to the throne for the sake of those liberties by violating which his predecessor had forfeited it.

The declaration of rights presented to the prince of Orange by the marquis of Halifax, as speaker of the lords, in the presence of both houses, on the 18th of February, consists of three parts: a recital of the illegal and arbitrary acts committed by the late king, and of their consequent vote of abdication; a declaration, nearly following the words of the former part, that such enumerated acts are illegal; and a resolution that the throne shall be filled by the prince and princess of Orange, according to the limitations mentioned in the last chapter. Thus the declaration of rights was indissolubly connected with the revolution-settlement, as its motive and its condition. *Declaration of rights.*

The lords and commons in this instrument declare: That the pretended power of suspending laws, and the execution of laws, by regal authority without consent of parliament, is illegal; That the pretended power of dispensing with laws by regal authority, as it hath been assumed and exercised of late, is illegal; That the commission for creating the late court of commissioners for ecclesiastical causes, and all other commissions and courts of the like nature, are illegal and pernicious; That levying of money for or to the use of the crown, by pretence of prerogative without grant of parliament, for longer time or in any other manner than the same is or shall be granted, is illegal; That it is the right of

* Parl. Hist. v. 54.

the subjects to petition the king, and that all commitments or prosecutions for such petitions are illegal; That the raising or keeping a standing army within the kingdom in time of peace, unless it be with consent of parliament, is illegal; That the subjects which are protestants may have arms for their defence suitable to their condition, and as allowed by law; That elections of members of parliament ought to be free; That the freedom of speech or debates, or proceedings in parliament, ought not to be impeached or questioned in any court or place out of parliament; That excessive bail ought not to be required, nor excessive fines imposed, nor cruel and unusual punishments inflicted; That juries ought to be duly impanelled and returned, and that jurors which pass upon men in trials of high treason ought to be freeholders; That all grants and promises of fines and forfeitures of particular persons, before conviction, are illegal and void; And that, for redress of all grievances, and for the amending, strengthening, and preserving of the laws, parliaments ought to be held frequently.[b]

Bill of rights.
This declaration was, some months afterwards, confirmed by a regular act of the legislature in the bill of rights, which establishes at the same time the limitation of the crown according to the vote of both houses, and adds the important provision, that all persons who shall hold communion with the church of Rome, or shall marry a papist, shall be excluded, and for ever incapable to possess, inherit, or enjoy, the crown and government of this realm; and in all such cases the people of these realms shall be absolved from their allegiance, and the crown shall descend to the next heir. This was as near an approach to a generalisation of the principle of resistance as could be admitted with any security for public order.

The bill of rights contained only one clause extending rather beyond the propositions laid down in the declaration. This relates to the dispensing power, which the lords had been unwilling absolutely to condemn. They softened the general assertion of its illegality sent up from the other house, by inserting the words "as it has

[b] Parl. Hist. v. 108.

been exercised of late."[c] In the bill of rights therefore a clause was introduced, that no dispensation by non obstante to any statute should be allowed, except in such cases as should be specially provided for by a bill to be passed during the present session. This reservation went to satisfy the scruples of the lords, who did not agree without difficulty to the complete abolition of a prerogative so long recognised, and in many cases so convenient.[d] But the palpable danger of permitting it to exist in its indefinite state, subject to the interpretation of time-serving judges, prevailed with the commons over this consideration of conveniency; and though in the next parliament the judges were ordered by the house of lords to draw a bill for the king's dispensing in such cases wherein they should find it necessary, and for abrogating such laws as had been usually dispensed with and were become useless, the subject seems to have received no further attention.[e]

Except in this article of the dispensing prerogative, we cannot say, on comparing the bill of rights with what is proved to be the law by statutes, or generally esteemed to be such on the authority of our best writers, that it took away any legal power of the crown, or enlarged the limits of popular and parliamentary privilege. The most questionable proposition, though at the same time one of the most important, was that which asserts the illegality of a standing army in time of peace, unless with consent of parliament. It seems difficult to perceive in what respect this infringed on any private man's right, or by what clear reason (for no statute could be pretended) the king was debarred from enlisting soldiers by voluntary contract for the defence of his dominions, especially after an express law had declared the sole power over the militia, without giving any definition of that word, to reside in the crown. This had never been expressly

Military force without consent declared illegal.

---

[c] Journals, 11th and 12th Feb. 1688-9.
[d] Parl. Hist. 345.
[e] Lords' Journals, 22nd Nov. 1689. [Pardons for murder used to be granted with a "non obstantibus statutis." After the Revolution it was contended that they were no longer legal: 1 Shower, 284. But Holt held "the power of pardoning all offences to be an inseparable incident of the crown and its royal power." This savours a little of old tory times. For there are certainly unrepealed statutes of Edward III. which materially limit the crown's prerogative of pardoning felonies. —1845.]

maintained by Charles II.'s parliaments; though the
general repugnance of the nation to what was certainly
an innovation might have provoked a body of men who
did not always measure their words to declare its illegality.' It was however at least unconstitutional, by
which, as distinguished from illegal, I mean a novelty
of much importance, tending to endanger the established
laws. And it is manifest that the king could never inflict penalties by martial law, or generally by any other
course, on his troops, nor quarter them on the inhabitants, nor cause them to interfere with the civil authorities; so that, even if the proposition so absolutely

f The guards retained out of the old army disbanded at the king's return have been already mentioned to have amounted to about 5000 men, though some assert their number at first to have been considerably less. No objection seems to have been made at the time to the continuance of these regiments. But in 1667, on the insult offered to the coasts by the Dutch fleet, a great panic arising, 12,000 fresh troops were hastily levied. The commons, on July 25, came to an unanimous resolution, that his majesty be humbly desired by such members as are his privy council, that, when a peace is concluded, the new-raised forces be disbanded. The king, four days after, in a speech to both houses, said, " he wondered what one thing he had done since his coming into England to persuade any sober person that he did intend to govern by a standing army; he said he was more an Englishman than to do so. He desired, for as much as concerned him, to preserve the laws," &c. Parl. Hist. iv. 363. Next session the two houses thanked him for having disbanded the late raised forces. Id. 369. But in 1673, during the second Dutch war, a considerable force having been levied, the house of commons, after a warm debate, resolved, Nov. 3, that a standing army was a grievance. ┌ 1. 604. And in February following, that the continuing of any standing forces in this nation, other than the militia, is a great grievance and vexation to the people; and that this house do humbly petition his majesty to cause immediately to be disbanded that part of them that were raised since Jan. 1, 1663. Id. 665. This was done not long afterwards; but early in 1678, on the pretext of entering into a war with France, he suddenly raised an army of 20,000 men, or more, according to some accounts, which gave so much alarm to the parliament, that they would only vote supplies on condition that those troops should be immediately disbanded. Id. 955. The king, however, employed the money without doing so, and maintained, in the next session, that it had been necessary to keep them on foot; intimating, at the same time, that he was now willing to comply, if the house thought it expedient to disband the troops, which they accordingly voted with unanimity to be necessary for the safety of his majesty's person and preservation of the peace of the government. Nov. 25. Id. 1049. James showed, in his speech to parliament, Nov. 9, 1685, that he intended to keep on foot a standing army. Id. 137L. But, though that house of commons was very differently composed from those in his brother's reign, and voted as large a supply as the king required, they resolved that a bill be brought in to render the militia more useful; an oblique and timid hint of their disapprobation of a regular force, against which several members had spoken.

I do not find that any one, even in debate, goes the length of denying that the king might by his prerogative maintain a regular army; none, at least, of the resolutions in the commons can be said to have that effect.

expressed may be somewhat too wide, it still should be considered as virtually correct.⁶ But its distinct assertion in the bill of rights put a most essential restraint on the monarchy, and rendered it in effect for ever impossible to employ any direct force or intimidation against the established laws and liberties of the people.

A revolution so thoroughly remedial, and accomplished with so little cost of private suffering, so little of angry punishment or oppression of the vanquished, ought to have been hailed with unbounded thankfulness and satisfaction. The nation's deliverer and chosen sovereign, in himself the most magnanimous and heroic character of that age, might have expected no return but admiration and gratitude. Yet this was very far from being the case. In no period of time under the Stuarts were public discontent and opposition of parliament more prominent than in the reign of William III.; and that high-souled prince enjoyed far less of his subjects' affection than Charles II. No part of our history perhaps is read upon the whole with less satisfaction than these thirteen years during which he sat upon his elective throne.

<small>Discontent with the new government.</small>

⁶ It is expressly against the petition of right to quarter troops on the citizens, or to inflict any punishment by martial law. No court-martial, in fact, can have any coercive jurisdiction except by statute; unless we should resort to the old tribunal of the constable and marshal. And that this was admitted, even in bad times, we may learn by an odd case in sir Thomas Jones's Reports, 147. (Pasch. 33 Car. 2, 1681. (An action was brought for assault and false imprisonment. The defendant pleaded that he was lieutenant-governor of the Isle of Scilly, and that the plaintiff was a soldier belonging to the garrison; and that it was the ancient custom of the castle that, if any soldier refused to render obedience, the governor might punish him by imprisonment for a reasonable time, which he had therefore done. The plaintiff demurred, and had judgment in his favour. By demurring, he put it to the court to determine whether this plea, which is obviously fabricated in order to cover the want of any general right to maintain discipline in this manner, were valid in point of law; which they decided, as it appears, in the negative.

In the next reign, however, an attempt was made to punish deserters capitally, not by a court-martial, but on the authority of an ancient act of parliament. Chief justice Herbert is said to have resigned his place in the king's bench rather than come in to this. Wright succeeded him; and two deserters, having been convicted, were executed in London. Ralph, 961. I cannot discover that there was anything illegal in the proceeding, and therefore question a little whether this were really Herbert's motive. See 3 Inst. 98.

[I have since observed, in a passage which had escaped me, that the cause of sir Edward Herbert's resignation, which was in fact no resignation, but only an exchange of places with Wright, chief justice of the common pleas, was his objection to the king's insisting on the execution of one of these deserters at Plymouth, the conviction having occurred at Reading. State Trials, xii. 262, from Heywood's Vindication of Fox.—1848.]

It will be sufficient for me to sketch generally the leading causes, and the errors both of the prince and people, which hindered the blessings of the Revolution from being duly appreciated by its contemporaries.

Its causes.

The votes of the two houses, that James had abdicated, or in plainer words forfeited, his royal authority, that the crown was vacant, that one out of the regular line of succession should be raised to it, were so untenable by any known law, so repugnant to the principles of the established church, that a nation accustomed to think upon matters of government only as lawyers and churchmen dictated could not easily reconcile them to its preconceived notions of duty. The first burst of resentment against the late king was mitigated by his fall; compassion, and even confidence, began to take place of it; his adherents—some denying or extenuating the faults of his administration, others more artfully representing them as capable of redress by legal measures—having recovered from their consternation, took advantage of the necessary delay before the meeting of the convention, and of the time consumed in its debates, to publish pamphlets and circulate rumours in his behalf.[h] Thus, at the moment when William and Mary were proclaimed (though it seems highly probable that a majority of the kingdom sustained the bold votes of its representatives), there was yet a very powerful minority who believed the constitution to be most violently shaken, if not irretrievably destroyed, and the rightful sovereign to have

Incompatibility of the Revolution with received principles.

---

[h] See several in the Somers Tracts, vol. x. One of these, a Letter to a Member of the Convention, by Dr. Sherlock, is very ably written, and puts all the consequences of a change of government, as to popular dissatisfaction, &c., much as they turned out, though, of course, falling to show that a treaty with the king would be less open to objection. Sherlock declined for a time to take the oaths; but, complying afterwards, and writing in vindication, or at least excuse, of the Revolution, incurred the hostility of the Jacobites, and impaired his own reputation by so interested a want of consistency; for he had been the most eminent champion of passive obedience. Even the distinction he found out, of the lawfulness of allegiance to a king de facto, was contrary to his former doctrine. [A pamphlet, entitled 'A Second Letter to a Friend,' in answer to the declaration of James II. in 1692 (Somers Tracts, x 378), which goes wholly on Revolution principles, is attributed to Sherlock by Scott, who prints the title as if Sherlock's name were in it, probably following the former edition of the Somers Tracts. But I do not find it ascribed to Sherlock in the Biographia Britannica, or in the list of his writings in Watt's Bibliotheca.—1845.]

been excluded by usurpation. The clergy were moved by pride and shame, by the just apprehension that their influence over the people would be impaired, by jealousy or hatred of the nonconformists, to deprecate so practical a confutation of the doctrines they had preached, especially when an oath of allegiance to their new sovereign came to be imposed; and they had no alternative but to resign their benefices, or wound their reputations and consciences by submission upon some casuistical pretext.[i] Eight bishops, including the primate and several of those who had been foremost in the defence of the church during the late reign, with about four hundred clergy, some of them highly distinguished, chose the more honourable course of refusing the new oaths; and thus began the schism of the nonjurors, more mischievous in its commencement than its continuance, and not so dangerous to the government of William III. and George I. as the false submission of less sincere men.[k]

[i] 1 W. & M. c. 8.

[k] The necessity of excluding men so conscientious, and several of whom had very recently sustained so conspicuously the brunt of the battle against king James, was very painful; and motives of policy, as well as generosity, were not wanting in favour of some indulgence towards them. On the other hand, it was dangerous to admit such a reflection on the new settlement as would be cast by its enemies, if the clergy, especially the bishops, should be excused from the oath of allegiance. The house of lords made an amendment in the act requiring this oath, dispensing with it in the case of ecclesiastical persons, unless they should be called upon by the privy council. This, it was thought, would furnish a security for their peaceable demeanour without shocking the people and occasioning a dangerous schism. But the commons resolutely opposed this amendment, as an unfair distinction, and derogatory to the king's title. Parl. Hist. 219. Lords' Journals, 17th April, 1689. The clergy, however, had six months more time allowed them, in order to take the oath, than the possessors of lay offices.

Upon the whole, I think the reasons for deprivation greatly preponderated. Public prayers for the king by name form part of our liturgy; and it was surely impossible to dispense with the clergy's reading them, which was as obnoxious as the oath of allegiance. Thus the beneficed priests must have been excluded; and it was hardly required to make an exception for the sake of a few bishops, even if difficulties of the same kind would not have occurred in the exercise of their jurisdiction, which hangs upon, and has a perpetual reference to, the supremacy of the crown.

The king was empowered to reserve a third part of the value of their benefices to any twelve of the recusant clergy. 1 W. & M. c. 8, s. 16. But this could only be done at the expense of their successors; and the behaviour of the nonjurors, who strained every nerve in favour of the dethroned king, did not recommend them to the government. The deprived bishops, though many of them through their late behaviour were deservedly esteemed, cannot be reckoned among the eminent characters of our church for learning or capacity. Sancroft, the most distinguished of them, had not made any remarkable figure; and none of the rest had any preten-

It seems undeniable that the strength of this Jacobite faction sprung from the want of apparent necessity for the change of government. Extreme oppression produces an impetuous tide of resistance, which bears away the reasonings of the casuists. But the encroachments of James II., being rather felt in prospect than much actual injury, left men in a calmer temper, and disposed to weigh somewhat nicely the nature of the proposed remedy. The Revolution was, or at least seemed to be, a case of political expediency; and expediency is always a matter of uncertain argument. In many respects it was far better conducted, more peaceably, more moderately, with less passion and severity towards the guilty, with less mixture of democratic turbulence, with less innovation on the regular laws, than if it had been that extreme case of necessity which some are apt to require. But it was obtained on this account with less unanimity and heartfelt concurrence of the entire nation.

Character and errors of William. The demeanour of William, always cold and sometimes harsh, his foreign origin (a sort of crime in English eyes) and foreign favourites, the natural and almost laudable prejudice against one who had risen by the misfortunes of a very near relation, conspired with a desire of power not very judiciously displayed by him to keep alive this disaffection; and the opposite party, regardless of all the decencies of political lying, took care to aggravate it by the vilest calumnies against one who, though not exempt from errors, must be accounted the greatest man of his own age. It is certain that his government was in very considerable danger for three or four years after the Revolution, and even to the peace of Ryswick. The change appeared so marvellous, and contrary to the bent of men's expectation, that it could not be permanent. Hence he was surrounded by the timid and the treasons to literary credit. Those who filled their places were incomparably superior. Among the nonjuring clergy a certain number were considerable men; but, upon the whole, the well-affected part of the church, not only at the Revolution, but for fifty years afterwards, contained by far its most useful and able members. Yet the effect of this expulsion was highly unfavourable to the new government; and it required all the influence of a latitudinarian school of divinity, led by Locke, which was very strong among the laity under William, to counteract it.

cherous; by those who meant to have merits to plead after a restoration, and those who meant at least to be secure. A new and revolutionary government is seldom fairly dealt with. Mankind, accustomed to forgive almost everything in favour of legitimate prescriptive power, exact an ideal faultlessness from that which claims allegiance on the score of its utility. The personal failings of its rulers, the negligences of their administration, even the inevitable privations and difficulties which the nature of human affairs or the misconduct of their predecessors create, are imputed to them with invidious minuteness. Those who deem their own merit unrewarded become always a numerous and implacable class of adversaries; those whose schemes of public improvement have not been followed think nothing gained by the change, and return to a restless censoriousness in which they have been accustomed to place delight. With all these it was natural that William should have to contend; but we cannot in justice impute all the unpopularity of his administration to the disaffection of one party, or the fickleness and ingratitude of another. It arose in no slight degree from errors of his own.

The king had been raised to the throne by the vigour and zeal of the whigs; but the opposite party were so nearly upon an equality in both houses that it would have been difficult to frame his government on an exclusive basis. It would also have been highly impolitic, and, with respect to some few persons, ungrateful, to put a slight upon those who had an undeniable majority in the most powerful classes. William acted, therefore, on a wise and liberal principle, in bestowing offices of trust on lord Danby, so meritorious in the Revolution, and on lord Nottingham, whose probity was unimpeached; while he gave the whigs, as was due, a decided preponderance in his council. Many of them, however, with that indiscriminating acrimony which belongs to all factions, could not endure the elevation of men who had complied with the court too long, and seemed by their tardy opposition[m] to be rather the patriots of the church than of civil liberty.

Jealousy of the whigs.

[m] Burnet. Ralph, 174, 179.

They remembered that Danby had been impeached as
a corrupt and dangerous minister; that Halifax had
been involved, at least by holding a confidential office
at the time, in the last and worst part of Charles's
reign. They saw Godolphin, who had concurred in the
commitment of the bishops, and every other measure of
the late king, still in the treasury; and, though they
could not reproach Nottingham with any misconduct,
were shocked that his conspicuous opposition to the
new settlement should be rewarded with the post of
secretary of state. The mismanagement of affairs in
Ireland during 1689, which was very glaring, furnished
specious grounds for suspicion that the king was betrayed." It is probable that he was so, though not at
that time by the chiefs of his ministry. This was the
beginning of that dissatisfaction with the government
of William, on the part of those who had the most zeal
for his throne, which eventually became far more harassing than the conspiracies of his real enemies. Halifax
gave way to the prejudices of the commons, and retired
from power. These prejudices were no doubt unjust,
as they respected a man so sound in principle, though
not uniform in conduct, and who had withstood the
arbitrary maxims of Charles and James in that cabinet
of which he unfortunately continued too long a member.
But his fall is a warning to English statesmen that they
will be deemed responsible to their country for measures
which they countenance by remaining in office, though
they may resist them in council.

The same honest warmth which impelled the whigs
to murmur at the employment of men sullied
by their compliance with the court, made them
unwilling to concur in the king's desire of a total amnesty. They retained the bill of indemnity in the
commons; and, excepting some by name, and many

Bill of
indemnity.

<small>" The parliamentary debates are full
of complaints as to the mismanagement
of all things in Ireland. These might
be thought hasty or factious; but marshal Schomberg's letters to the king yield
them strong confirmation. Dalrymple,
Appendix, 26, &c. William's resolution
to take the Irish war on himself saved
not only that country, but England. Our
own constitution was won on the Boyne.

The star of the house of Stuart grew pale
for ever on that illustrious day when
James displayed again the pusillanimity
which had cost him his English crown.
Yet the best friends of William dissuaded
him from going into Ireland, so imminent did the peril appear at home. Dalrymple, id. 97. "Things," says Burnet,
" were in a very ill disposition towards a
fatal turn."</small>

more by general clauses, gave their adversaries a pretext for alarming all those whose conduct had not been irreproachable. Clemency is indeed for the most part the wisest, as well as the most generous, policy; yet it might seem dangerous to pass over with unlimited forgiveness that servile obedience to arbitrary power, especially in the judges, which, as it springs from a base motive, is best controlled by the fear of punishment. But some of the late king's instruments had fled with him, others were lost and ruined; it was better to follow the precedents set at the Restoration than to give them a chance of regaining public sympathy by a prosecution out of the regular course of law.° In one instance, the expulsion of sir Robert Sawyer from the house, the majority displayed a just resentment against one of the most devoted adherents of the prerogative, so long as civil liberty alone was in danger. Sawyer had been latterly very conspicuous in defence of the church; and it was expedient to let the nation see that the days of Charles II. were not entirely forgotten.ᵖ

° See the debates on this subject in the Parliamentary History, which is a transcript from Anchitel Grey. The whigs, or at least some hot-headed men among them, were certainly too much actuated by a vindictive spirit, and consumed too much time on this necessary bill.

ᵖ The prominent instance of Sawyer's delinquency, which caused his expulsion, was his refusal of a writ of error to sir Thomas Armstrong. Parl. Hist. 516. It was notorious that Armstrong suffered by a legal murder; and an attorney-general in such a case could not be reckoned as free from personal responsibility as an ordinary advocate who maintains a cause for his fee. The first resolution had been to give reparation out of the estates of the judges and prosecutors to Armstrong's family, which was, perhaps rightly, abandoned.

The house of lords, who, having a power to examine upon oath, are supposed to sift the truth in such inquiries better than the commons, were not remiss in endeavouring to bring the instruments of Stuart tyranny to justice. Besides the committee appointed on the very second day of the convention, 23rd Jan. 1689, to investigate the supposed circumstances of suspicion as to the death of lord Essex (a committee renewed afterwards, and formed of persons by no means likely to have abandoned any path that might lead to the detection of guilt in the late king), another was appointed in the second session of the same parliament (Lords' Journals, 2nd Nov. 1689), " to consider who were the advisers and prosecutors of the murders of lord Russell, col. Sidney, Armstrong, Cornish, &c., and who were the advisers of issuing out writs of quo warrantos against corporations, and who were their regulators, and also who were the public assertors of the dispensing power." The examinations taken before this committee are printed in the Lords' Journals, 20th Dec. 1689; and there certainly does not appear any want of zeal to convict the guilty. But neither the law nor the proofs would serve them. They could establish nothing against Dudley North, the tory sheriff of 1683, except that he had named lord Russell's panel himself, which, though irregular and doubtless ill-designed, had unluckily a precedent in the conduct of the famous whig sheriff, Slingsby Bethell, a man who, like North, though on the opposite side,

Nothing was concluded as to the indemnity in this parliament; but in the next, William took the matter into his own hands by sending down an act of grace.

<small>Bill for restoring corporations.</small> I scarcely venture, at this distance from the scene, to pronounce an opinion as to the clause introduced by the whigs into a bill for restoring corporations, which excluded for the space of seven years all who had acted, or even concurred, in surrendering charters from municipal offices of trust. This was no doubt intended to maintain their own superiority by keeping the church or tory faction out of corporations. It evidently was not calculated to assuage the prevailing animosities. But, on the other hand, the cowardly submissiveness of the others to the quo warrantos seemed at least to deserve this censure; and the measure could by no means be put on a level in point of rigour with the corporation act of Charles II. As the dissenters, unquestioned friends of the Revolution, had been universally excluded by that statute, and the tories had lately been strong enough to prevent their readmission, it was not unfair for the opposite party, or rather for the government, to provide some security against men who, in spite of their oaths of allegiance, were not likely to have thoroughly abjured their former principles. This clause, which modern historians generally condemn as oppressive, had the strong support of Mr. Somers, then solicitor-general. It was, however, lost through the court's conjunction with the tories in the lower house, and the bill itself fell to the ground in the upper; so that those who had come into corporations by very ill means retained their power, to the great disadvantage of the Revolution party, as the next elections made appear.[q]

<small>cared more for his party than for decency and justice. Lord Halifax was a good deal hurt in character by this report, and never made a considerable figure afterwards. Burnet, 34. His mortification led him to engage in an intrigue with the late king, which was discovered; yet, I suspect that, with his usual versatility, he again abandoned that cause before his death. Ralph, 467. The act of grace (2 W. & M. c. 10) contained a small number of exceptions, too many indeed for its name; but probably there would have been difficulty in prevailing on the houses to pass it generally; and no one was ever molested afterwards on account of his conduct before the Revolution.

[q] Parl. Hist. 508, et post. Journals, 2nd and 10th Jan. 1689-90. Burnet's account is confused and inaccurate, as is very commonly the case: he trusted, I believe, almost entirely to his memory. Ralph and Somerville are scarce ever candid towards the whigs in this reign.</small>

But if the whigs behaved in these instances with too much of that passion which, though offensive and mischievous in its excess, is yet almost inseparable from patriotism and incorrupt sentiments in so numerous an assembly as the house of commons, they amply redeemed their glory by what cost them the new king's favour, their wise and admirable settlement of the revenue.

The first parliament of Charles II. had fixed on 1,200,000*l.* as the ordinary revenue of the crown, sufficient in times of no peculiar exigency for the support of its dignity and for the public defence. For this they provided various resources; the hereditary excise on liquors granted in lieu of the king's feudal rights, other excise and custom duties granted for his life, the post-office, the crown lands, the tax called hearth-money, or two shillings for every house, and some of smaller consequence. These in the beginning of that reign fell short of the estimate; but before its termination, by the improvement of trade and stricter management of the customs, they certainly exceeded that sum.' For the revenue of James from these sources, on an average of the four years of his reign, amounted to 1,500,964*l.*; to which something more than 400,000*l.* is to be added for the produce of duties imposed for eight years by his parliament of 1685.*

Settlement of the revenue.

William appears to have entertained no doubt that this great revenue, as well as all the power and prerogative of the crown, became vested in himself as king of England, or at least ought to be instantly settled by parliament according to the usual method.' There

---

' [Ralph puts the annual revenue about 1675 at 1,358,000*l.*; but with an anticipation, that is, debt, upon it to the amount of 866,954*l.* The expense of the army, navy, ordnance, and the fortress of Tangier, was under 700,000*l.* The rest went to the civil list, &c. Hist. of England, I. 290.—1845.]

* Parl. Hist. 150.

t Burnet, 13; Ralph, 138, 194. Some of the lawyers endeavoured to persuade the house that the revenue, having been granted to James for his life, devolved to William during the natural life of the former; a technical subtlety, against the spirit of the grant. Somers seems not to have come in to this; but it is hard to collect the sense of speeches from Grey's memoranda. Parl. Hist. 139. It is not to be understood that the tories universally were in favour of a grant for life, and the whigs against it. But as the latter were the majority, it was in their power, speaking of them as a party to have carried the measure.

could indeed be no pretence for disputing his right to
the hereditary excise, though this seems to have been
questioned in debate; but the commons soon displayed
a considerable reluctance to grant the temporary revenue for the king's life. This had usually been done
in the first parliament of every reign. But the accounts
for which they called on this occasion exhibited so considerable an increase of the receipts on one hand, so
alarming a disposition of the expenditure on the other,
that they deemed it expedient to restrain a liberality
which was not only likely to go beyond their intention,
but to place them, at least in future times, too much
within the power of the crown." Its average expenses
appeared to have been 1,700,000l. Of this 610,000l.
was the charge of the late king's army, and 83,493l. of
the ordnance. Nearly 90,000l. was set under the suspicious head of secret service, imprested to Mr. Guy,
secretary of the treasury.ᵛ Thus it was evident that,
far from sinking below the proper level, as had been
the general complaint of the court in the Stuart reigns,
the revenue was greatly and dangerously above it; and
its excess might either be consumed in unnecessary
luxury, or diverted to the worse purposes of despotism
and corruption. They had indeed just declared a standing army to be illegal. But there could be no such
security for the observance of this declaration as the
want of means in the crown to maintain one. Their
experience of the interminable contention about supply,
which had been fought with various success between
the kings of England and their parliaments for some
hundred years, dictated a course to which they wisely
and steadily adhered, and to which, perhaps above all
other changes at this revolution, the augmented authority of the house of commons must be ascribed.

Appropria-
tion of
supplies.

They began by voting that 1,200,000l. should be the
annual revenue of the crown in time of peace;
and that one half of this should be appropriated
to the maintenance of the king's government
and royal family, or what is now called the civil list,

" [Davenant, whom I quote at present
from Harris's Life of Charles II., p. 378,
computes the hereditary excise on beer
alone to have amounted, in 1689, to
694,498l. So extraordinarily good a
bargain had the crown made for giving
up the reliefs and wardships of military
tenure.]   ᵛ Parl. Hist. 187

the other to the public expense and contingent expenditure.* The breaking out of an eight years' war rendered it impossible to carry into effect these resolutions as to the peace establishment: but they did not lose sight of their principle, that the king's regular and domestic expenses should be determined by a fixed annual sum, distinct from the other departments of public service. They speedily improved upon their original scheme of a definite revenue, by taking a more close and constant superintendence of these departments, the navy, army, and ordnance. Estimates of the probable expenditure were regularly laid before them, and the supply granted was strictly appropriated to each particular service.

This great and fundamental principle, as it has long been justly considered, that the money voted by parliament is appropriated, and can only be applied, to certain specified heads of expenditure, was introduced, as I have before mentioned, in the reign of Charles II., and generally, though not in every instance, adopted by his parliament. The unworthy house of commons that sat in 1685, not content with a needless augmentation of the revenue, took credit with the king for not having appropriated their supplies.⁷ But from the Revolution it has been the invariable usage. The lords of the treasury, by a clause annually repeated in the appropriation act of every session, are forbidden, under severe penalties, to order by their warrant any moneys in the exchequer, so appropriated, from being issued for any other service, and the officers of the exchequer to obey any such warrant. This has given the house of commons so effectual a control over the executive power, or, more truly speaking, has rendered it so much a participator in that power, that no administration can possibly subsist without its concurrence; nor can the session of parliament be intermitted for an entire year, without leaving both the naval and military force of the kingdom unprovided for. In time of war, or in circumstances that may induce war, it has not been very uncommon to deviate a little from the rule of appropriation, by a grant of considerable sums on a vote of credit, which the crown is thus enabled to apply at its discre-

---

* Parl. Hist. 193.   ⁷ Id. iv. 1359

tion during the recess of parliament; and we have had also too frequent experience that the charges of public service have not been brought within the limits of the last year's appropriation. But the general principle has not perhaps been often transgressed without sufficient reason; and a house of commons would be deeply responsible to the country, if through supine confidence it should abandon that high privilege which has made it the arbiter of court factions, and the regulator of foreign connexions. It is to this transference of the executive government (for the phrase is hardly too strong) from the crown to the two houses of parliament, and especially the commons, that we owe the proud attitude which England has maintained since the Revolution, so extraordinarily dissimilar, in the eyes of Europe, to her condition under the Stuarts. The supplies, meted out with niggardly caution by former parliaments to sovereigns whom they could not trust, have flowed with redundant profuseness when they could judge of their necessity and direct their application. Doubtless the demand has always been fixed by the ministers of the crown, and its influence has retrieved in some degree the loss of authority; but it is still true that no small portion of the executive power, according to the established laws and customs of our government, has passed into the hands of that body which prescribes the application of the revenue, as well as investigates at its pleasure every act of the administration.[a]

The convention parliament continued the revenue as it already stood until December, 1690.[*] Their successors complied so far with the king's expectation as to grant the excise duties, besides those that were hereditary, for the lives of William and Mary, and that of the survivor.[b] The customs they only

Dissatisfaction of the king.

[a] Hatsell's Precedents, iii. 80, et alibi; Hargrave's Juridical Arguments, i. 394.

[*] 1 W. and M. sess. 2, c. 2. This was intended as a provisional act "for the preventing all disputes and questions concerning the collecting, levying, and assuring the public revenue due and payable in the reigns of the late kings Charles II. and James II., whilst the better settling the same is under the consideration of the present parliament."

[b] 2 W. and M. c. 3. As a mark of respect, no doubt, to the king and queen, it was provided that, if both should die, the successor should only enjoy this revenue of excise till December, 1693. In the debate on this subject in the new parliament, the tories, except Seymour, were for settling the revenue during the king's life; but many whigs spoke on the other side. Parl. Hist. 552. The latter justly urged that the amount of the revenue ought to be well known be-

continued for four years. They provided extraordinary
supplies for the conduct of the war on a scale of armament, and consequently of expenditure, unparalleled in
the annals of England. But the hesitation, and, as the
king imagined, the distrust they had shown in settling
the ordinary revenue, sunk deep into his mind, and
chiefly alienated him from the whigs, who were stronger
and more conspicuous than their adversaries in the two
sessions of 1689. If we believe Burnet, he felt so indignantly what appeared a systematic endeavour to reduce
his power below the ancient standard of the monarchy,
that he was inclined to abandon the government and
leave the nation to itself. He knew well, as he told the
bishop, what was to be alleged for the two forms of
government, a monarchy and a commonwealth, and
would not determine which was preferable; but of all
forms he thought the worst was that of a monarchy without the necessary powers.[e]

The desire of rule in William III. was as magnanimous
and public-spirited as ambition can ever be in a human
bosom. It was the consciousness not only of having
devoted himself to a great cause, the security of Europe,
and especially of Great Britain and Holland, against
unceasing aggression, but of resources in his own firmness and sagacity which no other person possessed. A
commanding force, a copious revenue, a supreme authority in councils, were not sought, as by the crowd of
kings, for the enjoyment of selfish vanity and covetousness, but as the only sure instruments of success in his
high calling in the race of heroic enterprise which Providence had appointed for the elect champion of civil
and religious liberty. We can hardly wonder that he
should not quite render justice to the motives of those
who seemed to impede his strenuous energies; that he
should resent as ingratitude those precautions against
abuse of power by him, the recent deliverer of the nation,
which it had never called for against those who had
sought to enslave it.

But, reasonable as this apology may be, it was still an
unhappy error of William that he did not sufficiently

---

fore they proceed to settle it for an indefinite time. The tories at that time had
great hopes of the king's favour, and
took this method of securing it.
[e] Burnet, 35.

weigh the circumstances which had elevated him to the English throne, and the alteration they had inevitably made in the relations between the crown and the parliament. Chosen upon the popular principle of general freedom and public good, on the ruins of an ancient hereditary throne, he could expect to reign on no other terms than as the chief of a commonwealth, with no other authority than the sense of the nation and of parliament deemed congenial to the new constitution. The debt of gratitude to him was indeed immense, and not sufficiently remembered; but it was due for having enabled the nation to regenerate itself and to place barriers against future assaults, to provide securities against future misgovernment. No one could seriously assert that James II. was the only sovereign of whom there had been cause to complain. In almost every reign, on the contrary, which our history records, the innate love of arbitrary power had produced more or less of oppression. The Revolution was chiefly beneficial as it gave a stronger impulse to the desire of political liberty, and rendered it more extensively attainable. It was certainly not for the sake of replacing James by William, with equal powers of doing injury, that the purest and wisest patriots engaged in that cause, but as the sole means of making a royal government permanently compatible with freedom and justice. The bill of rights had pretended to do nothing more than stigmatise some recent proceedings: were the representatives of the nation to stop short of other measures because they seemed novel and restrictive of the crown's authority, when for the want of them the crown's authority had nearly freed itself from all restriction? Such was their true motive for limiting the revenue, and such the ample justification of those important statutes enacted in the course of this reign, which the king, unfortunately for his reputation and peace of mind, too jealously resisted.

It is by no means unusual to find mention of a commonwealth or republican party, as if it existed in some force at the time of the Revolution, and throughout the reign of William III.; nay, some writers, such as Hume, Dalrymple, and Somerville, have, by putting them in a sort of balance against the Jacobites, as the extremes of the whig and tory factions,

No republican party in existence.

endeavoured to persuade us that the one was as substantial and united a body as the other. It may, however, be confidently asserted that no republican party had any existence, if by that word we are to understand a set of men whose object was the abolition of our limited monarchy. There might unquestionably be persons, especially among the independent sect, who cherished the memory of what they called the good old cause, and thought civil liberty irreconcilable with any form of regal government. But these were too inconsiderable, and too far removed from political influence, to deserve the appellation of a party. I believe it would be difficult to name five individuals to whom even a speculative preference of a commonwealth may with probability be ascribed. Were it otherwise, the numerous pamphlets of this period would bear witness to their activity. Yet, with the exception perhaps of one or two, and those rather equivocal, we should search, I suspect, the collections of that time in vain for any manifestations of a republican spirit. If indeed an ardent zeal to see the prerogative effectually restrained, to vindicate that high authority of the house of commons over the executive administration which it has in fact claimed and exercised, to purify the house itself from corrupt influence, if a tendency to dwell upon the popular origin of civil society, and the principles which Locke, above other writers, had brought again into fashion, be called republican (as in a primary but less usual sense of the word they may), no one can deny that this spirit eminently characterised the age of William III. And schemes of reformation emanating from this source were sometimes offered to the world, trenching more perhaps on the established constitution than either necessity demanded or prudence warranted. But these were anonymous and of little influence; nor did they ever extend to the absolute subversion of the throne.[d]

[d] See the Somers Tracts; but still more the collection of State Tracts in the time of William III., in three volumes folio. These are almost entirely on the whig side; and many of them, as I have intimated in the text, lean so far towards republicanism as to assert the original sovereignty of the people in very strong terms, and to propose various changes in the constitution, such as a greater equality in the representation. But I have not observed any one which recommends, even covertly, the abolition of hereditary monarchy. [It may even be suspected that some of these were really intended for the benefit of James.

William, however, was very early led to imagine, whether through the insinuations of lord Nottingham, as Burnet pretends, or the natural prejudice of kings against those who do not comply with them, that there not only existed a republican party, but that it numbered many supporters among the principal whigs. He dissolved the convention parliament, and gave his confidence for some time to the opposite faction.* But among these a real disaffection to his government prevailed so widely that he could with difficulty select men sincerely attached to it. The majority professed only to pay allegiance as to a sovereign de facto, and violently opposed the bill of recognition in 1690, both on account of the words "rightful and lawful king" which it applied to William, and of its declaring the laws passed in the last parliament to have been good and valid.† They had influence enough with the king to

<small>See one in Somers Tracts, x. 148, entitled 'Good Advice before it be too late, being a Breviate for the Convention.' The tone is apparently republican; yet we find the advice to be no more than imposing great restrictions on the king during his life, but not to prejudice a protestant successor; in other words, the limitation scheme proposed by Halifax in 1679. It may here be observed that the political tracts of this reign on both sides display a great deal of close and vigorous reasoning, and may well bear comparison with those of much later periods.—1845.]

* The sudden dissolution of this parliament cost him the hearts of those who had made him king. Besides several temporary writings, especially the Impartial Inquiry of the earl of Warrington, an honest and intrepid whig (Ralph, ii. 188), we have a letter from Mr. Wharton (afterwards marquis of Wharton) to the king, in Dalrymple, Appendix, p. 80, on the change in his councils at this time, written in a strain of bold and bitter expostulation, especially on the score of his employing those who had been the servants of the late family, alluding probably to Godolphin, who was indeed open to much exception. "I wish," says lord Shrewsbury, in the same year, "you could have established your party upon the moderate and honest-principled men of both factions; but, as there be a necessity of declaring, I shall make no difficulty to own my sense that your majesty and the government are much more safe depending upon the whigs, whose designs, if any against, are improbable and remoter, than with the tories, who many of them, questionless, would bring in king James; and the very best of them, I doubt, have a regency still in their heads; for, though I agree them to be the properest instruments to carry the prerogative high, yet I fear they have so unreasonable a veneration for monarchy, as not altogether to approve the foundation yours is built upon." Shrewsbury Correspond. 15.

† Parl. Hist. 575; Ralph, 194; Burnet, 41. Two remarkable protests were entered on the journals of the lords on occasion of this bill; one by the whigs, who were outnumbered on a particular division, and another by the tories on the passing of the bill. They are both vehemently expressed, and are among the not very numerous instances wherein the original whig and tory principles have been opposed to each other. The tory protest was expunged by order of the house. It is signed by eleven peers and six bishops, among whom were Stillingfleet and Lloyd. The whig protest has but ten signatures. The convention had already passed an act for preventing</small>

defeat a bill proposed by the whigs, by which an oath of abjuration of James's right was to be taken by all persons in trust.⁸ It is by no means certain that even those who abstained from all connexion with James after his loss of the throne would have made a strenuous resistance in case of his landing to recover it.ʰ But we know that a large proportion of the tories were engaged in a confederacy to support him. Almost every peer, in fact, of any consideration among that party, with the exception of lord Nottingham, is implicated by the secret documents which Macpherson and Dalrymple have brought to light; especially Godolphin, Carmarthen (Danby), and Marlborough, the second at that time prime minister of William (as he might justly be called), the last with circumstances of extraordinary and abandoned treacheryⁱ towards his country as well as

Intrigues with the late king.

doubts concerning their own authority, 1 W. & M. stat. 1, c. 1, which could, of course, have no more validity than they were able to give it. This bill had been much opposed by the tories. Parl. Hist. v. 122.

In order to make this clearer, it should be observed that the convention which restored Charles II., not having been summoned by his writ, was not reckoned by some royalist lawyers capable of passing valid acts; and consequently all the statutes enacted by it were confirmed by the authority of the next. Clarendon lays it down as undeniable that such confirmation was necessary. Nevertheless, this objection having been made in the court of king's bench to one of their acts, the judges would not admit it to be disputed, and said that the act, being made by king, lords, and commons, they ought not now to pry into any defects of the circumstances of calling them together, neither would they suffer a point to be stirred wherein the estates of so many were concerned. Heath v. Pryn, 1 Ventris, 15.

ᵍ Great indulgence was shown to the assertors of indefeasible right. The lords resolved that there should be no penalty in the bill to disable any person from sitting and voting in either house of parliament. Journals, May 5, 1690. The bill was rejected in the commons by 192 to 178. Journals, April 26; Parl. Hist. 594; Burnet, 41, ibid.

ʰ Some English subjects took James's commission, and fitted out privateers which attacked our ships. They were taken, and it was resolved to try them as pirates; when Dr. Oldys, the king's advocate, had the assurance to object that this could not be done, as if James had still the prerogatives of a sovereign prince by the law of nations. He was, of course, turned out, and the men hanged; but this is one instance among many of the difficulty under which the government laboured through the unfortunate distinction of *facto* and *jure*. Ralph, 423. The boards of customs and excise were filled by Godolphin with Jacobites. Shrewsb. Corresp. 51.

ⁱ The name of Carmarthen is perpetually mentioned among those whom the late king reckoned his friends. Macpherson's Papers, i. 457, &c. Yet this conduct was so evidently against his interest that we may perhaps believe him insincere. William was certainly well aware that an extensive conspiracy had been formed against his throne. It was of great importance to learn the persons involved in it and their schemes. May we not presume that lord Carmarthen's return to his ancient allegiance was feigned, in order to get an insight into the secrets of that party? This has already been conjectured by Somerville (p. 395) of lord Sunderland (who is also implicated by Macpherson's publication), and doubtless with higher probability;

his allegiance. Two of the most distinguished whigs (and if the imputation is not fully substantiated against

for Sunderland, always a favourite of William, could not without insanity have plotted the restoration of a prince he was supposed to have betrayed. It is evident that William was perfectly master of the cabals of St. Germain's. That little court knew it was betrayed, and the suspicion fell on lord Godolphin. Dalrymple, 189. But I think Sunderland and Carmarthen more likely.

I should be inclined to suspect that by some of this double treachery the secret of princess Anne's repentant letter to her father reached William's ear. She had come readily, or at least without opposition, into that part of the settlement which postponed her succession, after the death of Mary, for the remainder of the king's life. It would, indeed, have been absurd to expect that William was to descend from his throne in her favour; and her opposition could not have been of much avail. But, when the civil list and revenue came to be settled, the tories made a violent effort to secure an income of 70,000l. a-year to her and her husband. Parl. Hist. 492. As this on one hand seemed beyond all fair proportion to the income of the crown, so the whigs were hardly less unreasonable in contending that she should depend altogether on the king's generosity; especially as by letters patent in the late reign, which they affected to call in question, she had a revenue of about 30,000l. In the end the house resolved to address the king that he would make the princess's income 50,000l. in the whole. This, however, left an irreconcilable enmity, which the artifices of Marlborough and his wife were employed to aggravate. They were accustomed, in the younger sister's little court, to speak of the queen with severity, and of the king with rude and odious epithets. Marlborough, however, went much farther. He brought that narrow and foolish woman into his own dark intrigues with St. Germain's. She wrote to her father, whom she had grossly, and almost openly, charged with imposing a spurious child as prince of Wales, supplicating his forgiveness, and professing repentance for the part she had taken. Life of James, 476; Macpherson's Papers, i. 241.

If this letter, as cannot seem improbable, became known to William, we shall have a more satisfactory explanation of the queen's invincible resentment towards her sister than can be found in any other part of their history. Mary refused to see the princess on her deathbed, which shows more bitterness than suited her mild and religious temper, if we look only to their public squabbles about the Churchills as its motive. Burnet, 90; Conduct of Duchess of Marlborough, 41. But the queen must have deeply felt the unhappy, though necessary, state of enmity in which she was placed towards her father. She had borne a part in a great and glorious enterprise, obedient to a woman's highest duty, and had admirably performed those of the station to which she was called; but still with some violation of natural sentiments, and some liability to the reproach of those who do not fairly estimate the circumstances of her situation:—

Infelix! utcunque ferant ea facta minores.

Her sister, who had voluntarily trod the same path, who had misled her into a belief of her brother's illegitimacy, had now, from no real sense of duty, but out of pique and weak compliance with cunning favourites, solicited, in a clandestine manner, the late king's pardon, while his malediction resounded in the ears of the queen. This feebleness and duplicity made a sisterly friendship impossible.

As for lord Marlborough, he was among the first, if we except some Scots renegades, who abandoned the cause of the Revolution. He had so signally broken the ties of personal gratitude in his desertion of the king on that occasion, that, according to the severe remark of Hume, his conduct required for ever afterwards the most upright, the most disinterested, and most public-spirited behaviour to render it justifiable. What, then, must we think of it, if we find in the whole of this great man's political life nothing but ambition and rapacity in his motives,

others ᵏ by name, we know generally that many were liable to it) forfeited a high name among their contemporaries in the eyes of a posterity which has known them better; the earl of Shrewsbury, from that strange feebleness of soul which hung like a spell upon his nobler qualities, and admiral Russell, from insolent pride and sullenness of temper. Both these were engaged in the

nothing but treachery and intrigue in his means! He betrayed and abandoned James because he could not rise in his favour without a sacrifice that he did not care to make; he abandoned William and betrayed England because some obstacles stood yet in the way of his ambition. I do not mean only, when I say that he betrayed England, that he was ready to lay her independence and liberty at the feet of James II. and Louis XIV.; but that in one memorable instance he communicated to the court of St. Germain's, and through that to the court of Versailles, the secret of an expedition against Brest, which failed in consequence, with the loss of the commander and eight hundred men. Dalrymple, iii. 13; Life of James, 522; Macpherson, i. 497. In short, his whole life was such a picture of meanness and treachery, that one must rate military services very high indeed to preserve any esteem for his memory.

The private memoirs of James II., as well as the papers published by Macpherson, show us how little treason, and especially a double treason, is thanked or trusted by those whom it pretends to serve. We see that neither Churchill nor Russell obtained any confidence from the banished king. Their motives were always suspected; and something more solid than professions of loyalty was demanded, though at the expense of their own credit. James could not forgive Russell for saying that, if the French fleet came out, he must fight. Macpherson, i. 242. If Providence in its wrath had visited this island once more with a Stuart restoration, we may be sure that these perfidious apostates would have been no gainers by the change.

ᵏ During William's absence in Ireland in 1690, some of the whigs conducted themselves in a manner to raise suspicions of their fidelity, as appears by those most interesting letters of Mary, published by Dalrymple, which display her entire and devoted affection to a husband of cold and sometimes harsh manners, but capable of deep and powerful attachment, of which she was the chief object. I have heard that a late proprietor of these royal letters was offended by their publication, and that the black box of king William that contained them has disappeared from Kensington. The names of the duke of Bolton, his son the marquis of Winchester, the earl of Monmouth, lord Montague, and major Wildman, occur as objects of the queen's or her minister's suspicion. Dalrymple, Appendix, 107, &c. But Carmarthen was desirous to throw odium on the whigs; and none of these noblemen, except on one occasion lord Winchester, appear to be mentioned in the Stuart Papers. Even Monmouth, whose want both of principle and sound sense might cause reasonable distrust, and who lay at different times of his life under this suspicion of a Jacobite intrigue, is never mentioned in Macpherson, or any other book of authority within my recollection. Yet it is evident generally that there was a disaffected party among the whigs, or, as in the Stuart Papers they were called, republicans, who entertained the baseless project of restoring James upon terms. These were chiefly what were called compounders, to distinguish them from the thorough-paced royalists, or old tories. One person, whom we should least suspect, is occasionally spoken of as inclined to a king whom he had been ever conspicuous in opposing—the earl of Devonshire; but the Stuart agents often wrote according to their wishes rather than their knowledge; and it seems hard to believe what is not rendered probable by any part of his public conduct.

vile intrigues of a faction they abhorred; but Shrewsbury soon learned again to revere the sovereign he had contributed to raise, and withdrew from the contamination of Jacobitism. It does not appear that he betrayed that trust which William is said with extraordinary magnanimity to have reposed on him, after a full knowledge of his connexion with the court of St. Germain.[m] But Russell, though compelled to win the battle of La Hogue against his will, took care to render his splendid victory as little advantageous as possible. The credulity and almost wilful blindness of faction is strongly manifested in the conduct of the house of commons as to the quarrel between this commander and the board of admiralty. They chose to support one who was secretly a traitor, because he bore the name of whig, tolerating his infamous neglect of duty and contemptible excuses, in order to pull down an honest though not very able minister who belonged to the tories.[n] But they saw clearly that the king was betrayed, though mistaken, in this instance, as to the persons; and were right in concluding that the men who had effected the Revolution were in general most likely to maintain it; or, in the words of a committee of the whole house, "That his majesty be humbly advised, for the necessary support of his government, to employ in his councils and management of his affairs such persons only whose principles oblige them to stand by him and his right against the late king James, and all other pretenders whatsoever."[o] It is plain from this and other votes of the commons that the tories had lost that majority which they seem to have held in the first session of this parliament.[p]

[m] This fact apparently rests on good authority; it is repeatedly mentioned in the Stuart Papers, and in the Life of James. Yet Shrewsbury's letter to William, after Fenwick's accusation of him, seems hardly consistent with the king's knowledge of the truth of that charge in its full extent. I think that he served his master faithfully as secretary, at least after some time, though his warm recommendation of Marlborough, " who has been with me since this news [the failure of the attack on Brest] to offer his services with all the expressions of duty and fidelity imaginable" (Shrewsbury Correspondence, 47), is somewhat suspicious, aware as he was of that traitor's connexions.

[n] Commons' Journals, Nov. 28 et post; Dalrymple, ill. 11; Ralph, 346.

[o] Id. Jan. 11, 1692-3.

[p] Burnet says, "The elections of parliament (1690) went generally for men who would probably have declared for king James, if they could have known how to manage matters for him." P. 41. This is quite an exaggeration; though the tories, some of whom were at this time in place, did certainly succeed in several divisions. But parties had now

It is not, however, to be inferred, from this extensive combination in favour of the banished king, that his party embraced the majority of the nation, or that he could have been restored with any general testimonies of satisfaction. The friends of the Revolution were still by far the more powerful body. Even the secret emissaries of James confess that the common people were strongly prejudiced against his return. His own enumeration of peers attached to his cause cannot be brought to more than thirty, exclusive of catholics;[q] and the real Jacobites were, I believe, in a far less proportion among the commons. The hopes of that wretched victim of his own bigotry and violence rested less on the loyalty of his former subjects, or on their disaffection to his rival, than on the perfidious conspiracy of English statesmen and admirals, of lord-lieutenants and governors of towns, and on so numerous a French army as an ill-defended and disunited kingdom would be incapable to resist. He was to return, not as his brother, alone and unarmed, strong only in the consentient voice of the nation, but amidst the bayonets of 30,000 French auxiliaries. These were the pledges of just and constitutional rule which our patriot Jacobites invoked against the despotism of William III. It was from a king of the house of Stuart, from James II., from one thus encircled by the soldiers of Louis XIV., that we were to receive the guarantee of civil and religious liberty. Happily the determined love of arbitrary power, burning unextinguished amidst exile and disgrace, would not permit him to promise, in any distinct manner, those securities which a large portion of his own adherents required. The Jacobite faction was divided between compounders and non-compounders: the one insisting on the necessity of holding forth a promise of such new enactments upon the king's restoration as might remove all jealousies as

^{Schemes for his restoration.}

---

begun to be split; the Jacobite tories voting with the malecontent whigs. Upon the whole, this house of commons, like the next which followed it, was well affected to the revolution-settlement and to public liberty.

[q] Macpherson's State Papers, i. 459. These were all tories, except three or four. The great end James and his adherents had in view was to persuade Louis into an invasion of England; their representations, therefore, are to be taken with much allowance, and in some cases we know them to be false; as when James assures his brother of Versailles that three parts at least in four of the English clergy had not taken the oaths to William. Id. 409.

to the rights of the church and people; the other, more
agreeably to James's temper, rejecting every compromise
with what they called the republican party at the expense
of his ancient prerogative.' In a declaration which he
issued from St. Germain in 1692 there was so little acknowledgment of error, so few promises of security, so
many exceptions from the amnesty he offered, that the
wiser of his partisans in England were willing to insinuate
that it was not authentic.' This declaration, and the
virulence of Jacobite pamphlets in the same tone, must
have done harm to his cause.' He published another declaration next year at the earnest request of those who
had seceded to his side from that of the Revolution, in
which he held forth more specific assurances of consenting to a limitation of his prerogative." But no

---

' Macpherson, 433; Somers Tracts, xi. 94. This is a pamphlet of the time, exposing the St. Germain faction, and James's unwillingness to make conces- sions. It is confirmed by the most au- thentic documents.

' Ralph, 350; Somers Tracts, x. 211.

t Many of these Jacobite tracts are printed in the Somers Collection, vol. x. The more we read of them, the more cause appears for thankfulness that the nation escaped from such a furious party. They confess, in general, very little error or misgovernment in James, but abound with malignant calumnies on his successor. The name of Tullia is repeatedly given to the mild and pious Mary. The best of these libels is styled 'Great Britain's Just Complaint' (p. 429), by sir James Montgomery, the false and fickle proto-apostate of whiggism. It is written with singular vigour, and even elegance; and rather extenuates than denies the faults of the late reign.

" Ralph, 418; see the Life of James, 501. It contains chiefly an absolute pro- mise of pardon, a declaration that he would protect and defend the church of England as established by law, and secure to its members all the churches, universities, schools, and colleges, toge- ther with its immunities, rights, and privileges; a promise not to dispense with the test, and to leave the dispensing power in other matters to be explained and limited by parliament; to give the royal assent to bills for frequent parlia- ments, free elections, and impartial trials; and to confirm such laws made under the present usurpation as should be ten- dered to him by parliament. "The king," he says himself, " was sensible he should be blamed by several of his friends for submitting to such hard terms; nor was it to be wondered at if those who knew not the true condition of his affairs were scandalized at it; but, after all, he had nothing else to do." P. 505. He was so little satisfied with the articles in this declaration respecting the church of England, that he consulted several French and English divines, all of whom, including Bossuet, after some difference, came to an opinion that he could not in conscience undertake to protect and defend an erroneous church. Their objection, however, seems to have been rather to the expression than the plain sense; for they agreed that he might promise to leave the protestant church in possession of its endowments and privileges. Many, too, of the Eng- lish Jacobites, especially the nonjuring bishops, were displeased with the de- claration, as limiting the prerogative, though it contained nothing which they were not clamorous to obtain from Wil- liam. P. 514. A decisive proof how little that party cared for civil liberty, and how little would have satisfied them at the revolution, if James had put the church out of danger! The next para-

reflecting man could avoid perceiving that such promises wrung from his distress were illusory and insincere, that in the exultation of triumphant loyalty, even without the sword of the Gaul thrown into the scale of despotism, those who dreamed of a conditional restoration and of fresh guarantees for civil liberty would find, like the presbyterians of 1660, that it became them rather to be anxious about their own pardon, and to receive it as a signal boon of the king's clemency. The knowledge thus obtained of James's incorrigible obstinacy seems gradually to have convinced the disaffected that no hope for the nation or for themselves could be drawn from his restoration.* His connexions with the treacherous counsellors of William grew weaker; and even before the peace of Ryswick it was evident that the aged bigot could never wield again the sceptre he had thrown away. The scheme of assassinating our illustrious sovereign, which some of James's desperate zealots had devised without his privity, as may charitably and even reasonably be supposed,⁷ gave a fatal blow to the interests of that

---

graph is remarkable enough to be extracted for the better confirmation of what I have just said. "By this the king saw he had outshot himself more ways than one in this declaration; and therefore what expedient he would have found in case he had been restored, not to put a force either upon his conscience or honour, does not appear, because it never came to a trial; but this is certain, his church-of-England friends absolved him beforehand, and sent him word that, if he considered the preamble and the very terms of the declaration, he was not bound to stand by it, or to put it out verbatim as it was worded; that the changing some expressions and ambiguous terms, so long as what was principally aimed at had been kept to, could not be called a receding from his declaration, no more than a new edition of a book can be accounted a different work, though corrected and amended. And, indeed, the preamble showed his promise was conditional, which they not performing, the king could not be tied; for my lord Middleton had writ that, if the king signed the declaration, those who took it engaged to restore him in three or four months after; the king did his part, but their failure must needs take off the king's future obligation."

In a Latin letter, the original of which is written in James's own hand, to Innocent XII., dated from Dublin, Nov. 26. 1689, he declares himself "Catholicam fidem reducere in tria regna statuisse." Somers Tracts, x. 552. Though this may have been drawn up by a priest, I suppose the king understood what he said. It appears also by lord Balcarras's Memoir that lord Melfort had drawn up the declaration as to indemnity and indulgence in such a manner that the king might break it whenever he pleased. Somers Tracts, xi. 517.

* The protestants were treated with neglect and jealousy, whatever might have been their loyalty, at the court of James, as they were afterwards at that of his son. The incorrigibility of the Stuart family is very remarkable. Kennet, p. 638 and 738, enumerates many instances. Sir James Montgomery, the earl of Middleton, and others, were shunned at the court of St. Germain as guilty of this sole crime of heresy, unless we add that of wishing for legal securities.

⁷ James himself explicitly denies, in

faction. It was instantly seen that the murmurs of malecontent whigs had nothing in common with the dis-

the extracts from his Life published by Macpherson, all participation in the scheme of killing William, and says that he had twice rejected proposals for bringing him off alive; though it is not true that he speaks of the design with indignation, as some have pretended. It was very natural, and very conformable to the principles of kings, and others besides kings, in former times, that he should have lent an ear to this project: and as to James's moral and religious character, it was not better than that of Clarendon, whom we know to have countenanced similar designs for the assassination of Cromwell. In fact, the received code of ethics has been improved in this respect. We may be sure, at least, that those who ran such a risk for James's sake expected to be thanked and rewarded in the event of success. I cannot, therefore, agree with Dalrymple, who says that nothing but the fury of party could have exposed James to this suspicion. Though the proof seems very short of conviction, there are some facts worthy of notice. 1. Burnet positively charges the late king with privity to the conspiracy of Grandval, executed in Flanders for a design on William's life, 1692 (p. 95); and this he does with so much particularity and so little hesitation, that he seems to have drawn his information from high authority. The sentence of the court-martial on Grandval also alludes to James's knowledge of the crime (Somers Tracts, x. 580), and mentions expressions of his, which, though not conclusive, would raise a strong presumption in any ordinary case. 2. William himself, in a memorial intended to have been delivered to the ministers of all the allied powers at Ryswick, in answer to that of James (id. xi. 103; Ralph, 730), positively imputes to the latter repeated conspiracies against his life; and he was incapable of saying what he did not believe. In the same memorial he shows too much magnanimity to assert that the birth of the prince of Wales was an imposture. 3. A paper by Charnock, undeniably one of the conspirators, addressed to James, contains a marked allusion to William's possible death in a short time;

which even Macpherson calls a delicate mode of hinting the assassination-plot to him. Macpherson, State Papers, i. 519. Compare also State Trials, xii. 1323, 1327, 1329. 4. Somerville, though a disbeliever in James's participation, has a very curious quotation from Lamberti, tending to implicate Louis XIV. (p. 428); and we can hardly suppose that he kept the other out of the secret. Indeed, the crime is greater and less credible in Louis than in James. But devout kings have odd notions of morality; and their confessors, I suppose, much the same. I admit, as before, that the evidence falls short of conviction; and that the verdict, in the language of Scots law, should be, Not Proven; but it is too much for our Stuart apologists to treat the question as one absolutely determined. Documents may yet appear that will change its aspect.

I leave the above paragraph as it was written before the publication of M. Mazure's valuable History of the Revolution. He has therein brought to light a commission of James to Crosby, in 1693, authorising and requiring him "to seize and secure the person of the prince of Orange, and to bring him before us, taking to your assistance such other of our faithful subjects in whom you may place confidence." Hist. de la Révol. iii. 443. It is justly observed by M. Mazure that Crosby might think no renewal of his authority necessary in 1696 to do that which he had been required to do in 1693. If we look attentively at James's own language in Macpherson's extracts, without much regarding the glosses of Innes, it will appear that he does not deny in express terms that he had consented to the attempt in 1696 to seize the prince of Orange's person. In the commission to Crosby he is required not only to do this, but *to bring him before the king*. But is it possible to consider this language as anything else than an euphemism for assassination?

Upon the whole evidence, therefore, I now think that James was privy to the conspiracy, of which the natural and inevitable consequence must have been foreseen by himself; but I leave the text

affection of Jacobites. The nation resounded with an indignant cry against the atrocious conspiracy. An instrument of association abjuring the title of James, and pledging the subscribers to revenge the king's death after the mode of that in the reign of Elizabeth, was generally signed by both houses of parliament and throughout the kingdom.* The adherents of the exiled family dwindled into so powerless a minority that they could make no sort of opposition to the act of settlement, and did not recover an efficient character as a party till towards the latter end of the ensuing reign.

Perhaps the indignation of parliament against those who sought to bring back despotism through civil war and the murder of an heroic sovereign was carried too far in the bill for attainting sir John Fenwick of treason. Two witnesses required by our law in a charge of that nature, Porter and Goodman, had deposed before the grand jury to Fenwick's share in the scheme of invasion, though there is no reason to believe that he was privy to the intended assassination of the king. His wife subsequently prevailed on Goodman to quit the kingdom; and thus it became impossible to obtain a conviction in the course of law. This was the apology for a special act of the legislature, by which he suffered the penalties of treason. It did not, like some other acts of attainder, inflict a punishment beyond the offence, but supplied the deficiency of legal evidence. It was sustained by the production of Goodman's examination before the privy council, and by the evidence of two grand-jurymen as to the deposition he had made on oath before them, and on which they had found the bill of indictment. It was also shown that he had been tampered with by lady Mary Fenwick to leave the kingdom. This was undoubtedly as good secondary evidence as can well be imagined; and, though in criminal cases such evidence is not admissible by courts of law, it was plausibly urged that the legislature might prevent Fenwick from taking advantage of his own

<small>Attainder of sir John Fenwick.</small>

<small>as it stood, in order to show that I have not been guided by any prejudice against his character.

* Parl. Hist. 991. Fifteen peers and ninety-two commoners refused. The names of the latter were circulated in a printed paper, which the House voted to be a breach of their privilege, and destruction of the freedom and liberties of parliament. Oct. 30, 1696. This, however, shows the unpopularity of their opposition.</small>

underhand management, without transgressing the moral
rules of justice, or even setting the dangerous precedent
of punishing treason upon a single testimony. Yet, upon
the whole, the importance of adhering to the stubborn
rules of law in matters of treason is so weighty, and
the difficulty of keeping such a body as the house of
commons within any less precise limits so manifest, that
we may well concur with those who thought sir John
Fenwick much too inconsiderable a person to warrant
such an anomaly. The jealous sense of liberty prevalent
in William's reign produced a very strong opposition to
this bill of attainder: it passed in each house, especially
in the lords, by a small majority.* Nor, perhaps, would
it have been carried but for Fenwick's imprudent disclosure, in order to save his life, of some great statesmen's intrigues with the late king; a disclosure which
he dared not, or was not in a situation to confirm, but
which rendered him the victim of their fear and revenge.
Russell, one of those accused, brought into the commons
the bill of attainder; Marlborough voted in favour of
it, the only instance wherein he quitted the tories;
Godolphin and Bath, with more humanity, took the
other side; and Shrewsbury absented himself from the
house of lords.[b] It is now well known that Fenwick's

* Burnet; see the notes on the Oxford edition. Ralph, 692. The motion for bringing in the bill, Nov. 6, 1696, was carried by 169 to 61; but this majority lessened at every stage; and the final division was only 189 to 156. In the lords it passed by 68 to 61; several whigs, and even the duke of Devonshire, then lord steward, voting in the minority. Parl. Hist. 996-1154. Marlborough probably made prince George of Denmark support the measure. Shrewsbury Correspondence, 449. Many remarkable letters on the subject are to be found in this collection; but I warn the reader against trusting any part of the volume except the letters themselves. The editor has, in defiance of notorious facts, represented sir John Fenwick's disclosures as false; and twice charges him with prevarication (p. 404), using the word without any knowledge of its sense, in declining to answer questions put to him by members of the house of commons which he could not have answered without inflaming the animosity that sought his life.

It is said, in a note of lord Hardwicke on Burnet, that "the king, before the session, had sir John Fenwick brought to the cabinet council, where he was present himself. But sir John would not explain his paper." See also Shrewsbury Correspondence, 419, et post. The truth was, that Fenwick, having had his information at secondhand, could not prove his assertions, and feared to make his case worse by repeating them.

b Godolphin, who was then first commissioner of the treasury, not much to the liking of the whigs, seems to have been tricked by Sunderland into retiring from office on this occasion. Id. 415. Shrewsbury, secretary of state, could hardly be restrained by the king and his own friends from resigning the seals as soon as he knew of Fenwick's accusation. His behaviour shows either a conscious

discoveries went not a step beyond the truth. Their effect, however, was beneficial to the state; as, by displaying a strange want of secrecy in the court of St. Germains, Fenwick never having had any direct communication with those he accused, it caused Godolphin and Marlborough to break off their dangerous course of perfidy.*

Amidst these scenes of dissension and disaffection, and amidst the public losses and decline which aggravated them, we have scarce any object to contemplate with pleasure but the magnanimous and unconquerable soul of William. Mistaken in some parts of his domestic policy, unsuited by some failings of his character for the English nation, it is' still to his superiority in virtue and energy over all her own natives in that age that England is indebted for the preservation of her honour and liberty; not at the crisis only of the Revolution, but through the difficult period that elapsed until the peace of Ryswick. A war of nine years, generally unfortunate, unsatisfactory in its result, carried on at a cost unknown to former times, amidst the decay of trade, the exhaustion of resources, the decline, as there seems good reason to believe, of population itself, was the festering wound that turned a people's gratitude into factiousness and treachery. It was easy to excite the national prejudices against campaigns in Flanders, especially when so unsuccessful, and to inveigh against the neglect of our maritime power. Yet, unless we could have been secure against invasion, which Louis would infallibly have attempted, had not his whole force been occupied by the grand alliance, and which, in the feeble

---

ness of guilt, or an inconceivable cowardice. Yet at first he wrote to the king, pretending to mention candidly all that had passed between him and the earl of Middleton, which in fact amounted to nothing. P. 147. This letter, however, seems to show that a story which has been several times told, and is confirmed by the biographer of James II., and by Macpherson's Papers, that William compelled Shrewsbury to accept office in 1693, by letting him know that he was aware of his connexion with St. Germains, is not founded in truth. He could hardly have written in such a style to the king with that fact in his way. Monmouth, however, had some suspicion of it, as appears by the hints he furnished to sir J. Fenwick towards establishing the charges. P. 450. Lord Dartmouth, full of inveterate prejudices against the king, charges him with personal pique against sir John Fenwick, and with instigating members to vote for the bill. Yet it rather seems that he was, at least for some time, by no means anxious for it. Shrewsbury Correspondence, and compare Coxe's Life of Marlborough, i. 62.

° Life of James, ii. 558.

condition of our navy and commerce, at one time could not have been impracticable, the defeats of Steenkirk and Landen might probably have been sustained at home. The war of 1689, and the great confederacy of Europe, which William alone could animate with any steadiness and energy, were most evidently and undeniably the means of preserving the independence of England. That danger, which has sometimes been in our countrymen's mouths with little meaning, of becoming a province to France, was then close and actual; for I hold the restoration of the house of Stuart to be but another expression for that ignominy and servitude.

The expense therefore of this war must not be reckoned unnecessary; nor must we censure the government for that small portion of our debt which it was compelled to entail on posterity.[d] It is to the honour of William's administration, and of his parliaments, not always clear-sighted, but honest and zealous for the public weal, that they deviated so little from the praiseworthy, though sometimes impracticable, policy of providing a revenue commensurate with the annual expenditure. The supplies annually raised during the war were about five millions, more than double the revenue of James II. But a great decline took place in the produce of the taxes by which that revenue was

Its expenses.

[d] The debt at the king's death amounted to 16,394,702l., of which above three millions were to expire in 1710. Sinclair's Hist. of Revenue, L 425 (third edition).
Of this sum 664,263l. was incurred before the revolution, being a part of the money of which Charles II. had robbed the public creditor by shutting up the exchequer. Interest was paid upon this down to 1683, when the king stopped it. The legislature ought undoubtedly to have done justice more effectually and speedily than by passing an act in 1699, which was not to take effect till December 25, 1705; from which time the excise was charged with three per cent. interest on the principal sum of 1,328,526l., subject to be redeemed by payment of a moiety. No compensation was given for the loss of so many years' interest. 12 & 13 W. III. c. 12, § 15. Sinclair, L 397. State Trials, xiv. 1, et post. According to a particular statement in Somers Tracts, xii. 383, the receipts of the exchequer, including loans, during the whole reign of William, amounted to rather more than 72,000,000l. The author of the letter to the Rev. T. Carte, in answer to the latter's Letter to a Bystander, estimates the sums raised under Charles II., from Christmas 1660, to Christmas 1684, at 46,233,923l. Carte had made them only 32,474,265l. But his estimate is evidently false and deceptive. Both reckon the gross produce, not the exchequer payments. This controversy was about the year 1742. According to Sinclair, Hist. of Revenue, L 309, Carte had the last word; but I cannot conceive how he answered the above-mentioned letter to him. Whatever might be the relative expenditure of the two reigns, it is evident that the war of 1689 was brought on in a great measure by the corrupt policy of Charles II.

levied. In 1693 the customs had dwindled to less than half their amount before the Revolution, the excise duties to little more than half.* This rendered heavy impositions on land inevitable; a tax always obnoxious, and keeping up disaffection in the most powerful class of the community. The first land-tax was imposed in 1690, at the rate of three shillings in the pound on the rental; and it continued ever afterwards to be annually granted, at different rates, but commonly at four shillings in the pound, till it was made perpetual in 1798. A tax of twenty per cent. might well seem grievous; and the notorious inequality of the assessment in different counties tended rather to aggravate the burthen upon those whose contribution was the fairest. Fresh schemes of finance were devised, and, on the whole, patiently borne by a jaded people. The Bank of England rose under the auspices of the whig party, and materially relieved the immediate exigencies of the government, while it palliated the general distress by discounting bills and lending money at an easier rate of interest. Yet its notes were depreciated by twenty per cent. in exchange for silver; and exchequer tallies at least twice as much, till they were funded at an interest of eight per cent.' But these resources generally falling very short of calculation, and being anticipated at such an exorbitant discount, a constantly increasing deficiency arose; and public credit sunk so low, that about the year 1696 it was hardly possible to pay the fleet and army from month to month, and a total bankruptcy seemed near at hand. These distresses again were enhanced by the depreciation of the circulating coin, and by the bold remedy of a re-coinage, which made the immediate stagnation of commerce more complete. The mere operation of exchanging the worn silver coin for the new, which Mr. Montague had the courage to do without lowering the standard, cost the government two millions and a half. Certainly the vessel of our commonwealth

---

* Davenant, Essay on Ways and Means. In another of his tracts, vol. ii. 266, edit. 1771, this writer computes the payments of the state in 1688 at one shilling in the pound of the national income, but after the war at two shillings and sixpence.

f Godfrey's Short Account of Bank of England, in Somers' Tracts, xi. 5. Kennet's complete Hist. iii. 723. Ralph, 681. Shrewsbury Papers. Macpherson's Annals of Commerce, A.D. 1697. Sinclair's Hist. of Revenue.

has never been so close to shipwreck as in this period; we have seen the storm raging in still greater terror round our heads, but with far stouter planks and tougher cables to confront and ride through it.

Those who accused William of neglecting the maritime force of England, knew little what they said, or cared little about its truth.[g] A soldier, and a native of Holland, he naturally looked to the Spanish Netherlands as the theatre on which the battle of France and Europe was to be fought. It was by the possession of that country and its chief fortresses that Louis aspired to hold Holland in vassalage, to menace the coasts of England, and to keep the Empire under his influence. And if, with the assistance of those brave regiments who learned, in the well-contested though unfortunate battles of that war, the skill and discipline which made them conquerors in the next, it was found that France was still an overmatch for the allies, what would have been effected against her by the decrepitude of Spain, the perverse pride of Austria, and the selfish disunion of Germany? The commerce of France might, perhaps, have suffered more by an exclusively maritime warfare; but we should have obtained this advantage, which in itself is none, and would not have essentially crippled her force, at the price of abandoning to her ambition the quarry it had so long in pursuit. Meanwhile the naval annals of this war added much to our renown; Russell, glorious in his own despite at La Hogue, Rooke, and Shovel kept up the honour of the English flag. After that great victory the enemy never encountered us in battle; and the wintering of the fleet at Cadiz in 1694, a measure determined on by William's energetic mind, against the advice of his ministers, and in spite of the fretful insolence

---

[g] "Nor is it true that the sea was neglected; for I think during much the greater part of the war which began in 1689 we were entirely masters of the sea, by our victory in 1692, which was only three years after it broke out: so that for seven years we carried the *broom*. And for any neglect of our sea affairs otherwise, I believe I may in a few words prove that all the princes since the Conquest never made so remarkable an improvement to our naval strength as king William. He (Swift) should have been told if he did not know, what havoc the Dutch had made of our shipping in king Charles the Second's reign; and that his successor, king James the Second, had not in his whole navy, fitted out to defeat the designed invasion of the prince of Orange, an individual ship of the first or second rank, which all lay neglected, and mere skeletons of former services, at their moorings. These this abused prince repaired at an immense charge, and brought them to their pristine magnificence." Answer to Swift's Conduct of the Allies, in Somers' Tracts, xiii. 247.

of the admiral, gave us so decided a pre-eminence both in the Atlantic and Mediterranean seas, that it is hard to say what more could have been achieved by the most exclusive attention to the navy.[h] It is true that, especially during the first part of the war, vast losses were sustained through the capture of merchant-ships; but this is the inevitable lot of a commercial country, and has occurred in every war, until the practice of placing the traders under convoy of armed ships was introduced. And, when we consider the treachery which pervaded this service, and the great facility of secret intelligence which the enemy possessed, we may be astonished that our failures and losses were not still more decisive.

The treaty of Ryswick was concluded on at least as fair terms as almost perpetual ill fortune could warrant us to expect. It compelled Louis XIV. to recognise the king's title, and thus both humbled the court of St. Germains, and put an end for several years to its intrigues. It extinguished, or rather the war itself had extinguished, one of the bold hopes of the French court, the scheme of procuring the election of the dauphin to the Empire. It gave at least a breathing-time to Europe, so long as the feeble lamp of Charles II.'s life should continue to glimmer, during which the fate of his vast succession might possibly be regulated without injury to the liberties of Europe.[i] But to those who looked with the king's eyes on the prospects of the con-

Treaty of Ryswick.

---

[h] Dalrymple has remarked the important consequences of this bold measure; but we have learned only by the publication of lord Shrewsbury's Correspondence that it originated with the king, and was carried through by him against the mutinous remonstrances of Russell. See pp. 88, 104, 202, 210, 234. This was a most odious man; as ill-tempered and violent as he was perfidious. But the rudeness with which the king was treated by some of his servants is very remarkable. Lord Sunderland wrote to him at least with great bluntness. Hardwicke Papers, 444.

[i] The peace of Ryswick was absolutely necessary, not only on account of the defection of the duke of Savoy, and the manifest disadvantage with which the allies carried on the war, but because public credit in England was almost annihilated, and it was hardly possible to pay the army. The extreme distress for money is forcibly displayed in some of the king's letters to lord Shrewsbury. P. 114, &c. These were in 1696, the very nadir of English prosperity; from which, by the favour of Providence and the buoyant energies of the nation, we have, though not quite with an uniform motion, culminated to our present height (1824).

If the treaty could have been concluded on the basis originally laid down, it would even have been honourable. But the French rose in their terms during their negotiation; and through the selfishness of Austria obtained Strasburg, which they had at first offered to relinquish, and were very near getting Luxemburg. Shrewsbury Correspondence, 316, &c. Still the terms were better than those offered in 1693, which William has been censured for refusing.

tinent, this pacification could appear nothing else than a
preliminary armistice of vigilance and preparation. He
knew that the Spanish dominions, or at least as large a
portion of them as could be grasped by a powerful arm,
had been for more than thirty years the object of Louis
XIV. The acquisitions of that monarch at Aix-la-
Chapelle and Nimeguen had been comparatively trifling,
and seem hardly enough to justify the dread that Europe
felt of his aggressions. But in contenting himself for the
time with a few strong towns or a moderate district, he
constantly kept in view the weakness of the king of
Spain's constitution. The queen's renunciation of her
right of succession was invalid in the jurisprudence of
his court. Sovereigns, according to the public law of
France, uncontrollable by the rights of others, were incapable of limiting their own. They might do all things
but guarantee the privileges of their subjects or the
independence of foreign states. By the queen of France's
death, her claim upon the inheritance of Spain had devolved upon the dauphin; so that ultimately, and virtually in the first instance, the two great monarchies
would be consolidated, and a single will would direct a
force much more than equal to all the rest of Europe.
If we admit that every little oscillation in the balance of
power has sometimes been too minutely regarded by
English statesmen, it would be absurd to contend that
such a subversion of it as the union of France and Spain
under one head did not most seriously threaten both the
independence of England and Holland.

The house of commons which sat at the conclusion
of the treaty of Ryswick, chiefly composed of
whigs, and having zealously co-operated in the
prosecution of the late war, could not be supposed lukewarm in the cause of liberty, or indifferent to
the aggrandizement of France. But the nation's exhausted state seemed to demand an intermission of its
burthens, and revived the natural and laudable disposition to frugality which had characterised in all former
times an English parliament. The arrears of the war,
joined to loans made during its progress, left a debt of
about seventeen millions, which excited much inquie-
tude, and evidently could not be discharged but by
steady retrenchment and uninterruped peace. But, be-

Jealousy of the commons.

sides this, a reluctance to see a standing army established prevailed among the great majority both of whigs and tories. It was unknown to their ancestors—this was enough for one party; it was dangerous to liberty—this alarmed the other. Men of ability and honest intention, but, like most speculative politicians of the sixteenth and seventeenth centuries, rather too fond of seeking analogies in ancient history, influenced the public opinion by their writings, and carried too far the undeniable truth, that a large army at the mere control of an ambitious prince may often overthrow the liberties of a people.[k] It was not sufficiently remembered that the bill of rights, the annual mutiny bill, the necessity of annual votes of supply for the maintenance of a regular army, besides, what was far more than all, the publicity of all acts of government, and the strong spirit of liberty burning in the people, had materially diminished a danger which it would not be safe entirely to contemn.

Such, however, was the influence of what may be called the constitutional antipathy of the English in that age to a regular army, that the commons, in the first session after the peace, voted that all troops raised since 1680 should be disbanded, reducing the forces to about 7000 men, which they were with difficulty prevailed upon to augment to 10,000.[m] They resolved at the same time that, "in a just sense and acknowledgment of what great things his majesty has done for these kingdoms, a sum not exceeding 700,000*l*. be granted to his majesty during his life for the support of the civil list." So ample a gift from an impoverished nation is the strongest testimony of their affection to the king.[n] But he was justly disappointed by the former vote, which, in the hazardous condition of Europe, prevented this country from wearing a countenance of preparation, more likely to avert than to bring on a second conflict. He permitted himself, however, to carry this

Army reduced.

---

[k] Moyle now published his 'Argument, showing that a standing army is inconsistent with a free government, and absolutely destructive to the constitution of the English monarchy.' (State Tracts, temp. W. III., ii. 564); and Trenchard his History of Standing Armies in England. Id. 653. Other pamphlets of a similar description may be found in the same volume.

[m] Journals, 11th Dec. 1697. Parl. Hist. 1167.

[n] Journals, 21st Dec. 1697. Parl. Hist. v. 1168. It was carried by 226 to as

resentment too far, and lost sight of that subordination to the law which is the duty of an English sovereign, when he evaded compliance with this resolution of the commons, and took on himself the unconstitutional responsibility of leaving sealed orders, when he went to Holland, that 16,000 men should be kept up, without the knowledge of his ministers, which they as unconstitutionally obeyed. In the next session, a new parliament having been elected full of men strongly imbued with what the courtiers styled commonwealth principles, or an extreme jealousy of royal power,[o] it was found impossible to resist a diminution of the army to 7000 troops.[p] These too were voted to be natives of the British dominions; and the king incurred the severest mortification of his reign in the necessity of sending back his regiments of Dutch guards and French refugees. The messages that passed between him and the parliament bear witness how deeply he felt, and how fruitlessly he deprecated, this act of unkindness and ingratitude, so strikingly in contrast with the deference that parliament has generally shown to the humours and prejudices of the crown in matters of far higher moment.[q] The foreign troops

[o] "The elections fell generally," says Burnet, "on men who were in the interest of government; many of them had indeed some popular notions, which they had drank in under a bad government, and thought this ought to keep them under a good one; so that those who wished well to the public did apprehend great difficulties in managing them." Upon which speaker Onslow has a very proper note: "They might happen to think," he says, "a good one might become a bad one, or a bad one might succeed to a good one. They were the best men of the age, and were for maintaining the Revolution government by its own principles, and not by those of a government it had superseded," "The elections," we read in a letter of Mr. Montague, Aug. 1698, "have made a humour appear in the counties that is not very comfortable to us who are in business. But yet, after all, the present members are such as will neither hurt England nor this government, but I believe they must be handled very nicely." Shrewsbury Correspondence, 551. This parliament, however, fell into a great mistake about the reduction of the army; as Bolingbroke in his Letters on History very candidly admits, though connected with those who had voted for it.

[p] Journals, 17th Dec. 1698. Parl. Hist. 1191.

[q] Journals, 10th Jan., 18th, 20th, and 25th March. Lords' Journals, 8th Feb. Parl. Hist. 1167, 1191. Ralph, 808. Burnet, 219. It is now beyond doubt that William had serious thoughts of quitting the government and retiring to Holland, sick of the faction and ingratitude of this nation. Shrewsbury Correspondence, 571. Hardwicke Papers, 362. This was in his character, and not like the vulgar story which that retailer of all gossip, Dalrymple, calls a well-authenticated tradition, that the king walked furiously round his room, exclaiming, "If I had a son, by G— the guards should not leave me." It would be vain to ask how this son would have enabled him to keep them against the bent of the parliament and people.

were too numerous, and it would have been politic to conciliate the nationality of the multitude by reducing their number; yet they had claims which a grateful and generous people should not have forgotten: they were many of them the chivalry of protestantism, the Huguenot gentlemen who had lost all but their swords in a cause which we deemed our own; they were the men who had terrified James from Whitehall, and brought about a deliverance which, to speak plainly, we had neither sense nor courage to achieve for ourselves, or which at least we could never have achieved without enduring the convulsive throes of anarchy.

There is, if not more apology for the conduct of the commons, yet more to censure on the king's side, in another scene of humiliation which he passed through in the business of the Irish forfeitures. These confiscations of the property of those who had fought on the side of James, though, in a legal sense, at the crown's disposal, ought undoubtedly to have been applied to the public service. It was the intention of parliament that two-thirds at least of these estates should be sold for that purpose; and William had, in answer to an address (Jan. 1690), promised to make no grant of them till the matter should be considered in the ensuing session. Several bills were brought in to carry the original resolutions into effect, but, probably through the influence of government, they always fell to the ground in one or other house of parliament. Meanwhile the king granted away the whole of these forfeitures, about a million of acres, with a culpable profuseness, to the enriching of his personal favourites, such as the earl of Portland and the countess of Orkney.' Yet, as this

Irish forfeitures resumed.

' The prodigality of William in grants to his favourites was an undeniable reproach to his reign. Charles II. had, however, with much greater profuseness, though much less blamed for it, given away almost all the crown lands in a few years after the Restoration; and the commons could not now be prevailed upon to shake those grants, which was urged by the court, in order to defeat the resumption of those in the present reign. The length of time undoubtedly made a considerable difference. An enormous grant of the crown's demanial rights in North Wales to the earl of Portland excited much clamour in 1697, and produced a speech from Mr Price, afterwards a baron of the exchequer, which was much extolled for its boldness, not rather to say, virulence and disaffection. This is printed in Parl. Hist. 978, and many other books. The king, on an address from the house of commons, revoked the grant, which indeed was not justifiable. His answer on this occasion, it may here be remarked, was by its mildness and courtesy a striking contrast to the insolent rudeness with which the

had been done in the exercise of a lawful prerogative, it is not easy to justify the act of resumption passed in 1699. The precedents for resumption of grants were obsolete, and from bad times. It was agreed on all hands that the royal domain is not inalienable; if this were a mischief, as could not perhaps be doubted, it was one that the legislature had permitted with open eyes till there was nothing left to be alienated. Acts, therefore, of this kind shake the general stability of possession, and destroy that confidence in which the practical sense of freedom consists, that the absolute power of the legislature, which in strictness is as arbitrary in England as in Persia, will be exercised in consistency with justice and lenity. They are also accompanied for the most part, as appears to have been the case in this instance of the Irish forfeitures, with partiality and misrepresentation as well as violence, and seldom fail to excite an odium far more than commensurate to the transient popularity which attends them at the outset.[*]

But, even if the resumption of William's Irish grants could be reckoned defensible, there can be no doubt that the mode adopted by the commons, of tacking, as it was called, the provisions for this purpose to a money-bill, so as to render it impossible for the lords even to modify them without depriving the king of his supply, tended to subvert the constitution and annihilate the rights of a co-equal house of parliament. This most reprehensible device, though not an unnatural consequence of their pretended right to an exclusive concern in money-bills, had been employed in a former instance during this reign.[t] They were again successful on this occasion; the lords receded from their amendments, and passed the bill at the king's desire, who perceived that the fury of the commons was tending to a terrible convulsion.[u] But the precedent was infinitely dangerous to their legislative power. If the commons, after some more attempts of the same nature, desisted from so unjust an encroachment, it must be attributed to that which has

Stuarts, one and all, had invariably treated the house.
[t] Parl. Hist. 1171, 1202, &c. Ralph. Burnet. Shrewsbury Correspondence. See also Davenant's Essay on Grants and Resumptions, and sundry pamphlets in Somers Tracts, vol. II., and State Tracts, temp. W. III. vol. II.
[t] In Feb. 1692.
[u] See the same authorities, especially the Shrewsbury Letters, p. 602.

been the great preservative of the equilibrium in our government, the public voice of a reflecting people, averse to manifest innovation, and soon offended by the intemperance of factions.

The essential change which the fall of the old dynasty had wrought in our constitution displayed itself in such a vigorous spirit of inquiry and inter-ference of parliament with all the course of government as, if not absolutely new, was more uncontested and more effectual than before the Revolution. The commons indeed under Charles II. had not wholly lost sight of the precedents which the long parliament had established for them; though with continual resistance from the court, in which their right of examination was by no means admitted. But the tories throughout the reign of William evinced a departure from the ancient principles of their faction in nothing more than in asserting to the fullest extent the powers and privileges of the commons; and, in the coalition they formed with the malecontent whigs, if the men of liberty adopted the nickname of the men of prerogative, the latter did not less take up the maxims and feelings of the former. The bad success and suspected management of public affairs co-operated with the strong spirit of party to establish this important accession of authority to the house of commons. In June 1689 a special committee was appointed to inquire into the miscarriages of the war in Ireland, especially as to the delay in relieving Londonderry. A similar committee was appointed in the lords. The former reported severely against colonel Lundy, governor of that city; and the house addressed the king that he might be sent over to be tried for the treasons laid to his charge.[a] I do not think there is any earlier precedent in the Journals for so specific an inquiry into the conduct of a public officer, especially one in military command. It marks, therefore, very distinctly the change of spirit which I have so frequently mentioned. No courtier has ever since ventured to deny this general right of inquiry, though it is a frequent practice to elude it. The right to inquire draws with it the necessary means, the examination of witnesses, re-

Parliamentary inquiries.

[a] Commons' Journals, June 1, Aug. 12.

cords, papers, enforced by the strong arm of parliamentary privilege. In one respect alone these powers have fallen rather short; the commons do not administer an oath; and having neglected to claim this authority in the irregular times when they could make a privilege by a vote, they would now perhaps find difficulty in obtaining it by consent of the house of peers. They renewed this committee for inquiring into the miscarriages of the war in the next session.ʸ They went very fully into the dispute between the board of admiralty and admiral Russell after the battle of La Hogue;ᵃ and the year after, investigated the conduct of his successors, Killigrew and Delaval, in the command of the Channel fleet.ᵃ They went, in the winter of 1694, into a very long examination of the admirals and the orders issued by the admiralty during the preceding year; and then voted that the sending the fleet to the Mediterranean, and the continuing it there this winter, has been to the honour and interest of his majesty and his kingdoms.ᵇ But it is hardly worth while to enumerate later instances of exercising a right which had become indisputable, and, even before it rested on the basis of precedent, could not reasonably be denied to those who might advise, remonstrate, and impeach.

It is not surprising that, after such important acquisitions of power, the natural spirit of encroachment, or the desire to distress a hostile government, should have led to endeavours which by their success would have drawn the executive administration more directly into the hands of parliament. A proposition was made by some peers in December 1692 for a committee of both houses to consider of the present state of the nation, and what advice should be given to the king concerning it. This dangerous project was lost by 48 to 36, several tories and dissatisfied whigs uniting in a protest against its rejection.ᶜ The king had in his speech to parliament requested their advice in the most general terms; and this slight expression, though no more than is contained

---

ʸ Commons' Journals, Nov. 1.
ᵃ Parl. Hist. 657. Dalrymple. Commons' and Lords' Journals.
ᵃ Parl. Hist. 793. Delaval and Killigrew were Jacobites, whom William generously but imprudently put into the command of the fleet.
ᵇ Commons' Journals, Feb. 27, 1694-5
ᶜ Parl. Hist. 941. Burnet, 105

in the common writ of summons, was tortured into a pretext for so extraordinary a proposal as that of a committee of delegates, or council of state, which might soon have grasped the entire administration. It was at least a remedy so little according to precedent, or the analogy of our constitution, that some very serious cause of dissatisfaction with the conduct of affairs could be its only excuse.

Burnet has spoken with reprobation of another scheme engendered by the same spirit of inquiry and control, that of a council of trade, to be nominated by parliament, with powers for the effectual preservation of the interests of the merchants. If the members of it were intended to be immovable, or if the vacancies were to be filled by consent of parliament, this would indeed have encroached on the prerogative in a far more eminent degree than the famous India bill of 1783, because its operation would have been more extensive and more at home. And, even if they were only named in the first instance, as has been usual in parliamentary commissioners of account or inquiry, it would still be material to ask what extent of power for the preservation of trade was to be placed in their hands. The precise nature of the scheme is not explained by Burnet. But it appears by the journals that this council was to receive information from merchants as to the necessity of convoys, and send directions to the board of admiralty, subject to the king's control, to receive complaints and represent the same to the king, and in many other respects to exercise very important and anomalous functions. They were not however to be members of the house. But even with this restriction, it was too hazardous a departure from the general maxims of the constitution.[d]

The general unpopularity of William's administration, and more particularly the reduction of the forces, afford an ample justification for the two treaties of partition, which the tory faction, with scandalous injustice and inconsistency, turned to his reproach. No one could deny that the aggrandisement of France by both of these treaties was of serics conse-

Treaties of partition.

---

[d] Burnet, 163. Commons' Journals, Jan. 31, 1695-6. An abjuration of king James's title in very strong terms was proposed as a qualification for members of this council; but this was lost by 195 to 188.

quence. But, according to English interests, the first object was to secure the Spanish Netherlands from becoming provinces of that power; the next to maintain the real independence of Spain and the Indies. Italy was but the last in order; and though the possession of Naples and Sicily, with the ports of Tuscany, as stipulated in the treaty of partition, would have rendered France absolute mistress of that whole country and of the Mediterranean sea, and essentially changed the balance of Europe, it was yet more tolerable than the acquisition of the whole monarchy in the name of a Bourbon prince, which the opening of the succession without previous arrangement was likely to produce. They at least who shrunk from the thought of another war, and studiously depreciated the value of continental alliances, were the last who ought to have exclaimed against a treaty which had been ratified as the sole means of giving us something like security without the cost of fighting for it. Nothing, therefore, could be more unreasonable than the clamour of a tory house of commons in 1701 (for the malecontent whigs were now so consolidated with the tories as in general to bear their name) against the partition treaties; nothing more unfair than the impeachment of the four lords, Portland, Orford, Somers, and Halifax, on that account. But we must at the same time remark that it is more easy to vindicate the partition treaties themselves than to reconcile the conduct of the king and of some others with the principles established in our constitution. William had taken these important negotiations wholly into his own hands, not even communicating them to any of his English ministers, except lord Jersey, until his resolution was finally settled. Lord Somers, as chancellor, had put the great seal to blank powers, as a legal authority to the negotiators; which evidently could not be valid, unless on the dangerous principle that the seal is conclusive against all exception.[e] He had also sealed the ratification of the treaty, though not consulted upon it, and though he seems to have had objections to some of the terms; and in both instances he set up the king's

[e] See speaker Onslow's Note on Burnet (Oxf. edit. iv. 468), and lord Hardwicke's hint of his father's opinion. Id. 475. But see also lord Somers's plea as to this. State Trials, xiii. 267.

command as a sufficient defence. The exclusion of all those whom, whether called privy or cabinet councillors, the nation holds responsible for its safety, from this great negotiation, tended to throw back the whole executive government into the single will of the sovereign, and ought to have exasperated the house of commons far more than the actual treaties of partition, which may probably have been the safest choice in a most perilous condition of Europe. The impeachments, however, were in most respects so ill substantiated by proof, that they have generally been reckoned a disgraceful instance of party spirit.[f]

The whigs, such of them at least as continued to hold that name in honour, soon forgave the mistakes and failings of their great deliverer; and indeed a high regard for the memory of William III. may justly be reckoned one of the tests by which genuine whiggism, as opposed both to tory and republican principles, has always been recognised. By the opposite party he was rancorously hated; and their malignant calumnies still sully the stream of history.[g] Let us leave such as prefer Charles I. to William III. in

Improvements in constitution under William.

---

[f] Parl. Hist. State Trials, xlv. 233. The letters of William, published in the Hardwicke State Papers, are both the most authentic and the most satisfactory explanation of his policy during the three momentous years that closed the seventeenth century. It is said, in a note of lord Hardwicke on Burnet (Oxford edit. iv. 417) (from lord Somers's papers), that, when some of the ministers objected to parts of the treaty, lord Portland's constant answer was, that nothing could be altered; upon which one of them said, if that was the case, he saw no reason why they should be called together. And it appears by the Shrewsbury Papers, p. 371, that the duke, though secretary of state and in a manner prime minister, was entirely kept by the king out of the secret of the negotiations which ended in the peace of Ryswick; whether, after all, there remained some lurking distrust of his fidelity, or from whatever other cause this took place, it was very anomalous and unconstitutional. And it must be owned that by this sort of proceeding, which could have no sufficient apology but a deep sense of the unworthiness of mankind, William brought on himself much of that dislike which appears so ungrateful and unaccountable.

As to the impeachments, few have pretended to justify them; even Ralph is half ashamed of the party he espouses with so little candour towards their adversaries. The scandalous conduct of the tories in screening the earl of Jersey, while they impeached the whig lords, some of whom had really borne no part in a measure he had promoted, sufficiently displays the factiousness of their motives. See lord Haversham's speech on this. Parl. Hist. 1206.

[g] Bishop Fleetwood, in a sermon preached in 1703, says of William, "whom all the world of friends and enemies knew how to value, except a *few English wretches.*" Kennet, 840. Boyer, in his History of the Reign of Queen Anne, p. 12, says that the king spent most of his private fortune, computed at no less than two millions, in the service of the English nation. I should be glad to have found this vouched by better authority.

the enjoyment of prejudices which are not likely to be overcome by argument. But it must ever be an honour to the English crown that it has been worn by so great a man. Compared with him, the statesmen who surrounded his throne, the Sunderlands, Godolphins, and Shrewsburys, even the Somerses and Montagues, sink into insignificance. He was in truth too great, not for the times wherein he was called to action, but for the peculiar condition of a king of England after the Revolution; and as he was the last sovereign of this country whose understanding and energy of character have been very distinguished, so was he the last who has encountered the resistance of his parliament, or stood apart and undisguised in the maintenance of his own prerogative. His reign is no doubt one of the most important in our constitutional history, both on account of its general character, which I have slightly sketched, and of those beneficial alterations in our law to which it gave rise. These now call for our attention.

The enormous duration of seventeen years, for which Charles II. protracted his second parliament, turned the thoughts of all who desired improvements in the constitution towards some limitation on a prerogative which had not hitherto been thus abused. Not only the continuance of the same house of commons during such a period destroyed the connexion between the people and their representatives, and laid open the latter, without responsibility, to the corruption which was hardly denied to prevail; but the privilege of exemption from civil process made needy and worthless men secure against their creditors, and desirous of a seat in parliament as a complete safeguard to fraud and injustice. The term of three years appeared sufficient to establish a control of the electoral over the representative body, without recurring to the ancient but inconvenient scheme of annual parliaments, which men enamoured of a still more popular form of government than our own were eager to recommend. A bill for this purpose was brought into the house of lords in December, 1689, but lost by the prorogation.[b] It passed both houses early in 1693, the whigs generally supporting, and the tories

[b] Lords' Journals.

opposing it; but on this, as on many other great questions of this reign, the two parties were not so regularly arrayed against each other as on points of a more personal nature.[1] To this bill the king refused his assent: an exercise of prerogative which no ordinary circumstances can reconcile either with prudence or with a constitutional administration of government, but which was too common in this reign. But the commons, as it was easy to foresee, did not abandon so important a measure; a similar bill received the royal assent in November, 1694.[2] By the triennial bill it was simply provided that every parliament should cease and determine within three years from its meeting. The clause contained in the act of Charles II. against the intermission of parliaments for more than three years is repeated; but it was not thought necessary to revive the somewhat violent and perhaps impracticable provisions by which the act of 1641 had secured their meeting; it being evident that even annual sessions might now be relied upon as indispensable to the machine of government.

This annual assembly of parliament was rendered necessary, in the first place, by the strict appropriation of the revenue according to votes of supply. It was secured, next, by passing the mutiny bill, under which the army is held together, and subjected to military discipline, for a short term, seldom or never exceeding twelve months. These are the two effectual securities against military power: that no pay can be issued to the troops without a previous authorisation by the commons in a committee of supply, and by both houses in an act of appropriation; and that no officer or soldier can be punished for disobedience, nor any court-martial held, without the annual re-enactment of the mutiny bill. Thus it is strictly true that, if the king were not to summon parliament every year, his army would cease to have a legal existence; and the refusal of either house to concur in the mutiny bill would at once wrest the sword out of his grasp. By the bill of rights it is declared unlawful to keep any forces in time of peace without consent of parliament. This consent, by an invariable

---

[1] Parl Hist. 754.   [2] 6 W. & M.

and wholesome usage, is given only from year to year: and its necessity may be considered perhaps the most powerful of those causes which have transferred so much even of the executive power into the management of the two houses of parliament.

The reign of William is also distinguished by the pro-
<small>Law of treason.</small> visions introduced into our law for the security of the subject against iniquitous condemnations on the charge of high treason, and intended to perfect those of earlier times, which had proved insufficient against the partiality of judges. But upon this occasion it will be necessary to take up the history of our constitutional law on this important head from the beginning.

In the earlier ages of our law the crime of high treason appears to have been of a vague and indefinite nature, determined only by such arbitrary construction as the circumstances of each particular case might suggest. It was held treason to kill the king's father or his uncle; and Mortimer was attainted for accroaching, as it was called, royal power; that is, for keeping the administration in his own hands, though without violence towards the reigning prince. But no people can enjoy a free constitution unless an adequate security is furnished by their laws against this discretion of judges in a matter so closely connected with the mutual relation between the government and its subjects. A petition was accordingly presented to Edward III. by one of the best parliaments that ever sat, requesting that, "whereas the king's justices in different counties adjudge men indicted before them to be traitors for divers matters not known by the commons to be treasonable, the king would, by his council, and the nobles and learned men (les grands et sages) of the land, declare in parliament what should be held for treason." The answer to this petition is in the words of the existing statute, which, as it is by no means so prolix as it is important, I shall place before the reader's eyes.

"Whereas divers opinions have been before this time
<small>Statute of Edward III.</small> in what case treason shall be said, and in what not; the king, at the request of the lords and commons, hath made a declaration in the manner as hereafter followeth; that is to say, when a man doth

compass or imagine the death of our lord the king, of my lady his queen, or of their eldest son and heir; or if a man do violate the king's companion or the king's eldest daughter unmarried, or the wife of the king's eldest son and heir; or if a man do levy war against our lord the king in his realm, or be adherent to the king's enemies in his realm, giving to them aid and comfort in the realm or elsewhere, and thereof be proveably attainted of open deed by people of their condition; and if a man counterfeit the king's great or privy seal, or his money; and if a man bring false money into this realm, counterfeit to the money of England, as the money called Lusheburg, or other like to the said money of England, knowing the money to be false, to merchandise or make payment in deceipt of our said lord the king and of his people; and if a man slay the chancellor, treasurer, or the king's justices of the one bench or the other, justices in eyre, or justices of assize, and all other justices assigned to hear and determine, being in their place doing their offices; and it is to be understood that, in the cases above rehearsed, it ought to be judged treason which extends to our lord the king and his royal majesty. And of such treason the forfeiture of the escheats pertaineth to our lord the king, as well of the lands and tenements holden of others as of himself." ᵐ

It seems impossible not to observe that the want of distinct arrangement natural to so unphilosophical an age, and which renders many of our old statutes very confused, is eminently displayed in this strange conjunction of offences—where to counterfeit the king's seal, which might be for the sake of private fraud, and even his coin, which must be so, is ranged along with all that really endangers the established government, with conspiracy and insurrection. But this is an objection of little magnitude compared with one that arises out of an omission in enumerating the modes whereby treason could be committed. In most other offences the intention, however manifest, the contrivance, however deliberate, the attempt, however casually rendered abortive, form so many degrees of malignity, or at least of mischief, which the jurispru-

Its constructive interpretation.

ᵐ Rot. Parl. ii. 239. 3 Inst. 1.

dence of most countries, and none more, at least formerly, than England, has been accustomed to distinguish from the perpetrated action by awarding an inferior punishment, or even none at all. Nor is this distinction merely founded on a difference in the moral indignation with which we are impelled to regard an inchoate and a consummate crime, but is warranted by a principle of reason, since the penalties attached to the completed offence spread their terror over all the machinations preparatory to it; and he who fails in his stroke has had the murderer's fate as much before his eyes as the more dexterous assassin. But those who conspire against the constituted government connect in their sanguine hope the assurance of impunity with the execution of their crime, and would justly deride the mockery of an accusation which could only be preferred against them when their banners were unfurled and their force arrayed. It is as reasonable, therefore, as it is conformable to the usages of every country, to place conspiracies against the sovereign power upon the footing of actual rebellion, and to crush those by the penalties of treason who, were the law to wait for their opportunity, might silence or pervert the law itself. Yet in this famous statute we find it only declared treasonable to compass or imagine the king's death; while no project of rebellion appears to fall within the letter of its enactments unless it ripen into a substantive act of levying war.

We may be, perhaps, less inclined to attribute this material omission to the laxity which has been already remarked to be usual in our older laws, than to apprehensions entertained by the barons that, if a mere design to levy war should be rendered treasonable, they might be exposed to much false testimony and arbitrary construction. But strained constructions of this very statute, if such were their aim, they did not prevent. Without adverting to the more extravagant convictions under this statute in some violent reigns, it gradually became an established doctrine with lawyers that a conspiracy to levy war against the king's person, though not in itself a distinct treason, may be given in evidence as an overt act of compassing his death. Great as the authorities may be on which this depends, and reasonable as it surely is that such offences should be brought within the pale of high treason, yet it is almost necessary to confess that this doctrine appears utterly irreconcilable with any fair interpretation of the statute. It has, indeed, by some been chiefly confined to cases where the attempt meditated is directly against the king's person for the purpose of deposing him, or of compelling him, while under actual duress, to a change of measures; and this was construed into a compassing of his death, since any such violence must endanger his life, and because, as has been said, the prisons and graves of princes are not very distant.ª But it seems not very reasonable to found a capital conviction on such a sententious remark; nor is it by any means true that a design against a king's life is necessarily to be inferred from the attempt to get possession of his person. So far indeed is this from being a general rule, that in a multitude of instances, especially during the minority or imbecility of a king, the purposes of conspirators would be wholly defeated by the death of the sovereign whose name they designed to employ. But there is still less pretext for applying the same construction to schemes of insurrection when the royal person is not directly the object of attack, and where no circumstance indicates any hostile intention towards his safety. This ample extension of so penal a statute was first given, if I am not mistaken, by the judges in 1663, on occasion of a meeting by some persons at Farley Wood in Yorkshire,º in order to concert measures for a rising. But it was

---

ª 3 Inst. 12. 1 Hale's Pleas of the Crown, 120. Foster, 195. Coke lays it down positively, p. 14, that a conspiracy to levy war is not high treason, as an overt act of compassing the king's death. "For this were to confound the several classes or numbra dividentia." Hale objects that Coke himself cites the case of lords Essex and Southampton, which seems to contradict that opinion. But it may be answered, in the first place, that a conspiracy to levy war was made high treason during the life of Elizabeth; and secondly, that Coke's words as to that case are, that they " intended to go to the court where the queen was, and to have taken her into their power, and to have removed divers of her council, and for *that end did assemble a multitude of people*; this, being raised to the end aforesaid, was a sufficient overt act of compassing the death of the queen." The earliest case is that of Storie, who was convicted of compassing the queen's death on evidence of exciting a foreign power to invade the kingdom. But he was very obnoxious; and the precedent is not good. Hale, 122.

It is also held that an actual levying war may be laid as an overt act of compassing the king's death, which indeed follows à fortiori from the former proposition; provided it be not a constructive rebellion, but one really directed against the royal authority. Hale, 123

º Hale, 121.

afterwards confirmed in Harding's case, immediately after the Revolution, and has been repeatedly laid down from the bench in subsequent proceedings for treason, as well as in treatises of very great authority.[p] It has therefore all the weight of established precedent: yet I question whether another instance can be found in our jurisprudence of giving so large a construction, not only to a penal, but to any other statute.[q] Nor does it speak in favour of this construction, that temporary laws have been enacted on various occasions to render a conspiracy to levy war treasonable; for which purpose, according to this current doctrine, the statute of Edward III. needed no supplemental provision. Such acts were passed under Elizabeth, Charles II., and George III., each of them limited to the existing reign.[r] But it is very seldom that, in an hereditary monarchy, the reigning prince ought to be secured by any peculiar provisions; and though the remarkable circumstances of Elizabeth's situation exposed her government to unusual perils, there seems an air of adulation or absurdity in the two latter instances. Finally, the act of 57 G. III. c. 6, has confirmed, if not extended, what stood on rather a precarious basis, and rendered perpetual that of 36 G. III. c. 7, which enacts, " that if any person or persons whatsoever, during the life of the king, and until the end of the next session of parliament after a demise of the crown, shall, within the realm or without, compass, imagine, invent, devise, or intend death or destruction, or any bodily harm tending to death or destruction,

[p] Foster's Discourse on High Treason, 196. State Trials, xii. 646, 790, 818; xiii. 62 (sir John Friend's case) et alibi. This important question, having arisen on lord Russell's trial, gave rise to a controversy between two eminent lawyers, sir Bartholomew Shower and sir Robert Atkins; the former maintaining, the latter denying, that a conspiracy to depose the king and to seize his guards was an overt act of compassing his death. State Trials, ix. 719, 818.

See also Phillipps's State Trials, ii. 39, 76; a work to which I might have referred in other places, and which shows the well-known judgment and impartiality of the author.

[q] In the whole series of authorities, however, on this subject, it will be found that the probable danger to the king's safety from rebellion was the groundwork upon which this constructive treason rested; nor did either Hale or Foster, Pemberton or Holt, ever dream that any other death was intended by the statute than that of nature. It was reserved for a modern crown lawyer to resolve this language into a metaphysical personification, and to argue that, the king's person being interwoven with the state, and its sole representative, any conspiracy against the constitution must of its own nature be a conspiracy against his life. State Trials, xxiv. 1183.

[r] 13 Eliz. c. 1; 13 Car. 2, c. 1; 36 G. 3, c. 7.

maim or wounding, imprisonment or restraint of the person of the same our sovereign lord the king, his heirs and successors, or to deprive or depose him or them from the style, honour, or kingly name of the imperial crown of this realm, or of any other of his majesty's dominions or countries, or to levy war against his majesty, his heirs and successors, within this realm, in order, by force or constraint, to compel him or them to change his or their measures or counsels, or in order to put any force or constraint upon, or to intimidate or overawe, both houses or either house of parliament, or to move or stir any foreigner or stranger with force to invade this realm, or any other his majesty's dominions or countries under the obeisance of his majesty, his heirs and successors; and such compassings, imaginations, inventions, devices, and intentions, or any of them, shall express, utter, or declare, by publishing any printing or writing, or by any overt act or deed; being legally convicted thereof upon the oaths of two lawful and credible witnesses, shall be adjudged a traitor, and suffer as in cases of high treason."

This from henceforth will become our standard of law in cases of treason, instead of the statute of Edward III., the latterly received interpretations of which it sanctions and embodies. But it is to be noted, as the doctrine of our most approved authorities, that a conspiracy for many purposes which, if carried into effect, would incur the guilt of treason, will not of itself amount to it. The constructive interpretation of compassing the king's death appears only applicable to conspiracies whereof the intent is to depose or to use personal compulsion towards him, or to usurp the administration of his government.* But though insurrections in order to throw down all enclosures, to alter the established law or change religion, or in general for the reformation of alleged grievances of a public nature, wherein the insurgents have no special interests, are in themselves treasonable, yet the previous concert and conspiracy for such purpose could, under the statute of Edward III., only pass for a misdemeanor. Hence, while it has been positively laid down that an attempt by intimida-

* Hale, 123. Foster, 213.

tion and violence to force the repeal of a law is high treason,[t] though directed rather against the two houses of parliament than the king's person, the judges did not venture to declare that a mere conspiracy and consultation to raise a force for that purpose would amount to that offence.[u] But the statutes of 36 & 57 G. III. determine the intention to levy war, in order to put any force upon or to intimidate either house of parliament, manifested by any overt act, to be treason, and so far have undoubtedly extended the scope of the law. We may hope that so ample a legislative declaration on the law of treason will put an end to the preposterous interpretations which have found too much countenance on some not very distant occasions. The crime of compassing and imagining the king's death must be manifested by some overt act; that is, there must be something done in execution of a traitorous purpose. For, as no hatred towards the person of the sovereign, nor any longings for his death, are the imagination which the law here intends, it seems to follow that loose words or writings, in which such hostile feelings may be embodied, unconnected with any positive design, cannot amount to treason. It is now, therefore, generally agreed that no words will constitute that offence, unless as evidence of some overt act of treason; and the same appears clearly to be the case with respect at least to unpublished writings.[x]

The second clause of the statute, or that which declares the levying of war against the king within the realm to be treason, has given rise, in some instances, to constructions hardly less strained than those upon compassing his death. It would indeed be a very narrow interpretation, as little required by the letter as warranted by the reason of this law, to limit the ex-

[t] Lord George Gordon's case, State Trials, xxi. 649.

[u] Hanly's case, id. xxiv. 208. The language of chief justice Eyre is sufficiently remarkable.

[x] Foster, 198. He seems to concur in Hale's opinion that words which being spoken will not amount to an overt act to make good an indictment for compassing the king's death, yet, if reduced into writing, and published, will make such an overt act, "if the matters contained in them import such a compassing." Hale's Pleas of Crown, 118. But this is indefinitely expressed, the words marked as a quotation looking like a truism, and contrary to the first part of the sentence; and the case of Williams, under James I., which Hale cites in corroboration of this, will hardly be approved by any constitutional lawyer.

pression of levying war to rebellions whereof the deposition of the sovereign, or subversion of his government, should be the deliberate object. Force, unlawfully directed against the supreme authority, constitutes this offence; nor could it have been admitted as an excuse for the wild attempt of the earl of Essex, on this charge of levying war, that his aim was not to injure the queen's person, but to drive his adversaries from her presence. The only questions as to this kind of treason are: first, what shall be understood by force? and secondly, where it shall be construed to be directed against the government? And the solution of both these, upon consistent principles, must so much depend on the circumstances which vary the character of almost every case, that it seems natural to distrust the general maxims that have been delivered by lawyers. Many decisions in cases of treason before the Revolution were made by men so servile and corrupt, they violate so grossly all natural right and all reasonable interpretation of law, that it has generally been accounted among the most important benefits of that event to have restored a purer administration of criminal justice. But, though the memory of those who pronounced these decisions is stigmatized, their authority, so far from being abrogated, has influenced later and better men; and it is rather an unfortunate circumstance that precedents which, from the character of the times when they occurred, would lose at present all respect, having been transfused into text-books, and formed perhaps the sole basis of subsequent decisions, are still in not a few points the invisible foundation of our law. No lawyer, I conceive, prosecuting for high treason in this age, would rely on the case of the duke of Norfolk under Elizabeth, or that of Williams under James I., or that of Benstead under Charles I.; but he would certainly not fail to dwell on the authorities of sir Edward Coke and sir Matthew Hale. Yet these eminent men, and especially the latter, aware that our law is mainly built on adjudged precedent, and not daring to reject that which they would not have themselves asserted, will be found to have rather timidly exercised their judgment in the construction of this statute, yielding a deference to former authority which we have transferred to their own.

These observations are particularly applicable to that class of cases so repugnant to the general understanding of mankind, and, I believe, of most lawyers, wherein trifling insurrections for the purpose of destroying brothels or meeting-houses have been held treasonable under the clause of levying war. Nor does there seem any ground for the defence which has been made for this construction, by taking a distinction that, although a rising to effect a partial end by force is only a riot, yet, where a general purpose of the kind is in view, it becomes rebellion; and thus, though to pull down the enclosures in a single manor be not treason against the king, yet to destroy all enclosures throughout the kingdom would be an infringement of his sovereign power. For, however solid this distinction may be, yet, in the class of cases to which I allude, this general purpose was neither attempted to be made out in evidence, nor rendered probable by the circumstances; nor was the distinction ever taken upon the several trials. A few apprentices rose in London in the reign of Charles II., and destroyed some brothels.ʸ A mob of watermen and others, at the time of Sacheverell's impeachment, set on fire several dissenting meeting-houses.ᶻ Everything like a formal attack on the established government is so much excluded in these instances by the very nature of the offence and the means of the offenders, that it is impossible to withhold our reprobation from the original decision, upon which, with too much respect for un-

---

ʸ Hale, 134. State Trials, vi. 879. It is observable that Hale himself, as chief baron, differed from the other judges in this case.

ᶻ This is the well-known case of Damaree and Purchase, State Trials, xv. 520. Foster, 213. A rabble had attended Sacheverell from Westminster to his lodgings in the Temple. Some among them proposed to pull down the meeting-houses; a cry was raised, and several of these were destroyed. It appeared to be their intention to pull down all within their reach. Upon this overt act of levying war the prisoners were convicted; some of the judges differing as to one of them, but merely on the application of the evidence to his case. Notwithstanding this solemn decision, and the approbation with which sir Michael Foster has stamped it, some difficulty would arise in distinguishing this case, as reported, from many indictments under the riot act for mere felony; and especially from those of the Birmingham rioters in 1791, where the similarity of motives, though the mischief in the latter instance was far more extensive, would naturally have suggested the same species of prosecution as was adopted against Damaree and Purchase. It may be remarked that neither of these men was executed; which, notwithstanding the sarcastic observation of Foster, might possibly be owing to an opinion, which every one but a lawyer must have entertained, that their offence did not amount to treason.

reasonable and unjust authority, the later cases have been established. These, indeed, still continue to be cited as law; but it is much to be doubted whether a conviction for treason will ever again be obtained, or even sought for, under similar circumstances. One reason indeed for this, were there no weight in any other, might suffice: the punishment of tumultuous risings, attended with violence, has been rendered capital by the riot act of George I. and other statutes; so that, in the present state of the law, it is generally more advantageous for the government to treat such an offence as felony than as treason.

It might for a moment be doubted, upon the statute of Edward VI., whether the two witnesses whom the act requires must not depose to the same overt acts of treason. But, as this would give an undue security to conspirators, so it is not necessarily implied by the expression; nor would it be indeed the most unwarrantable latitude that has been given to this branch of penal law to maintain that two witnesses to any distinct acts comprised in the same indictment would satisfy the letter of this enactment. But a more wholesome distinction appears to have been taken before the Revolution, and is established by the statute of William, that, although different overt acts may be proved by two witnesses, they must relate to the same species of treason, so that one witness to an alleged act of compassing the king's death cannot be conjoined with another deposing to an act of levying war, in order to make up the required number.[a] As for the practice of courts of justice before the Restoration, it was so much at variance with all principles, that few prisoners were allowed the benefit of this statute;[b] succeeding judges fortunately deviated more from their predecessors in the method of conducting trials than they would have thought themselves at liberty to do in laying down rules of law.

Statute of William III.

Nothing had brought so much disgrace on the councils of government and on the administration of justice, nothing had more forcibly spoken the necessity of a great change, than the prosecutions for treason during the latter years of Charles II., and in truth during the

---

[a] 7 W. III. c 3, § 4. Foster, 257.   [b] Foster, 234.

whole course of our legal history. The statutes of
Edward III. and Edward VI., almost set aside by sophistical constructions, required the corroboration of
some more explicit law; and some peculiar securities
were demanded for innocence against that conspiracy of
the court with the prosecutor which is so much to be
dreaded in all trials for political crimes. Hence the
attainders of Russell, Sidney, Cornish, and Armstrong
were reversed by the convention parliament without
opposition; and men attached to liberty and justice,
whether of the whig or tory name, were anxious to prevent any future recurrence of those iniquitous proceedings, by which the popular frenzy at one time, the
wickedness of the court at another, and in each instance
with the co-operation of a servile bench of judges, had
sullied the honour of English justice. A better tone of
political sentiment had begun indeed to prevail, and the
spirit of the people must ever be a more effectual security
than the virtue of the judges; yet, even after the Revolution, if no unjust or illegal convictions in cases of
treason can be imputed to our tribunals, there was still
not a little of that rudeness towards the prisoner, and
manifestation of a desire to interpret all things to his
prejudice, which had been more grossly displayed by
the bench under Charles II. The Jacobites, against
whom the law now directed its terrors, as loudly complained of Treby and Pollexfen, as the whigs had of
Scroggs and Jefferies, and weighed the convictions of
Ashton and Anderton against those of Russell and
Sidney.[c]

Ashton was a gentleman who, in company with lord
Preston, was seized in endeavouring to go over to
France with an invitation from the Jacobite party. The
contemporary writers on that side, and some historians
who incline to it, have represented his conviction as

---

[c] "Would you have trials secured?"
says the author of the Jacobite Principles
Vindicated. (Somers Tracts, x. 526.)
"It is the interest of all parties care
should be taken about them, or all parties
will suffer in their turns. Plunket, and
Sidney, and Ashton were doubtless all
murdered, though they were never so
guilty of the crimes wherewith they
were charged; the one tried twice, the
other found guilty upon one evidence,
and the last upon nothing but presumptive proof." Even the prostitute lawyer,
sir Bartholomew Shower, had the assurance to complain of uncertainty in
the law of treason. Id. 572. And Roger
North, in his Examen, p. 411, labours
hard to show that the evidence in Ashton's
case was slighter than in Sidney's.

grounded upon insufficient, because only upon presumptive, evidence. It is true that, in most of our earlier cases of treason, treasonable facts have been directly proved; whereas it was left to the jury in that of Ashton, whether they were satisfied of his acquaintance with the contents of certain papers taken on his person. There does not, however, seem to be any reason why presumptive inferences are to be rejected in charges of treason, or why they should be drawn with more hesitation than in other grave offences; and if this be admitted, there can be no doubt that the evidence against Ashton was such as is ordinarily reckoned conclusive. It is stronger than that offered for the prosecution against O'Quigley at Maidstone, in 1798, a case of the closest resemblance; and yet I am not aware that the verdict in that instance was thought open to censure. No judge, however, in modern times, would question, much less reply to, the prisoner as to material points of his defence, as Holt and Pollexfen did in this trial; the practice of a neighbouring kingdom, which, in our more advanced sense of equity and candour, we are agreed to condemn.[d]

It is perhaps less easy to justify the conduct of chief justice Treby in the trial of Anderton for printing a treasonable pamphlet. The testimony came very short of satisfactory proof, according to the established rules of English law, though by no means such as men in general would slight. It chiefly consisted of a comparison between the characters of a printed work found concealed in his lodgings and certain types belonging to his press: a comparison manifestly less admissible than that of handwriting, which is always rejected, and indeed totally inconsistent with the rigour of English proof. Besides the common objections made to a comparison of hands, and which apply more forcibly to printed characters, it is manifest that types cast in the same font must always be exactly similar. But, on the other hand, it seems unreasonable absolutely to exclude, as our courts have done, the comparison of handwriting as inadmissible evidence: a rule which is every day eluded by fresh rules, not much more rational in themselves, which have been invented to get rid of its incon-

[d] State Trials, xii. 646.—See 668 and 799.

venience. There seems, however, much danger in the construction which draws printed libels, unconnected with any conspiracy, within the pale of treason, and especially the treason of compassing the king's death, unless where they directly tended to his assassination. No later authority can, as far as I remember, be adduced for the prosecution of any libel as treasonable under the statute of Edward III. But the pamphlet for which Anderton was convicted was certainly full of the most audacious jacobitism, and might perhaps fall, by no unfair construction, within the charge of adhering to the king's enemies; since no one could be more so than James, whose design of invading the realm had been frequently avowed by himself."

A bill for regulating trials upon charges of high treason passed the commons with slight resistance from the crown lawyers in 1691.' The lords introduced a provision in their own favour, that, upon the trial of a peer in the court of the high steward, all such as were entitled to vote should be regularly summoned, it having been the practice to select twenty-three at the discretion of the crown. Those who wished to hinder the bill availed themselves of the jealousy which the commons in that age entertained of the upper house of parliament, and persuaded them to disagree with this just and reasonable amendment.⁵ It fell to the ground, therefore, on this occasion, and, though more than once revived in subsequent sessions, the same difference between the two houses continued to be insuperable.ʰ In the new parliament that met in 1695 the commons had the good sense to recede from an irrational jealousy. Notwithstanding the reluctance of the ministry, for which perhaps the very dangerous position of the king's government furnishes an apology, this excellent statute was enacted as an additional guarantee (in such bad times as might again occur) to those who are prominent in their country's cause, against the great danger of false

---

* State Trials, xII. 1245. Ralph, 420. Somers Tracts, x. 472. The Jacobites took a very frivolous objection to the conviction of Anderton, that printing could not be treason within the statute of Edward III., because it was not invented for a century afterwards. According to this rule, it could not be treason to shoot the king with a pistol, or poison him with an American drug.

f Parl. Hist. v. 698.

⁵ Id. 675.

ʰ Id. 712, 737. Commons' Journals, Feb. 8, 1695.

accusers and iniquitous judges.¹ It provides that all persons indicted for high treason shall have a copy of their indictment delivered to them five days before their trial, a period extended by a subsequent act to ten days, and a copy of the panel of jurors two days before their trial; that they shall be allowed to have their witnesses examined on oath, and to make their defence by counsel. It clears up any doubt that could be pretended on the statute of Edward VI., by requiring two witnesses, either both to the same overt act, or the first to one, the second to another overt act of the same treason (that is, the same kind of treason), unless the party shall voluntarily confess the charge.ᵏ It limits prosecutions for treason to the term of three years, except in the case of an attempted assassination on the king. It includes the contested provision for the trial of peers by all who have a right to sit and vote in parliament. A later statute; 7 Anne, c. 21, which may be mentioned here as the complement of the former, has added a peculiar privilege to the accused, hardly less material than any of the rest. Ten days before the trial, a list of the witnesses intended to be brought for proving the indictment, with their professions and places of abode, must be delivered to the prisoner, along with the copy of the indictment. The operation of this clause was suspended till after the death of the pretended prince of Wales.

Notwithstanding a hasty remark of Burnet, that the design of this bill seemed to be to make men as safe in all treasonable practices as possible, it ought to be considered a valuable accession to our constitutional law; and no part, I think, of either statute will be reckoned inexpedient, when we reflect upon the history of all nations, and more especially of our own. The history of all nations, and more especially of our own, in the

---

¹ Parl. Hist. 965. Journal, 17th Feb. 1696. Stat. 7 W. III. c. 3. Though the court opposed this bill, it was certainly favoured by the zealous whigs as much as by the opposite party.

ᵏ When several persons of distinction were arrested on account of a Jacobite conspiracy in 1690, there was but one witness against some of them. The judges were consulted whether they could be indicted for a high misdemeanor on this single testimony, as Hampden had been in 1685; the attorney-general Treby maintaining this to be lawful. Four of the judges were positively against this, two more doubtfully the same way, one altogether doubtful, and three in favour of it. The scheme was very properly abandoned; and at present, I suppose, nothing can be more established than the negative. Dalrymple, Append. 186.

fresh recollection of those who took a share in these acts, teaches us that false accusers are always encouraged by a bad government, and may easily deceive a good one. A prompt belief in the spies whom they perhaps necessarily employ, in the voluntary informers who dress up probable falsehoods, is so natural and constant in the offices of ministers, that the best are to be heard with suspicion when they bring forward such testimony. One instance, at least, had occurred since the Revolution, of charges unquestionably false in their specific details, preferred against men of eminence by impostors who panted for the laurels of Oates and Turberville.ᵐ And, as men who are accused of conspiracy against a government are generally such as are beyond question disaffected to it, the indiscriminating temper of the prejudging people from whom juries must be taken is as much to be apprehended, when it happens to be favourable to authority, as that of the government itself; and requires as much the best securities, imperfect as the best are, which prudence and patriotism can furnish to innocence. That the prisoner's witnesses should be examined on oath will of course not be disputed, since by a subsequent statute that strange and unjust anomaly in our criminal law has been removed in all cases as well as in treason; but the judges had sometimes not been ashamed to point out to the jury, in derogation of the credit of those whom a prisoner called in his behalf, that they were not speaking under the same sanction as those for the crown. It was not less reasonable that the defence should be conducted by counsel; since that excuse which is often made for denying the assistance of counsel on charges of felony, namely, the moderation of prosecutors and the humanity of the bench, could never be urged in those political accusations wherein the advocates for the prosecution contend with all their strength for victory; and the impartiality of the court is rather praised when it is found than relied upon beforehand."

ᵐ State Trials, xii. 1051.
ⁿ The dexterity with which lord Shaftesbury (the author of the Characteristics), at that time in the house of commons, turned a momentary confusion which came upon him while speaking on this bill, into an argument for extending the aid of counsel to those who might so much more naturally be embarrassed on a trial for their lives, is well known. All well-informed writers ascribe this to Shaftesbury. But Johnson, in the Lives of the Poets, has, through inadvertence, as I believe, given lord Halifax (Mon-

Nor does there lie, perhaps, any sufficient objection even to that which many dislike, which is more questionable than the rest, the furnishing a list of the witnesses to the prisoner, when we set on the other side the danger of taking away innocent lives by the testimony of suborned and infamous men, and remember also that a guilty person can rarely be ignorant of those who will bear witness against him; or if he could, that he may always discover those who have been examined before the grand jury.

The subtlety of crown lawyers in drawing indictments for treason, and sometimes the willingness of judges to favour such prosecutions, have considerably eluded the chief difficulties which the several statutes appear to throw in their way. The government has at least had no reason to complain that the construction of those enactments has been too rigid. The overt acts laid in the indictment are expressed so generally that they give sometimes little insight into the particular circumstances to be adduced in evidence; and, though the act of William is positive that no evidence shall be given of any overt act not laid in the indictment, it has been held allowable, and is become the constant practice, to bring forward such evidence, not as substantive charges, but on the pretence of its tending to prove certain other acts specially alleged. The disposition to extend a constructive interpretation to the statute of Edward III. has continued to increase; and was carried, especially by chief-justice Eyre in the trials of 1794, to a length at which we lose sight altogether of the plain meaning of words, and apparently much beyond what l'emberton, or even Jefferies, had reached. In the vast mass of circumstantial testimony which our modern trials for high treason display, it is sometimes difficult to discern whether the great principle of our law, requiring two witnesses to overt acts, has been adhered to; for certainly it is not adhered to, unless such witnesses depose to acts of the prisoner from which an inference of his guilt is immediately deducible.* There can be no doubt that state

tagu) the credit of it; and some have since followed him. As a complete refutation of this mistake. It is sufficient to say that Mr. Montagu opposed the bill. His name appears as a teller on two divisions, 31st Dec. 1691, and 18th Nov. 1692.

* It was said by Scroggs and Jefferies that if one witness prove that A bought a knife, and another that he intended to

prosecutions have long been conducted with an urbanity and exterior moderation unknown to the age of the Stuarts, or even to that of William; but this may by possibility be compatible with very partial wresting of the law, and the substitution of a sort of political reasoning for that strict interpretation of penal statutes which the subject has a right to demand. No confidence in the general integrity of a government, much less in that of its lawyers, least of all any belief in the guilt of an accused person, should beguile us to remit that vigilance which is peculiarly required in such circumstances.ᵖ

For this vigilance, and indeed for almost all that keeps up in us, permanently and effectually, the spirit of regard to liberty and the public good, we must look to the unshackled and independent energies of the press. In the reign of William III., and through the influence of the popular principle in our constitution, this finally became free. The licensing act, suffered to expire in 1679, was revived in 1685 for seven years. In 1692 it was continued till the end of the session of 1693. Several attempts were afterwards made to renew its operation, which the less courtly whigs combined with the tories and Jacobites to defeat.ᑫ Both parties indeed employed the press with great diligence in this reign; but while one degenerated into malignant calumny and misrepresentation, the signal victory of liberal principles is manifestly due to the boldness and eloquence with which they were promulgated. Even during the existence of a censorship, a host of unlicensed publications, by the negligence or connivance of the officers employed to seize them, bore witness to the inefficacy of its restrictions. The bitterest invectives of jacobitism were circulated in the first four years after the Revolution.ʳ

kill the king with it, these are two witnesses within the statute of Edward VI. But this has been justly reprobated.

ᵖ Upon some of the topics touched in the foregoing pages, besides Hale and Foster, see Luders' Considerations on the Law of Treason in Levying War, and many remarks in Phillipps's State Trials; besides much that is scattered through the notes of Mr. Howell's great collection. Mr. Phillipps's work, however, was not published till after my own was written.

ᑫ Commons' Journals, 9th Jan. and 11th Feb. 1694-95. A bill to the same effect sent down from the lords was thrown out, 17th April, 1695. Another bill was rejected on the second reading in 1697. Id. 3rd April.

ʳ Somers Tracts, passim. John Dun-

The liberty of the press consists, in a strict sense, merely in an exemption from the superintendence of a licenser. But it cannot be said to exist in any security, or sufficiently for its principal ends, where discussions of a political or religious nature, whether general or particular, are restrained by too narrow and severe limitations. The law of libel has always been indefinite—an evil probably beyond any complete remedy, but which evidently renders the liberty of free discussion rather more precarious in its exercise than might be wished. It appears to have been the received doctrine in Westminster Hall before the Revolution, that no man might publish a writing reflecting on the government, nor upon the character or even capacity and fitness of any one employed in it. Nothing having passed to change the law, the law remained as before. Hence in the case of Tutchin, it is laid down by Holt that to possess the people with an ill opinion of the government, that is, of the ministry, is a libel. And the attorney-general, in his speech for the prosecution, urges that there can be no reflection on those that are in office under her majesty, but it must cast some reflection on the queen who employs them. Yet in this case the censure upon the administration, in the passages selected for prosecution, was merely general and without reference to any person, upon which the counsel for Tutchin vainly relied.*

Liberty of the press.

It is manifest that such a doctrine was irreconcilable with the interests of any party out of power, whose best hope to regain it is commonly by prepossessing the nation with a bad opinion of their adversaries. Nor would it have been possible for any ministry to stop the torrent of a free press, under the secret guidance of a powerful faction, by a few indictments for libel. They found it generally more expedient and more agreeable to borrow weapons from the same armoury, and retaliate with

---

ton the bookseller, in the History of his Life and Errors, hints that unlicensed books could be published by a douceur to Robert Stephens, the messenger of the press, whose business it was to inform against them.

* State Trials, xiv. 1103, 1128. Mr. Justice Powell told the rev. Mr. Stephens, in passing sentence on him for a libel on Harley and Marlborough, that to traduce the queen's ministers was a reflection on the queen herself. It is said, however, that this and other prosecutions were generally blamed; for the public feeling was strong in favour of the liberty of the press. Boyer's Reign of Queen Anne; p. 286.

unsparing invective and calumny. This was first practised (first, I mean, with the avowed countenance of government) by Swift, in the Examiner and some of his other writings. And both parties soon went such lengths in this warfare, that it became tacitly understood that the public characters of statesmen and the measures of administration are the fair topics of pretty severe attack.[t] Less than this, indeed, would not have contented the political temper of the nation, gradually and without intermission becoming more democratical, and more capable, as well as more accustomed, to judge of its general interests and of those to whom they were intrusted. The just limit between political and private censure has been far better drawn in these later times, licentious as we still may justly deem the press, than in an age when courts of justice had not deigned to acknowledge, as they do at present, its theoretical liberty. No writer, except of the most broken reputation, would venture at this day on the malignant calumnies of Swift.

Meanwhile the judges naturally adhered to their established doctrine; and, in prosecutions for political libels, were very little inclined to favour what they deemed the presumption, if not the licentiousness, of the press. They advanced a little farther than their predecessors; and, contrary to the practice both before and after the Revolution, laid it down at length as an absolute principle, that falsehood, though always alleged in the indictment, was not essential to the guilt of the libel; refusing to admit its truth to be pleaded, or given in evidence, or even urged by way of mitigation of punishment.[u] But as the defendant

Law of libel

---

[t] [In a tract called the 'Memorial of the State of England,' 1705 (Somers Tracts, xii. 526), written on the whig side, in answer to Drake's 'Memorial of the Church of England,' we find a vindication of the press, which had been attacked at that time by the tories:—" If the whigs have their Observator, have not the tories their Rehearsal? The Review does not take more liberty than the Whipping Post, nor is he a wilder politician than the Mercury. And many will think it a meaner character for Ridpath to be Atwood's antagonist than to be author of the Flying Post." The reign of Anne was the era of *periodical* politics. Gutta cavat lapidem, non vi, sed sæpe cadendo. We well know how forcibly this line describes the action of the regular press. It did not begin to operate much before 1704 or 1705, when the whigs came into office, and the rejection of the occasional conformity bill blew up a flame in the opposite party. But even then it was confined to periodical papers, such as the Observator or Rehearsal; for the common newspapers were as yet hardly at all political.—1848.]

[u] Pemberton, as I have elsewhere ob-

could only be convicted by the verdict of a jury, and jurors both partook of the general sentiment in favour of free discussion, and might in certain cases have acquired some prepossessions as to the real truth of the supposed libel, which the court's refusal to enter upon it could not remove, they were often reluctant to find a verdict of guilty; and hence arose by degrees a sort of contention which sometimes showed itself upon trials, and divided both the profession of the law and the general public. The judges and lawyers, for the most part, maintained that the province of the jury was only to determine the fact of publication; and also whether what are called the inuendoes were properly filled up, that is, whether the libel meant that which it was alleged in the indictment to mean, not whether such meaning were criminal or innocent, a question of law which the court were exclusively competent to decide. That the jury might acquit at their pleasure was undeniable; but it was asserted that they would do so in violation of their oaths and duty, if they should reject the opinion of the judge by whom they were to be guided as to the general law. Others of great name in our jurisprudence, and the majority of the public at large, conceiving that this would throw the liberty of the press altogether into the hands of the judges, maintained that the jury had a strict right to take the whole matter into their consideration, and determine the defendant's criminality or innocence according to the nature and circumstances of the publication. This controversy, which perhaps hardly arose within the period to which the present work relates, was settled by Mr. Fox's libel

---

served, permitted evidence to be given as to the truth of an alleged libel in publishing that sir Edmondbury Godfrey had murdered himself. And what may be reckoned more important, in a trial of the famous Fuller on a similar charge, Holt repeatedly (not less than five times) offered to let him prove the truth if he could. State Trials, xiv. 534. But, on the trial of Franklin, in 1731, for publishing a libel in the Craftsman, lord Raymond positively refused to admit of any evidence to prove the matters to be true, and said he was only abiding by what had been formerly done in other cases of the like nature. Id. xvii. 639. [" To make it a libel," says Powell in the case of the seven bishops, " it must be false, it must be scandalous, and it must tend to sedition." Id. xii. 427. In 1 Lord Raymond, 486, we find a case where judgment was arrested on an indictment for a libel on persons " to the jurors unknown;" because they could not properly say that the matter was false and scandalous, when they did not know the persons of whom it was spoken, nor could they say that any one was defamed by it.—1845.

bill in 1792. It declares the right of the jury to find a general verdict upon the whole matter; and though, from causes easy to explain, it is not drawn in the most intelligible and consistent manner, was certainly designed to turn the defendant's intention, as it might be laudable or innocent, seditious or malignant, into a matter of fact for their inquiry and decision.

The Revolution is justly entitled to honour as the era
Religious toleration. of religious, in a far greater degree than of civil liberty; the privileges of conscience having had no earlier magna charta and petition of right whereto they could appeal against encroachment. Civil, indeed, and religious liberty had appeared, not as twin sisters and co-heirs, but rather in jealous and selfish rivalry; it was in despite of the law, it was through infringement of the constitution, by the court's connivance, by the dispensing prerogative, by the declarations of indulgence under Charles and James, that some respite had been obtained from the tyranny which those who proclaimed their attachment to civil rights had always exercised against one class of separatists, and frequently against another.

At the time when the test-law was enacted, chiefly with a view against popery, but seriously affecting the protestant nonconformists, it was the intention of the house of commons to afford relief to the latter by relaxing in some measure the strictness of the act of uniformity in favour of such ministers as might be induced to conform, and by granting an indulgence of worship to those who should persist in their separation. This bill however dropped in that session. Several more attempts at an union were devised by worthy men of both parties in that reign, but with no success. It was the policy of the court to withstand a comprehension of dissenters; nor would the bishops admit of any concession worth the other's acceptance. The high-church party would not endure any mention of indulgence.ˣ In the parliament

---

ˣ See the pamphlets of that age, passim. One of these, entitled 'The Zealous and Impartial Protestant,' 1681, the author of which, though well known, I cannot recollect, after much invective, says, " Liberty of conscience and toleration are things only to be talked of and pretended to by those that are under; but none like or think it reasonable that are in authority. 'Tis an instrument of mischief and dissettlement to be courted by those who would have change, but no way desirable by such as would be quiet, and have the government undis-

of 1680 a bill to relieve protestant dissenters from the penalties of the 35th of Elizabeth, the most severe act in force against them, having passed both houses, was lost off the table of the house of lords at the moment that the king came to give his assent; an artifice by

turbed. For it is not consistent with public peace and safety without a standing army; conventicles being eternal nurseries of sedition and rebellion." P. 30. "To strive for toleration," he says in another place, "is to contend against all government. It will come to this,— whether there should be a government in the church or not? for if there be a government, there must be laws; if there be laws, there must be penalties annexed to the violation of those laws; otherwise the government is precarious and at every man's mercy; that is, it is none at all. ... The constitution should be made firm, whether with any alterations or without them, and laws put in punctual vigorous execution. Till that is done, all will signify nothing. The church hath lost all, through remissness and non-execution of laws; and by the contrary course things must be reduced, or they never will. To what purpose are parliaments so concerned to prepare good laws, if the officers who are intrusted with the execution neglect that duty, and let them lie dead? This brings laws and government into contempt, and it were much better the laws were never made; by these the dissenters are provoked, and, being not restrained by the exacting of the penalties, they are fiercer and more bent upon their own ways than they would be otherwise. But it may be said the execution of laws of conformity raiseth the cry of persecution; and will not that be scandalous? Not so scandalous as anarchy, schism, and eternal divisions and confusions both in church and state. Better that the unruly should clamour, than that the regular should groan, and all should be undone." P. 33. Another tract, 'Short Defence of the Church and Clergy of England, 1679,' declares for union (in his own way), but against a comprehension, and still more a toleration. "It is observable that, whereas the best emperors have made the severest laws

against all manner of sectaries, Julian the apostate, the most subtle and bitter enemy that Christianity ever had, was the man that set up this way of toleration." P. 87. Such was the temper of this odious faction. And at the time they were instigating the government to fresh severities, by which, I sincerely believe, they meant the pillory or the gallows (for nothing else was wanting), scarce a gaol in England was without nonconformist ministers. One can hardly avoid rejoicing that some of these men, after the Revolution, experienced, not indeed the persecution, but the poverty they had been so eager to inflict on others.

The following passage from a very judicious tract on the other side, 'Discourse of the Religion of England, 1667,' may deserve to be extracted:—" Whether cogent reason speaks for this latitude, be it now considered. How momentous in the balance of this nation those protestants are which are dissatisfied, in the present ecclesiastical polity. They are everywhere spread through city and country; they make no small part of all ranks and sorts of men; by relations and commerce they are so woven into the nation's interest, that it is not easy to sever them without unravelling the whole. They are not excluded from the nobility, among the gentry they are not a few; but none are of more importance than they in the trading part of the people and those that live by industry, upon whose hands the business of the nation lies much. It hath been noted that some who bear them no good will have said that the very air of corporations is infested with their contagion. And in whatsoever degree they are high of low, ordinarily for good understanding, steadiness, and sobriety, they are not inferior to others of the same rank and quality, neither do they want the national courage of Englishmen." P. 23.

which he evaded the odium of an explicit refusal.[r] Meanwhile the nonconforming ministers, and in many cases their followers, experienced a harassing persecution under the various penal laws that oppressed them; the judges, especially in the latter part of this reign, when some good magistrates were gone, and still more the justices of the peace, among whom a high-church ardour was prevalent, crowding the gaols with the pious confessors of puritanism.[s] Under so rigorous an administration of statute law, it was not unnatural to take the shelter offered by the declaration of indulgence; but the dissenters never departed from their ancient abhorrence of popery and arbitrary power, and embraced the terms of reconciliation and alliance which the church, in its distress, held out to them. A scheme of comprehension was framed under the auspices of archbishop Sancroft before the Revolution. Upon the completion of the new settlement it was determined, with the apparent concurrence of the church, to grant an indulgence to separate conventicles, and at the same time, by enlarging the terms of conformity, to bring back those whose differences were not irreconcilable within the pale of the Anglican communion.

The act of toleration was passed with little difficulty, though not without murmurs of the bigoted churchmen.[t] It exempts from the penalties of existing statutes against separate conventicles, or absence from the established worship, such as should take the oath of allegiance, and subscribe the declaration against popery, and such ministers of separate congregations as should subscribe the thirty-nine articles of the church of England, except three, and part of a fourth. It gives also an indulgence to quakers without this condition. Meeting-houses are required to be registered, and are protected from insult by a penalty. No part of this toleration is extended to papists, or to such as deny the Trinity. We may justly deem this act a very scanty measure of religious liberty; yet it proved more effectual through the lenient and liberal policy of the eighteenth

[r] Parl. Hist. iv. 1311. Ralph, 559.
[s] Baxter; Neal; Palmer's Nonconformist's Memorial.
Parl. Hist. v. 263. Some of the tories wished to pass it only for seven years. The high-church pamphlets of the age grumble at the toleration.

century; the subscription to articles of faith, which soon became as obnoxious as that to matters of a more indifferent nature, having been practically dispensed with, though such a genuine toleration as Christianity and philosophy alike demand had no place in our statute-book before the reign of George III.

It was found more impracticable to overcome the prejudices which stood against any enlargement of the basis of the English church. The bill of comprehension, though nearly such as had been intended by the primate, and conformable to the plans so often in vain devised by the most wise and moderate churchmen, met with a very cold reception. Those among the clergy who disliked the new settlement of the crown (and they were by far the greater part) played upon the ignorance and apprehensions of the gentry. The king's suggestion in a speech from the throne, that means should be found to render all protestants capable of serving him in Ireland, as it looked towards a repeal or modification of the test act, gave offence to the zealous churchmen.[b] A clause proposed in the bill for changing the oaths of supremacy and allegiance, in order to take away the necessity of receiving the sacrament in the church, as a qualification for office, was rejected by a great majority of the lords, twelve whig peers protesting.[c] Though the bill of comprehension proposed to parliament went no farther than to leave a few scrupled ceremonies at discretion, and to admit presbyterian ministers into the church without pronouncing on the invalidity of their former ordination, it was mutilated in passing through the upper house; and the commons, after entertaining it for a time, substituted an address to the king, that he would call the house of convocation, " to be advised with in ecclesiastical matters."[d] It was of course necessary to follow this recommendation. But the lower house of convocation, as might be foreseen, threw every obstacle in the way of their king's enlarged policy. They chose a man as their prolocutor who had been forward in the worst conduct of the university of Oxford. They displayed in everything a factious temper, which held the very

Attempt at comprehension.

[b] Burnet. Parl. Hist. 184.   [c] Parl. Hist. 196.
[d] Parl. Hist. ?, 2 .

names of concession and conciliation in abhorrence.^e Meanwhile a commission of divines, appointed under the great seal, had made a revision of the liturgy, in order to eradicate everything which could give a plausible ground of offence, as well as to render the service more perfect. Those of the high-church faction had soon seceded from this commission; and its deliberations were doubtless the more honest and rational for their absence. But, as the complacence of parliament towards ecclesiastical authority had shown that no legislative measure could be forced against the resistance of the lower house of convocation, it was not thought expedient to lay before that ill-affected body the revised liturgy which they would have employed as an engine of calumny against the bishops and the crown. The scheme of comprehension, therefore, fell absolutely and finally to the ground.^s

Schism of the nonjurors. A similar relaxation of the terms of conformity would, in the reign of Elizabeth, or even at the time of the Savoy conferences, have brought back so large a majority of dissenters that the separation of the remainder could not have afforded any colour of alarm to the most jealous dignitary. Even now it is said that two-thirds of the nonconformists would have embraced the terms of reunion. But the motives of dissent were already somewhat changed, and had come to turn less on the petty scruples of the elder puritans, and on the differences in ecclesiastical discipline, than on a dislike to all subscriptions of faith and compulsory uniformity. The dissenting ministers, accustomed to independence, and finding not unfrequently in the contributions of their disciples a better maintenance than court favour and private patronage have left for diligence

---

^e [The two houses of convocation differed about their address to the king, thanking him for his message about church reform. The lower house thought that proposed by the bishops too complimentary to the king and the Revolution; one was at last agreed upon, omitting the panegyrical passages. See both in Wilkin's Concilia, iv. 620.—1845.]

f [Ralph, ii. 167. The words high and low church are said by Swift in the Examiner to have come in soon after the Revolution. And probably they were not in common use before. But I find "high-church" named in a pamphlet of the reign of Charles II. It is in the Harleian Miscellany; but I have not got any more distinct reference.—1845.]

^g Burnet. Ralph. But a better account of what took place in the convocation and among the commissioners will be found in Kennet's Compl. Hist. 557, 558, &c.

and piety in the establishment, do not seem to have much regretted the fate of this measure. None of their friends, in the most favourable times, have ever made an attempt to renew it. There are indeed serious reasons why the boundaries of religious communion should be as widely extended as is consistent with its end and nature; and among these the hardship and detriment of excluding conscientious men from the ministry is not the least. Nor is it less evident that from time to time, according to the progress of knowledge and reason, to remove defects and errors from the public service of the church, even if they have not led to scandal or separation, is the bounden duty of its governors. But none of these considerations press much on the minds of statesmen; and it was not to be expected that any administration should prosecute a religious reform for its own sake, at the hazard of that tranquillity and exterior unity which is in general the sole end for which they would deem such a reform worth attempting. Nor could it be dissembled that, so long as the endowments of a national church are supposed to require a sort of politic organization within the commonwealth, and a busy spirit of faction for their security, it will be convenient for the governors of the state, whenever they find this spirit adverse to them, as it was at the Revolution, to preserve the strength of the dissenting sects as a counterpoise to that dangerous influence which in protestant churches, as well as that of Rome, has sometimes set up the interest of one order against that of the community. And though the church of England made a high vaunt of her loyalty, yet, as lord Shrewsbury told William of the tories in general, he must remember that he was not their king; of which indeed he had abundant experience.

A still more material reason against any alteration in the public liturgy and ceremonial religion at that feverish crisis, unless with a much more decided concurrence of the nation than could be obtained, was the risk of nourishing the schism of the nonjurors. These men went off from the church on grounds merely political, or at most on the pretence that the civil power was incompetent to deprive bishops of their ecclesiastical jurisdiction; to which none among the laity, who did not adopt the same political tenets, were likely to pay attention. But the established liturgy was, as it is at present in the eyes of the great majority, the distinguishing mark of the Anglican church, far more indeed than episcopal government, whereof so little is known by the mass of the people that its abolition, if we may utter such a paradox, would make no perceptible difference in their religion. Any change, though for the better, would offend those prejudices of education and habit which it requires such a revolutionary commotion of the public mind as the sixteenth century witnessed to subdue, and might fill the jacobite conventicles with adherents to the old church. It was already the policy of the nonjuring clergy to hold themselves up in this respectable light, and to treat the Tillotsons and Burnets as equally schismatic in discipline and unsound in theology. Fortunately, however, they fell into the snare which the established church had avoided; and deviating, at least in their writings, from the received standard of Anglican orthodoxy, into what the people saw with most jealousy, a sort of approximation to the church of Rome, gave their opponents an advantage in controversy, and drew farther from that part of the clergy who did not much dislike their political creed. They were equally injudicious and neglectful of the signs of the times, when they promulgated such extravagant assertions of sacerdotal power as could not stand with the regal supremacy, or any subordination to the state. It was plain, from the writings of Leslie and other leaders of their party, that the mere restoration of the house of Stuart would not content them, without undoing all that had been enacted as to the church from the time of Henry VIII.; and thus the charge of innovation came evidently home to themselves.[h]

[h] Leslie's Case of the Regale and Pontificate is a long, dull attempt to set up the sacerdotal order above all civil power, at least as to the exercise of its functions, and especially to get rid of the appointment of bishops by the crown, or, by parity of reasoning, of priests by laymen. He is indignant even at laymen choosing their chaplains, and thinks they ought to take them from the bishop; objecting also to the phrase my chaplain, as if they were servants: "otherwise the expression is proper enough to say my chaplain, as I say my parish priest, my bishop, my king, or my God; which argues my being under their care and direction, and that I belong to them, not they to me:" p. 182. [In another place he says, a man cannot serve two masters; therefore a peer should not have two chaplains." It

The convention parliament would have acted a truly politic, as well as magnanimous part, in extending this boon, or rather this right, of religious liberty to the members of that unfortunate church for whose sake the late king had lost his throne. It would have displayed to mankind that James had fallen, not as a catholic, nor for seeking to bestow toleration on catholics, but as a violator of the constitution. William, in all things superior to his subjects, knew that temporal, and especially military fidelity, would be in almost every instance proof against the seductions of bigotry. The Dutch armies have always been in a great measure composed of catholics; and many of that profession served under him in the invasion of England. His own judgment for the repeal of the penal laws had been declared even in the reign of James. The danger, if any, was now immensely diminished; and it appears in the highest degree probable that a genuine toleration of their worship, with no condition but the oath of allegiance, would have brought over the majority of that church to the protestant succession, so far at least as to engage in no schemes inimical to it. The wiser catholics would have perceived that, under a king of their own faith, or but suspected of an attachment to it, they must continue the objects of perpetual distrust to a protestant nation. They would have learned that conspiracy and jesuitical intrigue could but keep alive calumnious imputations, and diminish the respect which a generous people would naturally pay to their sincerity and their misfortune. Had the legislators of that age taken a still larger sweep, and abolished at once those tests and disabilities which, once necessary bulwarks against an insidious court, were no longer demanded in the more republican model of our government, the jacobite cause would have suffered, I believe, a more deadly wound

is full of enormous misrepresentation as to the English law. [Leslie, however, like many other controversialists, wrote impetuously and hastily for his immediate purpose. There is a great deal of contradiction between this 'Case of the Regale and Pontificate,' published in 1700 or 1701, and his 'Case stated between the Churches of Rome and England,' in 1713. In the latter the whole reasoning is strictly protestant; and while, in the Case of the Regale, he had set up the authority of the catholic church as binding not only on individuals but on national churches, he here even asserts the right of private judgment, and denies that any general council ever did or can exist.—1845.]

than penal statutes and double taxation were able to inflict. But this was beyond the philosophers, how much beyond the statesmen, of the time!

The tories, in their malignant hatred of our illustrious monarch, turned his connivance at popery into a theme of reproach.¹ It was believed, and probably with truth, that he had made to his catholic allies promises of relaxing the penal laws; and the jacobite intriguers had the mortification to find that William had his party at Rome, as well as her exiled confessor of St. Germains. After the peace of Ryswick many priests came over, and showed themselves with such incautious publicity as alarmed the bigotry of the house of commons, and produced the disgraceful act of 1700 against the growth of popery.ᵏ The admitted aim of this statute was to expel the catholic proprietors of land, comprising many very ancient and wealthy families, by rendering it necessary for them to sell their estates. It first offers a reward of 100*l.* to any informer against a priest exercising his functions, and adjudges the penalty of perpetual imprisonment. It requires every person educated in the popish religion, or professing the same, within six months after he shall attain the age of eighteen years, to take the oaths of allegiance and supremacy, and subscribe the declaration set down in the act of Charles II. against transubstantiation and the worship of saints; in default of which he is incapacitated, not only to purchase, but to inherit or take

Laws against Roman catholics.

ⁱ See Burnet (Oxf. iv. 409) and lord Dartmouth's note.

ᵏ No opposition seems to have been made in the house of commons; but we have a protest from four peers against it. Burnet, though he offers some shameful arguments in favour of the bill, such as might justify any tyranny, admits that it contained some unreasonable severities, and that many were really adverse to it. A bill proposed in 1705 to render the late act against papists effective was lost by 119 to 43 (Parl. Hist. vi. 514); which shows that men were ashamed of what they had done. A proclamation, however, was issued in 1711, immediately after Guiscard's attempt to kill Mr. Harley, for enforcing the penal laws against Roman catholics, which was very scandalous, as tending to impute that crime to them. Boyer's Reign of Anne, p. 429. And in the reign of Geo. 1. (1722) 100,000*l.* was levied by a particular act on the estates of papists and nonjurors. This was only carried by 188 to 172; sir Joseph Jekyll, and Mr. Onslow, afterwards speaker, opposing it, as well as lord Cowper in the other house. 9 G. I. c. 18. Parl. Hist. viii. 51, 353. It was quite impossible that those who sincerely maintained the principles of toleration should long continue to make any exception; though the exception in this instance was wholly on political grounds, and not out of bigotry, it did not the less contravene all that Taylor and Locke had taught men to cherish.

lands under any devise or limitation. The next of kin being a protestant shall enjoy such lands during his life.[m] So unjust, so unprovoked a persecution is the disgrace of that parliament. But the spirit of liberty and tolerance was too strong for the tyranny of the law; and this statute was not executed according to its purpose. The catholic landholders neither renounced their religion, nor abandoned their inheritances. The judges put such constructions upon the clause of forfeiture as eluded its efficacy; and, I believe, there were scarce any instances of a loss of property under this law. It has been said, and I doubt not with justice, that the catholic gentry during the greater part of the eighteenth century, were as a separated and half-proscribed class among their equals, their civil exclusion hanging over them in the intercourse of general society;[n] but their notorious, though not unnatural, disaffection to the reigning family will account for much of this, and their religion was undoubtedly exercised with little disguise or apprehension. The laws were perhaps not much less severe and sanguinary than those which oppressed the protestants of France; but, in their actual administration, what a contrast between the government of George II. and Louis XV., between the gentleness of an English court of king's bench, and the ferocity of the parliaments of Aix and Toulouse!

The immediate settlement of the crown at the Revolution extended only to the descendants of Anne and of William. The former was at that time pregnant, and became in a few months the mother of a son. Nothing therefore urged the convention parliament to go any farther in limiting the succession. But the king, in order to secure the elector of Hanover to the grand alliance, was desirous to settle the reversion of the crown on his wife the princess Sophia and her posterity. A provision to this effect was inserted in the bill of

Act of settlement.

---

[m] 11 & 12 W. III. c. 4. It is hardly necessary to add that this act was repealed in 1779. [According to a paper printed by Dalrymple, vol. ii. Appendix, p. 12, the number of papists in England above the age of sixteen was but 13,856. This was not long after the Revolution, though no precise date is given. The protestants, conformists and non-conformists, of the same age, are made to amount to 2,585,930. This would be not very far below the mark, as we know from other sources; but the number of catholics appears incredibly small.— 1845.]

[n] Butler's Memoirs of Catholics, ii. 64.

rights by the house of lords. But the commons rejected the amendment with little opposition; not, as Burnet idly insinuates, through the secret wish of a republican party (which never existed, or had no influence) to let the monarchy die a natural death, but from a just sense that the provision was unnecessary and might become inexpedient.° During the life of the young duke of Glocester the course of succession appeared clear. But upon his untimely death in 1700, the manifest improbability that the limitations already established could subsist beyond the lives of the king and princess of Denmark made it highly convenient to preclude intrigue, and cut off the hopes of the jacobites, by a new settlement of the crown on a protestant line of princes.ᴾ Though the choice was truly free in the hands of parliament, and no pretext of absolute right could be advanced on any side, there was no question that the princess Sophia was the fittest object of the nation's preference. She was indeed very far removed from any hereditary title. Besides the pretended prince of Wales, and his sister, whose legitimacy no one disputed, there stood in her way the duchess of Savoy, daughter of Henrietta duchess of Orleans, and several of the Palatine family. These last had abjured the reformed faith, of which their ancestors had been the strenuous assertors; but it seemed not improbable that some one might return to it; and, if all hereditary right of the ancient English royal line, the descendants of Henry VII., had not been extinguished, it would have been necessary to secure the succession of any prince who should profess the protestant religion at the time when the existing limitations should come to an end.ᑫ According to the tenor and

---

° While the bill regulating the succession was in the house of commons, a proviso was offered by Mr. Godolphin, that nothing in this act is intended to be drawn into example or consequence hereafter, to prejudice the right of any protestant prince or princess in their hereditary succession to the imperial crown of these realms. This was much opposed by the whigs; both because it tended to let in the son of James II. if he should become a protestant, and for a more secret reason, that they did not like to recognise the continuance of any hereditary right. It was rejected by 179 to 125. Parl. Hist. v. 249. The lords' amendment in favour of the princess Sophia was lost without a division. Id. 339.

ᴾ [It is asserted by lord Dartmouth, in a note on Burnet, iv. 520, that some of the whigs had a project of bringing in the house of Hanover at once on the king's death. But no rational man could have thought of this.—1845.]

ᑫ The duchess of Savoy put in a very foolish protest against anything that should be done to prejudice her right. Ralph, 924.

intention of the act of settlement, all prior claims of inheritance, save that of the issue of king William and the princess Anne, being set aside and annulled, the princess Sophia became the source of a new royal line.' The throne of England and Ireland, by virtue of the paramount will of parliament, stands entailed upon the heirs of her body, being protestants. In them the right is as truly hereditary as it ever was in the Plantagenets or the Tudors. But they derive it not from those ancient families. The blood indeed of Cerdic and of the Conqueror flows in the veins of his present majesty. Our Edwards and Henries illustrate the almost unrivalled splendour and antiquity of the house of Brunswic. But they have transmitted no more right to the allegiance of England than Boniface of Este or Henry the Lion. That rests wholly on the act of settlement, and resolves itself into the sovereignty of the legislature.

The majority of that house of commons which passed the bill of settlement consisted of those who, having long opposed the administration of William, though with very different principles both as to the succession of the crown and its prerogative, were now often called by the general name of tories. Some, no doubt, of these were adverse to a measure which precluded the restoration of the house of Stuart, even on the contingency that its heir might embrace the protestant religion.'

---

r [It might be urged against this, that the act of settlement *declares*, as well as enacts, the princess Sophia to be "next in succession, in the protestant line, to the imperial crown and dignity," &c., reciting also her descent from James I. But, if we take into consideration the public history of the transaction, and the necessity which was felt for a parliamentary settlement, we shall be led to think that this was merely the assertion of a fact, and not a recognition of an existing right. This also seems to be the opinion of Blackstone, who treats the princess Sophia as a new *stirps* of the royal family. But it is probable that those who drew the bill meant to show the world that we deviated as little as circumstances would admit from the hereditary line. The vote, in fact, of the convention parliament in January, 1689, that the throne was then *vacant*, put an end, according to any legal analogies, to the supposition of a subsisting reversionary right. Nor do I conceive that many persons conversant with our constitution imagine any one to have a right to the crown, on the happily most improbable supposition of the extinction of our royal family.—1846.]

s ["The whigs," says Bolingbroke, "had appeared zealous for the protestant succession, when king William proposed it after the death of the duke of Glocester. The tories voted for it then; and the acts that were judged necessary to secure it—some of them at least—were promoted by them. Yet were they not thought, nor did they affect, as the others did, to be thought extremely fond of it. King William did not come into this measure till *he found, upon trial, that there was no other safe and practicable,*

But this party could not show itself very openly; and Harley, the new leader of the tories, zealously supported the entail of the crown on the princess Sophia. But it was determined to accompany this settlement with additional securities for the subject's liberty.* The bill of rights was reckoned hasty and defective; some matters of great importance had been omitted, and, in the twelve years which had since elapsed, new abuses had called for new remedies. Eight articles were therefore inserted in the act of settlement, to take effect only from the commencement of the new limitation to the house of Hanover. Some of them, as will appear, sprung from a natural jealousy of this unknown and foreign line; some should strictly not have been postponed so long; but it is necessary to be content with what it is practicable to obtain. These articles are the following:—

Limitations of prerogative contained in it. That whosoever shall hereafter come to the possession of this crown shall join in communion with the church of England as by law established.

That in case the crown and imperial dignity of this realm shall hereafter come to any person, not being a native of this kingdom of England, this nation be not obliged to engage in any war for the defence of any dominions or territories which do not belong to the crown of England, without the consent of parliament.

That no person who shall hereafter come to the possession of this crown shall go out of the dominions of England, Scotland, or Ireland, without consent of parliament.

That from and after the time that the further limitation by this act shall take effect, all matters and things relating to the well-governing of this kingdom, which are properly cognizable in the privy council by the laws

and the tories had an air of coming into it for no other reason. Besides which, it is certain that there was at that time a much greater leaven of Jacobitism in the tory camp than at the time spoken of here." State of Parties at Accession of George I.—1845.]

† [It was resolved in a committee of the whole house, and agreed to by the house, that, " for the preserving the peace and happiness of this kingdom and the security of the protestant religion by law established, it is absolutely necessary a further declaration be made of the limitation and succession of the crown in the protestant line, after his majesty and the princess, and the heirs of their bodies respectively. Resolved that farther provision be first made for security of the rights and liberties of the people." Commons' Journals, 2nd March, 1700–1 - 1845.]

and customs of this realm, shall be transacted there, and all resolutions taken thereupon shall be signed by such of the privy council as shall advise and consent to the same.

That, after the said limitation shall take effect as aforesaid, no person born out of the kingdoms of England, Scotland, or Ireland, or the dominions thereunto belonging (although he be naturalized or made a denizen—except such as are born of English parents), shall be capable to be of the privy council, or a member of either house of parliament, or to enjoy any office or place of trust, either civil or military, or to have any grant of lands, tenements, or hereditaments, from the crown, to himself, or to any other or others in trust for him.

That no person who has an office or place of profit under the king, or receives a pension from the crown, shall be capable of serving as a member of the house of commons.

That, after the said limitation shall take effect as aforesaid, judges' commissions be made quamdiu se bene gesserint, and their salaries ascertained and established; but, upon the address of both houses of parliament, it may be lawful to remove them.

That no pardon under the great seal of England be pleadable to an impeachment by the commons in parliament."

The first of these provisions was well adapted to obviate the jealousy which the succession of a new dynasty, bred in a protestant church not altogether agreeing with our own, might excite in our susceptible nation. A similar apprehension of foreign government produced the second article, which so far limits the royal prerogative, that any minister who could be proved to have advised or abetted a declaration of war in the specified contingency would be criminally responsible to parliament.[x] The third article was repealed very soon

---

[u] 12 & 13 W. III. c. 2.

[x] It was frequently contended in the reign of George II. that subsidiary treaties for the defence of Hanover, or rather such as were covertly designed for that and no other purpose, as those with Russia and Hesse Cassel in 1755, were at least contrary to the spirit of the act of settlement. On the other hand it was justly answered that, although, in case Hanover should be attacked on the ground of a German quarrel, unconnected with English politics, we were not bound to defend her, yet, if a power at war with England should think fit to consider that electorate as part of the king's dominions

after the accession of George I., whose frequent journeys to Hanover were an abuse of the graciousness with which the parliament consented to annul the restriction.'

A very remarkable alteration that had been silently wrought in the course of the executive government gave rise to the fourth of the remedial articles in the act of settlement. According to the original constitution of our monarchy, the king had his privy council, composed of the great officers of state, and of such others as he should summon to it, bound by an oath of fidelity and secrecy, by whom all affairs of weight, whether as to domestic or exterior policy, were debated for the most part in his presence, and determined, subordinately of course to his pleasure, by the vote of the major part. It could not happen but that some councillors more eminent than the rest should form juntos or cabals, for more close and private management, or be selected as more confidential advisers of their sovereign; and the very name of a cabinet council, as distinguished from the larger body, may be found as far back as the reign of Charles I. But the resolutions of the crown, whether as to foreign alliances or the issuing of proclamations and orders at home, or any other overt act of government, were not finally taken without the deliberation and assent of that body whom the law recognised as its sworn and notorious councillors. This was first broken in upon after the Restoration, and especially after the fall of Clarendon, a strenuous assertor of the rights and dignity of the privy council. "The king," as he complains, "had in his nature so little reverence and esteem for antiquity, and did in truth so much contemn old orders, forms, and institutions, that the objection of novelty rather advanced than obstructed any proposition."ª He wanted to be absolute on the

Privy council superseded by a cabinet.

(which, perhaps, according to the law of nations might be done), our honour must require that it should be defended against such an attack. This is true; and yet it shows very forcibly that the separation of the two ought to have been insisted upon, since the present connexion engages Great Britain in a very disadvantageous mode of carrying on its wars, without any compensation of national wealth or honour, except indeed that of employing occasionally in its service a very brave and efficient body of troops.—1827.

y 1 G. I. c. 51.

ª Life of Clarendon, 319. [It was not usual to have any privy councillors except great officers of state, and a few persons of high rank. This was rather relaxed after the Restoration; but Clarendon opposed sir William Coventry's introduction into the council on this account. P. 565.—1845.]

French plan, for which both he and his brother, as the same historian tells us, had a great predilection, rather than obtain a power little less arbitrary, so far at least as private rights were concerned, on the system of his three predecessors. The delays and the decencies of a regular council, the continual hesitation of lawyers, were not suited to his temper, his talents, or his designs. And it must indeed be admitted that the privy council, even as it was then constituted, was too numerous for the practical administration of supreme power. Thus by degrees it became usual for the ministry or cabinet to obtain the king's final approbation of their measures, before they were laid, for a merely formal ratification, before the council.[a] It was one object of sir William Temple's short-lived scheme in 1679 to bring back the ancient course; the king pledging himself on the formation of his new privy council to act in all things by its advice.

During the reign of William this distinction of the cabinet from the privy council, and the exclusion of the latter from all business of state, became more fully established.[b] This, however, produced a serious consequence as to the re- *Exclusion of placemen and pensioners from parliament.*

---

[a] [Trenchard, in his Short History of Standing Armies, published about 1698, and again in 1731, says, "Formerly all matters of state and discretion were debated and resolved in the privy council, where every man subscribed his opinion, and was answerable for it. The late king Charles was the first who broke this most excellent part of our constitution, by settling a cabal or cabinet council, where all matters of consequence were debated and resolved, and then brought to the privy council to be confirmed. P. 9.— 1845.]

[b] "The method is this," says a member in debate: "things are concerted in the cabinet, and then brought to the council; such a thing is resolved in the cabinet, and brought and put on them for their assent, without showing any of the reasons. That has not been the method of England. If this method be, you will never know who gives advice." Parl. Hist. v. 731. [In the lords' house, Jan. 1711, "the earl of Scarsdale proposed the following question:—That it appears by the earl of Sunderland's letter to Mr. Stanhope that the design of an offensive war in Spain was approved and directed by the cabinet council." But the mover afterwards substituted the wor" "ministers" for "cabinet council," as better known. Lord Cowper sa' they were both terms of an uncertain signification, and the latter unknown to our law. Some contended that ministers and cabinet council were synonymous; others that there might be a difference. Peterborough said, "he had heard a distinction between the cabinet council and the privy council; that the privy council were such as were thought to know everything, and knew nothing, and those of the cabinet council thought nobody knew anything but themselves." Parl. Hist. vi. 971.

At a meeting of the privy council, April 7, 1713, the peace of Utrecht was laid before them, but merely for form's sake, the treaty being signed by all the powers four days afterwards. Chief justice Parker, however, and lord Cholmondeley were said to have spoken

sponsibility of the advisers of the crown; and at the very time when the controlling and chastising power of parliament was most effectually recognised, it was silently eluded by the concealment in which the objects of its inquiry could wrap themselves. Thus, in the instance of a treaty which the house of commons might deem mischievous and dishonourable, the chancellor setting the great seal to it would of course be responsible; but it is not so evident that the first lord of the treasury, or others more immediately advising the crown on the course of foreign policy, could be liable to impeachment, with any prospect of success, for an act in which their participation could not be legally proved. I do not mean that evidence may not possibly be obtained which would affect the leaders of the cabinet, as in the instances of Oxford and Bolingbroke; but that, the cabinet itself having no legal existence, and its members being surely not amenable to punishment in their simple capacity of privy councillors, which they generally share, in modern times, with a great number even of their adversaries, there is no tangible character to which responsibility is attached; nothing, except a signature or the setting of a seal, from which a bad minister need entertain any further apprehension than that of losing his post and reputation.[e] It may be that

against it. Id. 1192, from Swift's Journal.

If we may trust a party-writer at the beginning of Anne's reign, the archbishop of Canterbury was regularly a member of the cabinet council. Public Spirit of the Whigs, in Somers Tracts, ix. 22. But probably the fact was that he occasionally was called to their meetings, as took place much later. Coxe's Memoirs of Walpole, i. 637, et alibi.

Lord Mansfield said in the house of lords, in 1775, Parl. Hist. xviii. 274, that he had been a cabinet minister part of the late reign and the whole of the present; but there was a nominal and an efficient cabinet, and a little before lord Rockingham's administration he had asked the king's leave not to act in the latter.—1845.]

In sir Humphrey Mackworth's [or perhaps Mr. Harley's] Vindication of the Rights of the Commons of England, 1701, Somers Tracts, xi. 276, the constitutional doctrine is thus laid down, according to the spirit of the recent act of settlement:—" As to the setting of the great seal of England to foreign alliances, the lord chancellor, or lord keeper, for the time being, has a plain rule to follow; that is, humbly to inform the king that he cannot legally set the great seal of England to a matter of that consequence unless the same be first debated and resolved in council; which method being observed, the chancellor is safe, and the council answerable."—P. 293.

[e] This very delicate question as to the responsibility of the cabinet, or what is commonly called the ministry, *in solidum*, if I may use the expression, was canvassed in a remarkable discussion within our memory, on the introduction of the late chief justice of the king's bench into that select body; Mr. Fox strenuously denying the proposition, and lord Castle-

no absolute corrective is practicable for this apparent deficiency in our constitutional security; but it is expedient to keep it well in mind, because all ministers speak loudly of their responsibility, and are apt, upon faith of this imaginary guarantee, to obtain a previous confidence from parliament which they may in fact abuse with impunity. For should the bad success or detected guilt of their measures raise a popular cry against them, and censure or penalty be demanded by their opponents, they will infallibly shroud their persons in the dark recesses of the cabinet, and employ every art to shift off the burthen of individual liability.

William III., from the reservedness of his disposition, as well as from the great superiority of his capacity for affairs to any of our former kings, was far less guided by any responsible counsellors than the spirit of our constitution requires. In the business of the partition treaty, which, whether rightly or otherwise, the house of commons reckoned highly injurious to the public interest, he had not even consulted his cabinet; nor could any minister, except the earl of Portland and lord Somers, be proved to have had a concern in the transaction; for, though the house impeached lord Orford and lord Halifax, they were not in fact any farther parties to it than by being in the secret, and the former had shown his usual intractability by objecting to the whole measure. This was undoubtedly such a departure from sound constitutional usage as left parliament no control over the executive administration. It was endeavoured to restore the ancient principle by this provision in the act of settlement, that, after the accession of the house of Hanover, all resolutions as to government should be debated in the privy council, and signed by those present. But, whether it were that real objections were found to stand in the way of this article, or that ministers shrank back from so definite a responsibility,

---

reagh, with others now living, maintaining it. Parl. Debates, A.D. 1806. I cannot possibly comprehend how an article of impeachment, for sitting as a cabinet minister, could be drawn; nor do I conceive that a privy councillor has a right to resign his place at the board, or even to absent himself when summoned; so that it would be highly unjust and illegal to presume a participation in culpable measures from the mere circumstance of belonging to it. Even if notoriety be a ground, as has been sometimes contended, for impeachment, it cannot be sufficient for conviction.

they procured its repeal a very few years afterwards.[d] The plans of government are discussed and determined in a cabinet council, forming indeed part of the larger body, but unknown to the law by any distinct character or special appointment. I conceive, though I have not the means of tracing the matter clearly, that this change has prodigiously augmented the direct authority of the secretaries of state, especially as to the interior department, who communicate the king's pleasure in the first instance to subordinate officers and magistrates, in cases which, down at least to the time of Charles I., would have been determined in council. But proclamations and orders still emanate, as the law requires, from the privy council; and on some rare occasions, even of late years, matters of domestic policy have been referred to their advice. It is generally understood, however, that no councillor is to attend, except when summoned;[e] so that, unnecessarily numerous as the council has become, these special meetings consist only of a few persons besides the actual ministers of the cabinet, and give the latter no apprehension of a formidable resistance. Yet there can be no reasonable doubt that every councillor is as much answerable for the measures adopted by his consent, and especially when ratified by his signature, as those who bear the name of ministers, and who have generally determined upon them before he is summoned.

The experience of William's partiality to Bentinck and Keppel, in the latter instance not very consistent with the good sense and dignity of his character, led to a strong measure of precaution against the probable influence of foreigners under the new dynasty; the exclusion of all persons not born within the dominions of the British crown from every office of civil and military trust, and from both houses of parliament. No other country, as far as I recollect, has adopted so sweeping a disqualification; and it must, I think, be admitted that it goes a greater length than liberal policy can be said

---

[d] 4 Anne, c. 8. 6 Anne, c. 7.

[e] This is the modern usage, but of its origin I cannot speak. On one remarkable occasion, while Anne was at the point of death, the dukes of Somerset and Argyle went down to the council-chamber without summons to take their seats; but it seems to have been intended as an unexpected manœuvre of policy.

to warrant. But the narrow prejudices of George I. were well restrained by this provision from gratifying his corrupt and servile German favourites with lucrative offices.[f]

The next article is of far more importance; and would, had it continued in force, have perpetuated that struggle between the different parts of the legislature, especially the crown and house of commons, which the new limitations of the monarchy were intended to annihilate. The baneful system of rendering the parliament subservient to the administration, either by offices and pensions held at pleasure, or by more clandestine corruption, had not ceased with the house of Stuart. William, not long after his accession, fell into the worst part of this management, which it was most difficult to prevent: and, according to the practice of Charles's reign, induced by secret bribes the leaders of parliamentary opposition to betray their cause on particular questions. The tory patriot, sir Christopher Musgrave, trod in the steps of the whig patriot, sir Thomas Lee. A large expenditure appeared every year, under the head of secret-service money; which was pretty well known, and sometimes proved, to be disposed of, in great part, among the members of both houses.[g] No check was put

---

[f] It is provided by 1 G. I. st. 2, c. 4, that no bill of naturalization shall be received without a clause disqualifying the party from sitting in parliament, &c., "for the better preserving the said clause in the said act entire and inviolate." This provision, which was rather supererogatory, was of course intended to show the determination of parliament not to be governed, ostensibly at least, by foreigners under their foreign master.

[g] Parl. Hist. 807, 840. Burnet says, p. 42, that sir John Trevor, a tory, first put the king on this method of corruption. Trevor himself was so venal that he received a present of 1000 guineas from the city of London, being then speaker of the commons, for his service in carrying a bill through the house; and, upon its discovery, was obliged to put the vote that he had been guilty of a high crime and misdemeanor. This resolution being carried, he absented himself from the house, and was expelled. Parl. Hist. 900. Commons' Journals, 12 March, 1694-5. The duke of Leeds, that veteran of secret iniquity, was discovered about the same time to have taken bribes from the East India Company, and was impeached in consequence. I say discovered, for there seems little or no doubt of his guilt. The impeachment, however, was not prosecuted for want of evidence. Parl. Hist. 881, 911, 933. Guy, secretary of the treasury, another of Charles II.'s court, was expelled the house on a similar imputation. Id. 886. Lord Falkland was sent to the Tower for begging 2000l. of the king. Id. 841. A system of infamous peculation among the officers of government came to light through the inquisitive spirit of parliament in this reign; not that the nation was worse and more corrupt than under the Stuarts, but that a profligacy which had been engendered and had flourished under their administration was now dragged to light and punishment. Long

on the number or quality of placemen in the lower house. New offices were continually created, and at unreasonable salaries. Those who desired to see a regard to virtue and liberty in the parliament of England could not be insensible to the enormous mischief of this influence. If some apology might be offered for it in the precarious state of the Revolution government, this did not take away the possibility of future danger, when the monarchy should have regained its usual stability. But, in seeking for a remedy against the peculiar evil of the times, the party in opposition to the court, during this reign, whose efforts at reformation were too frequently misdirected, either through faction or some sinister regards towards the deposed family, went into the preposterous extremity of banishing all servants of the crown from the house of commons. Whether the bill for free and impartial proceedings in parliament, which was rejected by a very small majority of the house of lords in 1693, and, having in the next session passed through both houses, met with the king's negative, to the great disappointment and displeasure of the commons, was of this general nature, or excluded only certain specified officers of the crown, I am not able to determine; though the prudence and expediency of William's refusal must depend entirely upon that question.[h] But in the act of settlement the clause is quite without exception; and if it had ever taken effect, no

sessions of parliament and a vigilant party-spirit exposed the evil, and have finally in a great measure removed it; though Burnet's remark is still not wholly obsolete. "The regard," says that honest bishop, "that is shown to the members of parliament among us makes that few abuses can be inquired into or discovered."

[h] Parl. Hist. 748, 829. The house resolved, "that whoever advised the king not to give the royal assent to the act touching free and impartial proceedings in parliament, which was to redress a grievance, and take off a scandal upon the proceedings of the commons in parliament, is an enemy to their majesties and the kingdom." They laid a representation before the king, showing how few instances have been in former reigns of denying the royal assent to bills for redress of grievances, and the great grief of the commons "for his not having given the royal assent to several public bills, and particularly the bill touching free and impartial proceedings in parliament, which tended so much to the clearing the reputation of this house, after their having so freely voted to supply the public occasions." The king gave a courteous but evasive answer, as indeed it was natural to expect; but so great a flame was raised in the commons, that it was moved to address him for a further answer, which however there was still a sense of decorum sufficient to prevent.

Though the particular provisions of this bill do not appear, I think it probable that it went too far in excluding military as well as civil officers.

minister could have had a seat in the house of commons, to bring forward, explain, or defend the measures of the executive government. Such a separation and want of intelligence between the crown and parliament must either have destroyed the one or degraded the other. The house of commons would either, in jealousy and passion, have armed the strength of the people to subvert the monarchy, or, losing that effective control over the appointment of ministers which has sometimes gone near to their nomination, would have fallen almost into the condition of those states-general of ancient kingdoms, which have met only to be cajoled into subsidies, and give a passive consent to the propositions of the court. It is one of the greatest safeguards of our liberty that eloquent and ambitious men, such as aspire to guide the counsels of the crown, are from habit and use so connected with the houses of parliament, and derive from them so much of their renown and influence, that they lie under no temptation, nor could without insanity be prevailed upon, to diminish the authority and privileges of that assembly. No English statesman, since the Revolution, can be liable to the very slightest suspicion of an aim, or even a wish, to establish absolute monarchy on the ruins of our constitution. Whatever else has been done, or designed to be done amiss, the rights of parliament have been out of danger. They have, whenever a man of powerful mind shall direct the cabinet, and none else can possibly be formidable, the strong security of his own interest, which no such man will desire to build on the caprice and intrigue of a court. And, as this immediate connexion of the advisers of the crown with the house of commons, so that they are, and ever profess themselves, as truly the servants of one as of the other, is a pledge for their loyalty to the entire legislature, as well as to their sovereign (I mean, of course, as to the fundamental principles of our constitution), so has it preserved for the commons their preponderating share in the executive administration, and elevated them in the eyes of foreign nations, till the monarchy itself has fallen comparatively into shade The pulse of Europe beats according to the tone of our parliament; the counsels of our kings are there revealed, and, by that kind of previous sanction which it has been customary to obtain, become, as it were, the resolutions of a senate; and we enjoy the individual pride and dignity which belong to republicans, with the steadiness and tranquillity which the supremacy of a single person has been supposed peculiarly to bestow.¹

But, if the chief ministers of the crown are indispensably to be present in one or other house of parliament, it by no means follows that the doors should be thrown open to all those subaltern retainers, who, too low to have had any participation in the measures of government, come merely to earn their salaries by a sure and silent vote. Unless some limitation could be put on the number of such officers, they might become the majority of every parliament, especially if its duration were indefinite or very long. It was always the popular endeavour of the opposition, or, as it was usually denominated, the country party, to reduce the number of these dependents; and as constantly the whole strength of the court was exerted to keep them up. William, in truth, from his own errors, and from the disadvantage of the times, would not venture to confide in an unbiassed parliament. On the formation, however, of a new board of revenue, in 1694, for managing the stamp-duties, its members were incapacitated from sitting in the house of commons.ᵏ This, I believe, is the first instance of exclusion on account of employment; and a similar act was obtained in 1699, extending this disability to the commissioners and some other officers of excise.ᵐ But when the absolute exclusion of all civil and military officers by the act of settlement was found, on cool reflection, too impracticable to be maintained, and a revision of that article took place in the year 1706, the

---

¹ [The tories introduced a clause, according to Burnet, into the oath of abjuration, to maintain the government by king, lords, and commons. This was rejected by the lords; and Burnet calls it "a barefaced republican notion, which was wont to be condemned as such by the same persons who now pressed it." The lords and commons, he observes, are indeed part of the constitution and the legislative body, but not of the government. Vol. iv. p. 538. But speaker Onslow, coming half a century later, after the whig practice and theory had become established, sees little to object to in the phrase "government," which may be taken in a large sense. Burnet, however as Ralph points out, has misrepresented the clause. The words were, "constitution and government by king, lords, and commons, as by law established:" which he conjectures to be rather levelled at "barefaced republican notions" than borrowed from them. Ralph, ii. 1018. Burnet's memory was too deceitful to be trusted without reference to books; yet he seems rarely to have made any.—1845.]

ᵏ 4 & 5 W. & M. c. 21.
ᵐ 11 & 12 W. III. c. 2, § 50.

house of commons were still determined to preserve at least the principle of limitation as to the number of placemen within their walls. They gave way indeed to the other house in a considerable degree, receding, with some unwillingness, from a clause specifying expressly the description of offices which should not create a disqualification, and consenting to an entire repeal of the original article.ⁿ But they established two provisions of great importance, which still continue the great securities against an overwhelming influence: first, that every member of the house of commons accepting an office under the crown, except a higher commission in the army, shall vacate his seat, and a new writ shall issue; secondly, that no person holding an office created since the 25th of October, 1705, shall be capable of being elected or re-elected at all. They excluded at the same time all such as held pensions during the pleasure of the crown; and, to check the multiplication of placemen, enacted that no greater number of commissioners should be appointed to execute any office than had been employed in its execution at some time before that parliament.^o These restrictions ought to be rigorously and jealously maintained, and to receive a construction, in doubtful cases, according to their constitutional spirit; not as if they were of a penal nature towards individuals, an absurdity in which the careless and indulgent temper of modern times might sometimes acquiesce.^p

---

ⁿ The house of commons introduced into the act of security, as it was called, a long clause, carried on a division by 167 to 160, Jan. 24, 1706, enumerating various persons who should be eligible to parliament; the principal officers of state, the commissioners of treasury and admiralty, and a limited number of other placemen. The lords thought fit to repeal the whole prohibitory enactment. It was resolved in the commons, by a majority of 205 to 183, that they would not agree to this amendment. A conference accordingly took place, when the managers of the commons objected, Feb. 7, that a total repeal of that provision would admit such an unlimited number of officers to sit in their house as might destroy the free and impartial proceedings in parliament, and endanger the liberties of the commons of England. Those on the lords' side gave their reasons to the contrary at great length, Feb. 11. The commons determined, Feb. 18, to insert the provision vacating the seat of a member accepting office; and resolved not to insist on their disagreements as to the main clause. Three protests were entered in the house of lords against inserting the word " repealed " in reference to the prohibitory clause, instead of " regulated and altered," all by tory peers. It is observable that, as the provision was not to take effect till the house of Hanover should succeed to the throne, the sticklers for it might be full as much influenced by their ill-will to that family as by their zeal for liberty.

^o 4 Anne, c. 8. 6 Anne, c. 7.

^p This, it is to be observed, was writ-

It had been the practice of the Stuarts, especially in the last years of their dynasty, to dismiss judges, without seeking any other pretence, who showed any disposition to thwart government in political prosecutions. The general behaviour of the bench had covered it with infamy. Though the real security for an honest court of justice must be found in their responsibility to parliament and to public opinion, it was evident that their tenure in office must, in the first place, cease to be precarious, and their integrity rescued from the severe trial of forfeiting the emoluments upon which they subsisted. In the debates previous to the declaration of rights we find that several speakers insisted on making the judges' commissions *quamdiu se bene gesserint*—that is, during life or good behaviour, instead of *durante placito*, at the discretion of the crown. The former, indeed, is said to have been the ancient course till the reign of James I. But this was omitted in the hasty and imperfect bill of rights. The commissions, however, of William's judges ran *quamdiu se bene gesserint*. But the king gave an unfortunate instance of his very injudicious tenacity of bad prerogatives in refusing his assent, in 1692, to a bill that had passed both houses for establishing this independence of the judges by law, and confirming their salaries.[q] We owe this important provision to the act of settlement; not, as ignorance and adulation have perpetually asserted, to his late majesty George III. No judge can be dismissed from office, except in consequence of a conviction for some offence, or the address of both houses of parliament, which is tantamount to an act of the legislature.[r] It is always to be kept in mind that they are still accessible to the hope of further promotion, to the zeal of political attachment, to the flattery of princes and ministers; that the bias of their prejudices, as elderly and peaceable men, will, in a plurality of cases, be on

---

ten before the reform bill of 1832, which created a necessity, if any sort of balance is to be preserved in our constitution, of strengthening the executive power, and consequently dictated the expediency of relaxing many provisions which had been required in very different times.

[q] Burnet, 86. It was represented to the king, he says, by some of the judges themselves, that it was not fit they should be out of all dependence on the court.

[r] It was originally resolved that they should be removable on the address of either house, which was changed afterwards to both houses. Comm. Journ. 12th March and 10th May.

the side of power; that they have very frequently been trained, as advocates, to vindicate every proceeding of the crown: from all which we should look on them with some little vigilance, and not come hastily to a conclusion that, because their commissions cannot be vacated by the crown's authority, they are wholly out of the reach of its influence. I would by no means be misinterpreted, as if the general conduct of our courts of justice since the Revolution, and especially in later times, which in most respects have been the best times, were not deserving of that credit it has usually gained; but possibly it may have been more guided and kept straight than some are willing to acknowledge by the spirit of observation and censure which modifies and controls our whole government.

The last clause in the act of settlement, that a pardon under the great seal shall not be pleadable in bar of an impeachment, requires no particular notice beyond what has been said on the subject in a former chapter.*

In the following session, a new parliament having been assembled, in which the tory faction had less influence than in the last, and Louis XIV. having in the mean time acknowledged the son of James as king of England, the natural resentment of this insult and breach of faith was shown in a more decided assertion of Revolution principles than had hitherto been made. The pretended king was attainted of high treason; a measure absurd as a law, but politic as a denunciation of perpetual enmity.¹ It was made high treason to correspond with him, or remit money for his service. And a still more vigorous measure was adopted, an oath to be taken, not only by all civil officers, but by all ecclesiastics, members of the universities, and schoolmasters, acknowledging William as lawful and rightful king, and

Oath of abjuration.

---

* It was proposed in the lords, as a clause in the bill of rights, that pardons upon an impeachment should be void, but lost by 50 to 17; on which twelve peers, all whigs, entered a protest. Parl. Hist. 482.

¹ 13 W. III. c. 3. The lords introduced an amendment into this bill to attaint also Mary of Este, the late queen of James II. But the commons disagreed, on the ground that it might be of dangerous consequence to attaint any one by an amendment, in which case such due consideration cannot be had as the nature of an attainder requires. The lords, after a conference, gave way; but brought in a separate bill to attaint Mary of Este, which passed with a protest of the tory peers. Lords' Journals, Feb. 6, 12, 20, 1701-2.

denying any right or title in the pretended prince of Wales." The tories, and especially lord Nottingham, had earnestly contended, in the beginning of the king's reign, against those words in the act of recognition which asserted William and Mary to be rightfully and lawfully king and queen. They opposed the association at the time of the assassination-plot, on account of the same epithets, taking a distinction which satisfied the narrow understanding of Nottingham, and served as a subterfuge for more cunning men, between a king whom they were bound in all cases to obey and one whom they could style rightful and lawful. These expressions were in fact slightly modified on that occasion; yet fifteen peers and ninety-two commoners declined, at least for a time, to sign it. The present oath of abjuration therefore was a signal victory of the whigs who boasted of the Revolution over the tories who excused it.[x] The renunciation of the hereditary right, for at this time few of the latter party believed in the young man's spuriousness, was complete and unequivocal. The dominant faction might enjoy perhaps a charitable pleasure in exposing many of their adversaries, and especially the high-church clergy, to the disgrace and remorse of perjury. Few or none, however, who had taken the oath of allegiance refused this additional cup of bitterness, though so much less defensible, according to the principles they had employed to vindicate their compliance in the former instance; so true it is that in matters of conscience the first scruple is the only one which it costs much to overcome. But the imposition of this test, as was evident in a few years, did not check the boldness or diminish the numbers of the Jacobites; and I must confess that, of all sophistry that weakens moral obligation, that is the most pardonable which men employ to escape from this species of tyranny. The state may reasonably make an entire and heartfelt attachment to its authority the condition of civil trust; but nothing more than a promise of peaceable obedience can justly be exacted from those who ask only to obey in peace.

[u] 13 W. III. c. 6.
[x] Sixteen lords, including two bishops, Compton and Sprat, protested against the bill containing the abjuration oath. The first reason of their votes was afterwards expunged from the Journals by order of the house. Lords' Journals, 24th Feb. 3rd March, 1701-2.

There was a bad spirit abroad in the church, ambitious, factious, intolerant, calumnious; but this was not necessarily partaken by all its members, and many excellent men might deem themselves hardly dealt with in requiring their denial of an abstract proposition which did not appear so totally false according to their notions of the English constitution and the church's doctrine.[y]

[y] Whiston mentions that Mr. Baker, of St. John's, Cambridge, a worthy and learned man, as well as others of the college, had thoughts of taking the oath of allegiance on the death of king James; but the oath of abjuration, coming out the next year, had such expressions as he still scrupled. Whiston's Memoirs. Biog. Brit. (Kippis's edition), art. BAKER.

CHAPTER XVI.

ON THE STATE OF THE CONSTITUTION IN THE REIGNS OF ANNE, GEORGE I., AND GEORGE II.

Termination of Contest between the Crown and Parliament — Distinctive Principles of Whigs and Tories — Changes effected in these by Circumstances — Impeachment of Sacheverell displays them again — Revolutions in the Ministry under Anne — War of the Succession — Treaty of Peace broken off — Renewed again by the Tory Government — Arguments for and against the Treaty of Utrecht — the Negotiation mismanaged — Intrigues of the Jacobites — Some of the Ministers engage in them — Just Alarm for the Hanover Succession — Accession of George I. —Whigs come into Power — Great Disaffection in the Kingdom — Impeachment of Tory Ministers — Bill for Septennial Parliaments — Peerage Bill —Jacobitism among the Clergy — Convocation — Its Encroachments — Hoadley — Convocation no longer suffered to sit — Infringements of the Toleration by Statutes under Anne — They are repealed by the Whigs — Principles of Toleration fully established — Banishment of Atterbury — Decline of the Jacobites — Prejudices against the Reigning Family — Jealousy of the Crown — Changes in the Constitution whereon it was founded — Permanent Military Force — Apprehensions from it — Establishment of Militia — Influence over Parliament by Places and Pensions — Attempts to restrain it — Place Bill of 1743 — Secret Corruption —Commitments for Breach of Privilege — of Members for Offences — of Strangers for Offences against Members — or for Offences against the House — Kentish Petition of 1701 — Dispute with Lords about Aylesbury Election — Proceedings against Mr. Murray in 1751 — Commitments for Offences unconnected with the House — Privileges of the House not controllable by Courts of Law — Danger of stretching this too far — Extension of Penal Laws — Diminution of Personal Authority of the Crown — Causes of this — Party Connexions — Influence of Political Writings — Publication of Debates — Increased Influence of the Middle Ranks.

Termination of the contest between the crown and parliament. THE act of settlement was the seal of our constitutional laws, the complement of the Revolution itself and the bill of rights, the last great statute which restrains the power of the crown, and manifests, in any conspicuous degree, a jealousy of parliament in behalf of its own and the subject's privileges. The battle had been fought and gained; the statute-book, as it becomes more voluminous, is less interesting in the history of our constitution; the voice of petition, complaint, or remonstrance is seldom to be traced in the Journals; the crown in return desists altogether, not merely from the threatening or objurgatory tone of the Stuarts, but from that dissatisfaction sometimes apparent in the language of William; and the vessel seems riding in smooth water, moved by other impulses, and liable perhaps to other dangers, than those of the ocean-wave and the tempest. The reigns, accordingly, of Anne, George I., and George II., afford rather materials for dissertation, than consecutive facts for such a work as the present; and may be sketched in a single chapter, though by no means the least important, which the reader's study and reflection must enable him to fill up. Changes of an essential nature were in operation during the sixty years of these three reigns, as well as in that beyond the limits of this undertaking, which in length measures them all; some of them greatly enhancing the authority of the crown, or rather of the executive government, while others had so opposite a tendency, that philosophical speculators have not been uniform in determining on which side was the sway of the balance.

No clear understanding can be acquired of the political history of England without distinguishing, with some accuracy of definition, the two great parties of whig and tory. But this is not easy; because those denominations, being sometimes applied to factions in the state intent on their own aggrandizement, sometimes to the principles they entertained or professed, have become equivocal, and do by no means, at all periods and on all occasions, present the same sense; an ambiguity which has been increased by the lax and incorrect use of familiar language. We may consider the words, in the first instance, as expressive of a political theory or principle, applicable to the English government. They were originally employed at the time of the bill of exclusion, though the distinction of the parties they denote is evidently at least as old as the long parliament. Both of these parties, it is material to observe, agreed in the maintenance of the constitution; that is, in the administration of government by an hereditary sovereign, and in the concurrence of that sovereign with the two houses of parliament in legislation, as well as in those other institutions which have been reckoned most ancient and fundamental. A favourer of unlimited monarchy was not a tory, neither was a republican a whig. Lord Clarendon was a tory,

Distinctive principles of whigs and tories.

Hobbes was not; bishop Hoadley was a whig, Milton was not. But they differed mainly in this; that to a tory the constitution, inasmuch as it was the constitution, was an ultimate point, beyond which he never looked, and from which he thought it altogether impossible to swerve; whereas a whig deemed all forms of government subordinate to the public good, and therefore liable to change when they should cease to promote that object. Within those bounds which he, as well as his antagonist, meant not to transgress, and rejecting all unnecessary innovation, the whig had a natural tendency to political improvement, the tory an aversion to it. The one loved to descant on liberty and the rights of mankind, the other on the mischiefs of sedition and the rights of kings. Though both, as I have said, admitted a common principle, the maintenance of the constitution, yet this made the privileges of the subject, that the crown's prerogative, his peculiar care. Hence it seemed likely that, through passion and circumstance, the tory might aid in establishing despotism, or the whig in subverting monarchy. The former was generally hostile to the liberty of the press, and to freedom of inquiry, especially in religion; the latter their friend. The principle of the one, in short, was amelioration; of the other, conservation.

But the distinctive characters of whig and tory were less plainly seen, after the Revolution and act of settlement, in relation to the crown, than to some other parts of our polity. The tory was ardently, and in the first place, the supporter of the church in as much pre-eminence and power as he could give it. For the church's sake, when both seemed as it were on one plank, he sacrificed his loyalty; for her he was always ready to persecute the catholic, and if the times permitted not to persecute, yet to restrain and discountenance the nonconformist. He came unwillingly into the toleration which the whig held up as one of the great trophies of the Revolution. The whig spurned at the haughty language of the church, and treated the dissenters with moderation, or perhaps with favour. This distinction subsisted long after the two parties had shifted their ground as to civil liberty and royal power. Again, a predilection for the territorial aristocracy, and for a government chiefly conducted by

Changes effected in these by circumstances.

their influence, a jealousy of new men, of the mercantile interest, of the commonalty, never failed to mark the genuine tory. It has been common to speak of the whigs as an aristocratical faction. Doubtless the majority of the peerage from the Revolution downwards to the death of George II. were of that denomination. But this is merely an instance wherein the party and the principle are to be distinguished. The natural bias of the aristocracy is towards the crown; but, except in most part of the reign of Anne, the crown might be reckoned with the whig party. No one who reflects on the motives which are likely to influence the judgment of classes in society would hesitate to predict that an English house of lords would contain a larger proportion of men inclined to the tory principle than of the opposite school; and we do not find that experience contradicts this anticipation.

It will be obvious that I have given to each of these political principles a moral character; and have considered them as they would subsist in upright and conscientious men, not as we may find them "in the dregs of Romulus," suffocated by selfishness or distorted by faction. The whigs appear to have taken a far more comprehensive view of the nature and ends of civil society; their principle is more virtuous, more flexible to the variations of time and circumstance, more congenial to large and masculine intellects. But it may probably be no small advantage, that the two parties, or rather the sentiments which have been presumed to actuate them, should have been mingled, as we find them, in the complex mass of the English nation, whether the proportions may or not have been always such as we might desire. They bear some analogy to the two forces which retain the planetary bodies in their orbits; the annihilation of one would disperse them into chaos, that of the other would drag them to a centre. And, though I cannot reckon these old appellations by any means characteristic of our political factions in the nineteenth century, the names whig and tory are often well applied to individuals. Nor can it be otherwise; since they are founded not only on our laws and history, with which most have some acquaintance, but in the diversities of condition and of moral temperament generally subsisting among mankind.

It is however one thing to prefer the whig principle, another to justify, as an advocate, the party which bore that name. So far as they were guided by that principle, I hold them far more friendly to the great interests of the commonwealth than their adversaries. But, in truth, the peculiar circumstances of these four reigns after the Revolution, the spirit of faction, prejudice, and animosity, above all, the desire of obtaining or retaining power, which, if it be ever sought as a means, is soon converted into an end, threw both parties very often into a false position, and gave to each the language and sentiments of the other; so that the two principles are rather to be traced in writings, and those not wholly of a temporary nature, than in the debates of parliament. In the reigns of William and Anne, the whigs, speaking of them generally as a great party, had preserved their original character unimpaired far more than their opponents. All that had passed in the former reign served to humble the tories, and to enfeeble their principle. The Revolution itself, and the votes upon which it was founded, the bill of recognition in 1690, the repeal of the non-resisting test, the act of settlement, the oath of abjuration, were solemn adjudications, as it were, against their creed. They took away the old argument, that the letter of the law was on their side. If this indeed were all usurpation, the answer was ready; but those who did not care to make it, or by their submission put it out of their power, were compelled to sacrifice not a little of that which had entered into the definition of a tory. Yet even this had not a greater effect than that systematic jealousy and dislike of the administration, which made them encroach, according to ancient notions, and certainly their own, on the prerogative of William. They learned in this no unpleasing lesson to popular assemblies, to magnify their own privileges and the rights of the people. This tone was often assumed by the friends of the exiled family, and in them it was without any dereliction of their object. It was natural that a jacobite should use popular topics in order to thwart and subvert an usurping government. His faith was to the crown, but to the crown on a right head. In a tory who voluntarily submitted to the reigning prince, such an opposition to the prerogative was repugnant to the maxims of his creed, and placed him, as I have said, in a false position. This is of course applicable to the reigns of George I. and II., and in a greater degree in proportion as the tory and jacobite were more separated than they had been perhaps under William.

The tories gave a striking proof how far they might be brought to abandon their theories, in supporting an address to the queen that she would invite the princess Sophia to take up her residence in England; a measure so unnatural as well as imprudent, that some have ascribed it to a subtlety of politics which I do not comprehend. But we need not, perhaps, look farther than to the blind rage of a party just discarded, who, out of pique towards their sovereign, made her more irreconcilably their enemy, and, while they hoped to brand their opponents with inconsistency, forgot that the imputation would redound with tenfold force on themselves. The whigs justly resisted a proposal so little called for at that time; but it led to an act for the security of the succession, designating a regency in the event of the queen's decease, and providing that the actual parliament, or the last if none were in being, should meet immediately, and continue for six months, unless dissolved by the successor.[a]

In the conduct of this party, generally speaking, we do not, I think, find any abandonment of the cause of liberty. The whigs appear to have been zealous for bills excluding placemen from the house, or limiting their numbers in it; and the abolition of the Scots privy council, an odious and despotic tribunal, was owing in a great measure to the authority of lord Somers.[b] In these measures

---

[a] 4 Anne, c. 8; Parl. Hist. 457, et post; Burnet, 429.

[b] 6 Anne, c. 6; Parl. Hist. 613; Somerville, 296; Hardw. Papers, ii. 473. Cunningham attests the zeal of the whigs for abolishing the Scots privy council, though he is wrong in reckoning lord Cowper among them, whose name appears in the protest on the other side: ii. 135, &c. The distinction of old and modern whigs appeared again in this reign: the former professing, and in general feeling, a more steady attachment to the principles of civil liberty. Sir Peter King, sir Joseph Jekyll, Mr. Wortley, Mr. Hampden, and the historian himself, were of this description; and consequently did not always support Godolphin. P. 210, &c. Mr. Wortley brought in a bill, which passed the commons in 1710, for voting by ballot. It was opposed by Wharton and Godolphin in the lords, as dangerous to the constitution, and thrown out. Wortley, he says, went the next year to Venice, on purpose to inquire into the effects of the ballot, which prevailed universally in that republic. P. 285. I have since learned that no trace of such a bill can be found in the Journals; yet I think Cunningham must have had some foun-

however the tories generally co-operated; and it is certainly difficult in the history of any nation to separate the influence of sincere patriotism from that of animosity and thirst of power. But one memorable event in the reign of Anne gave an opportunity for bringing the two theories of government into collision, to the signal advantage of that which the whigs professed; I mean the impeachment of Dr. Sacheverell. Though, with a view to the interests of their ministry, this prosecution was very unadvised, and has been deservedly censured, it was of high importance in a constitutional light, and is not only the most authentic exposition, but the most authoritative ratification, of the principles upon which the Revolution is to be defended.[c]

Impeachment of Sacheverell displays them again.

The charge against Sacheverell was not for impugning what was done at the Revolution, which he affected to vindicate, but for maintaining that it was not a case of resistance to the supreme power, and consequently no exception to his tenet of an unlimited passive obedience. The managers of the impeachment had, therefore, not only to prove that there was resistance in the Revolution, which could not of course be sincerely disputed, but to assert the lawfulness, in great emergencies, or what is

---

dation for his circumstantial assertion. The ballot, however, was probably meant to be *in* parliament, not, or not wholly, in elections.

[On searching the Journals I find a bill " to prevent bribery, corruption, and other indecent practices, in electing of members to serve in parliament," ordered to be brought in, 17th Jan. 1708-9. Nothing further appears in this session; but in the next a bill with the same title is brought in, 15th Feb. 1709-10, and read a second time Feb. 18th; but no more appears about it. Mr. Wortley's name does not appear among those who were ordered to bring in either of these bills.

I have also found in a short tract, entitled 'A Patriot's Proposal to the People of England,' 1705, a recommendation of election by ballot. It is highly democratical in its principle, but came a full century too soon. The proceedings of the house of commons in the Aylesbury case seem to have produced it.

It seems, therefore, that I was mistaken in supposing the bill mentioned by Cunningham to have respected the mode of voting *in* parliament.—1845.]

[c] Parl. Hist. vI. 805; Burnet, 537; State Trials, xv. 1. It is said in Coxe's Life of Marlborough, iii. 141, that Marlborough and Somers were against this prosecution. This writer goes out of his way to make a false and impertinent remark on the managers of the impeachment, as giving encouragement by their speeches to licentiousness and sedition. Id. 166.

[Cunningham says that Marlborough was for prosecution at law, rather than impeachment; Somers against both: ii. 277. Harley spoke against the impeachment, as unworthy of the house, but condemned Sacheverell's sermon as foolish, calling it a "circumgyration of incoherent words;" which, the historian says, some thought was the character of his own speech. Vol. ii. p. 285.—1845.]

called in politics necessity, of taking arms against the
law—a delicate matter to treat of at any time, and not
least so by ministers of state and law officers of the
crown, in the very presence, as they knew, of their
sovereign.[d] We cannot praise too highly their speeches
upon this charge: some shades, rather of discretion than
discordance, may be perceptible; and we may distinguish
the warmth of Lechmere, or the openness of Stanhope,
from the caution of Walpole, who betrays more
anxiety than his colleagues to give no offence in the
highest quarter; but in every one the same fundamental
principles of the whig creed, except on which indeed the
impeachment could not rest, are unambiguously proclaimed.
"Since we must give up our right to the laws
and liberties of this kingdom," says sir Joseph Jekyll,
"or, which is all one, be precarious in the enjoyment of
them, and hold them only during pleasure, if this doctrine
of unlimited non-resistance prevails, the commons have
been content to undertake this prosecution."[e]—"The doctrine
of unlimited, unconditional passive obedience," says
Mr. Walpole, "was first invented to support arbitrary and
despotic power, and was never promoted or countenanced
by any government that had not designs some time or
other of making use of it."[f] And thus general Stanhope
still more vigorously: "As to the doctrine itself of absolute
non-resistance, it should seem needless to prove by

[d] "The managers appointed by the house of commons," says an ardent Jacobite, "behaved with all the insolence imaginable. In their discourse they boldly asserted, even in her majesty's presence, that, if the right to the crown was hereditary and indefeasible, the prince beyond seas, meaning the king, and not the queen, had the legal title to it, she having no claim thereto but what she owed to the people; and that by the Revolution principles, on which the constitution was founded, and to which the laws of the land agreed, tho people might turn out or lay aside their sovereigns as they saw cause. Though, no doubt of it, there was a great deal of truth in these assertions, it is easy to be believed that the queen was not well pleased to hear them maintained, even in her own presence and in so solemn a manner, before such a great concourse of her subjects. For, though princes do cherish these and the like doctrines whilst they serve as the means to advance themselves to a crown, yet, being once possessed thereof, they have as little satisfaction in them as those who succeed by an hereditary unquestionable title." Lockhart Papers, i. 312.

It is probable enough that the last remark has its weight, and that the queen did not wholly like the speeches of some of the managers; and yet nothing can be more certain than that she owed her crown in the first instance, and the preservation of it at that very time, to those insolent doctrines which wounded her royal ear; and that the genuine loyalists would soon have lodged her in the Tower.

[e] State Trials, xv. 95.
[f] Id. 115.

arguments that it is inconsistent with the law of reason, with the law of nature, and with the practice of all ages and countries. Nor is it very material what the opinions of some particular divines, or even the doctrine generally preached in some particular reigns, may have been concerning it. It is sufficient for us to know what the practice of the church of England has been, when it found itself oppressed. And indeed one may appeal to the practice of all churches, of all states, and of all nations in the world, how they behaved themselves when they found their civil and religious constitutions invaded and oppressed by tyranny. I believe we may further venture to say that there is not at this day subsisting any nation or government in the world, whose first original did not receive its foundation either from resistance or compact; and, as to our purpose, it is equal if the latter be admitted. For wherever compact is admitted, there must be admitted likewise a right to defend the rights accruing by such compact. To argue the municipal laws of a country in this case is idle. Those laws were only made for the common course of things, and can never be understood to have been designed to defeat the end of all laws whatsoever; which would be the consequence of a nation's tamely submitting to a violation of all their divine and human rights."[g] Mr. Lechmere argues to the same purpose in yet stronger terms.[h]

But, if these managers for the commons were explicit in their assertion of the whig principle, the counsel for Sacheverell by no means unfurled the opposite banner with equal courage. In this was chiefly manifested the success of the former. His advocates had recourse to the petty chicane of arguing that he had laid down a general rule of obedience without mentioning its exceptions, that the Revolution was a case of necessity, and that they fully approved what was done therein. They set up a distinction, which, though at that time perhaps novel, has sometimes since been adopted by tory writers; that resistance to the supreme power was indeed utterly illegal on any pretence whatever, but that the supreme power in this kingdom was the legislature, not the king; and that the Revolution took effect

[g] State Trials, 127. [h] Id. 61.

by the concurrence of the lords and commons.¹ This is of itself a descent from the high ground of toryism, and would not have been held by the sincere bigots of that creed. Though specious, however, the argument is a sophism, and does not meet the case of the Revolution. For, though the supreme power may be said to reside in the legislature, yet the prerogative within its due limits is just as much part of the constitution, and the question of resistance to lawful authority remains as before. Even if this resistance had been made by the two houses of parliament, it was but the case of the civil war which had been explicitly condemned by more than one statute of Charles II. But, as Mr. Lechmere said in reply, it was undeniable that the lords and commons did not join in that resistance at the revolution as part of the legislative and supreme power, but as part of the collective body of the nation.ᵏ And sir John Holland had before observed, " that there was a resistance at the revolution was most plain, if taking up arms in Yorkshire, Nottinghamshire, Cheshire, and almost all the counties of England; if the desertion of a prince's own troops to an invading prince, and turning their arms against their sovereign, be resistance." ᵐ It might in fact have been asked whether the dukes of Leeds and Shrewsbury, then sitting in judgment on Sacheverell (and who afterwards voted him not guilty), might not have been convicted of treason, if the prince of Orange had failed of success?" The advocates indeed of the prisoner made so many concessions as amounted to an abandonment of all the general question. They relied chiefly on numerous

---

¹ State Trials, 196, 229. It is observed by Cunningham, p. 286, that Sacheverell's counsel, except Phipps, were ashamed of him; which is really not far from the case. "The doctor," says Lockhart, "employed sir Simon, afterwards lord Harcourt, and sir Constantine Phipps, as his counsel, who defended him the best way they could, though they were hard put to it to maintain the hereditary right and unlimited doctrine of non-resistance, and not condemn the revolution. And the truth on it is, these are so inconsistent with one another, that the chief arguments alleged in this and other parallel cases came to no more than this:

that the revolution was an exception from the nature of government in general, and the constitution and laws of Britain in particular, which necessity in that particular case made expedient and lawful.' Ibid.

ᵏ State Trials, 407.
ᵐ Id. 110.
ⁿ Cunningham says that the duke of Leeds spoke strongly in favour of the revolution, though he voted Sacheverell not guilty. P. 298. Lockhart observes that he added success to necessity, as an essential point for rendering the revolution lawful.

passages in the homilies and most approved writers of the Anglican church, asserting the duty of unbounded passive obedience. But the managers eluded these in their reply with decent respect.º The lords voted Sacheverell guilty by a majority of 67 to 59; several voting on each side rather according to their present faction than their own principles. They passed a slight sentence, interdicting him only from preaching for three years. This was deemed a sort of triumph by his adherents; but a severe punishment on one so insignificant would have been misplaced; and the sentence may be compared to the nominal damages sometimes given in a suit instituted for the trial of a great right.

The shifting combinations of party in the reign of Anne, which affected the original distinctions of whig and tory, though generally known, must be shortly noticed. The queen, whose understanding and fitness for government were below mediocrity, had been attached to the tories, and bore an antipathy to her predecessor. Her first ministry, her first parliament, gave presage of a government to be wholly conducted by that party. But this prejudice was counteracted by the persuasions of that celebrated favourite, the wife of Marlborough, who, probably from some personal resentments, had thrown her influence into the scale of the whigs. The well-known records of their conversation and correspondence present a strange picture of good-natured feebleness on one side, and of ungrateful insolence on the other. But the in-

Revolution in the ministry under Anne.

º The homilies are so much more vehement against resistance than Sacheverell was, that it would have been awkward to pass a rigorous sentence on him. In fact, he or any other clergyman had a right to preach the homily against rebellion instead of a sermon. As to their laying down general rules without adverting to the exceptions, an apology which the managers set up for them, it was just as good for Sacheverell; and the homilies expressly deny all possible exceptions. Tillotson had a plan of dropping these old compositions, which in some doctrinal points, as well as in the tenet of non-resistance, do not represent the sentiments of the modern church, though, in a general way, it subscribes to them. But the times were not ripe for this, or some other of that good prelate's designs. Wordsworth's Eccles. Biog. vol. vi. The quotations from the homilies and other approved works by Sacheverell's counsel are irresistible, and must have increased the party spirit of the clergy. " No conjuncture of circumstances whatever," says bishop Sanderson, " can make that expedient to be done at any time that is of itself, and in the kind, unlawful. For a man to take up arms offensive or defensive against a lawful sovereign, being a thing in its nature simply and de toto genere unlawful, may not be done by any man, at any time, in any case, upon any colour or pretence whatsoever." State Trials, 231.

terior of a court will rarely endure daylight. Though Godolphin and Marlborough, in whom the queen reposed her entire confidence, had been thought tories, they became gradually alienated from that party, and communicated their own feelings to the queen. The house of commons very reasonably declined to make an hereditary grant to the latter out of the revenues of the postoffice in 1702, when he had performed no extraordinary services; though they acceded to it without hesitation after the battle of Blenheim.[p] This gave some offence to Anne; and the chief tory leaders in the cabinet, Rochester, Nottingham, and Buckingham, displaying a reluctance to carry on the war with such vigour as Marlborough knew to be necessary, were soon removed from office. Their revengeful attack on the queen, in the address to invite the princess Sophia, made a return to power hopeless for several years. Anne, however, entertained a desire very natural to an English sovereign, yet in which none but a weak one will expect to succeed, of excluding chiefs of parties from her councils. Disgusted with the tories, she was loth to admit the whigs; and thus Godolphin's administration, from 1704 to 1708, was rather sullenly supported, sometimes indeed thwarted, by that party. Cowper was made chancellor against the queen's wishes;[q] but the junto, as it was called, of five eminent whig peers, Somers, Halifax, Wharton, Orford, and Sunderland, were kept out through the queen's dislike, and in some measure, no question, through Godolphin's jealousy. They forced themselves into the cabinet about 1708; and effected the dismissal of Harley and St. John, who, though not of the regular tory school in connexion or principle, had already gone along with that faction in the late reign, and were now reduced by their dismissal to unite with it.[r] The whig ministry of queen

[p] Parl. Hist. vi. 57. They did not scruple, however, to say what cost nothing but veracity and gratitude, that Marlborough had retrieved the honour of the nation. This was justly objected to, as reflecting on the late king, but carried by 180 to 80. Id. 58; Burnet.

[q] Coxe's Marlborough, i. 463. Mr. Smith was chosen speaker by 248 to 205, a slender majority: but some of the ministerial party seem to have thought him too much a whig. Id. 485; Parl. Hist. 450. The whig pamphleteers were long hostile to Marlborough.

[r] Burnet rather gently slides over these jealousies between Godolphin and the whig junto; and Tindal, his mere copyist, is not worth mentioning. But Cunningham's history, and still more the letters published in Coxe's Life of Marlborough, show better the state of party intrigues; which the Parliamentary His-

Anne, so often talked of, cannot in fact be said to have existed more than two years, from 1708 to 1710; her previous administration having been at first tory, and afterwards of a motley complexion, though depending for existence on the great whig interest which it in some degree proscribed. Every one knows that this ministry was precipitated from power through the favourite's abuse of her ascendancy, become at length intolerable to the most forbearing of queens and mistresses, conspiring with another intrigue of the bedchamber, and the popular clamour against Sacheverell's impeachment.* It seems rather an humiliating proof of the sway which the feeblest prince enjoys even in a limited monarchy, that the fortunes of Europe should have been changed by nothing more noble than the insolence of one waiting-woman and the cunning of another. It is true that this was effected by throwing the weight of the crown into the scale of a powerful faction; yet the house of Bourbon would probably not have reigned beyond the Pyrenees, but for Sarah and Abigail at queen Anne's toilet.†

---

tory also illustrates, as well as many pamphlets of the time. Somerville has carefully compiled as much as was known when he wrote.

* [If we may believe Swift, the queen had become alienated from the duchess of Marlborough as far back as her accession to the throne; the ascendant of the latter being what "her majesty had neither patience to bear nor spirit to subdue." Memoirs relating to the Change in the Queen's Ministry. But Coxe seems to refer the commencement of the coldness to 1706. Life of Marlborough, p. 151.— 1845.]

† ("It is most certain that, when the queen first began to change her servants, it was not from a dislike of things but of persons, and those persons a very small number." Swift's Inquiry into the Behaviour of the Queen's last Ministry. Though this authority is not always trustworthy, I incline to credit what is here said, confirmed by his private letters to Stella at this time. "It was the issue," he goes on to inform us, "of Sacheverell's trial which encouraged her to proceed so far. She then determined to dissolve parliament, having previously only designed to turn out one family. The whigs on this resolved to resign, which she accepted unwillingly from Somers and Cowper, both of whom, especially the former, she esteemed as much as her nature was capable of." Her scheme was moderate and comprehensive, from which she never departed till near her death. She became very difficult to advise out of the opinion of having been too much directed. "So that few ministers had ever perhaps a harder game to play, between the jealousy and discontents of his [Oxford's] friends on one side, and the management of the queen's temper on the other." His friends were anxious for further changes, with which he was not unwilling to comply, had not the duchess of Somerset's influence been employed. The queen said, if she might not choose her own servants, she could not see what advantage she had got from the change of ministry; and so little was her heart set upon a tory administration, that many employments in court and country, and a great majority of all commissions, remained in the hands of the other party. She lost the government the vote on lord Nottingham's motion,

The object of the war, as it is commonly called, of the Grand Alliance, commenced in 1702, was, as expressed in an address of the house of commons, for preserving the liberties of Europe and reducing the exorbitant power of France." The occupation of the Spanish dominions by the duke of Anjou, on the authority of the late king's will, was assigned as its justification, together with the acknowledgment of the pretended prince of Wales as successor to his father James. Charles, archduke of Austria, was recognised as king of Spain; and as early as 1705 the restoration of that monarchy to his house is declared in a speech from the throne to be not only safe and advantageous, but glorious to England.ˣ Louis XIV. had perhaps at no time much hope of retaining for his grandson the whole inheritance he claimed; and on several occasions made overtures for negotiation, but such as indicated his design of rather sacrificing the detached possessions of Italy and the Netherlands than Spain itself and the Indies.ʸ After the battle of Oudenarde, however, and the loss of Lille in the campaign of 1708, the exhausted state of France and discouragement of his court induced him to acquiesce in the cession of the Spanish monarchy as a basis of treaty. In the conferences of the Hague, in 1709, he struggled for a time to preserve Naples and Sicily; but ultimately admitted the terms imposed by the allies, with the exception of the famous thirty-seventh article of the preliminaries, binding him to procure by force or persuasion the resignation of the Spanish crown by his grandson within two months. This proposition he declared to be both dishonourable and impracticable; and, the allies refusing to give way, the negotiation was broken off. It was renewed the next year at Gertruydenburg; but the same obstacle still proved insurmountable.ᶻ

War of the succession.

and seemed so little displeased, that she gave her hand to Somerset (who had voted against the court) to lead her out. But during her illness in the winter of 1713, the whigs were on the alert, which, he says, was so represented to her, that "she laid aside all schemes of reconciling the two opposite interests, and entered on a firm resolution of adhering to the old English principles." This passage is to be considered with a view to what we learn from other quarters about the "old English principles;" which, whether Swift was aware of it or no, meant with many nothing less than the restoration of the house of Stuart.—1845.]

ᵘ Parl. Hist. vi. 4.
ˣ Nov. 27; Parl. Hist. 477.
ʸ Coxe's Marlborough, i. 453, ii. 110; Cunningham, ii. 52, 83.
ᶻ Mémoires de Torcy, vol. ii. passim; Coxe's Marlborough, vol. iii.; Boling-

It has been the prevailing opinion in modern times that the English ministry, rather against the judgment of their allies of Holland, insisted upon a condition not indispensable to their security, and too ignominious for their fallen enemy to accept. Some may perhaps incline to think that, even had Philip of Anjou been suffered to reign in Naples, a possession rather honourable than important, the balance of power would not have been seriously affected, and the probability of durable peace been increased. This, however, it was not necessary to discuss. The main question is as to the power which the allies possessed of securing the Spanish monarchy for the archduke, if they had consented to waive the thirty-seventh article of the preliminaries. If indeed they could have been considered as a single potentate, it was doubtless possible, by means of keeping up great armies on the frontier, and by the delivery of cautionary towns, to prevent the king of France from lending assistance to his grandson. But, self-interested and disunited as confederacies generally are, and as the grand alliance had long since become, this appeared a very dangerous course of policy, if Louis should be playing an underhand game against his engagements. And this it was not then unreasonable to suspect, even if we should believe, in despite of some plausible authorities, that he was really sincere in abandoning so favourite an interest. The obstinate adherence of Godolphin and Somers to the preliminaries may possibly have been erroneous; but it by no means deserves the reproach that has been unfairly bestowed on it; nor can the whigs be justly charged with protracting the war to enrich Marlborough, or to secure themselves in power.*

broke's Letters on History, and Lord Walpole's Answer to them; Cunningham; Somerville, 840.

* The late biographer of Marlborough asserts that he was against breaking off the conferences in 1709, though clearly for insisting on the cession of Spain. (iii. 40.) Godolphin, Somers, and the whigs in general, expected Louis XIV. to yield the thirty-seventh article. Cowper, however, was always doubtful of this. Id. 176.

It is very hard to pronounce, as it appears to me, on the great problem of Louis's sincerity in this negotiation. No decisive evidence seems to have been brought on the contrary side. The most remarkable authority that way is a passage in the Mémoires of St. Phelipe, iii. 263, who certainly asserts that the king of France had, without the knowledge of any of his ministers, assured his grandson of a continued support. But the question returns as to St. Phelipe's means of knowing so important a secret. On the other hand, I cannot discover in the long correspondence between Madame de Maintenon and the Princesse des Ursins

The conferences at Gertruydenburg were broken off in July, 1710, because an absolute security for the evacuation of Spain by Philip appeared to be wanting; and within six months a fresh negotiation was secretly on foot, the basis of which was his retention of that kingdom. For the administration presided over by Godolphin had fallen meanwhile; new councillors, a new parliament, new principles of government. The tories had from the beginning come very reluctantly into the schemes of the grand alliance; though no opposition to the war had ever been shown in parliament, it was very soon perceived that the majority of that denomination had their hearts bent on peace.[b] But instead of renewing the negotiation in concert with the allies (which indeed might have been impracticable), the new ministers fell upon the course of a clandestine arrangement, in exclusion of all the other powers, which led to the signature of preliminaries in September, 1711, and afterwards to the public congress of Utrecht, and the celebrated treaty named from that town. Its chief provisions are too well known to be repeated.

Treaty of peace broken off.

Renewed again by the tory government.

the least corroboration of these suspicions, but much to the contrary effect. Nor does Torcy drop a word, though writing when all was over, by which we should infer that the court of Versailles had any other hopes left in 1709 than what still lingered in their heart from the determined spirit of the Castilians themselves.

It appears by the Mémoires de Noailles, iii. 10. (edit. 1777), that Louis wrote to Philip, 26th Nov. 1708, hinting that he must reluctantly give him up, in answer to one wherein the latter had declared that he would not quit Spain while he had a drop of blood in his veins. And on the French ambassador at Madrid, Amelot, remonstrating against the abandonment of Spain, with an evident intimation that Philip could not support himself alone, the King of France answered that he must end the war at any price. 15th April, 1709. Id. 34. In the next year, after the battle of Saragossa, which seemed to turn the scale wholly against Philip, Noailles was sent to Madrid, in order to persuade that prince to abandon the contest. Id. 107.

There were some in France who would even have accepted the thirty-seventh article, of whom Madame de Maintenon seems to have been. P. 117. We may perhaps think that an explicit offer of Naples, on the part of the allies, would have changed the scene; nay, it seems as if Louis would have been content at this time with Sardinia and Sicily. P. 108.

[b] A contemporary historian of remarkable gravity observes, "It was strange to see how much the desire of French wine, and the dearness of it, alienated many men from the duke of Marlborough's friendship." Cunningham, ii. 220. The hard drinkers complained that they were poisoned by port; these formed almost a party; Dr. Aldrich, dean of Christchurch, surnamed the Priest of Bacchus, Dr. Ratcliff, general Churchill, &c. "And all the bottle companions, many physicians, and great numbers of the lawyers and inferior clergy, and, in fine, the loose women too, were united together in the faction against the duke of Marlborough."

214 ARGUMENTS FOR AND AGAINST   CHAP. XVI.

The arguments in favour of a treaty of pacification, which should abandon the great point of contest, and leave Philip in possession of Spain and America, were neither few nor inconsiderable. 1. The kingdom had been impoverished by twenty years of uninterruptedly augmented taxation; the annual burthens being triple in amount of those paid before the Revolution. Yet amidst these sacrifices we had the mortification of finding a debt rapidly increasing, whereof the mere interest far exceeded the ancient revenues of the crown, to be bequeathed, like an hereditary curse, to unborn ages.[c] Though the supplies had been raised with less difficulty than in the late reign, and the condition of trade was less unsatisfactory, the landed proprietors saw with indignation the silent transfer of their wealth to new men, and almost hated the glory that was brought by their own degradation.[d] Was it not to be feared that they might hate also the Revolution, and the protestant succession that depended on it, when they tasted these fruits it had borne? Even the army had been recruited by violent means unknown to our constitution, yet such as the continual loss of men, with a population at the best stationary, had perhaps rendered necessary.[e]

Arguments for and against the treaty of Utrecht.

2. The prospect of reducing Spain to the archduke's obedience was grown unfavourable. It was at best an odious work, and not very defensible on any maxims of national justice, to impose a sovereign on a great people in despite of their own repugnance, and what they

[c] [The national debt, 31st Dec. 1714, amounted, according to Chalmers, to 50,644,306*l*. Sinclair makes it 52,145,363*l*. But about half of this was temporary annuities. The whole expenses of the war are reckoned by the former writer at 65,853,799*l*. The interest of the debt was, as computed by Chalmers, 2,811,903*l*.; by Sinclair, 3,351,358*l*.—1845.]

[d] ["Power," says Swift, "which, according to the old maxim, was used to follow land, is now gone over to money; so that, if the war continue some years longer, a landed man will be little better than a farmer of a rack-rent to the army and to the public funds." Examiner, No. 13, Oct. 1710.—1845.]

[e] A bill was attempted in 1704 to recruit the army by a forced conscription of men from each parish, but laid aside as unconstitutional. Boyer's Reign of Queen Anne, p. 123. It was tried again in 1707 with like success. P. 319. But it was resolved instead to bring in a bill for raising a sufficient number of troops out of such persons as have no lawful calling or employment. Stat. 4 Anne, c. 10; Parl. Hist. 335. The parish officers were thus enabled to press men for the land service; a method hardly less unconstitutional than the former, and liable to enormous abuses. The act was temporary, but renewed several times during the war. It was afterwards revived in 1757 (30 Geo. II. c. 8), but never, I believe, on any later occasion.

deemed their loyal obligation. Heaven itself might shield their righteous cause, and baffle the selfish rapacity of human politics. But what was the state of the war at the close of 1710? The surrender of 7000 English under Stanhope at Brihuega had ruined the affairs of Charles, which in fact had at no time been truly prosperous, and confined him to the single province sincerely attached to him, Catalonia. As it was certain that Philip had spirit enough to continue the war, even if abandoned by his grandfather, and would have the support of almost the entire nation, what remained but to carry on a very doubtful contest for the subjugation of that extensive kingdom? In Flanders, no doubt, the genius of Marlborough kept still the ascendant; yet France had her Fabius in Villars; and the capture of three or four small fortresses in a whole campaign did not presage a rapid destruction of the enemy's power.

3. It was acknowledged that the near connexion of the monarchs on the thrones of France and Spain could not be desired for Europe. Yet the experience of ages had shown how little such ties of blood determined the policy of courts; a Bourbon on the throne of Spain could not but assert the honour, and even imbibe the prejudices, of his subjects; and as the two nations were in all things opposite, and must clash in their public interests, there was little reason to fear a subserviency in the cabinet of Madrid, which, even in that absolute monarchy, could not be displayed against the general sentiment.

4. The death of the emperor Joseph, and election of the archduke Charles in his room, which took place in the spring of 1711, changed in no small degree the circumstances of Europe. It was now a struggle to unite the Spanish and Austrian monarchies under one head. Even if England might have little interest to prevent this, could it be indifferent to the smaller states of Europe that a family not less ambitious and encroaching than that of Bourbon should be so enormously aggrandized? France had long been to us the only source of apprehension; but to some states, to Savoy, to Switzerland, to Venice, to the principalities of the Empire, she might justly appear a very necessary bulwark against the aggressions of Austria. The alliance could not be expected to continue faithful and unani-

mous after so important an alteration in the balance of power.

5. The advocates of peace and adherents of the new ministry stimulated the national passions of England by vehement reproaches of the allies. They had thrown, it was contended, in despite of all treaties, an unreasonable proportion of expense upon a country not directly concerned in their quarrel, and rendered a negligent or criminal administration their dupes or accomplices. We were exhausting our blood and treasure to gain kingdoms for the house of Austria which insulted, and the best towns of Flanders for the States-General who cheated us. The barrier treaty of lord Townshend was so extravagant, that one might wonder at the presumption of Holland in suggesting its articles, much more at the folly of our government in acceding to them. It laid the foundation of endless dissatisfaction on the side of Austria, thus reduced to act as the vassal of a little republic in her own territories, and to keep up fortresses at her own expense which others were to occupy. It might be anticipated that, at some time, a sovereign of that house would be found more sensible to ignominy than to danger, who would remove this badge of humiliation by dismantling the fortifications which were thus to be defended. Whatever exaggeration might be in these clamours, they were sure to pass for undeniable truths with a people jealous of foreigners, and prone to believe itself imposed upon, from a consciousness of general ignorance and credulity.

These arguments were met by answers not less confident, though less successful at the moment, than they have been deemed convincing by the majority of politicians in later ages.

1. It was denied that the resources of the kingdom were so much enfeebled; the supplies were still raised without difficulty; commerce had not declined; public credit stood high under the Godolphin ministry; and it was especially remarkable that the change of administration, notwithstanding the prospect of peace, was attended by a great fall in the price of stocks. France on the other hand, was notoriously reduced to the utmost distress; and, though it were absurd to allege the misfortunes of our enemy by way of consolation for our own,

yet the more exhausted of the two combatants was naturally that which ought to yield; and it was not for the honour of our free government that we should be outdone in magnanimous endurance of privations for the sake of the great interests of ourselves and our posterity by the despotism we so boastfully scorned.' The king of France had now for half a century been pursuing a system of encroachment on the neighbouring states, which the weakness of the two branches of the Austrian house, and the perfidiousness of the Stuarts, not less than the valour of his troops and skill of his generals, had long rendered successful. The tide had turned for the first time in the present war; victories more splendid than were recorded in modern warfare had illustrated the English name. Were we spontaneously to relinquish these great advantages, and, two years after Louis had himself consented to withdraw his forces from Spain, our own arms having been in the mean time still successful on the most important scene of the contest, to throw up the game in despair, and leave him far more the gainer at the termination of this calamitous war than he had been after those triumphant campaigns which his vaunting medals commemorate? Spain of herself could not resist the confederates, even if united in support of Philip; which was denied as to the provinces composing the kingdom of Aragon, and certainly as to Catalonia; it was in Flanders that Castile was to be conquered; it was France that we were to overcome; and now that her iron barrier had been broken through, when Marlborough was preparing to pour his troops upon the defenceless plains of Picardy, could we doubt that Louis must in good earnest abandon the cause of his grandson, as he had already pledged himself in the conferences of Gertruydenburg?

2. It was easy to slight the influence which the ties of blood exert over kings. Doubtless they are often torn asunder by ambition or wounded pride. But it does not follow that they have no efficacy; and the practice of

---

f Every contemporary writer bears testimony to the exhaustion of France, rendered still more deplorable by the unfavourable season of 1709, which produced a famine. Madame de Maintenon's letters to the Princesse des Ursins are full of the public misery, which she did not soften, out of some vain hope that her inflexible correspondent might relent at length, and prevail on the king and queen of Spain to abandon their throne.

courts in cementing alliances by intermarriage seems to show that they are not reckoned indifferent. It might however be admitted that a king of Spain, such as she had been a hundred years before, would probably be led by the tendency of his ambition into a course of policy hostile to France. But that monarchy had long been declining: great rather in name and extent of dominion than intrinsic resources, she might perhaps rally for a short period under an enterprising minister; but with such inveterate abuses of government, and so little progressive energy among the people, she must gradually sink lower in the scale of Europe, till it might become the chief pride of her sovereigns that they were the younger branches of the house of Bourbon. To cherish this connexion would be the policy of the court of Versailles; there would result from it a dependent relation, an habitual subserviency of the weaker power, a family compact of perpetual union, always opposed to Great Britain. In distant ages, and after fresh combinations of the European commonwealth should have seemed almost to efface the recollection of Louis XIV. and the war of the succession, the Bourbons on the French throne might still claim a sort of primogenitary right to protect the dignity of the junior branch by interference with the affairs of Spain; and a late posterity of those who witnessed the peace of Utrecht might be entangled by its improvident concessions.

3. That the accession of Charles to the empire rendered his possession of the Spanish monarchy in some degree less desirable, need not be disputed; though it would not be easy to prove that it could endanger England, or even the smaller states, since it was agreed on all hands that he was to be master of Milan and Naples. But against this, perhaps imaginary mischief, the opponents of the treaty set the risk of seeing the crowns of France and Spain united on the head of Philip. In the year 1711 and 1712 the dauphin, the duke of Burgundy, and the duke of Berry were swept away. An infant stood alone between the king of Spain and the French succession. The king was induced, with some unwillingness, to sign a renunciation of this contingent inheritance. But it was notoriously the doctrine of the French court that such renunciations were invalid; and the

sufferings of Europe were chiefly due to this tenet of indefeasible royalty. It was very possible that Spain would never consent to this union, and that a fresh league of the great powers might be formed to prevent it; but, if we had the means of permanently separating the two kingdoms in our hands, it was strange policy to leave open this door for a renewal of the quarrel.

But whatever judgment we may be disposed to form as to the political necessity of leaving Spain and America in the possession of Philip, it is impossible to justify the course of that negotiation which ended in the peace of Utrecht. *The negotiation mismanaged.* It was at best a dangerous and inauspicious concession, demanding every compensation that could be devised, and which the circumstances of the war entitled us to require. France was still our formidable enemy; the ambition of Louis was still to be dreaded, his intrigues to be suspected. That an English minister should have thrown himself into the arms of this enemy at the first overture of negotiation; that he should have renounced advantages upon which he might have insisted; that he should have restored Lille, and almost attempted to procure the sacrifice of Tournay; that throughout the whole correspondence and in all personal interviews with Torcy he should have shown the triumphant queen of Great Britain more eager for peace than her vanquished adversary; that the two courts should have been virtually conspiring against those allies, without whom we had bound ourselves to enter on no treaty; that we should have withdrawn our troops in the midst of a campaign, and even seized upon the towns of our confederates while we left them exposed to be overcome by a superior force; that we should have first deceived those confederates by the most direct falsehood in denying our clandestine treaty, and then dictated to them its acceptance, are facts so disgraceful to Bolingbroke, and in somewhat a less degree to Oxford, that they can hardly be palliated by establishing the expediency of the treaty itself.[s]

[s] [Bolingbroke owns, in his Letters on the Study of History, Letter viii., that the peace of Utrecht was not what it should have been, and that France should have given up more; but singularly lays the blame of her not having done so on those who opposed the peace. It appears, on the contrary, from his correspondence, that the strength of this opposition at home was the only argument he used with Torcy to save Tournay and other places, as far as he cared to save them at all.—1845.]

For several years after the treaty of Ryswick the intrigues of ambitious and discontented statesmen, and of a misled faction, in favour of the exiled family, grew much colder; the old age of James and the infancy of his son being alike incompatible with their success. The jacobites yielded a sort of provisional allegiance to the daughter of their king, deeming her, as it were, a regent in the heir's minority, and willing to defer the consideration of his claim till he should be competent to make it, or to acquiesce in her continuance upon the throne, if she could be induced to secure his reversion.[h] Meanwhile, under the name of tories and high-churchmen, they carried on a more dangerous war by sapping the bulwarks of the revolution-settlement. The disaffected clergy poured forth sermons and libels, to impugn the principles of the whigs or traduce their characters. Twice a year especially, on the 30th of January and 29th of May, they took care that every stroke upon rebellion and usurpation should tell against the expulsion of the Stuarts, and the Hanover succession. They inveighed against the dissenters and the toleration. They set up pretences of loyalty towards the queen, descanting sometimes on her hereditary right, in order to throw a slur on the settlement. They drew a transparent veil over their designs, which might screen them from prosecution, but could not impose, nor was meant to impose, on the reader. Among these the most distinguished was Leslie, author of a periodical sheet called the Rehearsal, printed weekly from 1704 to 1708; and as he, though a nonjuror and unquestionable jacobite, held only the same language as Sacheverell, and others who affected obedience to the government, we cannot much be deceived in assuming that their views were entirely the same.[i]

The court of St. Germains, in the first years of the

[h] It is evident from Macpherson's Papers, that all hopes of a present restoration in the reign of Anne were given up in England. They soon revived, however, as to Scotland, and grew stronger about the time of the union.

[i] The Rehearsal is not written in such a manner as to gain over many proselytes. The scheme of fighting against liberty with her own arms had not yet come into vogue; or rather Leslie was too mere a bigot to practise it. He is wholly for arbitrary power; but the common stuff of his journal is high-church notions of all descriptions. This could not win many in the reign of Anne.

queen, preserved a secret connexion with Godolphin and Marlborough, though justly distrustful of their sincerity; nor is it by any means clear that they made any strong professions.[k] Their evident determination to reduce the power of France, their approximation towards the whigs, the averseness of the duchess to jacobite principles, taught at length that unfortunate court how little it had to expect from such ancient friends. The Scotch jacobites, on the other hand, were eager for the young king's immediate restoration; and their assurances finally produced his unsuccessful expedition to the coast in 1708.[l] This alarmed the queen, who at least had no thoughts of giving up any part of her dominions, and probably exasperated the two ministers.[m] Though Godolphin's partiality to the Stuart cause was always suspected, the proofs of his intercourse with their emissaries are not so strong as against Marlborough; who, so late as 1711, declared himself more positively than he seems hitherto to have done in favour of their restoration.[n] But the extreme selfishness and treachery of his character make it difficult to believe that he had any further view than

Some of the ministers engage in them.

---

[k] Macpherson, i. 608. If Carte's anecdotes are true, which is very doubtful, Godolphin, after he was turned out, declared his concern at not having restored the king; that he thought Harley would do it, but by French assistance, which he did not intend; that the tories had always distressed him, and his administration had passed in a struggle with the whig junto. Id. 170. Somerville says he was assured that Carte was reckoned credulous and ill-informed by the jacobites. P. 273. It seems, indeed, by some passages in Macpherson's Papers, that the Stuart agents either kept up an intercourse with Godolphin, or pretended to do so. Vol. ii. 2, et post. But it is evident that they had no confidence in him.

It must be observed, however, that lord Dartmouth, in his notes on Burnet, repeatedly intimates that Godolphin's secret object in his ministry was the restoration of the house of Stuart, and that with this view he suffered the act of security in Scotland to pass, which raised such a clamour that he was forced to close with the whigs in order to save himself. It is said also by a very good authority, lord Hardwicke (note on Burnet, Oxf. edit. v. 352), that there was something not easy to be accounted for in the conduct of the ministry, preceding the attempt on Scotland in 1708; giving us to understand in the subsequent part of the note that Godolphin was suspected of connivance with it. And this is confirmed by Ker of Kersland, who directly charges the treasurer with extreme remissness, if not something worse. Memoirs, i. 54. See also Lockhart's Commentaries (in Lockhart Papers, i. 308). Yet it seems almost impossible to suspect Godolphin of such treachery, not only towards the protestant succession, but his mistress herself.

[l] Macpherson, ii. 74, et post; Hooke's Negotiations; Lockhart's Commentaries; Ker of Kersland's Memoirs, i. 46; Burnet; Cunningham; Somerville.

[m] Burnet, 502.

[n] Macpherson, ii. 158, 228, 283; and see Somerville, 272.

to secure himself in the event of a revolution which he judged probable. His interest, which was always his deity, did not lie in that direction; and his great sagacity must have perceived it.

Just alarm for the Hanover succession. A more promising overture had by this time been made to the young claimant from an opposite quarter. Mr. Harley, about the end of 1710, sent the abbé Gaultier to marshal Berwick (natural son of James II. by Marlborough's sister), with authority to treat about the restoration; Anne of course retaining the crown for her life, and securities being given for the national religion and liberties. The conclusion of peace was a necessary condition. The jacobites in the English parliament were directed in consequence to fall in with the court, which rendered it decidedly superior. Harley promised to send over in the next year a plan for carrying that design into effect. But neither at that time, nor during the remainder of the queen's life, did this dissembling minister take any further measures, though still in strict connexion with that party at home, and with the court of St. Germains.º It was necessary, he said, to proceed gently, to make the army their own, to avoid suspicions which would be fatal. It was manifest that the course of his administration was wholly inconsistent with his professions; the friends of the house of Stuart felt that he betrayed, though he did not delude them; but it was the misfortune of this minister, or rather the just and natural reward of crooked counsels, that those he meant to serve could neither believe in his friendship, nor forgive his appearances of enmity. It is doubtless not easy to pronounce on the real intentions of men so destitute of sincerity as Harley and Marlborough; but in believing the former favourable to the protestant succession, which he had so eminently contributed to establish, we accede to the judgment of those contemporaries who were best able to form one, and especially of the very jacobites with whom he tampered. And this is so powerfully confirmed by most of his public measures, his averseness to the high tories, and their consequent hatred of him, his irreconcilable disagreement with those of his col-

---

º Memoirs of Berwick, 1778 (English Commentaries, p. 368; Macpherson, sub translation). And compare Lockhart's ann. 1712 and 1713, passim.

leagues who looked most to St. Germains, his frequent attempts to renew a connexion with the whigs, his contempt of the jacobite creed of government, and the little prospect he could have had of retaining power on such a revolution, that, so far at least as may be presumed from what has hitherto become public, there seems no reason for counting the earl of Oxford among those from whom the house of Hanover had any enmity to apprehend.[p]

The pretender, meanwhile, had friends in the tory government more sincere probably and zealous than Oxford. In the year 1712 lord Bolingbroke, the duke of Buckingham, president of the council, and the duke of Ormond, were engaged in this connexion.[q] The last

[p] The pamphlets on Harley's side, and probably written under his inspection, for at least the first year after his elevation to power, such as one entitled 'Faults on both Sides,' ascribed to Richard Harley, his relation ('Somers' Tracts, xii. 678), 'Spectator's Address to the Whigs on occasion of the Stabbing Mr. Harley,' or the 'Secret History of the October Club,' 1711 (I believe by De Foe), seem to have for their object to reconcile as many of the whigs as possible to his administration, and to display his aversion to the violent tories. There can be no doubt that his first project was to have excluded the more acrimonious whigs, such as Wharton and Sunderland, as well as the duke of Marlborough and his wife, and coalesced with Cowper and Somers, both of whom were also in favour with the queen. But the steadiness of the whig party, and their resentment of his duplicity, forced him into the opposite quarters, though he never lost sight of his schemes for reconciliation.

The dissembling nature of this unfortunate statesman rendered his designs suspected. The whigs, at least in 1713, in their correspondence with the court of Hanover, speak of him as entirely in the jacobite interest. Macpherson, ii. 472, 509. Cunningham, who is not on the whole unfavourable to Harley, says that "men of all parties agreed in concluding that his designs were in the pretender's favour. And it is certain that he affected to have it thought so." P. 363. Lockhart also bears witness to the reliance placed on him by the jacobites, and argues with some plausibility (p. 377) that the duke of Hamilton's appointment as ambassador to France, in 1712, must have been designed to further their object; though he believed that the death of that nobleman, in a duel with lord Mohun, just as he was setting out for Paris, put a stop to the scheme, and "questions if it was ever heartily reassumed by lord Oxford."—"This I know, that his lordship, regretting to a friend of mine the duke's death, next day after it happened, told him that it disordered all their schemes, seeing Great Britain did not afford a person capable to discharge the trust which was committed to his grace, which sure was somewhat very extraordinary; and what other than the king's restoration could there be of so very great importance, or require such dexterity in managing, is not easy to imagine. And indeed it is more than probable that, before his lordship could pitch upon one he might depend on in such weighty matters, the discord and division which happened betwixt him and the other ministers of state diverted or suspended his design of serving the king." Lockhart's Commentaries, p. 410. But there is more reason to doubt whether this design to serve the king ever existed.

[q] If we may trust to a book printed in 1717, with the title, 'Minutes of

of these being in the command of the army, little glory as that brought him, might become an important auxiliary. Harcourt, the chancellor, though the proofs are not, I believe, so direct, has always been reckoned in

Monsieur Mesnager's Negotiations with the Court of England towards the Close of the last Reign, written by himself,' that agent of the French cabinet entered into an arrangement with Bolingbroke in March, 1712, about the pretender. It was agreed that Louis should ostensibly abandon him, but should not be obliged, in case of the queen's death, not to use endeavours for his restoration. Lady Masham was wholly for this; but owned "the rage and irreconcilable aversion of the greatest part of the common people to her (the queen's) brother was grown to a height." But I must confess that, although Macpherson has extracted the above passage, and a more judicious writer, Somerville, quotes the book freely as genuine (Hist. of Anne, p. 581, &c.), I found in reading it what seemed to me the strongest grounds of suspicion. It is printed in England, without a word of preface to explain how such important secrets came to be divulged, or by what means the book was brought before the world; the correct information as to English customs and persons frequently botrays a native pen; the truth it contains, as to Jacobite intrigues, might have transpired from other sources, and in the main was pretty well suspected, as the Report of the Secret Committee on the Impeachments in 1715 shows; so that, upon the whole, I cannot but reckon it a forgery in order to injure the tory leaders. [In a note on Swift's Works, vol. xxv. p. 37 (1779), it is said, on the authority of Savage, that "no such book was ever printed in the French tongue, from which it is impudently said to be translated, as Mesnager's Negotiations." And, on reference to Savage's poem entitled False Historians, I find this couplet:—

"Some usurp names— an English garreteer,
From minutes forg'd, is Monsieur Mesnager."

I think that the book has been ascribed to De Foe.—1845.]
But however this may be, we find

Bolingbroke in correspondence with the Stuart agents in the latter part of 1712. Macpherson, 365. And his own correspondence with lord Strafford shows his dread and dislike of Hanover. (Bol. Corr. ii. 487, et alibi.) The duke of Buckingham wrote to St. Germains in July that year, with strong expressions of his attachment to the cause, and pressing the necessity of the prince's conversion to the protestant religion. Macpherson, 327. Ormond is mentioned in the duke of Berwick's letters as in correspondence with him; and Lockhart says there was no reason to make the least question of his affection to the king, whose friends were consequently well pleased at his appointment to succeed Marlborough in the command of the army, and thought it portended some good designs in favour of him. Id. 376.

Of Ormond's sincerity in this cause there can indeed be little doubt; but there is almost as much reason to suspect that of Bolingbroke as of Oxford: except that, having more rashness and less principle, he was better fitted for so dangerous a counter-revolution. But in reality he had a perfect contempt for the Stuart and tory notions of government, and would doubtless have served the house of Hanover with more pleasure if his prospects in that quarter had been more favourable. It appears that in the session of 1714, when he had become lord of the ascendant, he disappointed the zealous royalists by his delays as much as his more cautious rival had done before. Lockhart, 470. This writer repeatedly asserts that a majority of the house of commons, both in the parliament of 1710 and that of 1713, wanted only the least encouragement from the court to have brought about the repeal of the act of settlement. But I think this very doubtful; and I am quite convinced that the nation would not have acquiesced in it. Lockhart is sanguine, and ignorant of England.

It must be admitted that part of the cabinet were steady to the protestant

the same interest. Several of the leading Scots peers, with little disguise, avowed their adherence to it; especially the duke of Hamilton, who, luckily perhaps for the kingdom, lost his life in a duel at the moment when he was setting out on an embassy to France. The rage expressed by that faction at his death betrays the hopes they had entertained from him. A strong phalanx of tory members, called the October Club, though by no means entirely jacobite, were chiefly influenced by those who were such. In the new parliament of 1713 the queen's precarious health excited the Stuart partisans to press forward with more zeal. The mask was more than half drawn aside; and, vainly urging the ministry to fulfil their promises while yet in time, they cursed the insidious cunning of Harley and the selfish cowardice of the queen. Upon her they had for some years relied. Lady Masham, the bosom favourite, was entirely theirs; and every word, every look of the sovereign, had been anxiously observed, in the hope of some indication that she would take the road which affection and conscience, as they fondly argued, must dictate. But, whatever may have been the sentiments of Anne, her secret was never divulged, nor is there, as I apprehend, however positively the contrary is sometimes asserted, any decisive evidence whence we may infer that she even intended her brother's restoration.' The weakest of mankind have generally an

---

succession. Lord Dartmouth, lord Powlett, lord Trevor, and the bishop of London were certainly so; nor can there be any reasonable doubt, as I conceive, of the duke of Shrewsbury. On the other side, besides Ormond, Harcourt and Bolingbroke, were the duke of Buckingham, sir William Wyndham, and probably Mr. Bromley. [The impression which Bolingbroke's letter to sir William Wyndham leaves on the mind is, that, having no steady principle of action, he had been all along fluctuating between Hanover and St. Germains, according to the prospect he saw of standing well with one or the other, and in a great degree according to the politics of Oxford, being determined to take the opposite line. But he had never been able to penetrate a more dissembling spirit than his own. This letter, as is well known, though written in 1717, was not published till after Bolingbroke's death.—1845.]

' It is said that the duke of Leeds, who was now in the Stuart interest, had sounded her in 1711, but with no success in discovering her intention. Macpherson, 212. The duke of Buckingham pretended, in the above-mentioned letter to St. Germains, June, 1712, that he had often pressed the queen on the subject of her brother's restoration, but could get no other answer than, "You see he does not make the least step to oblige me;" or, "He may thank himself for it: he knows I always loved him better than the other." Id. 328. This alludes to the pretender's pertinacity, as the writer thought it, in adhering to his religion; and it may be very questionable whether he had ever such conversation with the queen at all. But, if he had, it does not lead

instinct of self-preservation which leads them right, and perhaps more than stronger minds possess; and Anne could scarcely help perceiving that her own deposition from the throne would be the natural consequence of once admitting the reversionary right of one whose claim was equally good to the possession. The asserters of hereditary descent could acquiesce in her usurpation no longer than they found it necessary for their object; if her life should be protracted to an ordinary duration, it was almost certain that Scotland first, and afterwards England, would be wrested from her impotent grasp. Yet, though I believe the queen to have been sensible of this, it is impossible to pronounce with certainty that, either through pique against the house of Hanover, or inability to resist her own counsellors, she might not have come into the scheme of altering the succession.

But, if neither the queen nor her lord treasurer were inclined to take that vigorous course which one party demanded, they at least did enough to raise just alarm in the other; and it seems strange to deny that the

---

to the supposition that under all circumstances she meditated his restoration. If the book under the name of Meanager is genuine, which I much doubt, Mrs. Masham had never been able to elicit anything decisive of her majesty's inclinations; nor do any of the Stuart correspondents in Macpherson pretend to know her intentions with certainty. The following passage in Lockhart seems rather more to the purpose:—On his coming to parliament in 1710, with a "high monarchical address," which he had procured from the county of Edinburgh, " the queen told me, though I had almost always opposed her measures, she did not doubt of my affection to her person, and hoped I would not concur in the design against Mrs. Masham, or for bringing over the prince of Hanover. At first I was somewhat surprised, but, recovering myself, I assured her I should never be accessary to the imposing any hardship or affront upon her; and as for the prince of Hanover, her majesty might judge from the address I had read that I should not be acceptable to my constituents if I gave my consent for bringing over any of that family either now or at any time hereafter. At that she smiled and withdrew; and then she said to the duke (Hamilton) she believed I was an honest man and a fair dealer; and the duke replied, he could assure her I liked her majesty and all her father's bairns." P. 317. It appears in subsequent parts of this book that Lockhart and his friends were confident of the queen's inclinations in the last year of her life, though not of her resolution.

The truth seems to be that Anne was very dissembling, as Swift repeatedly says in his private letters, and as feeble and timid persons in high station generally are; that she hated the house of Hanover, and in some measure feared them; but that she had no regard for the pretender (for it is really absurd to talk like Somerville of natural affection under all the circumstances), and feared him a great deal more than the other; that she had, however, some scruples about his right, which were counterbalanced by her attachment to the church of England; consequently, that she was wavering among opposite impulses, but with a predominating timidity which would have probably kept her from any change.

protestant succession was in danger. As lord Oxford's ascendancy diminished, the signs of impending revolution became less equivocal. Adherents of the house of Stuart were placed in civil and military trust; an Irish agent of the pretender was received in the character of envoy from the court of Spain; the most audacious manifestations of disaffection were overlooked.* Several even in parliament spoke with contempt and aversion of the house of Hanover.† It was surely not unreasonable in

* The duchess of Gordon, in June, 1711, sent a silver medal to the faculty of advocates at Edinburgh, with a head on one side, and the inscription, Cujus est; on the other, the British Isles, with the word Reddite. The dean of faculty, Dundas of Arniston, presented this medal; and there seems reason to believe that a majority of the advocates voted for its reception. Somerville, p. 452. Bolingbroke, in writing on the subject to a friend, it must be owned, speaks of the proceeding with due disapprobation. Bolingbroke Correspondence, i. 343. No measures, however, were taken to mark the court's displeasure.

"Nothing is more certain," says Bolingbroke, in his letter to sir William Wyndham, perhaps the finest of his writings, "than this truth, that there was at that time *no formed design* in the party, whatever views some particular men might have, against his majesty's accession to the throne." P. 22. This is in effect to confess a great deal; and in other parts of the same letter he makes admissions of the same kind; though he says that he and other tories had determined, before the queen's death, to have no connexion with the pretender, on account of his religious bigotry. P. 111.

† Lockhart gives us a speech of sir William Whitelock in 1714, bitterly inveighing against the elector of Hanover, who, he hoped, would never come to the crown. Some of the whigs cried out on this that he should be brought to the bar; when Whitelock said he would not recede an inch; he hoped the queen would outlive that prince, and in comparison to her he did not value all the princes of Germany one farthing. P. 469. Swift, in 'Some Free Thoughts upon the Present State of Affairs,' 1714, speaks with much contempt of the house of Hanover and its sovereign; and suggests, in derision, that the infant son of the electoral prince might be invited to take up his residence in England. He pretends in this tract, as in all his writings, to deny entirely that there was the least tendency towards jacobitism, either in any one of the ministry, or even any eminent individual out of it; but with so impudent a disregard to truth, that I am not perfectly convinced of his own innocence as to that intrigue. Thus, in his Inquiry into the Behaviour of the Queen's last Ministry, he says, "I remember, during the late treaty of peace, discoursing at several times with some very eminent persons of the opposite side with whom I had long acquaintance. I asked them seriously whether they or any of their friends did in earnest believe, or suspect, the queen or the ministry to have any favourable regards towards the pretender? They all confessed for themselves that they believed nothing of the matter," &c. He then tells us that he had the curiosity to ask almost every person in great employment whether they knew or had heard of any one particular man, except professed nonjurors, that discovered the least inclination towards the pretender; and the whole number they could muster up did not amount to above five or six; among whom one was a certain old lord, lately dead, and one a private gentleman, of little consequence and of a broken fortune, &c. (Vol. xv. p. 94, edit. 12mo. 1765.) This acute observer of mankind well knew that lying is frequently successful in the ratio of its effrontery and extravagance. There are, however, some passages in this tract, as in others written

the whig party to meet these assaults of the enemy with something beyond the ordinary weapons of an opposition. They affected no apprehensions that it was absurd to entertain. Those of the opposite faction who wished well to the protestant interest, and were called Hanoverian tories, came over to their side, and joined them on motions that the succession was in danger.ᵘ No one hardly, who either hoped or dreaded the consequences, had any doubts upon this score; and it is only a few moderns who have assumed the privilege of setting aside the persuasion of contemporaries upon a subject which contemporaries were best able to understand.ˣ Are we then to censure the whigs for urging on the elector of Hanover, who, by a strange apathy or indifference, seemed negligent of the great prize reserved for him; or is the bold step of demanding a writ of summons for the electoral prince as duke of Cambridge to pass for a factious insult on the queen, because, in her imbecility, she was leaving the crown to be snatched at by the first comer, even if she were not, as they suspected, in some conspiracy to bestow it on a proscribed heir?ʸ I am much inclined to believe that the great

---

by Swift, in relation to that time, which serve to illustrate the obscure machinations of those famous last years of the queen.

ᵘ On a motion in the house of lords that the protestant succession was in danger, April 5, 1714, the ministry had only a majority of 76 to 69, several bishops and other tories voting against them. Parl. Hist. vi. 1334. Even in the commons the division was but 256 to 208. d. 1347.

ˣ Somerville has a separate dissertation on the danger of the protestant succession, intended to prove that it was in no danger at all, except through the violence of the whigs in exasperating the queen. It is true that Lockhart's Commentaries were not published at this time; but he had Macpherson before him, and the Memoirs of Berwick, and even gave credit to the authenticity of Mesnager, which I do not. But this sensible, and on the whole impartial writer, had contracted an excessive prejudice against the whigs of that period as a party, though he seems to adopt their principles. His dissertation is a laboured attempt to explain away the most evident facts, and to deny what no one of either party at that time would probably have in private denied.

ʸ The queen was very ill about the close of 1713; in fact it became evident, as it had long been apprehended, that she could not live much longer. The Hanoverians, both whigs and tories, urged that the electoral prince should be sent for; it was thought that whichever of the competitors should have the start upon her death would succeed in securing the crown. Macpherson, 385, 546, 557, et alibi. Can there be a more complete justification of this measure, which Somerville and the tory writers treat as disrespectful to the queen? The Hanoverian envoy, Schutz, demanded the writ for the electoral prince without his master's orders; but it was done with the advice of all the whig leaders (id. 592), and with the sanction of the electress Sophia, who died immediately after. "All who are for Hanover believe the coming of the electoral prince to be advantageous; all those

majority of the nation were in favour of the protestant succession; but, if the princes of the house of Brunswic had seemed to retire from the contest, it might have been impracticable to resist a predominant faction in the council and in parliament, especially if the son of James, listening to the remonstrances of his English adherents, could have been induced to renounce a faith which, in the eyes of too many, was the sole pretext for his exclusion,[1] and was at least almost the only one which could have been publicly maintained with much success consistently with the general principles of our constitution.[a]

The queen's death, which came at last perhaps rather more quickly than was anticipated, broke for ever the fair prospects of her family. George I., unknown and absent, was proclaimed without a single

Accession of George I.

---

against it are frightened at it." Id. 590. It was doubtless a critical moment; and the court of Hanover might be excused for pausing in the choice of dangers, as the step must make the queen decidedly their enemy. She was greatly offended, and forbad the Hanoverian minister to appear at court. Indeed, she wrote to the elector, on May 19, expressing her disapprobation of the prince's coming over to England, and " her determination to oppose a project so contrary to her royal authority, however fatal the consequences may be." Id 621. Oxford and Bolingbroke intimate the same. Id. 593; and see Bolingbroke Correspondence, iv. 512, a very strong passage. The measure was given up, whether from unwillingness on the part of George to make the queen irreconcilable, or, as is at least equally probable, out of jealousy of his son. The former certainly disappointed his adherents by more apparent apathy than their ardour required; which will not be surprising when we reflect that, even upon the throne, he seemed to care very little about it. Macpherson, sub ann. 1714, passim.

[1] He was strongly pressed by his English adherents to declare himself a protestant. He wrote a very good answer. Macpherson, 436. Madame de Maintenon says some catholics urged him to the same course, " par une politique poussée un peu trop loin." Lettres à la Princesse des Ursins, ii. 428. [See also Bolingbroke's Letter to sir W. Wyndham: "I cannot forget, nor you either, what passed when, a little before the death of the queen, letters were conveyed from the chevalier to several persons, to myself among others. In the letter to me the article of religion was so awkwardly handled, that he made the principal motive of the confidence we ought to have in him to consist in his firm resolution to adhere to popery. The effect which this epistle had on me was the same which it had on those tories to whom I communicated it at that time—it made us resolve to have nothing to do with him." It seems to have been a sine quâ non with the tory leaders that the pretender should become a protestant. But others thought this an unreasonable demand. He would not even directly engage to secure the churches of England and Ireland, if we may believe Bolingbroke. Id.—1845.]

[a] [The whigs relied upon the army, in case of a struggle. Somerville, 565. Swift, in his Free Thoughts on the present State of Affairs, written in the spring of 1714, speaks with indignation of the disaffection of the guards towards the queen; taking care, at the same time, to deny the least inclination on the part of the ministry towards a change of succession.—1845.]

murmur, as if the crown had passed in the most regular descent. But this was a momentary calm. The jacobite party, recovering from the first consternation, availed itself of its usual arms, and of those with which the new king supplied it. Many of the tories who would have acquiesced in the act of settlement seem to have looked on a leading share in the administration as belonging of right to what was called the church party, and complained of the formation of a ministry on the whig principle. In later times also it has been not uncommon to censure George I. for governing, as it is called, by a faction. Nothing can be more unreasonable than this reproach. Was he to select those as his advisers who had been, as we know and as he believed, in a conspiracy with his competitor? Was lord Oxford, even if the king thought him faithful, capable of uniting with any public men, hated as he was on each side? Were not the tories as truly a faction as their adversaries, and as intolerant during their own power?[b] Was there not, above all, a danger that, if some of one denomination were drawn by pique and disappointment into the ranks of the jacobites, the whigs, on the other hand, so ungratefully and perfidiously recompensed for their arduous services to the house of Hanover, might think all royalty irreconcilable with the principles of freedom, and raise up a republican party, of which the scattered elements were sufficiently discernible in the nation?[c] The exclusion indeed of the whigs would have been so monstrous, both in honour and policy, that the censure has generally fallen on their alleged monopoly of public

[b] The rage of the tory party against the queen and lord Oxford for retaining whigs in office is notorious from Swift's private letters and many other authorities. And Bolingbroke, in his letter to sir William Wyndham, very fairly owns their intention "to fill the employments of the kingdom, down to the meanest, with tories."—"We imagined," he proceeds, "that such measures, joined to the advantages of our numbers and our property, would secure us against all attempts during her reign; and that we should soon become too considerable not to make our terms in all events which might happen afterwards; concerning which, to speak truly, I believe few or none of us had any very settled resolution." P. 11. It is rather amusing to observe that those who called themselves the tory or church party seem to have fancied they had a natural right to power and profit, so that an injury was done them when these rewards went another way; and I am not sure that something of the same prejudice has not been perceptible in times a good deal later.

[c] Though no republican party, as I have elsewhere observed, could with any propriety be said to exist, it is easy to perceive that a certain degree of provocation from the crown might have brought one together in no slight force. These two propositions are perfectly compatible.

offices. But the mischiefs of a disunited, hybrid ministry had been sufficiently manifest in the two last reigns; nor could George, a stranger to his people and their constitution, have undertaken without ruin that most difficult task of balancing parties and persons, to which the great mind of William had proved unequal. Nor is it true that the tories as such were proscribed; those who chose to serve the court met with court favour: and in the very outset the few men of sufficient eminence who had testified their attachment to the succession received equitable rewards; but, most happily for himself and the kingdom, most reasonably according to the principles on which alone his throne could rest, the first prince of the house of Brunswic gave a decisive preponderance in his favour to Walpole and Townshend above Harcourt and Bolingbroke.

The strong symptoms of disaffection which broke out in a few months after the king's accession, and which can be ascribed to no grievance, unless the formation of a whig ministry was to be termed one, prove the taint of the late times to have been deep-seated and extensive.[d] The clergy, in many

Great disaffection in the kingdom.

---

[d] This is well put by bishop Willis, in his speech on the bill against Atterbury. Parl. Hist. viii. 305. In a pamphlet entitled English Advice to the Freeholders (Somers Tracts, xiii. 521), ascribed to Atterbury himself, a most virulent attack is made on the government, merely because what he calls the church party had been thrown out of office. "Among all who call themselves whigs," he says, "and are of any consideration as such, name me the man I cannot prove to be an inveterate enemy to the church of England, and I will be a convert that instant to their cause." It must be owned perhaps that the whig ministry might better have avoided some reflections on the late times in the addresses of both houses; and still more, some not very constitutional recommendations to the electors, in the proclamation calling the new parliament in 1714. Parl. Hist. vi. 44, 50. "Never was prince more universally well received by subjects than his present majesty on his arrival; and never was less done by a prince to create a change in people's affections. But so it is, a very observable change hath happened. Evil infusions were spread on the one hand; and, it may be, there was too great a stoicism or contempt of popularity on the other." Argument to prove the Affections of the People of England to be the best Security for the Government, p. 11 (1716). This is the pamphlet written to recommend lenity towards the rebels, which Addison has answered in the Freeholder. It is invidious, and perhaps secretly Jacobite. Bolingbroke observes, in the letter already quoted, that the pretender's journey from Bar, in 1714, was a mere farce, no party being ready to receive him; but "the menaces of the whigs, backed by some very rash declarations [those of the king], and little circumstances of humour, which frequently offend more than real injuries, and by the entire change of all persons in employment, blew up the coals." P. 34. Then, he owns, the tories looked to Bar. "The violence of the whigs forced them into the arms of the pretender." It is to be remarked on all this, that, by Bolingbroke's own account, the tories, if they

instances, perverted, by political sermons, their influence over the people, who, while they trusted that from those fountains they could draw the living waters of truth, became the dupes of factious lies and sophistry. Thus encouraged, the heir of the Stuarts landed in Scotland; and the spirit of that people being in a great measure jacobite, and very generally averse to the union, he met with such success as, had their independence subsisted, would probably have established him on the throne. But Scotland was now doomed to wait on the fortunes of her more powerful ally; and, on his invasion of England, the noisy partisans of hereditary right discredited their faction by its cowardice. Few rose in arms to support the rebellion, compared with those who desired its success, and did not blush to see the gallant savages of the Highlands shed their blood that a supine herd of priests and country gentlemen might enjoy the victory. The severity of the new government after the rebellion has been often blamed; but I know not whether, according to the usual rules of policy, it can be proved that the execution of two peers and thirty other persons, taken with arms in flagrant rebellion, was an unwarrantable excess of punishment. There seems a latent insinuation in those who have argued on the other side, as if the jacobite rebellion, being founded on an opinion of right, was more excusable than an ordinary treason—a proposition which it would not have been quite safe for the reigning dynasty to acknowledge. Clemency, however, is the standing policy of constitutional governments, as severity is of despotism; and if the ministers of George I. might have extended it to part of the inferior sufferers (for surely those of higher rank were the first to be selected) with safety to their master, they would have done well in sparing him the odium that attends all political punishments.[e]

had no "formed design" or "settled resolution" that way, were not very determined in their repugnance before the queen's death; and that the chief violence of which they complained was, that George chose to employ his friends rather than his enemies.

[e] The trials after this rebellion were not conducted with quite that appearance of impartiality which we now exact from judges. Chief baron Montagu reprimanded a jury for acquitting some persons indicted for treason; and Tindal, an historian very strongly on the court side, admits that the dying speeches of some of the sufferers made an impression on the people, so as to increase rather than lessen the number of jacobites. Continuation of Rapin, p. 501 (folio edit.). There seems, however, upon the whole,

It will be admitted on all hands at the present day that the charge of high treason in the impeachments against Oxford and Bolingbroke was an intemperate excess of resentment at their scandalous dereliction of the public honour and interest. The danger of a sanguinary revenge inflamed by party spirit is so tremendous that the worst of men ought perhaps to escape rather than suffer by a retrospective, or, what is no better, a constructive extension of the law. The particular charge of treason was that in the negotiation for peace they had endeavoured to procure the city of Tournay for the king of France; which was maintained to be an adhering to the queen's enemies within the statute of Edward III.[f] But as this construction could hardly be brought within the spirit of that law, and the motive was certainly not treasonable or rebellious, it would have been incomparably more constitutional to treat so gross a breach of duty as a misdemeanor of the highest kind. This angry temper of the commons led ultimately to the abandonment of the whole impeachment against lord Oxford; the upper house, though it had committed Oxford to the Tower, which seemed to prejudge the question as to the treasonable character of the imputed offence, having two years afterwards resolved that the charge of treason should be first determined, before they would enter on the articles of less importance; a decision with which the commons were so ill satisfied that they declined to go forward with the prosecution. The resolution of the peers was hardly conformable to precedent, to analogy, or to the dignity of the house of commons, nor will it perhaps be deemed binding on any future

Impeachment of tory ministers.

---

to have been greater and less necessary severity after the rebellion in 1745; and upon this latter occasion it is impossible not to reprobate the execution of Mr. Ratcliffe (brother of that earl of Derwentwater who had lost his head in 1716), after an absence of thirty years from his country, to the sovereign of which he had never professed allegiance, nor could owe any, except by the fiction of our law.

[f] Parl. Hist. 73. It was carried against Oxford, by 247 to 127, sir Joseph Jekyll strongly opposing it, though he had said before (id. 67) that they had more than sufficient evidence against Bolingbroke on the statute of Edward III. A motion was made in the lords to consult the judges whether the articles amounted to treason, but lost by 84 to 52. Id. 154. Lord Cowper on this occasion challenged all the lawyers in England to disprove that proposition. The proposal of reference to the judges was perhaps premature; but the house must surely have done this before their final sentence, or shown themselves more passionate than in the case of lord Strafford.

occasion; but the ministers prudently suffered themselves to be beaten, rather than aggravate the fever of the people by a prosecution so full of delicate and hazardous questions.⁵

One of these questions, and by no means the least important, would doubtless have arisen upon a mode of defence alleged by the earl of Oxford in the House, when the articles of impeachment were brought up. "My lords," he said, "if ministers of state, acting by the immediate commands of their sovereign, are afterwards to be made accountable for their proceedings, it may, one day or other, be the case of all the members of this august assembly."ʰ It was indeed undeniable that the queen had been very desirous of peace, and a party, as it were, to all the counsels that tended to it. Though it was made a charge against the impeached lords that the instructions to sign the secret preliminaries of 1711 with M. Mesnager, the French envoy, were not under the great seal, nor countersigned by any minister, they were certainly under the queen's signet, and had all the authority of her personal command. This must have brought on the yet unsettled and very delicate question of ministerial responsibility in matters where the sovereign has interposed his own command; a question better reserved, it might then appear, for the loose generalities of debate than to be determined with the precision of criminal law. Each party, in fact, had in its turn made use of the queen's personal authority as a shield; the whigs availed themselves of it to parry the attack made on their ministry, after its fall, for an alleged mismanagement of the war in Spain before the battle of Almanza;ⁱ and the

---

⁵ Parl. Hist. vii. 486. The division was 88 to 56. There was a schism in the whig party at this time; yet I should suppose the ministers might have prevented this defeat if they had been anxious to do so. It seems, however, by a letter in Coxe's Memoirs of Walpole, vol. ii. p. 123, that the government were for dropping the charge of treason against Oxford, "it being very certain that there is not sufficient evidence to convict him of that crime," but for pressing those of misdemeanour.

ʰ Parl. Hist. vii. 105.

ⁱ Parl. Hist. vi. 972. Burnet, 560, makes some observations on the vote passed on this occasion, censuring the late ministers for advising an offensive war in Spain. "A resolution in council is only the sovereign's act, who, upon hearing his councillors deliver their opinions, forms his own resolution: a councillor may indeed be liable to censure for what he may say at that board; but the resolution taken there has been hitherto treated with a silent respect; but by that precedent it will be hereafter subject to a parliamentary inquiry." Speaker Onslow justly remarks that these general and indefinite sentiments are liable to

modern constitutional theory was by no means so established in public opinion as to bear the rude brunt of a legal argument. Anne herself, like all her predecessors, kept in her own hands the reins of power; jealous, as such feeble characters usually are, of those in whom she was forced to confide (especially after the ungrateful return of the duchess of Marlborough for the most affectionate condescension), and obstinate in her judgment from the very consciousness of its weakness, she took a share in all business, frequently presided in meetings of the cabinet, and sometimes gave directions without their advice.[k] The defence set up by lord Oxford would undoubtedly not be tolerated at present, if alleged in direct terms, by either house of parliament; however it may sometimes be deemed a sufficient apology for a minister, by those whose bias is towards a compliance with power, to insinuate that he must either obey against his conscience, or resign against his will.

Upon this prevalent disaffection, and the general dangers of the established government, was founded that measure so frequently arraigned in later times, the substitution of septennial for triennial parliaments.

Bill for septennial parliaments.

---

much exception, and that the bishop did not try them by his whig principles. The first instance where I find the responsibility of some one for every act of the crown strongly laid down is in a speech of the duke of Argyle in 1739. Parl. Hist. ix. 1138. "It is true," he says, "the nature of our constitution requires that public acts should be issued out in his majesty's name; but for all that, my lords, he is not the author of them." (But, in a much earlier debate, Jan. 12, 1711, the earl of Rochester said, "For several years they had been told that the queen was to answer for everything; but he hoped that time was over; that according to the fundamental constitution of this kingdom the ministers are accountable for all, and therefore he hoped nobody would—nay, nobody durst—name the queen in this debate." Parl. Hist. vi. 472. So much does the occasional advantage of urging an argument in debate lead men to speak against their own principles, for nothing could be more repugnant to those of the high tories, who reckoned Rochester their chief, than such a theory of the constitution as he here advances.—1845.]

[k] "Lord Bolingbroke used to say that the restraining orders to the duke of Ormond were proposed in the cabinet council, in the queen's presence, by the earl of Oxford, who had not communicated his intention to the rest of the ministers; and that lord Bolingbroke was on the point of giving his opinion against it, when the queen, without suffering the matter to be debated, directed these orders to be sent, and broke up the council. This story was told by the late lord Bolingbroke to my father." Note by lord Hardwicke on Burnet. (Oxf. edit. vi. 119.) The noble annotator has given us the same anecdote in the Hardwicke State Papers, ii. 482; but with this variance, that lord Bolingbroke there ascribes the orders to the queen herself, though he conjectured them to have proceeded from lord Oxford. [This fact is mentioned by Bolingbroke himself, in the Letters on the Study of History, Bolingbroke's Works, vol. iv. p. 129.—1845.]

triennial parliaments.[m] The ministry deemed it too perilous for their master, certainly for themselves, to encounter a general election in 1717; but the arguments adduced for the alteration, as it was meant to be permanent, were drawn from its permanent expediency. Nothing can be more extravagant than what is sometimes confidently pretended by the ignorant, that the legislature exceeded its rights by this enactment; or, if that cannot legally be advanced, that it at least violated the trust of the people, and broke in upon the ancient constitution. The law for triennial parliaments was of little more than twenty years' continuance. It was an experiment, which, as was argued, had proved unsuccessful; it was subject, like every other law, to be repealed entirely, or to be modified at discretion.[n] As a question of constitutional expediency, the septennial bill was doubtless open at the time to one serious objection. Every one admitted that a parliament subsisting indefinitely during a king's life, but exposed at all times to be dissolved at his pleasure, would become far too little dependent on the people, and far too much so upon the crown. But, if the period of its continuance should thus be extended from three to seven years, the natural course of encroachment, or some momentous circumstances like the present, might lead to fresh prolongations, and gradually to an entire repeal of what had been thought so important a safeguard of its purity. Time has happily put an end to apprehensions which are not on that account to be reckoned unreasonable.[o]

[m] ["Septennial parliaments were at first a direct usurpation of the rights of the people; for by the same authority that one parliament prolonged their own power to seven years, they might have continued it to twice seven, or, like the parliament of 1641, have made it perpetual." Priestley on Government 1771, p. 20. Similar assertions were common, grounded on the ignorant assumption that the septennial act prolonged the original duration of parliament, whereas it in fact only limited, though less than the triennial act which it repealed, the old prerogative of the crown to keep the same parliament during the life of the reigning King.—1845.]

[n] [The whole tory party, according to Bolingbroke, had become avowedly Jacobite by the summer of 1715. He lays this as far as he can on the impeachments of himself and others. But though these measures were too violent, and calculated to exasperate a fallen party, we have abundant proofs of the increase of Jacobitism in the preceding year.—1845.]

[o] Parl. Hist. vii. 292. The apprehension that parliament, having taken this step, might go on still farther to protract its own duration, was not quite idle. We find from Coxe's Memoirs of Walpole, ii. 217, that in 1720, when the first septennial house of commons had nearly run its term, there was a project of once more prolonging its life.

Many attempts have been made to obtain a return to triennial parliaments, the most considerable of which was in 1733, when the powerful talents of Walpole and his opponents were arrayed on this great question. It has been less debated in modern times than some others connected with parliamentary reformation. So long indeed as the sacred duties of choosing the representatives of a free nation shall be perpetually disgraced by tumultuary excess, or, what is far worse, by gross corruption and ruinous profusion (evils which no effectual pains are taken to redress, and which some apparently desire to perpetuate, were it only to throw discredit upon the popular part of the constitution), it would be evidently inexpedient to curtail the present duration of parliament. But, even independently of this not insuperable objection, it may well be doubted whether triennial elections would make much perceptible difference in the course of government, and whether that difference would on the whole be beneficial. It will be found, I believe, on a retrospect of the last hundred years, that the house of commons would have acted, in the main, on the same principles had the elections been more frequent; and certainly the effects of a dissolution, when it has occurred in the regular order, have seldom been very important. It is also to be considered whether an assembly which so much takes to itself the character of a deliberative council on all matters of policy, ought to follow with the precision of a weather-glass the unstable prejudices of the multitude. There are many who look too exclusively at the functions of parliament as the protector of civil liberty against the crown, functions, it is true, most important, yet not more indispensable than those of steering a firm course in domestic and external affairs, with a circumspectness and providence for the future which no wholly democratical government has ever yet displayed. It is by a middle position between an oligarchical senate and a popular assembly that the house of commons is best preserved both in its dignity and usefulness, subject indeed to swerve towards either character by that continual variation of forces which act upon the vast machine of our commonwealth. But what seems more important than the usual term of duration is that this should be permitted to take its course, except in cases where some great change of national policy may perhaps justify its abridgment. The crown would obtain a very serious advantage over the house of commons if it should become an ordinary thing to dissolve parliament for some petty ministerial interest, or to avert some unpalatable resolution. Custom appears to have established, and with some convenience, the substitution of six for seven years as the natural life of a house of commons; but an habitual irregularity in this respect might lead in time to consequences that most men would deprecate. And it may here be permitted to express a hope that the necessary dissolution of parliament within six months of a demise of the crown will not long be thought congenial to the spirit of our modern government.

Peerage bill.
A far more unanimous sentence has been pronounced by posterity upon another great constitutional question that arose under George I. Lord Sunderland persuaded the king to renounce his important prerogative of making peers; and a bill was supported by the ministry, limiting the house of lords, after the creation of a very few more, to its actual numbers. The Scots were to have twenty-five hereditary, instead of sixteen elective, members of the house, a provision neither easily reconciled to the union, nor required by the general tenor of the bill. This measure was carried with no difficulty through the upper house, whose interests were so manifestly concerned in it. But a similar motive, concurring with the efforts of a powerful malecontent party, caused its rejection by the commons.[p] It was justly thought a proof of the king's ignorance or indifference in everything that concerned his English crown, that he should have consented to so momentous a sacrifice, and Sunderland was reproached for so audacious an endeavour to strengthen his private faction at the expense of the fundamental laws of the monarchy. Those who maintained the expediency of limiting the peerage had recourse to uncertain theories as to the ancient constitution, and denied this prerogative to have been originally vested in the crown. A more plausible argument was derived from the abuse, as it was then generally accounted, of creating at once twelve peers in

[p] Parl. Hist. vii. 589.

the late reign, for the sole end of establishing a majority for the court, a resource which would be always at the command of successive factions, till the British nobility might become as numerous and venal as that of some European states. It was argued that there was a fallacy in concluding the collective power of the house of lords to be augmented by its limitation, though every single peer would evidently become of more weight in the kingdom; that the wealth of the whole body must bear a less proportion to that of the nation, and would possibly not exceed that of the lower house, while on the other hand it might be indefinitely multiplied by fresh creations; that the crown would lose one great engine of corrupt influence over the commons, which could never be truly independent while its principal members were looking on it as a stepping-stone to hereditary honours.[q]

Though these reasonings, however, are not destitute of considerable weight, and the unlimited prerogative of augmenting the peerage is liable to such abuses, at least in theory, as might overthrow our form of government, while, in the opinion of some, whether erroneous or not, it has actually been exerted with too little discretion, the arguments against any legal limitation seem more decisive. The crown has been carefully restrained by statutes, and by the responsibility of its advisers; the commons, if they transgress their boundaries, are annihilated by a proclamation; but against the ambition, or, what is much more likely, the perverse haughtiness of the aristocracy, the constitution has not furnished such direct securities. And, as this would be prodigiously enhanced by a consciousness of their power, and by a sense of self-importance which every peer would derive from it after the limitation of their numbers, it might break out in pretensions very galling to the people, and in an oppressive extension of privileges which were already sufficiently obnoxious and arbitrary. It is true that the resource of subduing an aristocratical faction by the creation of new peers could never be constitutionally employed, except in the case of a nearly equal balance; but it might usefully hang over the

---

[q] The arguments on this side are urged by Addison, in the Old Whig; and by the author of a tract entitled Six Questions Stated and Answered.

heads of the whole body, and deter them from any gross excesses of faction or oligarchical spirit. The nature of our government requires a general harmony between the two houses of parliament; and indeed any systematic opposition between them would of necessity bring on the subordination of one to the other in too marked a manner; nor had there been wanting, within the memory of man, several instances of such jealous and even hostile sentiments as could only be allayed by the inconvenient remedies of a prorogation or a dissolution. These animosities were likely to revive with more bitterness when the country gentlemen and leaders of the commons should come to look on the nobility as a class into which they could not enter, and the latter should forget more and more, in their inaccessible dignity, the near approach of that gentry to themselves in respectability of birth and extent of possessions.'

These innovations on the part of the new government were maintained on the score of its unsettled state and want of hold on the national sentiment. It may seem a reproach to the house of Hanover that, connected as it ought to have been with the names most dear to English hearts, the protestant religion and civil liberty, it should have been driven to try the resources of tyranny, and to demand more authority, to exercise more control, than had been necessary for the worst of its predecessors. Much of this disaffection was owing to the cold reserve of George I., ignorant of the language, alien from the prejudices of his people, and continually absent in his electoral dominions, to which he seemed to sacrifice the nation's interest and the security of his own crown. It is certain that the acquisition of the duchies of Bremen and Verden for Hanover in 1716* exposed Great Britain

---

' The speeches of Walpole and others, in the Parliamentary Debates, contain the whole force of the arguments against the peerage bill. Steele, in the Plebeian, opposed his old friend and coadjutor, Addison, who has been thought by Johnson to have forgotten a little in party and controversy their ancient friendship.

Lord Sunderland held out, by way of inducements to the bill, that the lords would part with scandalum magnatum, and permit the commons to administer an oath; and that the king would give up the prerogative of pardoning after an impeachment. Coxe's Walpole, ii. 172. Mere trifles, in comparison with the innovations projected.

* [These duchies had been conquered from Sweden by Denmark, who ceded them to George I., as elector of Hanover, though they had never been resigned by Charles XII. This is not consonant to the usage of nations, and at least was an act of hostility in George I. against a power

to a very serious danger, by provoking the king of Sweden to join in a league for the restoration of the pretender.ᵗ It might have been impossible (such was the precariousness of our revolution-settlement) to have made the abdication of the electorate a condition of the house of Brunswic's succession; but the consequences of that connexion, though much exaggerated by the factious and disaffected, were in various manners detrimental to English interests during those two reigns; and not the least, in that they estranged the affections of the people from sovereigns whom they regarded as still foreign.ᵘ The tory and jacobite factions, as I have observed, were powerful in the church. This had been the case ever since the Revolution. The avowed nonjurors were busy with the press, and poured forth, especially during the encouragement they received in part of Anne's reign, a multitude of pamphlets, sometimes argumentative, more often virulently libellous. Their idle cry that the church was in danger, which both houses in 1704 thought fit to deny by a formal vote, alarmed a senseless multitude. Those who took the oaths were frequently known partisans of the exiled

Jacobitism among the clergy.

who had not injured him. Yet Townshend affected to defend it, as beneficial to English interests; though the contrary is most evident, as it provoked Charles to espouse the pretender's cause. Coxe's Walpole, vol. i. p. 87.—1845.]

ᵗ The letters in Coxe's Memoirs of Walpole, vol. ii., abundantly show the German nationality, the impolicy and neglect of his duties, the rapacity and petty selfishness, of George I. The whigs were much dissatisfied; but fear of losing their places made them his slaves. Nothing can be more demonstrable than that the king's character was the main cause of preserving jacobitism, as that of his competitor was of weakening it.

The habeas corpus was several times suspended in this reign, as it had been in that of William. Though the perpetual conspiracies of the jacobites afforded a sufficient apology for this measure, it was invidiously held up as inconsistent with a government which professed to stand on the principles of liberty. Parl. Hist. v. 153, 267, 604; vii. 276; viii. 38. But some of these suspensions were too long, especially the last, from October 1722 to October 1723. Sir Joseph Jekyll, with his usual zeal for liberty, moved to reduce the time to six months.

ᵘ [The regent duke of Orleans not only assisted the pretender in his invasion of Scotland in 1715, but was concerned in the scheme of Charles XII. to restore him by arms in the next year, as appears by a despatch from the baron de Besenval, French envoy at Warsaw, dated Feb. 2, 1716, which is printed from the Dépôt des Affaires Etrangères, in Mém. de Besenval (his descendant), vol. i. p. 102. So much was Voltaire mistaken in his assertion that the regent, having discovered this intrigue through his spies, communicated it to George I. It was his own plot, though he soon afterwards allied himself to England, a remnant of the policy of 1715. But Sunderland and Stanhope, though too obsequious to their master's German views, had the merit of bringing over Dubois to a steady regard for the house of Hanover, which influenced the court of Versailles for many years.—1845.]

family; and those who affected to disclaim that cause defended the new settlement with such timid or faithless arms as served only to give a triumph to the adversary.* About the beginning of William's reign grew up the distinction of high and low churchmen: the first distinguished by great pretensions to sacerdotal power, both spiritual and temporal, by a repugnance to toleration, and by a firm adherence to the tory principle in the state, the latter by the opposite characteristics. These were pitched against each other in the two houses of convocation, an assembly which virtually ceased to exist under George I.

Convocation. The convocation of the province of Canterbury (for that of York seems never to have been important) is summoned by the archbishop's writ, under the king's direction, along with every parliament, to which it bears analogy both in its constituent parts and in its primary functions. It consists (since the Reformation) of the suffragan bishops, forming the upper house; of the deans, archdeacons, a proctor or proxy for each chapter, and two from each diocese, elected by the parochial clergy, who together constitute the lower house. In this assembly subsidies were granted, and ecclesiastical canons enacted. In a few instances under Henry VIII. and Elizabeth they were consulted as to momentous questions affecting the national religion; the supremacy of the former was approved in 1533, the articles of faith were confirmed in 1562, by the convocation. But their power to enact fresh canons without the king's licence was expressly taken away by a statute of Henry VIII.; and, even subject to this condition, is limited by several later acts of parliament (such as the acts of uniformity under Elizabeth and Charles II., that confirming, and therefore rendering unalterable, the thirty-nine articles, those relating to non-residence and other church matters), and still more perhaps by the doctrine established in Westminster Hall, that new ecclesiastical canons are not binding on the laity, so greatly that it will ever be impossible to exercise it in any effectual manner. The

---

* [The practice of using a collect before the sermon, instead of the form prescribed by the 55th canon, seems to have originated with the Jacobite clergy, to avoid praying for the king. It is prohibited by a royal proclamation of Dec. 11 1714. Hist. Reg. i. 78.—1845.]

convocation accordingly, with the exception of that in 1603, when they established some regulations, and that in 1640 (an unfortunate precedent), when they attempted some more, had little business but to grant subsidies, which however were from the time of Henry VIII. always confirmed by an act of parliament; an intimation, no doubt, that the legislature did not wholly acquiesce in their power even of binding the clergy in a matter of property. This practice of ecclesiastical taxation was discontinued in 1664, at a time when the authority and pre-eminence of the church stood very high, so that it could not then have seemed the abandonment of an important privilege. From this time the clergy have been taxed at the same rate and in the same manner with the laity.^y

^y Parl. Hist. iv. 310. "It was first settled by a verbal agreement between archbishop Sheldon and the lord chancellor Clarendon, and tacitly given into by the clergy in general as a great ease to them in taxations. The first public act of any kind relating to it was an act of parliament in 1665, by which the clergy were, in common with the laity, charged with the tax given in that act, and were discharged from the payment of the subsidies they had granted before in convocation; but in this act of parliament of 1665 there is an express saving of the right of the clergy to tax themselves in convocation if they think fit; but that has been never done since, nor attempted, as I know of, and the clergy have been constantly from that time charged with the laity in all public aids to the crown by the house of commons. In consequence of this (but from what period I cannot say), without the intervention of any particular law for it, except what I shall mention presently, the clergy (who are not lords of parliament) have assumed, and without any objection enjoyed, the privilege of voting in the election of members of the house of commons, in virtue of their ecclesiastical freeholds. This has constantly been practised from the time it first began; there are two acts of parliament which suppose it to be now a right. The acts are 10 Anne, c. 23; 18 Geo. II. c. 18. Gibson, bishop of London, said to me that this (the taxation of the clergy out of convocation) was the greatest alteration in the constitution ever made without an express law." Speaker Onslow's note on Burnet (Oxf. edit. iv. 508).

[In respect to this taxation of the clergy by parliament, and not by convocation, it is to be remembered that by far the greater part of modern taxes, being indirect, must necessarily fall on them in common with the laity. The convocation, like the parliament, were wont to grant tenths and fifteenths at fixed rates, supposed to arise from movable property. These being wholly disused from 1665 inclusive, other modes of taxation have supplied their place. But the clergy are charged to the land-tax for their benefices, and to the window-tax for their parsonages, as well as to occasional income-taxes. Exclusive of these, it does not appear that any imposts can be said to fall on them, from which they could have been exempt by retaining the right of convocation. They have not been losers in any manner by the alteration. The position of speaker Onslow, that the clergy have enjoyed the privilege of voting at county elections, in virtue of their ecclesiastical freeholds, only since their separate taxation has been discontinued, may be questioned: proofs of its exercise, as far as I remember, can be traced higher. In a conference between the two houses of parliament in 1671 on the subject of the lords' right to *alter* a money-bill, it is said "the clergy have a right to tax themselves, and it is part of

R 2

It was the natural consequence of this cessation of all business that the convocation, after a few formalities, either adjourned itself or was prorogued by a royal writ; nor had it ever, with the few exceptions above noticed, sat for more than a few days, till its supply could be voted. But, about the time of the Revolution, the party most adverse to the new order sedulously propagated a doctrine that the convocation ought to be advised with upon all questions affecting the church, and ought even to watch over its interests as the parliament did over those of the kingdom.² The commons had so far encouraged this faction as to refer to the convocation the great question of a reform in the liturgy for the sake of comprehension, as has been mentioned in the last chapter, and thus put a stop to the king's design. It was not suffered to sit much during the rest of that reign, to the great discontent of its ambitious leaders. The most celebrated of these, Atterbury, published a book, entitled the Rights and Privileges of an English Convocation, in answer to one by Wake, afterwards archbishop of Canterbury. The speciousness of the former, sprinkled with competent learning on the subject, a graceful style, and an artful employment of topics, might easily delude at least the willing reader. Nothing indeed could, on

the privilege of their estate. Doth the upper convocation house alter what the lower grant? Or do the lords or commons ever abate any part of their gift? Yet they have a power to reject the whole. But if abatement should be made, it would insensibly go to a raising, and deprive the clergy of their ancient right to tax themselves." Hatsell's Precedents, iii. 390. Thus we perceive that the change alleged to have taken place in 1665 was only *de facto*, and that the ancient practice of taxation by the convocation was not understood to be abrogated. The essential change was made by the introduction of new methods of raising money. In 1665 the sum of 2,477,000*l.* was granted, to be raised in three years, by an assessment in each county, on real and personal property of all kinds; but the old rates of subsidy are not mentioned in this or in any later tax-bill. Probably the arrangement with archbishop Sheldon was founded on the practical difficulty of ascertaining the proportion which the grant of the clergy ought to bear to the whole in the new mode of assessment. See Statutes of the Realm, 16 & 17 Car. II. c. 1.—1845.]

² The first authority I have observed for this pretension is an address of the house of lords, Nov. 19, 1675, to the throne, for the frequent meeting of the convocation, and that they do make to the king such representations as may be for the safety of the religion established. Lords' Journals. This address was renewed February 22, 1677. But what took place in consequence I am not apprised. It shows, however, some degree of dissatisfaction on the part of the bishops, who must be presumed to have set forward these addresses, at the virtual annihilation of their synod, which naturally followed from its relinquishment of self-taxation

reflection, appear more inconclusive than Atterbury's arguments. Were we even to admit the perfect analogy of a convocation to a parliament, it could not be doubted that the king may, legally speaking, prorogue the latter at his pleasure; and that, if neither money were required to be granted nor laws to be enacted, a session would be very short. The church had by pre-scription a right to be summoned in convoca- *Its encroachments.* tion; but no prescription could be set up for its longer continuance than the crown thought expedient; and it was too much to expect that William III. was to gratify his half-avowed enemies with a privilege of remonstrance and interposition they had never enjoyed. In the year 1701 the lower house of convocation pretended to a right of adjourning to a different day from that fixed by the upper, and consequently of holding separate sessions. They set up other unprecedented claims to independence, which were checked by a prorogation.[a] Their aim was in all respects to assimilate themselves to the house of commons, and thus both to set up the convocation itself as an assembly collateral to parliament, and in the main independent of it, and to maintain their co-ordinate power and equality in synodical dignity to the prelates' house. The succeeding reign, however, began under tory auspices, and the convocation was in more activity for some years than at any former period. The lower house of that assembly still distinguished itself by the most factious spirit, and especially by insolence towards the bishops, who passed in general for whigs, and whom, while pretending to assert the divine rights of episcopacy, they laboured to deprive of that pre-eminence in the Anglican synod which the ecclesiastical constitution of the kingdom had bestowed on them.[b] None was more prominent in their debates than Atterbury himself, whom, in the zenith of tory influence, at the close of her reign, the queen reluctantly promoted to the see of Rochester.

The new government at first permitted the convocation

[a] Kennet, 799, 842; Burnet, 280. This assembly had been suffered to sit, probably, in consequence of the tory maxims which the ministry of that year professed.

[b] Wilkins's Concilia, iv. Burnet, passim. Boyer's Life of Queen Anne, 225 Somerville, 82, 124

Hoadley. to hold its sittings; but they soon excited a flame which consumed themselves by an attack on Hoadley, bishop of Bangor, who had preached a sermon abounding with those principles concerning religious liberty of which he had long been the courageous and powerful assertor.[c] The lower house of convocation thought fit to denounce, through the report of a committee, the dangerous tenets of this discourse, and of a work not long before published by the bishop. A long and celebrated war of pens instantly commenced, known by the name of the Bangorian controversy, managed, perhaps on both sides, with all the chicanery of polemical writers, and disgusting both from its tediousness and from the manifest unwillingness of the disputants to speak ingenuously what they meant;[d] but as the principles of Hoadley and his advocates appeared in the main little else than those of protestantism and toleration, the sentence of the laity, in the temper that was then gaining ground as to ecclesiastical subjects, was soon pronounced in their favour; and the high-church party discredited themselves by an opposition to what now pass for the in-

[c] The lower house of convocation, in the late reign, among their other vagaries, had requested "that some synodical notice might be taken of the dishonour done to the church by a sermon preached by Mr. Benjamin Hoadley, at St. Lawrence Jewry, Sept. 29, 1705, containing positions contrary to the doctrine of the church, expressed in the first and second parts of the homily against disobedience and wilful rebellion." Wilkins, iv. 634.

[d] These qualities are so apparent that, after turning over some forty or fifty tracts, and consuming a good many hours on the Bangorian controversy, I should find some difficulty in stating with precision the propositions in dispute. It is, however, evident that a dislike, not perhaps exactly to the house of Brunswic, but to the tenor of George I.'s administration, and to Hoadley himself, as an eminent advocate for it, who had been rewarded accordingly, was at the bottom a leading motive with most of the church party; some of whom, such as Hare, though originally of a whig connexion, might have had disappointments to exasperate them.

There was nothing whatever in Hoadley's sermon injurious to the established endowments and privileges, nor to the discipline and government of the English church, even in theory. If this had been the case, he might be reproached with some inconsistency in becoming so large a partaker of her honours and emoluments. He even admitted the usefulness of censures for open immoralities, though denying all church authority to oblige any one to external communion, or to pass any sentence which should determine the condition of men with respect to the favour or displeasure of God. Hoadley's Works, ii. 465, 493. Another great question in this controversy was that of religious liberty, as a civil right, which the convocation explicitly denied. And another related to the much debated exercise of private judgment in religion, which, as one party meant virtually to take away, so the other perhaps unreasonably exaggerated. Some other disputes arose in the course of the combat, particularly the delicate problem of the value of sincerity as a plea for material errors.

controvertible truisms of religious liberty. In the ferment
of that age, it was expedient for the state to scatter a little
dust over the angry insects; the convocation Convocation
was accordingly prorogued in 1717, and has no longer suf-
never again sat for any business.* Those who fered to sit.
are imbued with high notions of sacerdotal power have
sometimes deplored this extinction of the Anglican great
council; and though its necessity, as I have already observed, cannot possibly be defended as an ancient part of
the constitution, there are not wanting specious arguments
for the expediency of such a synod. It might be urged
that the church, considered only as an integral member of
the commonwealth, and the greatest corporation within it,
might justly claim that right of managing its own affairs
which belongs to every other association; that the argument from abuse is not sufficient, and is rejected with indignation when applied, as historically it might be, to
representative governments and to civil liberty; that, in
the present state of things, no reformation even of secondary importance can be effected without difficulty,
nor any looked for in greater matters, both from the indifference of the legislature and the reluctance of the
clergy to admit its interposition.

It is answered to these suggestions that we must take
experience when we possess it, rather than analogy, for
our guide; that ecclesiastical assemblies have in all ages
and countries been mischievous where they have been
powerful, which those of our wealthy and numerous clergy
must always be; that if, notwithstanding, the convocation could be brought under the management of the state
(which by the nature of its component parts might seem
not unlikely), it must lead to the promotion of servile
men and the exclusion of merit still more than at present;
that the severe remark of Clarendon, who observes that
of all mankind none form so bad an estimate of human
affairs as churchmen, is abundantly confirmed by experience; that the representation of the church in the house
of lords is sufficient for the protection of its interests;
that the clergy have an influence which no other corpo
ration enjoys over the bulk of the nation, and may abuse
it for the purposes of undue ascendancy, unjust restraint,
or factious ambition; that the hope of any real good in

* Tindal, 539.

reformation of the church by its own assemblies, to whatever sort of reform we may look, is utterly chimerical; finally, that as the laws now stand, which few would incline to alter, the ratification of parliament must be indispensable for any material change. It seems to admit of no doubt that these reasonings ought much to outweigh those on the opposite side.

Infringements of the toleration by statutes under Anne. In the last four years of the queen's reign some inroads had been made on the toleration granted to dissenters, whom the high-church party held in abhorrence. They had for a long time inveighed against what was called occasional conformity, or the compliance of dissenters with the provisions of the test act in order merely to qualify themselves for holding office or entering into corporations. Nothing could, in the eyes of sensible men, be more advantageous to the church, if a reunion of those who had separated from it were advantageous, than this practice. Admitting even that the motive was self-interested, has an established government, in church or state, any better ally than the self-interestedness of mankind? Was it not what a presbyterian or independent minister would denounce as a base and worldly sacrifice? and if so, was not the interest of the Anglican clergy exactly in an inverse proportion to this? Any one competent to judge of human affairs would predict, what has turned out to be the case, that, when the barrier was once taken down for the sake of convenience, it would not be raised again for conscience; that the most latitudinarian theory, the most lukewarm dispositions in religion, must be prodigiously favourable to the reigning sect; and that the dissenting clergy, though they might retain, or even extend, their influence over the multitude, would gradually lose it with those classes who could be affected by the test. But even if the tory faction had been cool-headed enough for such reflections, it has unfortunately been sometimes less the aim of the clergy to reconcile those who differ from them than to keep them in a state of dishonour and depression. Hence, in the first parliament of Anne, a bill to prevent occasional conformity more than once passed the commons; and, on its being rejected by the lords, a great majority of William's bishops voting against the measure, an attempt was made to send it up again in a very reprehensible manner, tacked, as it was called, to a grant of money: so that, according to the pretension of the commons in respect to such bills, the upper house must either refuse the supply or consent to what they disapproved.[f] This, however, having miscarried, and the next parliament being of better principles, nothing farther was done till 1711, when lord Nottingham, a vehement high-churchman, having united with the whigs against the treaty of peace, they were injudicious enough to gratify him by concurring in a bill to prevent occasional conformity.[g] This was followed up by the ministry in a more decisive attack on the toleration, an act for preventing the growth of schism, which extended and confirmed one of Charles II., enforcing on all schoolmasters, and even on all teachers in private families, a declaration of conformity to the established church, to be made before the bishop, from whom a licence for exercising that profession was also to be obtained.[h] It is impossible to doubt for an instant, that, if the queen's life had preserved the tory government for a few years, every vestige of the toleration would have been effaced.

These statutes, records of their adversaries' power, the whigs, now lords of the ascendant, determined to abrogate. The dissenters were unanimously zealous for the house of Hanover and for the ministry; the church of very doubtful loyalty to the crown, and still less affection to the whig name. In the session of 1719, accordingly, the act against occasional conformity, and that restraining education, were repealed.[i] It had been the intention to have also repealed the test act; but the disunion then prevailing among the whigs had caused so formidable an opposition even to the former measures, that it was found necessary to abandon that project. Walpole, more cautious and mode-

They are repealed by the whigs.

---

[f] Parl. Hist. vi. 362.
[g] 10 Anne, c. 2.
[h] 12 Anne, c. 7. Parl. Hist. vi. 1349. The schism act, according to Lockhart, was promoted by Bolingbroke, in order to gratify the high tories, and to put lord Oxford under the necessity of declaring himself one way or other. "Though the earl of Oxford voted for it himself, he concurred with those who endeavoured to restrain some parts which they reckoned too severe; and his friends in both houses, particularly his brother, auditor Harley, spoke and voted against it very earnestly." P. 462.
[i] 5 Geo. I. c. 4. The whigs out of power, among whom was Walpole, factiously and inconsistently opposed the repeal of the schism act, so that it passed with much difficulty. Parl. Hist. vii. 569.

rate than the ministry of 1719, perceived the advantage of reconciling the church as far as possible to the royal family and to his own government; and it seems to have been an article in the tacit compromise with the bishops, who were not backward in exerting their influence for the crown, that he should make no attempt to abrogate the laws which gave a monopoly of power to the Anglican communion. We may presume also that the prelates undertook not to obstruct the acts of indemnity passed from time to time in favour of those who had not duly qualified themselves for the offices they held; and which, after some time becoming regular, have in effect thrown open the gates to protestant dissenters, though still subject to be closed by either house of parliament, if any jealousies should induce them to refuse their assent to this annual enactment.[k]

Principles of toleration fully established. Meanwhile the principles of religious liberty, in all senses of the word, gained strength by this eager controversy, naturally pleasing as they are to the proud independence of the English character, and congenial to those of civil freedom, which both parties, tory as much as whig, had now learned sedulously to maintain. The nonjuring and high-church factions among the clergy produced few eminent men; and lost credit, not more by the folly of their notions than by their general want of scholarship and disregard of their duties. The university of Oxford was tainted to the core with jacobite prejudices; but it must be added that it never stood so low in respectability as a place of education.[m] The government, on the other hand, was

---

[k] The first act of this kind appears to have been in 1727. 1 Geo. II. c. 23. It was repeated next year, intermitted the next, and afterwards renewed in every year of that reign except the fifth, the seventeenth, the twenty-second, the twenty-third, the twenty-sixth, and the thirtieth. Whether these occasional interruptions were intended to prevent the nonconformists from relying upon it, or were caused by some accidental circumstance, must be left to conjecture. I believe that the renewal has been regular every year since the accession of George III. It is to be remembered that the present work was first published before the repeal of the test act in 1828.

[m] We find in Gutch's Collectanea Curiosa, vol. i. p. 53, a plan, ascribed to lord chancellor Macclesfield, for taking away the election of heads of colleges from the fellows, and vesting the nomination in the great officers of state, in order to cure the disaffection and want of discipline which was justly complained of. This remedy would have been perhaps the substitution of a permanent for a temporary evil. It appears also that archbishop Wake wanted to have had a bill, in 1716, for asserting the royal supremacy, and better regulating the clergy of the two universities (Coxe's Walpole, ii. 122); but I do not know that the precise nature of this is anywhere men-

studious to promote distinguished men; and doubtless the hierarchy in the first sixty years of the eighteenth century might very advantageously be compared, in point of conspicuous ability, with that of an equal period that ensued. The maxims of persecution were silently abandoned, as well as its practice; Warburton, and others of less name, taught those of toleration with as much boldness as Hoadley, but without some of his more invidious tenets; the more popular writers took a liberal tone; the names of Locke and Montesquieu acquired immense authority; the courts of justice discountenanced any endeavour to revive oppressive statutes; and not long after the end of George II.'s reign, it was adjudged in the house of lords, upon the broadest principles of toleration laid down by lord Mansfield, that nonconformity with the established church is recognised by the law, and not an offence at which it connives.

Atterbury, bishop of Rochester, the most distinguished of the party denominated high-church, became the victim of his restless character and implacable disaffection to the house of Hanover. The pretended king, for some years after his competitor's accession, had fair hopes from different powers of Europe,—France, Sweden, Russia, Spain, Austria (each of whom, in its turn, was ready to make use of this instrument),—and from the powerful faction who panted for his restoration. This was unquestionably very numerous, though we have not as yet the means of fixing with certainty on more than comparatively a small number of names; but a conspiracy for an invasion from Spain and a simultaneous rising was detected in 1722, which implicated three or four peers, and among them the bishop of Rochester.[a]

Banishment of Atterbury

---

tioned. I can scarcely quote Amherst's Terræ Filius as authority; it is a very clever, though rather libellous, invective against the university of Oxford at that time; but, from internal evidence, as well as the confirmation which better authorities afford it, I have no doubt that it contains much truth.

Those who have looked much at the ephemeral literature of these two reigns must be aware of many publications fixing the charge of prevalent disaffection on this university down to the death of George II.; and Dr. King, the famous Jacobite master of St. Mary Hall, admits that some were left to reproach him for apostasy in going to court on the accession of the late king in 1760. The general reader will remember the Isis, by Mason, and the Triumph of Isis, by Warton; the one a severe invective, the other an indignant vindication: but in this instance, notwithstanding the advantages which satire is supposed to have over panegyric, we must award the laurel to the worse cause, and, what is more extraordinary, to the worse poet.

[a] Layer, who suffered on account of

The evidence, however, though tolerably convincing, being insufficient for a verdict at law, it was thought expedient to pass a bill of pains and penalties against this prelate, as well as others against two of his accomplices. The proof, besides many corroborating circumstances, consisted in three letters relative to the conspiracy, supposed to be written by his secretary Kelly, and appearing to be dictated by the bishop. He was deprived of his see, and banished the kingdom for life.[o] This met with strong opposition, not limited to the enemies of the royal family, and is open to the same objection as the attainder of sir John Fenwick—the danger of setting aside those precious securities against a wicked government which the law of treason has furnished. As a vigorous assertion of the state's authority over the church we may commend the policy of Atterbury's deprivation, but perhaps this was ill purchased by a mischievous precedent. It is, however, the last act of a violent nature in any important matter which can be charged against the English legislature.

No extensive conspiracy of the jacobite faction seems ever to have been in agitation after the fall of Atterbury. The pretender had his emissaries perpetually alert, and it is understood that an enormous mass of letters from his English friends is in

Decline of the Jacobites.

[o] State Trials, xvi. 324. Parl. Hist. this plot, had accused several peers, among others lord Cowper, who complained to the house of the publication of his name; and indeed, though he was at that time strongly in opposition to the court, the charge seems wholly incredible. Lord Strafford, however, was probably guilty; lords North and Orrery certainly so. Parl. Hist. viii. 203. There is even ground to suspect that Sunderland, to use Tindal's words, "in the latter part of his life, had entered into correspondences and designs which would have been fatal to himself or to the public." P. 657. This is mentioned by Coxe, i. 165; and certainly confirmed by Lockhart, ii. 68, 70. But the reader will hardly give credit to such a story as Horace Walpole has told, that he coolly consulted sir Robert, his political rival, as to the part they should take on the king's death. Lord Orford's Works, iv. 287.

viii. 195, et post. Most of the bishops voted against their restless brother; and Willis, bishop of Salisbury, made a very good but rather too acrimonious a speech on the bill. Id. 298. Hoadley, who was no orator, published two letters in the newspaper, signed Britannicus, in answer to Atterbury's defence; which, after all that had passed, he might better have spared. Atterbury's own speech is certainly below his fame, especially the peroration. Id. 267.

No one, I presume, will affect to doubt the reality of Atterbury's connexions with the Stuart family, either before his attainder or during his exile. The proofs of the latter were published by lord Hailes in 1768, and may be found also in Nicholls's edition of Atterbury's Correspondence, i. 148. Additional evidence is furnished by the Lockhart Papers, vol. ii. passim.

existence;[p] but very few had the courage, or rather folly, to plunge into so desperate a course as rebellion. Walpole's prudent and vigilant administration, without transgressing the boundaries of that free constitution for which alone the house of Brunswic had been preferred, kept in check the disaffected. He wisely sought the friendship of cardinal Fleury, aware that no other power in Europe than France could effectually assist the banished family. After his own fall and the death of Fleury, new combinations of foreign policy arose; his successors returned to the Austrian connexion; a war with France broke out; the grandson of James II. became master, for a moment, of Scotland, and even advanced to the centre of this peaceful and unprotected kingdom. But this was hardly more ignominious to the government than to the jacobites themselves; none of them joined the standard of their pretended sovereign; and the rebellion of 1745 was conclusive, by its own temporary success, against the possibility of his restoration.[q] From this time the

[p] The Stuart Papers obtained lately from Rome, and now in his majesty's possession, are said to furnish copious evidence of the Jacobite intrigues, and to affect some persons not hitherto suspected. We have reason to hope that they will not be long withheld from the public, every motive for concealment being wholly at an end. 1827.—Lord Mahon has communicated some information from these papers in his History of England; but the number of persons engaged in connexion with the pretender is rather less than had been expected. 1841.

It is said that there were not less than fifty jacobites in the parliament of 1728. Coxe, ii. 294.

[q] The tories, it is observed in the MS. Journal of Mr. Yorke (second earl of Hardwicke), showed no sign of affection to the government at the time when the invasion was expected in 1743, but treated it all with indifference. Parl. Hist. xiii. 668. In fact, a disgraceful apathy pervaded the nation; and according to a letter from Mr. Fox to Mr. Winnington in 1745, which I only quote from recollection, it seemed perfectly uncertain, from this general passiveness, whether the revolution might not be suddenly brought about. Yet very few comparatively, I am persuaded, had the slightest attachment or prejudice in favour of the house of Stuart; but the continual absence from England, and the Hanoverian predilections, of the two Georges, the feebleness and factiousness of their administration and of public men in general, and an indefinite opinion of misgovernment, raised through the press, though certainly without oppression or arbitrary acts, had gradually alienated the mass of the nation. But this would not lead men to expose their lives and fortunes; and hence the people of England, a thing almost incredible, lay quiet and nearly unconcerned, while the little army of Highlanders came every day nearer to the capital. It is absurd, however, to suppose that they could have been really successful by marching onward; though their defeat might have been more glorious at Finchley than at Culloden, 1827.—I should not have used, of course, the word absurd, if lord Mahon's History had been published, in which that acute and impartial writer inclines to the opinion of Charles Edward's probable success. I am still, however, persuaded that either the duke of Cumberland must have overtaken

government, even when in search of pretexts for alarm, could hardly affect to dread a name grown so contemptible as that of the Stuart party. It survived, however, for the rest of the reign of George II., in those magnanimous compotations which had always been the best evidence of its courage and fidelity.

Though the jacobite party had set before its eyes an object most dangerous to the public tranquillity, and which, could it have been attained, would have brought on again the contention of the seventeenth century; though, in taking oaths to a government against which they were in conspiracy, they showed a systematic disregard of obligation, and were as little mindful of allegiance, in the years 1715 and 1745, to the prince they owned in their hearts, as they had been to him whom they had professed to acknowledge, it ought to be admitted that they were rendered more numerous and formidable than was necessary by the faults of the reigning kings or of their ministers. They were not latterly actuated for the most part (perhaps with very few exceptions) by the slavish principles of indefeasible right, much less by those of despotic power.[r] They had been so long in opposition to the court, they had so often spoken the language of liberty, that we may justly believe them to have been its friends. It was the policy of Walpole to keep alive the strongest

Prejudices against the reigning family.

Jealousy of the crown.

---

him before he reached London, or that his small army would have been beaten by the king. 1842.

[r] [Even in 1715 this was not the case with the jacobite aristocracy. "When you were first driven into this interest," says Bolingbroke to sir W. Wyndham, "I may appeal to you for the notion which the party had. You thought of restoring him by the strength of the tories, and of opposing a tory king to a whig king. You took him up as the instrument of your revenge and of your ambition. You looked on him as your creature, and never once doubted of making what terms you pleased with him. This is so true that the same language is still held to the catechumens in jacobitism. Were the contrary to be avowed even now, the party in England would soon disunite. Instead of making the pretender their tool, they are his. Instead of having in view to restore him on their own terms, they are labouring to do it without any terms; that is, to speak properly, they are ready to receive him on his," &c. This was written in 1717, and seems to indicate that the real jacobite spirit of hereditary right was very strong among the people. And this continued through the reign of George I., as I should infer from the press. But Bolingbroke himself had great influence in subduing it afterwards, and, though of course not obliterated, we trace it less and less down to the extinction of the jacobite party in the last years of George II. Leslie's writings would have been received with scorn by the young jacobites of 1750. Church mobs were frequent in 1715; but we scarcely, I think, find much of them afterwards. In London, and the chief towns, the populace were chiefly whig.—1845.]

prejudice in the mind of George II., obstinately retentive of prejudice, as such narrow and passionate minds always are, against the whole body of the tories. They were ill received at court, and generally excluded not only from those departments of office which the dominant party have a right to keep in their power, but from the commission of the peace, and every other subordinate trust.[s] This illiberal and selfish course retained many, no doubt, in the pretender's camp, who must have perceived both the improbability of his restoration, and the difficulty of reconciling it with the safety of our constitution. He was indeed, as well as his son, far less worthy of respect than the contemporary Brunswic kings; without absolutely wanting capacity or courage, he gave the most undeniable evidence of his legitimacy by constantly resisting the counsels of wise men, and yielding to those of priests;[t] while his son, the fugitive of Culloden, despised and deserted by his own party, insulted by the court of France, lost with the advance of years even the respect and compassion which wait on unceasing misfortune, the last sad inheritance of the house of Stuart.[u] But they

---

[s] See Parl. Hist. xiii. 1244; and other proofs might be brought from the same work, as well as from miscellaneous authorities of the age of George II.

[t] [Bolingbroke's character of James is not wholly to be trusted. "He is naturally inclined to believe the worst, which I take to be a certain mark of a mean spirit and a wicked soul; at least I am sure that the contrary quality, when it is not due to weakness of understanding, is the fruit of a generous temper and an honest heart. Prone to judge ill of all mankind, he will rarely be seduced by his credulity; but I never knew a man so capable of being the bubble of his distrust and jealousy." Letter to sir W. Wyndham. Thus Bolingbroke, under the sting of his impetuous passions, threw away the scabbard when he quarrelled with the house of Stuart, as he had done with the whigs at home. But James was not a man altogether without capacity: his private letters are well and sensibly written. Like his father, he had a narrow and obstinate, but not a weak, understanding. His son, Charles Edward, appears to me inferior to him in this respect, as well as in his moral principle.—1845.]

[u] See in the Lockhart Papers, ii. 565, a curious relation of Charles Edward's behaviour in refusing to quit France after the peace of Aix-la-Chapelle. It was so insolent and absurd that the government was provoked to arrest him at the opera, and literally to order him to be bound hand and foot; an outrage which even his preposterous conduct could hardly excuse.

Dr. King was in correspondence with this prince for some years after the latter's foolish, though courageous, visit to London in September, 1750; which he left again in five days, on finding himself deceived by some sanguine friends. King says he was wholly ignorant of our history and constitution. "I never heard him express any noble or benevolent sentiment, the certain indications of a great soul and good heart; or discover any sorrow or compassion for the misfortune of so many worthy men who had suffered in his cause." Anecdotes of his own Times, p. 201. He goes on to charge him with love of money and

were little known in England, and from unknown princes men are prone to hope much: if some could anticipate a redress of every evil from Frederic prince of Wales, whom they might discover to be destitute of respectable qualities, it cannot be wondered at that others might draw equally flattering prognostics from the accession of Charles Edward. It is almost certain that, if either the

other faults. But his great folly in keeping a mistress, Mrs. Walkinshaw, whose sister was housekeeper at Leicester House, alarmed the Jacobites. "These were all men of fortune and distinction, and many of them persons of the first quality, who attached themselves to the P. as to a person who they imagined might be made the instrument of saving their country. They were sensible that by Walpole's administration the English government was become a system of corruption; and that Walpole's successors, who pursued his plan without any of his abilities, had reduced us to such a deplorable situation that our commercial interest was sinking, our colonies in danger of being lost, and Great Britain, which, if her powers were properly exerted, as they were afterwards in Mr. Pitt's administration, was able to give laws to other nations, was become the contempt of all Europe." P. 208. This is in truth the secret of the continuance of jacobitism. But possibly that party were not sorry to find a pretext for breaking off so hopeless a connexion, which they seem to have done about 1755. Mr. Pitt's great successes reconciled them to the administration; and his liberal conduct brought back those who had been disgusted by an exclusive policy. On the accession of a new king they flocked to St. James's; and probably scarcely one person of the rank of a gentleman, south of the Tweed, was found to dispute the right of the house of Brunswic after 1760. Dr. King himself, it may be observed, laughs at the old passive obedience doctrine (page 193); so far was he from being a jacobite of that school.

A few nonjuring congregations lingered on far into the reign of George III., presided over by the successors of some bishops whom Lloyd of Norwich, the last of those deprived at the Revolution, had consecrated in order to keep up the schism. A list of these is given in D'Oyly's Life of Sancroft, vol. ii. p. 34, whence it would appear that the last of them died in 1779. I can trace the line a little farther: a bishop of that separation, named Cartwright, resided at Shrewsbury in 1793, carrying on the business of a surgeon. State Trials, xxiii. 1073. I have heard of similar congregations in the west of England still later. He had, however, become a very loyal subject to king George: a singular proof of that tenacity of life by which religious sects, after dwindling down through neglect, excel frogs and tortoises; and that, even when they have become almost equally cold-blooded! [A late publication, Lathbury's History of the Nonjurors, gives several names of nonjuring bishops down to the close of the century; though it does not absolutely follow that all who frequented their congregations would have refused the oath of allegiance. Of such strict jacobites there were, as I have said, but few left south of the Tweed after the accession of George III. Still some there may have been, unknown by name, in the middling ranks; and Mr. Lathbury has quoted jacobite pamphlets as late as 1759, and probably the authors of these did not renounce their opinions in the next year. One or two writers in this strain have met my observation rather later. The last is in 1774, when, an absurd letter against the Revolution having been inadvertently admitted into the Morning Chronicle and Public Advertiser, Mr. Fox, with less good nature than belonged to him, induced the house of commons to direct a prosecution of the printers by the attorney-general; and they were sentenced to three months' imprisonment. Parl. Hist. xvii. 1054. Annual Register, 1774, p. 164.— 1845.]

claimant or his son had embraced the protestant religion, and had also manifested any superior strength of mind, the German prejudices of the reigning family would have cost them the throne, as they did the people's affections. Jacobitism, in the great majority, was one modification of the spirit of liberty burning strongly in the nation at this period. It gave a rallying point to that indefinite discontent which is excited by an ill opinion of rulers, and to that disinterested though ignorant patriotism which boils up in youthful minds. The government in possession was hated, not as usurped, but as corrupt; the banished line was demanded, not so much because it was legitimate, but because it was the fancied means of redressing grievances and regenerating the constitution. Such notions were doubtless absurd; but it is undeniable that they were common, and had been so almost from the Revolution. I speak only, it will be observed, of the English jacobites; in Scotland the sentiments of loyalty and national pride had a vital energy, and the Highland chieftains gave their blood, as freely as their southern allies did their wine, for the cause of their ancient kings.[x]

No one can have looked in the most cursory manner at the political writings of these two reigns, or at the debates of parliament, without being struck by the continual predictions that our liberties were on the point of extinguishment, or at least by apprehensions of their being endangered. It might seem that little or nothing had been gained by the Revolution, and by the substi-

---

[x] [Lord Mahon printed in 1842, but only for the Roxburghe Club, some extracts from despatches (in the State Paper Office) of the British envoy at Florence, containing information, from time to time, as to the motions and behaviour of Charles Edward. Were it not for the difficulty under which our minister at that court must generally labour to find any materials for a letter to the secretary of state, we might feel some wonder at the gravity with which sir Horace Mann seems to treat the table-talk and occasional journeys of the poor old exile, even down to 1786. It may be said that his excessive folly might render him capable of any enterprise, however extravagant, as long as he had bodily strength left; and that he is supposed to have kept up some connexion with the Irish priesthood to the end of his life, so as to recommend bishops to the court of Rome. But though sir Horace Mann, in a letter of the date Nov. 11, 1783, is "every day more convinced that something of importance is carrying on between the court of France and the pretender, and has reason to suspect that the latter either has a connexion with the king of Sweden, or is endeavouring to gain his friendship," he soon after discovers that this important matter was only an application to France for a pension, which Gustavus III., then in Italy, would out of compassion have been glad to promote.—1845.]

tution of an elective dynasty. This doubtless it was the
interest of the Stuart party to maintain or insinuate;
and, in the conflict of factions, those who, with far opposite views, had separated from the court, seemed to lend
them aid. The declamatory exaggerations of that able
and ambitious body of men who co-operated against the
ministry of sir Robert Walpole have long been rejected;
and perhaps, in the usual reflux of popular opinion, his
domestic administration (for in foreign policy his views,
so far as he was permitted to act upon them, appear to
have been uniformly judicious) has obtained of late rather
an undue degree of favour. I have already observed
that, for the sake of his own ascendancy in the cabinet,
he kept up unnecessarily the distinctions of the whig
and tory parties, and thus impaired the stability of the
royal house which it was his chief care to support. And
though his government was so far from anything oppressive or arbitrary that, considered either relatively to any
former times, or to the extensive disaffection known to
subsist, it was uncommonly moderate; yet, feeling or
feigning alarm at the jacobite intrigues on the one hand,
at the democratic tone of public sentiment and of popular
writings on the other, he laboured to preserve a more
narrow and oligarchical spirit than was congenial to so
great and brave a people, and trusted not enough, as
indeed is the general fault of ministers, to the sway of
good sense and honesty over disinterested minds. But,
as he never had a complete influence over his master,
and knew that those who opposed him had little else in
view than to seize the reins of power and manage them
worse, his deviations from the straight course are more
pardonable.

The clamorous invectives of this opposition, combined
with the subsequent dereliction of avowed principles by
many among them when in power, contributed more than
anything else in our history to cast obloquy and suspicion, or even ridicule, on the name and occupation of
patriots. Men of sordid and venal characters always
rejoice to generalise so convenient a maxim as the nonexistence of public virtue. It may not, however, be
improbable, that many of those who took a part in this
long contention were less insincere than it has been the
fashion to believe, though led too far at the moment by

their own passions, as well as by the necessity of colouring highly a picture meant for the multitude, and reduced afterwards to the usual compromises and concessions, without which power in this country is ever unattainable. But waiving a topic too generally historical for the present chapter, it will be worth while to consider what sort of ground there might be for some prevalent subjects of declamation; and whether the power of government had not, in several respects, been a good deal enhanced since the beginning of the century. By the power of government I mean not so much the personal authority of the sovereign as that of his ministers, acting perhaps without his directions; which, since the reign of William, is to be distinguished, if we look at it analytically, from the monarchy itself.

I. The most striking acquisition of power by the crown in the new model of government, if I may use such an expression, is the permanence of a regular military force. The reader cannot need to be reminded that no army existed before the civil war, that the guards in the reign of Charles II. were about 5000 men, that in the breathing-time between the peace of Ryswick and the war of the Spanish succession the commons could not be brought to keep up more than 7000 troops. Nothing could be more repugnant to the national prejudices than a standing army. The tories, partly from regard to the ancient usage of the constitution, partly, no doubt, from a factious or disaffected spirit, were unanimous in protesting against it. The most disinterested and zealous lovers of liberty came with great suspicion and reluctance into what seemed so perilous an innovation. But the court, after the accession of the house of Hanover, had many reasons for insisting upon so great an augmentation of its power and security. It is remarkable to perceive by what stealthy advances this came on. Two long wars had rendered the army a profession for men in the higher and middling classes, and familiarised the nation to their dress and rank; it had achieved great honour for itself and the English name; and in the nature of mankind the patriotism of glory is too often an overmatch for that of liberty. The two kings were fond of warlike policy, the second of war itself; their schemes, and those of their ministers, de-

Changes in the constitution whereon it was founded.

manded an imposing attitude in negotiation, which an army, it was thought, could best give; the cabinet was for many years entangled in alliances, shifting sometimes rapidly, but in each combination liable to produce the interruption of peace. In the new system which rendered the houses of parliament partakers in the executive administration, they were drawn themselves into the approbation of every successive measure, either on the propositions of ministers, or, as often happens more indirectly, but hardly less effectually, by passing a negative on those of their opponents. The number of troops for which a vote was annually demanded, after some variations, in the first years of George I., was, during the whole administration of sir Robert Walpole, except when the state of Europe excited some apprehension of disturbance, rather more than 17,000 men, independent of those on the Irish establishment, but including the garrisons of Minorca and Gibraltar. And this continued with little alteration to be our standing army in time of peace during the eighteenth century.

Permanent military force.

This army was always understood to be kept on foot, as it is still expressed in the preamble of every mutiny-bill, for better preserving the balance of power in Europe. The commons would not for an instant admit that it was necessary as a permanent force, in order to maintain the government at home. There can be no question, however, that the court saw its advantage in this light; and I am not perfectly sure that some of the multiplied negotiations on the continent in that age were not intended as a pretext for keeping up the army, or at least as a means of exciting alarm for the security of the established government. In fact, there would have been rebellions in the time of George I., not only in Scotland, which perhaps could not otherwise have been preserved, but in many parts of the kingdom, had the parliament adhered with too pertinacious bigotry to their ancient maxims. Yet these had such influence that it was long before the army was admitted by every one to be perpetual; and I do not know that it has ever been recognised as such in our statutes. Mr. Pulteney, so late as 1732, a man neither disaffected nor democratical, and whose views extended no farther than a

Apprehensions from it.

change of hands, declared that he "always had been, and always would be, against a standing army of any kind; it was to him a terrible thing, whether under the denomination of parliamentary or any other. A standing army is still a standing army, whatever name it be called by; they are a body of men distinct from the body of the people; they are governed by different laws; blind obedience and an entire submission to the orders of their commanding officer is their only principle. The nations around us are already enslaved, and have been enslaved by those very means; by means of their standing armies they have every one lost their liberties; it is indeed impossible that the liberties of the people can be preserved in any country where a numerous standing army is kept up."[y]

This wholesome jealousy, though it did not prevent what was indeed for many reasons not to be dispensed with, the establishment of a regular force, kept it within bounds which possibly the administration, if left to itself, would have gladly overleaped. A clause in the mutiny-bill, first inserted in 1718, enabling courts-martial to punish mutiny and desertion with death, which had hitherto been only cognizable as capital offences by the civil magistrate, was carried by a very small majority in both houses.[z] An act was passed in 1735, directing that no troops should come within two miles of any place, except the capital or a garrisoned town, during an election;[a] and on some occasions both the commons and the courts of justice showed that they had not forgotten the maxims of their ancestors as to the supremacy of the civil power.[b] A more important measure was projected by men of independent principles, at once to secure the kingdom against attack, invaded as it had been by rebels in 1745, and thrown into the most

[y] Parl. Hist. viii. 904.
[z] Id. vii. 536.
[a] 8 Geo. II. c. 30. Parl. Hist. viii. 883.
[b] The military having been called in to quell an alleged riot at Westminster election in 1741, it was resolved, Dec. 22, "that the presence of a regular body of armed soldiers at an election of members to serve in parliament is a high infringement of the liberties of the subject, a manifest violation of the freedom of elections, and an open defiance of the laws and constitution of this kingdom." The persons concerned in this, having been ordered to attend the house, received on their knees a very severe reprimand from the speaker. Parl. Hist. ix. 326. Upon some occasion, the circumstances of which I do not recollect, chief justice Willes uttered some laudable sentiments as to the subordination of military power.

ignominious panic on the rumours of a French armament in 1756, to take away the pretext for a large standing force, and perhaps to furnish a guarantee against any evil purposes to which in future times it might be subservient, by the establishment of a national militia, under the sole authority indeed of the crown, but commanded by gentlemen of sufficient estates, and not liable, except in war, to be marched out of its proper county. This favourite plan, with some reluctance on the part of the government, was adopted in 1757.[c] But though, during the long periods of hostilities which have unfortunately ensued, this embodied force has doubtless placed the kingdom in a more respectable state of security, it has not much contributed to diminish the number of our regular forces; and, from some defects in its constitution, arising out of too great attention to our ancient local divisions, and of too indiscriminate a dispensation with personal service, which has filled the ranks with the refuse of the community, the militia has grown unpopular and burthensome, rather considered of late by the government as a means of recruiting the army than as worthy of preservation in itself, and accordingly thrown aside in time of peace; so that the person who acquired great popularity as the author of this institution, lived to see it worn out and gone to decay, and the principles, above all, upon which he had brought it forward, just enough remembered to be turned into ridicule. Yet the success of that magnificent organization which, in our own time, has been established in France, is sufficient to evince the possibility of a national militia; and we know with what spirit such a force was kept up for some years in this country, under the name of volunteers and yeomanry, on its only real basis, that of property, and in such local distribution as convenience pointed out.

Nothing could be more idle, at any time since the Revolution, than to suppose that the regular army would pull the speaker out of his chair, or in any manner be employed to confirm a despotic power in the crown. Such power, I think, could never have been the waking

---

[c] Lord Hardwicke threw out the militia bill in 1756, thinking some of its clauses rather too republican, and, in fact, being adverse to the scheme. Parl. Hist. xv. 704. H. Walpole's Memoirs, ii. 45. Coxe's Memoirs of Lord Walpole, 450.

dream of either king or minister. But as the slightest inroads upon private rights and liberties are to be guarded against in any nation that deserves to be called free, we should always keep in mind not only that the military power is subordinate to the civil, but, as this subordination must cease where the former is frequently employed, that it should never be called upon in aid of the peace without sufficient cause. Nothing would more break down this notion of the law's supremacy than the perpetual interference of those who are really governed by another law; for the doctrine of some judges, that the soldier, being still a citizen, acts only in preservation of the public peace, as another citizen is bound to do, must be felt as a sophism, even by those who cannot find an answer to it. And, even in slight circumstances, it is not conformable to the principles of our government to make that vain display of 'military authority which disgusts us so much in some continental kingdoms. But, not to dwell on this, it is more to our immediate purpose that the executive power has acquired such a coadjutor in the regular army that it can in no probable emergency have much to apprehend from popular sedition. The increased facilities of transport, and several improvements in military art and science, which will occur to the reader, have in later times greatly enhanced this advantage.

II. It must be apparent to every one that since the Restoration, and especially since the Revolution, an immense power has been thrown into the scale of both houses of parliament, though practically in more frequent exercise by the lower, in consequence of their annual session during several months, and of their almost unlimited rights of investigation, discussion, and advice. But, if the crown should by any means become secure of an ascendancy in this assembly, it is evident that, although the prerogative, technically speaking, might be diminished, the power might be the same, or even possibly more efficacious; and that this result must be proportioned to the degree and security of such an ascendancy. A parliament absolutely, and in all conceivable circumstances, under the control of the sovereign, whether through intimidation or corrupt subservience, could not, *Influence over parliament by places and pensions.*

without absurdity, be deemed a co-ordinate power, or indeed, in any sense, a restraint upon his will. This is, however, an extreme supposition, which no man, unless both grossly factious and ignorant, will ever pretend to have been realised. But, as it would equally contradict notorious truth to assert that every vote has been disinterested and independent, the degree of influence which ought to be permitted, or which has at any time existed, becomes one of the most important subjects in our constitutional policy.

<small>Attempts to restrain it.</small> I have mentioned in the last chapter both the provisions inserted in the act of settlement, with the design of excluding altogether the possessors of public office from the house of commons, and the modifications of them by several acts of the queen. These were deemed by the country party so inadequate to restrain the dependents of power from overspreading the benches of the commons, that perpetual attempts were made to carry the exclusive principle to a far greater length. In the two next reigns, if we can trust to the uncontradicted language of debate, or even to the descriptions of individuals in the lists of each parliament, we must conclude that a very undue proportion of dependents on the favour of government were made its censors and counsellors. There was still, however, so much left of an independent spirit, that bills for restricting the number of placemen, or excluding pensioners, met always with countenance; they were sometimes rejected by very slight majorities; and, after a time, sir Robert Walpole found it expedient to reserve his opposition for the surer field of the other house.[d] After his

---

[d] By the act of 6 Anne, c. 7, all persons holding pensions from the crown during pleasure were made incapable of sitting in the house of commons; which was extended by 1 Geo. I. c. 56, to those who held them for any term of years. But the difficulty was to ascertain the fact; the government refusing information. Mr. Sandys accordingly proposed a bill in 1730, by which every member of the commons was to take an oath that he did not hold any such pension, and that, in case of accepting one, he would disclose it to the house within fourteen days. This was carried by a small majority through the commons, but rejected in the other house, which happened again in 1734 and in 1740. Parl. Hist. viii 789; ix. 369; xi. 510. The king, in an angry note to lord Townshend, on the first occasion, calls it "this villanous bill." Coxe's Walpole, ii. 537, 673. A bill of the same gentleman to limit the number of placemen in the house had so far worse success, that it did not reach the Serbonian bog. Parl. Hist. xi. 328. Bishop Sherlock made a speech against the prevention of corrupt practices by the pension bill, which, whether justly or not, excited much indignation, and even gave

fall, it was imputed with some justice to his successors, that they shrunk in power from the bold reformation which they had so frequently endeavoured to effect; the king was indignantly averse to all retrenchment of his power, and they wanted probably both the inclination and the influence to cut off all corruption. Yet we owe to this ministry the place-bill of 1743, which, derided as it was at the time, seems to have had a considerable effect; excluding a great number of inferior officers from the house of commons, which has never since contained so revolting a list of court-deputies as it did in the age of Walpole.[e]

Place-bill of 1743.

But while this acknowledged influence of lucrative office might be presumed to operate on many stanch adherents of the actual administration, there was always a strong suspicion, or rather a general certainty, of absolute corruption. The proofs in single instances could never perhaps be established; which, of course, is not surprising. But no one seriously called in question the reality of a systematic distribution of money by the crown to the representatives of the people; nor did the corrupters themselves, in whom the crime seems always to be deemed less heinous, disguise it in private.[f] It is true that the appropriation of supplies, and the established course of the exchequer, render the greatest part of the public revenue secure from misapplication; but, under the head of secret service money, a very large sum was annually expended without account, and some other parts of the civil list were equally free from all public examination.[g] The committee of secrecy

Secret corruption.

---

rise to the proposal of a bill for putting an end to the translation of bishops. Id. viii. 847.

[e] 25 Geo. II. c. 22. The king came very reluctantly into this measure: in the preceding session of 1742, Sandys, now become chancellor of the exchequer, had opposed it, though originally his own, alleging in no very parliamentary manner that the new ministry had not yet been able to remove his majesty's prejudices. Parl. Hist. xii. 896.

[f] Mr. Fox declared to the duke of Newcastle, when the office of secretary of state, and what was called the management of the house of commons, was offered to him, "that he never desired to touch a penny of the secret service money, or to know the disposition of it, farther than was necessary to *enable him to speak to the members without being ridiculous.*" Doddington's Diary, 15th March, 1754. H. Walpole confirms this in nearly the same words. Mem. of Last Ten Years, i. 332.

[g] In Coxe's Memoirs of Sir R. Walpole, iii. 609, we have the draught, by that minister, of an intended vindication of himself after his retirement from office, in order to show the impossibility of misapplying public money, which, however, he does not show; and his ela-

appointed after the resignation of sir Robert Walpole endeavoured to elicit some distinct evidence of this misapplication; but the obscurity natural to such transactions, and the guilty collusion of subaltern accomplices, who shrouded themselves in the protection of the law, defeated every hope of punishment, or even personal disgrace.[b] This practice of direct bribery continued, beyond doubt, long afterwards, and is generally supposed to have ceased about the termination of the American war.

There is hardly any doctrine with respect to our government more in fashion than that a considerable influence of the crown (meaning of course a corrupt influence) in both houses of parliament, and especially in the commons, has been rendered indispensable by the vast enhancement of their own power over the public administration. It is doubtless most expedient that many servants of the crown should be also servants of the people; and no man who values the constitution would separate the functions of ministers of state from those of legislators. The glory that waits on wisdom and eloquence in the senate should always be the great prize of an English statesman, and his high road to the sovereign's favour. But the maxim that private vices are public benefits is as sophistical as it is disgusting; and it is self-evident, both that the expectation of a clandestine recompence, or, what in effect is the same thing, of a lucrative office, cannot be the motive of an upright man in his vote, and that, if an entire parliament should be composed of such venal spirits, there would be an end of all control upon the crown. There is no real cause to apprehend that a virtuous and enlightened government would find difficulty in resting upon the reputation justly due to it; especially when we throw into the scale that species of influence which

---

borate account of the method by which payments are made out of the exchequer, though valuable in some respects, seems rather intended to lead aside the unpractised reader.

[b] This secret committee were checked at every step for want of sufficient powers. It is absurd to assert, like Mr. Coxe, that they advanced accusations which they could not prove, when the means of proof were withheld. Scrope and Paxton, the one secretary, the other solicitor, to the treasury, being examined about very large sums traced to their hands, and other matters, refused to answer questions that might criminate themselves; and a bill to indemnify evidence was lost in the upper house. Parl. Hist. xii. 626 et post.

must ever subsist, the sentiment of respect and loyalty to a sovereign, of friendship and gratitude to a minister, of habitual confidence in those intrusted with power, of averseness to confusion and untried change, which have in fact more extensive operation than any sordid motives, and which must almost always render them unnecessary.

III. The co-operation of both houses of parliament with the executive government enabled the latter to convert to its own purpose what had often in former times been employed against it, the power of inflicting punishment for breach of privilege. But as the subject of parliamentary privilege is of no slight importance, it will be convenient on this occasion to bring the whole before the reader in as concise a summary as possible, distinguishing the power, as it relates to offences committed by members of either house, or against them singly, or the houses of parliament collectively, or against the government and the public. *Committments for breach of privilege—*

1. It has been the constant practice of the house of commons to repress disorderly or indecent behaviour by a censure delivered through the speaker. Instances of this are even noticed in the Journals under Edward VI. and Mary; and it is in fact essential to the regular proceedings of any assembly. In the former reign they also committed one of their members to the Tower. But in the famous case of Arthur Hall in 1581, they established the first precedent of punishing one of their own body for a printed libel derogatory to them as a part of the legislature; and they inflicted the threefold penalty of imprisonment, fine, and expulsion.[l] From this time forth it was understood to be the law and usage of parliament that the commons might commit to prison any one of their members for misconduct in the house, or relating to it.[k] *of members for offences—*

---

[l] See vol. 1. pp. 272, 273.

[k] [In the case of Mr. Manley, committed Nov. 9, 1696, for saying, in the debate on sir John Fenwick's attainder, that it would not be the first time people have repented of making their court to the government at the hazard of the liberties of the people, the speaker issued his warrant to the lieutenant of the Tower to receive him. Commons' Journals. It will be remembered that in 1810, on the committal of sir F. Burdett, the governor of the Tower required the speaker's warrant to be backed by the secretary of state; with which the commons thought fit to put up, though it cut at the root of the privilege of imprisoning *proprio jure*.—1845.]

The right of imposing a fine was very rarely asserted after the instance of Hall. But that of expulsion, no earlier precedent whereof has been recorded, became as indubitable as frequent and unquestioned usage could render it. It was carried to a great excess by the long parliament, and again in the year 1680. These, however, were times of extreme violence; and the prevailing faction had an apology in the designs of the court, which required an energy beyond the law to counteract them. The offences too, which the whigs thus punished in 1680, were in their effect against the power and even existence of parliament. The privilege was far more unwarrantably exerted by the opposite party in 1714, against sir Richard Steele, expelled the house for writing The Crisis, a pamphlet reflecting on the ministry. This was, perhaps, the first instance wherein the house of commons so identified itself with the executive administration, independently of the sovereign's person, as to consider itself libelled by those who impugned its measures.^m

In a few instances an attempt was made to carry this farther, by declaring the party incapable of sitting in parliament. It is hardly necessary to remark that upon this rested the celebrated question of the Middlesex election in 1769. If a few precedents, and those not before the year 1680, were to determine all controversies of constitutional law, it is plain enough from the Journals that the house have assumed the power of incapacitation. But as such an authority is highly dangerous and unnecessary for any good purpose, and as, according to all legal rules, so extraordinary a power could not be supported except by a sort of prescription which cannot be shown, the final resolution of the house of commons, which condemned the votes passed in times of great excitement, appears far more consonant to just principles.

2. The power of each house of parliament over those who do not belong to it is of a more extensive consideration, and has lain open, in some respects, to more

---

^m Parl. Hist. vi. 1265. Walpole says, in speaking for Steele, "the liberty of the press is unrestrained; how then shall a part of the legislature dare to punish that as a crime which is not declared to be so by any law framed by the whole?"

doubt than that over its own members. It has been exercised, in the first place, very frequently, and from an early period, in order to protect the members personally, and in their properties, from anything which has been construed to interfere with the discharge of their functions. *[of strangers for offences against members.]* Every obstruction in these duties, by assaulting, challenging, insulting any single representative of the commons, has from the middle of the sixteenth century downwards, that is, from the beginning of their regular Journals, been justly deemed a breach of privilege, and an offence against the whole body. It has been punished generally by commitment, either to the custody of the house's officer, the sergeant-at-arms, or to the king's prison. This summary proceeding is usually defended by a technical analogy to what are called attachments for contempt, by which every court of record is entitled to punish by imprisonment, if not also by fine, any obstruction to its acts or contumacious resistance of them. But it tended also to raise the dignity of parliament in the eyes of the people, at times when the government, and even the courts of justice, were not greatly inclined to regard it; and has been also a necessary safeguard against the insolence of power. The majority are bound to respect, and indeed have respected, the rights of every member, however obnoxious to them, on all questions of privilege. Even in the case most likely to occur in the present age, that of libels, which by no unreasonable stretch come under the head of obstructions, it would be unjust that a patriotic legislator, exposed to calumny for his zeal in the public cause, should be necessarily driven to a troublesome and uncertain process at law, when the offence so manifestly affects the real interests of parliament and the nation. The application of this principle must of course require a discreet temper, which was not perhaps always observed in former times, especially in the reign of William III. Instances at least of punishment for breach of privilege by personal reflections are never so common as in the Journals of that turbulent period.

The most usual mode, however, of incurring the animadversion of the house was by molestations in regard to property. It was the most ancient privilege of the commons to be free from all legal process, during the term of the session and for forty days before and after, except on charges of treason, felony, or breach of the peace. I have elsewhere mentioned the great case of Ferrers, under Henry VIII., wherein the house first, as far as we know, exerted the power of committing to prison those who had been concerned in arresting one of its members; and have shown that, after some little intermission, this became their recognised and customary right. Numberless instances occur of its exercise. It was not only a breach of privilege to serve any sort of process upon them, but to put them under the necessity of seeking redress at law for any civil injury. Thus abundant cases are found in the Journals where persons have been committed to prison for entering on the estates of members, carrying away timber, lopping trees, digging coal, fishing in their waters. Their servants, and even their tenants, if the trespass were such as to affect the landlord's property, had the same protection.[n] The grievance of so unparalleled an immunity must have been notorious, since it not only suspended at least the redress of creditors, but enabled rapacious men to establish in some measure unjust claims in respect of property; the alleged trespasses being generally founded on some disputed right. An act, however, was passed, rendering the members of both houses liable to civil suits during the prorogation of parliament.[o] But they long continued to avenge the private injuries, real or pretended, of their members. On a complaint of breach of privilege by trespassing on a fishery (Jan. 25, 1768), they heard evidence on both sides, and determined that no breach of privilege had been committed; thus indirectly taking on them the decision of a freehold right. A few days after they came to a resolution, "that in case of any complaint of a breach of privilege, hereafter to be made by any member of this house, if the house shall adjudge there is no ground for such complaint, the house will order satisfaction to the person complained

margin: or for offences against the house.

---

[n] The instances are so numerous that to select a few would perhaps give an inadequate notion of the vast extension which privilege received. In fact, hardly anything could be done disagreeable to a member, of which he might not inform the house and cause it to be punished.

[o] 12 Will. III. c. 3.

of for his costs and expenses incurred by reason of such complaint."ᵖ But little opportunity was given to try the effect of this resolution, an act having passed in two years afterwards which has altogether taken away the exemption from legal process, except as to the immunity from personal arrest, which still continues to be the privilege of both houses of parliament.ᑫ

3. A more important class of offences against privilege is of such as affect either house of parliament collectively. In the reign of Elizabeth we have an instance of one committed for disrespectful words against the commons. A few others, either for words spoken or published libels, occur in the reign of Charles I. even before the long parliament; but those of 1641 can have little weight as precedents, and we may say nearly the same of the unjustifiable proceedings in 1680. Even since the Revolution we find too many proofs of encroaching pride or intemperate passion, to which a numerous assembly is always prone, and which the prevalent doctrine of the house's absolute power in matters of privilege has not contributed much to restrain. The most remarkable may be briefly noticed.

The commons of 1701, wherein a tory spirit was strongly predominant, by what were deemed its factious delays in voting supplies, and in seconding the measures of the king for the security of Europe, had exasperated all those who saw the nation's safety in vigorous preparations for war, and provoked at last the lords to the most angry resolution which one house of parliament in a matter not affecting its privileges has ever recorded against the other.ʳ The grand jury of Kent, and other freeholders of the county, presented accordingly a pe-

---

ᵖ Journals, 11th Feb. It had been originally proposed that the member making the complaint should pay the party's costs and expenses, which was amended, I presume, in consequence of some doubt as to the power of the house to enforce it.

ᑫ 10 G. III. c. 50.

ʳ Resolved, That whatever ill consequences may arise from the so long deferring the supplies for the year's service are to be attributed to the fatal counsel of putting off the meeting of a parliament so long, and to unnecessary delays of the house of commons. Lords' Journals, 23rd June, 1701. The commons had previously come to a vote, that all the ill consequences which may at this time attend the delay of the supplies granted by the commons for the preserving the public peace and maintaining the balance of Europe, are to be imputed to those who, to procure an indemnity for their own enormous crimes, have used their utmost endeavours to make a breach between the two houses. Commons' Journals, 20th June.

tition on the 8th of May, 1701, imploring them to turn their loyal addresses into bills of supply (the only phrase in the whole petition that could be construed into disrespect), and to enable his majesty to assist his allies before it should be too late. The tory faction was wrought to fury by this honest remonstrance. They voted that the petition was scandalous, insolent, and seditious, tending to destroy the constitution of parliament, and to subvert the established government of this realm; and ordered that Mr. Colepepper, who had been most forward in presenting the petition, and all others concerned in it, should be taken into custody of the sergeant.* Though no attempt was made on this occasion to call the authority of the house into question by habeas corpus or other legal remedy, it was discussed in pamphlets and in general conversation, with little advantage to a power so arbitrary, and so evidently abused in the immediate instance.¹

Kentish petition of 1701.

* Journals, 8th May; Parl. Hist. v. 1250; Ralph, 947. This historian, who generally affects to take the popular side, inveighs against this petition, because the tories had a majority in the commons. His partiality, arising out of a dislike to the king, is very manifest throughout the second volume. He is forced to admit afterwards that the house disgusted the people by their votes on this occasion. P. 976. [Colepepper having escaped from the custody of the sergeant, the house of commons addressed the king to cause him to be apprehended; upon which he surrendered himself. In the next parliament, which met Dec. 30, 1701, he had been a candidate for Maidstone, and, another being returned, petitioned the house, who, having resolved first in favour of the opposite party, proceeded to vote Colepeper guilty of "scandalous, villanous, and groundless reflections upon the late house of commons;" and, having committed him to Newgate, directed the attorney-general to prosecute him for the said offences. Parl. Hist. v. 1339. Ralph, 1015. Colepepper gave way to this crushing pressure, and having not long afterwards (Parl. Hist. vi. 95) petitioned the house, and acknowledged himself at the bar sorry for the scandalous and seditious practices by him acted against the honour and privileges of that house, &c., they addressed the queen to stop proceedings against him. But a resolution was passed, 16th Feb. 1702, at the same time with others directed against Colepepper, That it is the undoubted right of the people of England to petition or address *the king*, for the calling, sitting, or dissolving of parliaments, or for the redressing of grievances. Parl. Hist. v. 1340.—1845.]

¹ History of the Kentish Petition, Somers Tracts, xi. 242; Legion's Paper, id. 264; Vindication of the Rights of the Commons (either by Harley or sir Humphrey Mackworth), id. 276. This contains in many respects constitutional principles; but the author holds very strong language about the right of petitioning. After quoting the statute of Charles II. against tumults on pretence of presenting petitions, he says, "By this statute it may be observed, that not only the number of persons is restrained, but the occasion also for which they may petition; which is for the alteration of matters established in church or state, for want whereof some inconvenience may arise to that county from which the petition shall be brought. For it is plain by the express words and meaning of that statute that the grievance or matter of the petition must arise in the same county

A very few years after this high exercise of authority, it was called forth in another case, still more remarkable and even less warrantable. The house of commons had an undoubted right of determining all disputed returns to the writ of election, and consequently of judging upon the right

Dispute with lords about Aylesbury election.

as the petition itself. They may indeed petition the king for a parliament to redress their grievances; and they may petition that parliament to make one law that is advantageous, and repeal another that is prejudicial to the trade or interest of that county; but they have no power by this statute, nor by the constitution of the English government, to direct the parliament in the general proceedings concerning the whole kingdom; for the law declares that a general consultation of all the wise representatives of parliament is more for the safety of England than the hasty advice of a number of petitioners of a private county, of a grand jury, or of a few justices of the peace, who seldom have a true state of the case represented to them." P. 313.

These are certainly what must appear in the present day very strange limitations of the subject's right to petition either house of parliament. But it is really true that such a right was not generally recognised, nor frequently exercised, in so large an extent as is now held unquestionable. We may search whole volumes of the Journals, while the most animating topics were in discussion, without finding a single instance of such an interposition of the constituent with the representative body. In this particular case of the Kentish petition, the words in the resolution, that it tended to destroy the constitution of parliament and subvert the established government, could be founded on no pretence but its unusual interference with the counsels of the legislature. With this exception, I am not aware (stating this, however, with some diffidence) of any merely political petition before the septennial bill in 1717, against which several were presented from corporate towns; one of which was rejected on account of language that the house thought indecent; and as to these it may be observed, that towns returning members to parliament had a particular concern in the measure before the house.

They relate, however, no doubt, to general policy, and seem to establish a popular principle which stood on little authority. I do not of course include the petitions to the long parliament in 1640, nor one addressed to the convention, in 1689, from the inhabitants of London and Westminster, pressing their declaration of William and Mary; both in times too critical to furnish regular precedents. [It may be mentioned, however, that, a few months after the Revolution, the city of London added to a petition to have their ancient right of choosing their sheriffs restored to them, a prayer that the king might be enabled to make use of the service of all his protestant subjects; that is, that the test might be abrogated. Parl. Hist. v. 359. It was carried by 174 to 147 that this petition should be read.—1845.] But as the popular principles of government grew more established, the right of petitioning on general grounds seems to have been better recognised; and instances may be found, during the administration of sir Robert Walpole, though still by no means frequent. Parl. Hist. xii. 119. [In the South Sea crisis, 1721, many petitions were presented, praying for justice on the directors. Parl. Hist. vii. 763.—1845.] The city of London presented a petition against the bill for naturalization of the Jews, in 1753, as being derogatory to the Christian religion as well as detrimental to trade. Id. xiv. 1417. It caused however some animadversion; for Mr. Northey, in the debate next session on the proposal to repeal this bill, alluding to this very petition, and to the comments Mr. Pelham made on it, as "so like the famous Kentish petition, that if they had been treated in the same manner it would have been what they deserved," observes in reply, that the "right of petitioning either the king or the parliament in a decent and submissive manner, and without any riotous appearance, against any thing

VOL. III.

of every vote. But as the house could not pretend that it had given this right, or that it was not, like any other franchise, vested in the possessor by a legal title, no pretext of reason or analogy could be set up, for denying that it might also come, in an indirect manner at least, before a court of justice, and be judged by the common principles of law. One Ashby, however, a burgess of Aylesbury, having sued the returning officer for refusing his vote; and three judges of the king's bench, against the opinion of chief-justice Holt, having determined for different reasons that it did not lie, a writ of error was brought in the house of lords, when the judgment was reversed. The house of commons took this up indignantly, and passed various resolutions, asserting their exclusive right to take cognizance of all matters relating to the election of their members. The lords repelled these by contrary resolutions: That by the known laws of this kingdom, every person having a right to give his vote, and being wilfully denied by the officer who ought to receive it, may maintain an action against such officer to recover damage for the injury; That the contrary assertion is destructive of the property of the subject, and tends to encourage corruption and

they think may affect their religion and liberties, will never, I hope, be taken from the subject." Id. xv. 149; see also 376. And it is very remarkable that notwithstanding the violent clamour excited by that unfortunate statute, no petitions for its repeal are to be found in the Journals. They are equally silent with regard to the marriage act, another topic of popular obloquy. Some petitions appear to have been presented against the bill for naturalization of foreign protestants; but probably on the ground of its injurious effect on the parties themselves. The great multiplication of petitions on matters wholly unconnected with particular interests cannot, I believe, be traced higher than those for the abolition of the slave trade in 1787; though a few were presented for reform about the end of the American war, which would undoubtedly have been rejected with indignation in any earlier stage of our constitution. It may be remarked also that petitions against bills imposing duties are not received, probably on the principle that they are intended for the general interests, though affecting the parties who thus complain of them. Hatsell, iii. 200.

The convocation of public meetings for the debate of political questions, as preparatory to such addresses or petitions, is still less according to the practice and precedents of our ancestors; nor does it appear that the sheriffs or other magistrates are more invested with a right of convening or presiding in assemblies of this nature than any other persons; though, within the bounds of the public peace, it would not perhaps be contended that they have ever been unlawful. But that their origin can be distinctly traced higher than the year 1769, I am not prepared to assert. It will of course be understood, that this note is merely historical, and without reference to the expediency of that change in our constitutional theory which it illustrates.

partiality in returning officers; that the declaring persons guilty of breach of privilege for prosecuting such actions, or for soliciting and pleading in them, is a manifest assuming a power to control the law, and hinder the course of justice, and subject the property of Englishmen to the arbitrary votes of the house of commons. They ordered a copy of these resolutions to be sent to all the sheriffs, and to be communicated by them to all the boroughs in their respective counties.

A prorogation soon afterwards followed, but served only to give breathing time to the exasperated parties; for it must be observed, that though a sense of dignity and privilege no doubt swelled the majorities in each house, the question was very much involved in the general whig and tory course of politics. But Ashby, during the recess, having proceeded to execution on his judgment, and some other actions having been brought against the returning officer of Aylesbury, the commons again took it up, and committed the parties to Newgate. They moved the court of king's bench for a habeas corpus; upon the return to which, the judges, except Holt, thought themselves not warranted to set them at liberty against the commitment of the house.ª It was threatened to bring this by writ of error before the lords; and in the disposition of that assembly, it seems probable that they would have inflicted a severe wound on the privileges of the lower house, which must in all probability have turned out a sort of suicide upon their own. But the commons interposed by resolving to commit to prison the counsel and agents concerned in prosecuting the habeas corpus, and by addressing the queen not to grant a writ of error. The queen properly answered, that as this matter, relating to the course of judicial proceedings, was of the highest consequence, she thought it necessary to weigh very carefully what she should do. The lords came to some important resolutions: That neither house of parliament hath any power by any vote or declaration to create to themselves any new privilege that is not warranted by the known laws and customs of parliament; That the house of commons, in committing to Newgate certain persons for prosecuting an action at law, upon pretence that their so doing was

ª State Trials, xiv. 849.

contrary to a declaration, a contempt of the jurisdiction, and a breach of the privileges of that house, have assumed to themselves alone a legislative power, by pretending to attribute the force of law to their declaration, have claimed a jurisdiction not warranted by the constitution, and have assumed a new privilege, to which they can show no title by the law and custom of parliament; and have thereby, as far as in them lies, subjected the rights of Englishmen, and the freedom of their persons, to the arbitrary votes of the house of commons; That every Englishman, who is imprisoned by any authority whatsoever, has an undoubted right to a writ of habeas corpus, in order to obtain his liberty by the due course of law; That for the house of commons to punish any person for assisting a prisoner to procure such a writ is an attempt of dangerous consequence, and a breach of the statutes provided for the liberty of the subject; That a writ of error is not of grace but of right, and ought not to be denied to the subject when duly applied for, though at the request of either house of parliament.

These vigorous resolutions produced a conference between the houses, which was managed with more temper than might have been expected from the tone taken on both sides. But, neither of them receding in the slightest degree, the lords addressed the queen, requesting her to issue the writs of error demanded upon the refusal of the king's bench to discharge the parties committed by the house of commons. The queen answered the same day that she should have granted the writs of error desired by them, but finding an absolute necessity of putting an immediate end to the session, she was sensible there could have been no further proceeding upon them. The meaning of this could only be, that by a prorogation all commitments by order of the lower house of parliament are determined, so that the parties could stand in no need of a habeas corpus. But a great constitutional question was thus wholly eluded.[x]

We may reckon the proceedings against Mr. Alexander Murray, in 1751, among the instances wherein the house of commons has been hurried by passion to

---

[x] Parl. Hist. vi. 225 et post; State Trials, xiv. 695 et post.

an undue violence. This gentleman had been active in a contested Westminster election, on an anti-ministerial and perhaps Jacobite interest. In the course of an inquiry before the house, founded on a petition against the return, the high-bailiff named Mr. Murray as having insulted him in the execution of his duty. The house resolved to hear Murray by counsel in his defence, and the high-bailiff also by counsel in support of the charge, and ordered the former to give bail for his appearance from time to time. These, especially the last, were innovations on the practice of parliament, and were justly opposed by the more cool-headed men. After hearing witnesses on both sides, it was resolved that Murray should be committed to Newgate, and should receive this sentence upon his knees. This command he steadily refused to obey, and thus drew on himself a storm of wrath at such insolence and audacity. But the times were no more, when the commons could inflict whippings and pillories on the refractory; and they were forced to content themselves with ordering that no person should be admitted to him in prison, which, on account of his ill health, they soon afterwards relaxed. The public voice is never favourable to such arbitrary exertions of mere power: at the expiration of the session, Mr. Murray, thus grown from an intriguing Jacobite into a confessor of popular liberty, was attended home by a sort of triumphal procession amidst the applause of the people. In the next session he was again committed on the same charge; a proceeding extremely violent and arbitrary.⁷

<small>Proceedings against Mr. Murray in 1751.</small>

It has been always deemed a most important and essential privilege of the houses of parliament, that they may punish in this summary manner by commitment all those who disobey their orders to attend as witnesses, or for any purposes of their constitutional duties. No inquiry could go forward before the house at large or its committees, without this power to enforce obedience; especially when the information is to be extracted from public officers against the secret wishes of the court. It is equally necessary (or rather more so, since evidence

---

⁷ Parl. Hist. xiv. 838 et post, 1063; Walpole's Memoirs of the last Ten Years of George II., L 15 et post.

not being on oath in the lower house, there can be no punishment in the course of law), that the contumacy or prevarication of witnesses should incur a similar penalty. No man would seek to take away this authority from parliament, unless he is either very ignorant of what has occurred in other times and his own, or is a slave in the fetters of some general theory.

<small>Commitments for offences unconnected with the house.</small> But far less can be advanced for several exertions of power on record in the Journals, which under the name of privilege must be reckoned by impartial men irregularities and encroachments, capable only at some periods of a kind of apology from the unsettled state of the constitution. The commons began, in the famous or infamous case of Floyd, to arrogate a power of animadverting upon political offences, which was then wrested from them by the upper house. But in the first parliament of Charles I. they committed Montagu (afterwards the noted semi-popish bishop) to the serjeant on account of a published book containing doctrines they did not approve.[a] For this was evidently the main point, though he was also charged with reviling two persons who had petitioned the house, which bore a distant resemblance to a contempt. In the long parliament, even from its commencement, every boundary was swept away; it was sufficient to have displeased the majority by act or word; but no precedents can be derived from a crisis of force struggling against force. If we descend to the reign of William III., it will be easy to discover instances of commitments, laudable in their purpose, but of such doubtful legality and dangerous consequence, that no regard to the motive should induce us to justify the precedent. Graham and Burton, the solicitors of the treasury in all the worst state prosecutions under Charles and James, and Jenner, a baron of the exchequer, were committed to the Tower by the council immediately after the king's proclamation, with an intention of proceeding criminally against them. Some months afterwards, the suspension of the habeas corpus, which had taken place by bill, having ceased, they moved the king's bench to admit them to bail; but the house of commons took this up, and, after a report of a

---

[a] Journals, vii 9th July, 1725.

committee as to precedents, put them in custody of the serjeant-at-arms.[a] On complaints of abuses in victualling the navy, the commissioners of that department were sent for in the serjeant's custody, and only released on bail ten days afterwards.[b] But, without minutely considering the questionable instances of privilege that we may regret to find, I will select one wherein the house of commons appear to have gone far beyond either the reasonable or customary limits of privilege, and that with very little pretext of public necessity. In the reign of George I., a newspaper called Mist's Journal was notorious as the organ of the Jacobite faction. A passage full of the most impudent longings for the pretender's restoration having been laid before the house, it was resolved, May 28, 1721, "That the said paper is a false, malicious, scandalous, infamous, and traitorous libel, tending to alienate the affections of his majesty's subjects, and to excite the people to sedition and rebellion, with an intention to subvert the present happy establishment, and to introduce popery and arbitrary power." They went on after this resolution to commit the printer Mist to Newgate, and to address the king that the authors and publishers of the libel might be prosecuted.[c] It is to be observed that no violation of privilege either was, or indeed could be, alleged as the ground of this commitment; which seems to imply that the house conceived itself to be invested with a general power, at least in all political misdemeanors.

I have not observed any case more recent than this of Mist, wherein any one has been committed on a charge which could not possibly be interpreted as a contempt of the house, or a breach of its privilege. It became, however, the practice, without previously addressing the king, to direct a prosecution by the attorney-general for offences of a public nature, which the commons had learned in the course of any inquiry, or which had been formally laid before them.[d] This seems to have been introduced about the beginning of the reign of Anne, and is undoubtedly a far more constitutional course than that of arbitrary punishment by over-straining their

[a] Commons' Journals, 25th Oct. 1699.
[b] Id. 5th Dec.
[c] Parl. Hist. vii. 803.
[d] Lords' Journals, 10th Jun. 1702 Parl. Hist. vi. 21.

privilege. In some instances, libels have been publicly burned by the order of one or other house of parliament.

I have principally adverted to the powers exerted by the lower house of parliament, in punishing those guilty of violating their privileges. It will, of course, be understood that the lords are at least equal in authority. In some respects indeed they have gone beyond. I do not mean that they would be supposed at present to have cognizance of any offence whatever, upon which the commons could not animadvert. Notwithstanding what they claimed in the case of Floyd, the subsequent denial by the commons, and abandonment by themselves, of any original jurisdiction, must stand in the way of their assuming such authority over misdemeanors, more extensively at least than the commons, as has been shown, have in some instances exercised it. But, while the latter have, with very few exceptions, and none since the Restoration, contented themselves with commitment during the session, the lords have sometimes imposed fines, and on some occasions in the reign of George II., as well as later, have adjudged parties to imprisonment for a certain time. In one instance, so late as that reign, they sentenced a man to the pillory; and this had been done several times before. The judgments, however, of earlier ages, give far less credit to the jurisdiction than they take from it. Besides the ever-memorable case of Floyd, one John Blount, about the same time (27th Nov. 1621), was sentenced by the lords to imprisonment and hard labour in Bridewell during life.*

Privileges of the house not controllable by courts of law. It may surprise those who have heard of the happy balance of the English constitution, of the responsibility of every man to the law, and of the security of the subject from all unlimited power, especially as to personal freedom, that this power of awarding punishment at discretion of the houses of parliament is generally reputed to be universal and uncontrollable. This indeed was by no

---

* Hargrave's Juridical Arguments, vol. i. p. 1, &c. [In 1677, the lords having committed one Dr. Cary, for sending to the press a libel, asserting the illegality of the late prorogation, it was taken up warmly by the opposition commoners, on the ground that offences against the government could not be prosecuted in parliament. Nothing, however, was done by the house; so that the lords gained a victory. Parl. Hist. iv. 837.—1345.]

means received at the time when the most violent usurpations under the name of privilege were first made; the power was questioned by the royalist party who became its victims, and among others, by the gallant Welshman, judge Jenkins, whom the long parliament had shut up in the Tower. But it has been several times brought into discussion before the ordinary tribunals; and the result has been, that if the power of parliament is not unlimited in right, there is at least no remedy provided against its excesses.

The house of lords in 1677 committed to the Tower four peers, among whom was the earl of Shaftesbury, for a high contempt; that is, for calling in question, during a debate, the legal continuance of parliament after a prorogation of more than twelve months. Shaftesbury moved the court of king's bench to release him upon a writ of habeas corpus. But the judges were unanimously of opinion that they had no jurisdiction to inquire into a commitment by the lords of one of their body, or to discharge the party during the session, even though there might be, as appears to have been the case, such technical informality on the face of the commitment, as would be sufficient in an ordinary case to set it aside.[f]

Lord Shaftesbury was at this time in vehement opposition to the court. Without insinuating that this had any effect upon the judges, it is certain that a few years afterwards they were less inclined to magnify the privileges of parliament. Some who had been committed, very wantonly and oppressively by the commons in 1680, under the name of abhorrers, brought actions for false imprisonment against Topham, the serjeant-at-arms. In one of these he put in what is called a plea to the jurisdiction, denying the competence of the court of king's bench, inasmuch as the alleged trespass had been done by order of the knights, citizens, and burgesses of parliament. But the judges overruled this plea, and ordered him to plead in bar to the action. We do not find that Topham complied with this; at least judgments appear to have passed against him in these actions.[g] The commons, after the Revolution, entered on the sub-

[f] State Trials, vi. 1369; 1 Modern Reports, 159.   [g] State Trials, xii. 822; T. Jones, Reports, 208.

ject, and summoned two of the late judges, Pemberton and Jones, to their bar. Pemberton answered that he remembered little of the case; but if the defendant should plead that he did arrest the plaintiff by order of the house, and should plead that to the jurisdiction of the king's bench, he thought, with submission, he could satisfy the house that such a plea ought to be overruled, and that he took the law to be so very clearly. The house pressed for his reasons, which he rather declined to give. But on a subsequent day he fully admitted that the order of the house was sufficient to take any one into custody, but that it ought to be pleaded in bar, and not to the jurisdiction, which would be of no detriment to the party, nor affect his substantial defence. It did not appear, however, that he had given any intimation from the bench of so favourable a leaning towards the rights of parliament; and his present language might not uncharitably be ascribed to the change of times. The house resolved that the orders and proceedings of this house, being pleaded to the jurisdiction of the court of king's bench, ought not to be overruled; that the judges had been guilty of a breach of privilege, and should be taken into custody.[b]

I have already mentioned that, in the course of the controversy between the two houses on the case of Ashby and White, the commons had sent some persons to Newgate for suing the returning officer of Aylesbury in defiance of their resolutions; and that, on their application to the king's bench to be discharged on their habeas corpus, the majority of the judges had refused it. Three judges, Powis, Gould, and Powell, held that the courts of Westminster Hall could have no power to judge of the commitments of the houses of parliament; that they had no means of knowing what were the privileges of the commons, and consequently could not know their boundaries; that the law and custom of parliament stood on its own basis, and was not to be decided by the general rules of law; that no one had ever been discharged from such a commitment, which was an argument that it could not be done. Holt, the chief-justice, on the other hand, maintained that no privilege of parliament could destroy a man's right, such

[b] Journals, 10th, 12th, 19th July, 1689.

as that of bringing an action for a civil injury; that neither house of parliament could separately dispose of the liberty and property of the people, which could only be done by the whole legislature; that the judges were bound to take notice of the customs of parliament, because they are part of the law of the land, and might as well be learned as any other part of the law. "It is the law," he said, "that gives the queen her prerogative; it is the law gives jurisdiction to the house of lords, as it is the law limits the jurisdiction of the house of commons." The eight other judges having been consulted, though not judicially, are stated to have gone along with the majority of the court, in holding that a commitment by either house of parliament was not cognizable at law. But from some of the resolutions of the lords on this occasion which I have quoted above, it may seem probable that, if a writ of error had been ever heard before them, they would have leaned to the doctrine of Holt, unless indeed withheld by the reflection that a similar principle might easily be extended to themselves.[1]

It does not appear that any commitment for breach of privilege was disputed until the year 1751, when Mr. Alexander Murray, of whom mention has been made, caused himself to be brought before the court of king's bench on a habeas corpus. But the judges were unanimous in refusing to discharge him. "The house of commons," said Mr. justice Wright, "is a high court, and it is agreed on all hands that they have power to judge of their own privileges; it need not appear to us what the contempt is for; if it did appear, we could not judge thereof."—"This court," said Mr. justice Denison, "has no jurisdiction in the present case. We granted the habeas corpus, not knowing what the commitment was; but now it appears to be for a contempt of the privileges of the house of commons. What the privileges of either house are we do not know; nor need they tell us what the contempt was, because we cannot judge of it; for I must call this court inferior to the commons with respect to judging of their privileges and contempts against them." Mr. justice Foster agreed with the two others, that the house could commit for a

[1] State Trials, xiv. 849.

contempt, which, he said, Holt had never denied in such a case as this before them.[k] It would be unnecessary to produce later cases which have occurred since the reign of George II., and elicited still stronger expressions from the judges of their incapacity to take cognizance of what may be done by the houses of parliament.

Danger of stretching this too far. Notwithstanding such imposing authorities, there have not been wanting some who have thought that the doctrine of uncontrollable privilege is both eminently dangerous in a free country, and repugnant to the analogy of our constitution. The manly language of lord Holt has seemed to rest on better principles of public utility, and even perhaps of positive law.[m] It is not, however, to be inferred that the right of either house of parliament to commit persons, even not of their own body, to prison, for contempts or breaches of privilege, ought to be called in question. In some cases this authority is as beneficial, and even indispensable, as it is ancient and established. Nor do I by any means pretend that if the warrant of commitment merely recites the party to have been guilty of a contempt or breach of privilege, the truth of such allegation could be examined upon a return to a writ of habeas corpus, any more than in an ordinary case of felony. Whatever injustice may thus be done cannot have redress by any legal means; because the house of commons (or the lords, as it may be) are the fit judges of the fact, and must be presumed to have determined it according to right. But it is a more doubtful question, whether, if they should pronounce an offence to be a breach of privilege, as in the case of the Aylesbury

---

[k] State Trials, viii. 30.

[m] This is very elaborately and dispassionately argued by Mr. Hargrave in his Juridical Arguments, above cited: also vol. ii. p. 183. "I understand it," he says, "to be clearly part of the law and custom of parliament that each house of parliament may inquire into and imprison for breaches of privilege." But this he thinks to be limited by law; and after allowing it clearly in cases of obstruction, arrest, assault, &c., on members, admits also that "the judicative power as to writing, speaking, or publishing of gross reflections upon the whole parliament or upon either house, though perhaps originally questionable, seems now of too long a standing and of too much frequency in practice to be well counteracted." But after mentioning the opinions of the judges in Crosby's case, Mr. H. observes: "I am myself far from being convinced that commitment for contempts by a house of parliament, or by the highest court of judicature in Westminster Hall, either ought to be, or are, thus wholly privileged from all examination and appeal."

men, which a court of justice should perceive to be
clearly none, or if they should commit a man on a
charge of misdemeanor, and for no breach of privilege
at all, as in the case of Mist the printer, such excesses
of jurisdiction might not legally be restrained by the
judges. If the resolutions of the lords in the business
of Ashby and White are constitutional and true, neither
house of parliament can create to itself any new privilege; a proposition surely so consonant to the rules of
English law, which require prescription or statute as
the basis for every right, that few will dispute it; and
it must be still less lawful to exercise a jurisdiction
over misdemeanors, by committing a party who would
regularly be only held to bail on such a charge. Of
this I am very certain, that if Mist, in the year 1721,
had applied for his discharge on a habeas corpus, it
would have been far more difficult to have opposed it
on the score of precedent or of constitutional right,
than it was for the attorney-general of Charles I., nearly
one hundred years before, to resist the famous arguments of Selden and Littleton, in the case of the Buck-
inghamshire gentlemen committed by the council. If
a few scattered acts of power can make such precedents
as a court of justice must take as its rule, I am sure the
decision, neither in this case nor in that of ship-money,
was so unconstitutional as we usually suppose: it was
by dwelling on all authorities in favour of liberty, and
by setting aside those which made against it, that our
ancestors overthrew the claims of unbounded prerogative. Nor is this parallel less striking when we look
at the tone of implicit obedience, respect, and confidence with which the judges of the eighteenth century
have spoken of the houses of parliament, as if their
sphere were too low for the cognizance of such a trans-
cendent authority.[a] The same language, almost to the

---

[a] Mr. Justice Gould in Crosby's case, as reported by Wilson, observes: "It is true this court did, in the instance alluded to by the counsel at the bar (Wilkes's case, 2 Wilson, 151), deter- mine upon the privilege of parliament in the case of a libel; but then that privi- lege was promulged and known; it ex- isted in records and law-books, and was allowed by parliament itself. But even *in that case we now know that we were mistaken; for the house of commons have since determined, that privilege does not extend to matters of libel.*" It appears, therefore, that Mr. Justice Gould thought a declaration of the house of commons was better authority than a decision of the court of common pleas, as to a privi- lege which, as he says, existed in records and law-books.

words, was heard from the lips of the Hydes and Berkeleys in the preceding age, in reference to the king and to the privy council. But as, when the spirit of the government was almost wholly monarchical, so since it has turned chiefly to an aristocracy, the courts of justice have been swayed towards the predominant influence; not, in general, by any undue motives, but because it is natural for them to support power, to shun offence, and to shelter themselves behind precedent. They have also sometimes had in view the analogy of parliamentary commitments to their own power of attachment for contempt, which they hold to be equally uncontrollable, a doctrine by no means so dangerous to the subject's liberty, but liable also to no trifling objections.°

The consequences of this utter irresponsibility in each of the two houses will appear still more serious when we advert to the unlimited power of punishment which it draws with it. The commons indeed do not pretend to imprison beyond the session; but the lords have imposed fines and definite imprisonment, and attempts to resist these have been unsuccessful.ᴾ If the matter is to rest upon precedent, or upon what overrides precedent itself, the absolute failure of jurisdiction in the ordinary courts, there seems nothing (decency and discretion excepted) to prevent their repeating the sentences of James I.'s reign, whipping, branding, hard labour for life. Nay, they might order the usher of the black rod to take a man from their bar, and hang him up in the lobby. Such things would not be done, and, being done, would not be endured; but it is much that any sworn ministers of the law should, even by indefinite language, have countenanced the legal possibility of tyrannous power in England. The temper of government itself, in modern times, has generally been mild;

° "I am far from subscribing to all the latitude of the doctrine of attachments for contempts of the king's courts of Westminster, especially the king's bench, as it is sometimes stated, and it has been sometimes practised." Hargrave, ii. 213.

"The principle upon which attachments issue for libels on courts is of a more enlarged and important nature: it is *to keep a blaze of glory around them*, and to deter people from attempting to render them contemptible in the eyes of the people." Wilmot's Opinions and Judgments, p. 270. Yet the king, who seems as much entitled to this blaze of glory as his judges, is driven to the verdict of a jury before the most libellous insult on him can be punished.

ᴾ Hargrave, ubi supra.

and this is probably the best ground of confidence in the discretion of parliament; but popular, that is, numerous bodies, are always prone to excess, both from the reciprocal influences of their passions, and the consciousness of irresponsibility, for which reasons a democracy, that is the absolute government of the majority, is in general the most tyrannical of any. Public opinion, it is true, in this country, imposes a considerable restraint; yet this check is somewhat less powerful in that branch of the legislature which has gone the farthest in chastising breaches of privilege. I would not be understood, however, to point at any more recent discussions on this subject; were it not, indeed, beyond the limits prescribed to me, it might be shown that the house of commons, in asserting its jurisdiction, has receded from much of the arbitrary power which it once arrogated, and which some have been disposed to bestow upon it.q

q [This important topic of parliamentary privilege has been fully discussed, since the first publication of the present volumes, in the well-known proceedings to which the action Stockdale v. Hansard gave rise. In trying this case, lord Denman told the jury, that the order of the house of commons was not a justification for any man to publish a private libel. In consequence of this decision, the house of commons resolved, May 30, 1837, That, by the law and privilege of parliament, this house has the sole and exclusive jurisdiction to determine upon the existence and extent of its privileges, and that the institution or prosecution of any action, suit, or other proceeding, for the purpose of bringing them into discussion or decision, before any court or tribunal elsewhere than in parliament, is a high breach of such privilege, and renders all parties concerned therein amicuable to its just displeasure, and to the punishment consequent thereon. And, That for any court or tribunal to assume to decide upon matters of privilege inconsistent with the determination of either house of parliament, is contrary to the law of parliament, and is a breach and contempt of the privileges of parliament.

Of these resolutions, which, as is obvious, go far beyond what the particular case of Stockdale required, it has been well said, in an excellent pamphlet by Mr. Pemberton Leigh, which really exhausts the subject, and was never so much as tolerably answered, that "The question now is, whether each house of parliament has exclusive authority to decide upon the existence and extent of its own privileges, to pronounce at its pleasure upon the breach of those privileges, to bind by its declaration of law all the queen's subjects, between whom in a court of justice a question as to privilege may arise, and to punish at its discretion all persons, suitors, attorneys, counsel, and judges, who may be concerned in bringing those privileges into discussion in a court of justice directly or indirectly." Pemberton's Letter to Lord Langdale, p. 4.—1837.

In the debates which ensued in the house of commons, those who contended for unlimited privilege fell under two classes: such as availed themselves of the opinions of the eleven judges who dissented from Holt, in Ashby v. White, and of some later dicta; and such as, apparently indifferent to what courts of justice may have held, rested upon some paramount sovereignty of the houses of parliament, some uncontrollable right of exercising discretionary power for the public good, analogous to what was once

IV. It is commonly and justly said that civil liberty is not only consistent with, but in its terms implies, the restrictive limitations of natural liberty which are imposed by law. But, as these are not the less real limitations of liberty, it can hardly be maintained that the subject's condition is not impaired by very numerous restraints upon his will, even without reference to their expediency. The price may be well paid, but it is still a price that it costs some sacrifice to pay. Our statutes have been growing in bulk and multiplicity with the regular session of parliament, and with the new system of government; all abounding with prohibitions and penalties, which every man is presumed to know, but which no man, the judges themselves included, can really know with much exactness. We literally walk amidst the snares and pitfalls of the law. The very doctrine of the more rigid casuists, that men are bound in conscience to observe all the laws of their country, has become impracticable through their complexity and inconvenience; and most of us are content to shift off their penalties in the *mala prohibita* with as little scruple as some feel in risking those of graver offences. But what more peculiarly belongs to the present subject is the systematic encroachment upon ancient constitutional principles, which has for a long time been made through new enactments, proceeding from the crown, chiefly in respect to the revenue.' These may be traced indeed

---

supposed to be vested in the crown. If we but substitute prerogative of the crown for privileges of parliament in the resolutions of 1837, we may ask whether, in the worst times of the Tudors and Stuarts, such a doctrine was ever laid down in express terms by any grave authority. With these there could be no argument; the others had certainly as much right to cite legal authorities in their favour as their opponents.

The commitment of the sheriffs of London, in 1840, for executing a writ of the queen's bench, is recent in our remembrance; as well as that the immediate question was set at rest by a statute, 3 & 4 Vict. c. 9, which legalizes publications under the authority of either house of parliament, leaving, by a special proviso, their privileges as before.

But the main dispute between arbitrary and limited power is by no means determined; and, while great confidence may be placed in the caution which commonly distinguishes the leaders of parties, there will always be found many who, possessing individually a small fraction of despotic power, will not abandon it on any principle of respecting public liberty. It is observable, though easily to be accounted for, and conformable to what occurred in the long parliament, that, among the most strenuous asserters of unmeasured privilege, are generally found many, not celebrated for any peculiar sympathy with the laws, the crown, and the constitution.—1845.]

' This effect of continual new statutes is well pointed out in a speech ascribed to sir William Wyndham, in 1734:—
"The learned gentleman spoke (he says)

in the statute-book, at least as high as the Restoration, and really began in the arbitrary times of revolution which preceded it. They have, however, been gradually extended along with the public burthens, and as the severity of these has prompted fresh artifices of evasion. It would be curious, but not within the scope of this work, to analyze our immense fiscal law, and to trace the history of its innovations. These consist partly in taking away the cognizance of offences against the revenue from juries, whose partiality in such cases there was in truth much reason to apprehend, and vesting it either in commissioners of the revenue itself or in magistrates; partly in anomalous and somewhat arbitrary powers with regard to the collection; partly in deviations from the established rules of pleading and evidence, by throwing on the accused party in fiscal causes the burthen of proving his innocence, or by superseding the necessity of rigorous proof as to matters wherein it is ordinarily required; and partly in shielding the officers of the crown, as far as possible, from their responsibility for illegal actions, by permitting special circumstances of justification to be given in evidence without being pleaded, or by throwing impediments of various kinds in the way of the prosecutor, or by subjecting him to unusual costs in the event of defeat.

These restraints upon personal liberty, and, what is worse, these endeavours, as they seem, to prevent the fair administration of justice between the crown and the subject, have in general, more espe-

Extension of penal laws.

of the prerogative of the crown, and asked us if it had lately been extended beyond the bounds prescribed to it by law. Sir, I will not say that there have been lately any attempts to extend it beyond the bounds prescribed by law; but I will say that these bounds have been of late so vastly enlarged that there seems to be no great occasion for any such attempt. What are the many penal laws made within these forty years, but so many extensions of the prerogative of the crown, and as many diminutions of the liberty of the subject? And whatever the necessity was that brought us into the enacting of such laws, it was a fatal necessity; it has greatly added to the power of the crown, and particular care ought to be taken not to throw any more weight into that scale." Parl. Hist. ix. 463.

Among the modern statutes which have strengthened the hands of the executive power, we should mention the riot act, 1 Geo. I. stat. 2, c. 5, whereby all persons tumultuously assembled to the disturbance of the public peace, and not dispersing within one hour after proclamation made by a single magistrate, are made guilty of a capital felony. I am by no means controverting the expediency of this law; but, especially when combined with the prompt aid of a military force, it is surely a compensation for much that may seem to have been thrown into the popular scale.

cially in modern times, excited little regard as they have passed through the houses of parliament. A sad necessity has overruled the maxims of ancient law; nor is it my business to censure our fiscal code, but to point out that it is to be counted as a set-off against the advantages of the Revolution, and has in fact diminished the freedom and justice which we claim for our polity; and that its provisions have sometimes gone so far as to give alarm to not very susceptible minds, may be shown from a remarkable debate in the year 1737. A bill having been brought in by the ministers to prevent smuggling, which contained some unusual clauses, it was strongly opposed, among other peers, by lord chancellor Talbot himself, of course in the cabinet, and by lord Hardwicke, then chief justice, a regularly-bred crown lawyer, and in his whole life disposed to hold very high the authority of government. They objected to a clause subjecting any three persons travelling with arms to the penalty of transportation, on proof by two witnesses that their intention was to assist in the clandestine landing or carrying away prohibited or uncustomed goods. "We have in our laws," said one of the opposing lords, "no such thing as a crime by implication, nor can a malicious intention ever be proved by witnesses. Facts only are admitted to be proved, and from those facts the judge and jury are to determine with what intention they were committed; but no judge or jury can ever, by our laws, suppose, much less determine, that an action, in itself innocent or indifferent, was attended with a criminal and malicious intention. Another security for our liberties is, that no subject can be imprisoned unless some felonious and high crime be sworn against him. This, with respect to private men, is the very foundation-stone of all our liberties; and if we remove it, if we but knock off a corner, we may probably overturn the whole fabric. A third guard for our liberties is that right which every subject has, not only to provide himself with arms proper for his defence, but to accustom himself to the use of those arms, and to travel with them whenever he has a mind." But the clause in question, it was contended, was repugnant to all the maxims of free government. No presumption of a crime could be drawn from the mere wearing of arms—an act not only innocent, but highly commendable; and therefore the admitting of witnesses to prove that any of these men were armed in order to assist in smuggling, would be the admitting of witnesses to prove an intention which was inconsistent with the whole tenor of our laws.* They objected to another provision, subjecting a party against whom information should be given that he intended to assist in smuggling, to imprisonment without bail, though the offence itself were in its nature bailable; to another which made informations for assault upon officers of the revenue triable in any county of England; and to a yet more startling protection thrown round the same favoured class, that the magistrates should be bound to admit them to bail on charges of killing or wounding any one in the execution of their duty. The bill itself was carried by no great majority; and the provisions subsist at this day, or perhaps have received a further extension.

It will thus appear to every man who takes a comprehensive view of our constitutional history, that the executive government, though shorn of its lustre, has not lost so much of its real efficacy by the consequences of the Revolution as is often supposed—at least that with a regular army to put down insurrection, and an influence sufficient to obtain fresh statutes of restriction, if such should ever be deemed necessary, it is not exposed, in the ordinary course of affairs, to any serious hazard. But we must here distinguish the executive government, using that word in its largest sense, from the crown itself, or the personal authority of the sovereign: this is a matter of rather delicate inquiry, but too material to be passed by.

The real power of the prince, in the most despotic monarchy, must have its limits from nature, and bear some proportion to his courage, his activity, and his intellect. The tyrants of the East become puppets or slaves of their vizirs, or it turns to a game of cunning, wherein the winner is he who shall succeed in tying the bowstring round the other's neck. After some ages of feeble monarchs, the titular royalty is found wholly separated from the power of command, and glides on to posterity in its languid

Diminution of personal authority of the crown.

* 9 Geo. II. c. 35, sect. 10, 13. Parl. Hist. ix. 1729. I quote this as I find it; but probably the expressions are not quite correct, for the reasoning is not so.

channel till some usurper or conqueror stops up the stream for ever. In the civilized kingdoms of Europe, those very institutions which secure the permanence of royal families, and afford them a guarantee against manifest subjection to a minister, take generally out of the hands of the sovereign the practical government of his people. Unless his capacities are above the level of ordinary kings, he must repose on the wisdom and diligence of the statesmen he employs, with the sacrifice, perhaps, of his own prepossessions in policy, and against the bent of his personal affections. The power of a king of England is not to be compared with an ideal absoluteness, but with that which could be enjoyed in the actual state of society by the same person in a less bounded monarchy.

<small>Causes of this.</small>

The descendants of William the Conqueror on the English throne, down to the end of the seventeenth century, have been a good deal above the average in those qualities which enable, or at least induce, kings to take on themselves a large share of the public administration, as will appear by comparing their line with that of the house of Capet, or perhaps most others during an equal period. Without going farther back, we know that Henry VII., Henry VIII., Elizabeth, the four kings of the house of Stuart, though not always with as much ability as diligence, were the master-movers of their own policy, not very susceptible of advice, and always sufficiently acquainted with the details of government to act without it. This was eminently the case also with William III., who was truly his own minister, and much better fitted for that office than those who served him. The king, according to our constitution, is supposed to be present in council, and was in fact usually, or very frequently, present, so long as the council remained as a deliberative body for matters of domestic and foreign policy; but when a junto or cabinet came to supersede that ancient and responsible body, the king himself ceased to preside, and received their advice separately, according to their respective functions of treasurer, secretary, or chancellor, or that of the whole cabinet through one of its leading members. This change, however, was gradual; for cabinet councils were sometimes held in the presence of William and Anne, to which other councillors, not strictly of that select number, were occasionally summoned.

But on the accession of the house of Hanover this personal superintendence of the sovereign necessarily came to an end. The fact is hardly credible that, George I. being incapable of speaking English, as sir Robert Walpole was of conversing in French, the monarch and his minister held discourse with each other in Latin.[1] It is impossible that, with so defective a means of communication (for Walpole, though by no means an illiterate man, cannot be supposed to have spoken readily a language very little familiar in this country), George could have obtained much insight into his domestic affairs, or been much acquainted with the characters of his subjects. We know, in truth, that he nearly abandoned the consideration of both, and trusted his ministers with the entire management of this kingdom, content to employ its great name for the promotion of his electoral interests. This continued in a less degree to be the case with his son, who, though better acquainted with the language and circumstances of Great Britain, and more jealous of his prerogative, was conscious of his incapacity to determine on matters of domestic government, and reserved almost his whole attention for the politics of Germany.

The broad distinctions of party contributed to weaken the real supremacy of the sovereign. It had been usual before the Revolution, and in the two succeeding reigns, to select ministers individually at discretion; and, though some might hold themselves at liberty to decline office, it was by no means deemed a point of honour and fidelity to do so. Hence men in the possession of high posts had no strong bond of union, and frequently took opposite sides on public measures of no light moment. The queen particularly was always loth to discard a servant on account of his vote in parliament—a conduct generous perhaps, but feeble, inconvenient, when carried to such excess, in our constitution, and in effect holding out a reward to ingratitude

Party connexions.

---

[1] Coxe's Walpole, i. 206. H. Walpole's Works, iv. 476. The former, however, seems to rest on H. Walpole's verbal communication, whose want of accuracy, or veracity, or both, is so palpable that no great stress can be laid on his testimony. But I believe that the fact of George I. and his minister conversing in Latin may be proved on other authority.

and treachery. But the whigs having come exclusively into office under the line of Hanover (which, as I have elsewhere observed, was inevitable), formed a sort of phalanx which the crown was not always able to break, and which never could have been broken, but for that internal force of repulsion by which personal cupidity and ambition are ever tending to separate the elements of factions. It became the point of honour among public men to fight uniformly under the same banner, though not perhaps for the same cause—if indeed there was any cause really fought for, but the advancement of a party. In this preference of certain denominations, or of certain leaders, to the real principles which ought to be the basis of political consistency, there was an evident deviation from the true standard of public virtue; but the ignominy attached to the dereliction of friends for the sake of emolument, though it was every day incurred, must have tended gradually to purify the general character of parliament. Meanwhile the crown lost all that party attachments gained,—a truth indisputable on reflection, though, while the crown and the party in power act in the same direction, the relative efficiency of the two forces is not immediately estimated. It was seen, however, very manifestly in the year 1746, when, after long bickering between the Pelhams and lord Granville, the king's favourite minister, the former, in conjunction with a majority of the cabinet, threw up their offices, and compelled the king, after an abortive effort at a new administration, to sacrifice his favourite, and replace those in power whom he could not exclude from it. The same took place in a later period of his reign, when, after many struggles, he submitted to the ascendancy of Mr. Pitt."

" H. Walpole's Memoirs of the last Ten Years. Lord Waldegrave's Memoirs. In this well-written little book, the character of George II., in reference to his constitutional position, is thus delicately drawn: "He has more knowledge of foreign affairs than most of his ministers, and has good general notions of the constitution, strength, and interest of this country; but, being past thirty when the Hanover succession took place, and having since experienced the violence of party, the injustice of popular clamour, the corruption of parliaments, and the selfish motives of pretended patriots, it is not surprising that he should have contracted some prejudices in favour of those governments where the royal authority is under less restraint. Yet prudence has so far prevailed over these prejudices, that they have never influenced his conduct. On the contrary, many laws have been enacted in favour of public liberty; and in the course of a long

It seems difficult for any king of England, however conscientiously observant of the lawful rights of his subjects, and of the limitations they impose on his prerogative, to rest always very content with this practical condition of the monarchy. The choice of his councillors, the conduct of government, are intrusted, he will be told, by the constitution to his sole pleasure; yet both as to the one and the other he finds a perpetual disposition to restrain his exercise of power; and though it is easy to demonstrate that the public good is far better promoted by the virtual control of parliament and the nation over the whole executive government than by adhering to the letter of the constitution, it is not to be expected that the argument will be conclusive to a royal understanding. Hence he may be tempted to play rather a petty game, and endeavour to regain, by intrigue and insincerity, that power of acting by his own will which he thinks unfairly wrested from him. A king of England, in the calculations of politics, is little more than one among the public men of the day—taller indeed, like Saul or Agamemnon, by the head and shoulders, and therefore with no slight advantages in the scramble, but not a match for the many unless he can bring some dexterity to second his strength, and make the best of the

reign there has not been a single attempt to extend the prerogative of the crown beyond its proper limits. He has as much personal bravery as any man, though his political courage seems somewhat problematical: however, it is a fault on the right side; for had he always been as firm and undaunted in the closet as he showed himself at Oudenarde and Dettingen, he might not have proved quite so good a king in this limited monarchy." P. 5. This was written in 1757.

The real tories, those I mean who adhered to the principles expressed by that name, thought the constitutional prerogative of the crown impaired by a conspiracy of its servants. Their notions are expressed in some Letters on the English Nation, published about 1756, under the name of Battista Angeloni, by Dr. Shebbeare, once a Jacobite, and still so bitter an enemy of William III. and George I. that he stood in the pillory, not long afterwards, for a libel on those princes (among other things); on which Horace Walpole justly animadverts, as a stretch of the law by lord Mansfield destructive of all historical truth. Memoirs of the last Ten Years, ii. 328. Shebbeare, however, was afterwards pensioned, along with Johnson, by lord Bute, and, at the time when these letters were written, may possibly have been in the Leicester-house interest. Certain it is, that the self-interested cabal who belonged to that little court endeavoured too successfully to persuade its chief and her son that the crown was reduced to a state of vassalage, from which it ought to be emancipated; and the government of the duke of Newcastle, as strong in party connexion as it was contemptible in ability and reputation, afforded them no bad argument. The consequences are well known, but do not enter into the plan of this work.

self-interest and animosities of those with whom he has to deal; and of this there will generally be so much that in the long run he will be found to succeed in the greater part of his desires: thus George I. and George II., in whom the personal authority seems to have been at the lowest point it has ever reached, drew their ministers, not always willingly, into that course of continental politics which was supposed to serve the purposes of Hanover far better than of England. It is well known that the Walpoles and the Pelhams condemned in private this excessive predilection of their masters for their native country, which alone could endanger their English throne;[x] yet after the two latter brothers had inveighed against lord Granville, and driven him out of power for seconding the king's pertinacity in continuing the war of 1743, they

---

[x] Many proofs of this occur in the correspondence published by Mr. Coxe. Thus Horace Walpole, writing to his brother sir Robert, in 1739, says: "King William had no other object but the liberties and balance of Europe; but, good God! what is the case now? I will tell you in confidence; little, low, partial, electoral notions are able to stop or confound the best-conducted project for the public." Memoirs of sir R. Walpole, iii. 535. The Walpoles had, some years before, disapproved the policy of lord Townshend on account of his favouring the king's Hanoverian prejudices. Id. i. 331. And, in the preceding reign, both these whig leaders were extremely disgusted with the Germanism and continual absence of George I.; Id. ii. 116, 297; though first Townshend, and afterwards Walpole, according to the necessity, or supposed necessity, which controls statesmen, (that is, the fear of losing their places,) became in appearance the passive instruments of royal pleasure.

It is now, however, known that George II. had been induced by Walpole to come into a scheme, by which Hanover, after his decease, was to be separated from England. It stands on the indisputable authority of speaker Onslow. "A little while before sir Robert Walpole's fall, (and as a popular act to save himself, for he went very unwillingly out of his offices and power,) he took me one day aside, and said, 'What will you say, speaker, if this hand of mine shall bring a message from the king to the house of commons, declaring his consent to having any of his family, after his death, to be made, by act of parliament, incapable of inheriting and enjoying the crown, and possessing the electoral dominions at the same time?' My answer was, 'Sir, it will be as a message from heaven.' He replied, 'It will be done.' But it was not done; and I have good reason to believe, it would have been opposed, and rejected at that time, because it came from him, and by the means of those who had always been most clamorous for it; and thus perhaps the opportunity was lost: when will it come again? It was said that the prince at that juncture would have consented to it, if he could have had the credit and popularity of the measure, and that some of his friends were to have moved it in parliament, but that the design at St. James's prevented it. Notwithstanding all this, I have had some thoughts that neither court ever really intended the thing itself; but that it came on and went off, by a jealousy of each other in it, and that both were equally pleased that it did so, from an equal fondness (very natural) for their own native country." Notes on Burnet, (iv. 490. Oxf. edit.) This story has been told before, but not in such a manner as to preclude doubt of its authenticity.

went on themselves in the same track for at least two years, to the imminent hazard of losing for ever the Low Countries and Holland, if the French government, so indiscriminately charged with ambition, had not displayed extraordinary moderation at the treaty of Aix-la-Chapelle. The twelve years that ensued gave more abundant proofs of the submissiveness with which the schemes of George II. for the good of Hanover were received by his ministers, though not by his people; but the most striking instance of all is the abandonment by Mr. Pitt himself of all his former professions in pouring troops into Germany. I do not inquire whether a sense of national honour might not render some of these measures justifiable, though none of them were advantageous; but it is certain that the strong bent of the king's partiality forced them on against the repugnance of most statesmen, as well as of the great majority in parliament and out of it.

Comparatively, however, with the state of prerogative before the Revolution, we can hardly dispute that there has been a systematic diminution of the reigning prince's control, which, though it may be compensated or concealed in ordinary times by the general influence of the executive administration, is of material importance in a constitutional light. Independently of other consequences which might be pointed out as probable or contingent, it affords a real security against endeavours by the crown to subvert or essentially impair the other parts of our government; for though a king may believe himself and his posterity to be interested in obtaining arbitrary power, it is far less likely that a minister should desire to do so. I mean arbitrary, not in relation to temporary or partial abridgments of the subject's liberty, but to such projects as Charles I. and James II. attempted to execute. What indeed might be effected by a king, at once able, active, popular, and ambitious, should such ever unfortunately appear in this country, it is not easy to predict: certainly his reign would be dangerous, on one side or other, to the present balance of the constitution. But against this contingent evil, or the far more probable encroachments of ministers, which, though not going the full length of despotic power, might slowly undermine and contract the rights of the people, no positive statutes can be devised so effectual as the vigilance of the people themselves, and their increased means of knowing and estimating the measures of their government.

Influence of political writings. The publication of regular newspapers, not merely designed for the communication of intelligence, but for the discussion of political topics, may be referred to the latter part of the reign of Anne, when they obtained great circulation, and became the accredited organs of different factions.[y] The tory ministers were annoyed at the vivacity of the press, both in periodical and other writings, which led to a stamp-duty, intended chiefly to diminish their number, and was nearly producing more pernicious restrictions, such as renewing the licensing-act, or compelling authors to acknowledge their names.[z] These, however, did not take place, and the government more honourably coped with their adversaries in the same warfare; nor, with Swift and Bolingbroke on their side, could they require, except indeed through the badness of their cause, any aid from the arm of power.[a]

In a single hour these two great masters of language were changed from advocates of the crown to tribunes of the people; both more distinguished as writers in this altered scene of their fortunes, and certainly among the first political combatants with the weapons of the press whom the world has ever known. Bolingbroke's influence was of course greater in England; and, with all the signal faults of his public character, with all the factiousness which dictated most of his writings, and

---

[y] Upon examination of the valuable series of newspapers in the British Museum, I find very little expression of political feelings till 1710, after the trial of Sacheverell, and change of ministry. The Daily Courant and Postman then begin to attack the Jacobites, and the Post-boy the dissenters. But these newspapers were less important than the periodical sheets, such as the Examiner and Medley, which were solely devoted to party controversy.

[z] A bill was brought in for this purpose in 1712, which Swift, in his History of the Last Four Years, who never printed any thing with his name, naturally blames. It miscarried, probably on account of this provision. Parl. Hist. vi. 1141. But the queen, on opening the session, in April, 1713, recommended some new law to check the licentiousness of the press. Id. 1173. Nothing, however, was done in consequence.

[a] Bolingbroke's letter to the Examiner, in 1710, excited so much attention that it was answered by lord Cowper, then chancellor, in a letter to the Tatler. Somers Tracts, xiii. 75; where sir Walter Scott justly observes, that the fact of two such statesmen becoming the correspondents of periodical publications shows the influence they must have acquired over the public mind.

the indefinite declamation or shallow reasoning which they frequently display, they have merits not always sufficiently acknowledged. He seems first to have made the tories reject their old tenets of exalted prerogative and hereditary right, and scorn the high-church theories which they had maintained under William and Anne. His Dissertation on Parties, and Letters on the History of England, are in fact written on whig principles (if I know what is meant by that name), in their general tendency; however a politician, who had always some particular end in view, may have fallen into several inconsistencies.[b] The same character is due to the Craftsman, and to most of the temporary pamphlets directed against sir Robert Walpole. They teemed, it is true, with exaggerated declamations on the side of liberty; but that was the side they took; it was to generous prejudices they appealed, nor did they ever advert to the times before the Revolution but with contempt or abhorrence. Libels there were indeed of a different class, proceeding from the Jacobite school; but these obtained little regard; the Jacobites themselves, or such as affected to be so, having more frequently espoused that cause from a sense of dissatisfaction with the conduct of the reigning family than from much regard to the pretensions of the other. Upon the whole matter it must be evident to every person who is at all conversant with the publications of George II.'s reign, with the poems, the novels, the essays, and almost all the literature of the time, that what are called the popular or liberal doctrines of government were decidedly prevalent. The supporters themselves of the Walpole and Pelham administrations, though professedly whigs, and tenacious of Revolution principles, made complaints, both in parliament and in pamphlets, of the democratical spirit, the insubordination to authority, the tendency to republican sentiments, which they alleged to have gained ground among the people. It is certain that the tone of popular opinion gave some countenance to these assertions, though much exagge-

---

[b] ["A king of Great Britain," he says in his seventh Letter on the History of England, "is that supreme magistrate who has a negative voice in the legislature." This was in 1731. Nothing can be more unlike the original tone of toryism.—1845.]

rated, in order to create alarm in the aristocratical classes and furnish arguments against redress of abuses.

Publication of debates. The two houses of parliament are supposed to deliberate with closed doors. It is always competent for any one member to insist that strangers be excluded; not on any special ground, but by merely enforcing the standing order for that purpose. It has been several times resolved that it is a high breach of privilege to publish any speeches or proceedings of the commons;[c] though they have since directed their own votes and resolutions to be printed. Many persons have been punished by commitment for this offence; and it is still highly irregular, in any debate, to allude to the reports in newspapers, except for the purpose of animadverting on the breach of privilege.[d] Notwithstanding this pretended strictness, notices of the more interesting discussions were frequently made public; and entire speeches were sometimes circulated by those who had sought popularity in delivering them. After the accession of George I. we find a pretty regular account of debates in an annual publication, Boyer's Historical Register, which was continued to the year 1737. They were afterwards published monthly, and much more at length, in the London and the Gentleman's Magazines; the latter, as is well known, improved by the pen of Johnson, yet not so as to lose by any means the leading

---

[c] [The first instance seems to be Dec. 27th, 1694, when it is resolved, that no news-letter writers do, in their letters or other papers which they disperse, presume to intermeddle with the debates or other proceedings of this house. Journals.—1845.]

[d] It was resolved, nem. con., Feb. 26th, 1729, That it is an indignity to, and a breach of the privilege of, this house, for any person to presume to give, in written or printed newspapers, any account or minutes of the debates, or other proceedings of this house, or of any committee thereof; and that upon discovery of the authors, &c., this house will proceed against the offenders with the utmost severity. Parl. Hist. viii. 683. There are former resolutions to the same effect. The speaker having himself brought the subject under consideration some years afterwards, in 1738, the resolution was repeated in nearly the same words, but after a debate wherein, though no one undertook to defend the practice, the danger of impairing the liberty of the press was more insisted upon than would formerly have been usual; and sir Robert Walpole took credit to himself, justly enough, for respecting it more than his predecessors. Id. x. 800. Coxe's Walpole, i. 572. Edward Cave, the well-known editor of the Gentleman's Magazine, and the publisher of another Magazine were brought to the bar, April 30th, 1747, for publishing the house's debates; when the former denied that he retained any person in pay to make the speeches, and after expressing his contrition was discharged on payment of fees. Id. xlv. 57.

scope of the arguments. It follows of course that the restriction upon the presence of strangers had been almost entirely dispensed with. A transparent veil was thrown over this innovation by disguising the names of the speakers, or more commonly by printing only initial and final letters. This ridiculous affectation of concealment was extended to many other words in political writings, and had not wholly ceased in the American war.

It is almost impossible to overrate the value of this regular publication of proceedings in parliament, carried as it has been in our own time to nearly as great copiousness and accuracy as is probably attainable. It tends manifestly and powerfully to keep within bounds the supineness and negligence, the partiality and corruption, to which every parliament, either from the nature of its composition or the frailty of mankind, must more or less be liable. Perhaps the constitution would not have stood so long, or rather would have stood like an useless and untenanted mansion, if this unlawful means had not kept up a perpetual intercourse, a reciprocity of influence, between the parliament and the people. A stream of fresh air, boisterous perhaps sometimes as the winds of the north, yet as healthy and invigorating, flows in to renovate the stagnant atmosphere, and to prevent that *malaria* which self-interest and oligarchical exclusiveness are always tending to generate. Nor has its importance been less perceptible in affording the means of vindicating the measures of government, and securing to them, when just and reasonable, the approbation of the majority among the middle ranks, whose weight in the scale has been gradually increasing during the last and present centuries.

This augmentation of the democratical influence, using that term as applied to the commercial and industrious classes in contradistinction to the territorial aristocracy, was the slow but certain effect of accumulated wealth and diffused knowledge, acting, however, on the traditional notions of freedom and equality which had ever prevailed in the English people. The nation, exhausted by the long wars of William and Anne, recovered strength in thirty years of peace that ensued; and in that period, especially

Increased influence of the middle ranks.

under the prudent rule of Walpole, the seeds of our commercial greatness were gradually ripened. It was evidently the most prosperous season that England had ever experienced; and the progression, though slow, being uniform, the reign perhaps of George II. might not disadvantageously be compared, for the real happiness of the community, with that more brilliant but uncertain and oscillatory condition which has ensued. A distinguished writer has observed that the labourer's wages have never, at least for many ages, commanded so large a portion of subsistence as in this part of the eighteenth century.[e] The public debt, though it excited alarms, from its magnitude, at which we are now accustomed to smile, and though too little care was taken for redeeming it, did not press very heavily on the nation, as the low rate of interest evinces, the government securities at three per cent. having generally stood above par. In the war of 1743, which from the selfish practice of relying wholly on loans did not much retard the immediate advance of the country, and still more after the peace of Aix-la-Chapelle, a striking increase of wealth became perceptible.[f] This was shown in one circumstance directly affecting the character of the constitution. The smaller boroughs, which had been from the earliest time under the command of neighbouring peers and gentlemen, or sometimes of the crown, were attempted by rich capitalists, with no other connexion or recommendation than one which is generally sufficient.[g] This appears to have been first observed in the general elections of 1747 and 1754;[h] and though the prevalence of bribery is attested by the statute-book and

[e] Malthus, Principles of Political Economy (1820), p. 279.

[f] Macpherson (or Anderson), Hist. of Commerce. Chalmers's Estimate of Strength of Great Britain. Sinclair's Hist. of Revenue, *cum multis aliis.*

[g] [The practice of *treating* at elections, not with the view of obtaining votes, but as joyous hospitality, though carried to a ruinous extent, began with the country gentlemen themselves, and is complained of soon after the Restoration. Perhaps it was not older, at least so as to attract notice. Evelyn tells us of a county election which cost 2000*l*. In mere eating and drinking. The treating act, 7 W. III., c. 4, is very stringent in its provisions, and has dispossessed many of their seats on petition. Bribery came from a different quarter. Swift speaks, in the Examiner, of "influencing distant boroughs by powerful motives from the city."—1848.]

[h] Tindal, apud Parl. Hist. xiv. 66. I have read the same in other books, but know not at present where to search for the passages. Hogarth's pictures of the Election are evidence to the corruption in his time, so also are some of Smollett's novels. Addison, Swift, and Pope would

the journals of parliament from the Revolution, it seems not to have broken down all flood-gates till near the end of the reign of George II. But the sale of seats in parliament, like any other transferable property, is never mentioned in any book that I remember to have seen of an earlier date than 1760. We may dispense therefore with the inquiry in what manner this extraordinary traffic has affected the constitution, observing only that its influence must have tended to counteract that of the territorial aristocracy, which is still sufficiently predominant. The country gentlemen, who claimed to themselves a character of more independence and patriotism than could be found in any other class, had long endeavoured to protect their ascendancy by excluding the rest of the community from parliament. This was the principle of the bill which, after being frequently attempted, passed into a law during the tory administration of Anne, requiring every member of the commons, except those for the universities, to possess, as a qualification for his seat, a landed estate, above all incumbrances, of 300*l*. a year.[i] By a later act of George II., with which it was thought expedient by the government of the day to gratify the landed interest, this property must be stated on oath by every member on taking his seat, and, if required, at his election.[k] The law is, however, notoriously evaded; and, though much might be urged in favour of rendering a competent income the condition of eligibility, few would be found at present to maintain that the freehold qualification is not required both unconstitutionally, according to the ancient

not have neglected to lash this vice if it had been glaring in their age; which shews that the change took place about the time I have mentioned. [This is not quite accurately stated; both the election of strangers by boroughs, and its natural concomitant, bribery, had begun to excite complaint by their increasing frequency, as early as the reign of George I., and led to the act rendering elections void, and inflicting severe penalties, for bribery, in 1728. But still it is true that in the general election of 1747 much more of it took place than ever before.—1845.]

[i] 9 Anne, c. 5. A bill for this purpose had passed the commons in 1696; the city of London and several other places petitioning against it. Journals, Nov. 21, &c. The house refused to let some of these petitions be read: I suppose on the ground that they related to a matter of general policy. These towns, however, had a very fair pretext for alleging that they were interested; and in fact a rider was added to the bill, that any merchant might serve for a place where he should be himself a voter, on making oath that he was worth 5000*l*. Id. Dec. 19.

[k] 33 G. II. c. 20.

theory of representation, and absurdly, according to the present state of property in England. But I am again admonished, as I have frequently been in writing these last pages, to break off from subjects that might carry me too far away from the business of this history; and, content with compiling and selecting the records of the past, to shun the difficult and ambitious office of judging the present, or of speculating upon the future.

CHAPTER XVII.

ON THE CONSTITUTION OF SCOTLAND.

Early State of Scotland — Introduction of Feudal System — Scots Parliament — Power of the Aristocracy — Royal Influence in Parliament — Judicial Power — Court of Session — Reformation — Power of the Presbyterian Clergy — Their Attempts at Independence on the State — Andrew Melville — Success of James VI. in restraining them — Establishment of Episcopacy — Innovations of Charles I. — Arbitrary Government — Civil War — Tyrannical Government of Charles II. — Reign of James VII. — Revolution and Establishment of Presbytery — Reign of William III. — Act of Security — Union — Gradual Decline of Jacobitism.

IT is not very profitable to inquire into the constitutional antiquities of a country which furnishes no authentic historian, nor laws, nor charters, to guide our research, as is the case with Scotland before the twelfth century. The latest and most laborious of her antiquaries appears to have proved that her institutions were wholly Celtic until that era, and greatly similar to those of Ireland.[m] A total, though probably gradual, change must therefore have taken place in the next age, brought about by means which have not been satisfactorily explained. The crown became strictly hereditary, the governors of districts took the appellation of earls, the whole kingdom was subjected to a feudal tenure, the Anglo-Norman laws, tribunals, local and municipal magistracies were introduced as far as the royal influence could prevail; above all, a surprising number of families, chiefly Norman, but some of Saxon or Flemish descent, settled upon estates granted by the kings of Scotland, and became the founders of its aristocracy. It was, as truly as some time afterwards in Ireland, the encroachment of a Gothic and feudal polity upon the inferior civilisation of the Celts, though accomplished with far less resistance, and

Early state of Scotland.

Introduction of feudal system.

---

[m] Chalmers's Caledonia vol. i. passim.

not quite so slowly. Yet the Highland tribes long adhered to their ancient usages; nor did the laws of English origin obtain in some other districts two or three centuries after their establishment on both sides of the Forth.[a]

It became almost a necessary consequence from this adoption of the feudal system and assimilation to the English institutions, that the kings of Scotland would have their general council or parliament upon nearly the same model as that of the Anglo-Norman sovereigns they so studiously imitated. If the statutes ascribed to William the Lion, contemporary with our Henry II., are genuine, they were enacted, as we should expect to find, with the concurrence of the bishops, abbots, barons, and other good men (probi homines) of the land; meaning doubtless the inferior tenants in capite.[o] These laws, indeed, are questionable, and there is a great want of unequivocal records till almost the end of the thirteenth century. The representatives of boroughs are first distinctly mentioned in 1326, under Robert I.; though some have been of opinion that vestiges of their appearance in parliament may be traced higher; but they are not enumerated among the classes present in one held in 1315.[p] In the ensuing reign of David II., the three estates of the realm are expressly mentioned as the legislative advisers of the crown.[q]

A Scots parliament resembled an English one in the mode of convocation, in the ranks that composed it, in the enacting powers of the king, and the necessary consent of the three estates; but differed in several very important respects. No freeholders, except tenants in capite, had ever any right of suffrage; which may, not improbably, have been in some measure owing to the want of that Anglo-Saxon institution, the county-court. These feudal tenants of the crown came in person to parliament, as they did in England till the reign of Henry III., and sat together with the prelates and barons in one chamber. A prince arose in Scotland in the first part of the fifteenth century, resembling the English

---

[a] Chalmers's Caledonia, vol. 1. p. 500 et post; Dalrymple's Annals of Scotland, 29, 30, &c.

[o] Chalmers, 741; Wight's Law of Election in Scotland. 28.

[p] Id. 25; Dalrymple's Annals, f. 139, 235, 283; ii. 55, 116; Chalmers, 743 Wight thinks they may perhaps only have had a voice in the imposition of taxes

[q] Dalrymple, ii. 241; Wight, 26.

Justinian in his politic regard to strengthening his own prerogative and to maintaining public order. It was enacted by a law of James I., in 1427, that the smaller barons and free tenants "need not to come to parliament, so that of every sheriffdom there be sent two or more wise men, chosen at the head court," to represent the rest. These were to elect a speaker, through whom they were to communicate with the king and other estates.ʳ This was evidently designed as an assimilation to the English house of commons. But the statute not being imperative, no regard was paid to this permission; and it is not till 1587 that we find the representation of the Scots counties finally established by law; though one important object of James's policy was never attained, the different estates of parliament having always voted promiscuously, as the spiritual and temporal lords in England.

But no distinction between the national councils of the two kingdoms was more essential than what appears to have been introduced into the Scots parliament under David II. In the year 1367 a parliament having met at Scone, a committee was chosen by the three estates, who seem to have had full powers delegated to them, the others returning home on account of the advanced season. The same was done in one held next year without any assigned pretext. But in 1369 this committee was chosen only to prepare all matters determinable in parliament, or fit to be therein treated, for the decision of the three estates on the last day but one of the session.⁎ The former scheme appeared possibly, even to those careless and unwilling legislators, too complete an abandonment of their function. But even modified as it was in 1369, it tended to devolve the whole business of parliament on this elective committee, subsequently known by the appellation of lords of the articles. It came at last to be the general practice, though some exceptions to this rule may be found, that nothing was laid before parliament without their previous recommendation; and there seems reason to think that in the first parliament of James I., in 1424, such full powers were delegated to the committee as

Power of the aristocracy.

ʳ Statutes of Scotland, 1427; Pinkerton's History of Scotland, I. 120; Wight, 30.

⁎ Dalrymple, ii. 261; Stuart on Public Law of Scotland, 344; Robertson's History of Scotland, i. 84.

had been granted before in 1367 and 1368, and that the three estates never met again to sanction their resolutions.' The preparatory committee is not uniformly mentioned in the preamble of statutes made during the reign of this prince and his two next successors; but there may be no reason to infer from thence that it was not appointed. From the reign of James IV. the lords of articles are regularly named in the records of every parliament."

It is said that a Scots parliament, about the middle of the fifteenth century, consisted of near one hundred and ninety persons.* We do not find, however, that more than half this number usually attended. A list of those present in 1472 gives but fourteen bishops and abbots, twenty-two earls and barons, thirty-four lairds or lesser tenants in capite, and eight deputies of boroughs.' The royal boroughs entitled to be represented in parliament were above thirty; but it was a common usage to choose the deputies of other towns as their proxies.* The great object with them, as well as with the lesser barons, was to save the cost and trouble of attendance. It appears indeed that they formed rather an insignificant portion of the legislative body. They are not named as consenting parties in several of the statutes of James III.; and it seems that on some occasions they had not 'been summoned to parliament, for an act was passed in 1504, " that the commissaries and headmen of the burghs be warned when taxes or constitutions are given, to have their advice therein, as one of the three estates of the

---

t Wight, 62, 65.

u Id. 69. [A remarkable proof of the trust vested in the lords of articles will be found in the Scots Statutes, vol. ii. p. 340, which is not noticed by Pinkerton. Power was given to the lords of articles, after a prorogation of parliament in 1535, " to make acts, statutes, and constitutions for good rule, justice, and policy, conform to the articles to be given by the king's grace, and as shall please any other to give and present to them. And whatever they ordain or statute to have the same form, strength, and effect as if the same were made and statute by all the three estates being personally present. And if any greater matter occurs, that please his grace to have the greatest of his prelates' and barons' counsel, he shall advertise them thereof, by his special writings, to convene such day and place as he shall think most expedient." These lords of articles even granted a tax.—1845.]

x Pinkerton, i. 373.

y Id. 360. [In 1478 we find 24 spiritual and 32 temporal lords, with 22 tenants in capite, or lairds, and 201 commissioners of burghs. This was unusually numerous. But, as Robertson observes, in the reign of James III., public indignation brought to parliament many lesser barons and burgesses who were wont to stay away in peaceable times. Hist. of Scotland, i. 246.—1845.]

z Id. 372.

realm."[a] This, however, is an express recognition of their right, though it might have been set aside by an irregular exercise of power.

It was a natural result from the constitution of a Scots parliament, together with the general state of society in that kingdom, that its efforts were almost uniformly directed to augment and invigorate the royal authority. Their statutes afford a remarkable contrast to those of England in the absence of provisions against the exorbitancies of prerogative.[b] Robertson has observed that the kings of Scotland, from the time at least of James I., acted upon a steady system of repressing the aristocracy; and though this has been called too refined a supposition, and attempts have been made to explain otherwise their conduct, it seems strange to deny the operation of a motive so natural, and so readily to be inferred from their measures. The causes so well pointed out by this historian, and some that might be added; the defensible nature of great part of the country; the extensive possessions of some powerful families; the influence of feudal tenure and Celtic clanship; the hereditary jurisdictions, hardly controlled, even in theory, by the supreme tribunals of the crown; the custom of entering into bonds of association for mutual defence; the frequent minorities of the reigning princes; the necessary abandonment of any strict regard to monarchical supremacy during the struggle for

Royal influence in parliament.

---

[a] Pinkerton, ii. 83.

[b] In a statute of James II. (1440), "the three estates conclude *that it is speedful* that our sovereign lord the king ride throughout the realm incontinent as shall be seen to the council where any rebellion, slaughter, burning, robbery, outrage, or theft has happened," &c. Statutes of Scotland, ii. 32. Pinkerton (L 192), leaving out the words in italics, has argued on false premises. "In this singular decree we find the legislative body regarding the king in the modern light of a chief magistrate, bound equally with the meanest subject to obedience to the laws," &c. It is evident that the estates spoke in this instance as councillors, not as legislators. This is merely an oversight of a very well informed historian, who is by no means in the trammels of any political theory.

A remarkable expression, however, is found in a statute of the same king, in 1450; which enacts that any man rising in war against the king, or receiving such as have committed treason, or holding houses against the king, or assaulting castles or places where the king's power shall happen to be, *without the consent of the three estates*, shall be punished as a traitor. Pinkerton, i. 213. I am inclined to think that the legislators had in view the possible recurrence of what had very lately happened, that an ambitious cabal might get the king's person into their power. The peculiar circumstances of Scotland are to be taken into account when we consider these statutes, which are not to be looked at as mere insulated texts.

independence against England; the election of one great nobleman to the crown, and its devolution upon another; the residence of the two first of the Stuart name in their own remote domains; the want of any such effective counterpoise to the aristocracy as the sovereigns of England possessed in its yeomanry and commercial towns; all these together placed the kings of Scotland in a situation which neither for their own nor their people's interest they could be expected to endure. But an impatience of submitting to the insolent and encroaching temper of their nobles drove James I. (before whose time no settled scheme of reviving the royal authority seems to have been conceived) and his two next descendants into some courses which, though excused or extenuated by the difficulties of their position, were rather too precipitate and violent, and redounded at least to their own destruction. The reign of James IV., from his accession in 1488 to his unhappy death at Flodden, in 1513, was the first of tolerable prosperity; the crown having by this time obtained no inconsiderable strength, and the course of law being somewhat more established, though the aristocracy were abundantly capable of withstanding any material encroachment upon their privileges.

Though subsidies were of course occasionally demanded, yet from the poverty of the realm and the extensive domains which the crown retained, they were much less frequent than in England, and thus one principal source of difference was removed; nor do we read of any opposition in parliament to what the lords of articles thought fit to propound. Those who disliked the government stood aloof from such meetings, where the sovereign was in his vigour, and had sometimes crushed a leader of faction by a sudden stroke of power; confident that they could better frustrate the execution of laws than their enactment, and that questions of right and privilege could never be tried so advantageously as in the field. Hence it is, as I have already observed, that we must not look to the statute-book of Scotland for many limitations of monarchy. Even in one of James II., which enacts that none of the royal domains shall for the future be alienated, and that the king and his successors shall be sworn to observe this law, it may be conjectured that a provision rather derogatory in semblance to the king's dignity was introduced by his own suggestion as an additional security against the importunate solicitations of the aristocracy whom the statute was designed to restrain.[c] The next reign was the struggle of an imprudent and, as far as his means extended, despotic prince against the spirit of his subjects. In a parliament of 1487, we find almost a solitary instance of a statute that appears to have been directed against some illegal proceedings of the government. It is provided that all civil suits shall be determined by the ordinary judges, and not before the king's council.[d] James III. was killed the next year in attempting to oppose an extensive combination of the rebellious nobility. In the reign of James IV., the influence of the aristocracy shows itself rather more in legislation; and two peculiarities deserve notice, in which, as it is said, the legislative authority of a Scots parliament was far higher than that of our own. They were not only often consulted about peace or war, which in some instances was the case in England, but, at least in the sixteenth century, their approbation seems to have been necessary.[e] This, though not consonant to our modern notions, was certainly no more than the genius of the feudal system and the character of a great deliberative council might lead us to expect; but a more remarkable singularity was, that what had been propounded by the lords of articles, and received the ratification of the three estates, did not require the king's consent to give it complete validity. Such at least is said to have been the Scots constitution in the time of James VI.; though we may demand very full proof of such an anomaly, which the language of their statutes, expressive of the king's enacting power, by no means leads us to infer.[f]

The kings of Scotland had always their aula or curia regis, claiming a supreme judicial authority, at least in some causes, though it might be difficult to determine its boundaries, or how far they were respected. They had also bailiffs to administer justice in their own domains, and sheriffs in every county for the same purpose, wherever grants of regality did not exclude their jurisdiction. These regalities were here-

Judicial power.

[c] Pinkerton. 1. 234.
[d] Statutes of Scotland, ii. 177.
[e] Pinkerton, ii. 268.
[f] Pinkerton, i. 400; Laing, iii. 32.

ditary and territorial; they extended to the infliction of capital punishment; the lord possessing them might reclaim or repledge (as it was called, from the surety he was obliged to give that he would himself do justice) any one of his vassals who was accused before another jurisdiction. The barons, who also had cognizance of most capital offences, and the royal boroughs enjoyed the same privilege. An appeal lay, in civil suits, from the baron's court to that of the sheriff or lord of regality, and ultimately to the parliament, or to a certain number of persons to whom it delegated its authority.[g] This appellant jurisdiction of parliament, as well as that of the king's privy council, which was original, came, by a series of provisions from the year 1425 to 1532, into the hands of a supreme tribunal thus gradually constituted in its present form, the court of session. It was composed of fifteen judges, half of whom, besides the president, were at first churchmen, and soon established an entire subordination of the local courts in all civil suits. But it possessed no competence in criminal proceedings; the hereditary jurisdictions remained unaffected for some ages, though the king's two justiciaries, replaced afterwards by a court of six judges, went their circuits even through those counties wherein charters of regality had been granted. Two remarkable innovations seem to have accompanied, or to have been not far removed in time from, the first formation of the court of session; the discontinuance of juries in civil causes, and the adoption of so many principles from the Roman law as have given the jurisprudence of Scotland a very different character from our own.[h]

In the reign of James V. it might appear probable that by the influence of laws favourable to public order, better enforced through the council and court of session than before, by the final subjugation of the house of Douglas and of the earls of Ross in the North, and some slight increase of wealth in the towns, conspiring with the general tendency of the sixteenth century throughout Europe, the feudal spirit would be weakened and kept under in Scotland, or display itself only in a parlia-

---

[g] Kalms's Law Tracts; Pinkerton, i. 158, et alibi; Stuart on Public Law of Scotland. History of Scotland, i. 117, 237, 388; ii. 313; Robertson, i. 43; Stuart on Law of Scotland.

[h] Kalms's Law Tracts; Pinkerton's

mentary resistance to what might become in its turn dangerous, the encroachments of arbitrary power. But immediately afterwards a new and unexpected impulse was given; religious zeal, so blended with the ancient spirit of aristocratic independence that the two motives are scarcely distinguishable, swept before it in the first whirlwind almost every vestige of the royal sovereignty. The Roman catholic religion was abolished with the forms indeed of a parliament, but of a parliament not summoned by the crown, and by acts that obtained not its assent. The Scots church had been immensely rich; its riches had led, as everywhere else, to neglect of duties and dissoluteness of life; and these vices had met with their usual punishment in the people's hatred.[1] . The reformed doctrines gained a more rapid and general ascendancy than in England, and were accompanied with a more strenuous and uncompromising enthusiasm. It is probable that no sovereign retaining a strong attachment to the ancient creed would long have been permitted to reign; and Mary is entitled to every presumption, in the great controversy that belongs to her name, that can reasonably be founded on this admission. But without deviating into that long and intricate discussion, it may be given as the probable result of fair inquiry that to impeach the characters of most of her adversaries would be a far easier task than to exonerate her own.[k]

Reformation.

---

[1] Robertson, i. 149; M'Crie's Life of Knox, p. 15. At least one-half of the wea.th of Scotland was in the hands of the clergy, chiefly of a few individuals. Ibid. [Robertson thinks that James V. favoured the clergy as a counterpoise to the aristocracy, which may account for the eagerness of the latter, generally, in the reformation. History of Scotland, i. 88.—1845.]

[k] I have read a good deal on this celebrated controversy; but where so much is disputed it is not easy to form an opinion on every point. But, upon the whole, I think there are only two hypotheses that can be advanced with any colour of reason. The first is, that the murder of Darnley was projected by Bothwell, Maitland, and some others, without the queen's express knowledge, but with a reliance on her passion for the former, which would lead her both to shelter him from punishment, and to raise him to her bed; and that, in both respects, this expectation was fully realised by a criminal connivance at the escape of one whom she must believe to have been concerned in her husband's death, and by a still more infamous marriage with him. This, it appears to me, is a conclusion that may be drawn by reasoning on admitted facts, according to the common rules of presumptive evidence. The second supposition is, that she had given a previous consent to the assassination. This is rendered probable by several circumstances, and especially by the famous letters and sonnets, the genuineness of which has been so warmly disputed. I must confess that they seem

The history of Scotland from the reformation assumes a character, not only unlike that of preceding times, but to which there is no parallel in modern ages. It became a contest, not between the crown and the feudal aristocracy, as before, nor between the asserters of prerogative and of privilege, as in England, nor between the possessors of established power and those who deemed themselves oppressed by it, as is the usual source of civil discord, but between the temporal and spiritual authorities, the crown and the church—that in general supported by the legislature, this sustained by the voice of the people. Nothing of this kind, at least in anything like so great a degree, has occurred in other protestant countries—the Anglican church being, in its original constitution, bound up with the state as one of its component parts, but subordinate to the whole; and the ecclesiastical order in the kingdoms and commonwealths of the Continent being either destitute of temporal authority or at least subject to the civil magistrate's supremacy.

Power of the presbyterian clergy.

Knox, the founder of the Scots reformation, and those who concurred with him, both adhered to the theological system of Calvin, and to the scheme of polity he had introduced at Geneva, with such modifications as became necessary from the greater scale on which it was to be practised. Each parish had its minister, lay-elder, and deacon, who held their kirk-session for spiritual jurisdiction and other purposes; each ecclesiastical province its synod of ministers

Their attempts at independence on the state.

---

to me authentic, and that Mr. Laing's dissertation on the murder of Darnley has rendered Mary's innocence, even as to participation in that crime, an untenable proposition. No one of any weight, I believe, has asserted it since his time, except Dr. Lingard, who manages the evidence with his usual adroitness, but by admitting the general authenticity of the letters, qualified by a mere conjecture of interpolation, has given up what his predecessors deemed the very key of the citadel.

I shall dismiss a subject so foreign to my purpose with remarking a fallacy which affects almost the whole argument of Mary's most strenuous advocates. They seem to fancy that if the earls of Murray and Morton, and secretary Maitland of Lethington, can be proved to have been concerned in Darnley's murder, the queen herself is at once absolved. But it is generally agreed that Maitland was one of those who conspired with Bothwell for this purpose; and Morton, if he were not absolutely consenting, was, by his own acknowledgment at his execution, apprised of the conspiracy. With respect to Murray indeed there is not a shadow of evidence, nor had he any probable motive to second Bothwell's schemes; but, even if his participation were presumed, it would not alter in the slightest degree the proofs as to the queen.

and delegated elders presided over by a superintendent; but the supreme power resided in the general assembly of the Scots church, constituted of all ministers of parishes, with an admixture of delegated laymen, to which appeals from inferior judicatories lay, and by whose determinations or canons the whole were bound. The superintendents had such a degree of episcopal authority as seems implied in their name, but concurrently with the parochial ministers, and in subordination to the general assembly; the number of these was designed to be ten, but only five were appointed.[m] This form of church polity was set up in 1560; but according to the irregular state of things at that time in Scotland, though fully admitted and acted upon, it had only the authority of the church, with no confirmation of parliament, which seems to have been the first step of the former towards the independency it came to usurp. Meanwhile it was agreed that the Roman catholic prelates, including the regulars, should enjoy two-thirds of their revenues, as well as their rank and seats in parliament, the remaining third being given to the crown, out of which stipends should be allotted to the protestant clergy. Whatever violence may be imputed to the authors of the Scots reformation, this arrangement seems to display a moderation which we should vainly seek in our own. The new church was, however, but inadequately provided for; and perhaps we may attribute some part of her subsequent contumacy and encroachment on the state to the exasperation occasioned by the latter's parsimony, or rather rapaciousness, in the distribution of ecclesiastical estates.[n]

It was doubtless intended by the planners of a presbyterian model that the bishoprics should be extinguished by the death of the possessors, and their revenues be converted partly to the maintenance of the clergy, partly

---

[m] Spottiswood's Church History, 152; M'Crie's Life of Knox, ii. 6; Life of Melville, i. 143; Robertson's History of Scotland; Cook's History of the Reformation in Scotland. These three modern writers leave, apparently, little to require as to this important period of history; the first with an intenseness of sympathy that enhances our interest, though it may not always command our approbation; the two last with a cooler and more philosophical impartiality.

[n] M'Crie's Life of Knox, ii. 197, et alibi; Cook, iii. 308. According to Robertson, i. 291, the whole revenue of the protestant church, at least in Mary's reign, was about 24,000 pounds Scots, which seems almost incredible.

to other public interests. But it suited better the men in power to keep up the old appellations for their own benefit. As the catholic prelates died away, they were replaced by protestant ministers, on private compacts to alienate the principal part of the revenues to those through whom they were appointed. After some hesitation, a convention of the church, in 1572, agreed to recognise these bishops until the king's majority and a final settlement by the legislature, and to permit them a certain portion of jurisdiction, though not greater than that of the superintendent, and equally subordinate to the general assembly. They were not consecrated, nor would the slightest distinction of order have been endured by the church. Yet even this moderated episcopacy gave offence to ardent men, led by Andrew Melville, the second name to Knox in the ecclesiastical history of Scotland; and, notwithstanding their engagement to leave things as they were till the determination of parliament, the general assembly soon began to restrain the bishops by their own authority, and finally to enjoin them, under pain of excommunication, to lay down an office which they voted to be destitute of warrant from the word of God, and injurious to the church. Some of the bishops submitted to this decree; others, as might be expected, stood out in defence of their dignity, and were supported both by the king and by all who conceived that the supreme power of Scotland, in establishing and endowing the church, had not constituted a society independent of the commonwealth. A series of acts in 1584, at a time when the court had obtained a temporary ascendant, seemed to restore the episcopal government in almost its pristine lustre. But the popular voice was loud against episcopacy; the prelates were discredited by their simoniacal alienations of church revenues, and by their connexion with the court; the king was tempted to annex most of their lands to the crown by an act of parliament in 1587; Adamson, archbishop of St. Andrews, who had led the episcopal party, was driven to a humiliating retractation before the general assembly; and, in 1592, the sanction of the legislature was for the first time obtained to the whole scheme of presbyterian polity, and the laws of 1584 were for the most part abrogated.

The school of Knox, if so we may call the early presbyterian ministers of Scotland, was full of men breathing their master's spirit—acute in disputation, eloquent in discourse, learned beyond what their successors have been, and intensely zealous in the cause of reformation. They wielded the people at will, who, except in the Highlands, threw off almost with unanimity the old religion, and took alarm at the slightest indication of its revival. Their system of local and general assemblies infused, together with the forms of a republic, its energy and impatience of exterior control, combined with the concentration and unity of purpose that belongs to the most vigorous government. It must be confessed that the unsettled state of the kingdom, the faults and weakness of the regents Lennox and Morton, the inauspicious beginning of James's personal administration under the sway of unworthy favourites, 'the real perils of the reformed church, gave no slight pretext for the clergy's interference with civil policy. Not merely in their representative assemblies, but in the pulpits, they perpetually remonstrated, in no guarded language, against the misgovernment of the court, and even the personal indiscretions of the king. This they pretended to claim as a privilege beyond the restraint of law. Andrew Melville having been summoned before the council in 1584, to give an account of some seditious language alleged to have been used by him in the pulpit, declined its jurisdiction on the ground that he was only responsible, in the first instance, to his presbytery for words so spoken, of which the king and council could not judge without violating the immunities of the church. Precedents for such an immunity it would not have been difficult to find; but they must have been sought in the archives of the enemy. It was rather early for the new republic to emulate the despotism she had overthrown. Such, however, is the uniformity with which the same passions operate on bodies of men in similar circumstances; and so greedily do those whose birth has placed them far beneath the possession of power, intoxicate themselves with its unaccustomed enjoyments. It has been urged in defence of Melville, that he only denied the competence of a secular tribunal in the first instance; and that, after the ecclesiastical forum had pronounced on the spiritual offence, it was not disputed that the civil magistrate might vindicate his own authority.º But not to mention that Melville's claim, as I understand it, was to be judged by his presbytery in the first instance, and ultimately by the general assembly, from which, according to the presbyterian theory, no appeal lay to a civil court; it is manifest that the government would have come to a very disadvantageous conflict with a man to whose defence the ecclesiastical judicature had already pledged itself. For in the temper of those times it was easy to foresee the determination of a synod or presbytery.

James, however, and his councillors were not so feeble as to endure this open renewal of those extravagant pretensions which Rome had taught her priesthood to assert. Melville fled to England; and a parliament that met the same year sustained the supremacy of the civil power with that violence and dangerous latitude of expression so frequent in the Scots statute-book. It was made treason to decline the jurisdiction of the king or council in any matter, to seek the diminution of the power of any of the three estates of parliament, which struck at all that had been done against episcopacy, to utter, or to conceal, when heard from others in sermons or familiar discourse, any false or slanderous speeches to the reproach of the king, his council, or their proceedings, or to the dishonour of his parents and progenitors, or to meddle in the affairs of state. It was forbidden to treat or consult on any matter of state, civil or ecclesiastical, without the king's express command—thus rendering the general assembly for its chief purposes, if not its existence, altogether dependent on the crown. Such laws not only annihilated the pretended immunities of the church, but went very far to set up that tyranny which the Stuarts afterwards exercised in Scotland till their expulsion. These were in part repealed, so far as affected the church, in 1592; but the crown retained the exclusive right of convening its general assembly, to which the presby-

Success of James VI. in restraining them.

º M'Crie's Life of Melville, i. 287, 293. It is impossible to think without respect of this most powerful writer, before whom there are few living controversialists that would not tremble; but his presbyterian Hildebrandism is a little remarkable in this age.

terian hierarchy still gives but an evasive and reluctant obedience.ᵖ

These bold demagogues were not long in availing themselves of the advantages which they had obtained in the parliament of 1592, and through the troubled state of the realm. They began again to intermeddle with public affairs, the administration of which was sufficiently open to censure. This licence brought on a new crisis in 1596. Black, one of the ministers of St. Andrews, inveighing against the government from the pulpit, painted the king and queen, as well as their council, in the darkest colours, as dissembling enemies to religion. James, incensed at this attack, caused him to be summoned before the privy council. The clergy decided to make common cause with the accused. The council of the church, a standing committee lately appointed by the general assembly, enjoined Black to decline the jurisdiction. The king by proclamation directed the members of this council to retire to their several parishes. They resolved, instead of submitting, that since they were convened by the warrant of Christ, in a most needful and dangerous time, to see unto the good of the church, they should obey God rather than man. The king offered to stop the proceedings, if they would but declare that they did not decline the civil jurisdiction absolutely, but only in the particular case, as being one of slander, and consequently of ecclesiastical competence. For Black had asserted before the council, that speeches delivered in the pulpits, although alleged to be treasonable, could not be judged by the king until the church had first taken cognizance thereof. But these ecclesiastics, in the full spirit of the thirteenth century, determined by a majority not to recede from their plea. Their contest with the court soon excited the populace of Edinburgh, and gave rise to a tumult which, whether dangerous or not to the king, was what no government could pass over without utter loss of authority.

It was in church assemblies alone that James found opposition. His parliament, as had invariably been the case in Scotland, went readily into all that was proposed to them; nor can we doubt that the gentry must for the

---

ᵖ M'Crie's Life of Melville; Robertson; Spottiswood.

most part have revolted from these insolent usurpations of the ecclesiastical order. It was ordained in parliament that every minister should declare his submission to the king's jurisdiction in all matters civil and criminal, that no ecclesiastical judicatory should meet without the king's consent, and that a magistrate might commit to prison any minister reflecting in his sermons on the king's conduct. He had next recourse to an instrument of power more successful frequently than intimidation, and generally successful in conjunction with it—gaining over the members of the general assembly, some by promises, some by exciting jealousies, till they surrendered no small portion of what had passed for the privileges of the church. The crown obtained by their concession, which then seemed almost necessary to confirm what the legislature had enacted, the right of convoking assemblies, and of nominating ministers in the principal towns. James followed up this victory by a still more important blow. It was enacted that fifty-one ministers, on being nominated by the king to titular bishoprics and other prelacies, might sit in parliament as representatives of the church. This seemed justly alarming to the opposite party; nor could the general assembly be brought to acquiesce without such very considerable restrictions upon these suspicious commissioners, by which name they prevailed to have them called, as might in some measure afford security against the revival of that episcopal domination, towards which the endeavours of the crown were plainly directed. But the king paid little regard to these regulations; and thus the name and parliamentary station of bishops, though without their spiritual functions, were restored in Scotland after only six years from their abolition.[q]

Establishment of episcopacy.

[q] Spottiswood; Robertson; M'Crie. [In the 55th canon, passed by the convocation at London in 1603, the clergy are directed to bid the people to "pray for Christ's holy catholic church, that is, for the whole congregation of Christian people dispersed throughout the whole world, and especially for the churches of England, *Scotland*, and Ireland." A learned writer reckons this among the canons, the observance of which is *impossible*. Cardwell's Synodalia, preface, p. xxviii. By this singular word he of course means that it ought not to be done; and in fact I never heard the church of Scotland so distinguished, except once, by a Master of the Temple (Rennell). But it has evidently escaped Dr. Cardwell's recollection, that the church of Scotland was, properly speaking, as much presbyterian in 1603 as at present.—1845.]

A king like James, not less conceited of his wisdom than full of the dignity of his station, could not avoid contracting that insuperable aversion to the Scots presbytery which he expressed in his Basilicon Doron before his accession to the English throne, and more vehemently on all occasions afterwards. He found a very different race of churchmen, well trained in the supple school of courtly conformity, and emulous flatterers both of his power and his wisdom. The ministers of Edinburgh had been used to pray that God would turn his heart: Whitgift, at the conference of Hampton Court, falling on his knees, exclaimed, that he doubted not his majesty spoke by the special grace of God. It was impossible that he should not redouble his endeavours to introduce so convenient a system of ecclesiastical government into his native kingdom. He began, accordingly, to prevent the meetings of the general assembly by continued prorogations. Some hardy presbyterians ventured to assemble by their own authority, which the lawyers construed into treason. The bishops were restored by parliament, in 1606, to a part of their revenues, the act annexing these to the crown being repealed. They were appointed by an ecclesiastical convention, more subservient to the crown than formerly, to be perpetual moderators of provincial synods. The clergy still gave way with reluctance; but the crown had an irresistible ascendancy in parliament; and in 1610 the episcopal system was thoroughly established. The powers of ordination, as well as jurisdiction, were solely vested in the prelates; a court of high commission was created on the English model; and, though the general assembly of the church still continued, it was merely as a shadow, and almost mockery, of its original importance. The bishops now repaired to England for consecration—a ceremony deemed essential in the new school that now predominated in the Anglican church; and this gave a final blow to the polity in which the Scottish reformation had been founded.' With far more questionable prudence, James, some years afterwards, forced upon the people of Scotland what were called the five articles of Perth, reluctantly adopted by a general assembly held

---

' M'Crie's Life of Melville, ii. 378; Laing's Hist. of Scotland, iii. 20, 35, 42, 62.

there in 1617. These were matters of ceremony, such as the posture of kneeling in the eucharist, the right of confirmation, and the observance of certain holidays, but enough to alarm a nation fanatically abhorrent of every approximation to the Roman worship, and already incensed by what they deemed the corruption and degradation of their church.*

That church, if indeed it preserved its identity, was wholly changed in character, and became as much distinguished in its episcopal form by servility and corruption as during its presbyterian democracy by faction and turbulence. The bishops at its head, many of them abhorred by their own countrymen as apostates and despised for their vices, looked for protection to the sister church of England in its pride and triumph. It had long been the favourite project of the court, as it naturally was of the Anglican prelates, to assimilate in all respects the two establishments. That of Scotland still wanted one essential characteristic, a regular liturgy. But in preparing what was called the service book, the English model was not closely followed; the variations having all a tendency towards the Romish worship. It is far more probable that Laud intended these to prepare the way for a similar change in England, than that, as some have surmised, the Scots bishops, from a notion of independence, chose thus to distinguish their own ritual. What were the consequences of this unhappy innovation, attempted with that ignorance of mankind which kings and priests, when left to their own guidance, usually display, it is here needless to mention. In its ultimate results, it preserved the liberties and overthrew the monarchy of England. In its more immediate effects, it gave rise to the national covenant of Scotland; a solemn pledge of unity and perseverance in a great public cause, long since devised when the Spanish armada threatened the liberties and religion of all Britain, but now directed against the domestic enemies of both. The episcopal government had no friends, even among those who served the king. To him it was dear by the sincerest conviction, and by its connexion with absolute power, still more close and

* Laing, 74, 89

direct than in England. But he had reduced himself to a condition where it was necessary to sacrifice his authority in the smaller kingdom, if he would hope to preserve it in the greater; and in this view he consented, in the parliament of 1641, to restore the presbyterian discipline of the Scots church; an offence against his conscience (for such his prejudices led him to consider it) which he deeply afterwards repented, when he discovered how absolutely it had failed of serving his interests.

In the great struggle with Charles against episcopacy, the encroachments of arbitrary rule, for the sake of which, in a great measure, he valued that form of church polity, were not overlooked; and the parliament of 1641 procured some essential improvements in the civil constitution of Scotland. Triennial sessions of the legislature, and other salutary reformations, were borrowed from their friends and coadjutors in England. But what was still more important, was the abolition of that destructive control over the legislature, which the crown had obtained through the lords of articles. These had doubtless been originally nominated by the several estates in parliament, solely to expedite the management of business, and relieve the entire body from attention to it. But, as early as 1561, we find a practice established, that the spiritual lords should choose the temporal, generally eight in number, who were to sit on this committee, and conversely; the burgesses still electing their own. To these it became usual to add some of the officers of state; and in 1617 it was established that eight of them should be on the list. Charles procured, without authority of parliament, a further innovation in 1633. The bishops chose eight peers, the peers eight bishops; and these appointed sixteen commissioners of shires and boroughs. Thus the whole power was devolved upon the bishops, the slaves and sycophants of the crown. The parliament itself met only on two days, the first and last of their pretended session, the one time in order to choose the lords of articles, the other to ratify what they proposed.' So monstrous an anomaly could not

Innovations of Charles I.

¹ Wight, 69 et post.

long subsist in a high-spirited nation. This improvident assumption of power by low-born and odious men precipitated their downfall, and made the destruction of the hierarchy appear the necessary guarantee for parliamentary independence, and the ascendant of the aristocracy. But lest the court might, in some other form, regain this preliminary or initiative voice in legislation, which the experience of many governments has shown to be the surest method of keeping supreme authority in their hands, it was enacted in 1641, that each estate might choose lords of articles or not, at its discretion; but that all propositions should in the first instance be submitted to the whole parliament, by whom such only as should be thought fitting might be referred to the committee of articles for consideration.

This parliament, however, neglected to abolish one of the most odious engines that tyranny ever devised against public virtue, the Scots law of treason. It had been enacted by a statute of James I. in 1424, that all leasing-makers, and tellers of what might engender discord between the king and his people, should forfeit life and goods.[u] This act was renewed under James II., and confirmed in 1540.[x] It was aimed at the factious aristocracy, who perpetually excited the people by invidious reproaches against the king's administration. But in 1584, a new antagonist to the crown having appeared in the presbyterian pulpits, it was determined to silence opposition by giving the statute of leasing-making, as it was denominated, a more sweeping operation. Its penalties were accordingly extended to such as should "utter untrue or slanderous speeches, to the disdain, reproach, and contempt of his highness, his parents and progenitors, or should meddle in the affairs of his highness or his estate." The "hearers and not reporters thereof" were subjected to the same punishment. It may be remarked that these Scots statutes are worded with a latitude never found in England, even in the worst times of Henry VIII. Lord Balmerino, who had opposed the court in the parliament of 1633, retained in his possession a copy of an apology intended to have been presented by himself and other

Arbitrary government.

[u] Statutes of Scotland, vol. ii. p. 8; Pinkerton, I. 115; Laing, iii. 117.
[x] Statutes of Scotland, p. 360.

peers in their exculpation, but from which they had desisted, in apprehension of the king's displeasure. This was obtained clandestinely, and in breach of confidence, by some of his enemies; and he was indicted on the statute of leasing-making, as having concealed a slander against his majesty's government. A jury was returned with gross partiality; yet so outrageous was the attempted violation of justice that Balmerino was only convicted by a majority of eight against seven. For in Scots juries a simple majority was sufficient, as it is still in all cases except treason. It was not thought expedient to carry this sentence into execution; but the kingdom could never pardon its government so infamous a stretch of power.⁷ The statute itself, however, seems not to have shared the same odium; we do not find any effort made for its repeal; and the ruling party in 1641, unfortunately, did not scruple to make use of its sanguinary provisions against their own adversaries.ᶻ

The conviction of Balmerino is hardly more repugnant to justice than some other cases in the long reign of James VI. Eight years after the execution of the earl of Gowrie and his brother, one Sprot, a notary, having indiscreetly mentioned that he was in possession of letters, written by a person since dead, which evinced his participation in that mysterious conspiracy, was put to death for concealing them.ᵃ Thomas Ross suffered, in 1618, the punishment of treason for publishing at Oxford a blasphemous libel, as the indictment calls it, against the Scots nation.ᵇ I know not what he could have said worse than what their sentence against him enabled others to say, that, amidst a great vaunt of Christianity and civilization, they took away men's lives by such statutes, and such constructions of them, as could only be paralleled in the annals of the worst tyrants. By an act of 1584, the privy council were

---

⁷ Laing, ibid.
ᶻ Arnot's Criminal Trials, p. 122.
ᵃ The Gowrie conspiracy is well known to be one of the most difficult problems in history. Arnot has given a very good account of it, p. 20, and shown its truth, which could not reasonably be questioned, whatever motive we may assign for it. He has laid stress on Logan's letters, which appear to have been unaccountably slighted by some writers. I have long had a suspicion, founded on these letters, that the earl of Bothwell, a daring man of desperate fortunes, was in some manner concerned in the plot, of which the earl of Gowrie and his brother were the instruments.

ᵇ Arnot's Criminal Trials, p. 70.

empowered to examine an accused party on oath; and if he declined to answer any question, it was held denial of their jurisdiction, and amounted to a conviction of treason. This was experienced by two Jesuits, Crighton and Ogilvy, in 1610 and 1615, the latter of whom was executed.[c] One of the statutes upon which he was indicted contained the singular absurdity of "annulling and rescinding every thing done, or hereafter to be done, in prejudice of the royal prerogative, in any time bygone or to come."

Civil war.
It was perhaps impossible that Scotland should remain indifferent in the great quarrel of the sister kingdom. But having set her heart upon two things incompatible in themselves from the outset, according to the circumstances of England, and both of them ultimately impracticable, the continuance of Charles on the throne and the establishment of a presbyterian church, she fell into a long course of disaster and ignominy, till she held the name of a free constitution at the will of a conqueror. Of the three most conspicuous among her nobility in this period, each died by the hand of the executioner; but the resemblance is in nothing besides; and the characters of Hamilton, Montrose, and Argyle are not less contrasted than the factions of which they were the leaders. Humbled and broken down, the people looked to the re-establishment of Charles II. on the throne of his fathers, though brought about by the sternest minister of Cromwell's tyranny, not only as the augury of prosperous days, but as the obliteration of public dishonour.

Tyrannical government of Charles II.
They were miserably deceived in every hope. Thirty infamous years consummated the misfortunes and degradation of Scotland. Her factions have always been more sanguinary, her rulers more oppressive, her sense of justice and

---

[c] Arnot, p. 67, 329; State Trials, ii. 884. The prisoner was told that he was not charged for saying mass, nor for seducing the people to popery, nor for anything that concerned his conscience; but for declining the king's authority, and maintaining treasonable opinions, as the statutes libelled on made it treason not to answer the king or his council in any matter which should be demanded.

It was one of the most monstrous iniquities of a monstrous jurisprudence, the Scots criminal law, to debar a prisoner from any defence inconsistent with the indictment; that is, he might deny a fact, but was not permitted to assert that, being true, it did not warrant the conclusion of guilt. Arnot, 354.

humanity less active, or at least shown less in public acts, than can be charged against England. The parliament of 1661, influenced by wicked statesmen and lawyers, left far behind the royalist commons of London; and rescinded as null the entire acts of 1641, on the absurd pretext that the late king had passed them through force. The Scots constitution fell back at once to a state little better than despotism. The lords of articles were revived, according to the same form of election as under Charles I. A few years afterwards the duke of Lauderdale obtained the consent of parliament to an act, that whatever the king and council should order respecting all ecclesiastical matters, meetings, and persons, should have the force of law. A militia, or rather army, of 22,000 men, was established, to march wherever the council should appoint, and the honour and safety of the king require. Fines to the amount of 85,000*l.*, an enormous sum in that kingdom, were imposed on the covenanters. The earl of Argyle brought to the scaffold by an outrageous sentence, his son sentenced to lose his life on such a construction of the ancient law against leasing-making as no man engaged in political affairs could be sure to escape, the worst system of constitutional laws administered by the worst men, left no alternative but implicit obedience or desperate rebellion.

The presbyterian church of course fell by the act which annulled the parliament wherein it had been established. Episcopacy revived, but not as it had once existed in Scotland; the jurisdiction of the bishops became unlimited; the general assemblies, so dear to the people, were laid aside.[d] The new prelates were odious as apostates, and soon gained a still more indelible title to popular hatred as persecutors. Three hundred and fifty of the presbyterian clergy (more than one-third of the whole number) were ejected from their benefices.[e] Then began the preaching in conventicles, and the secession of the excited and exasperated multitude from the churches;

---

[d] Laing, iv. 20; Kirkton, p. 141. "Whoso shall compare," he says, "this set of bishops with the old bishops established in the year 1612, shall find that these were but a sort of pigmies compared with our new bishops."

[e] Laing, iv. 32. Kirkton says 300. P. 149. These were what were called the young ministers, those who had entered the church since 1649. They might have kept their cures by acknowledging the authority of bishops.

and then ensued the ecclesiastical commission with its inquisitorial vigilance, its fines and corporal penalties, and the free quarters of the soldiery, with all that can be implied in that word. Then came the fruitless insurrection, and the fanatical assurance of success, and the certain discomfiture by a disciplined force, and the consternation of defeat, and the unbounded cruelties of the conqueror. And this went on with perpetual aggravation, or very rare intervals, through the reign of Charles;. the tyranny of Lauderdale far exceeding that of Middleton, as his own fell short of the duke of York's. No part, I believe, of modern history for so long a period, can be compared for the wickedness of government to the Scots administration of this reign. In proportion as the laws grew more rigorous against the presbyterian worship, its followers evinced more steadiness; driven from their conventicles, they resorted sometimes by night to the fields, the woods, the mountains; and, as the troops were continually employed to disperse them, they came with arms which they were often obliged to use; and thus the hour, the place, the circumstance, deepened every impression, and bound up their faith with indissoluble associations. The same causes produced a dark fanaticism, which believed the revenge of its own wrongs to be the execution of divine justice; and, as this acquired new strength by every successive aggravation of tyranny, it is literally possible that a continuance of the Stuart government might have led to something very like an extermination of the people in the western counties of Scotland. In the year 1676 letters of intercommuning were published; a writ forbidding all persons to hold intercourse with the parties put under its ban, or to furnish them with any necessary of life, on pain of being reputed guilty of the same crime. But seven years afterwards, when the Cameronian rebellion had assumed a dangerous character, a proclamation was issued against all who had ever harboured or communed with rebels; courts were appointed to be held for their trial as traitors, which were to continue for the next three years. Those who accepted the test, a declaration of passive obedience repugnant to the conscience of the presbyterians and imposed for that reason in 1681, were excused from these penalties; and in this way they were eluded.

The enormities of this detestable government are far too numerous, even in species, to be enumerated in this slight sketch; and of course most instances of cruelty have not been recorded. The privy council was accustomed to extort confessions by torture; that grim divan of bishops, lawyers, and peers sucking in the groans of each undaunted enthusiast, in hope that some imperfect avowal might lead to the sacrifice of other victims, or at least warrant the execution of the present. It is said that the duke of York, whose conduct in Scotland tends to efface those sentiments of pity and respect which other parts of his life might excite, used to assist himself on these occasions.[f] One Mitchell having been induced, by a promise that his life should be spared, to confess an attempt to assassinate Sharp the primate, was brought to trial some years afterwards; when four lords of the council deposed on oath that no such assurance had been given him; and Sharp insisted upon his execution. The vengeance ultimately taken on this infamous apostate and persecutor, though doubtless in violation of what is justly reckoned an universal rule of morality, ought at least not to weaken our abhorrence of the man himself.

The test above mentioned was imposed by parliament in 1681, and contained, among other things, an engagement never to attempt any alteration of government in church or state. The earl of Argyle, son of him who had perished by an unjust sentence, and himself once before attainted by another, though at that time restored by the king, was still destined to illustrate the house of Campbell by a second martyrdom. He refused to subscribe the test without the reasonable explanation that he would not bind himself from attempting, in his station, any improvement in church or state. This exposed him to an accusation of leasing-making (the old mystery of iniquity in Scots law) and of treason. He was found guilty through the astonishing audacity of the crown lawyers and servility of the judges and jury. It is not perhaps certain that his immediate execution would have ensued; but no man ever trusted securely to the mercies of the Stuarts, and Argyle escaped in disguise by the aid of his daughter-in-law. The council proposed that this lady

[f] Laing, iv. 116.

should be publicly whipped; but there was an excess of atrocity in the Scots on the court side, which no Englishman could reach; and the duke of York felt as a gentleman upon such a suggestion.ᵍ The earl of Argyle was brought to the scaffold a few years afterwards on this old sentence; but after his unfortunate rebellion, which of course would have legally justified his execution.

The Cameronians, a party rendered wild and fanatical through intolerable oppression, published a declaration, wherein, after renouncing their allegiance to Charles, and expressing their abhorrence of murder on the score of religion, they announced their determination of retaliating, according to their power, on such privy councillors, officers in command, or others, as should continue to seek their blood. The fate of Sharp was thus before the eyes of all who emulated his crimes; and in terror the council ordered, that whoever refused to disown this declaration on oath, should be put to death in the presence of two witnesses. Every officer, every soldier, was thus entrusted with the privilege of massacre; the unarmed, the women and children, fell indiscriminately by the sword: and besides the distinct testimonies that remain of atrocious cruelty, there exists in that kingdom a deep traditional horror, the record, as it were, of that confused mass of crime and misery which has left no other memorial.ʰ

A parliament summoned by James on his accession, with an intimation from the throne that they were assembled not only to express their own duty, but to set an example of compliance to England, gave, without the least opposition, the required proofs of loyalty. They acknowledged the king's absolute power, declared their abhorrence of any principle derogatory to it, professed an unreserved obedience in all cases, bestowed a large revenue for life. They enhanced the penalties against sectaries; a refusal to give evidence against traitors or other delinquents was made equivalent to a conviction of the same offence; it was capital to preach even in houses, or to hear preachers in the fields. The persecution raged with still greater fury in the first

ᵍ Life of James II., i. 710.
ʰ Cloud of Witnesses, passim; De Foe's History of Church of Scotland; Kirkton; Laing; Scott's notes in Minstrelsy of Scottish Border, &c. &c.

part of this reign. But the same repugnance of the episcopal party to the king's schemes for his own religion, which led to his remarkable change of policy in England, produced similar effects in Scotland. He had attempted to obtain from parliament a repeal of the penal laws and the test; but, though an extreme servility or a general intimidation made the nobility acquiesce in his propositions, and two of the bishops were gained over, yet the commissioners of shires and boroughs, who voting promiscuously in the house had, when united, a majority over the peers, so firmly resisted every encroachment of popery, that it was necessary to try other methods than those of parliamentary enactment. After the dissolution the dispensing power was brought into play; the privy council forbade the execution of the laws against the catholics; several of that religion were introduced to its board; the royal boroughs were deprived of their privileges, the king assuming the nomination of their chief magistrates, so as to throw the elections wholly into the hands of the crown. A declaration of indulgence, emanating from the king's absolute prerogative, relaxed the severity of the laws against presbyterian conventicles, and, annulling the oath of supremacy and the test of 1681, substituted for them an oath of allegiance, acknowledging his power to be unlimited. He promised at the same time, that " he would use no force nor invincible necessity against any man on account of his persuasion, or the protestant religion, nor would deprive the possessors of lands formerly belonging to the church." A very intelligible hint that the protestant religion was to exist only by this gracious sufferance.

The oppressed presbyterians gained some respite by this indulgence, though instances of executions under the sanguinary statutes of the late reign are found as late as the beginning of 1688. But the memory of their sufferings was indelible; they accepted, but with no gratitude, the insidious mercy of a tyrant they abhorred. The Scots conspiracy with the prince of Orange went forward simultaneously with that of England; it included several of the council, from personal jealousy, dislike of the king's proceedings as to religion, or anxiety to secure an indemnity they had little deserved in the approaching crisis. The people

<small>Revolution and establishment of presbytery.</small>

rose in different parts; the Scots nobility and gentry in London presented an address to the prince of Orange, requesting him to call a convention of the estates; and this irregular summons was universally obeyed.

The king was not without friends in this convention; but the whigs had from every cause a decided preponderance. England had led the way; William was on his throne; the royal government at home was wholly dissolved; and, after enumerating in fifteen articles the breaches committed on the constitution, the estates came to a resolution—" That James VII., being a professed papist, did assume the royal power, and acted as king, without ever taking the oath required by law, and had, by the advice of evil and wicked counsellors, invaded the fundamental constitution of the kingdom, and altered it from a legal limited monarchy to an arbitrary despotic power, and hath exerted the same to the subversion of the protestant religion, and the violation of the laws and liberties of the kingdom, whereby he hath forfaulted (forfeited) his right to the crown, and the throne has become vacant." It was evident that the English vote of a constructive abdication, having been partly grounded on the king's flight, could not without still greater violence be applied to Scotland; and consequently the bolder denomination of forfeiture was necessarily employed to express the penalty of his mis-government. There was, in fact, a very striking difference in the circumstances of the two kingdoms. In the one, there had been illegal acts and unjustifiable severities; but it was, at first sight, no very strong case for national resistance, which stood rather on a calculation of expediency than an instinct of self-preservation or an impulse of indignant revenge. But in the other, it had been a tyranny, dark as that of the most barbarous ages; despotism, which in England was scarcely in blossom, had borne its bitter and poisonous fruits: no word of slighter import than forfeiture could be chosen to denote the national rejection of the Stuart line.

A declaration and claim of rights was drawn up, as in England, together with the resolution that the crown be tendered to William and Mary, and descend afterwards in conformity with the limitations enacted in the sister kingdom. This declaration excluded papists from the throne, and asserted the illegality of proclamations to dispense with statutes, of the inflicting capital punishment without jury, of imprisonment without special cause or delay of trial, of exacting enormous fines, of nominating the magistrates in boroughs, and several other violent proceedings in the two last reigns. These articles the convention challenged as their undoubted right, against which no declaration or precedent ought to operate. They reserved some other important grievances to be redressed in parliament. Upon this occasion a noble fire of liberty shone forth to the honour of Scotland, amidst those scenes of turbulent faction or servile corruption which the annals of her parliament so perpetually display. They seemed emulous of English freedom, and proud to place their own imperfect commonwealth on as firm a basis.

One great alteration in the state of Scotland was almost necessarily involved in the fall of the Stuarts. Their most conspicuous object had been the maintenance of the episcopal church; the line was drawn far more closely than in England; in that church were the court's friends, out of it were its opponents. Above all, the people were out of it, and in a revolution brought about by the people, their voice could not be slighted. It was one of the articles accordingly in the declaration of rights, that prelacy and precedence in ecclesiastical office were repugnant to the genius of a nation reformed by presbyters, and an unsupportable grievance which ought to be abolished. William, there is reason to believe, had offered to preserve the bishops, in return for their support in the convention. But this, not more happily for Scotland than for himself and his successors, they refused to give. No compromise, or even acknowledged toleration, was practicable in that country between two exasperated factions; but, if oppression was necessary, it was at least not on the majority that it ought to fall. But besides this, there was as clear a case of forfeiture in the Scots episcopal church as in the royal family of Stuart. The main controversy between the episcopal and presbyterian churches was one of historical inquiry, not perhaps capable of decisive solution; it was at least one as to which the bulk of mankind are absolutely incapable of forming a rational judgment for themselves. But, mingled up as it had always been, and most of all in Scotland, with faction, with revolution, with power and emolument, with courage and devotion, and fear, and hate, and revenge, this dispute drew along with it the most glowing emotions of the heart, and the question became utterly out of the province of argument. It was very possible that episcopacy might be of apostolical institution; but for this institution houses had been burned and fields laid waste, and the Gospel had been preached in wildernesses, and its ministers had been shot in their prayers, and husbands had been murdered before their wives, and virgins had been defiled, and many had died by the executioner, and by massacre, and in imprisonment, and in exile and slavery, and women had been tied to stakes on the sea-shore till the tide rose to overflow them, and some had been tortured and mutilated: it was a religion of the boots and the thumb-screw, which a good man must be very cool-blooded indeed if he did not hate and reject from the hands which offered it. For, after all, it is much more certain that the Supreme Being abhors cruelty and persecution, than that he has set up bishops to have a superiority over presbyters.

It was, however, a serious problem at that time, whether the presbyterian church, so proud and stubborn as she had formerly shown herself, could be brought under a necessary subordination to the civil magistrate, and whether the more fanatical part of it, whom Cargill and Cameron had led on, would fall again into the ranks of social life. But here experience victoriously confuted these plausible apprehensions. It was soon perceived that the insanity of fanaticism subsides of itself, unless purposely heightened by persecution. The fiercer spirit of the sectaries was allayed by degrees; and, though vestiges of it may probably still be perceptible by observers, it has never, in a political sense, led to dangerous effects. The church of Scotland, in her general assemblies, preserves the forms and affects the language of the sixteenth century; but the Erastianism, against which she inveighs, secretly controls and paralyses her vaunted liberties; and she cannot but acknowledge that the supremacy of the legislature is like the collar of the watch-dog, the price of food and shelter, and the condition upon which alone a religious society can be endowed and established by any prudent commonwealth.¹ The judicious admixture of laymen in these assemblies, and, in a far greater degree, the perpetual intercourse with England, which has put an end to everything like sectarian bigotry and even exclusive communion in the higher and middling classes, are the principal causes of that remarkable moderation which for many years has characterised the successors of Knox and Melville. [1827.]

The convention of estates was turned by an act of its own into a parliament, and continued to sit during the king's reign. This, which was rather contrary to the spirit of a representative government than to the Scots constitution, might be justified by the very unquiet state of the kingdom and the intrigues of the Jacobites. Many excellent statutes were enacted in this parliament, besides the provisions included in the declaration of rights; twenty-six members were added to the representation of the counties, the tyrannous acts of the two last reigns were repealed, the unjust attainders were reversed, the lords of articles were abolished. After some years an act was obtained against wrongous imprisonment, still more effectual perhaps in some respects than that of the habeas corpus in England. The prisoner is to be released on bail within twenty-four hours on application to a judge, unless committed on a capital charge, and in that case must be brought to trial within sixty days. A judge refusing to give full effect to the act is declared incapable of public trust.

Notwithstanding these great improvements in the constitution, and the cessation of religious tyranny, the Scots are not accustomed to look back on the reign of William with much complacency. The regeneration was far from perfect; the court of session continued to be corrupt and partial; severe and illegal proceedings might sometimes be imputed to the council; and in one lamentable instance, the massacre of the Macdonalds in Glencoe, the

---

¹ The practice observed in summoning or dissolving the great national assembly of the church of Scotland, which, according to the presbyterian theory, can only be done by its own authority, is rather amusing: "The moderator dissolves the assembly in the name of the Lord Jesus Christ, the head of the church; and, by the same authority, appoints another to meet on a certain day of the ensuing year. The lord high commissioner then dissolves the assembly in the name of the king, and appoints another to meet on the same day." Arnot's Hist. of Edin., p. 269.

deliberate crime of some statesmen tarnished not slightly the bright fame of their deceived master; though it was not for the adherents of the house of Stuart, under whom so many deeds of more extensive slaughter had been perpetrated, to fill Europe with their invectives against this military execution.[k] The episcopal clergy, driven out injuriously by the populace from their livings, were permitted after a certain time to hold them again in some instances under certain conditions; but William, perhaps almost the only consistent friend of toleration in his kingdoms, at least among public men, lost by this indulgence the affection of one party, without in the slightest degree conciliating the other.[m] The true cause, however, of the

[k] The king's instructions by no means warrant the execution, especially with all its circumstances of cruelty, but they contain one unfortunate sentence: "If Maclean [sic], of Glencoe, and that tribe can be well separated from the rest, it will be a proper vindication of the public justice to extirpate that seat of thieves." This was written, it is to be remembered, while they were exposed to the penalties of the law for the rebellion. But the massacre would never have been perpetrated, if lord Breadalbane and the master of Stair, two of the worst men in Scotland, had not used the foulest arts to effect it. It is an apparently great reproach to the government of William that they escaped with impunity; but political necessity bears down justice and honour. Laing, iv. 246; Carstares' State Papers.

[m] Those who took the oaths were allowed to continue in their churches without compliance with the presbyterian discipline, and many more who not only refused the oaths, but prayed openly for James and his family. Carstares, p. 40. But in 1693 an act for settling the peace and quiet of the church ordains that no person be admitted or continued to be a minister or preacher unless he have taken the oath of allegiance and subscribed the assurance that he held the king to be de facto et de jure, and also the confession of faith; and that he owns and acknowledges presbyterian church government to be the only government of this church, and that he will submit thereto and concur

therewith, and will never endeavour, directly or indirectly, the prejudice or subversion thereof. Id. 715; Laing, iv. 255.

This act seems not to have been strictly insisted upon; and the episcopal clergy, though their advocates did not forget to raise a cry of persecution, which was believed in England, are said to have been treated with singular favour. De Foe challenges them to show any one minister that ever was deposed for not acknowledging the church, if at the same time he offered to acknowledge the government and take the oaths; and says they have been often challenged on this head. Hist. of Church of Scotland, p. 319. In fact, a statute was passed in 1695, which confirmed all ministers who would qualify themselves by taking the oaths: and no less than 116 (according to Laing, iv. 259) did so continue; nay, De Foe reckons 165 at the time of the union. P. 320.

The rigid presbyterians inveighed against any toleration, as much as they did against the king's authority over their own church. But the government paid little attention to their bigotry; besides the above-mentioned episcopal clergymen, those who seceded from the church, though universally Jacobites, and most dangerously so, were indulged with meeting-houses in all towns; and by an act of the queen, 10 Anne, c. 7, obtained a full toleration on condition of praying for the royal family, with which they never complied. It was thought necessary to put them under some fresh re-

prevalent disaffection at this period was the condition of Scotland, an ancient, independent kingdom, inhabited by a proud, high-spirited people, relatively to another kingdom which they had long regarded with enmity, still with jealousy, but to which, in despite of their theoretical equality, they were kept in subordination by an insurmountable necessity. The union of the two crowns had withdrawn their sovereign and his court; yet their government had been national, and on the whole with no great intermixture of English influence. Many reasons, however, might be given for a more complete incorporation, which had been the favourite project of James I., and was discussed, at least on the part of Scotland, by commissioners appointed in 1670. That treaty failed of making any progress—the terms proposed being such as the English parliament would never have accepted. At the Revolution a similar plan was just hinted and abandoned. Meanwhile, the new character that the English government had assumed rendered it more difficult to preserve the actual connexion. A king of both countries, especially by origin more allied to the weaker, might maintain some impartiality in his behaviour towards each of them. But, if they were to be ruled, in effect, nearly as two republics; that is, if the power of their parliaments should be so much enhanced as ultimately to determine the principal measures of state (which was at least the case in England), no one who saw their mutual jealousy, rising on one side to the highest exasperation, could fail to anticipate that some great revolution must be at hand, and that an union, neither federal nor legislative, but possessing every inconvenience of both, could not long be endured. The well-known business of the Darien company must have undeceived every rational man who dreamed of any alternative but incorporation or separation. The Scots parliament took care to bring on the crisis by the act of security in 1704. It was enacted that, on the queen's death without issue, the estates should meet to name a successor of the royal line, and a protestant; but that this should not be the

strictions in 1748, their zeal for the pretender being notorious and universal, by an act 21 Geo. II. c. 34 which has very properly been repealed after the motive for it had wholly ceased, and even at first was not reconcilable with the general principles of religious liberty.

same person who would succeed to the crown of England, unless during her majesty's reign conditions should, be established to secure from English influence the honour and independence of the kingdom, the authority of parliament, the religion, trade, and liberty of the nation. This was explained to mean a free intercourse with the plantations, and the benefits of the navigation act. The prerogative of declaring peace and war was to be subjected for ever to the approbation of parliament, lest at any future time these conditions should be revoked.

Those who obtained the act of security were partly of the Jacobite faction, who saw in it the hope of restoring at least Scotland to the banished heir —partly of a very different description, whigs in principle and determined enemies of the pretender, but attached to their country, jealous of the English court, and determined to settle a legislative union on such terms as became an independent state. Such an union was now seen in England to be indispensable; the treaty was soon afterwards begun, and, after a long discussion of the terms between the commissioners of both kingdoms, the incorporation took effect on the 1st of May, 1707. It is provided by the articles of this treaty, confirmed by the parliaments, that the succession of the united kingdom shall remain to the princess Sophia, and the heirs of her body, being protestants; that all privileges of trade shall belong equally to both nations; that there shall be one great seal, and the same coin, weights, and measures; that the episcopal and presbyterian churches of England and Scotland shall be for ever established as essential and fundamental parts of the union; that the united kingdom shall be represented by one and the same parliament, to be called the parliament of Great Britain; that the number of peers for Scotland shall be sixteen, to be elected for every parliament by the whole body, and the number of representatives of the commons forty-five, two-thirds of whom to be chosen by the counties and one-third by the boroughs; that the crown be restrained from creating any new peers of Scotland; that both parts of the united kingdom shall be subject to the same duties of excise, and the same customs on export and import; but that, when England raises two

Act of security.

Union.

millions by a land-tax, 48,000*l.* shall be raised in Scotland, and in like proportion.

It has not been unusual for Scotsmen, even in modern times, while they cannot but acknowledge the expediency of an union and the blessings which they have reaped from it, to speak of its conditions as less favourable than their ancestors ought to have claimed. For this, however, there does not seem much reason. The ratio of population would indeed have given Scotland about one-eighth of the legislative body, instead of something less than one-twelfth; but no government, except the merest democracy, is settled on the sole basis of numbers; and if the comparison of wealth and of public contributions was to be admitted, it may be thought that a country, which stipulated for itself to pay less than one-fortieth of direct taxation, was not entitled to a much greater share of the representation than it obtained. Combining the two ratios of population and property, there seems little objection to this part of the union; and in general it may be observed of the articles of that treaty, what often occurs with compacts intended to oblige future ages, that they have rather tended to throw obstacles in the way of reformations for the substantial benefit of Scotland than to protect her against encroachment and usurpation.

This, however, could not be securely anticipated in the reign of Anne; and, no doubt, the measure was an experiment of such hazard, that every lover of his country must have consented in trembling, or revolted from it with disgust. No past experience of history was favourable to the absorption of a lesser state (at least where the government partook so much of the republican form) in one of superior power and ancient rivalry. The representation of Scotland in the united legislature was too feeble to give anything like security against the English prejudices and animosities, if they should continue or revive. The church was exposed to the most apparent perils, brought thus within the power of a legislature so frequently influenced by one which held her not as a sister, but rather a bastard usurper of a sister's inheritance; and, though her permanence was guaranteed by the treaty, yet it was hard to say how far the legal competence of parliament might hereafter be deemed to extend, or at least how far she might be abridged of her privileges and impaired in her dignity." If very few of these mischiefs have resulted from the union, it has doubtless been owing to the prudence of our government, and chiefly to the general sense of right and the diminution both of national and religious bigotry during the last century. But it is always to be kept in mind, as the best justification of those who came into so great a sacrifice of natural patriotism, that they gave up no excellent form of polity; that the Scots constitution had never produced the people's happiness; that their parliament was bad in its composition, and in practice little else than a factious and venal aristocracy; that they had before them the alternatives of their present condition, with the prospect of unceasing discontent, half suppressed by unceasing corruption, or of a more honourable but very precarious separation of the two kingdoms, the renewal of national wars and border-feuds, at a cost the poorer of the two could never endure, and at a hazard of ultimate conquest, which, with all her pride and bravery, the experience of the last generation had shown to be no impossible term of the contest.

The union closes the story of the Scots constitution. From its own nature not more than from the gross prostitution with which a majority had sold themselves to the surrender of their own legislative existence, it was long odious to both parties in Scotland. An attempt to dissolve it by the authority of the united parliament itself was made in a very few years, and not very decently supported by the whigs against the queen's last ministry. But, after the accession of the house of Hanover, the Jacobite party displayed such strength in Scotland, that to maintain the union was evidently indispensable for the reigning family. That party comprised a large proportion of the superior classes, and nearly the whole of the episcopal church, which, though fallen, was for some

---

" Archbishop Tenison said, in the debates on the union, he thought the narrow notions of all churches had been their ruin, and that he believed the church of Scotland to be as true a protestant church as the church of England, though he could not say it was as perfect. Carstares, 759. This sort of language was encouraging; but the exclusive doctrine, or jus divinum, was sure to retain many advocates, and has always done so. Fortunately for Great Britain, it has not had the slightest effect on the laity in modern times. [1827.]

years considerable in numbers. The national prejudices ran in favour of their ancient stock of kings, conspiring with the sentiment of dishonour attached to the union itself, and jealousy of some innovations which a legislature they were unwilling to recognise thought fit to introduce. It is certain that Jacobitism, in England little more after the reign of George I. than an empty word, the vehicle of indefinite dissatisfaction in those who were never ready to encounter peril or sacrifice advantage for its affected principle, subsisted in Scotland as a vivid emotion of loyalty, a generous promptitude to act or suffer in its cause; and, even when all hope was extinct, clung to the recollections of the past long after the very name was only known by tradition, and every feeling connected with it had been wholly effaced to the south of the Tweed. It is believed that some persons in that country kept up an intercourse with Charles Edward as their sovereign till his decease in 1787. They had given, forty years before, abundant testimonies of their activity to serve him. That rebellion is, in more respects than one, disgraceful to the British government; but it furnished an opportunity for a wise measure to prevent its recurrence and to break down in some degree the aristocratical ascendancy, by abolishing the hereditary jurisdictions which, according to the genius of the feudal system, were exercised by territorial proprietors under royal charter or prescription.

Gradual decline of Jacobitism.

CHAPTER XVIII.

ON THE CONSTITUTION OF IRELAND.

Ancient State of Ireland — Its Kingdoms and Chieftainships — Law of Tanistry and Gavel-kind — Rude State of Society — Invasion of Henry II. — Acquisitions of English Barons — Forms of English Constitution established — Exclusion of native Irish from them — Degeneracy of English Settlers — Parliament of Ireland — Disorderly State of the Island — The Irish regain Part of their Territories — English Law confined to the Pale — Poyning's Law — Royal Authority revives under Henry VIII. — Resistance of Irish to Act of Supremacy — Protestant Church established by Elizabeth — Effects of this Measure — Rebellions of her Reign — Opposition in Parliament — Arbitrary Proceedings of Sir Henry Sidney — James I. — Laws against Catholics enforced — English Law established throughout Ireland — Settlements of English in Munster, Ulster, and other Parts — Injustice attending them — Constitution of Irish Parliament — Charles I. promises Graces to the Irish — Does not confirm them — Administration of Strafford — Rebellion of 1641 — Subjugation of Irish by Cromwell — Restoration of Charles II. — Act of Settlement — Hopes of Catholics under Charles and James — War of 1689, and Final Reduction of Ireland — Penal Laws against Catholics — Dependence of Irish on English Parliament — Growth of a patriotic Party in 1753.

Ancient state of Ireland. The antiquities of Irish history, imperfectly recorded, and rendered more obscure by controversy, seem hardly to belong to our present subject. But the political order or state of society among that people at the period of Henry II.'s invasion must be distinctly apprehended and kept in mind before we can pass a judgment upon, or even understand, the course of succeeding events, and the policy of the English government in relation to that island.

It can hardly be necessary to mention (the idle traditions of a derivation from Spain having long been exploded) that the Irish are descended from one of those Celtic tribes which occupied Gaul and Britain some centuries before the Christian era. Their language, however, is so far dissimilar from that spoken in Wales, though evidently of the same root, as to render it probable that the emigration, whether from this island or from Armorica, was in a remote age; while its close resemblance to that of the Scottish Highlanders, which hardly can be called another dialect, as unequivocally demonstrates a nearer affinity of the two nations. It seems to be generally believed, though the antiquaries are far from unanimous, that the Irish are the parent tribe, and planted their colony in Scotland since the commencement of our era.

About the end of the eighth century some of those swarms of Scandinavian descent which were poured out in such unceasing and irresistible multitudes on France and Britain began to settle on the coasts of Ireland. These colonists were known by the name of Ostmen, or men from the east, as in France they were called Normans from their northern origin. They occupied the sea-coast from Antrim easterly round to Limerick; and by them the principal cities of Ireland were built. They waged war for some time against the aboriginal Irish in the interior; but, though better acquainted with the arts of civilized life, their inferiority in numbers caused them to fail at length in this contention; and the piratical invasions from their brethren in Norway becoming less frequent in the eleventh and twelfth centuries, they had fallen into a state of dependence on the native princes.

The island was divided into five provincial kingdoms, Leinster, Munster, Ulster, Connaught, and Meath; one of whose sovereigns was chosen king of Ireland in some general meeting, probably of the nobility or smaller chieftains and of the prelates. But there seems to be no clear tradition as to the character of this national assembly, though some maintain it to have been triennially held. The monarch of the island had tributes from the inferior kings, and a certain supremacy, especially in the defence of the country against invasion; but the constitution was of a federal nature, and each was independent in ruling his people, or in making war on his neighbours. Below the kings were the chieftains of different septs or families, perhaps in one or two degrees of subordination, bearing a relation which may be loosely called feudal, to each other and to the crown.°

Its kingdoms and chieftainships.

° Sir James Ware's Antiquities of Ireland; Leland's Hist. of Ireland (Introduction); Ledwich's Dissertations.

These chieftainships, and perhaps even the kingdoms themselves, though not partible, followed a very different rule of succession from that of primogeniture. They were subject to the law of tanistry, of which the principle is defined to be that the demesne lands and dignity of chieftainship descended to the eldest and most worthy of the same blood'; these epithets not being used, we may suppose, synonymously, but in order to indicate that the preference given to seniority was to be controlled by a due regard to desert. No better mode, it is evident, of providing for a perpetual supply of those civil quarrels in which the Irish are supposed to place so much of their enjoyment could have been devised. Yet, as these grew sometimes a little too frequent, it was not unusual to elect a tanist, or reversionary successor, in the lifetime of the reigning chief, as has been the practice of more civilized nations. An infant was never allowed to hold the sceptre of an Irish kingdom, but was necessarily postponed to his uncle or other kinsman of mature age; as was the case also in England, even after the consolidation of the Anglo-Saxon monarchy.^p

Law of tanistry.

The landowners who did not belong to the noble class bore the same name as their chieftain, and were presumed to be of the same lineage. But they held their estates by a very different and an extraordinary tenure, that of Irish gavel-kind. On the decease of a proprietor, instead of an equal partition among his children, as in the gavel-kind of English law, the chief of the sept, according to the generally received explanation, made, or was entitled to make, a fresh division of all the lands within his district; allotting to the heirs of the deceased a portion of the integral territory along with the other members of the tribe. It seems impossible to conceive that these partitions were renewed on every death of one of the sept. But they are asserted to have at least taken place so frequently as to produce a continual change of possession. The policy of this custom doubtless sprung from too jealous a solicitude as to the

and gavel-kind.

---

^p Id. Auct.: also Davis's Reports, 29, and his 'Discovery of the True Causes why Ireland was never entirely subdued till his Majesty's happy Reign,' 169. Sir John Davis, author of the philosophical poem, Γνῶθι Σεαυτὸν, was chief justice of Ireland under James I. The tract just quoted is well known as a concise and luminous exposition of the history of that country from the English invasion.

excessive inequality of wealth, and from the habit of looking on the tribe as one family of occupants, not wholly divested of its original right by the necessary allotment of lands to particular cultivators. It bore some degree of analogy to the institution of the year of jubilee in the Mosaic code; and, what may be thought more immediate, was almost exactly similar to the rule of succession which is laid down in the ancient laws of Wales.^q

In the territories of each sept, judges called Brehons, and taken out of certain families, sat with pri- meval simplicity upon turfen benches in some conspicuous situation, to determine controversies. Their usages are almost wholly unknown; for what have been published as fragments of the Brehon law seem open to great suspicion of having at least been interpolated.^r It is notorious that, according to the custom of many states in the infancy of civilization, the Irish admitted the composition or fine for murder, instead of capital punishment; and this was divided, as in other countries, between the kindred of the slain and the judge.

Rude state of society.

---

^q Ware; Leland; Ledwich; Davis's Discovery, Ibid.; Reports, 49. It is remarkable that Davis seems to have been aware of an analogy between the custom of Ireland and Wales, and yet that he only quotes the statute of Rutland, 12 Edw. I., which by itself does not prove it. It is however proved, if I understand the passage, by one of the Leges Walliæ, published by Wotton, p. 139. A gavel or partition was made on the death of every member of a family for three generations, after which none could be enforced. But these parceners were to be all in the same degree; so that nephews could not compel their uncle to a partition, but must wait till his death, when they were to be put on an equality with their cousins; and this, I suppose, is meant by the expression in the statute of Rutland, " quod hæreditates remaneant partibiles inter *consimiles hæredes.*"

^r Leland seems to favour the authenticity of the supposed Brehon laws published by Vallancey. Introduction, 29. The style is said to be very distinguishable from the Irish of the twelfth or thirteenth century, and the laws themselves to have no allusion to the settlement of foreigners in Ireland, or to coined money: whence some ascribe them to the eighth century. On the other hand, Ledwich proves that some parts must be later than the tenth century. Dissertations, i. 270. And others hold them to be not older than the thirteenth. Campbell's Historical Sketch of Ireland, 41. It is also maintained that they are very unfaithfully translated. But, when we find the Anglo-Saxon and Norman usages, relief, aid, wardship, trial by jury (and that unanimous), and a sort of correspondence in the ranks of society with those of England (which all we read elsewhere of the ancient Irish seems to contradict), it is impossible to resist the suspicion that they are either extremely interpolated, or were compiled in a late age, and among some of the septs who had most intercourse with the English. We know that the degenerate colonists, such as the earls of Desmond, adopted the Brehon law in their territories; but this would probably be with some admixture of that to which they had been used.

In the twelfth century it is evident that the Irish nation had made far less progress in the road of improvement than any other of Europe in circumstances of climate and position so little unfavourable. They had no arts that deserve the name, nor any commerce; their best line of sea-coast being occupied by the Norwegians. They had no fortified towns, nor any houses or castles of stone; the first having been erected at Tuam a very few years before the invasion of Henry.* Their conversion to Christianity, indeed, and the multitude of cathedral and conventual churches erected thoughout the island, had been the cause, and probably the sole cause, of the rise of some cities or villages with that name, such as Armagh, Cashel, and Trim. But neither the chiefs nor the people loved to be confined within their precincts, and chose rather to dwell in scattered cabins amidst the free solitude of bogs and mountains.† As we might expect, their qualities were such as belong to man by his original nature, and which he displays in all parts of the globe where the state of society is inartificial: they were gay, generous, hospitable, ardent in attachment and hate, credulous of falsehood, prone to anger and violence, generally crafty and cruel. With these very general attributes of a barbarous people, the Irish character was distinguished by a peculiar vivacity of imagination, an enthusiasm and impetuosity of passion, and a more than ordinary bias towards a submissive and superstitious spirit in religion.

This spirit may justly be traced in a great measure to the virtues and piety of the early preachers of the Gospel in that country. Their influence, though at this remote

---

* "The first pile of lime and stone that ever was in Ireland was the castle of Tuam, built in 1161 by Roderic O'Connor, the monarch." Introduction to Cox's History of Ireland. I do not find that any later writer controverts this, so far as the aboriginal Irish are concerned; but doubtless the Norwegian Ostmen had stone churches, and it used to be thought that some at least of the famous round towers so common in Ireland were erected by them, though several antiquaries have lately contended for a much earlier origin of these mysterious structures. See Ledwich's Dissertations, vii. 143; and the book called Grose's Antiquities of Ireland, also written by Ledwich. Piles of stone without mortar are not included in Cox's expression. In fact, the Irish had very few stone houses, or even regular villages and towns, before the time of James I. Davis, 170.

† ["I dare boldly say, that never any particular person, from the conquest till the reign of James I., did build any stone or brick house for his private habitation, but such as have lately obtained estates according to the course of the law of England." Davis.—1845.]

age, and with our imperfect knowledge, it may hardly be distinguishable amidst the licentiousness and ferocity of a rude people, was necessarily directed to counteract those vices, and cannot have failed to mitigate and compensate their evil. In the seventh and eighth centuries, while a total ignorance seemed to overspread the face of Europe, the monasteries and schools of Ireland preserved in the best manner they could such learning as had survived the revolutions of the Roman world. But the learning of monasteries had never much efficacy in dispelling the ignorance of the laity; and, indeed, even in them it had decayed long before the twelfth century. The clergy were respected and numerous, the bishops alone amounting at one time to no less than three hundred;" and it has been maintained by our most learned writers that they were wholly independent of the see of Rome till, a little before the English invasion, one of their primates thought fit to solicit the pall from thence on his consecration, according to the discipline long practised in other western churches.

It will be readily perceived that the government of Ireland must have been almost entirely aristocratical, and, though not strictly feudal, not very unlike that of the feudal confederacies in France during the ninth and tenth centuries. It was perhaps still more oppressive. The ancient condition of the common people of Ireland, says sir James Ware, was very little different from slavery.* Unless we believe this condition to have been greatly deteriorated under the rule of their native chieftains after the English settlement, for which there seems no good reason, we must give little credit to the fanciful pictures of prosperity and happiness in that period of aboriginal independence which the Irish, in their discontent with later times, have been apt to draw. They had, no doubt, like all other nations, good and wise princes, as well as tyrants and usurpers. But we find by their annals that, out of two hundred ancient kings, of whom some brief memorials are recorded, not more than thirty came to a natural death;⁷ while, for the later period, the oppression of the Irish chieftains, and of those degenerate English who trod in their steps, and

" Ledwich, i. 395.   * Antiquities of Ireland, ii. 76.
⁷ Ledwich, i. 260.

emulated the vices they should have restrained, is the one constant theme of history. Their exactions kept the peasants in hopeless poverty, their tyranny in perpetual fear. The chief claimed a right of taking from his tenants provisions for his own use at discretion, or of sojourning in their houses. This was called coshery, and is somewhat analogous to the royal prerogative of purveyance. A still more terrible oppression was the quartering of the lords' soldiers on the people, sometimes mitigated by a composition, called by the Irish bonaght.* For the perpetual warfare of these petty chieftains had given rise to the employment of mercenary troops, partly natives, partly from Scotland, known by the uncouth names of Kerns and Gallowglasses, who proved the scourge of Ireland down to its final subjugation by Elizabeth.

This unusually backward condition of society furnished but an inauspicious presage for the future. Yet we may be led by the analogy of other countries to think it probable that, if Ireland had not tempted the cupidity of her neighbours, there would have arisen in the course of time some Egbert or Harold Harfager to consolidate the provincial kingdoms into one hereditary monarchy; which, by the adoption of better laws, the increase of commerce, and a frequent intercourse with the chief courts of Europe, might have taken as respectable a station as that of Scotland in the commonwealth of Christendom. If the two islands had afterwards become incorporated through intermarriage of their sovereigns, as would very likely have taken place, it might have been on such conditions of equality as Ireland, till lately, has never known; and certainly without that long tragedy of crime and misfortune which her annals unfold.

The reduction of Ireland, at least in name, under the dominion of Henry II. was not achieved by his own efforts. He had little share in it, beyond receiving the homage of Irish princes, and granting charters to his English nobility. Strongbow, Lacy, Fitz-Stephen, were the real conquerors, through whom alone any portion of Irish territory was gained by arms or treaty; and, as they began the enterprise without

---

* Ware, ii. 74; Davis's Discovery, 174; Spenser's State of Ireland, 390.

the king, they carried it on also for themselves, deeming their swords a better security than his charters. This ought to be kept in mind, as revealing the secret of the English government over Ireland, and furnishing a justification for what has the appearance of a negligent abandonment of its authority. The few barons, and other adventurers, who, by dint of forces hired by themselves, and, in some instances, by conventions with the Irish, settled their armed colonies in the island, thought they had done much for Henry II. in causing his name to be acknowledged, his administration to be established in Dublin, and in holding their lands by his grant. They claimed in their turn, according to the practice of all nations and the principles of equity, that those who had borne the heat of the battle should enjoy the spoil without molestation. Hence, the enormous grants of Henry and his successors, though so often censured for impolicy, were probably what they could not have retained in their own hands; and, though not perhaps absolutely stipulated as the price of titular sovereignty, were something very like it.* But what is to be censured, and what at all hazards they were bound to refuse, was the violation of their faith to the Irish princes, in sharing among these insatiable barons their ancient territories; which, setting aside the wrong of the first invasion, were protected by their homage and submission, and sometimes by positive conventions. The whole island, in fact, with the exception of the county of Dublin and the maritime towns, was divided, before the end of the thirteenth century, and most of it in the twelfth, among ten English families: earl Strongbow, who had some colour of hereditary title, according to our notions of law, by his marriage with the daughter of Dermot, king of Leinster, obtaining a grant of that province; Lacy acquiring Meath, which was not reckoned a part of Leinster, in the same manner; the whole of Ulster being given to De Courcy; the whole of Connaught to De Burgh; and the rest to six others. These, it must be understood, they were to hold in a sort of feudal suzerainty, parcelling them among their tenants of English

marginal note: Acquisitions of English barons.

Davis, 135.

race, and expelling the natives, or driving them into the worst parts of the country by an incessant warfare.

<small>Forms of English constitution established.</small> The Irish chieftains, though compelled to show some exterior signs of submission to Henry, never thought of renouncing their own authority, or the customs of their forefathers; nor did he pretend to interfere with the government of their septs, content with their promise of homage and tribute, neither of which were afterwards paid. But in those parts of Ireland which he reckoned his own, it was his aim to establish the English laws, to render the lesser island, as it were, a counterpart in all its civil constitution, and mirror of the greater. The colony from England was already not inconsiderable, and likely to increase; the Ostmen, who inhabited the maritime towns, came very willingly, as all settlers of Teutonic origin have done, into the English customs and language; and upon this basis, leaving the accession of the aboriginal people to future contingencies, he raised the edifice of the Irish constitution. He gave charters of privilege to the chief towns, began a division into counties, appointed sheriffs and judges of assize to administer justice, erected supreme courts at Dublin, and perhaps assembled parliaments.[b] His successors pursued the same course of policy; the great charter of liberties, as soon as granted by John at Runnymede, was sent over to Ireland; and the whole common law, with all its forms of process, and every privilege it was deemed to convey, became the birthright of the Anglo-Irish colonists.[c]

These had now spread over a considerable part of the island. Twelve counties appear to have been established by John, comprehending most of Leinster and Munster; while the two ambitious families of Courcy and De Burgh encroached more and more on the natives in the other provinces.[d] But the same necessity, which grati-

---

[b] Leland, 80 et post. Davis, 100.
[c] 4 Inst. 349. Leland, 203. Harris's Hibernica, ii. 14.
[d] These counties are Dublin, Kildare, Meath (including Westmeath), Louth, Carlow, Wexford, Kilkenny, Waterford, Cork, Tipperary, Kerry, and Limerick. In the reign of Edward I. we find sheriffs also of Connaught and Roscommon. Leland, i. 19. Thus, except the northern province, and some of the central districts, all Ireland was shire-ground and subject to the crown in the thirteenth century, however it might fall away in the two next. Those who write confusedly about this subject pretend that

tude for the services or sense of the power of the great families had engendered, for rewarding them by excessive grants of territory, led to other concessions that rendered them almost independent of the monarchy.[e] The franchise of a county palatine gave a right of exclusive civil and criminal jurisdiction; so that the king's writ should not run, nor his judges come within it, though judgment in its courts might be reversed by writ of error in the king's bench. The lord might enfeoff tenants to hold by knight's service of himself; he had almost all regalian rights; the lands of those attainted for treason escheated to him; he acted in every thing rather as one of the great feudatories of France or Germany than a subject of the English crown. Such had been the earl of Chester, and only Chester, in England; but in Ireland this dangerous independence was permitted to Strongbow in Leinster, to Lacy in Meath, and at a later time to the Butlers and Geraldines in parts of Munster. Strongbow's vast inheritance soon fell to five sisters, who took to their shares, with the same palatine rights, the counties of Carlow, Wexford, Kilkenny, Kildare, and the district of Leix, since called the Queen's County.[f] In all these palatinates, forming by far the greater portion of the English territories, the king's process had its course only within the lands belonging to the church.[g] The English aristocracy of Ireland, in the thirteenth and fourteenth centuries, bears a much closer analogy to that of France in rather an earlier period than any thing which the history of this island can show.

Pressed by the inroads of these barons, and despoiled frequently of lands secured to them by grant or treaty, the native chiefs had recourse to the throne for protection, and would in all likelihood have submitted without repining to a sovereign who could have afforded it.[h] But John and Henry III., in whose reigns the

---

the authority of the king at no time extended beyond the pale; whereas that name was not known, I believe, till the fifteenth century. Under the great earl of Pembroke, who died in 1219, the whole island was perhaps nearly as much reduced under obedience as in the reign of Elizabeth. Leland, 205.

[e] Leland, 170.
[f] Davis, 140. William Marischal, earl of Pembroke, who married the daughter of earl Strongbow, left five sons and five daughters; the first all died without issue.
[g] Davis, 147. Leland, 291.
[h] Id. 194, 209.

independence of the aristocracy was almost complete, though insisting by writs and proclamations on a due observance of the laws, could do little more for their new subjects, who found a better chance of redress in standing on their own defence. The powerful septs of the north enjoyed their liberty. But those of Munster and Leinster, intermixed with the English, and encroached upon from every side, were the victims of constant injustice; and abandoning the open country for bog and mountain pasture, grew more poor and barbarous in the midst of the general advance of Europe. Many remained under the yoke of English lords, and in a worse state than that of villenage, because still less protected by the tribunals of justice. The Irish had originally stipulated with Henry II. for the use of their own laws.[i] They were consequently held beyond the pale of English justice, and regarded as aliens at the best, sometimes as enemies, in our courts. Thus, as by the Brehon customs murder was only punished by a fine, it was not held felony to kill one of Irish race, unless he had conformed to the English law.[k] Five septs, to which the royal families of Ireland belonged, the names of O'Neal, O'Connor, O'Brien, O'Malachlin, and Mac Murrough, had the special immunity of being within the protection of our law, and it was felony to kill one of them. I do not know by what means they obtained this privilege; for some of these were certainly as far from the king's

Exclusion of native Irish from them.

---

[i] Leland, 225.

[k] Davis, 100, 109. He quotes the following record from an assize at Waterford, in the 4th of Edward II. (1311), which may be extracted as briefly illustrating the state of law in Ireland better than any general positions. "Quod Robertus le Wayleys rectatus de morte Johannis filii Ivor Mac-Gillemory, felonicè per ipsum interfecti, &c. Venit et bene cognovit quod prædictum Johannem interfecit; dicit tamen quod per ejus interfectionem feloniam committere non potuit, quia dicit, quod prædictus Johannes fuit purus Hibernicus, et non de libero sanguine, &c. Et cum dominus dicti Johannis, cujus Hibernicus idem Johannes fuit, die quo interfectus fuit, solutionem pro ipso Johanne Hibernico suo sic interfecto petere voluerit, ipse Robertus paratus erit ad respondendum de solutione prædictâ prout justitia snadebit. Et super hoc venit quidam Johannes le Poer, et dicit pro domino rege, quod prædictus Johannes filius Ivor Mac-Gillemory, et antecessores sui de cognomine prædicto a tempore quo dominus Henricus filius imperatricis, quondam dominus Hiberniæ, tritavus domini regis nunc, fuit in Hiberniâ, legem Anglicanam in Hiberniâ usque ad hanc diem habere, et secundum ipsam legem judicari et deduci debent." We have here both the general rule, that the death of an Irishman was only punishable by a composition to his lord, and the exception in behalf of those natives who had conformed to the English law.

obedience as any in Ireland.ᵐ But besides these a vast
number of charters of denization were granted to particular persons of Irish descent from the reign of Henry II.
downwards, which gave them and their posterity the full
birthrights of English subjects; nor does there seem to
have been any difficulty in procuring these.ⁿ It cannot
be said, therefore, that the English government, or those
who represented it in Dublin, displayed any reluctance
to emancipate the Irish from thraldom. Whatever obstruction might be interposed to this was from that
assembly whose concurrence was necessary to every
general measure, the Anglo-Irish parliament. Thus, in
1278, we find the first instance of an application from
the community of Ireland, as it is termed, but probably
from some small number of septs dwelling among the
colony, that they might be admitted to live by the
English law, and offering 8000 marks for this favour.
The letter of Edward I. to the justiciary of Ireland on
this is sufficiently characteristic both of his wisdom and
his rapaciousness. He is satisfied of the expediency of
granting the request, provided it can be done with the
general consent of the prelates and nobles of Ireland;
and directs the justiciary, if he can obtain that concurrence, to agree with the petitioners for the highest fine
he can obtain, and for a body of good and stout soldiers.º
But this necessary consent of the aristocracy was withheld. Excuses were made to evade the king's desire.
It was wholly incompatible with their systematic encroachments on their Irish neighbours to give them the
safeguard of the king's writ for their possessions. The
Irish renewed their supplication more than once, both
to Edward I. and Edward III.; they found the same
readiness in the English court; they sunk at home
through the same unconquerable oligarchy.ᵖ It is not
to be imagined that the entire Irishry partook in this
desire of renouncing their ancient customs. Besides the
prejudices of nationality, there was a strong inducement
to preserve the Brehon laws of tanistry, which suited

ᵐ Davis, 104; Leland, 82. It was necessary to plead in bar of an action, that
the plaintiff was Hibernicus, et non de
quinque sanguinibus.
ⁿ Davis, 106. "If I should collect out
of the records all the charters of this kind,
I should make a volume thereof." They
began as early as the reign of Henry III.
Leland, 225.
º Leland, 243.   ᵖ Id. 239.

better a warlike tribe than the hereditary succession of England. But it was the unequivocal duty of the legislature to avail itself of every token of voluntary submission; which, though beginning only with the subject septs of Leinster, would gradually incorporate the whole nation in a common bond of co-equal privileges with their conquerors.

Degeneracy of English settlers. Meanwhile, these conquerors were themselves brought under a moral captivity of the most disgraceful nature; and, not as the rough soldier of Rome is said to have been subdued by the art and learning of Greece, the Anglo-Norman barons, that had wrested Ireland from the native possessors, fell into their barbarous usages, and emulated the vices of the vanquished. This degeneracy of the English settlers began very soon, and continued to increase for several ages. They intermarried with the Irish; they connected themselves with them by the national custom of fostering, which formed an artificial relationship of the strictest nature;[q] they spoke the Irish language; they affected the Irish dress and manner of wearing the hair;[r]

---

[q] "There were two other customs, proper and peculiar to the Irishry, which, being the cause of many strong combinations and factions, do tend to the utter ruin of a commonwealth. The one was *fostering*, the other *gossipred;* both which have ever been of greater estimation among this people than with any other nation in the Christian world. For *fostering*, I did never hear or read that it was in that use or reputation in any other country, barbarous or civil, as it hath been, and yet is, in Ireland, where they put away all their children to fosterers; the potent and rich men selling, the meaner sort buying, the alterage and nursing of their children; and the reason is, because, in the opinion of this people, *fostering* hath always been a stronger alliance than blood; and the foster-children do love and are beloved of their foster-fathers and their sept more than of their own natural parents and kindred, and do participate of their means more frankly, and do adhere to them in all fortunes with more affection and constancy. The like may be said of *gossipred* or compaternity, which though by the canon law it be a spiritual affinity, and a juror that was gossip to either of the parties might in former times have been challenged, as not indifferent, by our law, yet there was no nation under the sun that ever made so religious an account of it as the Irish." Davis, 179.

[r] "For that now there is no diversity in array between the English marchers and the Irish enemies, and so by colour of the English marchers, the Irish enemies do come from day to day into the English counties as English marchers, and do rob and kill by the highways, and destroy the common people by lodging upon them in the nights, and also do kill the husbands in the nights and do take their goods to the Irish men; wherefore it is ordained and agreed, that no manner man that will be taken for an Englishman shall have no beard above his mouth; that is to say, that he have no hairs upon his upper lip, so that the said lip be once at least shaven every fortnight, or of equal growth with the nether lip. And if any man be found among the English contrary hereunto, that then it shall be

they even adopted, in some instances, Irish surnames; they harassed their tenants with every Irish exaction and tyranny; they administered Irish law, if any at all; they became chieftains rather than peers; and neither regarded the king's summons to his parliaments, nor paid any obedience to his judges.* Thus the great family of De Burgh or Burke, in Connaught, fell off almost entirely from subjection; nor was that of the earls of Desmond, a younger branch of the house of Geraldine or Fitzgerald, much less independent of the crown; though by the title it enjoyed, and the palatine franchises granted to it by Edward III. over the counties of Limerick and Kerry, it seemed to keep up more show of English allegiance.

The regular constitution of Ireland was, as I have said, as nearly as possible a counterpart of that established in this country. The administration was vested in an English justiciary or lord deputy, assisted by a council of judges and principal officers, mixed with some prelates and barons, but subordinate to that of England, wherein sat the immediate advisers of the sovereign. The courts of chancery, king's bench, common pleas, and exchequer, were the same in both countries; but writs of error lay from judgments given in the second of these to the same court in England. For all momentous purposes, as to grant a subsidy, or enact a statute, it was as necessary to summon a parliament in the one island as in the other. An Irish parliament originally, like an English one, was but a more numerous council, to which the more distant as well as the neighbouring barons were summoned, whose consent, though dispensed with in ordinary acts of state, was both the pledge and the condition of their obedience to legislative provisions. Not long after 1295, the sheriff of each county and liberty is directed to return two knights to a parliament held by Wogan, an active and able deputy.‡ The date of the admission of burgesses cannot be

<small>*Parliament of Ireland.*</small>

<small>lawful to every man to take them and their goods as Irish enemies, and to ransom them as Irish enemies." Irish Statutes, 25 H. VI., c. 4.

² Davis, 152, 182; Leland, L. 256, &c. Ware, ii. 58.

‡ Leland, 253. [The precise year is not mentioned, but Wogan became deputy in 1295. Archbishop Usher, however (in Collectanea Curiosa, vol. i. p. 36), says that there had been a parliament as early as 48 H. III. (1264). Usher makes</small>

fixed with precision; but it was probably not earlier than the reign of Edward III. They appear in 1341; and the earl of Desmond summoned many deputies from corporations to his rebel convention held at Kilkenny in the next year." The commons are mentioned as an essential part of parliament in an ordinance of 1359; before which time, in the opinion of lord Coke, "the conventions in Ireland were not so much parliaments as assemblies of great men."ˣ This, as appears, is not strictly correct; but in substance they were perhaps little else long afterwards.

The earliest statutes on record are of the year 1310; and from that year they are lost till 1429, though we know many parliaments to have been held in the mean time, and are acquainted by other means with their provisions. Those of 1310 bear witness to the degeneracy of the English lords, and to the laudable zeal of a feeble government for the reformation of their abuses. They begin with an act to restrain great lords from taking of prises, lodging, and sojourning with the people of the country against their will. "It is agreed and assented," the act proceeds, "that no such prises shall be henceforth made without ready payment and agreement, and that none shall harbour or sojourn at the house of any other by such malice against the consent of him which is owner of the house to destroy his goods; and if any shall do the same, such prises, and such manner of destruction, shall be holden for open robbery, and the king shall have the suit thereof, if others will not, nor dare not sue. It is agreed also that none shall keep idle people nor kearn (foot soldiers) in time of peace to live upon the poor of the country, but that those which will have them shall keep them at their own charges, so that their free tenants, nor farmers, nor other tenants be not charged with them." The statute proceeds to restrain great lords or others, except such as have royal franchises, from giving protections, which they used to compel the people to purchase; and directs that there shall be com-

---

a distinction between small and great parliaments, calling the former rather *parlies.*—1845.]

ᵘ Cox's Hist. of Ireland, 117, 120.

ˣ Id. 125, 129; Leland, 313. [It may be probably thought that the *majores civitatum regalium*, whom Desmond summoned to Kilkenny, were mayors, rather than representatives. Usher, ibid.—1845.]

missions of assize and gaol delivery through all the counties of Ireland.[y]

These regulations exhibit a picture of Irish miseries. The barbarous practices of coshering and bonaght, the latter of which was generally known in later times by the name of coyne and livery, had been borrowed from those native chieftains whom our modern Hibernians sometimes hold forth as the paternal benefactors of their country.[z] It was the crime of the Geraldines and the De Courcys to have retrograded from the comparative humanity and justice of England, not to have deprived the people of freedom and happiness they had never known. These degenerate English, an epithet by which they are always distinguished, paid no regard to the statutes of a parliament which they had disdained to attend, and which could not render itself feared. We find many similar laws in the fifteenth century, after the interval which I have noticed in the printed records. And in the intervening period, a parliament held by Lionel duke of Clarence, second son of Edward III., at Kilkenny, in 1367, the most numerous assembly that had ever met in Ireland, was prevailed upon to pass a very severe statute against the insubordinate and degenerate colonists. It recites that the English of the realm of Ireland were become mere Irish in their language, names, apparel, and manner of living, that they had rejected the English laws, and allied themselves by intermarriage with the Irish. It prohibits under the penalties of high treason, or at least of forfeiture of lands, all these approximations to the native inhabitants, as well as the connexions of fostering and gossipred. The English are restrained from permitting the Irish to graze their lands, from presenting them to benefices, or receiving them into religious houses, and from entertaining their bards. On the other hand, they are forbidden to make war upon their Irish neighbours without the authority of the state. And, to enforce better these provisions, the king's sheriffs are empowered to enter all franchises for the apprehension of felons or traitors.[a]

---

[y] Irish Statutes.

[z] Davis, 174, 189; Leland, 281. Maurice Fitz-Thomas, earl of Desmond, was the first of the English, according to Ware, ii. 76, who imposed the exaction of coyne and livery.

[a] Irish Statutes; Davis, 202; Cox; Leland. [The statute of Kilkenny though

This statute, like all others passed in Ireland, so far from pretending to bind the Irish, regarded them not only as out of the king's allegiance, but as perpetually hostile to his government. They were generally denominated the Irish enemy. This doubtless was not according to the policy of Henry II., nor of the English government a considerable time after his reign. Nor can it be said to be the fact, though from some confusion of times the assertion is often made, that the island was not subject, in a general sense, to that prince and to the three next kings of England. The English were settled in every province; an imperfect division of counties and administration of justice subsisted; and even the Irish chieftains, though ruling their septs by the Brehon law, do not appear in that period to have refused the acknowledgment of the king's sovereignty. But, compelled to defend their lands against perpetual aggression, they justly renounced all allegiance to a government which could not redeem the original wrong of its usurpation by the benefits of protection. They became gradually stronger; they regained part of their lost territories; and after the era of 1315, when Edward Bruce invaded the kingdom with a Scots army, and, though ultimately defeated, threw the government into a disorder from which it never recovered, their progress was so rapid, that in the space of thirty or forty years the northern provinces, and even part of the southern, were entirely lost to the crown of England.[b]

It is unnecessary in so brief a sketch to follow the unprofitable annals of Ireland in the fourteenth and fifteenth centuries. Amidst the usual variations of war, the English interests were continually losing ground. Once only Richard II. appeared with a very powerful army, and the princes of Ireland crowded round his

Leland, i. 329, says that Edward was obliged to relax it in some particulars, as incapable of being enforced, restored the English government for a time, if we may believe Davis, p. 222, so that it did not fall back again till the war of the Roses. About this time Edward III. endeavoured to supersede the domestic legislature by causing the Anglo-Irish to attend his parliament at Westminster; and succeeded so far that, in 1375, not only prelates and peers, but proctors of the clergy, knights, and even burgesses from nine towns, actually sat there. But this was too much against the temper of the Irish to be repeated. Leland, i. 327, 363.—1845.]

[b] Leland, i. 276, 296, 324; Davis, 152, 197.

throne to offer homage.ᶜ But, upon his leaving the
kingdom, they returned of course to their former independence and hostility. The long civil wars of England
in the next century consummated the ruin of its power
over the sister island. The Irish possessed all Ulster,
and shared Connaught with the degenerate Burkes. The
sept of O'Brien held their own district of Thomond, now
the county of Clare. A considerable part of Leinster
was occupied by other independent tribes; while in the
south, the earls of Desmond, lords either by property
or territorial jurisdiction of the counties of Kerry and
Limerick, and in some measure those of Cork and Waterford, united the turbulence of English barons with the
savage manners of Irish chieftains; ready to assume
either character as best suited their rapacity and ambition; reckless of the king's laws or his commands, but
not venturing, nor, upon the whole probably, wishing,
to cast off the name of his subjects.ᵈ The elder branch
of their house, the earls of Kildare, and another illustrious family, the Butlers, earls of Ormond, were apparently more steady in their obedience to the crown; yet,
in the great franchises of the latter, comprising the counties of Kilkenny and Tipperary, the king's writ had no
course; nor did he exercise any civil or military authority but by the permission of this mighty peer.ᵉ
Thus in the reign of Henry VII., when the English law confined to the pale.
English authority over Ireland had reached its
lowest point, it was, with the exception of a
very few seaports, to all intents confined to the four
counties of the English pale, a name not older perhaps
than the preceding century; those of Dublin, Louth,
Kildare, and Meath, the latter of which at that time
included West Meath. But even in these there were
extensive marches, or frontier districts, the inhabitants
of which were hardly distinguishable from the Irish, and
paid them a tribute called black-rent; so that the real
supremacy of the English laws was not probably established beyond the two first of these counties, from

---

ᶜ Leland, 342. The native chieftains who came to Dublin are said to have been seventy-five in number; but the insolence of the courtiers, who ridiculed an unusual dress and appearance, disgusted them.

ᵈ [It appears by the rates paid to a subsidy granted in 1420, that most of Leinster, with a small part of Munster, still contributed. Cox, 152.—1845.]

ᵉ Davis, 193.

Dublin to Dundalk on the coast, and for about thirty miles inland.' From this time, however, we are to date its gradual recovery. The more steady counsels and firmer prerogative of the Tudor kings left little chance of escape from their authority, either for rebellious peers of English race, or the barbarous chieftains of Ireland.

I must pause at this place to observe that we shall hardly find in the foregoing sketch of Irish history, during the period of the Plantagenet dynasty (nor am I conscious of having concealed anything essential), that systematic oppression and misrule which is every day imputed to the English nation and its government. The policy of our kings appears to have generally been wise and beneficent; but it is duly to be remembered that those very limitations of their prerogative which constitute liberty, must occasionally obstruct the execution of the best purposes; and that the co-ordinate powers of parliament, so justly our boast, may readily become the screen of private tyranny and inveterate abuse. This incapacity of doing good as well as harm has produced, comparatively speaking, little mischief in Great Britain; where the aristocratical element of the constitution is neither so predominant, nor so much in opposition to the general interest, as it may be deemed to have been in Ireland. But it is manifestly absurd to charge the Edwards and Henrys, or those to whom their authority was delegated at Dublin, with the crimes they vainly endeavoured to chastise; much more to erect either the wild barbarians of the north, the O'Neals and O'Connors, or the degenerate houses of Burke and Fitzgerald, into patriot assertors of their country's welfare. The laws

---

f Leland, ii. 822 et post; Davis, 199, 229, 236; Hollingshed's Chronicles of Ireland, p. 4. Finglas, a baron of the exchequer in the reign of Henry VIII., in his Breviate of Ireland, from which Davis has taken great part of his materials, says expressly, that by the disobedience of the Geraldines and Butlers, and their Irish connexions, "the whole land is now of Irish rule, except the little English pale within the counties of Dublin and Meath, and Uriel [Louth], which pass not thirty or forty miles in compass." He afterwards includes Kildare. The English were also expelled from Munster, except the walled towns. The king had no profit from Ulster but the manor of Carlingford, nor any from Connaught. This treatise, written about 1530, is printed in Harris's Hibernica. The proofs that, in this age, the English law and government were confined to the four shires are abundant. It is even mentioned in a statute, 13 H. VIII., c. 2.

and liberties of England were the best inheritance to which Ireland could attain; the sovereignty of the English crown her only shield against native or foreign tyranny. It was her calamity that these advantages were long withheld; but the blame can never fall upon the government of this island.

In the contest between the houses of York and Lancaster, most of the English colony in Ireland had attached themselves to the fortunes of the White Rose; they even espoused the two pretenders, who put in jeopardy the crown of Henry VII.; and thus became of course obnoxious to his jealousy, though he was politic enough to forgive in appearance their disaffection. But as Ireland had for a considerable time rather served the purposes of rebellious invaders than of the English monarchy, it was necessary to make her subjection, at least so far as the settlers of the pale were concerned, more than a word. This produced the famous statute of Drogheda, in 1495, known by the name of Poyning's law, from the lord deputy through whose vigour and prudence it was enacted. *Poyning's law.* It contains a variety of provisions to restrain the lawlessness of the Anglo-Irish within the pale (for to no others could it immediately extend), and to confirm the royal sovereignty. All private hostilities without the deputy's licence were declared illegal; but to excite the Irish to war was made high treason. Murders were to be prosecuted according to law, and not in the manner of the natives, by pillaging, or exacting a fine from the sept of the slayer. The citizens or freemen of towns were prohibited from receiving wages or becoming retainers of lords and gentlemen; and, to prevent the ascendancy of the latter class, none who had not served apprenticeships were to be admitted as aldermen or freemen of corporations. The requisitions of coyne and livery, which had subsisted in spite of the statutes of Kilkenny, were again forbidden, and those statutes were renewed and confirmed. The principal officers of state and the judges were to hold their patents during pleasure, "because of the great inconveniences that had followed from their being for term of life, to the king's grievous displeasure." A still more important provision, in its permanent consequence, was made, by enacting that all statutes lately made in England be deemed good and effectual in Ireland.⁸ It has been remarked that the same had been done by an Irish act of Edward IV. Some question might also be made, whether the word "lately" was not intended to limit this acceptation of English law. But in effect this enactment has made an epoch in Irish jurisprudence; all statutes made in England prior to the eighteenth year of Henry VII. being held equally valid in Ireland, while none of later date have any operation, unless specially adopted by its parliament; so that the law of the two countries has begun to diverge from that time, and after three centuries has been in several respects differently modified.

But even these articles of Poyning's law are less momentous than one by which it is peculiarly known. It is enacted that no parliament shall in future be holden in Ireland till the king's lieutenant shall certify to the king, under the great seal, the causes and considerations, and all such acts as it seems to them ought to be passed thereon, and such be affirmed by the king and his council, and his licence to hold a parliament be obtained. Any parliament holden contrary to this form and provision should be deemed void. Thus by securing the initiative power to the English council, a bridle was placed in the mouths of every Irish parliament. It is probable also that it was designed as a check on the lord-deputies, sometimes powerful Irish nobles, whom it was dangerous not to employ, but still more dangerous to trust. Whatever might be its motives, it proved in course of time the great means of preserving the subordination of an island, which, from the similarity of constitution, and the high spirit of its inhabitants, was constantly panting for an independence which her more powerful neighbour neither desired nor dared to concede.ʰ

---

⁸ [It had been common to extend the operation of English statutes to Ireland, even when not particularly named, if the judges thought that the subject was sufficiently general to require it; as in the statute of Merchants, 13 E. I.; the statute Westminster 2, the same year; and many others under Edward II. and Edward III. But in the reign of Richard III. a question was debated in the exchequer chamber, "Si villæ corporatæ in Hibernia et alii habitantes in Hibernia erunt ligati per statutum factum in Anglia." And this was resolved affirmatively by a majority of the English judges, though some differed. Usher, in Collectanea Curiosa, p. 29; citing Fitzherbert and Broke.—1845.]

ʰ Irish Statutes; Davis, 230; Leland, ii. 102.

No subjects of the crown in Ireland enjoyed such influence at this time as the earls of Kildare, whose possessions lying chiefly within the pale, they did not affect an ostensible independence, but generally kept in their hands the chief authority of government, though it was the policy of the English court, in its state of weakness, to balance them in some measure by the rival family of Butler. But the self-confidence with which this exaltation inspired the chief of the former house laid him open to the vengeance of Henry VIII.; he affected, while lord-deputy, to be surrounded by Irish lords, to assume their wild manners, and to intermarry his daughters with their race. The councillors of English birth or origin dreaded this suspicious approximation to their hereditary enemies; and Kildare, on their complaint, was compelled to obey his sovereign's order by repairing to London. He was committed to the Tower: on a premature report that he had suffered death, his son, a young man to whom he had delegated the administration, took up arms under the rash impulse of resentment; the primate was murdered by his wild followers, but the citizens of Dublin and the reinforcement sent from England suppressed this hasty rebellion, and its leader was sent a prisoner to London. Five of his uncles, some of them not concerned in the treason, perished with him on the scaffold; his father had been more fortunate in a natural death; one sole surviving child of twelve years old, who escaped to Flanders, became afterwards the stock from which the great family of the Geraldines was restored.[1]

Royal authority revives under Henry VIII.

The chieftains of Ireland were justly attentive to the stern and systematic despotism which began to characterise the English government, displayed, as it thus was, in the destruction of an ancient and loyal house. But their intimidation produced contrary effects; they became more ready to profess allegiance and to put on the exterior badges of submission, but more jealous of the crown in their hearts, more resolute to preserve their independence, and to withstand any change of laws. Thus, in the latter years of Henry, after the northern Irish had been beaten by an able deputy, lord Leonard

[1] Leland.

Grey, and the lordship of Ireland, the title hitherto borne by the successors of Henry II., had been raised by act of parliament to the dignity of a kingdom,[k] the native chiefs came in and submitted; the earl of Desmond, almost as independent as any of the natives, attended parliament, from which his ancestors had for some ages claimed a dispensation; several peerages were conferred, some of them on the old Irish families; fresh laws were about the same time enacted to establish the English dress and language, and to keep the colonists apart from Irish intercourse;[m] and after a disuse of two hundred years, the authority of government was nominally recognised throughout Munster and Connaught.[n] Yet we find that these provinces were still in nearly the same condition as before; the king's judges did not administer justice in them, the old Brehon usages continued to prevail even in the territories of the new peers, though their primogenitary succession was evidently incompatible with Irish tanistry. A rebellion of two septs in Leinster under Edward VI. led to a more complete reduction of their districts, called Leix and O'Fally, which in the next reign were made shireland, by the names of King's and Queen's county.[o] But, at the accession of Elizabeth, it was manifest that an arduous struggle would ensue between law and liberty; the one too nearly allied to cool-blooded oppression, the other to ferocious barbarism.

It may be presumed, as has been already said, from the analogy of other countries, that Ireland, if left to

---

[k] Irish Statutes, 33 H. VIII., c. 1.

[m] Ibid. 28 H. VIII., c. 15, 28. The latter act prohibits intermarriage or fostering with the Irish; which had indeed been previously restrained by other statutes. In one passed five years afterwards, it is recited that "the king's English subjects, by reason that they are inhabited in so little compass or circuit and restrained by statute to marry with the Irish nation, and therefore of necessity must marry themselves together, so that in effect they all for the most part must be allied together: and therefore it is enacted that consanguinity or affinity beyond the fourth degree shall be no cause of challenge on a jury." 33 H. VIII., c. 4. These laws were for many years of little avail, so far at least as they were meant to extend beyond the pale. Spenser's State of Ireland, p. 384 et post.

[n] Leland, ii. 178, 184.

[o] Ibid. ii. 189, 211; 3 and 4 P. and M. c. 1 & 2. Meath had been divided into two shires, by separating the western part. 34 H. VIII., c. 1. "Forasmuch as the shire of Methe is great and large in circuit, and the west part thereof laid about or beset with divers of the king's rebels." Baron Finglas says, "Half Meath has not obeyed the king's laws these one hundred years or more." Breviate of Ireland, apud Harris, p. 85.

herself, would have settled in time under some one line of kings, and assumed, like Scotland, much of the feudal character, the best transitional state of a monarchy from rudeness and anarchy to civilization. And, if the right of female succession had been established, it might possibly have been united to the English crown on a juster footing, and with far less of oppression or bloodshed than actually took place. But it was too late to dream of what might have been: in the middle of the sixteenth century Ireland could have no reasonable prospect of independence; nor could that independence have been any other than the most savage liberty, perhaps another denomination of servitude. It was doubtless for the interest of that people to seek the English constitution, which, at least in theory, was entirely accorded to their country, and to press with spontaneous homage round the throne of Elizabeth. But this was not the interest of their ambitious chieftains, whether of Irish or English descent, of a Slanes O'Neil, an earl of Tyrone, an earl of Desmond. Their influence was irresistible among a nation ardently sensible to the attachments of clanship, averse to innovation, and accustomed to dread and hate a government that was chiefly known by its severities. But the unhappy alienation of Ireland from its allegiance in part of the queen's reign would probably not have been so complete, or at least led to such permanent mischiefs, if the ancient national animosities had not been exasperated by the still more invincible prejudices of religion.

Henry VIII. had no sooner prevailed on the lords and commons of England to renounce their spiritual obedience to the Roman see, and to acknowledge his own supremacy, than, as a natural consequence, he proceeded to establish it in Ireland. *Resistance of Irish to act of supremacy.* In the former instance, many of his subjects, and even his clergy, were secretly attached to the principles of the Reformation; as many others were jealous of ecclesiastical wealth, or eager to possess it. But in Ireland the reformers had made no progress; it had been among the effects of the pernicious separation of the two races, that the Irish priests had little intercourse with their bishops, who were nominated by the king, so that their synods are commonly recited to have been holden *inter Anglicos;* the bishops themselves were sometimes intruded by violence, more often dispossessed by it; a total ignorance and neglect prevailed in the church; and it is even found impossible to recover the succession of names in some sees.[p] In a nation so ill predisposed, it was difficult to bring about a compliance with the king's demand of abjuring their religion: ignorant, but not indifferent, the clergy, with Cromer the primate at their head, and most of the lords and commons, in a parliament held at Dublin in 1536, resisted the act of supremacy; which was nevertheless ultimately carried by the force of government.[q] Its enemies continued to withstand the new schemes of reformation, more especially in the next reign, when they went altogether to subvert the ancient faith. As it appeared dangerous to summon a parliament, the English liturgy was ordered by a royal proclamation; but Dowdall, the new primate, as stubborn an adherent of the Romish church as his predecessor, with most of the other bishops and clergy, refused obedience; and the Reformation was never legally established in the short reign of Edward.[r] His eldest sister's accession reversed of course what had been done, and restored tranquillity in ecclesiastical matters; for the protestants were too few to be worth persecution, nor were even those molested who fled to Ireland from the fires of Smithfield.

Another scene of revolution ensued in a very few years. Elizabeth, having fixed the protestant church on

---

[p] Leland, ii. 158.

[q] [Ibid 165. An act in this year, reciting that " proctors of the clergy had been used and accustomed to be summoned and warned to be at parliament, which were never by the order of the law, usage, custom, or otherwise, any member or parcel of the whole body of the parliament, nor have had of right any voice or suffrage in the same, but only to be there as councillors and assistants to the same," and proceeding to admit that these proctors "have usually been privy and consulted about laws," asserts and enacts that they have no right, as they " temerariously presume, and usurpedly take on themselves, to be parcel of the body, in manner claiming that without their assents nothing can be enacted at any parliament within this land." Irish Statutes, 28 H. VIII., c. 12. This is followed by c. 13, enacting the oath of supremacy; the refusal of which, by any person holding an office temporal or spiritual, is made treason. See Gilbert's Treatise of the Exchequer, p. 58, for the proctors of the clergy assisting in parliament.—1845.]

[r] [The famous Bail was made bishop of Ossory, and insisted on being consecrated according to the protestant form, though not established. He lived in a perpetual state of annoyance, brought on in great measure by his rash zeal. Leland, ii. 202. At the accession of Mary, those of the clergy who had taken wives were ejected: 207.—1845.]

a stable basis in England, sent over the earl of Sussex to hold an Irish parliament in 1560. The disposition of such an assembly might be presumed hostile to the projected reformations; but contrary to what had occurred on this side of the channel, though the peers were almost uniformly for the old religion, a large majority of the bishops are said to have veered round with the times, and supported, at least by conformity and acquiescence, the creed of the English court. In the house of commons pains had been taken to secure a majority; ten only out of twenty counties, which had at that time been formed, received the writ of summons; and the number of seventy-six representatives of the Anglo-Irish people was made up by the towns, many of them under the influence of the crown, some perhaps containing a mixture of protestant population. The English laws of supremacy and uniformity were enacted in nearly the same words; and thus the common prayer was at once set up instead of the mass, but with a singular reservation, that in those parts of the country where the minister had no knowledge of the English language, he might read the service in Latin. All subjects were bound to attend the public worship of the church, and every other was interdicted.*

Protestant church established by Elizabeth.

There were doubtless three arguments in favour of this compulsory establishment of the protestant church, which must have appeared so conclusive to Elizabeth and her council, that no one in that age could have disputed them without incurring, among other hazards, that of being accounted a lover of unreasonable paradoxes. The first was, that the protestant religion being true, it was the queen's duty to take care that her subjects should follow no other; the second, that, being an absolute monarch, or something like it, and a very wise princess, she had a better right to order what doctrine they should believe, than they could have to choose for themselves; the third, that Ireland, being as a handmaid, and a conquered country, must wait, in all important matters, on the pleasure of the greater island, and be accommodated to its revolutions. And, as it was natural that the queen and her advisers should not

---

* Leland, 224; Irish Statutes, 2 Eliz.

reject maxims which all the rest of the world entertained, merely because they were advantageous to themselves, we need not perhaps be very acrimonious in censuring the laws whereon the church of Ireland is founded. But it is still equally true that they involve a principle essentially unjust, and that they have enormously aggravated, both in the age of Elizabeth and long afterwards, the calamities and the disaffection of Ireland. An ecclesiastical establishment, that is, the endowment and privileges of a particular religious society, can have no advantages (relatively at least to the community where it exists) but its tendency to promote in that community good order and virtue, religious knowledge and edification. But, to accomplish this end in any satisfactory manner, it must be their church, and not that merely of the government; it should exist for the people, and in the people, and with the people. This indeed is so manifest that the government of Elizabeth never contemplated the separation of a great majority as licensed dissidents from the ordinances established for their instruction. It was undoubtedly presumed, as it was in England, that the church and commonwealth, according to Hooker's language, were to be two denominations of the same society; and that every man in Ireland who appertained to the one ought to embrace, and in due season would embrace, the communion of the other. There might be ignorance, there might be obstinacy, there might be feebleness of conscience for a time; and perhaps some connivance would be shown to these; but that the prejudices of a majority should ultimately prevail so as to determine the national faith, that it should even obtain a legitimate indulgence for its own mode of worship, was abominable before God, and incompatible with the sovereign authority.

This sort of reasoning, half bigotry, half despotism, was nowhere so preposterously displayed as in Ireland. The numerical majority is not always to be ascertained with certainty; and some regard may fairly, or rather necessarily, be had to rank, to knowledge, to concentration. But in that island the disciples of the Reformation were in the most inconsiderable proportion among the Anglo-Irish colony, as well as among the natives their church was a govern-

Effects of this measure.

ment without subjects, a college of shepherds without sheep. I am persuaded that this was not intended nor expected to be a permanent condition; but such were the difficulties which the state of that unhappy nation presented, or such the negligence of its rulers, that scarce any pains were taken in the age of Elizabeth, nor indeed in subsequent ages, to win the people's conviction, or to eradicate their superstitions, except by penal statutes and the sword. The Irish language was universally spoken without the pale; it had even made great progress within it; the clergy were principally of that nation; yet no translation of the Scriptures, the chief means through which the Reformation had been effected in England and Germany, nor even of the regular liturgy, was made into that tongue; nor was it possible, perhaps, that any popular instruction should be carried far in Elizabeth's reign, either by public authority or by the ministrations of the reformed clergy. Yet neither among the Welsh nor the Scots Highlanders, though Celtic tribes, and not much better in civility of life at that time than the Irish, was the ancient religion long able to withstand the sedulous preachers of reformation.

It is evident from the history of Elizabeth's reign that the forcible dispossession of the catholic clergy, and their consequent activity in deluding a people too open at all times to their counsels, aggravated the rebellious spirit of the Irish, and rendered their obedience to the law more unattainable. But, even independently of this motive, the Desmonds and Tyrones would have tried, as they did, the chances of insurrection, rather than abdicate their unlicensed but ancient chieftainship. It must be admitted that, if they were faithless in promises of loyalty, the crown's representatives in Ireland set no good example; and when they saw the spoliations of property by violence or pretext of law, the sudden executions on alleged treasons, the breaches of treaty, sometimes even the assassinations, by which a despotic policy went onward in its work of subjugation, they did but play the usual game of barbarians in opposing craft and perfidy, rather more gross perhaps and notorious, to the same engines of a dissembling government.' Yet if we can put any trust in our own testimonies, the great families were, by mismanagement and dissension, the curse of their vassals. Sir Henry Sidney represents to the queen, in 1567, the wretched condition of the southern and western counties in the vast territories of the earls of Ormond, Desmond, and Clanricarde." " An unmeasurable tract," he says, " is now waste and uninhabited, which of late years was well tilled and pastured." " A more pleasant nor a more desolate land I never saw than from Youghall to Limerick."[t] "So far hath that policy, or rather lack of policy, in keeping dissension among them prevailed, as now, albeit all that are alive would become honest and live in quiet, yet are there not left alive in those two provinces the twentieth person necessary to inhabit the same."[y] Yet this was but the first scene of

[t] Leland gives several instances of breach of faith in the government. A little tract, called a Brief Declaration of the Government of Ireland, written by captain Lee, in 1594, and published in Desiderata Curiosa Hibernica, vol. i., censures the two last deputies (Grey and Fitzwilliams) for their ill-usage of the Irish, and unfolds the despotic character of the English government. "The cause they (the lords of the north) have to stand upon those terms, and to seek for better assurance, is the harsh practices used against others by those who have been placed in authority to protect men for your majesty's service, which they have greatly abused in this sort. They have drawn unto them by protection three or four hundred of the country people, under colour to do your majesty service, and brought them to a place of meeting, where your garrison soldiers were appointed to be, who have there most dishonourably put them all to the sword; and this hath been by the consent and practice of the lord deputy for the time being. If this be a good course to draw those savage people to the state to do your majesty service, and not rather to enforce them to stand on their guard, I leave to your majesty." P. 90. He goes on to enumerate more cases of hardship and tyranny; many being arraigned and convicted of treason on slight evidence; many assaulted and killed by the sheriffs on commissions of rebellion; others imprisoned and kept in irons; among others, a youth, the heir of a great estate. He certainly praises Tyrone more than, from subsequent events, we should think just, which may be thought to throw some suspicion on his own loyalty; yet he seems to have been a protestant, and in 1594 the views of Tyrone were ambiguous, so that captain Lee may have been deceived.

[u] Sidney Papers, L 20. [This is in a long report to the queen, which contains an interesting view of the state of the country during its transition from Irish to English law. Athenry, he says, had once 300 good householders, and in his own recollection twenty, who are reduced to four, and those poor. It had been mixed by the Clanricardes. But, "as touching all Leinster and Meath, I dare affirm on my credit unto your majesty, as well for the English pale and the justice thereof, it was never in the memory of the oldest man that now liveth in greater quiet and obedience."— 1845.]

[x] Ibid. 24.

[y] Sidney Papers, i. 29. Spenser descants on the lawless violence of the superior Irish, and imputes, I believe with much justice, a great part of their crimes to his own brethren, if they might claim so proud a title, the bards:—" whomsoever they find to be most licentious of

calamity. After the rebellion of the last earl of Desmond, the counties of Cork and Kerry, his ample patrimony, were so wasted by war and military executions, and famine and pestilence, that, according to a contemporary writer, who expresses the truth with hyperbolical energy, "the land itself, which before those wars was populous, well inhabited, and rich in all the good blessings of God, being plenteous of corn, full of cattle, well stored with fruit and sundry other good commodities, is now become waste and barren, yielding no fruits, the pastures no cattle, the fields no corn, the air no birds, the seas, though full of fish, yet to them yielding nothing. Finally, every way the curse of God was so great, and the lands so barren both of man and beast, that whosoever did travel from the one end unto the other of all Munster, even from Waterford to the head of Limerick, which is about six-score miles, he should not meet any man, woman, or child, saving in towns and cities; nor yet see any beast but the very wolves, the foxes, and other like ravening beasts."[z] The severity of sir Arthur Grey, at this time deputy, was such that Elizabeth was assured he had left little for her to reign over but ashes and carcasses; and, though not by any means of too indulgent a nature, she was induced to recall him.[a] His successor, sir John Perrott, who held the viceroyalty only from 1584 to 1587, was distinguished for a sense of humanity and justice, together with an active zeal for the enforcement of law. Sheriffs were now appointed for the five counties into which Connaught had some years before been parcelled; and even for Ulster, all of which, except Antrim and Down, had hitherto been undivided, as well as ungoverned.[b]

life, most bold and lawless in his doings, most dangerous and desperate in all parts of disobedience and rebellious disposition, him they set up and glorify in their rhymes, him they praise to the people, and to young men make an example to follow." P. 394.

[z] Hollingshed, 460.

[a] Leland, 287; Spenser's Account of Ireland, p. 430 (vol. viii. of Todd's edition, 1805). Grey is the Arthegal of the Faery Queen, the representative of the virtue of justice in that allegory, attended by Talus with his iron flail, which indeed was unsparingly employed to crush rebellion. Grey's severity was signalised in putting to death seven hundred Spaniards who had surrendered at discretion in the fort of Smerwick. Though this might be justified by the strict laws of war (Philip not being a declared enemy), it was one of those extremities which justly revolt the common feelings of mankind. The queen is said to have been much displeased at it. Leland, 283. Spenser undertakes the defence of his patron Grey. State of Ireland, p. 434.

[b] Leland, 247, 293. An Act had

Yet even this apparently wholesome innovation aggravated at first the servitude of the natives, whom the new sheriffs were prone to oppress.[c] Perrott, the best of Irish governors, soon fell a sacrifice to a court intrigue and the queen's jealousy; and the remainder of her reign was occupied with almost unceasing revolts of the earl of Tyrone, head of the great sect of O'Neil in Ulster, instigated by Rome and Spain, and endangering, far more than any preceding rebellion, her sovereignty over Ireland.

The old English of the pale were little more disposed to embrace the reformed religion, or to acknowledge the despotic principles of a Tudor administration, than the Irish themselves; and though they did not join the rebellions of those they so much hated, the queen's deputies had sometimes to encounter a more legal resistance. A new race of colonists had begun to appear in their train, eager for possessions, and for the rewards of the crown, contemptuous of the natives, whether aboriginal or of English descent, and in consequence the objects of their aversion or jealousy.[d]

Opposition in parliament. Hence in a parliament summoned by sir Henry Sidney in 1569, the first after that which had reluctantly established the protestant church, a strong country party, as it may be termed, was formed in opposition to the crown. They complained with much justice of the management by which irregular returns of members had been made; some from towns not incorporated, and which had never possessed the elective right; some self-chosen sheriffs and magistrates; some mere English strangers, returned for places which they had never seen. The judges, on reference to their opinion, declared the elections illegal in the two former cases; but confirmed the non-resident burgesses, which still left a majority for the court.

---

passed, 11 Eliz. c. 9, for dividing the whole island into shire-ground, appointing sheriffs, justices of the peace, &c.; which however was not completed till the time of sir John Perrott. Hollingshed, p. 457.

[c] Leland, 305. Their conduct provoked an insurrection both in Connaught and Ulster. Spenser, who shows always a bias towards the most rigorous policy, does injustice to Perrott. "He did tread down and disgrace all the English, and set up and countenance the Irish all that he could." P. 437. This has in all ages been the language, when they have been placed on an equality, or anything approaching to an equality, with their fellow-subjects.

[d] Leland, 248.

The Irish patriots, after this preliminary discussion, opposed a new tax upon wines and a bill for the suspension of Poyning's law. Hooker, an Englishman, chosen for Athenry, to whose account we are chiefly indebted for our knowledge of these proceedings, sustained the former in that high tone of a prerogative lawyer which always best pleased his mistress. "Her Majesty," he said, "of her own royal authority, might and may establish the same without any of your consents, as she hath already done the like in England; saving of her courtesy, it pleaseth her to have it pass with your own consents by order of law, that she might thereby have the better trial and assurance of your dutifulness and goodwill towards her." This language from a stranger, unusual among a people proud of their birthright in the common constitution, and little accustomed even to legitimate obedience, raised such a flame that the house was adjourned; and it was necessary to protect the utterer of such doctrines by a guard. The duty on wines, laid aside for the time, was carried in a subsequent session in the same year; and several other statutes were enacted, which, as they did not affect the pale, may possibly have encountered no opposition. A part of Ulster, forfeited by Slanes O'Neil, a rebel almost as formidable in the first years of this reign as his kinsman Tyrone was near its conclusion, was vested in the crown; and some provisions were made for the reduction of the whole island into shires. Connaught, in consequence, which had passed for one county, was divided into five.[e]

In sir Henry Sidney's second government, which began in 1576, the pale was excited to a more strenuous resistance by an attempt to subvert their liberties. It had long been usual to obtain a sum of money for the maintenance of the household and of the troops by an assessment settled between the council and principal inhabitants of each district. This, it was contended by the government, was instead of the contribution of victuals which the queen, by her prerogative of purveyance, might claim at a fixed rate, much lower than the current price.[f] It was

Arbitrary proceedings of sir Henry Sidney.

---

[e] Hollingshed's Chronicles of Ireland, 342. This part is written by Hooker himself. Leland, 240; Irish Statutes, 11 Eliz.
[f] Sidney Papers, i. 153.

maintained on the other side to be a voluntary benevolence. Sidney now devised a plan to change it for a cess or permanent composition for every plough-land, without regard to those which claimed exemption from the burden of purveyance; and imposed this new tax by order of council, as sufficiently warrantable by the royal prerogative. The landowners of the pale remonstrated against such a violation of their franchises, and were met by the usual arguments. They appealed to the text of the laws; the deputy replied by precedents against law. "Her majesty's prerogative," he said, "is not limited by Magna Charta, nor found in Littleton's Tenures, nor written in the books of Assizes, but registered in the remembrances of her majesty's exchequer, and remains in the rolls of records of the Tower."[g] It was proved, according to him, by the most ancient and credible records in the realm, that such charges had been imposed from time to time, sometimes by the name of cess, sometimes by other names, and more often by the governor and council, with such of the nobility as came on summons, than by parliament. These irregularities did not satisfy the gentry of the pale, who refused compliance with the demand, and still alleged that it was contrary both to reason and law to impose any charge upon them without parliament or grand council. A deputation was sent to England in the name of all the subjects of the English pale. Sidney was not backward in representing their behaviour as the effect of disaffection; nor was Elizabeth likely to recede where both her authority and her revenue were apparently concerned. But, after some demonstrations of resentment in committing the delegates to the Tower, she took alarm at the clamours of their countrymen; and, aware that the king of Spain was ready to throw troops into Ireland, desisted with that prudence which always kept her passion in command, accepting a voluntary composition for seven years in the accustomed manner.[h]

[g] Sidney Papers, l. 179.
[h] Id. 84, 117, &c., to 236; Hollingshed, 389; Leland, 261. Sidney was much disappointed at the queen's want of firmness; but it was plain by the correspondence that Walsingham also thought he had gone too far. P. 192. The sum required seems to have been reasonable, about 2000l. a-year from the five shires of the pale; and, if they had not been stubborn, he thought all Munster also, except the Desmond territories, would have submitted to the payment. P. 183 "I have great cause," he writes,

James I. ascended the throne with as great advantages in Ireland as in his other kingdoms. That island was already pacified by the submission of Tyrone; and all was prepared for a final establishment of the English power upon the basis of equal laws and civilised customs; a reformation which in some respects the king was not ill fitted to introduce. His reign is perhaps on the whole the most important in the constitutional history of Ireland, and that from which the present scheme of society in that country is chiefly to be deduced.

James I.

1. The laws of supremacy and uniformity, copied from those of England, were incompatible with any exercise of the Roman catholic worship, or with the admission of any members of that church into civil trust. It appears indeed that they were by no means strictly executed during the queen's reign;[i] yet the priests were of course excluded, so far as the English authority prevailed, from their churches and benefices; the former were chiefly ruined; the latter fell to protestant strangers or to conforming ministers of native birth, dissolute and ignorant, as careless to teach as the people were predetermined not to listen.[k] The priests, many of them,

---

" to mistrust the fidelity of the greatest number of the people of this country's birth of all degrees; they be papists, as I may well term them, body and soul. For not only in matter of religion they be Romish, but for government they will change, to be under a prince of their own superstition. Since your highness' reign the papists never showed such boldness as now they do." P. 184. This, however, hardly tallies with what he says afterwards (p. 208): " I do believe, for far the greatest number of the inhabitants of the English pale, her highness hath as true and faithful subjects as any she hath subject to the crown;" unless the former passage refer chiefly to those without the pale, who, in fact, were exclusively concerned in the rebellions of this reign.

i Leland, ii. 381.

k " The church is now so spoiled," says sir Henry Sidney in 1576. " as well by the ruin of the temples, as the dissipation and embezzling of the patrimony, and most of all for want of sufficient ministers, as so deformed and overthrown a church there is not, I am sure, in any region where Christ is professed." Sidney Papers, i. 109. In the diocese of Meath, being the best inhabited country of all the realm, out of 224 parish churches, 105 were impropriate, having only curates, of whom but 18 could speak English, the rest being " Irish rogues who used to be papists," 52 other churches had vicars, and 52 more were in better state than the rest, yet far from well. Id. 112. Spenser gives a bad character of the protestant clergy, p. 412. [It was chiefly on this account that the university of Dublin was founded in 1591. Leland, ii. 319.—1845.]

An act was passed, 12 Eliz. c. 1, for erecting free schools in every diocese under English masters; the ordinary paying one-third of the salary, and the clergy the rest. This, however, must have been nearly impracticable. Another act, 13 Eliz. c. 4, enables the archbishop of Armagh to grant leases of his lands out of the pale for a hundred years

engaged in a conspiracy with the court of Spain against the queen and her successor, and, all deeming themselves unjustly and sacrilegiously despoiled, kept up the spirit of disaffection, or at least of resistance to religious innovation, throughout the kingdom.ᵐ The accession of James seemed a sort of signal for casting off the yoke of heresy; in Cork, Waterford, and other cities, the people, not without consent of the magistrates, rose to restore the catholic worship; they seized the churches, ejected the ministers, marched in public processions, and shut their gates against the lord deputy. He soon reduced them to obedience; but almost the whole nation was of the same faith, and disposed to struggle for a public toleration. This was beyond every question their natural right, and as certainly was it the best policy of England to have granted it; but the king-craft and the priest-craft of the day taught other lessons. Priests

without assent of the dean and chapter, to persons of English birth, " or of the English and civil nation, born in this realm of Ireland," at the rent of 4d. an acre. It recites the chapter to be " except a very few of them, both by nation, education, and customs, Irish, Irishly affectioned, and small hopes of their conformities or assent unto any such devices as would tend to the placing of any such number of civil people there, to the disadvantage or bridling of the Irish." In these northern parts the English and protestant interests had so little influence, that the pope conferred three bishoprics, Derry, Clogher, and Raphoe, throughout the reign of Elizabeth. Davis, 254; Leland, II. 248. What is more remarkable is, that two of these prelates were summoned to parliament in 1585 (Id. 295); the first in which some Irish were returned among the commons.

The reputation of the protestant church continued to be little better in the reign of Charles I., though its revenues were much improved. Strafford gives the clergy a very bad character in writing to Laud. Vol. I. 187. And Burnet's Life of Bedell, transcribed chiefly from a contemporary memoir, gives a detailed account of that bishop's diocese (Kilmore), which will take off any surprise that might be felt at the slow progress of the Reformation. He had about fifteen pro-

testant clergy, but all English, unable to speak the tongue of the people, or to perform any divine offices, or converse with them, " which is no small cause of the continuance of the people in popery still." P. 47. " The bishop observed," says his biographer, " with much regret, that the English had all along neglected the Irish as a nation, not only conquered but undisciplinable; and that the clergy had scarce considered them as a part of their charge; but had left them wholly into the hands of their own priests, without taking any other care of them but the making them pay their tithes. And, indeed, their priests were a strange sort of people, that knew generally nothing but the reading their offices, which were not so much as understood by many of them; and they taught the people nothing but the saying their paters and aves in Latin." P. 114. Bedell took the pains to learn himself the Irish language; and, though he could not speak it, composed the first grammar ever made of it, had the common prayer read every Sunday in Irish, circulated catechisms, engaged the clergy to set up schools, and even undertook a translation of the Old Testament, which he would have published, but for the opposition of Laud and Strafford. P. 121.

ᵐ Leland, 413.

were ordered by proclamation to quit the realm; the magistrates and chief citizens of Dublin were committed to prison for refusing to frequent the protestant church. The gentry of the pale remonstrated at the court of Westminster; and, though their delegates atoned for their self-devoted courage by imprisonment, the secret menace of expostulation seems to have produced, as usual, some effect, in a direction to the lord deputy that he should endeavour to conciliate the recusants by instruction. These penalties of recusancy, from whatever cause, were very little enforced, but the catholics murmured at the oath of supremacy, which shut them out from every distinction: though here again the execution of the law was sometimes mitigated, they justly thought themselves humiliated, and the liberties of their country endangered, by standing thus at the mercy of the crown. And it is plain that even within the pale the compulsory statutes were at least far better enforced than under the queen; while in those provinces within which the law now first began to have its course, the difference was still more acutely perceived.[a]

Laws against catholics enforced.

2. The first care of the new administration was to perfect the reduction of Ireland into a civilised kingdom. Sheriffs were appointed throughout Ulster; the territorial divisions of counties and baronies were extended to the few districts that still wanted them; the judges of assize went their circuits everywhere; the customs of tanistry and gavelkind were determined by the court of king's bench to be void; the Irish lords surrendered their estates to the crown, and received them back by the English tenures

English law established throughout Ireland.

---

[a] Leland, 414, &c. In a letter from six catholic lords of the pale to the king in 1613, published in Desiderata Curiosa Hibernica, i. 158, they complain of the oath of supremacy, which they say had not been much imposed under the queen, but was now for the first time enforced in the remote parts of the country; so that the most sufficient gentry were excluded from magistracy, and meaner persons, if conformable, put instead. It is said, on the other side, that the laws against recusants were very little enforced, from the difficulty of getting juries to present them. Id. 359; Carte's Ormond, 33. But this at least shows that there was some disposition to molest the catholics on the part of the government; and it is admitted that they were excluded from offices, and even from practising at the bar, on account of the oath of supremacy. Id. 320; and compare the letter of six catholic lords with the answer of lord deputy and council, in the same volume.

of knight-service or soccage; an exact account was taken of the lands each of these chieftains possessed, that he might be invested with none but those he occupied; while his tenants, exempted from those uncertain Irish exactions, the source of their servitude and misery, were obliged only to an annual quit-rent, and held their own lands by a free tenure. The king's writ was obeyed, at least in profession, throughout Ireland; after four centuries of lawlessness and misgovernment a golden period was anticipated by the English courtiers, nor can we hesitate to recognise the influence of enlightened, and sometimes of benevolent minds, in the scheme of government now carried into effect.º But two unhappy maxims debased their motives, and discredited their policy; the first, that none but the true religion, or the state's religion, could be suffered to exist in the eye of the law; the second, that no pretext could be too harsh or iniquitous to exclude men of a different race or erroneous faith from their possessions.

3. The suppression of Slanes O'Neil's revolt in 1567 seems to have suggested the thought, or afforded the means, of perfecting the conquest of Ireland by the same methods that had been used to commence it, an extensive plantation of English colonists. The law of forfeiture came in very conveniently to further this great scheme of policy. O'Neil was attainted in the parliament of 1569; the

Settlements of English in Munster, Ulster, and other parts.

º Davis's Reports, ubi supra; Discovery of Causes, &c., 260; Carte's Life of Ormond, i. 14; Leland, 418. It had long been an object with the English government to extinguish the Irish tenures and laws. Some steps towards it were taken under Henry VIII.; but at that time there was too great a repugnance among the chieftains. In Elizabeth's instructions to the earl of Sussex on taking the government in 1560, it is recommended that the Irish should surrender their estates, and receive grants in tail male, but no greater estate. Desiderata Curiosa Hibernica, i. 1. This would have left a reversion in the crown, which could not have been cut off by suffering a recovery. But as those who held by Irish tenure had probably no right to alienate their lands, they had little cause to complain. An act in 1569, 12 Eliz. c. 4, reciting the greater part of the Irish to have petitioned for leave to surrender their lands, authorises the deputy, by advice of the privy council, to grant letters patent to the Irish and degenerate English, yielding certain reservations to the queen. Sidney mentions, in several of his letters, that the Irish were ready to surrender their lands. Vol. i. 94, 105, 165.

The act 11 Jac. I. c. 5 repeals divers statutes that treat the Irish as enemies, some of which have been mentioned above. It makes all the king's subjects under his protection to live by the same law. Some vestiges of the old distinctions remained in the statute-book, and were eradicated in Strafford's parliament. 10 & 11 Car. L, c. 6.

territories which acknowledged him as chieftain, comprising a large part of Down and Antrim, were vested in the crown; and a natural son of sir Thomas Smith, secretary of state, who is said to have projected this settlement, was sent with a body of English to take possession of the lands thus presumed in law to be vacant. This expedition however failed of success; the native occupants not acquiescing in this doctrine of our lawyers.[p] But fresh adventurers settled in different parts of Ireland; and particularly after the earl of Desmond's rebellion in 1583, whose forfeiture was reckoned at 574,628 Irish acres, though it seems probable that this is more than double the actual confiscation.[q] These lands in the counties of Cork and Kerry, left almost desolate by the oppression of the Geraldines themselves, and the far greater cruelty of the government in subduing them, were parcelled out among English undertakers at low rents, but on condition of planting eighty-six families on an estate of 12,000 acres, and in like proportion for smaller possessions. None of the native Irish were to be admitted as tenants; but neither this nor the other conditions were strictly observed by the undertakers, and the colony suffered alike by their rapacity and their neglect.[r] The oldest of the second race of English families in Ireland are found among the descendants of these Munster colonists. We find among them also some distinguished names that have left no memorial in their posterity; sir Walter Raleigh, who here laid the foundation of his transitory success, and one not less in glory, and hardly less in misfortune, Edmund Spenser. In a country house once belonging to the Desmonds on the banks of the Mulla, near Doneraile, the first three books of the 'Faery Queen' were written; and here too the poet awoke to the sad realities of life, and has left us, in his 'Account of the State of Ireland,' the most full and authentic document that illustrates its condition. This treatise abounds with judicious observations; but we regret the disposition to recommend an extreme

[p] Leland, ii. 254.
[q] See a note in Leland, ii. 302. The truth seems to be, that in this, as in other Irish forfeitures, a large part was restored to the tenants of the attainted parties.
[r] Leland, ii. 301.

severity in dealing with the native Irish, which ill becomes the sweetness of his muse.

The two great native chieftains of the north, the earls of Tyrone and Tyrconnel, a few years after the king's accession, engaged, or were charged with having engaged, in some new conspiracy, and flying from justice were attainted of treason. Five hundred thousand acres in Ulster were thus forfeited to the crown; and on this was laid the foundation of that great colony which has rendered that province, from being the seat of the wildest natives, the most flourishing, the most protestant, and the most enlightened part of Ireland. This plantation, though projected no doubt by the king and by lord Bacon, was chiefly carried into effect by the lord deputy, sir Arthur Chichester, a man of great capacity, judgment, and prudence. He caused surveys to be taken of the several counties, fixed upon proper places for building castles or founding towns, and advised that the lands should be assigned, partly to English or Scots undertakers, partly to servitors of the crown, as they were called, men who had possessed civil or military offices in Ireland, partly to the old Irish, even some of those who had been concerned in Tyrone's rebellion. These and their tenants were exempted from the oath of supremacy imposed on the new planters. From a sense of the error committed in the queen's time by granting vast tracts to single persons, the lands were distributed in three classes, of 2000, 1500, and 1000 English acres; and in every county one half of the assignments was to the smallest, the rest to the other two classes. Those who received 2000 acres were bound within four years to build a castle and bawn, or strong court-yard; the second class within two years to build a stone or brick house with a bawn; the third class a bawn only. The first were to plant on their lands within three years forty-eight able men, eighteen years old or upwards, born in England or the inland parts of Scotland; the others to do the same in proportion to their estates. All the grantees were to reside within five years, in person or by approved agents, and to keep sufficient store of arms; they were not to alienate their lands without the king's licence, nor to let them for less than twenty-one years; their tenants were to live in houses built in the English manner, and not dispersed, but in villages. The natives held their lands by the same conditions, except that of building fortified houses; but they were bound to take no Irish exactions from their tenants, nor to suffer the practice of wandering with their cattle from place to place. In this manner were these escheated lands of Ulster divided among a hundred and four English and Scots undertakers, fifty-six servitors, and two hundred and eighty-six natives. All lands which through the late anarchy and change of religion had been lost to the church were restored; and some further provision was made for the beneficed clergy. Chichester, as was just, received an allotment in a far ampler measure than the common servants of the crown.*

This noble design was not altogether completed according to the platform. The native Irish, to whom some regard was shown by these regulations, were less equitably dealt with by the colonists, and by those other adventurers whom England continually sent forth to enrich themselves and maintain her sovereignty. Pretexts were sought to establish the crown's title over the possessions of the Irish; they were assailed through a law which they had but just adopted, and of which they knew nothing, by the claims of a litigious and encroaching prerogative, against which no prescription could avail, nor any plea of fairness and equity obtain favour in the sight of English-born judges. Thus, in the King's and Queen's counties, and in those of Leitrim, Longford, and Westmeath, 385,000 acres were adjudged to the crown, and 66,000 in that of Wicklow. The greater part was indeed regranted to the native owners on a permanent tenure; and some apology might be found for this harsh act of power in the means it gave of civilising those central regions, always the shelter of rebels and robbers; yet this did not take off the sense of forcible spoliation which every foreign tyranny renders so intolerable. Surrenders were extorted by menaces; juries refusing to find the crown's title were fined by the council; many were dispossessed without any compensation, and

Injustice attending them.

---

* Carte's Life of Ormond, l. 15; Leland, 429; Farmer's Chronicle of sir Arthur Chichester's government in Desiderata Curiosa Hibernica, l. 32—an important and interesting narrative; also vol. ii. of the same collection 37; Bacon's Works, i. 657.

sometimes by gross perjury, sometimes by barbarous cruelty. It is said that in the county of Longford the Irish had scarcely one third of their former possessions assigned to them, out of three-fourths which had been intended by the king. Those who had been most faithful, those even who had conformed to the protestant church, were little better treated than the rest. Hence, though in many new plantations great signs of improvement were perceptible, though trade and tillage increased, and towns were built, a secret rankling for those injuries was at the heart of Ireland; and in these two leading grievances, the penal laws against recusants, and the inquisition into defective titles, we trace, beyond a shadow of doubt, the primary source of the rebellion in 1641.[1]

4. Before the reign of James, Ireland had been regarded either as a conquered country or as a mere colony of English, according to the persons or the provinces which were in question. The whole island now took a common character, that of a subordinate kingdom, inseparable from the English crown, and dependent also, at least as was taken for granted by our lawyers, on the English legislature; but governed after the model of our constitution, by nearly the same laws, and claiming entirely the same liberties. It was a natural consequence

[1] Leland, 437, 466; Carte's Ormond, 22; Desiderata Curiosa Hibernica, 238, 243, 378, et alibi; ii. 37, et post. In another treatise published in this collection, entitled a Discourse on the State of Ireland, 1614, an approaching rebellion is remarkably predicted. "The next rebellion, whensoever it shall happen, doth threaten more danger to the state than any that hath preceded; and my reasons are these:—1. They have the same bodies they ever had; and therein they have and had advantage over us. 2. From their infancies they have been and are exercised in the use of arms. 3. The realm, by reason of long peace, was never so full of youth as at this present. 4. That they are better soldiers than heretofore, their continual employments in the wars abroad assure us; and they do conceive that their men are better than ours. 5. That they are more politic, and able to manage rebellion with more judgment and dexterity than their elders, their experience and education are sufficient. 6. They will give the first blow, which is very advantageous to them that will give it. 7. The quarrel for which they rebel will be under the veil of religion and liberty, than which nothing is esteemed so precious in the hearts of men. 8. And, lastly, their union is such, as not only the old English dispersed abroad in all parts of the realm, but the inhabitants of the pale cities and towns, are as apt to take arms against us, which no precedent time hath ever seen, as the ancient Irish." Vol. i. 432. "I think that little doubt is to be made, but that the modern English and Scotch would in an instant be massacred in their houses." P. 438. This rebellion the author expected to be brought about by a league with Spain, and with aid from France.

that an Irish parliament should represent, or affect to represent, every part of the kingdom. None of Irish blood had ever sat, either lords or commoners, till near the end of Henry VIII.'s reign. The representation of the twelve counties into which Munster and part of Leinster were divided, and of a few towns, which existed in the reign of Edward III., if not later, was reduced by the defection of so many English families to the limits of the four shires of the pale.[u] The old counties, when they returned to their allegiance under Henry VIII., and those afterwards formed by Mary and Elizabeth, increased the number of the commons; though in that of 1567, as has been mentioned, the writs for some of them were arbitrarily withheld. The two queens did not neglect to create new boroughs, in order to balance the more independent representatives of the old Anglo-Irish families by the English retainers of the court. Yet it is said that in seventeen counties out of thirty-two into which Ireland was finally parcelled, there was no town that returned burgesses to parliament before the reign of James I., and the whole number in the rest was but about thirty.[x] He created at once forty new boroughs, or possibly rather more; for the number of the commons, in 1613, appears to have been 232.[y] It was several times afterwards augmented, and reached its complement of 300 in 1692.[z] These grants of the elective franchise

Constitution of Irish Parliament.

---

[u] The famous parliament of Kilkenny, in 1367, is said to have been very numerously attended. Leland, i. 319. We find, indeed, an act, 10 H. VII. c. 23, annulling what was done in a preceding parliament, for this reason, among others, that the writs had not been sent to all the shires, but to four only. Yet it appears that the writs would not have been obeyed in that age.

[x] Speech of sir John Davis (1612) on the parliamentary constitution of Ireland, in Appendix to Leland, vol. ii. p. 490, with the latter's observations on it. Carte's Ormond, i. 18; Lord Mountmorres's Hist. of Irish Parliament.

[y] In the letter of the lords of the pale to king James above mentioned, they express their apprehension that the erecting so many insignificant places to the rank of boroughs was with the view of bringing on fresh penal laws in religion; " and so the general scope and institution of parliament frustrated; they being ordained for the assurance of the subjects not to be pressed with any new edicts or laws, but such as should pass with their general consents and approbations." P. 158. The king's mode of replying to this constitutional language was characteristic. " What is it to you whether I make many or few boroughs? My council may consider the fitness, if I require it. But what if I had created 40 noblemen and 400 boroughs? The more the merrier, the fewer the better cheer." Desid. Cur. Hib. 308.

[z] Mountmorres, i. 166. The whole number of peers in 1634 was 122, and those present in parliament that year

were made, not indeed improvidently, but with very sinister intents towards the freedom of parliament; two-thirds of an Irish house of commons, as it stood in the eighteenth century, being returned with the mere farce of election by wretched tenants of the aristocracy.

The province of Connaught, with the adjoining county of Clare, was still free from the intrusion of English colonists. The Irish had complied, both under Elizabeth and James, with the usual conditions of surrendering their estates to the crown in order to receive them back by a legal tenure. But, as these grants, by some negligence, had not been duly enrolled in chancery (though the proprietors had paid large fees for that security), the council were not ashamed to suggest, or the king to adopt, an iniquitous scheme of declaring the whole country forfeited, in order to form another plantation as extensive as that of Ulster. The remonstrances of those whom such a project threatened put a present stop to it; and Charles, on ascending the throne, found it better to hear the proposals of his Irish subjects for a composition.

Charles I. promises graces to the Irish. After some time it was agreed between the court and the Irish agents in London, that the kingdom should voluntarily contribute 120,000*l.* in three years by equal payments, in return for certain graces, as they were called, which the king was to bestow. These went to secure the subject's title to his lands against the crown after sixty years' possession, and gave the people of Connaught leave to enrol their grants, relieving also the settlers in Ulster or other places from the penalties they had incurred by similar neglect. The abuses of the council-chamber in meddling with private causes, the oppression of the court of wards, the encroachments of military authority, and excesses of the soldiers were restrained. A free trade with the king's dominions or those of friendly powers was admitted. The recusants were allowed to sue for livery of their estates in the court of wards, and to practise in courts of law, on taking an oath of mere allegiance instead of that of supremacy. Unlawful exactions and severities of the clergy were prohibited. These reformations of unquestionable and intolerable evils, as bene-

---

were 66. They had the privilege not proxy; and those who sent none were only of voting, but even protesting by sometimes fined. Id. vol. i. 318.

ficial as those contained nearly at the same moment in the Petition of Right, would have saved Ireland long ages of calamity, if they had been as faithfully completed as they seemed to be graciously conceded. But Charles I. emulated on this occasion the most perfidious tyrants. It had been promised by an article in these graces that a parliament should be held to confirm them. Writs of summons were accordingly issued by the lord deputy; but with no consideration of that fundamental rule established by Poyning's law, that no parliament should be held in Ireland until the king's licence be obtained. This irregularity was of course discovered in England, and the writs of summons declared to be void. It would have been easy to remedy this mistake, if such it were, by proceeding in the regular course with a royal licence. But this was withheld; no parliament was called for a considerable time; and, when the three years had elapsed during which the voluntary contribution had been payable, the king threatened to straiten his graces if it were not renewed.[a]

Does not confirm them.

He had now placed in the viceroyalty of Ireland that star of exceeding brightness, but sinister influence, the willing and able instrument of despotic power, lord Strafford. In his eyes the country he governed belonged to the crown by right of conquest; neither the original natives, nor even the descendants of the conquerors themselves, possessing any privileges which could interfere with its sovereignty. He found two parties extremely jealous of each other, yet each loth to recognise an absolute prerogative, and thus in some measure having a common cause. The protestants, not a little from bigotry, but far more from a persuasion that they held their estates on the tenure of a rigid religious monopoly, could not endure to hear of a toleration of popery, which, though originally demanded, was not even mentioned in the king's graces; and disapproved the indulgence shown by those graces to recusants, which is said to have been followed by an impolitic ostentation of the Romish worship.[b] They

Administration of Strafford.

[a] Carte's Ormond, i. 48; Leland, ii. 475, et post.
[b] Leland, iii. 4, et post. A vehement protestation of the bishops about this time, with Usher at their head, against any connivance at popery, is a disgrace to their memory. It is to be met with in many books. Strafford, however, was

objected to a renewal of the contribution, both as the price of this dangerous tolerance of recusancy and as debarring the protestant subjects of their constitutional right to grant money only in parliament. Wentworth, however, insisted upon its payment for another year, at the expiration of which a parliament was to be called.[c]

The king did not come without reluctance into this last measure, hating, as he did, the very name of parliament; but the lord deputy confided in his own energy to make it innoxious and serviceable. They conspired together how to extort the most from Ireland, and concede the least; Charles, in truth, showing a most selfish indifference to anything but his own revenue and a most dishonourable unfaithfulness to his word.[d] The parliament met in 1634, with a strong desire of insisting on the confirmation of the graces they had already paid for; but Wentworth had so balanced the protestant and recusant parties, employed so skilfully the resources of fair promises and intimidation, that he procured six subsidies to be granted before a prorogation, without any mutual concession from the crown.[e] It had been agreed that a

---

far from any real liberality of sentiment. His abstinence from religious persecution was intended to be temporary, as the motives whereon it was founded. " It will be ever far forth of my heart to conceive that a conformity in religion is not above all other things principally to be intended. For undoubtedly till we be brought all under one form of divine service the crown is never safe on this side, &c. It were too much at once to distemper them by bringing plantations upon them, and disturbing them in the exercise of their religion, so long as it be without scandal; and so, indeed, very inconsiderate, as I conceive, to move in this latter, till that former be fully settled, and by that means the protestant party become by much the stronger, which in truth I do not yet conceive it to be." Straff. Letters, ii. 39. He says, however, and I believe truly, that no man had been touched for conscience-sake since he was deputy. Id. 112. Every parish, as we find by Bedell's Life, had its priest and mass-house; in some places mass was said in the churches; the Romish bishops exercised their jurisdiction, which was fully obeyed; but " the priests were grossly ignorant and openly scandalous, both for drunkenness and all sort of lewdness." P. 41, 76. More than ten to one in his diocese, the county of Cavan, were recusants.

[c] Some of the council-board having intimated a doubt of their authority to bind the kingdom, " I was then put to my last refuge, which was plainly to declare that there was no necessity which induced me to take them to counsel in this business, for, rather than fail in so necessary a duty to my master, I would undertake, upon the peril of my head, to make the king's army able to subsist, and to provide for itself amongst them, without their help." Strafford Letters, i. 98.

[d] Id. i. 183; Carte, 61.

[e] The protestants, he wrote word, had a majority of eight in the commons. He told them " it was very indifferent to him what resolution the house might take; that there were two ends he had in view, and one he would infallibly attain,—either a submission of the people to his majesty's just demands, or a just

second session should be held for confirming the graces; but in this, as might be expected, the supplies having been provided, the request of both houses that they might receive the stipulated reward met with a cold reception; and ultimately the most essential articles, those establishing a sixty years' prescription against the crown, and securing the titles of proprietors in Clare and Connaught, as well as those which relieved the catholics in the court of wards from the oath of supremacy, were laid aside. Statutes, on the other hand, were borrowed from England, especially that of uses, which cut off the methods they had hitherto employed for evading the law's severity.[f]

Strafford had always determined to execute the project of the late reign with respect to the western counties. He proceeded to hold an inquisition in each county of Connaught, and summoned juries in order to preserve a mockery of justice in the midst of tyranny. They were required to find the king's title to all the lands, on such evidence as could be found and was thought fit to be laid before them; and were told that what would be

---

occasion of breach, and either would content the king; the first was undeniably and evidently best for them." Id. 277, 278. In his speech to the two houses, he said, "His majesty expects not to find you muttering, or, to name it more truly, mutinying in corners. I am commanded to carry a very watchful eye over these private and secret conventicles, to punish the transgression with a heavy and severe hand; therefore it behoves you to look to it." Id. 289. "Finally," he concludes, "I wish you had a right judgment in all things; yet let me not prove a Cassandra amongst you, to speak truth and not be believed. However, speak truth I will, were I to become your enemy for it. Remember, therefore, that I tell you, you may easily make or mar this parliament. If you proceed with respect, without laying clogs and conditions upon the king, as wise men and good subjects ought to do, you shall infallibly set up this parliament eminent to posterity, as the very basis and foundation of the greatest happiness and prosperity that ever befell this nation. But, if you meet a great king with narrow circumscribed hearts,

if you will needs be wise and cautious above the moon [sic], remember again that I tell you, you shall never be able to cast your mists before the eyes of a discerning king; you shall be found out; your sons shall wish they had been the children of more believing parents; and in a time when you look not for it, when it will be too late for you to help, the sad repentance of an unadvised heart shall be yours, lasting honour shall be my master's."

These subsidies were reckoned at near 41,000l. each, and were thus apportioned: Leinster paid 13,000l. (of which 1000l. from the city of Dublin), Munster 11,000l., Ulster 10,000l., Connaught 6800l. Mountmorres, ii. 16.

[f] Irish Statutes, 10 Car. I. c. 1, 2, 3, &c.; Strafford Letters, i. 279, 312. The king expressly approved the denial of the graces, though promised formerly by himself. Id. 345; Leland, iii. 20.

"I can now say," Strafford observes (Id. 344), "the king is as absolute here as any prince in the whole world can be; and may still be, if it be not spoiled on that side.

best for their own interest would be to return such a verdict as the king desired; what would be best for his, to do the contrary; since he was able to establish it without their consent, and wished only to invest them graciously with a large part of what they now unlawfully withheld from him. These menaces had their effect in all counties except that of Galway, where a jury stood out obstinately against the crown, and being in consequence, as well as the sheriff, summoned to the castle in Dublin, were sentenced to an enormous fine. Yet the remonstrances of the western proprietors were so clamorous that no steps were immediately taken for carrying into effect the designed plantation; and the great revolutions of Scotland and England which soon ensued gave another occupation to the mind of lord Strafford.[a] It has never been disputed that a more uniform administration of justice in ordinary cases, a stricter coercion of outrage, a more extensive commerce, evidenced by the augmentation of customs, above all, the foundation of the great linen manufacture in Ulster, distinguished the period of his government.[b] But it is equally manifest that neither the reconcilement of parties, nor their affection to the English crown, could be the result of his arbitrary domination; and that, having healed no wound he found, he left others to break out after his removal. The despotic violence of this minister towards private persons, and those of great eminence, is in some instances well known by the proceedings on his impeachment, and in others is sufficiently familiar by our historical and biographical literature. It is indeed remarkable that we find among the objects of his oppression and insult all that most illustrates the contemporary annals of Ireland, the venerable learning of Usher, the pious integrity of Bedell, the experienced wisdom of Cork, and the early virtue of Clanricarde.

The parliament assembled by Strafford in 1640 began with loud professions of gratitude to the king for the

[a] Strafford Letters, i. 353, 370, 402, 442, 451, 454, 473; ii. 113, 139, 366; Leland, iii. 30, 39; Carte, 82.

[b] It is, however, true that he discouraged the woollen manufacture, in order to keep the kingdom more dependent, and that this was part of his motive in promoting the other. Strafford Letters, ii. 19.

excellent governor he had appointed over them; they voted subsidies to pay a large army raised to serve against the Scots, and seemed eager to give every manifestation of zealous loyalty.[i] But after their prorogation, and during the summer of that year, as rapid a tendency to a great revolution became visible as in England; the commons, when they met again, seemed no longer the same men; and, after the fall of their great viceroy, they coalesced with his English enemies to consummate his destruction. Hate long smothered by fear, but inflamed by the same cause, broke forth in a remonstrance of the commons presented through a committee, not to the king, but a superior power, the long parliament of England. The two houses united to avail themselves of the advantageous moment, and to extort, as they very justly might, from the necessities of Charles that confirmation of his promises which had been refused in his prosperity. Both parties, catholic as well as protestant, acted together in this national cause, shunning for the present to bring forward those differences which were not the less implacable for being thus deferred. The catalogue of temporal grievances was long enough to produce this momentary coalition: it might be groundless in some articles, it might be exaggerated in more, it might in many be of ancient standing; but few can pretend to deny that it exhibits a true picture of the misgovernment of Ireland at all times, but especially under the earl of Strafford. The king, in May, 1641, consented to the greater part of their demands, but unfortunately they were never granted by law.[k]

But the disordered condition of his affairs gave encouragement to hopes far beyond what any parliamentary remonstrances could realize; hopes long cherished when they had seemed vain to the world, but such as courage and bigotry and resentment would never lay aside. The court of Madrid had not abandoned its connexion with

---

[i] Leland, iii. 51. Strafford himself (il. 397) speaks highly of their disposition.

[k] Carte's Ormond, 100, 140; Leland, iii. 54, et post; Mountmorres, il. 29. A remonstrance of the commons to lord-deputy Wandesford against various grievances was presented 7th November, 1640, before lord Strafford had been impeached. Id. 39. As to confirming the graces, the delay, whether it proceeded from the king or his Irish representatives, seems to have caused some suspicion. Lord Clanricarde mentions the ill consequences that might result, in a letter to lord Bristol. Carte's Ormond iii 40.

the disaffected Irish, especially of the priesthood; the son of Tyrone, and many followers of that cause, served in its armies; and there seems much reason to believe that in the beginning of 1641 the project of insurrection was formed among the expatriated Irish, not without the concurrence of Spain, and perhaps of Richelieu.[m] The government had passed from the vigorous hands of Strafford into those of two lords justices, sir William Parsons and sir John Borlase, men by no means equal to the critical circumstances wherein they were placed, though possibly too severely censured by those who do not look at their extraordinary difficulties with sufficient candour. The primary causes of the rebellion are not to be found in their supineness or misconduct, but in the two great sins of the English government; in the penal laws as to religion which pressed on almost the whole people, and in the systematic iniquity which despoiled them of their possessions. They could not be expected to miss such an occasion of revolt; it was an hour of revolution, when liberty was won by arms, and ancient laws were set at nought; the very success of their worst enemies, the covenanters in Scotland, seemed the assurance of their own victory, as it was the reproach of their submission.[n]

[m] Sir Henry Vane communicated to the lords justices, by the king's command, March 16, 1640-41, that advice had been received and confirmed by the ministers in Spain and elsewhere, which "deserved to be seriously considered, and an especial care and watchfulness to be had therein: that of late there have passed from Spain (and the like may well have been from other parts) an unspeakable number of Irish churchmen for England and Ireland, and some good old soldiers, under pretext of asking leave to raise men for the king of Spain; whereas, it is observed among the Irish friars there, a whisper was, as if they expected a rebellion in Ireland, and particularly in Connaught." Carte's Ormond, iii. 30. This letter, which Carte seems to have taken from a printed book, is authenticated in Clarendon State Papers, ii. 143. I have mentioned in another part of this work, Chap. VIII., the provocations which might have induced the cabinet of Madrid to foment disturbances in Charles's dominions. The lords justices are taxed by Carte with supineness in paying no attention to this letter (vol. i. 166); but how he knew that they paid none seems hard to say.

Another imputation has been thrown on the Irish government and on the parliament, for objecting to permit levies to be made for the Spanish service out of the army raised by Strafford, and disbanded in the spring of 1641, which the king had himself proposed. Carte, i. 133; and Leland, 82, who follows the former implicitly, as he always does. The event, indeed, proved that it would have been far safer to let those soldiers, chiefly catholics, enlist under a foreign banner; but, considering the long connexion of Spain with that party, and the apprehension always entertained that the disaffected might acquire military experience in her service, the objection does not seem so very unreasonable.

[n] The fullest writer on the Irish rebellion is Carte, in his Life of Ormond,

The rebellion broke out, as is well known, by a sudden massacre of the Scots and English in Ulster, designed no doubt by a vindictive and bigoted people to extirpate those races, and, if contemporary authorities are to be credited, falling little short of this in its execution. Their evident exaggeration has long been acknowledged; but possibly the scepticism of later writers has extenuated rather too much the horrors of this massacre.° It was certainly not the

_{Rebellion of 1641.}

who had the use of a vast collection of documents belonging to that noble family, a selection from which forms his third volume. But he is extremely partial against all who leaned to the parliamentary or puritan side, and especially the lords justices, Parsons and Borlase; which renders him, to say the least, a very favourable witness for the catholics. Leland, with much candour towards the latter, but a good deal of the same prejudice against the presbyterians, is little more than the echo of Carte. A more vigorous though less elegant historian is Warner, whose impartiality is at least equal to Leland's, and who may perhaps, upon the whole, be reckoned the best modern authority. Sir John Temple's History of Irish Rebellion, and lord Clanricarde's Letters, with a few more of less importance, are valuable contemporary testimonies.

The catholics themselves might better leave their cause to Carte and Leland than excite prejudices instead of allaying them by such a tissue of misrepresentation and disingenuousness as Curry's Historical Account of the Civil Wars in Ireland.

° Sir John Temple reckons the number of protestants murdered, or destroyed in some manner, from the breaking out of the rebellion in October, 1641, to the cessation in September, 1643, at three hundred thousand, an evident and enormous exaggeration; so that the first edition being incorrectly printed, and with numerals, we might almost suspect a cipher to have been added by mistake, p. 15 (edit. Maseres). Clarendon says forty or fifty thousand were murdered in the first insurrection. Sir William Petty, in his Political Anatomy of Ireland, from calculations too vague to deserve confidence, puts the number massacred at thirty-seven thousand. Warner has scrutinized the examinations of witnesses, taken before a commission appointed in 1643, and now deposited in the library of Trinity College, Dublin; and, finding many of the depositions unsworn, and others founded on hearsay, has thrown more doubt than any earlier writer on the extent of the massacre. Upon the whole, he thinks twelve thousand lives of protestants the utmost that can be allowed for the direct or indirect effects of the rebellion, during the two first years, except losses in war (History of Irish Rebellion, p. 397), and of these only one-third by murder. It is to be remarked, however, that no distinct accounts could be preserved in formal depositions of so promiscuous a slaughter, and that the very exaggerations show its tremendous nature. The Ulster colony, a numerous and brave people, were evidently unable to make head for a considerable time against the rebels, which could hardly have been if they had only lost a few thousands. It is idle to throw an air of ridicule (as is sometimes attempted) on the depositions because they are mingled with some fabulous circumstances, such as the appearance of the ghosts of the murdered on the bridge at Cavan; which, by the way, is only told, in the depositions subjoined to Temple, as the report of the place, and was no cold-blooded fabrication, but the work of a fancy bewildered by real horrors.

Carte, who dwells at length on every circumstance unfavourable to the opposite party, despatches the Ulster massacre in a single short paragraph, and coolly remarks, that there were not many murders, " *considering the nature of such an affair*," in the first week of the insurrec-

crime of the catholics generally; nor, perhaps, in the other provinces of Ireland are they chargeable with more cruelty than their opponents.[p] Whatever may have been the original intentions of the lords of the pale, or of the Anglo-Irish professing the old religion in general (which has been a problem in history), a few months only elapsed before they were almost universally engaged in the war.[q] The old distinctions of Irish and

---

tion. Life of Ormond, i. 175-177. This is hardly reconcilable to fair dealing. Curry endeavours to discredit even Warner's very moderate estimate, and affects to call him, in one place (p. 164), " a writer highly prejudiced against the insurgents," which is grossly false. He praises Carte and Nalson, the only protestants he does praise, and bestows on the latter the name of impartial. I wonder he does not say that no one protestant was murdered. Dr. Lingard has lately given a short account of the Ulster rebellion (Hist. of England, x. 154), omitting all mention of the massacre, and endeavouring, in a note at the end of the volume, to disprove, by mere scraps of quotation, an event of such notoriety, that we must abandon all faith in public fame if it were really unfounded.

[p] Carte, i. 253, 266; iii. 51; Leland, 154. Sir Charles Coote and sir William St. Leger are charged with great cruelties in Munster. The catholic confederates spoke with abhorrence of the Ulster massacre. Leland, 161; Warner, 203. They behaved in many parts with humanity; nor, indeed, do we find frequent instances of violence, except in those counties where the proprietors had been dispossessed. [It has been not unfrequent with catholic writers to allege that 3000 Irish had been massacred by the protestants in Isle Magee, near Carrickfergus, before the rebellion broke out. Curry, in his grossly unfair History of the Civil Wars, and Plowden, in his not less unfair and more superficial Historical Review of the State of Ireland, are among these; the latter having been misled, or affecting to be persuaded, by a passage in the appendix to Clarendon's Historical Account of Irish Affairs, which appendix evidently was not written by that historian himself, but subjoined by some one to the posthumous work. Carte, though he seems to be staggered by the numbers, gives some credit to, or at least states as not improbable, the main fact, that this massacre occurred antecedently to any committed by the Irish themselves. Life of Ormond, i. 188. But Leland refers to the original depositions in Trinity College, Dublin, whence it appears that some Scots soldiers in garrison at Carric-fergus sallied out in January, when the rebellion was at its height, and slaughtered a few families of unoffending natives in Isle Magee. Leland, iii. 129. Dr. Lingard, it must in justice be added, does not repeat this slander.—1845.]

[q] Carte and Leland endeavour to show that the Irish of the pale were driven into rebellion by the distrust of the lords justices, who refused to furnish them with arms, after the revolt in Ulster, and permitted the parliament to sit for one day only, in order to publish a declaration against the rebels. But the prejudice of these writers is very glaring. The insurrection broke out in Ulster, October 23, 1641; and in the beginning of December the lords of the pale were in arms. Surely this affords some presumption that Warner has reason to think them privy to the rebellion, or, at least, not very averse to it. P. 146. And with the suspicion that might naturally attach to all Irish catholics, could Borlase and Parsons be censurable for declining to intrust them with arms, or rather for doing so with some caution? Temple, 56. If they had acted otherwise, we should certainly have heard of their incredible imprudence. Again, the catholic party in the house of commons were so cold in their loyalty, to say the least that they objected to giving any appellation to the rebels worse than that of discontented gentlemen. Leland, 140; see too Clanricarde's Letters, p. 33, &c. In fact,

English blood were obliterated by those of religion; and it became a desperate contention whether the majority of the nation should be trodden to the dust by forfeiture and persecution, or the crown lose every thing beyond a nominal sovereignty over Ireland. The insurgents, who might once perhaps have been content with a repeal of the penal laws, grew naturally in their demands through success, or rather through the inability of the English government to keep the field, and began to claim the entire establishment of their religion; terms in themselves not unreasonable, nor apparently disproportionate to their circumstances, and which the king was, in his distresses, nearly ready to concede, but such as never could have been obtained from a third party, of whom they did not sufficiently think, the parliament and people of England. The commons had, at the very beginning of the rebellion, voted that all the forfeited estates of the insurgents should be allotted to such as should aid in reducing the island to obedience; and thus rendered the war desperate on the part of the Irish.' No great efforts were made, however, for some years; but, after the king's person had fallen into their

several counties of Leinster and Connaught were in arms before the pale.

It has been thought by some that the lords justices had time enough to have quelled the rebellion in Ulster before it spread farther. Warner, 130. Of this, as I conceive, we should not pretend to judge confidently. Certain it is that the whole army in Ireland was very small, consisting of only nine hundred and forty-three horse, and two thousand two hundred and ninety-seven foot. Temple, 32; Carte, 194. I think sir John Temple has been unjustly depreciated; he was master of the rolls in Ireland at the time, and a member of the council — no bad witness for what passed in Dublin; and he makes out a complete justification, as far as appears, for the conduct of the lords justices and council towards the lords of the pale and the catholic gentry. Nobody alleges that Parsons and Borlase were men of as much energy as lord Strafford; but those who sit down in their closets, like Leland and Warner, more than a century afterwards, to lavish the most indignant contempt on their memory, should have reflected a little on the circumstances.

ʳ "I perceived (says Preston, general of the Irish, writing to lord Clanricarde), that the catholic religion, the rights and prerogatives of his majesty, my dread sovereign, the liberties of my country, and whether there should be an Irishman or no, were the prizes at stake." Carte, iii. 120. Clanricarde himself expresses to the king, and to his brother, lord Essex, in January 1642, his apprehension that the English parliament meant to make it a religious war. Clanricarde's Letters, 61 et post. The letters of this great man. perhaps the most unsullied character in the annals of Ireland, and certainly more so than even his illustrious contemporary, the duke of Ormond, exhibit the struggles of a noble mind between love of his country and his religion on the one hand, loyalty and honour on the other. At a later period of that unhappy war, he thought himself able to conciliate both principles.

hands, the victorious party set themselves in earnest to effect the conquest of Ireland. This was achieved by Cromwell and his powerful army after several years, with such bloodshed and rigour that, in the opinion of lord Clarendon, the sufferings of that nation, from the outset of the rebellion to its close, have never been surpassed but by those of the Jews in their destruction by Titus.

Subjugation of the Irish by Cromwell.

At the restoration of Charles II. there were in Ireland two people, one either of native or old English blood, the other of recent settlement; one catholic, the other protestant; one humbled by defeat, the other insolent with victory; one regarding the soil as his ancient inheritance, the other as his acquisition and reward. There were three religions—for the Scots of Ulster and the army of Cromwell had never owned the episcopal church, which for several years had fallen almost as low as that of Rome. There were claims, not easily set aside on the score of right, to the possession of lands, which the entire island could not satisfy. In England, little more had been necessary than to revive a suspended constitution; in Ireland, it was something beyond a new constitution and code of law that was required—it was the titles and boundaries of each man's private estate that were to be litigated and adjudged. The episcopal church was restored with no delay, as never having been abolished by law; and a parliament, containing no catholics and not many vehement nonconformists, proceeded to the great work of settling the struggles of opposite claimants by a fresh partition of the kingdom.*

Restoration of Charles II.

The king had already published a declaration for the settlement of Ireland, intended as the basis of an act of parliament. The adventurers, or those who, on the faith of several acts passed in England in 1642, with the assent of the late king, had advanced money for quelling the rebellion, in consideration of lands to be allotted to them in certain stipulated proportions, and who had, in general, actually received them from Cromwell, were confirmed in all the lands possessed by them on the 7th of May, 1659; and all the deficiencies

Act of settlement.

---

* Carte, II. 221. Leland, 420.

were to be supplied before the next year. The army was confirmed in the estates already allotted for their pay, with an exception of church lands and some others. Those officers who had served in the royal army against the Irish before 1649 were to be satisfied for their pay, at least to the amount of five-eighths, out of lands to be allotted for that purpose. Innocent papists, that is, such as were not concerned in the rebellion and whom Cromwell had arbitrarily transplanted into Connaught, were to be restored to their estates, and those who possessed them to be indemnified. Those who had submitted to the peace of 1648, and had not been afterwards in arms, if they had not accepted lands in Connaught, were also to be restored as soon as those who now possessed them should be satisfied for their expenses. Those who had served the king abroad, and thirty-six enumerated persons of the Irish nobility and gentry, were to be put on the same footing as the last. The precedency of restitution, an important point where the claims exceeded the means of satisfying them, was to be in the order above specified.[1]

This declaration was by no means pleasing to all concerned. The loyal officers who had served before 1649 murmured that they had little prospect of more than twelve shillings and sixpence in the pound, while the republican army of Cromwell would receive the full value. The Irish were more loud in their complaints; no one was to be held innocent who had been in the rebel quarters before the cessation of 1643, and other qualifications were added so severe that hardly any could expect to come within them. In the house of commons the majority, consisting very much of the new interests, that is, of the adventurers and army, were in favour of adhering to the declaration. In the house of lords it was successfully urged that, by gratifying the new men to the utmost, no fund would be left for indemnifying the loyalists or the innocent Irish. It was proposed that, if the lands not yet disposed of should not be sufficient to satisfy all the interests for which the king had meant to provide by his declaration, there should be a proportional defalcation out of every class for the benefit of the whole. These discussions were adjourned to London, where

[1] Carte, II. 216; Leland, 414.

delegates of the different parties employed every resource of intrigue at the English court. The king's bias towards the religion of the Irish had rendered him their friend, and they seemed, at one time, likely to reverse much that had been intended against them; but their agents grew rash with hope, assumed a tone of superiority which ill became their condition, affected to justify their rebellion, and finally so much disgusted their sovereign that he ordered the act of settlement to be sent back with little alteration, except the insertion of some more Irish nominees."

The execution of this act was intrusted to English commissioners, from whom it was reasonable to hope for an impartiality which could not be found among the interested classes. Notwithstanding the rigorous proofs nominally exacted, more of the Irish were pronounced innocent than the commons had expected; and the new possessors having the sway of that assembly, a clamour was raised that the popish interest had prevailed: some talked of defending their estates by arms, some even meddled in fanatical conspiracies against the government; it was insisted that a closer inquisition should be made and stricter qualifications demanded. The manifest deficiency of lands to supply all the claimants for whom the act of settlement provided, made it necessary to resort to a supplemental measure, called the act of explanation. The adventurers and soldiers relinquished one-third of the estates enjoyed by them on the 7th of May, 1659. Twenty Irish nominees were added to those who were to be restored by the king's favour; but all those who had not already been adjudged innocent, more than three thousand in number, were absolutely cut off from any hope of restitution. The great majority of these no question were guilty; yet they justly complained of this confiscation without a trial.[x] Upon the whole result, the Irish catholics, having previously held about two-thirds of the kingdom, lost more than one-half of their possessions by forfeiture on account of their rebellion. If we can rely at all on the calculations, made almost in the infancy of political arithmetic by one of its most diligent investigators, they were diminished also by

[u] Carte, 222 et post; Leland, 420 et post.
[x] Carte, 258-316; Leland, 431 et post.

much more than one-third through the calamities of that period.[y]

It is more easy to censure the particular inequalities, or even in some respects injustice of the act of settlement, than to point out what better course was to have been adopted. The re-adjustment of all private rights after so entire a destruction of their landmarks, could only be effected by the coarse process of general rules. Nor does it appear that the catholics, considered as a great mass, could reasonably murmur against the confiscation of half their estates, after a civil war wherein it is evident that so large a proportion of themselves were concerned.[z] Charles, it is true, had not been personally resisted by the insurgents; but, as chief of England, he stood in the place of Cromwell, and equally represented the sovereignty of the greater island over the lesser, which under no form of government it would concede.

---

[y] The statements of lands forfeited and restored, under the execution of the act of settlement, are not the same in all writers. Sir William Petty estimates the superficies of Ireland at 10,500,000 Irish acres (each being to the English measure nearly as thirteen to eight), whereof 7,500,000 are of good land, the rest being moor, bog, and lake. In 1641, the estates of the protestant owners and of the church were about one third of these cultivable lands, those of catholics two thirds. The whole of the latter were seized or sequestered by Cromwell and the parliament. After summing up the allotments made by the commissioners under the act of settlement, he concludes that, in 1672, the English, protestants, and church have 5,140,000 acres, and the papists nearly half as much. Political Anatomy of Ireland, c. 1. In lord Orrery's letters, i. 187 et post, is a statement which seems not altogether to tally with sir William Petty's; nor is that of the latter clear and consistent in all its computations. Lawrence, author of 'The Interest of Ireland stated,' a treatise published in 1682, says, "Of 10,868,949 acres, returned by the last survey of Ireland, the Irish papists are possessed but of 2,041,108 acres, which is but a small matter above the fifth part of the whole." Part ii. p. 48. But, as it is evidently below one fifth, there must be some mistake. It appears that in one of these sums he reckoned the whole extent, and in the other only cultivable lands. Lord Clare, in his celebrated speech on the Union, greatly overrates the confiscations. [It is stated in the English Journals of Commons, 12th Jan. 1694, that the court of claims (that is, the commissioners appointed as in the text) allotted 4,560,037 acres to the English, 2,323,809 to the Irish, and left 824,391 undisposed. This, by supposing the last to have been afterwards divided, would very closely tally with sir William Petty's estimate.—1845.]

Petty calculates that above 500,000 of the Irish "perished and were wasted by the sword, plague, famine, hardship, and banishment, between the 23rd day of October 1641 and the same day 1652;" and conceives the population of the island in 1641 to have been nearly 1,500,000, including protestants. But his conjectures are prodigiously vague.

[z] Petty is as ill satisfied with the restoration of lands to the Irish as they could be with the confiscations. "Of all that claimed innocency, seven in eight obtained it. The restored persons have more than what was their own in 1641 by at least one fifth. Of those adjudged innocents not one in twenty were really so."

The catholics, however, thought themselves oppressed by the act of settlement, and could not forgive the duke of Ormond for his constant regard to the protestant interests and the supremacy of the English crown. They had enough to encourage them in the king's bias towards their religion, which he was able to manifest more openly than in England. Under the administration of Lord Berkely in 1670, at the time of Charles's conspiracy with the king of France to subvert religion and liberty, they began to menace an approaching change, and to aim at revoking, or materially weakening, the act of settlement. The most bigoted and insolent of the popish clergy, who had lately rejected with indignation an offer of more reasonable men to renounce the tenets obnoxious to civil governments, were countenanced at Dublin; but the first alarm of the new proprietors, as well as the general apprehension of the court's designs in England, soon rendered it necessary to desist from the projected innovations.[a] The next reign, of course, reanimated the Irish party; a dispensing prerogative set aside all the statutes; every civil office, the courts of justice and the privy council, were filled with catholics; the protestant soldiers were disbanded; the citizens of that religion were disarmed; the tithes were withheld from their clergy; they were suddenly reduced to feel that bitter condition of a conquered and proscribed people which they had long rendered the lot of their enemies.[b] From these enemies, exasperated by bigotry and revenge, they could have nothing but a full and exceeding measure of retaliation to expect; nor had they even the last hope that an English king, for the sake of his crown and country, must protect those who formed the strongest link between the two islands. A man violent and ambitious, without superior capacity, the earl of Tyrconnel, lord-lieutenant in 1687 and commander of the army, looked only to his master's interests, in subordination to those of his countrymen and of his own. It is now ascertained that, doubtful of the king's success in the struggle for restoring popery in England, he had made secret overtures to some of the French agents for casting off all connexion with that

Side-notes: Hopes of the catholics under Charles and James.

[a] Carte, ii. 414 et post. Leland, 458   [b] Leland, 493 et post. Mazure, Hist. de la Révolut. ii. 113.

kingdom in case of James's death, and, with the aid of Louis, placing the crown of Ireland on his own head.[c] The Revolution in England was followed by a war in Ireland of three years' duration, and a war on both sides, like that of 1641, for self-preservation. In the parliament held by James at Dublin in 1690, the act of settlement was repealed, and above 2000 persons attainted by name—both, it has been said perhaps with little truth, against the king's will, who dreaded the impetuous nationality that was tearing away the bulwarks of his throne.[d] But the magnanimous defence of Derry and the splendid victory of the Boyne restored the protestant cause: though the Irish, with the succour of French troops, maintained for two years a gallant resistance, they could not ultimately withstand the triple superiority of military talents, resources, and discipline. Their bravery, however, served to obtain the articles of Limerick on the surrender of that city—conceded by their noble-minded conqueror, against the disposition of those who longed to plunder and persecute their fallen enemy. By the first of these articles, "the Roman catholics of this kingdom shall enjoy such privileges in the exercise of their religion as are consistent with the laws of Ireland, or as they did enjoy in the reign of king Charles II.; and their majesties, as soon as their affairs will permit them to summon a parliament in this kingdom, will endeavour to procure the said Roman catholics such further security in that particular as may preserve them from any disturbance upon the account of their said religion." The second secures to the inhabitants of Limerick and other places then in possession of the Irish, and to all officers and soldiers then in arms who should return to their majesties' obedience, and to all such as should be under their protection in the counties of Limerick, Kerry, Clare, Galway, and Mayo,

War of 1689, and final reduction of Ireland.

[c] M. Mazure has brought this remarkable fact to light. Bonrepos, a French emissary in England, was authorised by his court to proceed in a negotiation with Tyrconnel for the separation of the two islands, in case that a protestant should succeed to the crown of England. He had accordingly a private interview with a confidential agent of the lord lieutenant at Chester, in the month of October 1687. Tyrconnel undertook that in less than a year every thing should be prepared. Id. ii. 281, 288; iii. 430.

[d] Leland, 537. This seems to rest on the authority of Leslie, which is by no means good. Some letters of Barillon, in 1687, show that James had intended the repeal of the act of settlement. Dalrymple 257, 263.

all their estates and all their rights, privileges, and immunities, which they held in the reign of Charles II., free from all forfeitures or outlawries incurred by them.*

This second article, but only as to the garrison of Limerick or other persons in arms, is confirmed by statute some years afterwards.[f] The first article seems, however, to be passed over. The forfeitures on account of the rebellion, estimated at 1,060,792 acres, were somewhat diminished by restitutions to the ancient possessors under the capitulation; the greater part were lavishly distributed to English grantees.[g] It appears from hence that at the end of the seventeenth century the Irish or Anglo-Irish catholics could hardly possess above one-sixth or one-seventh of the kingdom.[h] They were still formidable from their numbers and their sufferings; and the victorious party saw no security but in a system of oppression, contained in a series of laws during the reigns of William and Anne, which have scarce a parallel in European history, unless it be that of the protestants in France, after the revocation of the edict of Nantes, who yet were but a feeble minority of the whole people. No papist was allowed to keep a school, or to teach any in private houses, except the children of the family.[i] Severe penalties were denounced against such as should go themselves or send others for education beyond seas in the Romish religion; and, on probable information given to a magistrate, the burden of proving the contrary was thrown on the accused—the offence not to be tried by a jury, but by justices at quarter sessions.[k] Intermarriages between persons of different religion, and possessing any estate in Ireland, were forbidden; the children, in case of either parent being protestant, might be taken from the other, to be educated in that faith.[m] No papist could be guardian to any child; but the court of chancery might appoint some relation or other person to bring up the ward in the protestant religion.[n] The eldest son,

---

* See the articles at length in Leland, 619.

[f] Irish Stat. 9 Will. III., c. 2.

[g] Parl. Hist. v. 1202.

[h] [Vide supra. But of cultivable lands, if their forfeitures are to be reckoned in these alone, they may have retained about one fifth. As their freehold property at the time of the union was very much less than this, we must attribute the difference partly to the conversion of the wealthier families, and partly to the pressure of the penal laws, which induced men to sell their lands.—1845.]

[i] 7 Will. III., c. 4.

[k] Id.

[m] 9 Will. III., c. 3. 2 Anne, c 6.

[n] 9 Will. III., c. 3. 2 Anne, c. 6.

being a protestant, might turn his father's estate in fee simple into a tenancy for life, and thus secure his own inheritance. But if the children were all papists, the father's lands were to be of the nature of gavelkind, and descend equally among them. Papists were disabled from purchasing lands except for terms of not more than thirty-one years, at a rent not less than two-thirds of the full value. They were even to conform within six months after any title should accrue by descent, devise, or settlement, on pain of forfeiture to the next protestant heir—a provision which seems intended to exclude them from real property altogether, and to render the others almost supererogatory.° Arms, says the poet, remain to the plundered; but the Irish legislature knew that the plunder would be imperfect and insecure while arms remained: no papist was permitted to retain them, and search might be made at any time by two justices.ᴾ The bare celebration of catholic rites was not subjected to any fresh penalties; but regular priests, bishops, and others claiming jurisdiction, and all who should come into the kingdom from foreign parts, were banished on pain of transportation in case of neglecting to comply, and of high treason in case of returning from banishment. Lest these provisions should be evaded, priests were required to be registered; they were forbidden to leave their own parishes, and rewards were held out to informers who should detect the violations of these statutes, to be levied on the popish inhabitants of the country.ᵠ To have exterminated the catholics by the sword, or expelled them, like the Moriscoes of Spain, would have been little more repugnant to justice and humanity, but incomparably more politic.

It may easily be supposed that no political privileges would be left to those who were thus debarred of the common rights of civil society. The Irish parliament had never adopted the act passed in the fifth of Elizabeth, imposing the oath of supremacy on the members of the commons. It had been full of catholics under the queen and her two next successors. In the second session of 1641, after the flames of rebellion had enveloped almost all the

Dependence of the Irish upon the English parliament.

° 9 Will III., c. 3; 2 Anne, c. 6
ᴾ 7 W. III., c. 5.
ᵠ 9 W. III., c. 1 ; 2 Anne, c. 3, s. 7; 8 Anne, c. 3.

island, the house of commons were induced to exclude, by a resolution of their own, those who would not take that oath; a step which can only be judged in connexion with the general circumstances of Ireland at that awful crisis.ʳ In the parliament of 1661 no catholic, or only one, was returned;ˢ but the house addressed the lords justices to issue a commission for administering the oath of supremacy to all its members. A bill passed the commons in 1663 for imposing that oath in future, which was stopped by a prorogation; and the duke of Ormond seems to have been adverse to it.ᵗ An act of the English parliament after the Revolution, reciting that " great disquiet and many dangerous attempts have been made to deprive their majesties and their royal predecessors of the said realm of Ireland by the liberty which the popish recusants there have had and taken to sit and vote in parliament," requires every member of both houses of parliament to take the new oaths of allegiance and supremacy, and to subscribe the declaration against transubstantiation before taking his seat.ᵘ This statute was adopted and enacted by the Irish parliament in 1782, after they had renounced the legislative supremacy of England under which it had been enforced. The elective franchise, which had been rather singularly spared in an act of Anne, was taken away from the Roman catholics of Ireland in 1715, or, as some think, not absolutely till 1727.ˣ

These tremendous statutes had in some measure the effect which their framers designed. The wealthier families, against whom they were principally levelled, conformed in many instances to the protestant church.ʸ The catholics were extinguished as a political body; and, though any willing allegiance to the house of

---

ʳ Carte's Ormond, i. 328; Warner, 212. These writers censure the measure as illegal and impolitic.

ˢ Leland says none; but by lord Orrery's Letters, i. 35, it appears that one papist and one anabaptist were chosen for that parliament, both from Tuam.

ᵗ Mountmorres, i. 158.

ᵘ Ibid. 3 W. & M. c. 2.

ˣ Mountmorres, i. 163. Plowden's Hist. Review of Ireland, i. 263. The terrible act of the second of Anne prescribes only the oaths of allegiance and abjuration for voters at elections, § 24.

ʸ Such conversions were naturally distrusted. Boulter expresses alarm at the number of pseudo-protestants who practised the law; and a bill was actually passed to disable any one, who had not professed that religion for five years, from acting as a barrister or solicitor. Letters, i. 226. "The practice of the law, from the top to the bottom, is almost wholly in the hands of these converts."

Hanover would have been monstrous, and it is known that their bishops were constantly nominated to the pope by the Stuart princes,[a] they did not manifest at any period, or even during the rebellions of 1715 and 1745, the least movement towards a disturbance of the government. Yet for thirty years after the accession of George I. they continued to be insulted in public proceedings under the name of the common enemy, sometimes oppressed by the enactment of new statutes, or the stricter execution of the old; till in the latter years of George II. their peaceable deportment, and the rise of a more generous spirit among the Irish protestants, not only sheathed the fangs of the law, but elicited expressions of esteem from the ruling powers, which they might justly consider as the pledge of a more tolerant policy. The mere exercise of their religion in an obscure manner had long been permitted without molestation.[a]

Thus in Ireland there were three nations, the original natives, the Anglo-Irish, and the new English; the two former catholic, except some, chiefly of the upper classes, who had conformed to the church; the last wholly protestant. There were three religions, the Roman catholic, the established or Anglican, and the Presbyterian; more than one-half of the protestants, according to the computation of those times, belonging to the latter denomination.[b] These, however, in a less degree were under the ban of the law as truly as the catholics themselves; they were excluded from all civil and military offices by a test act, and even their religious

---

[a] Evidence of State of Ireland in Sessions of 1824 and 1825, p. 325 (as printed for Murray). In a letter of the year 1755, from a clergyman in Ireland to archbishop Herring, in the British Museum (Sloane MSS. 4164, 11), this is also stated. The writer seems to object to a repeal of the penal laws, which the catholics were supposed to be attempting; and says they had the exercise of their religion as openly as the protestants, and monasteries in many places.

[a] Plowden's Historical Review of State of Ireland, vol. i. passim.

[b] Sir William Petty, in 1672, reckons the inhabitants of Ireland at 1,100,000; of whom 200,000 English, and 100,000 Scots; above half the former being of the established church. Political Anatomy of Ireland, chap. ii. It is sometimes said in modern times, though erroneously, that the presbyterians form a majority of protestants in Ireland; but their proportion has probably diminished since the beginning of the eighteenth century. [It appears by a late census, in 1837, that the established church reckoned near 800,000 souls, the presbyterians 660,000; the catholics were above six millions.—1845.]

meetings were denounced by penal statutes. Yet the house of commons after the Revolution always contained a strong presbyterian body, and being unable, as it seems, to obtain an act of indemnity for those who had taken commissions in the militia, while the rebellion of 1715 was raging in Great Britain, had recourse to a resolution, that whoever should prosecute any dissenter for accepting such a commission is an enemy to the king and the protestant interest.[c] They did not even obtain a legal toleration till 1720.[d] It seems as if the connexion of the two islands, and the whole system of constitutional laws in the lesser, subsisted only for the sake of securing the privileges and emoluments of a small number of ecclesiastics, frequently strangers, who rendered very little return for their enormous monopoly. A great share, in fact, of the temporal government under George II. was thrown successively into the hands of two primates, Boulter and Stone: the one a worthy but narrow-minded man, who showed his egregious ignorance of policy in endeavouring to promote the wealth and happiness of the people, whom he at the same time studied to depress and discourage in respect of political freedom; the other an able, but profligate and ambitious statesman, whose name is mingled, as an object of odium and enmity, with the first great struggles of Irish patriotism.

The new Irish nation, or rather the protestant nation, since all distinctions of origin have, from the time of the great rebellion, been merged in those of religion, partook in large measure of the spirit that was poured out on the advocates of liberty and the revolution in the sister kingdom. Their parliament was always strongly whig, and scarcely manageable during the later years of the queen. They began to assimilate themselves more and more to the English model, and to cast off by degrees the fetters that galled and degraded them. By Poyning's celebrated law, the initiative power was reserved to the English council. This act, at one time popular in Ireland, was afterwards justly regarded as destructive of the rights of their parliament, and a badge of the nation's dependence. It was attempted by the commons in 1641,

[c] Plowden, 243   [d] Irish Stat. 6 G. I., c. 5

and by the catholic confederates in the rebellion, to procure its repeal, which Charles I. steadily refused, till he was driven to refuse nothing. In his son's reign it is said that " the council framed bills altogether; a negative alone on them and their several provisoes was left to parliament; only a general proposition for a bill by way of address to the lord lieutenant and council came from parliament; nor was it till after the revolution that heads of bills were presented; these last in fact resembled acts of parliament or bills, with only the small difference of ' We pray that it may be enacted,' instead of ' Be it enacted.'"[e] They assumed about the same time the examination of accounts, and of the expenditure of public money.[f]

Meanwhile, as they gradually emancipated themselves from the ascendancy of the crown, they found a more formidable power to contend with in the English parliament. It was acknowledged, by all at least of the protestant name, that the crown of Ireland was essentially dependent on that of England, and subject to any changes that might affect the succession of the latter. But the question as to the subordination of her legislature was of a different kind. The precedents and authorities of early ages seem not decisive; so far as they extend, they rather countenance the opinion that English statutes were of themselves valid in Ireland. But from the time of Henry VI. or Edward IV. it was certainly established that they had no operation, unless enacted by the Irish parliament.[g] This, however, would not legally prove that they might not be binding, if express words to that effect were employed; and such was the doctrine of lord Coke and of other English lawyers. This came into discussion about the eventful period of 1641. The Irish in general protested against the legislative authority of England as a novel theory which could not be maintained;[h] and two treatises on the subject, one ascribed to lord chancellor Bolton, or more probably to an eminent lawyer, Patrick Darcy, for the

[e] Mountmorres, II. 142. As one house could not regularly transmit heads of bills to the other, the advantage of a joint recommendation was obtained by means of conferences, which were consequently much more usual than in England. Id. 179.
[f] Id. 184.
[g] Vide supra.
[h] Carte's Ormond, III. 55.

independence of Ireland, another, in answer to it, by serjeant Mayart, may be read in the Hibernica of Harris.[i] Very few instances occurred before the Revolution wherein the English parliament thought fit to include Ireland in its enactments, and none perhaps wherein they were carried into effect. But after the Revolution several laws of great importance were passed in England to bind the other kingdom, and acquiesced in without express opposition by its parliament. Molyneux, however, in his celebrated 'Case of Ireland's being bound by Acts of Parliament in England stated,' published in 1697, set up the claim of his country for absolute legislative independency. The house of commons at Westminster came to resolutions against this book; and, with their high notions of parliamentary sovereignty, were not likely to desist from a pretension which, like the very similar claim to impose taxes in America, sprung in fact from the semi-republican scheme of constitutional law established by means of the revolution.[k] It is evident that while the sovereignty and enacting power was supposed to reside wholly in the king, and only the power of consent in the two houses of parliament, it was much less natural to suppose a control of the English legislature over other dominions of the crown, having their own representation for similar purposes, than after they had become, in effect and in general sentiment, though not quite in the statute book, co-ordinate partakers of the supreme authority. The Irish parliament, however, advancing as it were in a parallel line, had naturally imbibed the same sense of its own supremacy, and made at length an effort to assert it. A judgment from the court of exchequer in 1719 having been reversed by the house of lords, an appeal was brought before the lords in England, who affirmed the judgment of the exchequer. The Irish

---

[i] Vol. II. Mountmorres, i. 360.

[k] Journals, 27th June, 1698. Parl. Hist. v. 1181. They resolved at the same time that the conduct of the Irish parliament, in pretending to re-enact a law made in England expressly to bind Ireland, had given occasion to these dangerous positions. On the 30th of June they addressed the king in consequence, requesting him to prevent any thing of the like kind in future. In this address as first drawn, the legislative authority of the *kingdom of England* is asserted. But this phrase was omitted afterwards, I presume, as rather novel; though by doing so they destroyed the basis of their proposition, which could stand much better on the new theory of the constitution than the ancient.

lords resolved that no appeal lay from the court of exchequer in Ireland to the king in parliament in Great Britain; and the barons of that court, having acted in obedience to the order of the English lords, were taken into the custody of the black rod. That house next addressed the king, setting forth their reasons against admitting the appellant jurisdiction. But the lords in England, after requesting the king to confer some favour on the barons of the exchequer who had been censured and illegally imprisoned for doing their duty, ordered a bill to be brought in for better securing the dependency of Ireland upon the crown of Great Britain, which declares " that the king's majesty, by and with the advice and consent of the lords spiritual and temporal, and commons of Great Britain, in parliament assembled, had, hath, and of right ought to have, full power and authority to make laws and statutes of sufficient force and validity to bind the people and the kingdom of Ireland; and that the house of lords of Ireland have not, nor of right ought to have, any jurisdiction to judge of, reverse, or affirm any judgment, sentence, or decree given or made in any court within the said kingdom; and that all proceedings before the said house of lords upon any such judgment, sentence, or decree, are, and are hereby declared to be, utterly null and void, to all intents and purposes whatsoever." ᵐ

The English government found no better method of counteracting this rising spirit of independence than by bestowing the chief posts in the state and church on strangers, in order to keep up what was called the English interest.ⁿ This wretched policy united the natives of Ireland in jealousy and discontent, which the latter years of Swift were devoted to inflame. It was impossible that the kingdom should become, as it did

---

ᵐ 6 G. I., c. 5. Plowden, 244. [There was some opposition made to this bill by lord Molesworth, and others not so much connected as he was with Ireland: it passed by 140 to 83. Parl. Hist. vii. 642.—1845.] The Irish house of lords had, however, entertained writs of error as early as 1644, and appeals in equity from 1661. Mountmorres, i. 339. The English peers might have remembered that their own precedents were not much older.

ⁿ See Boulter's Letters, passim. His plan for governing Ireland was to send over as many English-born bishops as possible. " The bishops," he says, " are the persons on whom the government must depend for doing the public business here " (i. 238). This of course disgusted the Irish church.

under George II., more flourishing through its great natural fertility, its extensive manufacture of linen, and its facilities for commerce, though much restricted, the domestic alarm from the papists also being allayed by their utter prostration, without writhing under the indignity of its subordination; or that a house of commons, constructed so much on the model of the English, could hear patiently of liberties and privileges it did not enjoy.

Growth of a patriotic party in 1753. These aspirations for equality first, perhaps, broke out into audible complaints in the year 1753. The country was in so thriving a state that there was a surplus revenue after payment of all charges. The house of commons determined to apply this to the liquidation of a debt. The government, though not unwilling to admit of such an application, maintained that the whole revenue belonged to the king, and could not be disposed of without his previous consent. In England, where the grants of parliament are appropriated according to estimates, such a question could hardly arise; nor would there, I presume, be the slightest doubt as to the control of the house of commons over a surplus income. But in Ireland the practice of appropriation seems never to have prevailed, at least so strictly;° and the constitutional right might perhaps not unreasonably be disputed. After long and violent discussions, wherein the speaker of the commons and other eminent men bore a leading part on the popular side, the crown was so far victorious as to procure some motions to be carried, which seemed to imply its authority; but the house took care, by more special applications of the revenue, to prevent the recurrence of an undisposed surplus.ᵖ From this era the great parliamentary history of Ireland begins, and is terminated after half a century by the Union: a period fruitful of splendid eloquence, and of ardent, though not always uncompromising, patriotism, but which, of course, is beyond the limits prescribed to these pages.

° Mountmorres, l. 424.
ᵖ Plowden, 306 et post. Hardy's Life of Lord Charlemont.

INDEX.

₊ *The Roman Numerals refer to the Volumes — the Arabic Figures to the Pages of each Volume.*

ABBEY LANDS.

ABBEY LANDS, appropriation of them considered, i. 74, 79, note h—lawfulness of seizing, 75—distribution of, 77—retained by the parliament under Mary, 78—increase the power of the nobility, &c., 79—charity of the early possessors of, 80—confirmed by the pope to their new possessors, 104.

Abbot (George, archbishop of Canterbury) sequestered, i. 417 and note e—his Calvinistic zeal, ii. 55—Popish tracts in his library, 67, note P.

Abbots, surrenders of, to Henry VIII probably unlawful, i. 72—seats of, in parliament, and their majority over the temporal peers, 73 and note b.

Abjuration, oath of, clause introduced into, by the tories, iii. 192, note l.

Abolition of military tenures, ii. 312.

Act of Indemnity, ii. 304—exclusion of the regicides from the, ib.—commons vote to exclude seven, yet add several more, 305, and notes d e f g.

Act of Uniformity, ii. 338 — clauses against the presbyterians, 339 — no person to hold any preferment in England without episcopal ordination, ib. and 340, note d—every minister compelled to give his assent to the Book of Common Prayer on pain of being deprived of his benefice, ib. and note e —schoolmasters obliged to subscribe to, ib.

Act for suppressing conventicles, ii. 348, 386—opposed by bishop Wilkins, ib.—supported by Sheldon and others, ib.

Act of Supremacy, particulars of the, ii. 393.

Act of Security, persons eligible to parliament by the, iii. 190 and note b—in Scotland, 338.

Act of 1700 against the growth of popery, iii. 178 and note k—severity of its penalties, ib.—not carried into effect, 179.

Act of Settlement, iii. 179—limitations of the prerogative contained in it, 182—remarkable cause of the fourth remedial article, 184—its precaution against the influence of foreigners, 188, 189 and note f—importance of its sixth article, ib.

ANNE.

Act of Toleration, a scanty measure of religious liberty, iii. 172.

Act against wrongous imprisonment in Scotland, iii. 333.

Act for settlement of Ireland, iii. 394—its insufficiency, 396.

Act of explanation, iii. 396.

Acts, harsh, against the native Irish in settlement of colonies, iii. 381.

Acts replacing the crown in its prerogatives, ii. 328. See Bills and Statutes.

Adamson, archbishop of St. Andrews, obliged to retract before the general assembly of the church of Scotland, iii. 316.

Addresses, numerous servile, from all parties to James II., iii. 72 and note u.

Administration of Ireland, in whom vested, iii. 355.

Adultery, canon laws concerning, i. 102, note.

Agitators established in every regiment, ii. 210.

Aix-la-Chapelle, peace of, ii. 376.

Alienation, ancient English laws on, i. 12.

Allegiance, extent and power of, i. 307, note r.

Allegiance, oath of, administered to papists under James I., i. 407.

Allen (——), his treacherous purposes against Elizabeth, i. 144 and note f.

Almanza, battle of, iii. 234.

Altars removed in churches, i. 87.

Alva (duke of) his designed invasion of England, i. 134 and note d, 139.

Ambassadors, exempt from criminal process, i. 160—extent of their privilege examined, ib. note l.

Andrews (Dr. Launcelot, bishop of Winchester), his sentiments on transubstantiation, ii. 63, note e—singular phrase in his epitaph, ib. note d.

Anecdotes, two, relating to king Charles I. and Cromwell, ii 211, note y.

Anglesea (lord privy seal), statement of, in the case of lord Danby, ii. 413, note k.

Anglican church, ejected members of, their claims, ii. 3 8.

Anjou (duke of), his proposed marriage with queen Elizabeth, i. 125, note k 136, 232, note u.

Anne (princess of Denmark), her re-

410   INDEX.

ANNE.

pentant letter to James II., iii. 123, 124, *note* f — a narrow-minded, foolish woman, *ib.*—her dark intrigues with the court of St. Germain's, *ib.*
Anne (queen of Great Britain), her incapacity for government, iii. 208 — her confidence in Godolphin and Marlborough, 209—revolutions in her ministry, *ib.* 210—alarmed at the expedition of the pretender, 221 — her secret intentions with respect to the pretender never divulged, 225 and *note* f — her death, 229.
Appeals in civil suits in Scotland lay from the baron's court to that of the sheriff or lord of regality, and ultimately to the parliament, iii. 312.
Argyle (earl of), refuses to subscribe the test, iii. 329—convicted of treason upon the statute of leasing-making, and escapes, *ib.*—is executed after his rebellion upon his old sentence, 330.
Aristocracy, English, in Ireland, analogy of, to that of France, iii. 351.
Aristocracy of Scotland, influence of the, in the reign of James IV., iii. 311—system of repressing the, *ib.*
Arlington (Henry Bennett, earl of), one of the Cabal, ii. 372—obliged to change his policy, 396.
Arminian controversy, view of the, i. 400-404 and *notes.*
Arms, provided by freeholders, &c., for defence of the nation, ii. 133, *note* P.
Armstrong (sir Thomas), given up by the States, and executed without trial, ii. 461.
Army, conspiracy for bringing in, to overawe the parliament, ii. 125 and *note* e.
Army of Scotland enters England, ii. 167.
Army, parliamentary, new modelled, ii. 181—advances towards London, 206.
Army, proposals of the, to king Charles I. at Hampton-court, ii. 209—rejected by him, 210—innovating spirit in, 219—publishes a declaration for the settlement of the nation, 221 — principal officers of, determine to bring the king to justice, 223 and *note* b, 224.
Army disbanded, ii. 314—origin of the present, 315.
Army, great, suddenly raised by Charles II., ii. 401, 402 and *note* i.
Army, intention of James II. to place the, under the command of catholic officers, iii. 54.
Army, standing, Charles II.'s necessity for, ii. 380 — its illegality in time of peace, iii. 105, 106 and *note* f. (See Standing army)—Apprehensions from it, 260.
Army reduced by the commons, iii. 139.
Army recruited by violent means, iii. 214 and *note* e.
Array, commissions of, ii. 133.

AYLMER.

Arrest, exemption from, claimed by the house of commons, i. 268-272—parliamentary privilege of exemption from, 303.
Articles, lords of the, their origin and power, iii. 307—regularly named in the records of every parliament from the reign of James IV., 308—what they propounded, when ratified by the three estates, did not require the king's consent to give it validity, 311—abolished, 335.
Articles of the church of England, real presence denied in the, i. 91—subsequently altered, *ib.* and *note* s—original drawing up of the, 101 and *note* u—brought before parliament, 191—statute for subscribing, 192 — ministers deprived for refusing, 193, *note* x.
Articles, thirty-nine, denial of any of the, made excommunication, i. 303, *note* k.
Articles of the church on predestination, i. 400.
Articuli Cleri, account of the, i. 324.
Artillery company established, ii. 133.
Arundel (Thomas Howard, earl of), his committal to the Tower, i. 378.
Arundel (Henry Howard, earl of), his case in parliament, iii. 35, *note* a.
Ashby, a burgess of Aylesbury, sues the returning officer for refusing his vote, iii. 274.
Ashley (Anthony, lord, afterwards earl of Shaftesbury), one of the Cabal, ii. 374.
Ashley (serjeant), his speech in favour of prerogative, i. 390, *note* c.
Ashton (John), remarks on his conviction for high treason on presumptive evidence, iii. 160, 161.
Association abjuring the title of James II., and pledging the subscribers to revenge the death of William III., generally signed, iii. 131 and *note* z.
Atkinson (——), his speech in the house of commons against the statute for the queen's power, i. 117, *note* q.
Attainders against Russell, Sidney, Cornish, and Armstrong, reversed, iii. 160.
Atterbury (Dr.), an account of his book entitled *Rights and Privileges of an English Convocation,* iii. 244 — promoted to the see of Rochester, 245—disaffection to the house of Hanover, 251—deprived of his see, and banished for life, 252 and *note.*
Augsburg Confession, consubstantiation acknowledged in the, i. 90.
Augsburg, league of, iii. 86.
Aylmer (John, bishop of London), his persecution of papists, i. 183, *note* d—his covetousness and prosecution of the puritans, i. 203 and *note* s—Elizabeth's tyranny to, 225, *note* m—his answer to Knox against female monarchy, 280—

BACON.

passage from his book on the limited power of the English crown, 280, 281.

Bacon (sir Francis, lord Verulam), his praise of the laws of Henry VII, i. 11—his error concerning the act of benevolence, 14, *note* ¹—his account of causes belonging to the court of starchamber, 54—his apology for the execution of catholics, 164, *note* ᵠ—his character of lord Burleigh, 204—excellence and moderation of his *Advertisement on the Controversies of the Church of England*, 227, and *note* ᴾ—disliked agreeing with the house of lords on a subsidy, 276—his advice to James I. on summoning a parliament, 338—acquainted with the particulars of Overbury's murder, 352 and 353, *note* ˢ—impeached for bribery, 358—extenuation of, 359, *note* ˣ—his notice of the puritans, 396, *note* ᵐ—recommends mildness towards the papists, 409, *note* ᵐ¹.

Bacon (sir Nicholas), great seal given to, i. 110, *note* ᵛ—abilities of, 110—suspected of favouring the house of Suffolk, 128—his reply to the speaker of the house of commons, 252.

Baillie (Robert), his account of the reception and impeachment of the earl of Strafford in England, ii. 104, *note* ᵠ.

Ball (bishop of Ossory), persists in being consecrated according to the protestant form, iii. 366, *note* ʳ.

Ballot, the, advocated in the reign of Anne, iii. 203, *note* ᵇ.

Balmerino (lord), tried for treason on the Scottish statute of leasing-making, iii. 324, 325.

Bancroft (Richard), archbishop of Canterbury, endeavours to increase the ecclesiastical jurisdiction, i. 324, 325 and *note* ˢ—puritan clergymen deprived by, 394 and *note* ᵏ—defence of episcopacy, 395, 396 and *note* ᵐ.

Bangorian controversy, iii. 246—character of it, *ib.* and *note* ᵈ.

Bank of England, its origin and depreciation of its notes, iii. 135.

Banks (sir John), attorney-general, his defence of the king's absolute power, ii. 21.

Baptism by midwives abolished, i. 181, *note* ⁿ.

Barebone's parliament, ii. 243—apply themselves with vigour to reform abuses, *ib.*—vote for the abolition of the court of chancery, *ib.*—alarm the clergy, *ib.*—surrender their power to Cromwell, 244.

Barillon (the French ambassador), favours the opposition, ii. 405, *note* ᵠ—sums given to members of parliament mentioned by, 406—remarks on that corruption, *ib.*—suspicions against, 446

BERKLEY.

—extract from, concerning an address from the commons to the king, iii. 50, 51, *note* ᵉ.

Barnes (Dr. Thomas), appointed to defend the marriage of Henry VIII. with Catherine of Aragon, i. 66, *note* ᵈ.

Baronets created by James I. to raise money, i. 338, and *note* ˣ.

Barons of parliament, the title of, objected to, i. 361, *note* ⁿ.

Barons, English, their acquisitions in Ireland, iii. 349.

Barrier treaty of lord Townshend, iii. 216.

Baxter, extract from his Life, descriptive of the episcopalians of his day, ii. 320, *note* ᵠ.

Beal (——), his book against the ecclesiastical system of England, i. 148, *note* ʳ.

Beauchamp (William Seymour, lord), honours of his family restored to, i. 293, and *note* ¹.

Bedford (Francis Russell, second earl of), imprisoned under queen Mary, on account of his religion, i. 103.

Bedford (Francis Russell, fourth earl of), plan to bring back popular leaders frustrated by his death, ii. 120, and *note* ʳ.

Bedford (William Russell, fifth earl of), joins king Charles I. at Oxford, ii. 153—is ill received, 159—returns to the parliament, *ib.*

Beggars caused by the alms of monasteries, i. 80—statute against giving to, *ib.*, *note* ¹.

Bell (Mr.), his attack on licences, i. 254—elected speaker, *ib.* and 255, *note* ʳ.

Bellarmine (Cardinal Robert), opposes the test-oath of James I., i. 407.

Bellay (Joachim du, bishop of Bayonne), reports that a revolt was expected in England on the divorce of Henry VIII., i. 67.

Benefices, first fruits of, taken from the pope, i. 65.

Benevolence, exaction so called, in 1545, i. 24—consequences of refusing to contribute to it, 25—taken by queen Elizabeth, 244, and *note* ᵘ.

Benevolences, oppression of, under Edward IV., i. 14—abolished under Richard III., and revived by Henry VII., *ib.*—granted by private persons, *ib.*, *note* ¹—required under James I., 342.

Bennet (Dr.), his proposal on the divorce of Henry VIII., i. 66, *note* ᵏ.

Bennet (——), an informer against papists, i. 154, *note* ⁿ.

Benison (——), his imprisonment by bishop Aylmer, i. 203.

Berkley (sir John), justice of the king's bench, defends ship-money, ii. 17 and *note* ¹—and the king's absolute power, 22—parliamentary impeachment of, 140, *note* ᶜ

BERKELY.

Berkely (Charles, first earl of), his administration in Ireland in 1670, iii. 398.
Berwick, right of election extended to, by Henry VIII., iii. 38.
Best (Paul), ordinance against, for writing against the Trinity, ii. 201, note *e*.
Bible, 1535, church translation of the proscribed, i. 83—liberty of reading, procured by Cromwell, and recalled by Henry VIII., *ib.*, and note *n*.
Bill of exclusion drawn in favour of the duke of York's daughters, ii. 432—of rights, iii. 104—of indemnity, 112—for regulating trials upon charges of high treason, 160—of 7th of queen Anne, affording peculiar privileges to the accused, 163—to prevent occasional conformity, passes the commons, and is rejected by the lords, 248—passed by next parliament, 249—repealed by the whigs, *ib.* and note *l*.
Birch (Dr. Thomas), confirms the genuineness of Glamorgan's commissions, ii. 193.
Birth of the pretender, suspicions attending the, iii. 81, 82.
Bishops of England, authority of the pope in their election taken away, i. 66—their adherence to Rome the cause of their abolition by the Lutherans, 100—less offensive in England than Germany, *ib.*—defend church property in England, *ib.*—some inclined to the puritans, 182—conference with the house of commons, 210—commons opposed to the, 211—puritans object to their title, 224, note *e*—character of, under Elizabeth, 225 and note *k*—tyranny of the queen towards them, *ib.* and note *m*—conference of with the puritans at Hampton Court, 297—proceedings of the against the puritans, 394—jurisdiction of the, ii. 47 and note *y*—moderate government of, proposed, 114, 115 and notes *d e f*—proceedings on abolishing, 116—excluded from parliament, 117 and note *a*—reflections on that measure, 118, 119—impeachment of the twelve, 142, note *m*—restored to their seats in the house of lords, 329—their right of voting denied by the commons, in the case of lord Danby, 414—discussion of the same, 415—restored to Scotland after six years' abolition, iii. 320—and to part of their revenues, 321—their protestations against any connivance at popery, 385, note *b*.
Bishops, popish, endeavour to discredit the English Scriptures, i. 83, note *n*—refuse to officiate at Elizabeth's coronation, 110 and note *c*—deprived under Elizabeth, 111—their subsequent treatment, 115.
Bishoprics despoiled in the reformation under Henry VIII., i. 94.

BOROUGHS.

Black, one of the ministers of St. Andrew's, summoned before the privy council of Scotland, iii. 319.
Blackstone (sir William), his misunderstanding of the statute of allegiance, 11th Henry VII., i. 10, note *f*—inadvertent assertion of, ii. 448.
Blair (sir Adam), impeached for high treason, ii. 448.
Bland (———), fined by authority of parliament, i. 274.
Blount (John), sentenced by the lords to imprisonment and hard labour in Bridewell for life, iii. 280.
Boleyn (Anne), her weakness of character, i. 31, note *n*—undoubted innocence of; her indiscretion; infamous proceedings upon her trial; her levities in discourse brought as charges against her; confesses a precontract with lord Percy; her marriage with the king annulled, 32—act settling the crown on the king's children by, or any subsequent wife, 34—time of her marriage with Henry VIII. considered, 62, note *s*—interested in the reformed faith, 68.
Bolingbroke (Henry St. John, lord), remarkable passage in his Letters on History, ii. 383, note *x*—engaged in correspondence with the pretender, iii. 223, 224 and note *q*—impeached of high treason, 233—his letters in the Examiner answered by lord Cowper, 298, note *s*—character of his writings, 298, 299.
Bolton (lord chancellor), his treatise on the Independence of Ireland, iii. 405
Bonaght, usage of, explained, iii. 348.
Bonaght and coshering, barbarous practice of, iii. 357.
Bonner (Edmund, bishop of London), his persecution, i. 96—treatment of by Edward VI.'s council, 97, note *o*—royal letter to, for the prosecution of heretics, 105, note *f*—imprisoned in the Marshalsea, 118—denies bishop Horn to be lawfully consecrated, *ib.*
Books of the reformed religion imported from Germany and Flanders, i. 82—statute against, *ib.* note *m*—books against the queen prohibited by statute, 138.
Books, restrictions on printing, selling, possessing, and importing, i. 238, 239, and notes *i k l m n*.
Booth (sir George), rises in Cheshire in favour of Charles II., ii. 277.
Boroughs and burgesses, elections and wages of, under Elizabeth, i. 264 and note *o*.
Boroughs, twenty-two created in the reign of Edward VI., i. 45—fourteen added to the number under Mary, *ib.*—state of those that return members to parliament, iii. 37—fourteen created

BOROUGHS.

by Edward VI., 38—twenty-one members for, added by Mary, *ib.*—many more by Elizabeth and James, *ib.*
Boroughs royal of Scotland, common usage of the, to choose the deputies of other towns as their proxies, iii. 308.
Bossuet (Jacques), his invective against Cranmer, i. 98.
Boucher (Joan), execution and speech of, i. 96 and *note* ⁿ.
Boulter, primate of Ireland, his great share in the government of Ireland in the reign of George II., iii. 404—his character, *ib.*
Bound (Dr.), founder of the Sabbatarians, i. 397, *note* ᵒ.
Boyne, splendid victory of the, gained by William III., iii. 399.
Brady (Dr. Thomas), remarks on his writings, ii. 464—on his treatise on boroughs, iii. 41.
Brehon, customs of, murder not held felony by the, iii. 345 and *note* ʳ.
Brewers complain of an imposition on malt, i. 363, *note* ᵈ—proclamation concerning, ii. 25.
Bribery, first precedent for a penalty on, i. 268—impeachments for, 358—prevalent in the court of Charles II., ii. 356—its prevalence at elections, iii. 44.
Bridgeman (sir Orlando), succeeds Clarendon, ii. 374.
Brihuega, seven thousand English under Stanhope surrender at, iii. 215.
Bristol (John, lord Digby, earl of), refusal of summons to, &c., i. 379, 380 and *note* ᵏ.
Bristol (George Digby, earl of), converted to popery, ii. 344—attacks Clarendon, 365, *note* ᵍ.
Brodie (Mr.), his exposure of the misrepresentations of Hume, i. 284, *note* ʲ.
Browne (sir Thomas), his abilities, ii. 74.
Brownists and Barrowists, most fanatic of the puritans, i. 214—emigrate to Holland, *ib.*—execution of, *ib.* 215 and *note* ᵃ.
Bruce (Edward), his invasion of Ireland, iii. 358.
Bucer (Martin), his permission of a concubine to the landgrave of Hesse, i. 68, *note* ᵒ—his doctrines concerning the Lord's Supper, 90—politic ambiguity of, *ib. note* ʲ—assists in drawing up the forty-two articles, 97, *note* ᵖ—objected to the English vestments of priests, 102.
Buckingham (Edward Stafford, duke of), his trial and execution under Henry VIII, i. 27 and *note* ᶠ.
Buckingham (George Villiers, duke of), his connexion with lord Bacon's impeachment, i. 359 and *note* ˣ—sets aside the protracted match with Spain, 371—deceit of, 376 and *note* ᶜ—his impeachment, 377-378—his enmity to

CALVINISM.

Spain, 409, 410 and *notes* ᵐ ᵒ—his scheme of seizing on American gold-mines, 409, *note* ⁿ.
Buckingham (son of the preceding), one of the cabal ministry, ii. 370—driven from the king's councils, 396—administration of, during the reign of Charles II., iii. 10.
Buckingham (John Sheffield, duke of), engaged in the interest of the pretender, iii. 224, 225, *note*.
Bull of Pius V. deposing Elizabeth, i. 137—prohibited in England by statute, *ib.*
Bullinger (Henry) objected to the English vestments of priests, i. 103.
Buonaparte (Napoleon), character of, compared with that of Oliver Cromwell, ii. 263-265, and *note* ᵘ.
Burchell (Peter), in danger of martial law under Elizabeth, i. 241 and *note* ᵒ.
Burgage tenure, iii. 37—opinion of the author concerning ancient, 40, 41.
Burgesses, wages of boroughs to, i. 264, *note* ᵒ—debate on non-resident, in the house of commons, 266.
Burgundy (duke of), effect of his death on the French succession, iii. 218.
Burnet (Dr. Gilbert, bishop of Salisbury), denies the answer of Henry VIII. to Luther, i. 59, *note* ᵇ—and the king's bribery of the universities on his divorce, 61, *note* ᶠ—his doubts on the time of Anne Boleyn's marriage, 62, *note* ᵍ—his valuation of the suppressed monasteries, 76—his observations on the persecutions of Mary, 106, *note* ᵍ—anecdote related by, ii. 364, *note* ᵈ—his remarkable conversation with Bentinck, iii. 99, *note* ᵖ—remark of, on the statute for regulating trials in cases of high treason, 163.
Burton (Henry), and Edward Bastwick, prosecuted by the star-chamber, ii. 38.
Bushell, a juryman, committed for non-payment of his fine imposed on him in the case of Penn and Mead, iii. 9.
Butler (Mr. Charles), his candid character of Cranmer, i. 99, *note* ᶠ—his discussion of the oath of supremacy, 112, *note* ᵍ.

Cabal ministry, account of the, ii. 374.
Cabinet council, question of its responsibility, iii. 185 and *note* ᵃ—members of the, answerable for the measures adopted by its consent, 187.
Calais, right of election extended to, iii. 38.
Calamy (Edmund), irregularly set at liberty by the king's order, ii. 347.
Calvin (John), adopts Bucer's doctrine on the Lord's Supper, i. 91 and *note* ˣ—malignity of, 96—objected to the English vestments of priests, 103.
Calvinism in England, i. 401-403, and *note* ᵒ.

CALVINISTS.

Calvinists, severe act against the, ii. 349.
Cambridge University, favourable to protestantism, i. 184.
Camden (William, Clarenceux king of arms), remarks of, concerning Elizabeth's appointment of a successor, i. 126, note a.
Cameronian rebellion, iii. 328—the Cameronians publish a declaration renouncing their allegiance to Charles II., 330.
Campian (Edmund), executed for popery, i. 146—his torture justified by lord Burleigh, 150.
Canon laws, commissioners appointed for framing a new series, i. 100, 101, notes t u—character of the canons, which were never enacted, ib.—amendments of, attempted, 191.
Canons, ecclesiastical, new code of, under James I., i. 303 and notes k m—defending the king's absolute power, 322 and note x.
Cardwell's 'Annals of the Church,' remarks upon a passage in, i. 396, note m.
Carleton (sir Dudley), his unconstitutional speech on parliaments, i. 377, note k.
Carne (sir Edward), ambassador at Rome, to queen Mary, i. 109 and note b.
Carte (Thomas), his censure of the character, &c. of queen Mary, i. 105, note e —his anecdotes of Godolphin and Harley, iii. 221, note k—his Life of the Duke of Ormond, 390, note n—the fullest writer on the Irish rebellion, ib.
Carte and Leland, their account of the causes of the rebellion in Ireland in 1641, iii. 392, note q.
Cartwright (Thomas), founder of the puritans, i. 185—his character, ib.—his Admonition, 186—his opposition to civil authority in the church, ib.—his probable intent of its overthrow, 187, note n—design of his labours, 188— objected to the seizure of church property, ib. note p—summoned before the ecclesiastical commission, 207—disapproved of the puritan libels, 208— assertions of, concerning Scripture, 216, note h.
Catherine of Aragon, queen of Henry VIII., his marriage with her, and cause of dislike, i. 60 and note d, 61— divorce from, 62—feelings of the nation in her favour, 67.
Catholic religion, presumption of the establishment of, ii. 381—remarks on James II.'s intention to re-establish, iii. 52-55.
Catholics, laws of Elizabeth respecting the, i. chap. iii. 108-169—a proud and obnoxious faction in the reign of Charles I., ii. 169—natural enemies to peace, ib.—hated by both parties,

CEREMONIES.

175—Charles I. gave much offence by accepting their proffered services, ib. —promises of Charles II. to, 342— Loyalty of, ib.—Charles II.'s bias in favour of, 344—laws against, enforced in Ireland, iii. 377—claim the re-establishment of their religion, 393— aim at revoking the act of settlement, 397 · their hopes under Charles II. and James II., 398—their possessions at the end of the seventeenth century, 400— severity of the laws against them during the reigns of William III. and Anne, ib.—severe penalties imposed upon them, ib.
Cavaliers, ruined, inadequate relief voted to, ii. 325.
Cavendish (Richard), proceedings concerning his office for Writs, i. 279, note s.
Cecil, William (lord Burleigh), his great talents, i. 110—paper of, on religious reform, ib. note d—his memoranda concerning the debates on the succession under Elizabeth, 126, note B—his conduct concerning Elizabeth's marriage, 124—arguments of, relating to the archduke Charles and the Earl of Leicester, ib. note h—procures an astrological judgment on her marriage with the duke of Anjou, 125, note i— favours her marriage with the archduke Charles, 125, note m—suspected of favouring the house of Suffolk, 128 and note r—memorandum of, concerning the queen of Scots, 132—fears of, concerning the nation, 136—his proceedings against Mary Stuart restrained by Elizabeth, 139—pamphlets of, in defence of Elizabeth, 149, 150 and note t —answered by cardinal Allen, and supported by Stubbe, 150, note t—his memorial on the oath of supremacy, 151—his advice for repressing of papists, 152—fidelity of his spies on Mary queen of Scots, 156—continues his severity to the papists, 167—his strictness over Cambridge University, 185, note i — averse to the severity of Whitgift, 202—his apology for the puritans, 204—his constant pliancy towards Elizabeth, ib.—his spoliation of church property, 224—project of, for raising money, 245—interests himself in affairs of private individuals, 246 and note s —his policy in doing so, ib.—foresight the character of his administration, 247.
Cecil, Robert (earl of Salisbury), his innocence of the gunpowder conspiracy, i. 406, note.
Celibacy of priests, its origin and evils considered, i. 91 and note e.
Census of 1837, results of the, in Ireland, iii. 403, note b.
Ceremonies, superstitious, abolished in England, i. 86.

CHAMBERS.

Chambers (Rich.L.), proceedings against, for refusing to pay customs, &c., ii. 7.
Chancery, court of, its practice concerning charitable bequests, i. 79, *note* b.
Chancery, origin and power of the court of, i. 344—dispute on the extent of its jurisdiction, 345—its abolition voted, ii. 243.
Chantries, acts for abolishing, i. 94—disposition of their revenues, *ib.*
Charles I. (king of England), constitution of England under, from 1625-1629, i. chap. vii. 374-419—favourable features of his character, 374 and *note* a—succeeds to the throne in preparations for war, 375—privileges of parliament infringed by, 378, 379—determines to dissolve it, 380 and *note* b—demands a loan, and consequent tumult, 381 and *note* b—arbitrary proceedings of his council, 382, 383 and *note* f—summons a new parliament, 387 and *note* x—his dislike to the petition of right, 389-392—answer concerning tonnage and poundage, and prorogues the parliament, 393—his engagement to the Spanish papists when prince of Wales, 410—conditions for his marriage with the princess Henrietta Maria, 412—view of his third parliament compared with his character, 418—constitution of England under from 1629-1640, ii. chap. viii. 1-93—declaration of, after the dissolution, 2, and *note* a—his proclamations, 24—proceedings against the city, 25—offer of London to build the king a palace, 27, *note* d—principal charges against his government, 29—his court, &c., suspected of favouring popery, 58-61—supposed to have designed restoration of church lands, 66—attempts to draw him into the Romish church, 71—aversion to calling a parliament, 87—vain endeavour to procure a supply from, 89—dissolved, 91—his means for raising money, 92—summons the council of York, *ib.*—assents to calling a parliament, 93—constitution of England under, from 1640-1642, chap. ix. 94-150—his desire of saving Lord Strafford, 108, *note* u—recovers a portion of his subjects' confidence, 120—his sincerity still suspected, 123—his attempt to seize members of parliament, 125, 126, *notes* c d—effects of, on the nation, 127—his sacrifices to the parliament, 135—nineteen propositions offered to, 137—powers claimed by, in the nineteen propositions, *ib.*—comparative merits of his contest with the parliament, 138-150—his concessions important to his cause, 148—his intentions of levying war considered, 147, *note* p—probably too soon abandoned the parliament, 148-150—his success in the first part of the civil war, 153—his error in besieging Gloucester, *ib.*—affair at Brentford

CHARLES II.

injurious to his reputation, 154—his strange promise to the queen—155—denies the two houses the name of a parliament, 158—Earls of Holland, Bedford, and Clare join, *ib.*—their bad reception, and return to the parliament, 159—is inferior in substantial force, 160—yeomanry and trading classes general against him, 167—remarks on the strength and resources of the two parties, 168—loses ground during winter, *ib.*—makes a truce with the rebel catholics, who are beaten at Namptwich, *ib.*—success over Essex in the west, *ib.*—summons the peers and commons to meet at Oxford, 170—vote of parliament summoning him to appear at Westminster, 171—his useless and inveterate habit of falsehood, 175 and *note* a—does not sustain much loss in the west, 179—defeat of, at Naseby, 181—observations on his conduct after his defeat, 182, 183—surrenders himself to the Scots, 184—reflections on his situation, 185—fidelity to the English church, 186—thinks of escaping, 188—imprudence of preserving the queen's letters, which fell into the hands of parliament, 189 and *note* e—disavows the power granted to Glamorgan, 192—is delivered up to the parliament, 194—remarks on that event, 195 and *notes* n o—offers made by the army to, 205—taken by Joyce, *ib.*—treated with indulgence, 207—his ill reception of the proposals of the army at Hampton Court, 208—escapes from Hampton Court, 212—declines passing four bills, 213—placed in solitary confinement, *ib.*—remarks on his trial, 223—reflections on his execution, character, and government, 225, 226 and *note* s—his innovations on the law of Scotland, iii. 321, 322—his promise of graces to the Irish, 384—his perfidy on the occasion, *ib.*—state of the church in Ireland in the reign of, 385 and *note* b.
Charles II. (king of England), seeks foreign assistance, ii. 248—attempts to interest the pope in his favour, *ib.*—his court at Brussels, 275 - receives pledges from many friends in England, 276—pressed by the royalists to land in England, 278—fortunate in making no public engagements with foreign powers, 279—hatred of the army to, 287—his restoration considered imminent, early in the year 1660, 288 and *note* t—constitution of the convention parliament greatly in his favour, 292, 293 and *notes* c d—his declaration from Breda, 304—proclamation soon after landing, 306 - re-enters on the crown lands 309—income settled on, 311—character of, by opposite parties, 316 and *note* k—promises to grant liberty of conscience,

CHARLES II.

317—his declaration in favour of a compromise, 321—violates his promise by the execution of Vane, 327—his speech to parliament concerning the triennial act, 331—violates the spirit of his declarations, 342—wishes to mitigate the penal laws against the catholics, 344—his inclination toward that mode of faith, *ib.* and *note* P—publishes a declaration in favour of liberty of conscience, 346—private life of, 354—commons jealous of his designs, 356—not averse to a commission of inquiry into the public accounts, 357—solicits money from France, 371—intrigues with France, 376—his desire of absolute power, 377—complains of the freedom of political conversations, 378—advice of some courtiers to, on the fire of London, 379—unpopularity of, 380—endeavours to obtain aid from France, 381—desires to testify publicly his adherence to the Romish communion, *ib.*—his conference with the duke of York, Clifford, and Arlington, for the advancement of the catholic faith, *ib.*—his personal hatred to the Dutch, 384—joins with Louis to subvert Holland, *ib.*—confesses to Louis XIV's. ambassador the national dislike to French alliance, 385—his evasive conduct towards Louis XIV., 386—hopes of his court, 387—his prerogative opposed by the commons, 392—complains to the lords of the opposition of the commons, *ib.*—gives way to the public voice about the suspension bill, *ib.* and *note* u—compelled to make peace with Holland, 397—his attachment to French interests, *ib.*—receives money from France, 401—his secret treaties with France, 409—his insincerity, *ib.* —his proposal to Louis XIV. of a league to support Sweden, 410—his death anxiously wished for by the Jesuits, 424—his unsteadiness, 434 and *note* t —tells Hyde it will not be in his power to protect the duke of York, 435—his offers in the case of exclusion, 436—implores the aid of Louis XIV. against his council and parliament, 441—his dissimulation, 443—consultations against his government begin to be held, 455—his connexion with Louis XIV. broken off, 467—his death, 468—no general infringements of public liberty during his reign, iii. 1—tyrannical form of his government in Scotland, 326—state of the protestants and catholics in Ireland at his restoration, 394—state, character, and religion of the parties in Ireland at the restoration of, *ib.*—his declaration for the settlement of Ireland, *ib.*—claims of the different parties, 395—not satisfactory to all concerned, *ib.* —disgusted with the Irish agents, 396.

CHURCH.

Charles IX. (king of France), his persecution of the protestant faith, i. 136.

Charles V. (emperor of Germany), his influence over the pope on Henry VIII.'s divorce, i. 63—intercedes for the princess Mary to enjoy her religion, 95.

Charles (archduke of Austria), a suitor for the hand of Elizabeth, i. 123, 141 —Cecil's arguments in his favour, 124, *note* b—recognised as king of Spain, iii. 211—elected emperor, 215.

Charles Louis (elector palatine), suspected of aspiring to the throne, ii. 218, *note* a.

Charnock, one of the conspirators to assassinate William III., iii. 130, *note*.

Chatelherault, verses displayed at the entry of Francis II. at, i. 130, *note* u.

Chester, county of, right of election extended to, iii. 38.

Chichester (sir Arthur, lord deputy), his capacity, iii. 380—the great colony of Ulster carried into effect by his means, *ib.*, 381.

Chieftains (Irish), compelled to defend their lands, iii. 358.

Chillingworth (Dr. William), his examination of popery, ii. 75—effect of the covenant upon his fortunes, 166.

Cholmley (sir Henry), his letter to the mayor of Chester on a loan to queen Elizabeth, I. 244, *note* u.

Christ Church College, Oxford, endowed by Wolsey from the suppressed monasteries, i. 70.

Church of England, view of, under Henry VIII., Edward VI., and queen Mary, i. chap. ii. 57-107.

Church ceremonies and liturgy disliked by the reformers, i. 171—proposal for abolishing, 175, *note* P—concession of, beneficial, 177—irregularly observed by the clergy, 178. Elizabeth's reported offer of abolishing, 226, *note* o.

Church of England, its tenets and homilies altered under Edward VI., i. 86 —liturgy of, chiefly a translation of the Latin rituals, *ib.* and *note* r—images removed from, *ib.* and *note* s—altars taken down and ceremonies abolished in the, 87—principally remodelled by Cranmer, 97—alterations in the, under Elizabeth, 108, *note* a—its liturgy amended, 111 and *note* e—Entirely separated from Rome, 112—opposition of Cartwright to the, 187, *note* o—moderate party of, the least numerous under Elizabeth, 189—attack on, by Strickland, 190—its abuses, *ib.*—articles of, brought before parliament, 191— innovations meditated in the, ii. 114-118, and *notes*—parliamentary orders for protecting, 317, 318 and *notes* i k.

Church of Scotland, its immense wealth, iii. 313—wholly changed in character

INDEX. 417

CHURCH.

since the restoration of the bishops, 322—in want of a regular liturgy, *ib.*—English model not closely followed; consequences of this, *ib.*
Church lands restored at the Restoration, ii. 310.
Church plate stolen in the Reformation under Edward VI., i. 94, note ⁸.
Church revenues, spoliation of, in England, i. 224.
Civil war under Charles I., commencement of, ii. 150—great danger of, in the reign of Charles II., 445.
Clanricarde (marquis of), his unsullied character, iii. 393, note ᶠ.
Clare (earl of), joins the king, is ill received, and returns to the parliament, ii. 158, 159.
Clarence (Lionel, duke of), parliament held by, at Kilkenny, for reform of abuses, iii. 357.
Clarendon (Edward Hyde, earl of), character of his talents and works, ii. 78—MSS. and interpolation of his history and life, *ib.* note b—imperfections and prejudices of the work, 78-81 and notes b ᶜ, 86, note ᵃ, 93, note ᵍ—observations on, 183, note k—against Monk, 289—resolution of, to replace the church in its property at the Restoration, 310—his integrity, 325 and note ᵒ—the principal adviser of Charles II., 332—prejudices of, 335, note ʸ—against any concession to the catholics, 345—averse to some of the clauses in the Act of uniformity, *ib.*—his account of the prevailing discontents of his time, 353, note ᵃ—inveighs against a proviso in a money bill, 358—his bigotry to the tory party, *ib.*—opposes the commission of inquiry, 359—clandestine marriage of his daughter with the duke of York, 361 and note b—decline of his power, *ib.*—suspected of promoting the marriage of Miss Stewart and the duke of Richmond, 363—his notions of the English constitution, 364—strongly attached to protestant principles, 365—will not favour the king's designs against the established religion, *ib.*—coalition against, 365, 366 and note h—his loss of the king's favour, *ib.*—severity of his treatment, *ib.*—his impeachment, 367—unfit for the government of a free country, *ib.*—articles of his impeachment greatly exaggerated, 368—fears the hostility of the commons, *ib.*—charged with effecting the sale of Dunkirk, 369—his close connection with France, 370—conjectures on his policy, *ib.*—advises Charles to solicit money from France, 371—his faults as a minister, *ib.*—further remarks on his History of the Rebellion, *ib.* and note ᵘ—his disregard for truth, and pusillanimous flight, 373—banishment, *ib.*—

VOL. III.

CLERGY.

justification of it, *ib.* and note ᶻ—severe remark of, on the clergy, iii. 247.
Clarendon (Henry, earl of), succeeded by Tyrconnel in the government of Ireland, iii. 65.
Clark (baron of the exchequer), his speech on the royal power, i. 318.
Clement VII. (cardinal Julius), pope, his artful conduct towards Henry VIII., . 61—difficulties of deciding on the king's divorce, 62—forced to give sentence against him, 63—probably could not have recovered his authority in England, 64—last bulls of, in the reign of Henry VIII., 66—advice to the king on his divorce, 68, note ᵒ.
Clement VIII. (pope), favours Arabella Stuart's title to the English crown, i. 287—his project of conquering England, *ib.* note b,
Clergy, levy on their possessions under Henry VIII., i. 19, 20—immunity of the, from civil authority, 58 - compelled to plead their privilege, *ib.*—to be branded for felony, *ib.*—benefit of, taken from robbers, &c., with exemptions, *ib.*—their privileges tried and defeated, *ib.*—popular opposition to the, 59—attacked in the house of commons, 64—convicted of præmunire, *ib.*—petition the king for mercy, and acknowledge him supreme head of the church, 65—cause of their dislike of the king's divorce, 67—unwilling to quit the catholic church, 68—jealousy excited by their wealth, 69—subdued by separation from Rome, and the dissolution of monasteries, 81—dramatic satires on the, 84 and note ᵒ—their answers to libels against them, *ib.*—their importance aided by the Latin ritual, 86—their celibacy abolished by statute, 92—conciliated by this measure, *ib.*—conforming, but averse to the innovations of the Reformation, 92, 93, note d—the superior, in England, less offensive than in Germany, 100—expelled from their cures by Queen Mary for having married, 104 and note ᶜ—the same restored under Elizabeth, 111. note f—protestant, emigration of, to Germany, 171—division of, on the church service, *ib.*—marriage of, disapproved by Elizabeth, 173—her injunctions concerning it, and illegitimacy of their children, *ib.* 174, and notes k ᵐ—their irregular observance of church ceremonies, 178—archbishop Parker's orders for their discipline, 180—the puritan advised not to separate from the church of England, 181—deficiency and ignorance of, in the English church, 183 and notes f ᵍ—certificates ordered of, *ib.* note ᵏ—endeavours to supply their deficiency by meetings called prophesyings, 197—

2 E

CLEVES.

ex-officio oath given to the, 202—aid raised on the, under Elizabeth, 244 and *note* t—support the doctrine of absolute power in the king, 324—to promote their own authority, *ib.*—disliked, from their doctrine of non-resistance, ii. 56—deprived for refusing the Book of Sports, *ib.*—oath imposed on the, by the convocation, 114—episcopal, restored to their benefices at the Restoration, 315—national outcry against the catholics raised by the, 428—refuse the oath of allegiance to William and Mary, iii. 109 and *note* k—their Jacobite principles, 173 - remarks on the taxation of, 243, *note* y—presbyterian, of Scotland, three hundred and fifty ejected from their benefices, 327—of Ireland, their state, 366.

Cleves and Juliers, disputed succession in the duchies of, i. 334 and *note* n.

Clifford, sir Thomas, one of the Cabal ministry, ii. 374.

Clifford, Thomas, lord treasurer, obliged to retire, ii. 394.

Cloths, impositions on, without consent of parliament, i. 316, 317 and *note* b.

Club-men, people so called, who united to resist the marauders of both parties during the troubles, ii. 178, *note* s.

Coffee-houses, proclamation for shutting up, iii. 6, 7 and *note* a.

Coke (sir Edward), his statement of the number of catholic martyrs under Elizabeth, i. 163, *note* q—his defection from the court, and summary of his character, 334—defence of laws, and treatment of, by James, 335 and *note* p—his report concerning arbitrary proclamations, 336—his sentiments on benevolences, 342—objects to the privately conferring with judges, 343—opposes the extended jurisdiction of the court of chancery, 346—his defence of the twelve judges, 348 - suspension, restoration, and subsequent life and character, 349—his MSS., &c., seized, ii. 28—extract from his fourth Institute, iii. 45—his explanation of the law regarding the king's prerogative, 60—his timid judgment in the law of treason, 157.

Coleman (Edward), remarkable confession of, ii. 407—seizure of his letters, 423.

Colepepper (Lord), dictatorial style of his letters to Charles I., ii. 183.

Colepepper (Mr.), ordered into custody of the serjeant at arms for presenting the Kentish petition, iii. 272 and *notes* s t.

College (——), gross iniquity practised on his trial, ii. 450 and *note* 6.

Collier, Jeremy, vindicates the practice of praying for the dead, i. 87, *note* t—advocates auricular confession,80, *note* u.

COMMONS.

Commendam, royal power of granting, disputed, i. 347.

Commerce, its stagnation in the reign of William III., iii. 133.

Commission of public accounts, ii. 358.

Commission of divines revise the liturgy, iii. 174.

Commitments for breach of privilege, iii. 267-271.

Committee of secrecy appointed after the resignation of sir Robert Walpole, iii. 265, 266 and *notes* s b.

Commonalty, risings of the, highly dangerous, i. 47—in Cornwall, *ib.*—in consequence of Wolsey's taxation, *ib.*—simultaneous in several counties, *ib.*

Commoners of England, ancient extent of the, i. 5.

Common council, two acts of the, considered as sufficient misdemeanors to warrant a forfeiture of the charter of the city of London, ii. 453.

Common-law right of election, iii. 41.

Commons of Ireland, their remonstrance of the long parliament of England, iii. 388.

Commons, house of, rejects bills sent from the lords, i. 44—two witnesses required by the, in treason, *ib.*—rejects a bill for attainting Tunstal, bishop of Durham, *ib.*—unwilling to coincide with court measures, *ib.*—increased weight of, 45—persons belonging to the court elected as knights of shires, 46—persons in office form a large part of the, *ib.*—oath of supremacy imposed on the, 112—desirous that queen Elizabeth should marry, 123, *note* c, 125—address of, to her to settle the succession, 129—puritan members address Elizabeth against the queen of Scots, 138—against the papists, 144—papists excluded from, and chiefly puritanical, 190—articles of the church examined by the, 191—dissatisfied with the church, 210—articles, &c., for reforming, prepared by the, 211—its disposition and duties, 247—character of, under Elizabeth, 248—imperfection of early parliamentary history, *ib.*—more copious under Elizabeth, 249—dispute of, with the queen on the succession, &c. 250—Mr. Yelverton's defence of its privileges, 253—vainly interferes in the reformation of ecclesiastical abuses, 254—first complaint on abuses in her government, *ib.*—proceedings concerning queen Mary, 255—restricted as to bills on religious matters, *ib.*—its privileges defended by Peter Wentworth, *ib.*—examines him, &c. on his speech, 256—puritanical measures of reform in, 257—members of the, imprisoned, 258—triumphant debate of, on monopolies, 263—subsidies solicited from the, *ib.*—general view of its members under

INDEX. 419

COMMONS.

Elizabeth, 264—increased by her, *ib.* and *note* °—influence of the crown in, 265, *note* P—bill against non-resident burgesses in, 266—exemption of, from arrest during session claimed by, 268—power of committal for contempt, &c. 270, 272—right of expulsion and determining its own elections, 273—privileges of, concerning money bills, 276—debate on the election of Goodwin and Fortescue, 300—proceedings of, on the arrest of sir Thomas Shirley, 302—remonstrances of, against grievances, 303—proceedings of, on purveyance, 304—temper of the, concerning grants of money, 305—vindication of its privileges to the king, 307—proceedings of, on the design of an union with Scotland, 309, *note* ⁰—continual bickerings of, with the king, 311—proceedings of, concerning Spanish grievances, 313—debate and remonstrance on imposition of James I., 320, 322—proceedings of, against Cowell's *Interpreter*, 324—grievances brought forward by, to be redressed, 327—complaint of, against proclamations, 328—negotiation with the king for giving up feudal tenures, 329—dissolution of parliament, 331—customs again disputed in the, 340—parliament dissolved without a bill passing, 341—proceedings against Mompesson, 356—against lord Bacon, 358, 359 and *note*—against Floyd, 360—lords disagree to titles assumed by the, 361 and *note* ˢ—proceedings of, for reformation, 363—sudden adjournment of, by the king, and unanimous protestation, *ib.*—meets and debates on a grant for the German war, *ib.*—petition and remonstrance against popery, 365—king's letter on, to the speaker, *ib.*—petition in reply, 366—debate and protestation in consequence of the king's answer, *ib.*—adjourned and dissolved, 368—subsidies voted by the, 371—summary of its proceedings under James I., 372, 373—first one of Charles I., 375—penurious measures and dissolution of, 376—ill temper of, continued in the second, *ib.* and *note* f—dissolution of, 380 and *note* ᵇ—a new parliament summoned, 387—proceedings of, on the petition of right, 389—disputes the king's right to tonnage and poundage, 392—prorogued, 393—assembled again and dissolved, 394—religious disputes commenced by, *ib.*—proceedings on bill for observance of Sunday, 599—remonstrates against Arminianism and popery, 404—view of the third parliament of Charles I., 418, 419 and *note* °—the king's declaration after its dissolution, il. 1—members of it committed and proceeded against, 5—parliament of 1640 summoned, 88—cha-

COMMONS.

racter of the members, 88, *note* ˣ—confer upon grievances, 89—opposition of, to ship-money, *ib.*—dissolution of, 91—desire of the nation for a parliament, 93—the long parliament convoked, *ib.* (see Long Parliament)—attempt to seize five members of the, 126 and *note* ᵈ—proceedings on the militia question, 128, *note* f, 135 and *notes* ˢ ᵗ ᵘ—estimate of the dispute between Charles I. and the parliament, 138-150—faults of, in the contest, 138—resolve to disband part of the army, 204—form schemes for getting rid of Cromwell, *ib.* and *notes* ⁿ °—vote not to alter the fundamental government, 215—restore eleven members to their seats, *ib.*—large body of new members admitted, 220—favourable to the army, *ib.*—petition to, ordered to be burnt by the hangman, *ib.*—resolution of against any further addresses to the king, 221—lords agree to this vote, *ib.*—observations on the members who sat on the trial of Charles, 223—vote that all just power is in the people, and for the abolition of monarchy, 232—constitutional party secluded from the, 234—resolve that the house of peers is useless, 235—protected by the army, 236—members do not much exceed one hundred, 239—retain great part of the executive government, *ib.*—charges of injustice against, *ib.*—vote for their own dissolution, 242 and *note* ᵏ—give offence to the republicans, *ib.*—their faults aggravated by Cromwell, *ib.*—question the protector's authority, 246—agree with the lords, on the restoration, that the government ought to be in king, lords, and commons, 300—pass several bills of importance, *ib.*—prepare a bill for restoring ministers, 319 and *note* ᵐ—object to the scheme of indulgence, 347—establish two important principles with regard to taxation, 357—appoint a committee to inspect accounts and nominate commissioners, with full powers of inquiring into public accounts, 358—extraordinary powers of, *ib.*—important privilege of right of impeachment established, 373—address of, to Charles II., about disbanding the army, 380—not unfriendly to the court, 389—the court loses the confidence of, 390—testify their sense of public grievances, 398—strongly adverse to France and popery, 399 and *note* ᵉ—connexion of the popular party with France, 402 and *notes* ᵏ ᵐ—many leaders of the opposition receive money from France, 406—impeach lord Danby, 410—culpable violence of the, 414—deny the right of the bishops to vote, 415—remarks on the jurisdiction of, 416—expel Withens.

2 E 2

COMMONWEALTH.

444—take Thompson, Can, and others, into custody, 445—their impeachment of Fitzharris, and their right to impeach discussed, 446—its dispute with, and resistance to, the lords, iii. 15-21—its proceedings in the case of Skinner and the East India Company, 21-24—its proceedings in the case of Shirley and Fagg, 25—its violent dispute with the lords, 25-27 and *notes*—its exclusive right as to money bills, 27—its originating power of taxation, 30—its state from the earliest records, 36—its numbers from Edward I. to Henry VIII., and unequal representation, *ib.*—accession of its members not derived from popular principle, 38—address of, to James II., concerning unqualified officers, 59—its augmented authority, 117, 118—its true motive for limiting the revenue, 120—its jealousy of a standing army, 139—its conduct with regard to the Irish forfeitures, 142—special committee to inquire into the miscarriages of the war in Ireland, 143—power of the, to direct a prosecution by the attorney-general, for offences of a public nature, 279.

Commonwealth, engagement to live faithful to the, taken with great reluctance, ii. 236.

Companies, chartered, established in evasion of the statute of monopolies, ii. 11—revoked, *ib.*

Compositions for knighthood, ii. 9 and 10, and *notes* o p—taken away, 99.

Comprehension, bill of, clause proposed in the, for changing the oaths of supremacy and allegiance, rejected, iii. 173.

Compton (sir William), expense of proving his will, i. 64, *note* i.

Confession, auricular, consideration of its benefits and mischiefs, i. 88.

Confessions extorted by torture in Scotland, iii. 329.

Confirmatio chartarum, statute of, i. 315—cited in the case of Hampden, ii. 19.

Conformity, proclamation for, by king James I., i. 298.

Conformity, bill to prevent occasional, rejected by the lords, iii. 248.

Connaught, divided into five counties, iii. 371—province of, infamously declared forfeited, 384—inquisition held in each county of, by Strafford, 387.

Con, nuncio from the court of Rome, ii. 60, 72.

Conscience, treatment and limits of, in government, i. 228, *note* q.

Consecration of churches and burial-grounds, ii. 62, and *note* b.

Conspiracy supposed to be concerted by the Jesuits at St. Omers, ii. 424.

Conspiracy to levy war against the king's person, may be given in evidence as an overt act of treason, iii. 152—not recon-

CONVENTS.

cilable to the interpretation of the statute, 153 and *note* n—first instance of this interpretation, *ib.*—confirmed in Harding's case, 154—for an invasion from Spain, 251, and *note* n.

Conspirators, military, destitute of a leader, ii. 272.

Constitution of England from Henry III. to Mary I., i. chap. i. 1-56—under James I., chap. vi. 285-373—under Charles I., chap. vii. 1625-29, 374-419—chap. viii. 1629-40, ii. 1-93—chap. ix. 1640-42, 94-150—from the commencement of the Civil War to the Restoration, ch. x. 151-302—from the Restoration to the death of Charles II., chaps xi. xii. 303-468; iii. chap. xiii. 1-47—from the accession of James II. to the Revolution, chap. xiv. 48-101—under William III., chap. xv. 102-197—under Queen Anne, and George I. and II. chap. xvi. 198-304—design of a party to change, ii. 220—nothing so destructive to, as the exclusion of the electoral body from their franchises, 455—original, highly aristocratical, iii. 17—improvements in the, under William III., 147.

Constitution, forms of the English, established in Ireland, iii. 350.

Constitutional law, important discussions on the, in the case of lord Danby, ii. 412.

Constructive treason, first case of, iii. 153 and *note* n—confirmed in Harding's case, 154 and *note* q—its great latitude, *ib.*, 165—confirmed and rendered perpetual by 36 and 57 George III., 154, 156—Hardy's case of, *ib. note* u.

Consubstantiation, Luther's doctrine, so called, i. 90.

Controversy, religious conduct of, by the Jesuits, &c., ii. 74.

Controversy between the episcopal and presbyterian churches of Scotland, iii. 314.

Conventicles, act against, ii. 348, 349 and *note* b—its severity, *ib.*

Convention parliament, the proceedings of, ii. 304—balance of parties in, 309, *note* r—dissolved, 323—attack on its legality, *ib. note* s—convention of 1688, proceedings of the, iii. 93, 94—question of the best and safest way to preserve the religion and laws of the kingdom, 95—conference between the lords and commons, 96—house of lords give way to the commons, 98—summary of its proceedings, 99—its impolicy in not extending the act of toleration to the catholics, 172.

Convents, inferior, suppressed, i. 72—vices of, greater than in large abbeys, &c. *ib. note* s—evils of their indiscriminate suppression, 75—excellence of several at the dissolution, 76

CONVOCATION.

Convocation (houses of), to be advised with in ecclesiastical matters, iii. 174.
Convocation of the province of Canterbury, its history, iii. 242 — commons refer to it the question of reforming the liturgy, 244—its aims to assimilate itself to the house of commons, 245—finally prorogued in 1717, 247.
Cope (Mr.), his measures for ecclesiastical reform in the house of commons, i. 257—committed to the Tower, 258.
Copley (Mr.), power of the parliament over, I. 272.
Coronation oath, dispute on its meaning and construction, ii. 138 and *note* ⁸.
Corporate property, more open than private to alteration, I. 75.
Corporation act, ii. 329—severely affects the presbyterian party, 330.
Corporations, informations brought against several, ii. 453 — forfeiture of their charters, 454—receive new ones, 455—freemen of, primary franchise attached to the, iii. 41—their great preponderance in elections, 44—their forfeiture and re-grant under restrictions, 50—new modelling of the, 74—bill for restoring particular clause in, 114.
Cosbery, custom of, in Ireland, iii. 348, 357.
Cotton (sir Robert), his books, &c. seized, ii. 28.
Council of State, under the commonwealth, consisted principally of presbyterians, ii. 290.
Counsellors (Oxford) of Charles I., solicit the king for titles, ii. 160—their motives, *ib.*
Court, inns of, examined, concerning religion, i. 141.
Court of parliament, the title disputed, i. 361, *note* ⁸.
Court of supremacy, commission for, in 1583, i. 201, *note* ᵏ.
Court of Charles II., wicked and artful policy of, to secure itself from suspicion of popery, ii. 451.
Courts of law, the three, under the Plantagenets, how constituted, i. 5—mode of pleading in, 6, *note* ᵇ.
Courts, inferior, under the Plantagenets, county courts, hundred courts, manor courts, their influence, i. 7.
Courts of Star-chamber, origin and powers of, i. 50, *note* ᵍ, 51 and *note* ʰ. See Star-chamber.
Courts, ecclesiastical, their character and abuses, i. 213 and *note* ᵘ.
Covenant, solemn league and negotiations concerning the, ii. 163—particular account of, *ib.*—want of precision in the language of, 164—imposed on all civil and military officers, *ib.*—number of the clergy ejected by, among whom were the most learned and virtuous men of that age, 165, 166—burnt by the common hangman, 324.

CRICHTON.

Covenant of Scotland, national, its origin, iii. 322.
Covenanters (Scotch), heavily fined, iii 327.
Coventry (Thomas), lord keeper, his address to the house of commons, i. 376 *note* f.
Coventry (sir William), his objection to the arbitrary advice of Clarendon, ii 378—outrageous assault on, 389, 390 and *note* ᵠ.
Coverdale (Miles), his translation of the Bible, i. 83.
Cowell (Dr. John), attributes absolute power to the king in his *Interpreter*, 1607, i. 325 and *note* ˢ—the book suppressed, 326 and *note* ᵃ.
Cowper (William), lord, made chancellor, iii. 209.
Cox (Richard), bishop of Ely, defends church ceremonies and habits, i. 173, 175—Elizabeth's violence to, 224 and *note* ᵇ.
Coyne and livery, or coshering and bonaght, barbarous practice of, iii. 357.
Cranfield (lord), his arguments to the commons on a grant for German war, i. 364, *note* ⁱ.
Cranmer (Thomas), archbishop of Canterbury, probably voted for the death of Cromwell, I. 30, *note* ᵐ—his part in the execution of Catherine Howard, 33, *note* ᵖ—letter on the marriage of Anne Boleyn, 62, *note* ᵍ—made archbishop, 66—active in Henry VIII.'s divorce, 68—induces Henry VIII. to sanction the principles of Luther, 82—procured Edward VI. to burn Joan Boucher, 85, *note* ᵠ—marriage of, 91—compelled to separate from his wife, *ib.*—protests against the destruction of chantries, 94, *note* ᶫ—recommended the abolition of the collegiate clergy, 94, *note* ᵘ—liberality of, to the princess Mary, 95 and *note* ˣ—censurable concerning Joan Boucher, &c., 96—one of the principal reformers of the English church, 97—his character variously depicted, *ib.*—articles of the church drawn up by, *ib.* *note* ᵖ—disingenuousness of his character, 98—protest of, before his consecration, *ib.* and *note* ᵠ—his recantations and character, 99 and *note* ʳ—his moderation in the measures of reform, *ib.* —compliance of, with the royal supremacy, 100—some church ceremonies and habits retained by, 102.
Cranmer's Bible, 1539, peculiarities of, i. 83, *note* ᵘ.
Cranmer (bishop), his sentiments on episcopacy, i. 396, *note*.
Craven (earl of), unjust sale of his estates, ii. 240, *note* ᵈ.
Crichton (——), his memoir for invading England on behalf of the papists, i. 155, *note* ᵈ.

CRIGHTON.

Crighton and Ogilvy, their case, iii. 326.
Croke (sir George), his sentence for Hampden in the cause of ship-money, ii. 23, note º.
Cromwell (earl of Essex), his question to the judges respecting condemnations for treason, i. 29—himself the first victim of their opinion, 30—causes which led to his execution, ib.—his visitation and suppression of the monastic orders, 71—advises the distribution of abbey lands, &c., to promote the Reformation, 78—his plan for the revenues of the lesser monasteries, ib. note f—procures the dispersion of the Scriptures, with liberty to read them, 83, note n.
Cromwell (Oliver), rising power of, ii. 171—excluded from the commons, but continues lieutenant-general, 181—historical difficulties in the conduct of, 207—wavers as to the settlement of the nation, 221, 222—victory at Worcester, its consequences to, 237—two remarkable conversations of, with Whitelock and others, ib., 238—his discourse about taking the title of king, ib.—policy of, 242 and note m—assumes the title of protector, 244—observations on his ascent to power, 245—calls a parliament, 246—his authority questioned, ib.—dissolves the parliament, 247—project to assassinate, 250—divides the kingdom into districts, 251—appoints military magistrates, ib.—his high court of justice, 253—executions by, ib. and note x—summons a parliament in 1656, 254—excludes above ninety members, ib. and note u—aspires to the title of king, 255—scheme fails through opposition of the army, 257—abolishes the civil power of the major-generals, ib.—refuses the crown, 258 and note h—the charter of the commonwealth under, changed to the " Petition and Advice," 258—particulars of that measure, 259 and note i—his unlimited power, ib.—oath of allegiance taken by members of parliament, 259—his house of lords described, 260—dissolves the parliament, 261—his great design an hereditary succession, ib.—referred to a council of nine, ib.—his death and character, and foreign policy, 262—management of the army, 263—paralleled with Buonaparte, 264, 265 and note u—his conquest of Ireland, iii. 394.
Cromwell (Richard), succeeds his father, ii. 266—inexperience of, ib.—no proof of his appointment by his father, ib. and note a—gains some friends, 267—steadily supported by Pierpoint and St. John, ib.—his conduct commended by Thurloe, 268, 269 and note b—summons a parliament, which takes the

DEATHS.

oath of allegiance to him as protector, ib.—proceedings of the parliament under, 270 and notes—disappoints the hopes of the royalists, 271—does not refuse to hear the agents of Charles II., 276 and note u—hopes entertained of his relinquishing the government, 277.
Crown (officers of the), under the Plantagenets, violence used by, i. 5—juries influenced by, ib.
Crown of England, uncertain succession of the, between the houses of Scotland and Suffolk, i. 123, 129, 285, 288.
Crown and parliament, termination of the contest between the, iii. 198.
Crown, the, personal authority of, its diminution, iii. 291—the reason of it, 292—of material constitutional importance, 297.
Crown (the), its jealousy of the prerogative, iii. 254, 255.
Crucifix, its lawfulness in the English churches discussed, i. 172—Elizabeth's partiality for the, 173 and notes.
Customs on woad and tobacco, i. 237 and note º—on cloths and wines, 243—treble, against the English law, 317, note l—arbitrary, imposed by James I., 318 and note n.
Cy Pres, proceeding of, in the court of chancery, i. 79, note b.

Damaree (Daniel), and George Purchase, their trial for high treason, iii. 158, note z.
Damport (Mr.), his cautious motion concerning the laws, i. 258.
Danby (Thomas Osborne, earl of), his administration, ii. 397—his virtues as a minister, 399—marriage of the prince of Orange and princess Mary owing to his influence, 400 and note f—concerned in the king's receipt of money from France, 401 and note h—cause of his fall and his impeachment, 410—argument urged in defence of, 411—questions arising from his impeachment, 412—intemperance of the proceedings against him, 413—important discussions in the case of, ib. and note g—committed to the Tower, ib.—pleads his pardon, 414—lords resist this plea, ib.—confined in the Tower three years, 420—admitted to bail by judge Jeffries, ib.
Darien company, the business of the, iii. 337.
Dauphin (son of Louis XIV.), effect of his death on the French succession, iii. 218, 219.
David II., parliament at Scone under him, iii. 307.
Dead, prayers for the, in the first liturgy of Edward VI., i. 87—omitted on its revisal, ib.
Deaths of the dauphin and dukes of Bur-

DEBT.

gundy and Berry, iii. 218—effect of their deaths on the French succession, ib. 219.

Debt (public), its amount in 1714, iii. 214, note ᵇ—alarm excited at its magnitude, 302.

De Burgh, or Burke, family of, in Ireland, fall off from their subjection to the crown, iii. 355.

Declaration published by the army for the settlement of the nation, ii. 221—in favour of a compromise, 321—in favour of liberty of conscience, 346—of indulgence, 390—opposed by parliament, 392—of rights, iii. 103.

Denization, charters of, granted to particular persons, iii. 353.

Dependence of Irish on English parliament, iii. 405.

Derry, noble defence of, iii. 399.

Desiderata Curiosa Hibernica, extract from that work, concerning the prediction of the rebellion in 1641, iii. 381, note ᵗ.

Desmond (earl of), attends the Irish parliament, iii. 364—his rebellion in 1583, and forfeiture of his lands, 379—his lands parcelled out among English undertakers, ib.

Difference between the lords and commons on the *Habeas Corpus* bill, iii. 11.

Digby (John, lord), his speech concerning Strafford, ii. 110—letters taken on the rout of, at Sherborne, 192, note ᵏ.

Digges (Sir Dudley), his committal to the Tower, i. 378.

Discontent of the royalists, ii. 310.

Discontent of the nation with the government of William III., iii. 107.

Discontent of the nation at the conduct of Charles II., ii. 352.

Discussions between the two houses of parliament on the exclusion of the regicides and others, ii. 304-307.

Dispensation, power of, preserved after the Reformation, i. 190—attempt to take away, 191.

Dispensations granted by Charles I., ii. 28.

Dissensions between lords and commons of rare occurrence, iii. 16.

Divinity, study of, in the seventeenth century, ii. 64 and note ᶜ.

Divorce of Henry VIII. from queen Catherine, historical account of its rise, progress, and effects, i. 60-66.

Divorces, canon law concerning, under Edward VI., i. 102, note—Henry VIII.'s two, creating an uncertainty in the line of succession, parliament enable the king to bequeath the kingdom by his will, 34.

Dodd's Church History, important letters to be found in, relative to the Catholic intrigues on the succession, i. 286, note.

EFFECT.

Domesday Book, burgesses of, were inhabitants within the borough, iii. 42.

Dort, synod of, king James's conduct to the, i. 402, 403, note ᵇ.

Douay College, intrigues of the priests of, i. 137—account of the foundation, ib., note ᵃ.

Downing (sir George), proviso introduced by, into the subsidy bill, ii. 357.

Drury (——), execution of, i. 467, note ᵏ.

Dublin, citizens of, committed to prison for refusing to frequent the protestant church, iii. 377.

Dugdale (sir William), garter king at arms, his account of the earl of Hertford's marriage, i. 292 and note ʰ.

Dunkirk, sale of, by Charles II., ii. 353—particulars relating to the sale of, 369, 370 and note ʳ.

Durham, county and city of, right of election granted to the, iii. 39.

Dutch, mortgaged towns restored to the, i. 342—fleet insults our coasts, ii. 368—armies mostly composed of catholics, iii. 177.

Ecclesiastical commission court, i. 201 and note ᵏ.

Ecclesiastical courts, their character and abuses, i. 213, note ᵘ—restrained by those of law, 327—their jurisdiction, ii. 47, note ʸ—commission of 1686 issued by James II., iii. 63.

Ecclesiastics of Ireland, their enormous monopoly, iii. 404.

Edgehill, battle of, ii. 152—its consequences in favour of Charles, ib.

Edward I., his letter to the justiciary of Ireland, granting permission to some septs to live under English law, iii. 353.

Edward II. (king of England), legislature established by statute of, i. 4 and note ᵃ.

Edward III. (king of England), remarkable clause relating to treason in the act of, ii. 413.

Edward VI. (king of England), attached to the reformed religion, i. 85—abilities of his letters and journal, ib. note ᵈ—harsh treatment of his sister Mary, and reluctance to execute Joan Boucher, ib.—alterations in the English church under, 85—the Reformation in his minority conducted with violence and rapacity, 93—denies the princess Mary enjoying her own religion, 95—positive progress of the Reformation under, 103—his laws concerning religion reenacted, 111—omission of a prayer in his liturgy, ib. note ᵉ—differences between the protestants commenced under, 170—his death prevented the Genevan system from spreading in the English church, 171.

Effect of the press, ii. 464—restrictions

EJECTION.

upon it in the reign of Henry VIII., iii. 2—before and after the Restoration, 3, 4.
Ejection of non-conformist clergy, ii. 340.
Election, rights of, iii. 36-47—four different theories relating to the, 40—their relative merits considered, 41.
Elections, regulated by Elizabeth's ministers, i. 265 and note P—debate concerning, 266—first penalty for bribery in, 268—right of determining, claimed by parliament, 274—interference of James I. in, 301.
Elections, remarks on their management, iii. 44, 45 and notes d e.
Elective franchise in ancient boroughs, difficult to determine by what class of persons it was possessed, iii. 37—different opinions regarding the, 40.
Eliot (sir John), his committal to the Tower, i. 378—committal and proceedings against, ii. 2.
Elizabeth (princess), treasonable to assert her legitimacy, i. 34.
Elizabeth (queen of England), population of the realm under, i. 8, note c—revision of church articles under, 91—a dangerous prisoner to queen Mary, 105, note e—easily re-establishes protestantism, 107—laws of, respecting catholics, chap. iii. 108-169—her popularity and protestant feelings, 108—suspected of being engaged in Wyatt's conspiracy, ib. note s—announces her accession to the pope, but proceeds slowly in her religious reform, 109—her council and parliament generally protestant, 110—her acts of supremacy and uniformity, 112—oath of supremacy to, explained, ib. note g—restraint of Roman catholic worship in her first years, 113—embassy to, from Pius IV., 114—her death prophesied by the Romanists, 115 and note B—statute preventing, ib.—conspiracy against, ib. note o—letters of the emperor Ferdinand to, on behalf of the English catholics, 119 and note x—her answer against them, ib.—circumstances of her reign affected her conduct towards them, 122—the crown settled on her by act 35th Henry VIII., ib —uncertainty of her succession, 123—her marriage desired by the nation, ib.—suitors to her, the archduke Charles, and Dudley earl of Leicester, ib.—her unwillingness to marry, and coquetry, 124, 249—astrological prediction on her marriage, 125, note I—objects with her council to tolerate popery, 125 and note k, 142—improbability of her having issue, 125 and note m—pressed to decide on her successor, 126, 249—proceedings of, against lady Grey, 127—offended by the queen of Scots bearing the arms, &c. of England, 129—intrigues with the

ELIZABETH.

malcontents of France and Scotland to revenge herself on Mary, 130, note u—not unfavourable to her succession, ib. —courses open to, after Mary's abdication, 131—Bull of excommunication and deposition published against her by pope Pius V., 134—insurrections against, and dangerous state of England had she died, 135—her want of foreign alliances, 136—statutes for her security against the papists, 137, 138 and note o—addressed by the puritans against the queen of Scots, 138—restrains the parliament's proceedings against her, 139, 255—advised to provide for her security, 139—inclined and encouraged to proceed against the papists, 140—her declaration for uniformity of worship, 141—on doubtful terms with Spain, 143—foreign policy of, justifiable, 144, note f—her intention to avoid capital penalties on account of religion, 145—papists executed on her statutes, ib.—acknowledged queen by Campian the Jesuit, 146—torture used in her reign, 148—persecutions of, procure her to be published as a tyrant, 149—lord Burleigh's defences of, ib.—her persecutions an argument against the reign of Henry IV. of France, ib. note s—commands the torture to be disused, 151—an inquisition made after her enemies, and some executed, 154—her assassination contemplated, 155 and note c—disaffection of the papists to, caused by her unjust aggressions on their liberty of conscience, 155, note d—an association formed to defend her person, 156—her affectation concerning the death of queen Mary, 158—number of catholic martyrs under, 163—character of her religious restraints, 168—her laws respecting protestant non-conformists, chap. iv. 170-228—her policy to maintain her ecclesiastical power, 170—protestants recalled by her accession, 172—difference of her tenets and ceremonies, ib. and note d—disapproves of the clergy marrying, 173—coarse treatment of archbishop Parker's wife, 174, note m—probable cause of her retaining some ceremonies, 177—prevents the abolishing of licences and dispensations, 191—orders for suppression of prophesyings, 197, 198—supported the Scottish clergy, 210—omits to summon parliament for five years, ib.—anxious for the good government of church and state, but jealous of interference, 211—her violence towards bishop Cox, 224 and note h—tyranny of, towards her bishops, 225 and note m—her reported offer to the puritans, 226, note o—Walsingham's letter in defence of her government, 228 and note—view of her civil government, chap. v. 229-284—

EMPSON.

character of her administration chiefly religious, 229—her advantages for acquiring extensive authority, 230—her course of government illustrated, 234, note ˢ—unwarranted authority of some of her proclamations, 236—disposition to adopt martial law, 240—her illegal commission to sir Thomas Wilford, 242—did not assert arbitrary taxation, 243—her singular frugality, 244—borrowed money by privy seals, but punctual in repayment, ib.—instance of her returning money illegally collected, 245, note ˣ—dispute of, with the parliament, on her marriage and succession, and the common prayer, 249-253—instances of her interference and authority over her parliaments, 253-261—resigned monopolies, 262—compelled to solicit subsidies of her later parliaments, 263—added to the members of the house of commons, 264—her monarchy limited, 277 and note ᵠ—supposed power of her crown, 282—Philip II. attempts to dethrone her, 286, note—intended James I. for her successor, 288, note ˢ—her popularity abated in her latter years, 295 and note ᵠ—probable causes of, ib.—probable reasons for her not imposing customs on foreign goods, 318—mutilation ordered by the star-chamber during her reign, ll. 34—alienation of part of Ireland in the reign of, iii. 365—reasons for establishing the protestant religion in Ireland in the reign of, 367.
Empson (sir Richard), and Edmund Dudley, prostitute instruments of the avarice of Henry VII., i. 15—put to death on a frivolous charge of high treason, 16, 17 and note ᴾ.
Enclosures, rebellion concerning, i. 92.
England, state of religion in, at the beginning of the 16th century, i. 57—preparations in, for a reformation of the church, ib.—means of its emancipation from the papal power, 68—foreign politics of, under James I., 333
England, view of, previous to the long parliament, ii. 81-93—divided into districts by Cromwell, 251—state of, since the Revolution in 1688, compared with its condition under the Stuarts, iii. 117, 118—its danger of becoming a province to France, 134.
England, New, proclamation against emigrations to, ii. 58.
English nation not unsuited to a republican form of government, ii. 274—unwillingness of the, to force the reluctance of their sovereign, 432—English settlers in Ireland, their degeneracy, iii. 354—settlements of, in Munster, Ulster, and other parts, 378—justice attending them, 381.
Episcopacy, house of commons opposed to, i. 210—divine right of, maintained,

FAIRFAX.

395, 396 and note ᵐ, ii. 64 and note ᵍ—moderation of, designed, 115 and note ᵉ—bill for abolishing, 162—revived in Scotland, iii. 327—jurisdiction of the bishops unlimited, ib.
Episcopal discipline revives with the monarchy, ii. 318—clergy driven out injuriously by the populace from their livings, iii. 315—permitted to hold them again, ib.
Episcopalians headed by Selden, ii. 195 and note ʸ.
Erastianism, the church of England in danger of, i. 113, note.
Erudition of a Christian Man, 1540, reformed doctrines contained in, by authority of Henry VIII., i. 82—character of, ib. note ᵏ.
Escheats, frauds of, under Henry VII.; i. 15—act for amending, 16.
Essex (county of), extent of royal forests in, ii. 10.
Essex (Robert Devereux, earl of), injudicious conduct of, after the battle of Edgehill, ii. 152, note ᵇ—raises the siege of Gloucester, 181—suspected of being reluctant to complete the triumph of the parliament, 179 and note ᵈ.
Estates, the convention of, turned into a parliament, iii. 335—forfeited in Ireland, allotted to those who would aid in reducing the island to obedience, 394.
Et cæteru oath imposed on the clergy, ii. 114.
Europe, absolute sovereigns of, in the sixteenth century, i. 283.
Exchequer, court of, trial in, on the king's prerogative of imposing duties, i. 315, 316 and note ᵇ—cause of ship-money tried in the court of, ii. 18 and note ᵐ—court of, an intermediate tribunal between the king's bench and parliament, iii. 19.
Excise on liquor, first imposition of, in England, ii. 178 and note ᵇ—granted in lieu of military tenures, 312—prerogative of the crown reduced by the, 313—amount of duty on beer, under William III., iii. 116, note ᵘ.
Exclusion of the duke of York proposed and discussed, ii. 430-433—of placemen and pensioners from parliament, iii. 192, 193 and note ᵇ.
Exeter, bishopric of, despoiled in the Reformation, i. 94.
Ex officio oath, in the high commission court, i. 202—attacked in the house of commons, 211.
Expulsion, right of, claimed by parliament, i. 273.

Factions of Pym and Vane, ii. 160—cause of their aversion to pacific measures ¹ᵉ—at Oxford, '69.
Fairfax (sir Thomas), and Oliver Crom

FALKLAND.

well, superiority of their abilities for war, ii. 180.
Falkland (Henry Carey, lord), account of, ii. 170, note ⁿ.
Family of Love, said to have been employed by the papists, i. 122, note ᶜ.
Feckenham (John), abbot of Westminster), imprisoned under Elizabeth, i. 118, note ᶠ.
Felton (——), executed for fixing the pope's bull on the bishop of London's palace, i. 137.
Fenwick (sir John), strong opposition to his attainder in parliament, iii. 131 —his imprudent yet true disclosure, 132.
Ferdinand (emperor of Germany), writes to Elizabeth on behalf of the English catholics, i. 118 and note ᵘ—his liberal religious policy, 119, note ˣ.
Ferrers (George), his illegal arrest, i. 269, note ᵗ.
Festivals in the church of England, i. 397.
Feudal rights perverted under Henry VII., i. 15—system in Scotland, introduction of, iii. 305—remarks on the probable cause of its decline, 312.
Filmer (sir Robert), remarks on his scheme of government, ii. 465.
Finch (Heneage), chief justice of the common pleas, adviser of ship-money, ii. 15—defends the king's absolute power, 22—parliamentary impeachment of, 140, note ᵉ.
Fines, statute of, misunderstood, i. 13 and note ᵍ.
Fire of London, ii. 378—advice to Charles on the, ib.—papists suspected, 379—odd circumstance connected with, ib. and note ᵏ.
Fish, statutes and proclamations for the eating of, in Lent, i. 397, note ᵖ.
Fisher (John, bishop of Rochester), his defence of the clergy, i. 64—beheaded for denying the ecclesiastical supremacy, 27.
Fitzharris (Edward), his impeachment, ii. 446—constitutional question on, discussed, ib. 447.
Fitzstephen, his conquests in Ireland, iii. 348.
Flanders, books of the reformed religion printed in, i. 82.
Fleetwood (lieutenant-general Charles), opposes Cromwell's assuming the title of king, ii. 258—the title of lord-general, with power over all commissions, proposed to be conferred on, 268 —his character, 279 and note ᵉ.
Fleming (Thomas), chief baron of the exchequer, his speech on the king's power, i. 318.
Flesh, statutes, &c. against eating, in Lent, i. 397 and note ᵒ.
Fletcher (John, bishop of London), suspended by Elizabeth, i. 225, note ᵐ.

GARRAWAY.

Floyd (Mr.), violent proceedings of the parliament against, i. 360-362, and note ᶜ—the infamous case of, conduct of the commons in, iii. 278.
Forbes (sir David), fined by the star-chamber, ii. 35.
Forest laws, enforcement and oppression of, under Charles I., ii. 10, 11 and note ᵗ —extent of forests fixed by act of parliament, 99, 100.
Forfeiture of the charter of London, ii. 453—observations on the proceedings on, ib.
Fortescue (sir John), question of his election, i. 300.
Fostering, Irish custom of, explained, iii. 354, note ᵠ—severe penalty against, 357.
Fox (Edward, bishop of Hereford), excites Wolsey to reform the monasteries, i. 70.
Fox (right honourable C. J.), his doubt whether James II. aimed at subverting the protestant establishment examined, iii. 52-55 and notes ⁱ ᵏ ᵐ ⁿ — anecdote of, and the duke of Newcastle, concerning secret service money, 265, note ᶠ.
France, its government despotic when compared with that of England, i. 277 —authors against the monarchy of, 278, note ʳ—public misery of, iii. 216, 217 and note ᶠ.
Franchise, elective, taken away from the catholics of Ireland, iii. 402 and note ˣ.
Francis I. (king of France), his mediation between the pope and Henry VIII., i. 62.
Francis II. (king of France), display of his pretensions to the crown of England, i. 130 and note ᵘ.
Frankfort, divisions of the protestants at, i. 171 and 172 note ᶜ.
Freeholder, privileges of the English, ii. 27—under the Saxons bound to defend the nation, 132.
French government, moderation of the, at the treaty of Aix-la-Chapelle, iii. 297.
Fresh severities against dissenters, ii. 388.
Fulham, destruction of trees, &c. at the palace of, by bishop Aylmer, i. 203, note ᵇ.
Fuller (Mr.), imprisonment of, by the star-chamber, i. 349.

Gardiner (Stephen, bishop of Winchester), prevails on Henry VIII. to prohibit the English Bible, i. 83, note ᵇ—forms a list of words in it unfit for translation, ib.—a supporter of the popish party, 85—in disgrace at the death of Henry VIII., ib.—character and virtues of, 97, note ᵒ—his persecution palliated, ib.
Garnet (Henry), his probable guilt in the gunpowder plot, i. 406, note ᵈ.
Garraway and Lee take money from the

GARRISONS.

court for softening votes, ii. 399 and note ᶜ.
Garrisons, ancient military, force kept in, ii. 131.
Gauden (Dr. John), the supposed author of Icon Basiliké, ii. 230, 231 and note ᵏ.
Gavelkind, tenure of Irish, explained, iii. 344, 345 and note ᑫ—determined to be void, 377.
Gentry, or landowners, under the Plantagenets, without any exclusive privilege, i. 5—disordered state of under Henry VI. and Edward IV., 9—of the north of England, their turbulent spirit, 52—repressed by Henry VIII. and the court of star-chamber, 53, 54 and note ᵏ —why inclined to the Reformation, 68 —of England, became great under the Tudors, deriving their estates from the suppressed monasteries, 79.
George I. (king of England), his accession to the crown, iii. 229—chooses a whig ministry, 230—great dissa..ection in the kingdom, 231 and note ᵈ—causes of his unpopularity, 240 — Habeas Corpus Act several times suspended in his reign, 241, note ᶤ— incapable of speaking English, trusted his ministers with the management of the kingdom, 293.
George I. and George II. (kings of England), their personal authority at the lowest point, iii. 296.
George II., character of, iii. 294, note ᵘ.
Geraldines, family of the, restored, iii. 363.
Gerard (Mr.), executed for plotting to kill Cromwell, ii. 248.
Germany, less prepared for a religious reformation than England, i. 57—books of the reformed religion printed in, 82 —celibacy of priests rejected by the protestants of, 91—troops of, sent to quell commotions, 93 and note ᵈ—mass not tolerated by the Lutheran princes of, 95 and note ᵇ—reformation caused by the covetousness and pride of superior ecclesiastics, 99—war with, commons' grant for, in 1621, 304.
Gertruydenburg, conferences broken off and renewed at, iii. 213 — remark of Cunningham on the, ib., note ᵇ.
Glamorgan (Edward Somerset, earl of), discovery of a secret treaty between him and the Irish catholics, ii. 191— certainty of, confirmed by Dr. Birch, 193 and note l.
Godfrey (sir Edmondbury), his very extraordinary death, ii. 425—not satisfactorily accounted for, ib., 426 and notes ᵈ ᵘ ᵍ.
Godolphin (Sidney, earl of), preserves a secret connexion with the court of James, iii. 221, note ᵏ—his partiality to the Stuart cause suspected, ib.
Godstow nunnery interceded for at the dissolution, i. 76.

GREY.

Godwin (William), important circumstances, omitted by other historians, respecting the self-denying ordinance, pointed out by, in his history of the commonwealth, ii. 181, note ᶠ—his book characterised as a work in which great attention has been paid to the order of time, 196, note ᵖ.
Gold coin, Dutch merchants fined for exporting, i. 342.
Goodwin (sir Francis), question of his election, i. 302 and note ᶦ.
Gossipred, iii. 354, note ᑫ—severe penalty against, 357.
Government of England, ancient form of, a limited monarchy, i. 276-281, and 279, note ᵃ — erroneously asserted to have been absolute, 279—consultations against the, of Charles II. begin to be held, ii. 455—difficult problem in the practical science of, iii. 91—always a monarchy limited by law, 100—its predominating character aristocratical, 101 —new and revolutionary, remarks on a, 111—Locke and Montesquieu, authority of their names on that subject, 251—studious to promote distinguished men, ib. — executive, not deprived of so much power by the Revolution as is generally supposed, 291—arbitrary, of Scotland, 325.
Government, Irish, its zeal for the reformation of abuses, iii. 357—of Ireland, benevolent scheme in the, 378 and note ᵒ.
Governors of districts in Scotland take the title of earls, iii. 305.
Gowrie (earl of), and his brother, executed for conspiracy, iii. 325 and note ᵃ.
Grafton (Thomas), his *Chronicle* imperfect, i. 18, note ᶠ.
Graham and Burton, solicitors to the treasury, committed to the Tower by the council, and afterwards put in custody of the serjeant by the commons, iii. 278.
Granville (lord), favourite minister of George II., iii. 294—bickering between him and the Pelhams, ib., 290.
Gregory XIII., his explanation of the bull of Pius V., i. 147.
Grenville (right honourable George), his excellent statute respecting controverted elections, iii. 47.
Grey (lady Catherine), presumptive heiress to the English throne at the beginning of Elizabeth's reign, i. 123, 230—proceedings of the queen against her, 128 and note ᵒ—her party deprived of influence by their ignoble connexions, 129—legitimacy of her marriage and issue, 291, 292—present representative of this claim, 293, note ⁿ — her former marriage with the earl of Pembroke, ib.

GREY.

Grey (Leonard, lord deputy of Ireland), defeats the Irish, iii. 363.
Grey (sir Arthur), his severity in the government of Ireland, iii. 371.
Griffin (——), star-chamber information against, ii. 33, note *a*.
Grimston (sir Harbottle), extract from his speech, ii. 286, note *a* — elected speaker, 293.
Grindal (Edmund, bishop of London), his letter concerning a private priest, i 114.
Grindal (Edmund, archbishop of Canterbury), prosecutes the puritans, i. 194 — tolerates their meetings called "prophesyings," 198 — his consequent sequestration and independent character, 199 and note d.
Gunpowder plot, probable conspirators in the, i. 405, 406 and note g.

Habeas Corpus, trial on the right of, i. 383-387, 390, ii. 2—act of, first sent up to the lords, 398—passed, iii. 12—no new principle introduced by it, *ib.*—power of the court of common pleas to issue writs of, *ib.* and note c—particulars of the, 13—its effectual remedies, 14, 15.
Hale (sir Matthew), and other judges, decide on the illegality of fining juries, iii. 8, 9—his timid judgment in cases of treason, 157.
Hales (John), his defence of lady Catherine Grey, i. 128 and note *l*—his character and *Treatise on Schism*, ii. 76, 77.
Hales (sir Edward), case of, iii. 61, 62.
Halifax (George Savile, marquis of), gives offence to James II., iii. 49 — declaration of rights, presented by, to the prince of Orange, 103, 104—retires from power, 112.
Hall (Arthur), proceedings of parliament against, i. 273 and note d—famous case of, the first precedent of the commons punishing one of their own members, 274.
Hall (Edward), his *Chronicle* contains the best account of the events of the reign of Henry VIII., i. 18, note *r*—his account of the levy of 1525, 19, note *t*.
Hall (Dr. Joseph, bishop of Exeter), his defence of episcopacy, ii. 64, note g.
Hamilton (James, duke of), engaged in the interest of the pretender, iii. 224—killed in a duel with lord Mohun, *ib.*
Hampden (John), levy on, for ship-money, ii. 17, and note k—trial of, for refusing payment, 17-23, and notes m o—mentioned by lord Strafford, 51.
Hampton Court conference with the puritans, i. 297.
Hanover, settlement of the crown on the house of, iii. 179—limitations of the prerogative contained in it, 180 and

HENRY VI.

note o—remarkable cause of the fourth remedial article, 184.
Hanover, the house of, spoken of with contempt, iii. 227 and note l—acquires the duchies of Bremen and Verden in 1716, 240 and note s.
Hanoverian succession in danger from the ministry of queen Anne, iii. 227 and note e.
Harcourt (Simon, lord Chancellor), engaged in the interest of the pretender, iii. 224.
Harding's case, constructive treason in, iii. 154, and notes p q.
Hardwicke (lord chief justice), his arguments in opposing a bill to prevent smuggling, iii. 290.
Harley (sir Robert), puritan spoliations of, ii. 119 and note q.
Harley (Robert, earl of Oxford), his censure on the parliamentary proceedings against Floyd, i. 362, note c.
Harmer, his valuation of monastic property in England, i. 69, and 76, note d.
Harrington (sir John), notice of James I. by, i. 296, note v.
Hatton (sir Christopher), his lenity towards papists, i. 167 and note y—an enemy to the puritans, 200—his spoliation of church property, 224—attempt to assassinate, 241—his forest amercement, ii. 11.
Heath (Robert), attorney-general, his speech on the case of habeas corpus, i. 385—on the petition of right, *ib.*—denies the criminal jurisdiction of parliament, ii. 3.
Heath, Thomas, seized with sectarian tracts, i. 122, note c.
Henrietta Maria (queen of Charles I.), conditions of her marriage with him, i. 412—letter of, concerning the religion of Charles I., ii. 70, note u—her imprudent zeal for popery, 124, note a—fear of impeachment, 127, note d—sent from England with the crown jewels, 139 and note b—Charles I.'s strange promise not to make any peace without her mediation, 156—impeachment of, for high treason, the most odious act of the long parliament, 157—her conduct, 183—and advice to Charles, *ib.*—writes several imperious letters to the king, 187—forbids him to think of escaping, *ib.* note x—ill conduct of, 188—abandons all regard to English interest, *ib.*—plan formed by to deliver Jersey up to France, 189—anecdote of the king's letters to her, *ib.* note e—power given her by the king to treat with the catholics, 190.
Henry II. (king of England), institutes itinerant justices, i. 6, 7—invasion of Ireland by, iii. 342.
Henry VI., clerical laws improved under, i. 58.

HENRY VII.

Henry VII. (king of England), state of the kingdom at his accession, i. 8—parliament called by, not a servile one, ib.—proceedings for securing the crown to his posterity, ib.—his marriage, and vigilance in guarding the crown, made his reign reputable but not tranquil, 9—statute of the 11th of, concerning the duty of allegiance, ib.—Blackstone's reasoning upon it erroneous, that of Hawkins correct, 10, note f—did not much increase the power of the crown, ib.—laws enacted by, over-rated by lord Bacon, 11—his mode of taxation, 13—subsidies being unpopular, he has recourse to benevolence, 14—and to amercements and forfeitures, 15—made a profit of all offices, even bishoprics, ib.—wealth amassed by him soon dissipated by his son, 16—council court formed by, existing at the fall of Wolsey, 54—not that of star-chamber, nor maintainable by his act, 55, note º—his fatal suspicion, 56—enacts the branding of clerks convicted of felony, 58—probable policy of, in the marriage of Henry VIII., 60 and note d—low point of his authority over Ireland, iii. 359—confined to the four counties of the English pale, ib.

Henry VIII., his foreign policy, i. 16—his profusion and love of magnificence, ib.—acts passed by, to conciliate the discontents excited by his father, ib.—extensive subsidies demanded of parliament by him, 17—exaction by miscalled benevolence, in 1525, 21—instance of his ferocity of temper, 27, 29, 31—reflections on his government and character, 36—did not conciliate his people's affections, ib.—was open and generous, but his foreign politics not sagacious, ib.—memory revered on account of the Reformation, ib.—was uniformly successful in his wars, ib.—as good a king as Francis I., 37, note ª—suppresses the turbulence of the northern nobility, &c., 52—star-chamber in full power under, 54 and 55, note º—his intention of beheading certain members of parliament, 55—fierce and lavish effects of his wayward humour, 56—religious contests the chief support of his authority, 56—Lollards burnt under, 57—controversial answer to Luther, 59—ability of, for religious dispute, ib. note b—apparent attachment of, to the Romish church, 60—his marriage, and aversion to Catherine of Aragon, ib.—time of his marriage with Anne Boleyn, 62 and note b—sends an envoy with his submission to Rome, 63—throws off its authority on receiving the papal sentence, ib.—his previous measures preparatory to doing so, 64—takes away

HIGH.

the first fruits from Rome, 65—becomes supreme head of the English church, 66 and note m—delays his separation from queen Catherine, from the temper of the nation, 67—expedient concerning his divorce, 68, note º—proceeds in the Reformation from policy and disposition, 69—the history of his time written with partiality, ib. note q—not enriched by the revenues of suppressed monasteries, 74—his alienation of their lands beneficial to England, ib.—should have diverted rather than have confiscated their revenues, 76—doubtful state of his religious doctrines, and his inconsistent cruelty in consequence, 81—sanctions the principles of Luther, 82—bad policy of his persecutions, 83—prohibits the reading of Tindal's Bible, ib. note ⁿ—state of religion at his death, 85—his law on the celibacy of priests, 91—his reformed church most agreeable to the English, 104, note d—his provisions for the succession of the crown, 123—supports the commons in their exemption from arrest, 269—his will disposing of the succession, 289—doubt concerning the signature of it, ib.—account of his death, and of that instrument, ib. note d—disregarded on the accession of James, 294—institution of the council of the north by, ii. 43.

Henry IV. (king of France), opposes the claim of Arabella Stuart on the English crown, i. 287, note b.

Henry (prince of Wales, son of James I.), his death, suspicion concerning it, i. 352, 353 and notes f g—design of marrying him to the infanta, 355 and note ⁱº.

Herbert (chief justice), his judgment in the case of sir Edward Hales, iii. 62—remarks on his decision, ib. 63—reasons of his resignation, 107, note g.

Herbert (Edward, lord, of Cherbury), fictitious speeches in his *History of Henry VIII.*, i. 17, note q.

Heresy, canon laws against, framed under Edward VI., i. 101, note u.

Hertford (Edward Seymour, earl of), his private marriage with lady Grey, i. 127—imprisonment and subsequent story of, ib. and 128, note º—inquiry into the legitimacy of his issue, 291, 292 and note k—Dugdale's account of it, 293, note l.

Hexham Abbey interceded for at the dissolution, i. 76.

Heyle, serjeant, his speech on the royal prerogative, i. 263, note.

Heylin (Dr. Peter), his notice of the Sabbatarian bill, i. 400, note s—his conduct towards Prynne, ii. 38.

Heywood (Mr. serjeant), his *Vindication of Mr. Fox's History*, iii. 52, note i.

High commission, court of, 1583, its

HIGH.

powerful nature, i. 201 and *note* k—act for abolishing the, ii. 98 and *note* e.
High and low churchmen, their origin and description, iii. 174, *note* f, 242.
Histriomastix, volume of invectives so called, ii. 37.
Hoadley (Benjamin, bishop of Bangor), attacked by the convocation, iii. 246—his principles, *ib.*
Hobby (sir Philip), recommends the bishops' revenues being decreased, i. 94, *note* g.
Hobby (sir Edward), his bill concerning the exchequer, i. 258, 259.
Holland (Henry Rich, earl of), chief justice in eyre, ii. 10—joins the king at Oxford, 158—is badly received, 159—returns to the parliament, *ib.*
Holland, war with, great expense of the, ii. 377—Charles II. receives large sums from France during the, 386—infamy of the, 390.
Holles (Denzil), committal and proceedings against, ii. 2, 4.
Hollingshed (Raphael), his savage account of the persecution of the papists, i. 146, *note* p—his description of the miserable state of Ireland, iii. 371.
Hollis (lord), sincerely patriotic in his clandestine intercourse with France, ii. 405 and *note* q.
Holt (chief justice), his opinion concerning the power of the commons to commit, iii. 282, 283.
Homilies, duty of non-resistance maintained in the, i. 415, *note* z.
Hooker (Richard), excellence of his *Ecclesiastical Polity*, i. 215—character and force of his argument, 216—relative perfection of the various books, 217—imperfections of, 218—justness and liberality of, in his views of government, 219—interpolations in the posthumous books considered, 220 and *note* d—his view of the national constitution and monarchy, 221, 222——dangerous view of the connexion of church and state, 222-227.
Hooker, member for Athenry, extract from his speech in the Irish parliament, iii. 373.
Hopes of the presbyterians from Charles II., ii. 316.
Houses built of timber forbidden to be erected in London after the great fire, iii. 6.
Howard (Catherine), her execution not an act of tyranny, her licentious habits probably continued after marriage, i. 33 and *notes* p q r.
Howard (sir Robert), and sir R. Temple, become placemen, ii. 308.
Howard (lord, of Escrick), his perfidy caused the deaths of Russell and Essex, ii. 456, 457.
Howell (James), letters concerning the

INDEPENDENT.

elevation of bishop Juxon, ii. 40, *note* i.
Hugonots of France, their number, i. 176, *note* q.
Huic (——), physician to queen Elizabeth, accused of dissuading her from marrying, i. 123, *note* m.
Hume (David), his estimate of the value of suppressed monasteries, i. 76, *note* d—perversion in his extracts of parliamentary speeches, 263, *note*—his erroneous assertion on the government of England, 279, *note* s—his partial view of the English constitution under Elizabeth, 284, *note* y—his account of Glamorgan's commission, ii. 191.
Hun (Richard), effects of his death in the Lollards' tower, i. 59.
Huntingdon (George Hastings, earl of), his title to the English crown, i. 286.
Hutchinson (Mrs.), her beautiful expression of her husband's feelings at the death of the regicides, ii. 326.
Hutchinson (colonel), died in confinement, ii. 368.
Hutton (Mr. justice), his statement concerning a benevolence collected for Elizabeth, i. 245, *note* x.
Hyde (sir Nicholas, chief justice), his speech on the trial of habeas corpus, i. 386.
Hyde and Keeling (chief justices), exercise a pretended power with regard to juries, iii. 8 and *note* o.
Hyde, lord chancellor, extract from his speech at the prorogation of the convention parliament, ii. 323, *note* y.

Icon Basiliké, account of, ii. 230.
Images, destruction of, under Edward VI., i. 86 and *note* s.
Impeachment, parliamentary character and instances of, i. 357, 358, 371—question on the king's right of pardon in cases of, ii. 416—decided by the act of settlement against the king's right, 417—abatement of, by dissolution of parliament, *ib.*—decided in the case of Hastings, 422—of commons for treason, constitutional, 446, 447.
Impositions on merchandise without consent of parliament, i. 316, 317 and *note* l—argument on, 318-320—again disputed in the house of commons, 340.
Impressment, statute restraining, ii. 100.
Imprisonment, illegal, banished from the English constitution, i. 234—flagrant instances of, under Elizabeth, 235—remonstrances of the judges against, *it*
Incident (transaction in Scotland so called), alarm excited by the, ii. 124.
Independence of judges, iii. 194—this important provision owing to the act of settlement, *ib.*
Independent party (the), their first

INDEX. 431

INDEPENDENTS.

great victory the self-denying ordinance, ii. 180—new-model the army, 181—two essential characters of, 197 and *note* t—first bring forward principles of toleration, 202.

Independents, liability of the, to severe laws, i. 213—origin of the name, 214 —emigrate to Holland, *ib.*—and to America, ii. 57.

Influence of the crown in both houses of parliament, remarks on the, iii. 266.

Innes, father, the biographer of James II., extract from, iii. 74.

Innocent VIII. (pope), his bull for the reformation of monasteries, i. 72, note J.

Institution of a Christian Man, 1537, reformed doctrines contained in, by authority of Henry VIII., i. 82—character of, *ib.*, *note* k.

Insurgents in the rebellion of 1641, their success, iii. 393—claim the re-establishment of the catholic religion, *ib.*

Insurrections on account of forced loans, i. 21—on the king's supremacy, 28, 29 —concerning enclosures, 92—of sir Thomas Wyatt, &c., 108, *note* n.

Intercommuning, letters of, published in Scotland, iii. 328.

Intrigues of Charles II. with France, ii. 376.

Ireland, mismanagement of the affairs of, iii. 112 and *note* D—ancient state of, 342—necessity of understanding the state of society at the time of Henry the Second's invasion, *ib.*—its division, 343—king of, how chosen, *ib.*—its chieftains, 344—rude state of society there, 345—state of the clergy in, 347 —ancient government of, nearly aristocratical, *ib.*—its reduction by Henry II., 348—its greatest part divided among ten English families, 349—the natives of, expelled, 350—English laws established in, *ib.*—natives of, claim protection from the throne, 351— its disorderly state, 354—miseries of the natives, 357—its hostility to the government, 358—its northern provinces, and part of the southern, lost to the crown of England, 359—its conduct during the contest between the houses of York and Lancaster, 361—royal authority over it revives under Henry VIII., 363—raised to the dignity of a kingdom, 364—elections declared illegal in, 372—rising of the people to restore the catholic worship, 376—priests ordered to quit, 377— English laws established throughout, *ib.*, 378—scheme for perfecting its conquest, *ib.* 379—Edmund Spenser, his account of the state of Ireland, *ib.* —constitution of its parliament, 383— its voluntary contribution for certain graces, 384—free trade to be admitted,

JAMES I.

ib.—rebellion of 1640, 389—its misgovernment at all times, 390—its fresh partition, 394—declaration for its settlement by Charles II., *ib.*—different parties in, their various claims, 395—declaration not satisfactory, *ib.* —complaints of the Irish, *ib.*—natural bias of Charles II. to the religion of, 396—unpopularity of the duke of Ormond with the Irish Catholics, 398— lord Berkeley's administration in 1670, *ib.*—the civil offices of, filled with catholics in the reign of James II., *ib.* —civil war of, in 1689, 399—treaty of Limerick, *ib.*—oath of supremacy imposed on the parliament of, 402— three nations and their religions in, 403—its dependence on the English parliament, 406—rising spirit of independence in, 407—jealousy and discontent of the natives of, against the English government, *ib.*—result of the census of 1837, as showing the relative numbers belonging to the different religious bodies, 403, *note* b.

Irish agents for the settlement of Ireland disgust Charles II., iii. 396.

Irish catholics, penal laws against, iii. 400.

Irish forfeitures resumed, iii. 141.

Irish lords surrender their estates to the crown, iii. 377.

Irish natives, origin of the, iii. 343— their character, 346—their ancient condition, 347—claim the protection of the throne, 351—not equitably treated in the settlement of the colonies, 352 —disaffected, their connexion with Spain, 390.

Jacobite faction, origin of the, iii. 109— party rendered more formidable by the faults of government, 254—their strength, 257—strength of, in Scotland, in the reigns of George I. and II., 340, 341.

Jacobites, intrigues of the, iii. 220— their disaffected clergy send forth libels, *ib.*—decline of the, 252.

Jacobitism of the ministers of queen Anne, iii. 225, 226, *note* r—of Swift, 227, *note* t—its general decline, 341.

James I. (king of England), view of the English constitution under, i. chap. vi. 285-373—his quiet accession, notwithstanding the numerous titles to the crown, 285—his and the other claims considered, 286-294 and *notes*— Elizabeth's intrigues against, 287, 288, *note* e—four proofs against his title, 289—his affection for hereditary right, 294—posture of England at his accession, *ib.*—his early unpopularity, 295— hasty temper and disregard of law, 296, *note* f—his contempt for Elizabeth, *ib. note* s—the Millenary petition pre-

JAMES II.

sented to, *ib.* and *note* ᵗ—his conduct to the puritans at the Hampton Court conference, 297 and *notes* ᵘ ᵛ ʷ—proclamation for conformity, 298—employed in publishing his maxims on the power of princes, 299—his first parliament summoned by irregular proclamation, 300—dispute with, on the election of Fortescue and Goodwin, 301—artifice of, towards the commons on a subsidy, 305—discontent of, at their proceedings, *ib.*, 331, *note* ᶠ—his scheme of an union with Scotland, 309, 310 and *notes* ᵘ ˣ—his change of title, 311, *note* ᶻ—continual bickerings with his parliaments, 312—his impolitic partiality for Spain, *ib.* and *notes* ᵈ ᵉ, 313, 355, 369, 370 and *notes* ʸ ᶻ, 408—duties imposed by, 315, 316 and *note* ᵍ—defects of his character, 331, 332 and *notes* ᵍ ʰ—foreign politics of England under, 333—his treatment of lord Coke, 335, *note* ᵖ—his use of proclamations, 337, *note* ˢ—his endeavours to raise money by loans, titles, &c., *ib.*, 338 and *note* ˣ—dissolves the parliament, 341 and *note* ᶦ—his letter and conduct to the twelve judges, 347, 348—his unpopularity increased by the circumstances of Arabella Stuart, Overbury, and Raleigh, 352-355—his probable knowledge of the murder of Overbury, 352 and *note* ᵍ—calls a new parliament, 356—his sudden adjournment of it, 363—his letter to the speaker of the commons on petitions against popery, 365—reply of, to a second petition, *ib.*—adjournment, dissolution, and proceedings against members of both houses, 368. 369 and *note* ˣ—libels against, 370 and *note* ʸ—his declaration of sports, 399—opposes the Arminian heresy, 402, 403 and *notes* ᵃ ᵇ—suspected of inclination to the papists, 404 and *note* ᵈ—answers cardinal Bellarmine, 407—state of papists under, 404-415 and *notes*—his reign the most important in the constitutional history of Ireland, iii. 375.

James II. (king of England), attributes his return to popery to the works of Hooker, i. 219, *note* ᶜ—his schemes of arbitrary power, iii. 49—issues a proclamation for the payment of customs, *ib.* and *note* ᵇ—his prejudice in favour of the catholic religion, 51—his intention to repeal the habeas corpus and test acts, 52—his remarkable conversation with Barillon, *ib.* and 53, *note* ᵏ —deceived in the disposition of his subjects, 55—supported by his brother's party, 57 and *note* ᵠ—prorogues the parliament, 59—his scheme for subverting the established religion, 64—his success against Monmouth inspires him with false confidence, 67, 68—rejects the plan for excluding the princess of Orange, 69—dissolves the parliament, 73—attempts to violate the right of electors, 74—solicits votes for repealing the test and penal laws, 75—expels the fellows from Magdalen college, 76—his infatuation, 77—his impolicy, 78—received 500,000 livres from Louis XIV., 79—his coldness to Louis XIV., *ib.*—his uncertain policy discussed, *ib.*—his character, 79 and *note* ᵠ, 80—reflections on his government, 83—compared with his father, *ib.*—has a numerous army, 85—influenced by his confessor Petre, 87—considered an enemy to the prince of Orange and the English nation, *ib.*—his sudden flight, 88—his return to London and subsequent flight, 89 and *note* ᵈ, 90—vote against him in the convention, 94—compassion excited for him by his fall, 108—large proportion of the tories engaged to support him, 123—various schemes for his restoration, and conspiracy in his favour, 127—issues a declaration from St. Germain's, 128 and *notes* ᵗ ᵘ—charged by Burnet with privity to the scheme of Grandval, 130, *note*—his commission to Crosby to seize the prince of Orange, *ib.*—civil offices, courts of justice, and the privy council in Ireland, filled with catholics in the reign of, 398.

James II. (king of Scotland), statute of, to prevent the alienation of the royal domains, iii. 311.

James VI. (king of Scotland), his success in restraining the presbyterians, iii. 318—his aversion to the Scottish presbytery, 321—forces on the people of Scotland the five articles of Perth, *ib.*

James VII. (king of Scotland), his reign, iii. 330—his cruelties, *ib.*—attempts to introduce popery, 331—national rejection of him from that kingdom, 332.

Jefferies (judge), violence of, iii. 64.

Jenkes, committed by the king in council for a mutinous speech, iii. 10, 11.

Jenkins (judge), confined in the Tower by the long parliament, iii. 281.

Jenner (a baron of the exchequer), committed to the Tower by the council, and afterwards to the custody of the serjeant by the commons, iii. 278.

Jermyn (Henry, lord), dictatorial style assumed by him in his letters to Charles I., ii. 187.

Jesuits, their zeal for the catholic faith, i. 165—missionaries of, in England, ii. 61 and *note* ˢ.

Jewell (John, bishop of Salisbury), opposes church ceremonies and habits, i. 172, *note* ᵈ, 173, 175, *note* ᵒ.

JEWS.

Jews permitted to settle in England, ii. 316.
Johnson (Dr. Samuel), error of, with respect to lord Shaftesbury, iii. 164, *note* ⁿ.
Joseph (emperor of Germany), his death, iii. 215.
Joyce, seizure of Charles by, ii. 205.
Judges in the reign of Henry VIII., their opinion that attainders in parliament could not be reversed in a court of law, i. 29—of the court of starchamber, 54 and *note* ᵐ—of Elizabeth, remonstrate against illegal imprisonments, 234—privately conferred with, to secure their determination for the crown, 343 and *note* ᵖ—the twelve disregard the king's letters for delay of judgment, 347, 348—their answers on the petition of right, 390—instances of their independence in their duty, ii. 4 —their sentiments on ship-money, 16 —sentence in Hampden's case, 22— —account Strafford guilty, 106, 107 and *note* ᵗ—their conduct on the trial of Vane, 326, 327—in the reign of Charles II. and James II., their brutal manners and gross injustice, 426 and *note* ˢ—Scroggs, North, and Jones, their conduct, 427 and *note* ⁱ—devise various means of subjecting juries to their own direction, iii. 7—their general behaviour infamous under the Stuarts, 194—independence of the, *ib.* —this important constitutional provision owing to the act of settlement, *ib.* —Pemberton and Jones, two late judges, summoned by the commons in the case of Topham, 282—Powis, Gould, and Powell, their opinions concerning the power of the commons to commit, *ib.*
Juries governed by the crown under Elizabeth, i. 233—fined for verdicts, i. 49; iii. 7—question of the right of, to return a general verdict, 8, 9.
Jury, trial by, its ancient establishment, i. 6, *note* ᵇ.
Jury, grand, their celebrated ignoramus on the indictment against Shaftesbury, ii. 450 and *note* ᵉ.
Justice, open administration of, the best security of civil liberty in England, i. 231—courts of, sometimes corrupted and perverted, 233, 234.
Justices of the peace under the Plantagenets, their jurisdiction, i. 7—limitation of their power, 16.
Juxon (Dr. William, bishop of London), made lord-treasurer, ii. 40 and *note* ⁱ— well treated in the parliament, 187, *note* ˢ.

Keeling (chief justice), strong resolutions of the commons against, for fining juries, iii. 8.
Kentish petition of 1701, ɴo. 272.

VOL. III.

LANDOWNERS.

Kerns and gallowglasses, names of mercenary troops in Ireland, iii. 348.
Kildare (earls of), their great influence in Ireland, iii. 363—(earl of), his son takes up arms, *ib.*—sent prisoner to London and committed to the Tower, *ib.*—executed with five of his uncles, *ib.*
Killigrew and Delaval, parliamentary inquiry into their conduct, iii. 144.
King, ancient limitations of his authority in England, i. 2—his prerogative of restraining foreign trade, 320 and *note* ᶠ—ecclesiastical canons on the absolute power of the, 322—his authority styled absolute, 325—command of the cannot sanction an illegal act, 385— his power of committing, 383, 386, 387 and *note* ᵗ, ii. 2—power of the, over the militia considered, 134, 135, and *note* ᵏ.
Kings of England, vote of the commons against the ecclesiastical prerogative of, ii. 392—their difficulties in the conduct of government, iii. 295—their comparative power in politics, *ib.*—of Scotland always claim supreme judicial power, 311.
King's Bench (court of), its order prohibiting the publishing a pamphlet, iii. 5—formed an article of impeachment against Scroggs, *ib.*
Knight (———), proceedings against, by the University of Oxford, i. 416 and *note* ⁿ.
Knight's service, tenure of, ii. 128-130, and *note* ᵍ—statutes amending, 129.
Knighthood, conferred by James I., &c., to raise money, i. 334, *note* ˣ; ii. 9, 10, and *note* ⁿ—compulsory, abolished, 99.
Knollys (sir Francis), friendly to the puritans, i. 138, *note* ᵒ, 200—opposed to episcopacy, 209, *note* ᵐ, 212.
Knox (John), persecuting spirit of, against the papists, i. 140, *note* ⁿ—supports the dissenting innovations at Frankfort, 171—his book against female monarchy, 280—founder of the Scots reformation, particulars of his scheme of church polity, iii. 314.

Lacy, his conquests in Ireland, iii. 348.
Lambert (general), refuses the oath of allegiance to Cromwell, ii. 259, *note* ᵏ— ambitious views of, 268—a principal actor in expelling the commons, 273— cashiered by parliament, *ib.*—his character, 280—panic occasioned by his escape from the Tower, 296—sent to Guernsey, 328—suspected to have been privately a catholic, 343.
Landed proprietors, their indignation at the rise of new men, iii. 214.
Landowners of England, became great under the Tudors, many of their estates acquired from the suppressed monasteries, i. 79.

2 F

LAND-TAX.

Land-tax, its origin, iii. 135 — its inequality, ib.
Lands, ancient English laws concerning their alienation, i. 12 — crown and church, restoration of, ii. 309—in Ireland act for their restitution, iii. 394—its insufficiency, 395—three thousand claimants unjustly cut off from any hope of restitution, 396.
Latimer (Hugh, bishop of Worcester), intercedes for Malvern priory at the dissolution, i. 76—zealous speech of, against the temporising clergy, 92, note c.
Latin ritual, antiquity and excellence of the, i. 86.
Latitudinarian divines, men most conspicuous in their writings in the reign of King Charles II., iii. 56.
Laud (William, archbishop of Canterbury), his assertion concerning bishops, i. 396, note; ii. 46, note f—high religious influence of, i. 403, note c—his talents and character, ii. 39, 40, and notes g h—his correspondence with lord Strafford, 45, &c., 60, note g, 85 and note h—accused of prosecuting Prynne, &c., 46—his conduct in the church prosecution of the puritans, 55, 56 and note o — procures a proclamation to restrain emigrants, 58 and note s—cardinal's hat offered to, 59, note x—charges of popery against, 62 and note b, 63—union with the catholics intended by, 66—turns against them, 73 and note s—impeached for high treason, 166—confined in the Tower, and in great indigence, ib.—particulars of the charges against him, ib.—defends himself with courage and ability, ib.—judges determine the charges contain no legal treason, 167—commons change their impeachment into an ordinance for his execution, ib. — peers comply, ib. — number of peers present, ib.
Lauderdale (duke of), one of the cabal, ii. 374—obliged to confine himself to Scotch affairs, 396—act of the, respecting the order of king and council to have the force of law in Scotland, iii. 327—his tyranny, 328.
Law, the ecclesiastical, reformed, i. 100-103, and notes t u—less a security for the civil liberty of England than the open administration of justice, 231—its ordinances for regulating the press, 239.
Laws, severity of, against theft, i. 7—of England, no alteration of ever attempted without the consent of parliament, 278—not enacted by kings of England without the advice of their great council, ib.—penal, extension of the, iii. 288 and note r—their gradual progress and severity, 289—have excited little attention as they passed through the houses of parliament, 290

LIBERTY.

—several passed in England to bind Ireland, 406.
Lawyers, their jealous dislike of the ecclesiastical courts, i. 212—Whitgift's censure of, ib. note t—dislike of the common lawyers by archbishop Laud and the earl of Strafford, ii. 46.
Layer (——), accuses several peers of conspiring in Atterbury's plot, iii. 251, note b.
Leeds (Henry Osborn, duke of), in the Stuart interest, iii. 225, note r.
Leicester (Robert Dudley, earl of), a suitor for the hand of Elizabeth, i. 123 —Cecil's arguments against him, 124, note h—assumes an interest in the queen, 124—connection with, broken off, 125—combines with the catholic peers against Cecil, 128, note r.
Leicester (Robert Sidney, earl of), archbishop Laud's dislike to, ii. 65, note k.
Leighton (Alexander), prosecution of by the court of star-chamber, ii. 37.
Leinster, rebellion of two septs in, leads to a reduction of their districts, now called King's and Queen's counties, iii. 364.
Lent, proclamations of Elizabeth for observing of, i. 238 and note s—statutes and proclamations for the observance of, 397, note p—licenses for eating flesh in, ib.
Lesley (bishop of Ross, ambassador of Mary queen of Scots), his answer concerning Elizabeth, i. 147, note q.
Leslie, remarks on his writings, iii. 176, note h—author of the Rehearsal, a periodical paper in favour of the Jacobites, 220.
L'Estrange (sir Roger), business of licensing books intrusted to him, iii. 4.
Lethington (Maitland of), his arguments on the title of Mary Stuart to the English crown, i. 131 and note x—his account of the death and will of Henry VIII., 289 and note d.
Levellers, and various sects, clamorous for the king's death, ii. 223—favourably spoken of by Mrs. Hutchinson, 240, note e.
Levies of 1524-5, letters on the difficulty of raising, i. 18, note r.
Libel, law of, indefinite, iii. 167—falsehood not essential to the law of, 168 and note u, 169—Powell's definition of a libel in the case of the seven bishops, ib. note—settled by Mr. Fox's libel bill in 1792, 169, 170.
Libels published by the puritans, i. 205, 206 and notes a b c—against James I., 370 and note y.
Liberty of the subject, comparative view of the, in England and France in the reign of Henry VIII., i. 22—civil, its securities in England, 230—of conscience, declaration for, iii. 71 — its motive, ib.—observations on its effects,

LICENSES.

ib.—similar to that published in Scotland, 72—of the press, 166—particulars relating to the, 167.
Licenses granted for eating flesh in Lent, i. 398, *note*.
Licensing acts, iii. 3—act, particulars relating to the, 166.
Lichfield (bishopric of), despoiled in the Reformation, i. 94.
Limerick, treaty of, iii. 399—its articles, *ib.*
Lincoln (Theophilus Clinton, earl of), refuses to take the covenant, and is excluded from the house of peers, ii. 164, *note* t.
Lingard (Dr. John), artifice of, in regard to the history of Anne Boleyn, i. 31, *note* n—his insinuation with regard to Catherine Howard and Lady Rochford, 33, *note* q—his notice of the bill on the papal supremacy, 66, *note* m—his estimate of the value of suppressed monasteries, 76, *note* d—his observations on the canon laws, and on Cranmer, 101, *note* u—his extenuations of queen Mary's conduct, 105, *note* e.
Litany, translated in 1542, i. 86, *note* r.
Littleton (lord keeper), carries away the great seal, ii. 161.
Liturgy, chiefly translated from the Latin service book, i. 86, and *note* r—prayers for the departed kept in, 87—taken out on its first revisal, *ib.*—amendments of the English, under Elizabeth, 110 and *note* c—statute defending, 111—revised, iii. 174—the, established the distinguishing marks of the Anglican church, 176.
Llandaff (bishopric of), despoiled in the Reformation, i. 94.
Loans, on property in 1524-25, raised by cardinal Wolsey, i. 18-22, and *notes* r s t u—remitted to Henry VII. by parliament, 23—to Elizabeth, not quite voluntary, nor without intimidation, 244 and *note* u—always repaid, 246—solicited under James I., 337—demanded by Charles I., and conduct of the people on it, 381-383, and *notes* p r—committal and trial of several refusing to contribute, 383—their demand of a habeas corpus, *ib.*—their right to it debated and denied, 383-387.
Lollards, the origin of the Protestant church of England, i. 57—their reappearance and character before Luther, *ib.*
London Gazette, amusing extract from, ii. 441, *note* i.
London, levies on the city of, i. 18, 25—citizens of, inclined to the Reformation, 68—increase of, prohibited by proclamation, 237—tumultuous assemblies of, resigned to martial law, 241—remonstrates against paying shipmoney, ii. 12—proclamation against buildings near, 26 and *note* y—proposed

LORDS.

improvements in, *ib.*—lands in Derry granted to, 27—offer of, to erect the king a palace in lieu of a fine, &c., 28, *note* d — corporation of, information against the, and forfeiture of their charter, 453—purchases the continued enjoyment of its estates at the expense of its municipal independence, 454.
Long (Thomas), member for Westbury, pays 4*l*. to the mayor, &c., for his return in 1571, i. 268.
Long parliament summoned, ii. 93—different political views of the, 94—its measures of reform, 94-97—made but little change from the constitution under the Plantagenets, 101—errors of the, 102, 112—bill of, enacting their not being dissolved against their own consent, 113 and *note* s.
Lord-lieutenant, institution of the office of, ii. 134.
Lords Portland, Oxford, Somers, and Halifax, impeached on account of the treaties of partition, iii. 146.
Lords, singularity of their sentence pronounced upon Anne Boleyn, i. 33, *note* o—house of, cold reception of the articles on religious reform prepared by the commons, 210—disagreements of the house of commons with the, 277, *note* o—impeachment of lord Latimer at the bar of the, 357—sentence of the, on Mompesson, 358—object to titles assumed by the commons, 361, *note* n—unable to withstand the inroads of democracy, ii. 233—reject a vote of the commons, 234—motion to take into consideration the settlement of the government on the death of the king, *ib.*— their messengers refused admittance by the commons, *ib.*—retain their titles, 235—Cromwell's description of, 260—embarrassing question concerning the eligibility of peers, 298—commons desire a conference with the, 299 and *note* n—receive a letter from Charles II., *ib.*—declare the government ought to be in the king, lords, and commons, 300—vote to exclude all who signed the death-warrant of Charles I. from act of indemnity, 306 and *note* i—in the case of lord Danby, not wrong in refusing to commit, 413 and *note* g—inquiry of the, in cases of appeals, 419—their judicial power historically traced, iii. 17—make orders on private petitions of an original nature, 18—antiquity of their ultimate jurisdiction, 19—pretensions of the, about the time of the Restoration, *ib.*, 20—their conduct in the case of Skinner and the East India Company, 21-24—state of, under the Tudors and Stuarts, 33—numbers from 1454 to 1661, 34; and of the spiritual lords, *ib.*, 35—every peer of full age entitled to his writ of summons, *ib.*— privilege of

2 F 2

LORD'S SUPPER.

voting by proxy, originally by special permission of the king, *ib.*—proceedings of the, in the convention of 1688, 93—dispute with, about Aylesbury election, 273-276—spiritual, in Scotland, choose the temporal to be number of eight, 323.

Lord's Supper, controversies and four theories on the, i. 89-91—modern Romish doctrines on the, 90, *note.*

Loudon (Dr. ——), his violent proceedings towards the monasteries, i. 71, *note* x.

Louis XIV., his object in the secret treaty with Charles II., ii. 382—mutual distrust between them, 386—secret connections formed by the leaders of opposition with, 402, *note* k—his motives for the same, 404 and *note* o—secret treaties with Charles, 409—mistrusts Charles's inclinations, and refuses him the pension stipulated for in the private treaty, 410—connexion between Charles II. and, broken off, 467—his views in regard to Spain dangerous to the liberties of Europe, iii. 137, 153—acknowledges the son of James II. as king of England, 195—makes overtures for negociations, 211, 212 and *note* a—exhausted state of his country, 216.

Love (Christopher), executed for a conspiracy, ii. 236—effects of his trial and execution, *ib.* and *note* x.

Luders (Mr.), observations in his report of election cases, iii. 43, *note* c.

Ludlow (general), and Algernon Sidney, project an insurrection, ii. 367, 368.

Lundy (colonel), inquiry into his conduct, iii. 143.

Luther (Martin), his doctrines similar to those of Wicliffe, i. 57—treatise of, answered by Henry VIII., 59—his rude reply and subsequent letter to the king, 60 and *note* c—his allowance of double marriages, 68, *note* u—his doctrine of consubstantiation, 90—rejects the belief of Zuingle, *ib.*

Lutherans of Germany, less disposed than the catholics to the divorce of Henry VIII., i. 68 and *note* o.

M'Crie (Dr.), his misconception of a passage in Hooker's Ecclesiastical Polity, i. 220, *note* d.

Macdiarmid (John), his Lives of British Statesmen, ii. 41, *note* k.

Macdonalds, their massacre in Glencoe, iii. 336 and *note* k.

Mackenzie (sir George), account of his Jus Regium, ii. 465.

Macpherson (John), extract from his Collection of State Papers, iii. 123, *note* l.

Madox (Dr. ——, bishop of Worcester), his answer to Neal's History of the Puritans, i. 206, *note* c.

MARY.

Magdalen college, Oxford, expulsion of the fellows from, iii. 76—mass said in the chapel of, *ib.*

Magistrates under Elizabeth inclined to popery, i. 143 and *note* e.

Mainwaring (——), his assertion of kingly power, i. 417.

Malt, imposition set upon, i. 363, *note* d.

Malvern priory interceded for at the dissolution, i. 76.

Manchester (Edward Montagu, earl of), suspected of being reluctant to complete the triumph of the parliament in the contest with Charles I., ii. 179.

Mann, sir Horace, notice of his letters from Florence, iii. 257, *note* x.

Maritime glory of England first traced from the commonwealth, ii. 262.

Markham (chief justice), his speech on the trial of habeas corpus, i. 385.

Marlborough (John, earl of), and Sidney (earl of Godolphin), Fenwick's discoveries obliged them to break off their course of perfidy, iii. 133.

Marlborough (John, duke of), abandons the cause of the Revolution, iii. 124, *note*—his whole life fraught with meanness and treachery, *ib.*, 125—preserves a secret connection with the court of James, 221—extreme selfishness and treachery of his character, *ib.*

Marlborough (Sarah, duchess of), her influence over queen Anne, iii. 208.

Marriages, ordered to be solemnized before justices of the peace, ii. 244.

Martial law, origin, benefits, and evils of, i. 240—instances of its use, *ib.*, 241—ordered under Charles I., 389, *note* a—restrained by the petition of right, 389, 392.

Martin Mar-prelate, puritan libels so called, i. 205, 206 and *notes* a b.

Martyr (Peter), assists the Reformation in England, i. 91—and in drawing up the forty-two articles, 97, *note* p—objected to the English vestments of priests, 102.

Martyrs under queen Mary, their number considered, i. 105, *note* f.

Mary (princess), unnatural and unjust proceedings in regard to, i. 34—denied the enjoyment of the privileges of her own religion, 85, *note* q, 95.

Mary (queen of England), restores the Latin liturgy, i. 41—married clergy expelled, *ib.*—averse to encroach on the privileges of the people, 42—her arbitrary measures attributed to her counsellors, *ib.*—duty on foreign cloth without assent of parliament, *ib.*—torture more frequent than in all former ages, *ib.*—unprecedented act of tyranny, 43—sends a knight to the Tower for his conduct in parliament, 55—her re-establishment of popery pleasing to a large portion of the nation, 103—pro-

MARY.

testant services to, *ib.*—her unpopularity, 105—her marriage with Philip of Spain disliked, *ib.*—cruelty of her religion productive of aversion to it, *ib.* —and of many becoming protestants, 106—her dislike of Elizabeth, and desire of changing the succession, 108, *note* ⁿ—origin of the high commission court under, 201, *note* ᵏ—use of martial law by, 241—Knox's attack on her government, and Aylmer's defence of, 280—imposes duties on merchandise without consent of parliament, 317.

Mary (queen of William III.), letters of, published by Dalrymple, iii. 125, *note* ᵏ.

Mary Stuart (queen of Scots), her prior right to the throne of England, i. 123— her malevolent letter to Elizabeth, 125, *note* ᵐ — her offensive and peculiar manner of bearing her arms, 130 and *note* ᵘ—her claim to the English throne, *ib.*—Elizabeth intrigues against, though not unfavourable to her succession, *ib.* —her difficulties in Scotland, and imprudent conduct, 131 — Elizabeth's treatment of, considered, *ib.*, 132 — strength of her party claim to England, *ib.*—her attachment to popery, and intent of restoring it, 133 and *note* ᵇ—combination in favour of, *ib.*— statute against her supporters, and allusion to herself, 138 and *note* ᵒ—bill against her succession considered, 138 —her succession feared by the puritans, 140 and *note* ᵘ—in confinement, and her son educated a protestant, 144— her deliverance designed by the catholics, 156—her correspondence regularly intercepted, *ib.* — statute intended to procure her exclusion, 158—her danger from the common people, *ib.*—reflections on her trial, imprisonment, death, and guilt, *ib.*—her regal title and privileges examined, 159.

Masham (lady), in the interest of pretender, iii. 225.

Mass (service of the), not tolerated in Germany and England, i. 95—performance of the, interdicted by the act of uniformity, 113—secretly permitted, *ib.* —instances of severity against catholics for hearing, 114—penalty for, and imprisonments, probably illegal, 114, *note* ˡ.

Massacre of the Scots and English, in Ulster, iii. 391.

Massachusetts bay, granted by charter, ii. 58.

Massey, a catholic, collated to the deanery of Christ Church, iii. 64 and *note* ᵉ.

Matthews's Bible, 1537, Coverdale's so-called, i. 83—notes against popery in, *ib. note* ⁿ.

Maximilian, his religious toleration in Germany, i. 119, *note* —said to have

MINISTERS.

leagued against the protestant faith, 136 and *note* ᵏ.

Mayart (serjeant), his treatise in answer to lord Bolton, iii. 406.

Mayne (—), persecution of, for popery i. 145.

Mazure (F. A. J.), extracts from his *Histoire de la Révolution*, relating to James II. and the prince of Orange, iii. 68, 69, *notes* ᵐ ⁿ—to the vassalage of James II. to Louis XIV., 79, 80, *notes* ᵠ ʳ —another extract concerning James II.'s order to Crosby to seize the prince of Orange, 130, *note*—his account of the secret negotiations between lord Tyrconnel and the French agent Bonrepos, for the separation of England and Ireland, 399, *note* ᵉ.

Melancthon (Philip), his permission of a concubine to the landgrave of Hesse, i. 68, *note* ᵉ—allowed of a limited episcopacy, 100—declared his approbation of the death of Servetus, 122, *note* ᵈ.

Melville (Andrew), and the general assembly of Scotland, restrain the bishops, iii. 316—some of the bishops submit, *ib.*—he is summoned before the council for seditious language, 317 —flies to England, 318.

Members of parliament, free from personal arrest, i. 302, 303; iii. 271.

Merchants, petition on grievances from Spain, i. 315 and *note* ᶠ—petition against arbitrary duties on goods, 316.

Merchandise, impositions on, not to be levied but by parliament, i. 316—book of rates on, published, 319.

Michele (Venetian ambassador), his slander of the English, i. 104, *note* ᵇ— states that Elizabeth was suspected of protestantism, 109, *note* ᵃ.

Michell (—), committed to the Tower by the house of commons, i. 357.

Middlesex (Lionel Cranfield, earl of), his parliamentary impeachment, i. 371, 372 and *note* ᵈ.

Military force in England, historical view of, ii. 128-135 and *notes*.

Military excesses committed by Maurice and Goring's armies, ii. 177, 178, and *notes* ʸ ᶻ—by the Scotch, 179.

Military power, the two effectual securities against, iii. 149—always subordinate to the civil, 263.

Militia, dispute on the question of, between Charles I. and the parliament ii. 128 and *note* ᶠ, 134, 135—its origin, iii. 262—considered as a means of recruiting the army, *ib.*—established in Scotland, 327.

Millenary petition, treatment of, by James I., i. 296 and *note* ᵗ.

Ministers of the crown, responsibility of, ii. 411; iii. 237, *note* ⁱ—necessity of their presence in parliament, 191.

Ministers, mechanics admitted to bene-

MIST'S JOURNAL.

Sees in England, i. 183—early presbyterian, of Scotland, were eloquent, learned, and zealous in the cause of the Reformation, iii. 317—their influence over the people, *ib.*—interfere with the civil policy, *ib.*

Mist's Journal, the printer Mist committed to Newgate by the commons for libel in, iii. 279.

Mitchell, confessing upon promise of pardon, executed in Scotland at the instance of Archbishop Sharp, iii. 329.

Molyneux, his celebrated "*Case of Ireland's being bound by acts of parliament in England stated,*" iii. 406—resolutions of the house of commons against his book, *ib.*

Mompesson (sir Giles), his patents questioned, i. 356.

Monarchy of England limited, i. 2—erroneously asserted to have been absolute, 277.

Monarchy, established, tendency of the English government towards, from Henry VI. to Henry VIII., i. 46—not attributable to military force, *ib.*—abolished, ii. 232—extraordinary change in our, at the Revolution, iii. 99 and *note* p—absolute power of, defined, 291.

Monasteries, their corruptions exposed by the visitations of, i. 71—resignation and suppression of, 72—papal bull for reforming, *ib. note* y—act reciting their vices, *ib. note* z—feelings and effects of their suppression, 72—might lawfully and wisely have been abolished, 74—several interceded for at the dissolution, 76—evils of their indiscriminate destruction, *ib.*—immense wealth procured by their suppression, *ib.* and *note* d—how bestowed and distributed, 77 and *note* e—alms of the, erroneously supposed to support the poor, 80—in Ireland, in the 7th and 8th centuries, learning preserved by, iii. 347.

Monastic orders averse to the Reformation, i. 69—their possessions great but unequal, *ib.* and *note* f—evils of, in the reign of Henry VIII., 70—reformed and suppressed by Wolsey, *ib.* and *note* u—visitations of the, truly reported, 71—protestant historians in favour of, *ib. note* y—pensions given to the, on their suppression, 73, *note* u.

Money-bills, privilege of the commons concerning, i. 276—ancient mode of proceeding in, discussed, iii. 27.

Monk (general George), his strong attachment to Cromwell, ii. 281—his advice to Richard Cromwell, *ib.*—observations on his conduct, *ib.*, 282 and *notes* i k—takes up his quarters in London, 283—his first tender of service to the king, 285—can hardly be said to have restored Charles II., but did not oppose him so long as he might have done,

MOYLE.

286, *note* n—not secure of the army, 287—represses a mutinous spirit, and writes to the gentry of Devon, *ib. note* q—his slowness in declaring for Charles, 288—urges the most rigid limitations to the monarchy, 291—suggests the sending the king's letter to the two houses of parliament, *ib.*—his character, 301—advises the exclusion of only four regicides from the act of indemnity, 305.

Monks, pensions given to, on their suppression, i. 73 and *note* a.

Monmouth (James, duke of), remark on the death of, iii. 58 and *note* f.

Monmouth's rebellion, numbers executed for, iii. 67, *note* k.

Monmouth (county), right of election extended to, iii. 67.

Monopolies, nature of, i. 261—victorious debate on, in the house of commons, 262—parliamentary proceedings against, 356-359.

Montagu (abbé), committed by the commons for publishing a book, iii. 278.

Montagu (Dr. Richard, bishop of Chichester), his Roman catholic tenets, ii. 63—his intrigues with Panzani, 69-72.

Montagu (lord), his speech in the house of lords against the statute for the queen's power, i. 116, and 117, *note* q—brings a troop of horse to Elizabeth at Tilbury, 162 and *note* m.

Monteagle (lord), his suit with the earl of Hertford, i. 292 and *note* k.

Montreuil, his opinion on the plan of flight contemplated by Charles I., ii. 182, *note* b—negotiation of, 188 and *notes* a b.

Mordaunt (lord), charges against, ii. 373.

More (sir Thomas), opposes the granting a subsidy to Henry VII., i. 13, *note* b—his conduct upon another motion for a large grant, 17—apology for his proceedings against Wolsey, 22—beheaded for denying the king's ecclesiastical supremacy, 28—inclined to the divorce of Henry VIII., 65, 66 and *note* k.

Morgan (Thomas), his letter to Mary Stuart, i. 159, *note* g.

Morice (——), attorney of the court of wards), attacks the oath *ex officio*, i. 212—his motion on ecclesiastical abuses, 260—his imprisonment and letter, *ib.*

Mortmain, effect of the statutes of, on the clergy, i. 69.

Morton (John, archbishop of Canterbury), his mode of soliciting benevolences, called "Morton's fork," i. 14—his charge against the abbey of St. Alban's, 72, *note* y.

Mortuaries, fees of the clergy on, limited, i. 64.

Mountnorris (lord), conduct of lord Strafford to, ii. 44, 45 and *notes* r s.

Moyle (Walter), his *Argument against a standing Army*, iii. 139, *note* k.

MURDERERS.

Murderers and robbers deprived of the benefit of clergy, i. 58—the question of pardons to, considered, iii. 105, *note* ᵉ.

Murray (William), employed by 'king Charles to sound the parliamentary leaders, ii. 187.

Murray (Mr. Alexander), arbitrary proceedings of the commons against him, iii. 277—causes himself to be brought by habeas corpus before the king's bench, 283.

Mutiny bill passed, iii. 149.

Naseby, defeat of Charles I. at, ii. 181—consequences of, 182.

Nation, state of the, proposition for an inquiry into the, iii. 144.

National antipathy to the French not so great before the reign of Charles II., ii. 375.

National debt at the death of William III., iii. 134, *note* ᵈ—rapid increase of the, 214 and *note* ᶜ.

Nations, three, and three religions, in Ireland, iii. 403.

Naval transactions in the reign of William III., iii. 126.

Navy of Charles I., reasons for increasing, ii. 12.

Neal (Daniel), his *History of the Puritans* and *Answer to Bishop Maddox*, i. 206, *note* ᶜ—statement of the puritan controversy under Elizabeth, *ib.*

Netherlands, Charles I. negotiates with the disaffected in the, ii. 13.

Neville (sir Henry), his memorial to James I. on summoning a parliament, i. 339.

Newark, charter granted to, enabling it to return two members, iii. 40.

Newbury, battle of, its consequences to the prevailing party, ii. 161.

Newport, treaty of, ii. 215—observations on the, *ib.*, 216 and *note* ˡ.

News, to publish any without authority, determined by the judges in 1680 to be illegal, iii. 5 and *note* ᶠ.

Newspapers, their great circulation in the reign of Anne, iii. 298—stamp duty laid on, *ib.*

Neyle (Dr. Richard, bishop of Lichfield), proceedings of the house of commons against, i. 340.

Nicholas (Henry), a fanatic leader, i. 122, *note* ᶜ.

Nicolas (sir Harris), notice of his "Proceedings and Ordinances of the Privy Council of England," i. 53, *note*.

Nimeguen, treaty of, hasty signature of the, ii. 410.

Nine, council of, ii. 261 and *note* ᵠ.

Noailles (ambassador in England from Henry II. of France), his conduct secures the national independence, i. 46, *note* ᵇ—unpopularity of queen Mary reported by, 103—his account of her persecutions, 106, *note* ᵍ.

Noailles (marshal de), extract from his memoirs relating to Philip of Anjou, iii. 213, *note* ᵃ.

Nobility, pliant during the reign of Henry VIII., i. 48—responsible for various illegal and sanguinary acts, *ib.*—of the north, repressed by Henry VIII. and the court of star-chamber, 52—why inclined to the Reformation, 68—of England become great under the Tudors, deriving their estates from the suppressed monasteries, 79—averse to the bill against the celibacy of priests, 92—and to the Reformation, *ib.*—such advanced into power under Mary, 103—censured, &c. for religion under that queen, *ib.* and *note* ᵇ—combination of the catholic, for Mary Stuart, 133.

Nonconformists, protestant, laws of Elizabeth respecting, i. ch. iv. 170-228—summoned and suspended by archbishop Parker, 180—number of, in the clergy, 183, *note* ᵉ—deprived by archbishop Whitgift, 200 and *note* ᵇ—increased under Elizabeth, 226—remarks on acts against, ii. 350—avail themselves of the toleration held out by James II., iii. 73.

Nonjurors, schism of the, its beginning, iii. 109—send forth numerous libellous pamphlets, 220.

Non-resistance preached by the clergy and enforced in the Homilies, i. 415 and *note* ᵃ.

Norfolk (Thomas Howard, duke of), his letter to Wolsey on the grant of 1525, i. 18, *note* ᶠ—letter of the council to, during the rebellion, 28, *note* ʰ—combines with the catholic peers against Cecil, 128, *note* ʳ.

Norfolk (John, lord Howard, duke of), confidential minister of Henry VIII., ruined by the influence of the two Seymours; execution prevented by the death of Henry, i. 31—continued in prison during Edward's reign, and is restored under Mary, *ib.*—prevails on Henry VIII. to prohibit the English Scriptures, 83, *note* ᵃ—a supporter of the popish party, 85—in prison at the death of Henry VIII., *ib.*—proposed union of, with Mary Stuart, 133—character, treason, and trial of, 134.

Norfolk, county of, assists to place Mary on the throne, and suffers greatly from persecution, i. 103 and *note* ᵃ—parliamentary inquiry into the returns for, 275.

Norman families, great number of, settle in Scotland, and become the founders of its aristocracy, iii. 305.

North of England, slow progress of the Reformation in, i. 92—council of the, its institution and power, ii. 42—act for abolishing, 99 and *note* ᵇ.

NORTH.

North (chief justice), proclamation drawn up by, against petitions, ii. 442.
North and Rich (sheriffs) illegally put into office, ii. 458.
Northampton (Henry Howard, earl of) declines to forward the merchants' petitions against Spain, i. 314.
Northampton, payment of ship-money complained of in, ii. 86, *note* °.
Northumberland (Algernon Percy, earl of), his connexion with the gunpowder conspiracy, i. 406, *note*—and others, take measures against a standing army, ii. 380.
Norton (Mr.), his defence of the bill against non-resident burgesses, i. 266.
Nottingham (Daniel Finch, earl of), holds offices of trust under William III., iii. 111—unites with the whigs against the treaty of peace, 249.
Nowell (Alexander), parliamentary inquiry into his election, i. 275.
Noy (William), discovers an early tax imposed for shipping, ii. 12.
"Nuisance," introduction of this word into the Irish bill, iii. 61, *note* ʸ.

Oath, called *ex officio*, in the high commission court, i. 201—attacked in the house of commons, 212—administered to papists under James I., 407—to the clergy, 1640, ii. 114—of abjuration, iii. 195.
October club, generally Jacobites, iii. 225.
Œcolampadius (John), his doctrines on the Lord's Supper, i. 90.
Offices, new, created at unreasonable salaries, as bribes to members of parliament, iii. 190.
Officers of the crown, undue power exerted by, i. 3.
O'Neil, attainted in the parliament of 1569, and his land forfeited to the crown, iii. 378, 379.
Onslow (speaker), his assertion of the property of the subject, i. 279.
Opposition to the court of Charles II., ii. 330.
O'Quigley (Patrick), his case compared with Ashton's, iii. 181.
Orange (William, Prince of), declares against the plan of restrictions, ii. 438—remarks on his conduct before the Revolution, iii. 66—derived great benefit from the rebellion of Monmouth, 67—overtures of the malcontents to, 69—receives assurances of attachment from men of rank in England, 81—invitation to him, *ib.* and *note* ˣ—his design of forming an alliance against Louis XIV., 86—requested to take the administration of the government of England upon himself, 91—vote of the convention declaring him and the princess of Orange king and queen of England, 92.

PALGRAVE.

Ordinance, a severe one of Cromwell, ii. 316.
Ordinance, self-denying, judiciously conceived, ii. 180, 181 and *notes* ᵉ ᶠ.
Origin of the present regular army, ii. 315.
Orkney (countess of), receives large grants from William III., iii. 141.
Orleans (duchess of, sister of Charles II.) her famous journey to Dover, ii. 384.
Orleans (duke of), favours the pretender, iii. 241, *note* ᵘ.
Ormond (duke of), engaged in the interests of the pretender, iii. 223 and *note* ᵠ—his unpopularity with the Irish catholics, 398.
Ormond (James Butler, marquis of), sent to England by Charles II., ii. 276.
Orrery (Roger Boyle, earl of), a catholic, ii. 387.
Overbury (sir Thomas), his murder, i. 352—examination of, 353, *note* ᵇ.
Oxford (university of), measure adopted to procure its judgment in favour of the divorce of Henry VIII., i. 67—attached to popery, 183, and 184, *note* ᵇ—proceedings on doctrine of non-resistance, 416—decree of the, against pernicious books, ii. 466—opposes the measures of James II., iii. 77—tainted with Jacobite prejudices, 250 and *note* ᵐ.
Oxford, short parliament held at, in March, 1681, ii. 446.
Oxford (John de Vere, earl of), fined for his retainers, i. 15—censured by queen Mary's council for his religion, 104, *note* ᵇ.
Oxford (Robert Harley, earl of), sends abbé Gaultier to marshal Berwick to treat of the Restoration, iii. 222—promises to send a plan for carrying it into effect, *ib.*—account of pamphlets written on his side, 223, *note* ᵖ—hated by both parties, 230—impeached of high treason, 233—committed to the Tower, *ib.*—impeachment against him abandoned, 234 and *note* ˢ—his speech when the articles were brought up, *ib.*

Paget (William, first lord), his remark on the doubtful state of religion in England, i. 93, *note* ᵈ—advises the sending for German troops to quell commotions, *ib.*—his lands increased by the bishopric of Lichfield, 94.
Palatinate, negotiation of Charles I. for its restoration, ii. 14.
Palatine jurisdiction of some counties under the Plantagenets, i. 7.
Pale, old English of the, ill disposed to embrace the reformed religion in Ireland, iii. 372—deputation sent from Ireland to England, in the name of all the subjects of the, 374—delegates from, committed to the Tower, *ib.* and *note* ʰ.
Palgrave (sir Francis), notice of his

INDEX. 441

PAMPHLETS.

"Essay upon the Original Authority of the King's Council," i. 53, *note*.
Pamphlets, account of some in the reign of Charles and James II., iii. 170, *note* ˣ —and political tracts, their character and influence on the public mind at the commencement of the last century, 299.
Panzani, a priest, ambassador to Charles I., ii. 59—his report to the pope of Papists in England, 68, *note* ʳ.
Papists proceeded against for hearing mass, I. 114—tracts and papers to recall the people of England to their faith, 115 and *note* ⁿ.
Papists of England, the Emperor Ferdinand's intercession for, I. 118—subsequent persecution of, 119-122 and *notes*—attended the English church, 120—combinations of, under Elizabeth, 132—more rigorously treated, and emigration of, 140, *note* ᵘ—their strength and encouragement under Elizabeth, 143—emissaries from abroad, numbers and traitorous purposes of, *ib.*—executed for their religion under Elizabeth, 145—concealment of their treacherous purposes, 148—lord Burleigh's provisions against, in the oath of supremacy, 151, 152—his opinion that they were not reduced by persecution, but severity against, productive of hypocrites, *ib.*—petition against the banishment of priests, 153—heavy penalties on, 154 and *note* b—the queen's death contemplated by, 155—become disaffected to Elizabeth, *ib.* *note* d—excellent conduct of at the Spanish invasion, 156, *note*, 162 and *note* ᵐ—depressed state of, *ib.*—continued persecution of, between 1588 and 1603, 163 and *note* ᵠ—statute restricting their residence, *ib.*—executed for safety of the government, and not their religion, 164—their simple belief construed into treason, *ib.*—the nature of their treason considered, *ib.* *note* ˢ—proportion of, in England, under Elizabeth, 176, *note* ᵠ—excluded from the house of commons, 190—treatment of, under James I., 404-414 and *notes*—state and indulgence of, under Charles I., 413 and *note*, 414; ii. 59—inclined to support the king, 60 and *note* ᶻ—report of, in England, by Panzani, 68, *note* ʳ—contributions raised by the gentry, 85.
Parker (Matthew), made archbishop of Canterbury, i. 110, *note* ᶜ—his liberal treatment of bishop Tunstall, 118, *note* ˢ—his consecration admitted, *ib.* *note* ᵗ—his sentence against lady Grey, 127—his advice against Mary queen of Scots, 139—speech of, against the papists, 141—Elizabeth's coarse treatment of his wife, 174, *note* ᵐ—defends the church liturgy and ceremonies, 175, 179 and *note* ᵗ, 182, 136—his order for

PARLIAMENT

the discipline of the clergy, 179, *note* ᵗ 180—summons nonconformists, *ib.*—orders certificates of the clergy, 183, *note* ˢ—discussion of church authority with Mr. Wentworth, 192—prosecutes the puritans, 194—suppresses their "prophesyings," 197—defends the title of bishops, 224, *note* ᵉ.
Parker (Samuel, bishop of Oxford), account of his *History of his Own Time*, ii. 388, *note* ᵒ.
Parliament, the present constitution of, recognised in the reign of Edward II., i. 3—of Henry VII. secure the crown to his posterity, 8—anxious for his union with Elizabeth of York, 9—power of the privy council over the members of, 55—struggles of, against the crown, *ib.*—complaint of the house of commons against Fisher, 64—divorce of Henry VIII. brought before the houses of, 65—address of, moved for Henry VIII. to receive back queen Catherine, 67—influence of the crown over, 264—statutes for holding, ii. 95, 96 and *note* ˢ—enormous extension of its privileges, 141 and *note* ʳ—few acts of justice, humanity, generosity, or of wisdom from, manifested by, from their quarrel with the king to their expulsion, 152—deficient in military force, 154—offers terms of peace to Charles I. at Newcastle, 185—deficient in political courage, 205—eleven members charged with treason, 206—duration of, proposed, 209—has no means to withstand the power of Cromwell, 239—is strongly attached to the established church, 241—new one called decidedly royalist, 324—its implacable resentment against the sectaries, 345—session of, held at Oxford in 1665, 349—tendency of long sessions to form opposition in, 355—supplies granted by, only to be expended for specific objects, 357—strenuous opposition made by to Charles II. and the duke of York, 386—convention dissolved, iii. 122—its spirit of inquiry after the Revolution, 143—annual assembly of, rendered necessary, 149—its members influenced by bribes, 189—its rights out of danger since the Revolution, 191—influence over it by places and pensions, 264, 265—its practice to repress disorderly behaviour, 267—assumed the power of incapacitation, 268—debates in account of their first publication, 300—their great importance, 301—seat in, necessary qualification for, 303.
Parliament of 1685, remarks on its behaviour, iii. 50.
Parliament (convention), accused of abandoning public liberty at the Restoration ii. 293—pass several bills of importance, 304.

PARLIAMENT.

Parliament (long), called back by the council of officers, ii. 272—expelled again, 273—of seventeen years' duration dissolved, 429 and *note* °—long prorogation of, 440.

Parliaments, probable effect of Wolsey's measures for raising supplies without their intervention, i. 21—bill for triennial, iii. 148—for septennial, 235, 236.

Parliament of Scotland, its model nearly the same as that of the Anglo-Norman sovereigns, iii. 306—its mode of convocation, *ib.*—law enacted by James I. relating to, 307—royal boroughs in the fifteenth century, 308—its legislative authority higher than that of England, 311—summoned at his accession by James II., acknowledges the king's absolute power, 330.

Parliament of Ireland, similar to an English one, iii. 355—its constitution, 383—meet in 1634; its desire to insist on the confirmation of the graces, 386—opposition in the, to the crown, 401—in 1661, only one catholic returned to, 402.

Parliament of the new protestant nation of Ireland always whig, iii. 404.

Parliamentary party (old), assemble to take measures against a standing army, ii. 380.

Parliamentary privilege, observations respecting, iii. 287, *note* q.

Parry (Dr. William), executed for a plot against Elizabeth, i. 155—account of him, *ib. note* c.

Parry (Dr.), committal and expulsion of, by parliament, i. 274.

Parry (Thomas), his letter concerning the papists under James ..i. 406, *note* b.

Parsons (sir William), and sir John Borlase (lords justices), succeed lord Strafford in the government of Ireland, iii. 390.

Partition treaty, earl of Portland and lord Somers the only ministers proved to be concerned in the, iii. 187.

Party (moderate), endeavour to bring about a pacification with Charles, ii. 152—negotiation with the king, broken off by the action at Brentford, 154—three peers of the, go over to the king, 158.

Passive obedience (doctrine of), passed from the Homilies into the statutes, ii. 330—remarks on the doctrine of, 463.

Paul IV. (pope), his arrogant reply to the message of Elizabeth, i. 109 and *note* b, 114.

Paulet (sir Amias), his honourable and humane conduct to Mary Stuart, i. 169, *note* b.

Peacham (Rev. ——), prosecution of, for a libellous sermon, i. 343.

PERSONS.

Pearce (Dr. Zachary, bishop of Rochester) his right to a seat in parliament after resigning his see, i. 73, *note* b.

Peasantry of England under the Plantagenets, i. 5.

Peers of England, under the Plantagenets, a small body, i. 5—their privileges not considerable, *ib.*—disordered state of, under Henry VI. and Edward IV., 9—authority and influence of abbots, &c. in the house of, 71—freedom of the, from the oath of supremacy, 116—their interference with elections opposed, 267—proceedings of James I. against, for conduct in parliament, 369 and *note* x—not of the council could not sit in the star-chamber, ii. 30, *note*.

Peerage of England, probably supported the commons against the crown, i. 55.

Peerages, several conferred on old Irish families, iii. 361.

Peerage bill, particulars of the, iii. 238.

Pelhams (the), resign their offices, and oblige George II. to give up lord Granville, iii. 296.

Pemberton (sir Francis, chief justice), unfair in all trials relating to popery, ii. 427, 428—his conduct on the trial of lord Russell, 458.

Pembroke (William Herbert, earl of), peers' proxies held by, i. 378, *note* h.

Pembroke (Philip Herbert, earl of), sits in the house of commons, ii. 235.

Penal statutes, power of the crown to dispense with, ii. 391—severity of the, 393—laws enforced against some unfortunate priests, 443—against catholics in Ireland, iii. 400, 401.

Penruddock enters Salisbury, and seizes the judge and sheriff, ii. 250 and *note* °.

Penry (John, Martin Mar-prelate), tried and executed for libels against queen Elizabeth, &c., i. 205 and *note* z, 232.

Pensioners during the pleasure of the crown, excluded from the commons, iii. 193.

Pepys (Samuel), his *Diary* — extract from, concerning money expended by Charles II., ii. 359, *note* a.

Permanent military force, national repugnance to, iii. 259—its number during the administration of sir Robert Walpole, 268. (See Army, and Standing Army.)

Perrot (sir John), his justice in the government of Ireland, iii. 371—falls a sacrifice to court intrigue, 372.

Persecution, religious, greater under Charles II. than during the commonwealth, ii. 353.

Persons (father), his book on the succession to the English crown, i. 285, *note* a—his *Leicester's Commonwealth*, *ib.*

PETITION.

Petition of Right, its nature and proceedings in, i. 316, 359 and *notes*, ii. 3.
Petition and Advice, particulars of the, ii. 259—empowers Cromwell to appoint a successor, 266.
Petitions, law relating to, ii. 329—for the meeting of parliament checked by a proclamation of Charles II., drawn up by chief justice North, 442—interfering with the prerogative repugnant to the ancient principles of our monarchy, *ib*.
Petre (father), with a few catholics, takes the management of affairs under James II., iii. 65 and *note* ᵍ—James II.'s intention of conferring the archbishopric of York on, 77 and *note* ᵏ.
Petty (sir William), his account of the lands forfeited and restored in Ireland, iii. 397, *note* ʲ.
Philip II. (king of Spain), his temptation to the English to dethrone Elizabeth, i. 286, *note*.
Philopater (Andreas Persons), his account of the confederacy against Cecil, i. 128, *note* ʳ—justifies deposing a heretic sovereign, 147, *note* ᵠ.
Pickering (lord-keeper), his message to the house of commons, i. 259.
Pierpoint (Henry, lord), hopes to settle the nation under Richard Cromwell, ii. 267—his aversion to the recall of Charles II., 289.
Pitt (William, earl of Chatham), the inconsistency of his political conduct, iii. 297.
Pius IV. (pope), his embassy to Elizabeth, i. 114—moderation of his government, 115—falsely accused of sanctioning the murder of Elizabeth, 115, *note* ᵒ.
Pius V. (pope), his bull deposing Elizabeth, i. 134—most injurious to its own party, 137—his bull explained by Gregory XIII., 147.
Place bill of 1743, iii. 265 and *note* ᵉ.
Plague in 1665, ii. 378.
Plan for setting aside Mary, princess of Orange, at the period of the Revolution, iii. 68 and *note* ᵐ.
Plantagenets, state of the kingdom under the, i. 4-8—privileges of the nation under the, 4—violence used by their officers of the crown, 5—inconsiderable privileges of the peers, gentry, and yeomanry, *ib*.—their courts of law, *ib*. —constitution of England under the, 284 ; ii. 101—conduct of with regard to the government of Ireland, iii. 360.
Plays and interludes satirising the clergy, i. 84—suppression of plays reflecting on the conduct of the king, 370, *note* ʲ.
Pleadings, their nature and process explained, i. 6, *note* ᵇ.
Plunket (titular archbishop of Dublin), executed, ii. 452 and *note* ⁱ—sacrificed to the wicked policy of the court, *ib*.

PRESBYTERIAN.

Pluralities, the greatest abuse of the church, i. 210—bill for restraining, 211.
Pole (cardinal Reginald), actively employed by the pope in fomenting rebellion in England, i. 29 and *note* ⁱ—procures the pope's confirmation of grants of abbey lands, 104—conspiracy of his nephew against queen Elizabeth, 115 and *note* ᵒ.
Polity of England at the accession of Henry VII., i. 2.
Political writings, their influence, iii. 299.
Poor, the, erroneously supposed to have been maintained by the alms of monasteries, i. 80—statutes for their provision, *ib*. and *note* ⁱ.
Pope, his authority in England, how taken away, i. 64-69—his right of deposing sovereigns, 147.
Popery preferred by the higher ranks in England, i. 103—becomes disliked under queen Mary, 105.
Popish plot, great national delusion of the, ii. 423.
Popular party, in the reign of Charles II., its connection with France, ii. 402.
Population, state of, under the Plantagenets, i. 8 and *note* ᶜ.
Portland (William Bentinck, earl of), receives large grants from William III., iii. 141.
Pound (Mr.), sentenced by the starchamber, ii. 34, *note* ᵛ.
Power, despotic, no statutes so effectual against, as the vigilance of the people, iii. 298.
Poyning's Law, or Statute of Drogheda, provisions of, iii. 361—its most momentous article, 362—bill for suspending, 373—attempts to procure its repeal, 404.
Predestination, canon law against, under Edward VI., i. 104, *note* ᵘ—dispute on, 400-403 and *notes*.
Prerogative, confined nature of the royal, i. 2—strengthened by Henry VII., 10—undue assumption of, on the dissolution of parliament, by Charles I., 414—of a catholic king, act for limiting the, ii. 436—of the kings of England in granting dispensations, iii. 60.
Prejudices against the house of Hanover, iii. 254.
Presbyterians, their attempt to set up a government of their own, i. 207—erroneous use of scripture by, 216—consider the treaty of Newport as a proper basis for the settlement of the kingdom, ii. 294—received by the king, 335—remarks on Charles II.'s conduct to, 345 —implore his dispensation for their nonconformity, *ib*.
Presbyterian party, supported by the

PRESBYTERIAN.

city of London, ii. 200—regain their ascendancy, 215—ministry solicit a revision of the liturgy, 320—clergy of Scotland, their power and attempts at independence, iii. 314—restrained by James VI., 318—intermeddle again with public affairs, 319—church, its obstinacy, 336.

Presbyterian discipline of the Scottish church, restored, iii. 323.

Presence, the real, zeal of Henry VIII. in defending, i. 81—principal theories concerning the, 89-92 and *notes* only two doctrines in reality, 90, *note* J—believed in England in the seventeenth century, ii. 63 and *note* c.

Press, liberty of the, iii. 168, 169, *note* t.

Pretender (James Stuart, the), acknowledged king of England by France, and attainted of high treason by parliament, iii. 195—has friends in the tory government, 223 and *note* q, 224—lands in Scotland, and meets with great success, 232—invades England, *ib.*—the king of Sweden leagues with, for his restoration, 241 and *note* t—becomes master of Scotland, and advances to the centre of England, 253—rebellion of 1745 conclusive against the possibility of his restoration, *ib.* and *note* q—deserted by his own party, 255—insulted by France, *ib.* and *note* u.

Priests, antiquity and evils of their celibacy, i. 91, *note* a—catholic, resigned or deprived under Elizabeth, 111—pensions granted to, *ib. note* f—Romish, persecution for harbouring and supporting, 120—the most essential part of the Romish ritual, 121—secret travels and deceitful labours of, *ib.*—unite with sectarians, *ib.*—ordered to depart from England unless they acknowledge the queen's allegiance, 166.

Priests and Jesuits, intrigues of, against Elizabeth, i. 137—statute against, *ib.*

Priests (popish seminary), executed under Elizabeth, i. 145—lord Burleigh's justification of their persecution, 149—ordered to quit the kingdom, 153.

Priests (Romish), in Ireland, engaged in a conspiracy with the court of Spain, iii. 376—ordered to quit Ireland by proclamation, *ib*

Prince of Wales (son of James II.), suspicions attending the birth of, unfounded, iii. 81 and *note* x.

Principles of toleration fully established, iii. 250, 251.

Printing, bill for the regulation of, iii. 3.

Printing and bookselling, regulated by proclamations, i. 238 and *notes* k l m n.

Priors, pensions given to, on their suppression, i. 73, *note* a.

Prisoners of war made amenable to the laws of England, i. 160.

PROTESTANTS.

Privilege, breach of, members of parliament committed for, iii. 267—punishment of, extended to strangers, 269—never so frequent as in the reign of William III., *ib.*

Privilege of parliament, discussed, iii. 25—not controllable by courts of law, 274—important, the power of committing all who disobey its orders to attend as witnesses, 277—danger of stretching too far, 284 and *note* m—uncontrollable, draws with it unlimited power of punishment, 286, 287 and *note* q.

Privy council, illegal jurisdiction exercised by the, i. 48—the principal grievance under the Tudors, *ib.*—its probable connexion with the court of star-chamber, 52—authority of, over parliament, 55—illegal committments of the, under Elizabeth, 234—power of its proclamations considered, 236—all matters of state formerly resolved in, 348 and *note*—its power of imprisoning, 383 and *note* r—commission for enabling it to interfere with courts of justice, ii. 9, *note* n—without power to tax the realm, 21—of Ireland, filled with catholics by James II., iii. 398.

Privy-seal, letter of, for borrowing money, i. 244, 245 and *notes* u s, 381.

Proceedings against Shaftesbury and College, ii. 448 and *note* c.

Proclamation of Henry VII., controlling the subject's right of doing all things not unlawful, i. 4—of the sovereign in council, authority attached to, 237—unwarranted power of some of those under Elizabeth, 236, 238—of martial law against libels, &c., 241—of James I. for conformity, 298—for summoning his first parliament, 299—house of commons' complaint against, 327—debate of judges, &c. on, 335—illegality of, *ib.* and *note* q—issued under Charles I., ii. 24, 25.

Projects of lord William Russell and colonel Sidney, ii. 455.

Prophesyings, religious exercises so called, i. 197—suppression of, *ib.*—tolerated by some prelates, *ib.*

Propositions (the nineteen), offered to Charles I. at York, ii. 137 and *note* y.

Protestants, origin of the name, i. 95, *note* b—number of, executed under queen Mary, 105, *note* f—increased by her persecution, 106—never approved of religious persecution, 122, *note* d—faith, league of the catholic princes against the, 136, *note* k—origin of the differences between, 170—emigration of, to Germany, 171—dislike of, to the English liturgy and ceremonies, 171-175 and *notes*—proportion of, in England, under Elizabeth, 176, *note* t—

PROTESTANTISM.

favour Arabella Stuart's claim on the crown, 287, *note* b—dissenters, bill to relieve, lost off the table of the house of lords, iii. 171—succession in danger, 221, *note* k, 222—church established by Elizabeth in Ireland, 367—many of the wealthier families conform to the, 403.

Protestantism, dissolution of the monasteries essential to its establishment, i. 74—strengthened by the distribution of their revenues, &c., 79—slow progress of, in the north of England, 92.

Protestation of the house of commons against adjournment in 1621, i. 367.

Prynne (William), prosecution of, by the star-chamber, ii. 37 and *note* d, 38.

Pulteney (Mr.), his remark on the standing army, iii. 260, 261.

Purgatory, doctrine of, abolished by the reformers, i. 87.

Puritans address Elizabeth against the queen of Scots, i. 138—laws of Elizabeth respecting, i. chap. iv. 170-228—rapid increase of, under Elizabeth, 179—begin to form conventicles, 181—advised not to separate, *ib.*, *note* a—first instance of their prosecution, 182—supporters and opposers of, in the church and state, *ib.*—their opposition to civil authority in the church, 185 — not all opposed to the royal supremacy, 189 and *note* q—predominance of, under Elizabeth, *ib.* and *note* r—prosecuted by the prelates, 194—partly supported by the privy council, *ib.*—tolerated to preserve the protestant religion, 196—deprived by archbishop Whitgift, 200 and *note* b—lord Burleigh favourable to, 202—libels published by, 205, 206 and *notes* a b c—their church government set up, 207—dangerous extent of their doctrines, 208—their sentiments on civil government, *ib.*—severe statute against, 213—state of their controversy with the church under Elizabeth, 214, *note* j—object to the title of bishops, 224, *note* o — Elizabeth's reported offer to, 226, *note* o—civil liberty preserved by the, 230—their expectations on the accession of James I., 297, *note* u—summoned to a conference at Hampton Court, *ib.*—alarmed at the king's proceedings, 303—ministers of the, deprived by archbishop Bancroft, 394 and *note* k—character of the, 395—difference with the sabbatarians, 397 — doctrinal puritans, *ib.* and *note* o.

Purveyance, abuses of, i. 304—proceedings of parliament against, *ib.*; ii. 313—taken away, 99.

Pyrenees, treaty of the, ii. 279.

Quartering of soldiers (compulsory), treason of, ii. 107.

REFORMERS.

Raleigh (sir Walter), instances of his flattery of monarchy, i. 277 and *note* q—his execution, character, and probable guilt considered, 354 and *notes* h i—his first success in the Munster colonies, iii. 379.

Ranke's 'History of the Popes,' notice of, i. 119, *note* x.

Reading, a Romish attorney, trial of, ii. 426.

Real presence denied in the articles of the church of England, i. 91—the term not found in the writers of the 16th age, except in the sense of "corporal," ii. 63, *note* e.

Rebellion (northern), excited by the harsh innovations of Henry VIII.; appeased by conciliatory measures, but made a pretext for several executions of persons of rank, i. 28—in Ireland, in 1641, iii. 382, 391—success of the insurgents in the, 393—of 1690, forfeitures on account of the, 400.

Recovery (common), for cutting off the entail of estates, its origin and establishment, i. 12.

Recusancy, persecutions for, under Elizabeth, i. 118—heavy penalties on, under Elizabeth, 144, 145—annual fines paid for, 154, *note* b.

Recusants, severity against, productive of hypocrites, i. 153 — annual fines paid by, 154, *note* b—statute restraining their residence, 163—penalties upon, under James I., 405, *note* e, 406, *note* g.

Reed (alderman Richard), his treatment for refusing to contribute to the benevolence in 1545, i. 25.

Reeves (John), his History of English Law, character of, i. 13, *note* s.

Reformation of the church gradually prepared and effected, i. 57—disposition of the people for a, 68—uncertain advance of the, after the separation from Rome and dissolution of monasteries, 81—spread of, in England, 82—promoted by translating the Scriptures, 83, 84—principal innovations of the, in the church of England, 88-92—chiefly in towns and eastern counties of England, 92—German troops brought over at the time of, 93, *note* d—measures of, under Edward VI., too zealously conducted, 94—toleration not considered practicable in the, 95—in Germany, caused by vices of the superior ecclesiastics, 99—its actual progress under Edward VI., 103.

Reformatio Legum Ecclesiasticûm, account of the compilation and canons of, i. 101, *note* u—extract from, 102, *note.*

Reformers, their predilection for satirical libels, i. 205—for the Mosaic polity, 208, *note* g—of Scotland, their extreme moderation, iii. 315 and *note* o.

REFUGEES.

Refugees, popish, their exertions against Elizabeth, i. 137, 143.
Regalities of Scotland, their power, iii. 311.
Regicides, execution of the, ii. 308—some saved from capital punishment, 325.
Religion, reformation of, gradually prepared and effected, i. 57—state of, in England, at the beginning of the sixteenth century, 58—different restraints of governments on, 94—Roman catholic, abolished in Scotland, iii. 313.
Religious toleration, iii. 170—infringement of, 248.
Remonstrance on the state of the kingdom under Charles I., ii. 122 and note u.
Republican party, first decisive proof of a, ii. 219 — composed of two parties, levellers and anabaptists, 240—government by, ill-suited to the English in 1659, 274—no, in the reign of William III., iii. 120, 121.
Reresby (sir John), his conversation with lord Halifax, ii. 446 and note u.
Restitution of crown and church lands, ii. 309.
Restoration of Charles II., remarks on the unconditional, ii. 293—popular joy at the, 303—chiefly owing to the presbyterians, 324.
Revenue, settlement of the, iii. 115—statement of the, by Ralph, ib. note r—surplus, in Ireland, dispute between the commons and the government concerning its appropriation, 408.
Revolution in 1688, its true basis, iii. 63—its justice and necessity, 83—argument against it, 84—favourable circumstances attending the, 88, 89—salutary consequences resulting from the, 91—its great advantage, 92—its temperate accomplishment, 107 — in Scotland, and establishment of presbytery, 331.
Reynolds (Dr.), at the Hampton Court conference, i. 297, note w.
Richard II., statute of, restraining the papal authority, i. 64—supply raised under, ii. 20—his invasion of Ireland, iii. 358.
Richard III., first passed the statute of fines, i. 11.
Richelieu (cardinal, Armand du Plessis), his intrigues against England, ii. 15, note e.
Richmond (Charles Stuart, duke of), his marriage with Miss Stewart, ii. 363.
Richmond Park extended, ii. 11, note t.
Ridley (Nicholas, bishop of London), liberality of, to the princess Mary, i. 95—assists in remodelling the English church, 97, note p—firmness of, in the cause of lady Jane Grey, 99—moderation in the measures of reform, ib.

SALISBURY.

Right of the commons as to money bills i. 276, iii. 27.
Robbers and murderers deprived of the benefit of clergy, i. 58.
Rochester (Laur. Hyde, lord), his dismissal, iii. 65, 66 and note t—creates great alarm, ib. and note b.
Rockingham Forest increased, ii. 11.
Rockisane (archbishop of Prague), his reply to cardinal Carjaval at the council of Basle, i. 192, note u.
Rockwood (——), persecution of, for popery, i. 142, note d.
Roman catholic prelates of Scotland, including the regulars, allowed two thirds of their revenues, iii. 315.
Romish priests, address to the king to send them out of the kingdom, ii. 347, 348 and note x—their policy, 388—superstition, general abhorrence of the, iii. 55.
Root and branch party, ii. 116.
Ross (Thomas), executed for publishing at Oxford a blasphemous libel, iii. 325.
Royal families of Ireland (O'Neal, O'Connor, O'Brien, O'Malachlin, and Mac Murrough), protected by the English law, iii. 352.
Royal power, its constitutional boundaries well established, iii. 1.
Royalists, decimation of the, by Cromwell, ii. 252 and note t—discontent of the, 310, 311 and note x.
Rump, the parliament commonly so called, ii. 238 and note d—fanatical hatred of, to the king, ib.
Rupert (prince), Bristol taken by, ii. 161—and Newcastle defeated at Marston Moor, 168—consequences of the same, ib.
Russel (Admiral), engaged in intrigues, iii. 125, 126—his conduct at the battle of La Hogue, and quarrel with the board of admiralty, ib.—parliamentary inquiry into their dispute, 144.
Russell (lord), sincerely patriotic in his clandestine intercourse with France, ii. 405 and note q—and the earl of Essex concert measures for a resistance to the government, 456—they recede from the councils of Shaftesbury, ib.—evidence on his trial not sufficient to justify his conviction, 457 and note r.
Rye-house plot, ii. 423 and note s.
Ryswick (treaty of), particulars relating to, iii. 137, 138.

Sabbatarians, origin and tenets of, i. 397 and note o.
Salisbury (countess of), her execution, causes of, i. 29—not heard in her defence, 30, note k.
Salisbury (Robert Cecil, earl of), exteriates the wrongs imputed to Spain, i. 314—his scheme for procuring an annual revenue from the commons, 330—

SAMPSON.

his death and character, 332, 333 and *notes* ᵐ ⁿ.—(William Cecil, earl of), his forest amerciament, ii. 11.
Sampson, the puritan, his remonstrance against the papists, i. 140.
Sancroft (Thomas, archbishop of Canterbury), his scheme of comprehension, iii. 172.
Sandys (sir Edwin), his commitment to the Tower, i. 363, 364 and *note* l, 372.
Savoy, conference at the, in 1661, ii. 336 —animosity between the parties, 337 —conduct of the churchmen not justifiable, *ib.* and *note* ᵃ—only productive of a more exasperated disunion, *ib.*— general remarks on, *ib.* 338.
Sawyer (sir Robert), expelled from the house of commons, iii. 113 and *notes* ᵒ ᴾ.
Scambler (Edmund, bishop of Norwich), his character, i. 225.
Scandinavia, colonists from, settle on the coasts of Ireland, iii. 343.
Scheme of comprehension and indulgence, ii. 374—observations on the, iii. 173.
Schism in the constitutional party under Charles I., ii. 120 and *notes* ˢ ᵗ—of the nonjurors, iii. 174-176.
Schools (free), in Ireland, act passed in the reign of Elizabeth for erecting, iii. 375, *note* k.
Scotland, uncertain succession of the English crown in the royal family of, i. 123, 161—its claims not favoured, 129—puritanical church government established in, 209—union with England brought forward, 309-311 and *notes* ᵘ ˣ ʸ ᶻ—troubles commenced in, ii. 84, 85 and *note* b—privy council of, abolished, iii. 203 and *note* b—its early state wholly Celtic before the twelfth century, 305—its want of records, 306 —its wealth, 312—character of its history from the Reformation, 314— church of, still preserves the forms of the sixteenth century, 315, 334—establishment of episcopacy in, 320— could not remain indifferent during the civil war in England, 326—crown of, tendered to William and Mary, 332— episcopal and presbyterian, chief controversy between, 333 — practice observed in summoning the national assembly of the, 334, 335 and *note* l— assemblies of the, judicious admixture of laymen in, *ib.*
Scots, the, conduct of, to Charles I., ii. 194, 195, and *notes* ᵐ ⁿ ᵒ—conclude a treaty with Charles, and invade England, 214.
Scots presbyterians sincerely attached to king Charles, ii. 203 and *note* l.
Scot and lot boroughs, very opposite species of franchise in, iii. 43 and *note* ᵒ.
Scripture, English translation of pro-

SHEFFIELD.

scribed, i. 83—permitted to be read, and prohibited, *ib.* and *note* ᵃ—effect of their general use, *ib.*
Scroggs (chief justice), impeached for treason, ii. 447.
Scudamore (lord), anecdote of, ii. 65 and *note* k.
Seal, great, lord keeper Littleton carries it to the king, ii. 161—new one ordered to be made by the parliament, 162.
Seats in parliament, sale of, iii. 303.
Secret corruption, iii. 265.
Secret historical documents brought to light by Macpherson and Dalrymple, iii. 123.
Secret-service money disposed of to corrupt the parliament, iii. 189 and *note* ᵍ.
Secret treaty of 1670, anecdotes and particulars relating to, ii. 382 and *note* ᵠ— differences between Charles and Louis as to the mode of its execution, 383, 384.
Sectaries, persecution or toleration the only means of dealing with, i. 205.
Selden (John), summoned before the starchamber, i. 350.
Septs of the north of Ireland, liberty enjoyed by, iii. 352—of Munster and Leinster, their oppression, *ib.*—offers made by some for permission to live under the English law, 353.
Serjeant of the house of commons, authority of the, i. 268-272.
Session, court of, of Scotland, its origin and judicature, iii. 312.
Settlement, act of, rights of the reigning monarch emanate from the parliament and people, by the, iii. 92—Blackstone's view of, 181, *note* ᶠ.
Settlement of the revenue, ii. 311.
Seymour (lord), of Sudeley, courts the favour of the young king, Edward VI., i. 38—entertains a hope of marrying princess Elizabeth, 39—accused of treason, and not heard in his defence, *ib.*— warrant for his execution signed by his brother, *ib.*
Seymour (William, marquis of Hertford), married to lady Arabella Stuart, i. 351.
Seymour (sir Francis), his refusal to pay ship-money, ii. 86 and *note* P.
Shaftesbury (Anthony, third earl of), declaration of indulgence projected by, ii. 390—fall of, and his party, 395— bad principles of, 433—desperate counsels of, 456—committed to the Tower with three other peers, by the lords for calling in question the legal continuance of parliament, after a prorogation of twelve months, iii. 281.
Shaftesbury and College, impeachment of, ii. 448-450 and *notes* ᵈ ᵉ ᶠ ᵍ.
Sharp (James), archbishop of St. Andrew's, an infamous apostate and persecutor iii. 329.
Sheffield (sir Robert), confined in the

SHELLEY.

Tower for his complaint against Wolsey, i. 54, *note* k.
Shelley (sir Richard), reluctantly permitted to enjoy his religion, i. 141.
Shepherd (Mr.), expelled the house of commons, i. 400.
Sherfield (——), recorder of Salisbury, star-chamber prosecution of, ii. 65, *note* k.
Sherlock (Dr.), his work entitled *Case of Resistance to the Supreme Powers*, ii. 463 and *note* e—his Inconsistency, iii. 108, *note* h—a pamphlet, entitled *A Second Letter to a Friend*, attributed to him, *ib*.
Ship-money, its origin and imposition, ii. 12—extended to the whole kingdom, 15—trials concerning, 16-18 and *notes* i k m—case of Hampden, 17 and *note* k—the king's proposal of resigning for a supply, 90, *note* b—declared illegal, 97.
Shirley (sir Thomas), parliamentary proceedings on his arrest, i. 302.
Shirley (Dr.), and sir John Fagg, case between, iii. 25.
Shower, infamous address of the barristers of the Middle Temple under the direction of, iii. 72.
Shrewsbury (earl of), engaged in intrigues, iii. 125—his letter to king William after Fenwick's accusation of him, 126 and *note* m.
Shrewsbury (lady), fine and imprisonment of, i. 351.
Sibthorp (——), his assertion of kingly power, i. 417.
Sidney (sir Philip), writes a remonstrance against Elizabeth's match with the duke of Anjou, i. 232.
Sidney (Algernon), receives pecuniary gratifications from France, ii. 406—was a distressed man, 408—his dislike to the prince of Orange, *ib*.—his conviction illegally obtained, 459 and *note* z—observations on his character and conduct, 460.
Sidney (sir Henry), his representation to queen Elizabeth of the wretched condition of the Irish, iii. 370 and *note* u—his second government in Ireland excites resistance by an attempt to subvert the liberties of the pale, 373—his disappointment at the want of firmness in queen Elizabeth, 374, *note* h—account of the protestant church in Ireland, 375, *note* k.
Silenced preachers set at liberty, i. 180, *note* y.
Six articles, law of, on the celibacy of priests, i. 91.
Skinner (Thomas), case of, against the East India Company, iii. 21—committed by the commons for breach of privilege, 23.
Smith (sir Thomas), his Treatise on the Commonwealth of England, cited concerning the star-chamber, i. 49—his account of causes belonging to the court of star-chamber, 53—his natural son sent with a body of English to settle in Ireland, iii. 379.

SPIES.

Soap, chartered company for making, ii. 11.
Somers (lord chancellor), puts the great seal to blank powers, iii. 146, 147 and *notes* e f.
Somers, Halifax, Wharton, Oxford, and Sunderland, kept out of administration by the dislike of queen Anne, iii. 209.
Somerset (Edward Seymour), duke of, obtains a patent constituting him protector; discovers a rival in his brother, lord Seymour; signs his warrant for execution, i. 39—deprived of his authority, 40—accused of a conspiracy to murder some of the privy councillors, *ib*.—evidence not insufficient, *ib*.—inclined to the Reformation, and powerful in the council, 85—his destruction of churches to erect his palace, 94—designed the demolition of Westminster Abbey, *ib*.—his liberality to the princess Mary, 95, *note* k.
Somerset (Robert Car, earl of), his guilt of the murder of Overbury examined, i. 352, 353 and *note* g.
Somerville, executed for a plot against Elizabeth, i. 155.
Southampton (Thomas Wriothesley, earl of), his estate in the New Forest seized, ii. 10—his opposition to the statute against nonconformists, 350.
Southey (Robert), his assertion on persecution and toleration in the church of England, i. 122, *note* d.
Sovereigns, their inviolability to criminal process examined, i. 159, 160—their power weakened by the distinction of party, iii. 294.
Spain, design of transferring England to the yoke of, i. 46—dislike of the English to, under queen Mary, 105—king James's partiality for, 313 and *notes* d e—connexion with England under James I., 333—his unhappy predilection for, 355 and *note* m—treaty of royal marriage with, 365, 369—policy of Charles I. with, ii. 15 and *notes* d e—decline of the power of, after the treaty of the Pyrenees, 376.
Speaker of the house of commons, power of, concerning bills, i. 263, *note*.
Speech, freedom of, in parliament, ii. 4.
Speed (John), his valuation of the suppressed monasteries, i. 76, *note* d.
Spenser (Edmund), his *Account of Ireland*, iii. 371, *note* a, 379—the first three books of his *Faery Queen*, where written, *ib*.
Spies should be heard with suspicion in cases of treason, iii. 164.

SPIRE.

Spire, protestation of, by the Lutheran princes against mass, i. 95, note b.
Sports, declaration of, by James I., i. 399—by Charles I., ii. 56.
Sprot, a notary, executed in Scotland for concealing letters, iii. 325.
Stafford (William Howard, lord), convicted of the popish plot, ii. 428 and note k.
Standing army, without consent of parliament, declared illegal, iii. 105, 106 and note f—national repugnance to its rise, 260, 261.
Standish (Dr. ——), denies the divine privileges of the clergy, i. 58—censured in the Journals, 7 Hen. VIII., 59, note a.
St. Bartholomew (day of), 2000 persons resign their preferments, ii. 341.
St. Germain's (court of), preserve a secret connexion with Godolphin and Marlborough, iii. 220, 221.
St. John (Oliver), declines to contribute to the benevolences, i. 342—his statement of means for defence of the royal prerogative, ii. 18, 19.
St. John's College, Cambridge, nonconformists of, in 1565, i. 185, note i.
St. Paul's Cathedral, proposed improvement of, ii. 27.
St. Phelipe, remarkable passage in his Memoirs, iii. 212, note e.
Star-chamber, court of, the same as the ancient *Concilium Regis*, or *Ordinarium*, i. 50 and note g—account of the powers of, 51—augmented by cardinal Wolsey, 52—original limitation and judges of the, 54 and note m—causes within the cognizance of the, *ib.*—its arbitrary and illegal powers, 55—not the court erected by Henry VII., *ib.* note o—examination of papists in the, 120—security of the, 230—power of, 233—instances of its extended authority, 349—informations in the, against London, ii. 27—jurisdiction of the, 29-33—caution of, in cases of inheritance, 31—offences belonging to, *ib.*—mode of process in the, 33—punishments inflicted by the, 33, 34 and notes u v—fines and sentences of the, 35—corrupt and partial, 36, note y—act for abolishing, 97 and 98, note o—attempt to revive the, 333—report of committee of the lords concerning the, *ib.*
State, council of, consists of forty-one members, ii. 235—tests proposed to the, to which only nineteen subscribed, *ib.*
Stationers, company of, power given to, over printers and booksellers, i. 239.
Statute of the 15th of Edward II., recognising the existence of the present constitution of parliament, i. 3—of 11th Henry VII. protecting persons in the king's service, 9—extraordinary,

STATUTE.

giving to Henry VIII. all moneys paid by way of loan, &c., 23—similar act releasing to him all moneys he had subsequently borrowed, 24—11th Henry VII. for payment of arrears of benevolences, 14 and note i—of fines enacted by Henry VII. merely a transcript from one of Richard III., 11—object of this enactment, *ib.*—of Edward I. *de donis conditionalibus*, 12—revived under Henry VII., and their penalties enforced, 15—of 1st Henry VIII. for amendment of escheats, 16—of 11th Henry VII. giving power to justices of the peace, *ib.*—for the exclusion of princess Mary from the succession in 1534, 34—of Henry VII. concerning the court of star-chamber, 53-55, and notes m o—of Henry VI. for compelling clerks to plead their privilege, 58—of 4th Henry VII. for branding clerks convicted of felony, *ib.*—of Richard II. restraining the papal jurisdiction, 64—of Henry VIII. taking away appeals to Rome, 66—of ditto on the consecration of bishops, *ib.*—of mortmain of Edward I. and III., 69—of 27th Henry VIII. censures the vices of monasteries, 72, note z—of Henry VIII., 1st Edward VI., 14th Elizabeth, for support of the poor, 80 and note l—of 34th Henry VIII. against the sale and reading of Tindal's Bible, 83 and note a—of 2nd, 3rd, and 6th of Edward VI. on the celibacy of priests, 92—of 2nd Edward VI. against irreverently speaking of the sacrament, 93—for abolishing chantries, 94 and note l—of 2nd and 3rd Edward VI. against hearing mass, 95—of 25th Henry VIII. against importation of foreign books, 82, note m—of supremacy and uniformity, 1st of Elizabeth, 112—of 5th Elizabeth against fantastical prophecies, 115, note n—for the assurance of the queen's power, 116—opposed by Mr. Atkinson and lord Montagu, *ib.*—arguments for it, 117, note q—of 8th of Elizabeth on behalf of the bishops, 118 and note t—of 28th and 35th Henry VIII. on the succession, 122—of 13th of Elizabeth on altering the succession, 129—13th Elizabeth against papists, 137, 149 and note—of 23rd ditto against recusancy, 145—of 25th Edward III. against treason, 146—of Elizabeth, commanding papists to depart the kingdom, 153—of 27th Elizabeth for her security, 157—of 33rd Elizabeth restricting the residence of popish recusants, 163—of 13th Elizabeth for subscribing church articles, 192—of 23rd Elizabeth against seditious books of seminary priests, wrested against the puritan libels, 206, 214—of 35th Elizabeth for imprisoning nonconformists

STATUTE.

214—of 1st of Elizabeth, restraining the grant of ecclesiastical lands, 224—of 14th Elizabeth on recusants, 244, note—of *Confirmatio Chartarum* and *Magna Charta*, 315—of 45th Edward III. against new customs, 319, 320—of 34th Henry VIII. for court of council of Wales, 328, note d—of 34th of Henry VIII. on making laws for Wales, 339, 340—of 2nd and 3rd Edward VI. for preserving Lent, 398, note—of 5th, 27th, and 35th of Elizabeth, for increase of the fishery, *ib.*—of 1st and 3rd Charles I. for observance of Sunday, 400, note s—of 1st Edward II., *De Militibus*, ii. 10, note o—of 4th Edward III. for holding parliaments, 95, 96 and note a—of 16th Charles I. for abolishing court of star-chamber, &c., 98, 99 and notes e f—for determining forests, restraining purveyance, amending the stannary courts, levying troops, 99, 100—of 1st and 25th of Edward III., and 4th Henry IV., amending military service, 130 — of Winchester, for defence of the nation, 132—of 1st James I. on furnishing soldiers, 133, note p—of Edward IV., constructive interpretation of, by chief justice Eyre, iii. 165 —of leasing-making in Scotland, 324— English, question on their validity in Ireland, 405.

Statute of Kilkenny, its influence on the government of Ireland, iii. 357, note s.

Statutes, Irish, account of the, iii. 356— English, extended to Ireland, 362 and note g.

Stawell, a gentleman of Devonshire, refuses compliance to the speaker's warrant, ii. 445.

Steele (sir Richard), expelled the house of commons for writing a pamphlet reflecting on the ministry, iii. 268.

Stephens (Rev. Mr.), justice Powell's observations in passing sentence on him for a libel on ministers, iii. 167, note e.

Stewart (Miss), her marriage with the duke of Richmond, ii. 363 and note e.

Stone (primate of Ireland), his great share in the government of Ireland in the reign of George II., iii. 404.

Storie (John), his committal by authority of parliament, i. 271.

Stow (John), his library seized, i. 238.

Strafford (Thomas Wentworth earl of), character of, ii. 41 and note k—made president of the council of the north, 42—lord-deputy of Ireland, 44—his correspondence with archbishop Laud, 45-48 and notes—his sentiments and practice on ship-money, 51—advice to Charles I. against war with Spain, 52 —his sentiments and use of parliaments, 53, 54—summary of his conduct, &c., *ib.*, 55 and note a—his im-

SUNDAY.

peachment, 103 and note p—its justice discussed, 105-112 and notes—his able government of Ireland, iii. 385, 386 and notes b c—procures six subsidies, 386.

Strangers amenable to law wherever they dwell, i. 160.

Strickland (Mr.), his attack on the abuses of the church of England, i. 190—taken from his seat in the house of commons, 253—restored to it, 254.

Strongbow (earl), his acquisitions in Ireland, iii. 348, 349 — his possessions divided among his five sisters, 351.

Stuart (Arabella), her title to the English crown, i. 287 and note b—her unhappy life and persecutions, 350, 351 and note d.

Stuart (house of), want of legal title to the crown, i. 288, 289 and note d.

Stuart, Henry VII., Henry VIII., Elizabeth, and the four kings of the house of, master-movers of their own policy, iii. 292.

Stuart papers in the hands of George IV., iii. 253, note p.

Stubbe, his pamphlet against Elizabeth's marriage with the duke of Anjou, i. 232, 233.

Subsidies, popular aversion to, i. 13— grant of, in 1588, 261—in 1593-1601, 263, 264—less frequent in Scotland than in England, iii. 310.

Subsidy, value of, examined, i. 370, note a.

Succession, difficulties in regard to the, created by Henry's two divorces, i. 34—princesses Mary and Elizabeth, nominated in the entail after the king's male issue; crown devised to the heirs of Mary, duchess of Suffolk, to the exclusion of the royal family of Scotland, *ib.*

Suffolk (Frances Brandon, duchess of), emigrates on account of her religion, i. 103, note b.

Suffolk (family of Brandon, duke of), succession of the crown settled in, i. 123, 129, 285—title of, nearly defeated by Elizabeth, 127—descendants of, living at the death of Elizabeth, 290, 293—present representatives of their claim, *ib.*, note a.

Suffolk (Edmund de la Pole, earl of), conspires against Henry VII., attainted, flies to the Netherlands, given up by the archduke Philip on condition of safety: Henry VIII. causes him to be executed, i. 26.

Suffolk, county of, assists in placing Mary on the throne, and suffers greatly from her persecution, i. 103 and note s.

Sully (duc de), wears mourning for Elizabeth at the court of James I., i. 296, note e.

Sunday, differences on the observance of, i. 397 and note o—statutes for, 400 and note e.

INDEX. 451

SUNDERLAND.

Sunderland (Robert Spencer, earl of), early mention of his inclination to adopt the catholic religion, ii. 387—his intentions, iii. 59, note ᵗ—enters into secret negotiation with the prince of Orange, 70—reproached for his conduct in the peerage bill, 238.

Supply to the crown, ancient mode of, iii. 27—the commons are the granting and the lords the consenting power, 28—present practice of, 29.

Supplies, origin of the estimates of, ii. 357—remarks on the appropriation of, iii. 116, 117.

Supremacy of the church given to Henry VIII., i. 66—difficulty of repealing the act of, under queen Mary, 104—restored to the crown under Elizabeth, 111—character and power of the act of, 112—oath of, ib., 43.—penalty for refusing, ib.—lord Burleigh's memorial on the oath of, 151—act of, links the church with the temporal constitution, 170—the sovereign's, rejected by Cartwright and the puritans, 185—acknowledged by some of the puritans, 209—executions for denial of, 215, note ⁿ—act of resistance of the Irish to it, iii. 365—oath of, catholics murmur at the, 377, note ⁿ.—imposed on the commons by the 5th of Elizabeth, never adopted by the Irish parliament, 401—resolution of commons of Ireland to exclude those who would not take the oath of the, 402.

Surrey (Thomas Howard, earl of), futile charges against, of the crime of quartering the royal arms, i. 31—ignominious behaviour of his father, ib.

Sussex (Henry Ratcliffe, earl of), writes to the burgesses of Yarmouth and others, requesting them to vote for the person he should name, i. 46.

Sussex (Thomas Ratcliffe, earl of), his letter concerning the imprisonment of Mary Stuart, i. 132, note ʸ.

Sweden (king of), leagues with the pretender, iii. 241.

Swift (Dr. Jonathan), employed by government to retaliate on libellers, iii. 168.

Talbot (lord chancellor), bill to prevent smuggling strongly opposed by him, iii. 290—his arguments against it, ib.

Tanistry, law of, defined, iii. 344—strong inducement of the native Irish to preserve the, 353—custom of, determined to be void, 377.

Tax upon property in the reign of Henry VIII., mode of its assessment, i. 19, note ᵗ—discontents excited by it, 21—opposed tumultuously, and finally abandoned, ib.

Taxation under Henry VIII., mode of, i.

TORTURES.

13—arbitrary, under the two Henries 25.

Taxation, arbitrary, restrained by the Petition of Right, i. 392; ii. 21.

Taxations not attempted by Elizabeth, i. 244, note ᵗ.

Taxes not to be levied in England without consent of parliament, i. 315—larger in amount in the reign of Charles II. than at any former period, ii. 353.

Temple (sir John), his relation of the number of protestants massacred in Ireland, iii. 391, note ᵒ—his *History of the Irish Rebellion* unjustly depreciated, 393, note ᵠ.

Temple (sir William), his views of government, ii. 378, note ⁿ—new council formed by, 439, 440 and notes ᵉ ᶠ ᵍ.

Tenancy from year to year, of very recent introduction, iii. 43.

Tenison, archbishop, extract from his speech on the union, iii. 340, note ⁿ.

Test act, dissenters give their support to the, ii. 393-395 and notes ʸ ᶻ ᵃ ᵇ.

Testament, New, 1526, translated into English, and proscribed, i. 83.

Thompson (Richard), taken into custody for preaching virulent sermons at Bristol, and impeached upon strange charges, ii. 445.

Thorough, a phrase used by archbishop Laud and the earl of Strafford to express their system of government, ii. 45 *et seq.*

Thurloe, John, letter from, to Henry Cromwell, ii. 269, note ᵇ.

Tindal (William), his translations of the Scriptures, i. 83 and note ⁿ.

Tithes, subsisted during the commonwealth, ii. 315.

Toleration, ancient avowal of the principle of, i. 122, note ᵈ—religious, iii. 170, 171, note ˣ—act, a measure of religious liberty, 172—no part of the, extended to papists or such as deny the Trinity, ib.—anti-toleration statutes repealed by the whigs, 249—natural right of the Irish, 376.

Tom Tell-truth, a libel against James I., i. 370, note ʸ.

Tonnage and poundage, granted to Henry VIII. by his first parliament, mistaken assertion of Hume and Lingard respecting it, i. 19, note ʳ—the king's right to, disputed, 392—declaration in the act for, 393.

Topcliffe (———), his persecution of papists under Elizabeth, i. 142, note ᵈ.

Topham (serjeant at arms), actions brought against him for false imprisonment, iii. 281.

Torture, use of, denied by the judges, ii. 8—instances of, in England, ib. note ⁱ—strictures on Mr. Jardine's views of this subject, ib.

Tortures, used under the horse of Tudor,

2 G 2

TORY.

i. 148 and *note* ʳ—under Elizabeth, denied by Lord Burleigh, 150.
Tory principles of the clergy, ii. 462—firmly adhere to the established religion, *ib.*—party, their rage against the queen and lord Oxford for retaining whigs, iii. 230, *note* ᵇ—ministry annoyed by the vivacity of the press, 298.
Tories, their inconsistency, iii. 203—111 received at court, and excluded from office, 209.
Toryism, its real character, ii. 442—cardinal maxim of, *ib.*
Tower of London, historical associations connected with the, i. 148.
Towns, chartered, their jurisdiction, i. 7.
Tracts, political, extraordinary number published from the meeting of the long parliament, iii. 2.
Trade, foreign, proclamations of Elizabeth restricting, i. 237—the king's prerogative of restraining, 316, *note* ᵍ—project for a council of, iii. 145.
Transubstantiation, persecutions concerning, i. 82, 92—metaphysical examination of, 89, 90—modern Romish doctrine of, *ib. note.*
Treason, consideration of the law of, as applied to the papists under Elizabeth, i. 165, *note*—trials for, unjustly conducted under Elizabeth, 231—perversions of the law of, under James I., 344, *note* ᑫ—law of, iii. 148—statute of Edward III., 150—its constructive interpretation and material omission, 151—various strained constructions of the, 152, 153—statute of William III., 159—prosecutions for, under Charles II., disgraceful to government, 160—Scots law of, its severity and odium, 324, 325.
Treasury, reduced state of the, in 1639, ii. 84-86 and *notes.*
Treaty begun at Oxford, ii. 154—pretended, signed with France, secret between Charles II. and Louis XIV., 409—of peace broken off and renewed by the tory government, iii. 213.
Treaties of partition, two, iii. 145—impeachment of four lords on account of the, 146.
Treating at elections, origin of, iii. 302, *note* ᵏ.
Treby (chief justice), his conduct in the case of Anderton, iii. 161.
Trial by jury, its ancient establishment, i. 6, *note* ᵇ.
Trials for treason, &c., unjustly conducted under Elizabeth, i. 231—of Russell and Sidney, ii. 457.
Triennial bill, its constitution and privileges, ii. 95, 96 and *note* ⁿ—act, repeal of, 330—and of the act for its repeal, 331.
Trinity, denial of the, or of the inspira-

UXBRIDGE.

tion of any book of the Bible, made felony, ii. 201, *note.*
Triple alliance, public satisfaction at the, ii. 375.
Trust estates, view of the laws relating to, i. 344, 345.
Tudor, house of, difficulty experienced by, in raising supplies, i. 13—one of the most important constitutional provisions of, 40—strengthened by Mary, *ib.*
Tudors, military levies under the, ii. 133, 134.
Tunstal (Cuthbert), bishop of Durham, liberally entertained by Parker, i. 118, *note* ˢ.
Tutchin (John), law laid down by Holt in the case of, iii. 167.
Tyrconnel (earl of), charged with conspiracy, and attainted of treason, iii. 380—lord-lieutenant of Ireland in 1687, his secret overtures with the French agents, 398.
Tyrone (earl of), charged with conspiracy and attainted of treason, iii. 380.
Tyrrel (Anthony), an informer against papists, i. 154, *note* ᵃ.

Udal (——), tried and imprisoned for a libel on the bishops, i. 206 and *note* ᶜ, 232.
Ulster, the most enlightened part of Ireland, iii. 380—the colonisation of, first carried into effect by sir Arthur Chichester in the reign of James I., *ib.*—linen manufacture first established by Strafford, 388.
Undertakers, agents between the king and the parliament so called, i. 339, 356, *note* ᵒ.
Uniformity, act of, passed under Elizabeth, i. 111 and *note* ᵒ—its character and extent, 112—links the church with the temporal constitution, 170.
Union of the two crowns, sovereign and court withdrawn by, from Scotland, iii. 337—general observations on the same, *ib.*-340.
Universities, foreign, bribed on the subject of Henry VIII.'s divorce, i. 61, *note* ᶠ—difficulty of procuring the judgment of Oxford and Cambridge against the marriage, 67.
Usher (James), archbishop of Armagh, his scheme for a moderate episcopacy, ii. 115 and *note* ᶠ—model of church government, 319 and *notes* ᵒ ᴾ—scheme of church government not inconvenient or impracticable, 335.
Utrecht, treaty of, arguments for and against the, iii. 214-219—negotiations mismanaged, 219—advantages lost by the, *ib.*—misconduct of lords Bolingbroke and Oxford in the management of it, *ib., note* ᵍ.
Uxbridge, negotiations at, ii. 171, 172 and *note* ᵐ—rupture of the, 177.

INDEX. 453

VAGABONDS.

Vagabonds, act of state against, under Elizabeth, i. 242.
Vane (sir Henry), his message to the commons, 1640, ii. 90—and general Lambert, excepted from act of indemnity, 325—injustice of his condemnation, 326, 327 and note f—execution and character, 327, 328—his communication to the lords justices relating to the connexion between Spain and the disaffected Irish, iii. 390, note m.
Vaughan (chief justice), his argument with regard to the power of juries, iii. 9.
Venner, insurrection of in 1660, ii. 314.
Verdict, general, question of the right of juries to return a, discussed, iii. 8, 9.
Vestments of priests retained in England, i. 102—dislike of the German reformers to, ib.
Vintners' company fined by the starchamber, ii. 35, 36 and note y.
Visitations of monasteries, character and truth of, i. 72.
Vote of parliament, to prevent the meeting of caballing officers, ii. 271 and note i—the parliament dissolved in consequence, 272 and note k.
Vowell's Treatise on the Order of Parliament, extract from, iii. 44, note d.

Waldegrave (sir Edward), and his lady imprisoned for hearing mass, i. 114.
Wales, court of the council of, its jurisdiction, i. 323 and note d—court and council abolished, ii. 99—right of election extended to, by Henry VIII., iii. 38.
Waller's plot, ii. 157—oath taken by both houses in consequence of, ib.
Wallingford House, cabal of, form a coalition with the republicans, ii. 271—oblige Richard Cromwell to dissolve his parliament, 272.
Walpole (sir Robert), reconciles the church to the royal family, iii. 249, 250—remarks on his administration, 254—character of the opposition to him, 257—the successors of, did not carry reform to the extent they previously aimed at, 265—and Pelham, condemn the excessive partiality of their masters for their Hanoverian dominions, 293 and note x—his prudent administration, 298.
Walsingham (sir Francis), deceived by Charles IX., i. 137—his advice against Mary queen of Scots, 139—fidelity of his spies upon her, 156—his enmity to her, 159 and note b—his moderation and protection towards the puritans, 194—his disinterested liberality, 224—his letter in defence of Elizabeth's government, 228 and note.
Walton (Dr. Brian), ejected by the covenant, ii. 166

WHITAKER.

War with Holland, infamy of the, ii. 390 and note r—between William III. and Louis XIV., its ill success and expenses, iii. 133, 134—of the succession, its object, ib. 137.
Wards, extraordinary liveries taken for, i. 15.
Warham (William), archbishop of Canterbury, his letter to Wolsey, on the grants, &c., of 1525, i. 19, note u.
Warrant of committal, form and power of, debated, i. 384, 387; ii. 3.
Warwick (Edward Plantagenet, earl of), his long captivity, attempt to escape with Perkin Warbeck, his trial for conspiracy, induced to confess himself guilty in the hope of pardon, his execution, and the probable motive for it, i. 26—(John Dudley, earl of), a concealed papist, 95, note k.
Wenlock, the first charter for returning members to parliament, iii. 42.
Wentworth (Paul), his discussion of the church authority with archbishop Parker, i. 192—his bold motion on a command of Elizabeth, 251—(Peter), his motion on the succession, 255—his bold defence of the privileges of parliament against Elizabeth, ib.—examined concerning it, 256—committed to the Tower, ib.—questions of, on the privileges, &c., of parliament, 257—again committed to the Tower, 258.
Westbury, borough of, fined for bribery, i. 268.
Westminster, ancient courts of law held at, i. 5—abbey, preserved from destruction in the reformation under Edward VI., 94—hall, tumult in, on demand of a loan by Charles I., 381 and note p.
Westmoreland (Mildmay Fane, earl of), his forest amerciament, ii. 11.
Whalley (abbey of), Dr. Whitaker's scheme for distributing its revenues, i. 79, note b.
Whig and tory, first heard of in the year 1679, ii. 439—their first meeting, 442—necessity of accurately understanding their definition, 199—their distinctive principles, ib., 200—changes effected in them by circumstances, ib. 201.
Whiggism, genuine, one of the tests of, iii. 147.
Whig party, justified in their distrust of Charles II., ii. 451.
Whigs, remarkable triumph of the, iii. 94—their influence in the councils of William III., 111—oppose a general amnesty, 112—bold measure of the, 228—come into power, 230.
Whiston, extract from his Memoirs, iii. 197, note 7.
Whitaker (Dr. Thomas Dunham), his plan for distributing the revenues of the abbey of Whalley, i. 79, note b.

WHITBREAD.

Whitbread, a Jesuit, his trial, ii. 426, 427.
White (John, bishop of Winchester), speaks against the protestants in his funeral sermon for queen Mary, i. 110, note c.
Whitelock (sir James), cited before the star-chamber, i. 350 — (Bulstrode), palliation of his father's pliancy, ii. 3, note c—curious anecdote recorded by, 285.
Whitgift (John, archbishop of Canterbury), orders given to, concerning papists in Denbigh, i. 142—his allowance of torture, 148, note r—his answer to Cartwright, 199 and note c—rigour of his ecclesiastical government, 200 and note b—ex officio oath tendered by, 202—his intercession for Udal, 206—his censure of lawyers, 213 and note t—his bigoted sway over the press, 239, note n—his exclamation at Hampton Court, iii. 321.
Wicliffe (John), effect of his doctrines in England, i. 57.
Wildman (major), unites the republicans and royalists against the power of Cromwell, ii. 249.
Wilford (sir Thomas), Elizabeth's illegal commission of martial law to, i. 242.
Wilkins (bishop), opposes the act for suppressing conventicles, ii. 388.
William the Conqueror, capacity of his descendants to the seventeenth century described, iii. 292.
William the Lion, statutes ascribed to him, iii. 306.
William III. receives the crown conjointly with his wife, iii. 98—discontent with his government, 107—his character and errors, 110—his government in danger, ib.—his dissatisfaction, 118—his magnanimous and public-spirited ambition, 119—dissolves the convention parliament, and gives his confidence to the tories, 122 and notes e t—scheme for his assassination, 129, 130, and note r—his magnanimous conduct, 133—unjustly accused of neglecting the navy, 136 and note g—skill and discipline acquired by the troops under his command, ib.—aware of the intentions of Louis XIV. on the Spanish dominions, 138 — 700,000l. granted him during life, 139—leaves a sealed order to keep up the army, 140—obliged to reduce his army, and send home his Dutch guards, ib.—his conduct censurable with regard to the Irish forfeitures, 142, note s—unpopularity of his administration, 144—his conduct with respect to the two treaties of partition, 146 – his superiority over the greatest men of the age, 148—improvements in the English constitution under him, ib.—his statute of treason, 150—hatred of the tories to, 178—distinction of the cabinet from the privy council during his reign, 184—reservedness of his disposition, 187—his partiality to Bentinck and Keppel not consistent with the good sense and dignity of his character, 188—influences members of parliament by bribes, 189—refuses to pass a bill for rendering the judges independent, 194—truly his own minister, 292—never popular in Scotland, 335—the only consistent friend of toleration, 336 and note m.
Williams (——), his prediction of king James's death, i. 344, note q—(Dr. John, bishop of Lincoln), suspicion of corruption in, 389, note b—fined by the star-chamber, ii. 36—made lord keeper, 40—suspected of popish principles, 70, note t.
Wills, fees of the clergy on the probates of, limited, i. 64.
Winchester, statutes of, on defence of the nation, ii. 132.
Wines, duties imposed on their importation, i. 317, note i.
Wisbech castle, factions of the prisoners in, i. 166, note t.
Withens (sir Francis), expelled the house of commons, ii. 444.
Woad, proclamation of Elizabeth, prohibiting its culture, i. 237 and note c.
Wolsey (cardinal Thomas), his motion for a supply of 800,000l. to be raised by a tax on lands and goods, i. 17—opposed by the commons, ib.—circumstantial account of this transaction, ib. and note q—his arbitrary modes of raising money without the intervention of parliament, 18—letters to, concerning, 19, note u—obloquy incurred by these measures, 21—estimate of his character, 22—articles against him never intended to be proceeded upon by the king, 23, note s—cause of the duke of Buckingham's execution, 27 and note t—augments the authority of the court of star-chamber, 52—rigid in restraining the turbulence of the nobility, &c., 54, note k—Luther's attack on, 60, note c—a delegate of Clement VII. on Henry VIII.'s divorce, 61—increases the fees of the clergy on wills, 64, note l—his reformation and suppression of the monastic orders, 70—did not persecute, but proscribed heretic writings, 82.
Wool, &c., ancient unjust tolls on, i. 319, 320, note r.
Wotton (sir Henry), his palliation of impositions, i. 340, note c.
Worcester, victory of, its consequences to the future power of Cromwell, ii. 237.
Wright (——), his case of conscience and confinement, i. 144, note l.
Wright (Mr. Thomas), notice of his edition of 'Letters relating to the Suppression of Monasteries,' i. 72, note y.

Wyatt (sir Thomas), insurrection of, i. 108, *note* ª.

Yelverton (Mr.), his defence of the privileges of parliament, i. 253.
Yeomen of the guard, establishment of the, ii. 131.
Yeomanry of England, under the Plantagenets, described, i. 5.
York, council of, summoned, ii. 92, 93, *notes* 5 k.
York (James, duke of), protests against a clause in act of uniformity, ii. 341—suspected of being a catholic before the Restoration, 344 and *note* P—his marriage with lady Anne Hyde, 361 and *note* b, 362—converted to the Romish faith, 381—particulars relating to his conversion, *ib.* and *note* º—always strenuous against schemes of comprehension, 388—obliged to retire from the office of lord admiral, 394 and *note* ʳ

—dangerous enemy of the constitution, 398—his accession to the throne viewed with great apprehension, 428—engaged in a scheme of general conversion, 431—resolved to excite a civil war rather than yield to the exclusion, 435—plan for banishing him for life, 438 and *note* d—his unpopularity among the middling classes, 443—his tyranny in Scotland, iii. 328.
Yorke (Philip, second earl of Hardwicke), his account of the tories in 1745, iii. 253, *note* q.
Yorkshire, levy of ship-money refused in, ii. 86.

Zeal, religious, in Scotland, its furious effects, iii. 313.
Zwingle (Ulric), his belief concerning the Lord's Supper nearly fatal to the Reformation, i. 90.

THE END.

LONDON: PRINTED BY WILLIAM CLOWES AND SONS, STAMFORD STREET,
AND CHARING CROSS.

www.ingramcontent.com/pod-product-compliance
Lightning Source LLC
Chambersburg PA
CBHW031959300426
44117CB00008B/824